THE GOSPEL OF MARK

THE GOSPEL OF MARK

A Commentary

FRANCIS J. MOLONEY, S.D.B.

© 2002 by Hendrickson Publishers, Inc.
P. O. Box 3473
Peabody, Massachusetts 01961–3473

ISBN 13   978-1-56563-682-8
ISBN 10   1-56563-682-1

Printed in China

Second Printing—May 2006

Cover art: St. Mark from the Lindisfarne Gospels, British Library, Cotton Nero D. IV, c. 698. Copyright Art Resource, N.Y.

Library of Congress Cataloging-in-Publication Data

Moloney, Francis J.
    The Gospel of Mark : a commentary / Francis J. Moloney.
        p. cm.
    Includes bibliographical references and index.
        ISBN 1-56563-682-1
        1. Bible. N.T. Mark—Commentaries.   I. Title.
        BS2585.53 .M65 2002
        226.3′07—dc21

                                        2002004912

For
Morna Hooker and Brendan Byrne

Bella memorized, repeating phrases until her fingers were so tired they gave up resisting and got it right. . . . But when she finished memorizing—bar by bar, section by section—and played the piece without stopping, I was lost; no longer aware of a hundred accumulated fragments but only of one long story, after which the house would fall silent for what seemed a very long time.

Anne Michael, *Fugitive Pieces*
See Mark 16:8.

TABLE OF CONTENTS

SECTION 4
Epilogue: Mark 16:1–8

ABBREVIATIONS

AB	Anchor Bible
ABD	*Anchor Bible Dictionary.* Edited by D. N. Freedman. 6 vols. New York: Doubleday, 1992
ABRL	Anchor Bible Reference Library
AGSU	Arbeiten zur Geschichte des Spätjudentums und Urchristentums
AnBib	Analecta biblica
BDAG	Danker, F. W. *Greek-English Lexicon of the New Testament and Other Early Christian Literature.* 3d ed. Chicago: University of Chicago Press, 2000.
BDF	Blass, F., A. Debrunner, and R. W. Funk. *A Greek Grammar of the New Testament and Other Early Christian Literature.* Chicago: University of Chicago Press, 1961.
BETL	Bibliotheca ephemeridum theologicarum lovaniensium
BEvT	Beiträge zur evangelischen Theologie
BHT	Beiträge zur historischen Theologie
Bib	*Biblica*
BibInt	*Biblical Interpretation*
BibIntS	Biblical Interpretation Series
BibSciRel	Biblioteca di scienze religiose
BJRL	*Bulletin of the John Rylands University Library of Manchester*
BJS	Brown Judaica Studies
BNTC	Black's New Testament Commentaries
BTB	*Biblical Theology Bulletin*
BZ	*Biblische Zeitschrift*
BZNW	Beihefte zur Zeitschrift für die neutestamentliche Wissenschaft
CahRB	Cahiers de la Revue biblique
CBQ	*Catholic Biblical Quarterly*
CBQMS	Catholic Biblical Quarterly Monograph Series
CGTC	Cambridge Greek Testament Commentary
ConBNT	Coniectanea biblica: New Testament Series
DRev	*Downside Review*
EBib	Etudes bibliques
EDNT	*Exegetical Dictionary of the New Testament.* Edited by H. Balz and G. Schneider. ET. Grand Rapids: Eerdmans, 1990–1993.
EKKNT	Evangelisch-katholischer Kommentar zum Neuen Testament
ETL	*Ephemerides theologicae lovanienses*

ETR	*Etudes théologiques et religieuses*
ExpTim	*Expository Times*
FB	Forschung zur Bibel
FRLANT	Forschungen zur Religion und Literatur des Alten und Neuen Testaments
FTS	Frankfurter theologische Studien
GNS	Good News Studies
HNT	Handbuch zum Neuen Testament
HTKNT	Herders theologischer Kommentar zum Neuen Testament
HTR	*Harvard Theological Review*
HUCA	*Hebrew Union College Annual*
IBS	*Irish Biblical Studies*
ICC	International Critical Commentary
Int	*Interpretation*
IRT	Issues in Religion and Theology
ITS	International Theological Studies
JBL	*Journal of Biblical Literature*
JR	*Journal of Religion*
JSNT	*Journal for the Study of the New Testament*
JSNTSup	Journal for the Study of the New Testament: Supplement Series
JSOT	*Journal for the Study of the Old Testament*
JSOTSup	Journal for the Study of the Old Testament: Supplement Series
JSPSup	Journal for the Study of the Pseudepigrapha: Supplement Series
JTS	*Journal of Theological Studies*
Jud	*Judaica*
LD	Lectio divina
LSJ	Liddell, H. G., R. Scott, and H. S. Jones, *A Greek-English Lexicon*. 9th ed. with revised supplement. Oxford: Clarendon Press, 1996.
MNTC	Moffatt New Testament Commentary
NCB	New Century Bible
NEB	New English Bible
NS	New series
NICNT	New International Commentary on the New Testament
NovT	*Novum Testamentum*
NovTSupp	Novum Testamentum Supplements
NRTh	*La nouvelle revue théologique*
NTAbh	Neutestamentliche Abhandlungen
NTG	New Testament Guides
NTS	*New Testament Studies*
OTP	*Old Testament Pseudepigrapha*. Edited by J. H. Charlesworth. 2 vols. New York: Doubleday, 1983.
PG	Patrologiae cursus completus: Series graeca. Edited by J.-P. Migne. 162 vols. Paris, 1857–1886.
PL	Patrologiae cursus completus: Series latina. Edited by J.-P. Migne. 217 vols. Paris, 1844–1864.
PNTC	Pelican New Testament Commentaries
RB	*Revue biblique*
RevQ	*Revue de Qumran*

RGG	*Religion in Geschichte und Gegenwart: Handwörterbuch fur Theologie und Religionswissenschaft.* Edited by H. D. Betz, D. S. Browning, B. Janowski, and W. Jüngel. 4th ed. Tübingen: J. C. B. Mohr (Paul Siebeck), 1999–.
RNT	Regensburger Neues Testament
RSR	*Recherches de science religieuse*
SANT	Studien zum Alten und Neuen Testaments
SBLDS	Society of Biblical Literature Dissertation Series
SBS	Stuttgarter Bibelstudien
SBT	Studies in Biblical Theology
Sem	*Semeia*
SNTSMS	Society for New Testament Studies Monograph Series
SP	Sacra pagina
Str-B	H. Strack and P. Billerbeck, *Kommentar zum Neuen Testament aus Talmud und Midrasch.* 6 vols. Munich: C. H. Beck, 1922–1961.
SUNT	Studien zur Umwelt des Neuen Testaments
TDNT	*Theological Dictionary of the New Testament.* Edited by G. Kittel and G. Friedrich. Translated by G. W. Bromiley. 10 vols. Grand Rapids: Eerdmans, 1964–1976.
THKNT	Theologischer Handkommentar zum Neuen Testament
TQ	*Theologische Quartalschrift*
TS	*Theological Studies*
TTZ	*Trierer theologische Zeitschrift*
TZ	*Theologische Zeitschrift*
WBC	Word Biblical Commentary
WUNT	Wissenschaftliche Untersuchungen zum Neuen Testament
ZKT	*Zeitschrift für katholische Theologie*
ZNW	*Zeitschrift für die neutestamentliche Wissenschaft und die Kunde der älteren Kirche*
ZTK	*Zeitschrift für Theologie und Kirche*

PREFACE

In 1985, at Catholic Theological College, Clayton, Victoria, Australia, I was teaching the Gospel of Mark to a mixed group of students. Some were students for the ordained ministry; others were lay people taking the course as preparation for Christian ministries in classrooms, hospitals, and parishes. Also present was a strikingly attractive woman, an academic from the neighboring Monash University. As she had a senior academic post at Monash, I wondered why she would bother to take an undergraduate course in the Gospel of Mark. After my introductory remarks about the Gospel, I asked the group to introduce themselves. She shared that she had been diagnosed with terminal cancer, and wished to follow the Markan Jesus to the Cross as she made her journey down that same path. Accompanying that woman through the last months of her life with the text of the Gospel of Mark in our hands left a lasting impression on all who shared that semester. One of my Salesian brothers, Peter Rankin, S.D.B., was in that class. For years he has insisted that I "write something on Mark." The book that follows is that "something on Mark."

Administrative responsibilities and other major publishing commitments have prevented me from turning my mind and heart to this task until now. Two events coincided to make the study possible. Initially there was a request for a work on Mark from the then editorial director at Hendrickson Publishers, Patrick Alexander. Then followed my appointment as professor of New Testament at the Catholic University of America in Washington, D.C. With Patrick's promise of publication, and the resources of the Catholic University and the city of Washington available, the way was clear for me to realize my wish: to do "something on Mark."

Heavily dependent upon the great commentaries of the last century, and some of the monographic literature written in recent decades, this commentary records my understanding of the Gospel of Mark as a unified, theologically driven narrative. Despite my interest in narrative, I avoid the specialized literary terminology that surrounds many narrative-critical readings of biblical texts. I also pay more attention to exegetical and theological problems that emerge from a close reading of the Gospel of Mark than is common to narrative commentaries. It remains true that many commentators' attempts to read the text in the light of its original setting produce forced, and sometimes artificial, interpretations that make little impact upon a contemporary reader. I wish to marry the rich contribution made by traditional historical scholarship with the contemporary focus on narrative as such. The Gospel of Mark, as with the rest of the biblical literature, is read today because of almost two thousand years of reading. The ongoing relevance of the narrative, as well as its original setting, will be a concern of the following study. Contemporary biblical commentary sometimes either ignores the literary contribution of a document, or disregards the historical-critical questions that must be asked in the interpretation of any ancient text.

No interpretative context can claim to have exhausted all the possible interpretations of any text. I have no doubt that my experiences, including the one mentioned above, have shaped my reading of the Gospel of Mark. My peers may judge some of it as maverick, the imposition of my world upon the world of the Markan text. But we all do that as we strive, even if unconsciously, to fit everything together in a consistent pattern. I have attempted to lessen that risk by recording other scholarly positions as I wend my way through the text.

My aim has been to trace what Mark's story said to an early Christian community perplexed by failure and suffering. The author presents Jesus as a suffering Messiah, Son of God, and highlights the failure of the Markan disciples. Failure and suffering continue to perplex all who believe that God has acted definitively and uniquely in the person of Jesus Christ. We all know that 1 John 3:9, extrapolated from its literary and historical context, is simply untrue: "No one born of God commits sin; for God's nature abides in him, and he cannot sin because he is born of God." What God has done in and through Jesus of Nazareth, and the ambiguity of our response to God's action, is the "stuff" of our everyday Christian lives. Christians today, facing the biblical text in its third millennium, resonate with the perplexity found behind and within the text of the Gospel of Mark.

The members of my doctoral seminars on the Gospel of Mark at the Catholic University of America in the fall semesters of 1999 and 2000 provided a fine testing ground for much that follows. I am particularly grateful to Rekha Chennattu, R.A., who provided hard-working support in her role as my research assistant at the university, and Nerina Zanardo, F.S.P., whose interest in my writing has not flagged, despite the distance between Washington, D.C., and Adelaide, South Australia. My editor, Dr. James Ernest, and the production team at Hendrickson have left no stone unturned to produce this book. I am very grateful for their diligent and friendly attention to my work. The staffs of the Mullen Library at the Catholic University of America and the Woodstock Library at Georgetown made research possible. The Sisters of the Visitation Convent, Georgetown, always provided me with the warmth of Salesian hospitality.

This study is dedicated to two people who, in different ways, have been an important part of my life, both scholarly and otherwise, for three decades. The three of us first met in late 1972 at the University of Oxford, England. Brendan and I, both from Australia, met Dr. Morna Hooker (later Lady Margaret Professor of Divinity at the University of Cambridge), who had agreed to direct our doctoral research at the university. Morna taught us more than biblical scholarship and has remained a good friend to us both since that time. As the commentary will show, I still have a lot to learn from her. Brendan has been my dear friend and colleague since those days. His influence on my life and scholarship cannot be measured. The dedication is a token of my gratitude to Morna and Brendan for all that they have been to me and done for me over many years.

Francis J. Moloney, S.D.B.
The Catholic University of America
Washington, D.C. 20064, U.S.A.

INTRODUCTION TO THE GOSPEL OF MARK

The Gospel of Mark was neglected by early Christian tradition, rarely—if ever—used in preaching. The Gospel of Matthew surpassed it in both length and detail. Mark was seen as something of a poor cousin to the great Gospel of Matthew, used so consistently by the fathers of the church. Already at the turn of the first Christian century authors were citing Matthew (the *Didache* [90s C.E.], *1 Clement* [96–98 C.E.], *Barnabas* [about 110 C.E.], and Ignatius of Antioch [110 C.E.]). Toward the middle of the second century (circa 130 C.E.) Papias, the bishop of Hierapolis in South Phrygia in the province of Asia, associated the Second Gospel with a certain "Mark" and the Apostle Peter, and Clement of Alexandria located that association in the city of Rome. Irenaeus, Clement of Alexandria, Origen, Jerome, and Tertullian agree: the Gospel of Mark appeared in Rome, and reports a Petrine story of Jesus, interpreted by his associate, Mark. But the great fathers of the church scarcely use this gospel in their writings.

Augustine articulated most clearly an understanding of the Gospel of Mark that has endured till the modern era: "Marcus eum subsecutus tamquam pedisequus et breviator eius videtur."[1] As the emerging Christian church looked consistently to Matthew for its instruction, no commentary on the Gospel of Mark appeared until the turn of the sixth century. From 650 to 1000 C.E. thirteen major commentaries were written on Matthew, and four on Mark. This neglect continued down to the end of the eighteenth century.[2] The Gospel of Mark maintained its place in the Christian canon because of its traditional relationship with Peter and the city of Rome. But it has been well described as "present but absent."[3] As the Christian church became an increasingly unified political, social, and ideological phenomenon in the early centuries, "biblical texts were not used as narratives in themselves but as sources for proofs of doctrinal and ecclesiastical positions. In this enterprise, Mark was a weak contender."[4]

---

[1] Augustine, *De consensu evangelistarum*, 1.2 (PL 34:1044): "Mark appears only as his follower and abbreviator." See E. Massaux, *The Influence of the Gospel of Saint Matthew on Christian Literature before Saint Irenaeus* (trans. N. J. Belval and S. Hecht; ed. A. J. Bellinzoni; New Gospel Studies 5; Macon: Mercer, 1993), and B. D. Schildgen, *Power and Prejudice: The Reception of the Gospel of Mark* (Detroit: Wayne State University Press, 1999), 35–42. Through a rebirth of interest in J. J. Griesbach's theory (see Schildgen, *Power and Prejudice*, 111–23), a number of contemporary scholars continue to claim that Mark abbreviated Matthew. See below, note 8.

[2] See R. H. Lightfoot, *The Gospel Message of St. Mark* (Oxford: Clarendon Press, 1950), 1–14; S. P. Kealy, *Mark's Gospel: A History of Its Interpretation* (New York: Paulist Press, 1982), 7–57; Schildgen, *Power and Prejudice*, 43–110.

[3] This is the title of Schildgen's first chapter (*Power and Prejudice*, 35–42).

[4] Schildgen, *Power and Prejudice*, 41.

The First Gospel

Things have changed since that time, and it could be claimed that gospel scholarship over the past 150 years has been dominated by a fascination with the Gospel of Mark.[5] The turn to the Gospel of Mark was initiated by the so-called source critics who began to question the long-held tradition that Matthew was the first of the gospels to appear. In the latter half of the nineteenth century, the source critics established the priority of Mark over Matthew and Luke. The traditional "Second Gospel" became the first gospel. The modern era, ushered in by the Enlightenment, saw a rapid development of critical thought. The English deists, themselves products of the Enlightenment, demanded that the biblical tradition be subjected to the scrutiny of hard logic. The doublets, contradictions, and non sequiturs had to be explained.[6] A "higher criticism" emerged, especially in Germany, but also in England and France, applying more rational criteria to biblical studies. The source critics were part of the "higher criticism." Their work, especially that of H. J. Holtzmann,[7] sought to establish a firm historical basis for the life of Jesus. Holtzmann argued that Mark, the most primitive of all the gospels, took us back to a reliable "framework" for the life of Jesus: Jesus' messianic consciousness developed over a period of preaching in Galilee, and reached its high point at Caesarea Philippi. There he made known to his followers his belief that he was the expected Jewish Messiah. His journey to Jerusalem and his end there were the result of the Jewish leadership's rejection of his claim.

Contemporary scholarship is skeptical about Holtzmann's discovery of a framework for the life of Jesus in the Gospel of Mark. But close and detailed study of the use of individual passages in each of the three Synoptic Gospels (Matthew, Mark, and Luke) suggests that Mark's Gospel is the most ancient. Although the so-called Synoptic Question, i.e., the order of appearance and the related question of the literary dependence of one Synoptic Gospel upon another, is still debated,[8] the priority of Mark is the best explanation for a number of the features of Mark, Matthew, and Luke. Matthew and Luke had their own sources for their accounts of the life, teaching, death, and resurrection of Jesus. Some material is found only in Matthew (sometimes called M; see, for example, Matt 16:16–18), or only in Luke (sometimes called L; see, for example, Luke 15:1–32). A large amount of ma-

---

[5] For a survey down to 1985, see W. Telford, "Introduction: The Gospel of Mark," in *The Interpretation of Mark* (IRT 7; ed. W. Telford; Philadelphia: Fortress, 1985), 1–41.

[6] See Shildgen, *Power and Prejudice*, 111–23.

[7] H. J. Holtzmann, *Die synoptischen Evangelien: Ihr Ursprung und geschichtlicher Charakter* (Leipzig: Wilhelm Engelmann, 1863). For a full discussion of this period, see Kealy, *Mark's Gospel*, 58–89. Other important figures were K. Lachmann, C. H. Weisse, J. Hawkins, and P. Wernle. See also U. Schnelle, *The History and Theology of the New Testament Writings* (trans. M. E. Boring; Minneapolis: Fortress, 1998), 162–79.

[8] See, for example, W. R. Farmer, "Modern Developments of Griesbach's Hypothesis," *NTS* 23 (1976–1977): 275–95; T. R. W. Longstaff, *Evidence of Conflation in Mark? A Study in the Synoptic Problem* (SBLDS 28; Missoula: Scholars Press, 1977); H.-H. Stoldt, *History and Criticism of the Markan Hypothesis* (Edinburgh: T. & T. Clark, 1980); *J. J. Griesbach: Synoptic and Text-Critical Studies* (ed. B. Orchard and T. R. Longstaff; SNTSMS 34; Cambridge: Cambridge University Press, 1978); M. D. Goulder, *Luke: A New Paradigm* (2 vols.; JSNTSup 20: Sheffield: Sheffield Academic Press, 1989). See, however, the critical response to these proposals by C. M. Tuckett, *The Revival of the Griesbach Hypothesis* (SNTSMS 44; Cambridge: Cambridge University Press, 1982), and idem, *Q and the History of Early Christianity: Studies on Q* (Peabody: Hendrickson, 1996), 1–39.

terial in both Matthew and Luke is not present in Mark (sometimes called "Q," from the German word *Quelle,* meaning "source"; see, for example, teachings in Matt 5:1–7:28 found in Luke 6:12–49 and elsewhere in Luke, but nowhere in Mark). It appears that the authors of both Matthew and Luke had the Gospel of Mark before them as they penned their particular stories of Jesus.[9]

On this supposition, it was Mark who invented the literary form which we call gospel: a narrative telling the story of the life, teaching, death, and resurrection of Jesus of Nazareth, proclaiming the good news (Greek: εὐαγγέλιον;[10] Old English: *god-spel*) that Jesus is the Christ, the Son of God (see Mark 1:1). Only about forty of Mark's 675 verses are not found somewhere in Matthew.[11] The presence of material from the Gospel of Mark in the Gospel of Luke is not so obvious. But this can be accounted for by Luke's very skillful storytelling techniques. He uses the tradition in a creative way and has some memorable material not found in either Mark or Matthew, especially some parables, e.g., the Good Samaritan (10:25–37) and the Father with the Two Sons (15:11–32). Yet, both Matthew and Luke have accepted the basic story line of the Gospel of Mark: beginnings in Galilee; a journey to Jerusalem; a brief presence in the city, leading to his arrest, trial, crucifixion, burial, and resurrection. Only the Gospel of John dares to break from this story line, as the Johannine Jesus journeys from Galilee to Jerusalem, especially for the Jewish feasts of Passover, Tabernacles, and Dedication.[12] When Matthew and Luke agree in sequence, they also

---

[9] The greatest difficulty, and the departure point for those who deny Markan priority, are the so-called "minor agreements." These are passages where Matthew and Luke agree almost word for word, over against Mark. See F. Neirynck, T. Hansen, and F. van Segbroeck, *The Minor Agreements of Matthew and Luke against Mark, with a Cumulative List* (BETL 37; Leuven: Leuven University Press, 1974), and the briefer survey of Schnelle, *History and Theology,* 170–72. The solution lies in the vitality of the oral tradition and not, as Schnelle and others suggest, in a *Deuteromark,* a second edition of the canonical Mark used by Matthew and Luke (thus the minor agreements). If there was a second edition of our Gospel of Mark, what happened to it? It has left no trace in early Christianity, except in the "minor agreements." This is unlikely.

[10] The verb εὐαγγελίζομαι and the noun εὐαγγέλιον are found in the LXX and in secular Greek. Second Isaiah uses it to present the one who brings glad tidings (see LXX Isa 52:6–7). But it is a rare word; among the Greeks the expression is used in contexts that announce great events: a victory in battle, deliverance from powers of evil, the birth of a son to the King, etc. Paul applies it to the "good news" of what God has done in and through the death and resurrection of Jesus (see, for example, Rom 1:1; 10:15; 15:12; 1 Cor 9:14, 18; 15:1–2; 2 Cor 2:12; 8:18; 10:16; 11:7; Gal 1:8, 11; 4:13; Phil 4:3, 15). Thus, the appearance of the word εὐαγγέλιον in Mark 1:1 ("The beginning of the *good news* [τοῦ εὐαγγελίου]") is not new in early Christian tradition. What is new, however, is the use of the word to describe the story of the life, teaching, death, and resurrection of Jesus of Nazareth, and to use that story to proclaim him as "the Christ, the Son of God" (Mark 1:1). Indeed, it is this use of the Greek εὐαγγέλιον (English: *gospel*) which is most common today. For contemporary Christians, a "gospel" is a life story. On this, see G. Friedrich, "εὐαγγελίζομαι κτλ," *TDNT* 2:707–37; W. Marxsen, *Mark the Evangelist: Studies on the Redaction History of the Gospel* (trans. R. A. Harrisville; Nashville: Abingdon, 1969), 117–50.

[11] The chapters and verses, so much a part of modern Bibles, and of our citation of the biblical text, are recent additions. Various divisions of the books and passages had been attempted in antiquity, but present chapter divisions were created by Stephen Langton in the thirteenth century. Verse divisions were added by Robert Estienne in the sixteenth century. They are not always a sure guide to the original literary design of a biblical author, but are useful in locating specific texts.

[12] See F. J. Moloney, *Signs and Shadows: Reading John 5–12* (Minneapolis: Fortress, 1996). This may be one of several elements in the Fourth Gospel that reflect more accurately what actually took place during the life and ministry of Jesus. On this, see F. J. Moloney, "The Fourth Gospel and the Jesus of History," *NTS* 46 (2000): 42–58.

agree with Mark.[13] Matthew's order of events is closer to that of Mark's, but even Luke, who intersperses his account more systematically with other material, follows the Markan order of events. This fact points to the possibility that the authors of Matthew and Luke both had the same text, the Gospel of Mark, before them as they wrote their versions of the life of Jesus.[14]

These are but some of the reasons for the widespread scholarly consensus on the priority of Mark. Perhaps the most significant factor, however, is not found in the Synoptic Tradition's use of the same material in terms of words, style, and the location of each single, self-contained passage, called "pericopes" by critics. If Matthew was the first gospel, as Augustine suggested, and Mark derived his account from Matthew, it is difficult to find good reasons why Mark would have performed such a radical operation on Matthew's carefully assembled work. It is, on the other hand, easier to find satisfactory reasons for a Matthean or a Lukan reworking of the Gospel of Mark. It takes a deal of imagination and mental gymnastics to read the Gospel of Mark *in its entirety* as a deliberately shortened version of the Gospel of Matthew.[15] However, as Fitzmyer has pointed out " 'the truth' of the matter is largely inaccessible to us, and we are forced to live with a hypothesis or a theory."[16]

Mark the Historian

But does the primitive nature of the Gospel of Mark give us privileged access to a framework for the life of Jesus of Nazareth, as Holtzmann claimed?[17] At the turn of last century two scholars almost single-handedly brought such speculations to an end and thus established a new era for the study of the Gospel of Mark. In 1901 William Wrede, among other things, addressed the thesis of those who, like Holtzmann, regarded the Gospel of Mark as a faithful record of Jesus' life. In his book, titled *The Messianic Secret in the Gospels*, he demolished the suggestion that the Gospel of Mark represented a primitive portrait of Jesus' story.[18] He argued, on the basis of Jesus' continual commands to silence in the Gos-

---

[13] For a thorough presentation of the case for Markan priority and the existence of Q, see J. A. Fitzmyer, "The Priority of Mark and the 'Q' Source in Luke," in *To Advance the Gospel: New Testament Studies* (New York: Crossroad, 1981), 3–40. For a more recent and equally thorough discussion, see Tuckett, *Q and the History of Early Christianity*, 1–39; J. Marcus, *Mark 1–8* (AB 27; New York: Doubleday, 2000), 40–47, and R. E. Brown, *The Death of the Messiah: From Gethsemane to the Grave: A Commentary on the Passion Narratives in the Four Gospels* (ABRL; 2 vols.; New York: Doubleday, 1994), 1:40–46.

[14] See the useful summaries of the "argument from order" in Fitzmyer, "The Priority of Mark," 7–9, and Tuckett, *Q and the History of Early Christianity*, 8–10.

[15] I stress *in its entirety* as it is possible to pick scattered Markan pericopes and show that they can be understood as an abbreviated rewriting of the Matthean parallel. Then there is the further problem of those places where both Matthew and Luke omit Markan material (e.g., Mark 1:1; 2:27; 3:20–21, etc.), and other sayings where there are minor verbal agreements (omissions or alterations) of Matthew and Luke against Mark. See Fitzmyer, "The Priority of Mark," 11–16; Marcus, *Mark*, 45–47. However, such an exercise must be extended to show how *all* the pericopes *in their Markan order* make theological and literary sense as an abbreviation of Matthew. No contemporary return to Matthean (or Lukan) priority has done this convincingly. See Tuckett's survey in *Q and the History of Early Christianity*, 11–34.

[16] Fitzmyer, "The Priority of Mark," 4.

[17] For a helpful survey of all the issues surrounding this question, see W. R. Telford, *Mark* (NTG; Sheffield: Sheffield Academic Press, 1995), 36–85.

[18] W. Wrede, *Das Messiasgeheimnis in den Evangelien: Zugleich ein Beitrag zum Verständnis des Markusevangeliums* (Göttingen: Vandenhoeck & Ruprecht, 1901). The book, reprinted four times

pel of Mark, that Jesus made no messianic claims. They were added to the story by the early church, and the Gospel of Mark was clear evidence of this process. Jesus was not the Messiah, and never made such a claim. Many were surprised to hear early Christian preachers claim that he was. In the Gospel of Mark the nonmessianic Jesus was explained by Jesus' repeated insistence that no one be told of his messianic words and deeds. He was not widely known as the Messiah because he himself forbade any such proclamation in his own time. This meant that the Gospel of Mark was not a reliable historical report; it was part of the theological creativity of the early church. "The Gospel of Mark belongs to the history of dogma."[19]

Shortly after Wrede's epoch-making study, Albert Schweitzer's *The Quest of the Historical Jesus* reviewed nineteenth-century scholars' portrayal of the historical Jesus.[20] He showed that each "life of Jesus" was more a projection of German scholarship than an objective historical reconstruction.

> The Jesus of Nazareth who came forth publicly as the Messiah, who preached the ethic of the kingdom of God, who founded the Kingdom of Heaven on earth, and died to give His work its final consecration, never had any existence. He is a figure designed by rationalism, endowed with life by liberalism, and clothed by modern theology in an historical garb.[21]

For Schweitzer, Jesus preached the imminent end of time and must be judged to have failed in terms of his own understanding of his God-ordained mission, however much the four gospels and subsequent Christian culture had reinterpreted his person and message.

These debates were not limited to the studies and the lecture rooms of German universities. Critical biblical scholarship had its origins in an attempt to put the study of the Bible on the same scholarly footing as the emerging sciences in a post-Enlightenment world. Its activities and conclusions captured the imagination of many, especially those responsible for the preaching of the word of God, so central to the Christian tradition. But a gulf was opening between the critical biblical scholars and those involved in a ministry of the word because, like many of their contemporaries, in their search for the scholarly excellence of their time, the biblical scholars had lost touch with the primacy of the story itself. This problem was to deepen with the passing of time.[22] The turmoil, suffering, and death which marked the First World War (1914–1918) did not lessen the growing skepticism among German scholars. Between World War I and World War II Karl Ludwig Schmidt, Martin Dibelius, and Rudolf Bultmann founded a new approach to the Synoptic Gospels

---

since then (last reprint 1969), is now available in English: *The Messianic Secret* (trans. J. C. G. Grieg; Cambridge & London: James Clarke, 1971). See the critical discussion of Wrede's contribution, and responses to him, in G. Minette de Tillesse, *Le secret messianique dans l'Evangile de Marc* (LD 47; Paris: Cerf, 1968), 9–34.

[19] Wrede, *The Messianic Secret*, 131.

[20] A. Schweitzer, *The Quest of the Historical Jesus* (trans. W. Montgomery; London: A. & C. Black, 1910). This was an English translation of Schweitzer's original book: *Von Reimarus zu Wrede: Eine Geschichte der Leben-Jesu-Forschung* (Tübingen: J. C. B. Mohr [Paul Siebeck], 1906]). A considerably enlarged second edition, titled simply *Geschichte der Leben-Jesu-Forschung,* was published in 1913 and has only recently appeared in English: *The Quest of the Historical Jesus* (first complete edition; ed. J. Bowden; London: SCM, 2000; Minneapolis: Fortress, 2001).

[21] Schweitzer, *The Quest*, 396 (1910 edition).

[22] For an analysis of this phenomenon, see H. W. Frei, *The Eclipse of Biblical Narrative: A Study in Eighteenth and Nineteenth Century Hermeneutics* (New Haven: Yale University Press, 1974). See also the interesting (but debatable) remarks of Schildgen (*Power and Prejudice,* 29) on the impact of the shift from biblical exegesis done in the church to biblical exegesis done in the universities.

that focused upon the identifiable prehistory of the individual pericopes that had been as-sembled by an editor to produce the gospels as we now have them.[23]

This approach was called form criticism. It focused its attention on the literary form of each single pericope and attempted to locate its origin in the life of Jesus or the life of the early church. Using an increasing bank of knowledge about other ancient religions, the form critics traced parallel "forms" in the parables, the miracle stories, the conflict stories, the pronouncements, and the stories of suffering found in those religions. They identified (somewhat speculatively, and often with insufficient support) the "situation in the life" of Jesus or the church where such passages were born. From this comes the well-known ex-pression, widely used even by non-German scholars, *Sitz im Leben* (the situation in life). The title of Schmidt's study, *Der Rahmen der Geschichte Jesu*, stated a truth by now ac-cepted by all form critics: the "framework" *(Rahmen)* of Jesus' story cannot be recovered from the Gospel of Mark. This had already been made clear by Wrede's work on the messi-anic secret and quickly became a bedrock point of departure for all subsequent study. The first evangelist, Mark, was little more than an editor, gathering pericopes from various tra-ditional sources, placing them side by side to form the Gospel as it now stands.[24] A fascina-tion with the world behind the text led to an ever-decreasing interest in the story of Jesus *as it is told in the Gospel of Mark*. Matthew and Luke were also editors but were strongly in-fluenced by decisions already made by Mark. Thus, a form-critical approach to Matthew or Luke looked to the "forms" and the *Sitz im Leben* of passages in the Gospel of Mark that had been taken over and modified in these *later* uses of the *same* traditions. Because of the emerging scholarly unanimity that Mark was the first gospel, all gospel studies had to take the story of Jesus as Mark tells it as an essential point of departure.

Mark the Theologian

The establishment of the priority of Mark and the advent of form criticism moved this gospel to center stage. It has never moved far from that privileged position since the early decades of the twentieth century. After the Second World War (1939–1945) an issue raised by Wrede, largely ignored by the form critics, returned to dominate gospel studies.[25] Wrede had insisted that Mark did not write history but had told a story of Jesus of Naza-reth and deliberately imposed a Christian dogma upon the narrative. The Gospel of Mark and the gospels that followed, insisted Wrede, were theologically motivated. German New

---

[23] K. L. Schmidt, *Der Rahmen der Geschichte Jesu: Literarkritische Untersuchungen zur ältesten Jesusüberlieferung* (Darmstadt: Wissenschaftliche Buchgesellschaft, 1964 [original: 1919]); M. Di-belius, *From Tradition to Gospel* (trans. B. L. Woolf; Library of Theological Translations; Cambridge & London: James Clarke, 1971 [original German: 1919]); R. Bultmann, *History of the Synoptic Tradi-tion* (trans. John Marsh; Oxford: Basil Blackwell, 1968 [original German: 1921]). For further detail, see Kealy, *Mark's Gospel,* 115–58.

[24] See Bultmann, *History,* 338, 350: "In Mark we can still see clearly, and most easily in compari-son with Luke, that the most ancient tradition consisted of individual sections, and that the connect-ing together is secondary.... Mark is not sufficiently master of his material to be able to venture on a systematic construction himself."

[25] The issue was not entirely ignored. Bultmann (*History,* 337–67) devotes attention to the edit-ing of the narrative material and the composition of the Gospels in a larger section (pp. 321–67) on the editing of traditional material. His approach, however, is still more concerned with sources than with the theology of each evangelist.

Testament scholars again led the way as Hans Conzelmann (Luke), Willi Marxsen (Mark) and Günther Bornkamm (Matthew) investigated the theological perspectives that inspired the evangelists to gather the material traditions and shape them in a particular way. [26] This movement, called redaction criticism, focused upon each particular gospel as a whole utterance, rather than upon the form, history, and *Sitz im Leben* of the pericopes that formed it. The redaction critics, however, depended heavily upon the form critics for their conclusions. The latter provided the necessary *historical* evidence for the *theological* conclusions drawn by the redaction critics. The project has been well described by Hans Conzelmann, widely regarded as the founder of redaction criticism (although it could be argued that this honor rightly belongs to Wrede):

> Our aim is to elucidate Luke's work in its present form, not to enquire into possible sources or into the historical facts which provide the material. A variety of sources does not necessarily imply a similar variety in the thought and composition of the author. How did it come about that he brought together these particular materials? Was he able to imprint on them his own views? It is here that the analysis of the sources renders the *necessary service* of helping to distinguish what comes from the source from what belongs to the author. [27]

The Gospel of Mark has no small part to play in all such considerations, since "what comes from the source" for Matthew and Luke is largely determined by this first of all gospels. If the major source used by Matthew and Luke is the Gospel of Mark, then redaction critics must look carefully at the original theological perspective of the text that acts as matrix for the other two Synoptic Gospel accounts. When the interpreter finds that a particular Markan theological perspective is *consistently* reworked in either Matthew or Luke, then, it can be claimed, this is clear evidence for the theological point of view of either Matthew or Luke. The same could be said for the use of Q, and material unique to Matthew (M) or Luke (L). The canonical gospels' use of these reconstructed "sources" is often subjected to intense analysis in an attempt to rediscover its pre-Matthean or pre-Lukan form so that the redactional tendencies of each gospel author can be traced. Redaction criticism continued the tendency to shift the Gospel of Mark from the margin of scholarly interest to the center.

If redaction criticism determines the unique theological perspective of a single author by analyzing the way he has worked with traditions that preexisted the gospel under consideration, how do redaction critics approach the Gospel of Mark? How do they determine what came to Mark in his Christian tradition, and what Mark invented? [28] This is a perennial problem for contemporary redactional studies of the Gospel of Mark. Recent decades

---

[26] H. Conzelmann, *The Theology of St. Luke* (trans. G. Buswell; London: Faber & Faber, 1961 [original German: 1957]); W. Marxsen, *Mark the Evangelist* (originally published in German in 1956); G. Bornkamm, G. Barth and H. J. Held, *Tradition and Interpretation in Matthew* (trans. P. Scott; London: SCM, 1963 [original German: 1960]). For a helpful study of the early years of redaction criticism, and the major contributors, see J. Rohde, *Rediscovering the Teaching of the Evangelists* (trans. D. M. Barton; London: SCM, 1968).

[27] Conzelmann, *The Theology of St. Luke*, 9. The italics are mine, as I wish to stress the fact that redaction criticism does not disregard the historical work of the form critics, and their determination of various historically and culturally determined literary forms and *Sitze im Leben*. Such work performs a "necessary service" for the redaction critics. See further, Kealy, *Mark's Gospel*, 159–97.

[28] For a balanced analysis of Mark as an author who was conditioned by a received tradition, yet creative in his shaping of it, see Marcus, *Mark*, 59–62.

have seen sophisticated studies of how Mark dealt with pre-Markan traditions that told of Jesus' family, his miracle-working activity, his conflicts with Jewish leaders, the two bread miracles, journeys in a boat, and the passion narrative, to mention only some major Markan themes.[29] It could be said that source criticism is not dead. The difference between nineteenth-century source criticism and the source criticism that is a necessary part of redactional studies of Mark is that the former worked with the texts of the gospels. Today's redaction critics must reconstruct a hypothetical pre-Markan text.[30]

This is a speculative task. Scholars examine passages with great detail, determine typically Markan words and expressions, and eliminate them as the result of editorial activity on the part of the author. The process runs the danger of being circular. Everything "Markan" is eliminated from a given passage, so that what remains is "pre-Markan." What each scholar regards as "Markan" is eliminated, and thus (surprisingly!) a non-Markan (pre-Markan) fragment remains. This process also assumes that Mark was not influenced by the tradition in any way so that it is easy to peel away the Markan elements from what came to the author in the tradition. This is to assume too much, as many reviewers of contemporary Markan studies have said.[31] As we shall see in our reading of the Gospel, there are places where signs of a pre-Markan tradition emerge.[32] However, much redaction criticism of the Gospel of Mark is fragile because it is based upon the frail hypothetical reconstruction of a pre-Markan source, established by means of the elimination of all that is Markan according to each redaction critic's criteria.[33]

More Recent Developments

Redactional critical scholarship has generated a large number of publications on the Gospel of Mark.[34] It is impossible to wend our way through those many and interesting

---

[29] See the summary of major works in Telford, "The Gospel of Mark," 6–15. There are other important redactional studies not mentioned in this valuable article. See the fuller list in M. R. Mansfield, *"Spirit and Gospel" in Mark* (Peabody: Hendrickson, 1987), 1–2, 10–12.

[30] Some have suggested that Mark knew 'Q,' or *The Gospel of Thomas,* or the so-called *Secret Gospel of Mark.* For a consideration and rejection of these "sources" for Mark, see Marcus, *Mark,* 47–56.

[31] See C. C. Black, *The Disciples according to Mark: Markan Redaction in Current Debate* (JSNTSup 27; Sheffield: Sheffield Academic Press, 1989), 159–81; W. R. Telford, "The Pre-Markan Tradition in Recent Research (1980–1990)," in *The Four Gospels, 1992: Festschrift Frans Neirynck* (ed. F. van Segbroeck, C. M. Tuckett, G. van Belle, and J. Verheyden; BETL 100; 3 vols.; Leuven: Leuven University Press, 1992), 2:695–723. This study also contains an excellent bibliography (pp. 713–23).

[32] See J. Ernst, *Das Evangelium nach Markus* (RNT; Regensburg: Pustet-Verlag, 1981), 10–13; Marcus, *Mark,* 56–59.

[33] A telling criticism of redaction critics who use these methods of establishing a pre-Markan tradition is that so many who analyze the same passages come up with different Markan and pre-Markan elements. This has led many to suggest that too much Markan, Matthean, and Lukan theology has its roots in the mind of the interpreter. See, for example, M. D. Hooker, "In His Own Image?" in *What About the New Testament? Studies in Honour of Christopher Evans* (ed. M. D. Hooker and C. Hickling; London: SCM, 1975), 28–44.

[34] For a summary, down to 1985, see Telford, "The Gospel of Mark," 15–28. For studies since then, see idem, *The Theology of the Gospel of Mark* (New Testament Theology; Cambridge: Cambridge University Press, 1999), 29–163, and idem, *Mark,* 86–119, with special attention given to more literary approaches to the Gospel. Introducing his 1985 study, Telford remarks, "In evaluating the major contributions to Marcan scholarship in recent years . . . , the present reviewer was faced

studies. Some will appear as we read the Gospel of Mark. Studies of individual passages, and books and articles that attempt to trace the Markan redactional activity across the narrative as a whole, have rightly focused upon major themes in the Gospel. They include the secrecy motif, disciples, the kingdom of God, the Son of Man, the Son of God, Jewish leadership, the crowds, the function of Galilee, the significance of the crossings of the sea of Galilee, the Gentile mission, eschatology and apocalyptic (see Mark 13), discipleship, suffering, the cross, martyrdom, and the strange ending of the Gospel at 16:8 with the expression ἐφοβοῦντο γάρ ("for they were afraid"). As most redactional studies depend upon speculatively reconstructed pre-Markan tradition, it is not surprising that the conclusions reached by contemporary redactional studies of the Gospel of Mark have not met with universal acceptance among Markan scholars.[35]

There is a discernible movement from one approach to the Gospel to another. Source criticism, form criticism, and redaction criticism are all interrelated, and one leads to the other. The same could be said for more recent approaches to the Gospel of Mark. Difficulties are created by the speculative reconstruction of *the world behind the text* (sometimes called a "diachronic" analysis of the text). Recent scholarship focuses upon *the world in the text* (sometimes called a "synchronic" analysis of the text) and how it addresses *the world in front of the text*. An interest in the impact that the whole utterance of a narrative makes upon a readership is but a logical consequence of the work of the redaction critics. Redaction criticism attempts to trace the theological themes that determine the shape and message of a gospel. Newer approaches ask how a narrative's use of these themes impacts upon a readership. It is not an easy task to classify recent Markan scholarship that has turned to these newer approaches. Some of it uses the techniques developed in the study of modern narratives, tracing an implied author's manipulation of an implied reader by means of characters, plot, descriptions of place, the use of time, and the many other elements of a "good story." This approach is generally called "narrative criticism."[36] It opens the possibility of a greater focus upon the impact of the narrative upon the reader *in the text* and subsequently upon the reader *of the text*.[37]

---

with the formidable task of assessing over two hundred and fifty essays, articles and books on the Gospel, ninety percent of which were written after 1960." See also, Kealy, *Mark's Gospel*, 198–237.

[35] Particularly helpful in this regard is the study of Black, *The Disciples according to Mark*. Black looks at the redactional critical work of R. P. Meye, E. Best, and T. J. Weeden, and shows that each of these studies of the Markan disciples is limited by the recourse to assumptions outside the text itself which are not open to empirical analysis. See also C. C. Black, "The Quest of Mark the Redactor: Why Has It Been Pursued, and What Has It Taught us," *JSNT* 22 (1989): 19–39; R. H. Stein, "The Proper Methodology for Ascertaining a Markan Redaction History," in *The Composition of Mark's Gospel: Selected Studies from Novum Testamentum* (ed. D. E. Orton; Brill's Readers in Biblical Studies 3; Leiden: Brill, 1999), 34–51.

[36] For an introduction to this approach to a gospel, see F. J. Moloney, "Narrative Criticism of the Gospels," in *"A Hard Saying": The Gospel and Culture* (Collegeville: The Liturgical Press, 2001), 85–105, and for its application to the Markan narrative, see E. S. Malbon, "Narrative Criticism: How Does the Story Mean?" in *In the Company of Jesus: Characters in Mark's Gospel* (Louisville: Westminster John Knox, 2000), 1–40. Early attempts to apply narrative criticism to the Gospel of Mark are F. Kermode, *The Genesis of Secrecy: On the Interpretation of Narrative* (Cambridge: Harvard University Press, 1969); N. Petersen, *Literary Criticism for New Testament Critics* (Philadelphia: Fortress, 1978); and D. Rhoads, J. Dewey, and D. Michie, *Mark as Story: An Introduction to the Narrative of a Gospel* (2d ed.; Philadelphia: Fortress, 1999).

[37] While they cannot be regarded as methodologically identical, a sample of recent narrative-critical studies of the Gospel of Mark can be found in W. H. Kelber, *Mark's Story of Jesus* (Philadelphia:

A further development of this focus upon the reader, again adopting the terminology of contemporary literary criticism, has been called reader-response criticism. The turn toward the reader has opened the way to a number of further so-called postmodern approaches. This is something of a caricature, but one could say that an increased focus upon the reader lessens focus upon the text itself. Such readings become more subversive, finding surprising and new interpretations in a never-ending interplay of possible meanings, many of them strongly determined by the fragile and highly fragmented situation of the postmodern reader. Indeed, granted the all-determining role of the reader, the givenness of an ancient text can almost disappear, as all that matters is the reader.[38] Side by side with the growth in interest in the *literary* world which generated the text, and the ongoing impact of the Gospel as "story," has been the study of the cultural and especially the *sociopolitical* world that determined the shape of the narrative, its plot, and its characterization. Drawing upon cross-cultural studies, the Gospel of Mark is found to be rich in its portrayal of marginalized artisans, farmers, and tradesmen, a wandering charismatic preacher, an oppressive taxation system, corrupt Jewish leadership exploiting those lower on the social scale, and the presence in the nation of an unscrupulous army of occupation. As with narrative criticism, reader-response criticism, and the more postmodern readings, a sociopolitical approach to the Gospel of Mark shows that the perennial problems of the use and abuse of power, subverted by the Markan understanding of the person and message of Jesus, are still eloquently addressed in our contemporary world.[39] Far from its former situation as the Cinderella of the New Testament, the Gospel of Mark has been the subject of intense focus from the days of the source critics till our contemporary scholarly world, marked by a multiplication of interpretative methods. There is no sign of any waning of this interest.

Fortress, 1979); A. Stock, *Call to Discipleship: A Literary Study of Mark's Gospel* (GNS 1; Wilmington: Michael Glazier, 1982); B. M. F. van Iersel, *Reading Mark* (Collegeville: The Liturgical Press, 1988); M. A. Tolbert, *Sowing the Gospel: Mark's World in Literary-Historical Perspective* (Minneapolis: Fortress, 1989); J. D. Kingsbury, *Conflict in Mark: Jesus, Authority, Disciples* (Minneapolis: Fortress, 1989); D. H. Juel, *A Master of Surprise: Mark Interpreted* (Minneapolis: Fortress, 1994); *Der Erzähler des Evangeliums: Methodische Neuansätze in der Markusforschung* (ed. F. Hahn; SBS 118–119; Stuttgart: Katholisches Bibelwerk, 1985). The list is by no means exhaustive. Markan interpretation has shifted considerably from Bultmann's view that "Mark is not sufficiently master of his material to be able to venture on a systematic construction himself" (*History,* 350). It is Mark's "systematic construction" that interests these scholars.

[38] An excellent introduction to these less stable readings, as well as to a reader-response approach to the Gospel of Mark, is R. M. Fowler, *Let the Reader Understand: Reader-Response Criticism and the Gospel of Mark* (Minneapolis: Fortress, 1991). For a general introduction to the more subversive, postmodern, readings of biblical texts, see The Bible and Culture Collective, *The Postmodern Bible* (London and New Haven: Yale University Press, 1996). As a contemporary literary critic puts it: "Once you take seriously the notion that readers 'construct' (even partially) the texts that they read, then the canon (any canon) is not (or not only) the product of the inherent qualities of the text; it is also (at least partly) the product of particular choices of the arbiters of choice who create it—choices always grounded in ideological and cultural values, always enmeshed in class, race, and gender" (P. J. Rabinowitz, "Whirl without End: Audience-Oriented Criticism," in *Contemporary Literary Theory* [ed. C. D. Atkins and L. Morrow; London: Macmillan, 1989], 94).

[39] Three important and instructive sociocultural readings of the Gospel of Mark are F. Belo, *A Materialist Reading of the Gospel of Mark* (New York: Orbis, 1981); H. C. Waetjen, *A Reordering of Power: A Socio-Political Reading of Mark's Gospel* (Minneapolis: Fortress, 1989); and C. Myers, *Binding the Strong Man: A Political Reading of Mark's Story of Jesus* (Maryknoll: Orbis, 1990). More general, but useful, studies are: K. C. Hanson and D. E. Oakman, *Palestine in the Time of Jesus: Social Structures and Social Conflicts* (Minneapolis: Fortress, 1998); E. W. Stegemann and W. Stegemann,

Who, Where, and When?

Who wrote these 675 terse verses telling of Jesus' ministry, death, and burial? Where and when were they written? The Gospel itself gives no hint, although many have identified the author as the young man dressed only in a white robe who flees from Jesus' arrest in Gethsemane (14:51–52). Even if this suggestion were true, it would tell us only that the author was an eyewitness. It does not tell us his name or his role in the life of Jesus and the early church. At a later date, when the gospels were given titles, this gospel was given the title "according to Mark" (κατὰ Μάρκον).[40] The first witness to Mark as the author of this gospel comes from Papias, the bishop of Hierapolis who, in about 130 C.E., wrote a five-volume work titled *Exposition of the Oracles of the Lord.* We no longer have the works of Papias, but they are cited by the historian Eusebius of Caesarea in his *Ecclesiastical History* (about 303 C.E.). He quotes Papias as follows:

> This also the elder (John) used to say. When Mark became Peter's interpreter (ἑρμηνευτής), he wrote down accurately (ἀκριβῶς), though by no means in order (οὐ μέντοι τάξει), as much as he remembered of the words and deeds of the Lord; [*what follows is probably from Papias, and not "the elder"*] for he had neither heard the Lord nor been in his company, but subsequently joined Peter as I said. Now Peter did not intend to give a complete exposition of the Lord's ministry but delivered his instructions to meet the needs of the moment. It follows, then, that Mark was guilty of no blunder if he wrote, simply to the best of his recollections, an incomplete account (Eusebius, *Ecclesiastical History* 3.39.15).[41]

This identification of Mark as the secretary or interpreter or translator (ἑρμηνευτής is open to a number of translations) of Peter was accepted almost without question until the modern era. Possibly this ancient association of the Gospel of Mark with the figure of Peter assured its place over the early Christian centuries. As Morna Hooker remarks, "Since almost all of Mark's material is found in either Matthew or Luke, it is remarkable that the Gospel survived."[42] According to Eusebius (*Ecclesiastical History* 6.14.6), Clement of Alexandria (circa 150–215) located the association between Mark and Peter in the city of Rome.[43]

Papias's insistence upon Mark's accuracy (ἀκριβῶς), and his having written the Gospel in its entirety on the basis of Peter's account of Jesus' story, although not in order (οὐ μέντοι τάξει), flies in the face of the form critics' conclusions that the work is the result of a

---

The Jesus Movement: A Social History of Its First Century (trans. O. C. Dean Jr.; Minneapolis: Fortress, 1999).

[40] Just how late has now become the subject of a minor debate. It was widely accepted that the titles were not given to the Gospels until late in the second century. However, M. Hengel (*Studies in the Gospel of Mark* [London: SCM, 1985], 64–84) has argued that Mark's highly innovative use of εὐαγγέλιον to introduce a new literary form into Christian literature may have led to its being called εὐαγγέλιον κατὰ Μάρκον from the beginning. The titles given to Matthew, Luke, and John, at a later stage, imitated that of Mark's Gospel.

[41] Translation from Kealy, *Mark's Gospel*, 12. The explanatory parentheses are mine.

[42] M. D. Hooker, *The Gospel according to St. Mark* (BNTC; Peabody: Hendrickson, 1991), 7.

[43] Modern scholars continue to support the witness of Papias. See, for example, V. Taylor, *The Gospel according to St. Mark* (2d ed.; London: Macmillan, 1966), 26–31; W. L. Lane, *Commentary on the Gospel of Mark* (NICNT; Grand Rapids: Eerdmans, 1974), 21–23; R. P. Martin, *Mark: Evangelist and Theologian* (Exeter: Paternoster Press, 1972), 51–79; Mansfield, *"Spirit and Gospel,"* 8–10, 145–63; Hengel, *Studies in the Gospel of Mark,* 1–6.

process of editing and that the various pericopes originated in different times and places. Some may have come from the life of Jesus, and others may have been developed in the life of the early church. However, there is nothing inherently impossible in the claim that an authoritative "Mark" in an early Christian community "authored" the Gospel.[44] Mark was a very common name at the time, but the association between Peter and Mark ("my son") found in 1 Pet 5:13 quickly became attached to the tradition. Other occurrences of the name "Mark" in the New Testament were gathered around this figure, especially the "John Mark" of Acts 12:12, 25; 15:37–39, and the "Mark" of Col 4:10; Phlm 24; and 2 Tim 4:11. In the end, we cannot be sure who "Mark" was. Perhaps we should respect the author's concern to keep his name and association with either Jesus or Peter out of the account, but we have no cause not to refer to the book as the Gospel of Mark, and to its author as "Mark."[45]

Recent Markan scholarship is returning to the traditional view that the Gospel was written in Rome.[46] The association of Mark with Peter in Rome, the inelegant Greek style, the number of Latin loan words, and the author's vague knowledge of the geography of first-century Palestine incline some scholars to locate the Gospel in a Roman setting.[47] In addition, many have pointed to the Markan theology of the cross and the failure of the disciples, read as indications that the community addressed is exposed to persecution and death, and has to deal with faintheartedness, fear, and failure in the community. For many, this admirably suits the church in Rome during and immediately after the Neronic persecution (65 C.E.).[48]

---

[44] See R. Pesch, *Das Markusevangelium* (2d ed.; HTKNT 2.1–2; 2 vols.; Freiburg: Herder, 1977), 1:3–11. This would also allow for Hengel's thesis that the Gospel was attached to "Mark," whoever he might have been, from the beginning. For the form critics his "authoring" would have been more editorial than authorial. As the commentary will show, Mark may have edited sources, but he is to be regarded as a creative author in the best sense. Not only has he written a compelling narrative, but he created the gospel "form," which has given Christianity its founding narrative. This is no small achievement.

[45] For a recent detailed discussion of the evidence, devoting particular attention to the question of "John Mark," but deciding in the end that the case is "not proven," see Marcus, *Mark*, 17–24.

[46] See, for example, Ernst, *Markus*, 21–22; Pesch, *Markusevangelium*, 1:112–14; J. Gnilka, *Das Evangelium nach Markus* (5th ed.; EKKNT 2.1–2; 2 vols.; Zurich/Neukirchen/Vluyn: Benziger Verlag/Neukirchener Verlag, 1998–1999), 1:34–35; R. E. Brown and J. P. Meier, *Antioch and Rome: New Testament Cradles of Catholic Christianity* (New York: Paulist Press, 1983), 191–97; R. A. Guelich, *Mark 1–8:26* (WBC 34A; Dallas: Word Books, 1989), xxix–xxxi; J. Donahue, "Windows and Mirrors: The Setting of Mark's Gospel," *CBQ* 57 (1995): 1–26; Hengel, *Studies in the Gospel of Mark*, 1–30; D. Senior, " 'With Swords and Clubs . . .'—The Setting of Mark's Community and His Critique of Abusive Power," *BTB* 17 (1987): 10–20. C. C. Black (*Mark: Images of an Apostolic Interpreter* [Studies on Personalities of the New Testament; Columbia: University of South Carolina, 1994], 238) remarks that a Roman origin for the Gospel of Mark "if not proven, is, at least, not improbable." See also his "Was Mark a Roman Gospel?" *ExpTim* 105 (1993–1994): 36–40. For a survey of contemporary opinion on the place of origin for the Gospel of Mark, see J. Donahue, "The Quest for the Community of Mark's Gospel," in *The Four Gospels, 1992: Festschrift Frans Neirynck* (ed. F. van Segbroeck, C. M. Tucker, G. van Belle, and J. Verheyden; BETL 100; 3 vols.; Leuven: Leuven University Press, 1992), 2:819–34. Recent popular studies of Mark are now adopting this position. See P. J. Flanagan, *The Gospel of Mark Made Easy* (New York: Paulist Press, 1997); P. J. Cunningham, *Mark: The Good News Preached to the Romans* (New York: Paulist Press, 1998).

[47] See, for example, Taylor, *St. Mark*, 44–54; Martin, *Mark*, 63–65.

[48] See, for example, Martin, *Mark*, 61–70. For a summary of the case for the contemporary interest in Rome as the Gospel's place of origin, and its rejection, see Marcus, *Mark*, 30–33.

Redaction critics, however, have focused upon the use of Galilee in the narrative. The Gospel begins in Galilee, where Jesus exercises his ministry. As he moves to Jerusalem the disciples become increasingly timid, and Jesus goes alone to the cross as the disciples flee. Yet the Gospel ends with the command from the young man in the tomb, recalling Jesus' promise of 14:28: he is going before them into Galilee (16:7). This message is not delivered (16:8), and thus the Markan community waits in Galilee, experiencing the absence of the Lord, waiting for his promised return. According to this reading, the Gospel was written either during or shortly after the destruction of Jerusalem in 70 C.E., somewhere in Galilee.[49] The social science critics locate the Gospel in a setting where the exploitation and suffering of the Jesus story is found in the life experience of the original readers of the Gospel. For example, Waetjen locates it somewhere in Syria, also early in the 70s of the first Christian century,[50] while Myers suggests that life in first-century Palestine best responds to the Markan narrative.[51]

Three elements must be taken into account and held together in these discussions.[52] In the first place, the syntax and the loanwords that indicate a Roman setting must be explained.[53] Second, there is a concern in the Gospel of Mark for the Gentile mission. Jesus heals a demoniac in Gentile territory and tells him to go to his hometown to announce what the Lord has done (see 5:1–20). After a bitter encounter with Israel (7:1–23) Jesus journeys outside the borders of Israel to the region of Tyre and Sidon, again to bring healing, this time to a Syrophoenician woman (7:24–30). His passage from the region of Tyre and Sidon back to the eastern side of the lake deliberately keeps him in Gentile lands (see 7:31). There he again heals a Gentile, and for the first time in the narrative his actions are recognized by others—Gentiles—as the work of the expected Messiah (7:31–37). He immediately nourishes Gentiles, who "have come a long way" (8:1–10). As he defuses anxiety about the end of time, in the midst of many false signs, he tells disciples that "the gospel must first be preached to all the nations" (13:10). The end will come, however, and at that time the Son of Man "will send out the angels and gather his elect from the four winds, from the ends of the earth to the ends of heaven" (13:27). At his death the veil that "hid" the Holy of Holies from the rest of the world is rent asunder (15:37–38) and a Roman centurion confesses that Jesus was the Son of God.[54]

Finally, although not all would agree, the discourse in Mark 13 presupposes that Jerusalem has fallen.[55] Many details *look back* to that dramatic experience for both Israel and the

---

[49] Although differing in their approach to this issue, Marxsen (*Mark the Evangelist,* 54–116), N. Perrin ("Towards an Interpretation of the Gospel of Mark," in *Christology and a Modern Pilgrimage* [ed. H. D. Betz; Claremont: Society of Biblical Literature, 1971], 1–78), T. J. Weeden (*Mark: Traditions in Conflict* [Philadelphia: Fortress, 1971]), and H. C. Kee (*Community of the New Age: Studies in Mark's Gospel* [Philadelphia: Westminster, 1977]) have adopted this position.

[50] Waetjen, *A Reordering of Power,* 1–26.

[51] Myers, *Binding the Strong Man,* 39–87.

[52] Some reader-oriented studies neglect these issues, but they must be raised. See, for example, van Iersel (*Reading Mark,* 15): "The fact that the author time and time again warns his audience so seriously of the danger of persecutions says much about their situation but little or nothing about the time when the book was written." As one element among several, it may be a very helpful indicator of when the book was written.

[53] See J. Marcus, "The Jewish War and the *Sitz im Leben* of Mark," *JBL* 111 (1992): 441–46.

[54] See Marcus, "The Jewish War," 453–54; Pesch, *Markusevangelium,* 1:10–11.

[55] See Marcus, "The Jewish War," 446–48. As Pesch (*Markusevangelium,* 1:14) remarks: "Thus the dating of the Gospel of Mark depends upon the interpretation of Mark 13." (Here and throughout I have translated into English quotations from German and French works.) Myers (*Binding the*

early Christian church: false prophets (see 13:5–6; 21–22), wars and rumors of wars (see 13:7, 14–20), events that took place at the fall of the temple (13:14). Mark 13 is "rather like a window which allows a close view of Markan circumstances."[56] The Gospel of Mark must have reached its final shape in the period just after 70 C.E., as the horror and significance of the destruction of Jerusalem and its temple made its impact upon the Markan community.[57]

These three elements leave us with some hard facts, which can, in turn, lead to a suggestion (which nevertheless remains speculative) about the time and the place of the Gospel of Mark. I would regard the following details as hard facts:

1. The author is familiar with the Roman world, its language, and its mode of government.

2. The author and the community for whom he was writing were concerned about the mission to the Gentiles.

3. The community is exposed to suffering and persecution, and its members are probably discouraged by the failure of some to commit themselves, unto death, to the gospel of Jesus Christ.[58]

4. The Gospel was written shortly after the fall of Jerusalem in 70 C.E.

The traditional location of Rome has much to offer, but the background of the fall of Jerusalem to Mark 13 suggests a location closer to these events. Were the Roman Christians in need of severe warnings not to listen to false prophets, rising up in the midst of the postwar chaos to declare that the end time had come (see 13:5–6, 21–22)? Was it necessary to tell Roman Christians, who lived at the center of the known world, that they must calm their apocalyptic fever because before the final coming of the Son of Man the gospel must be preached to all the nations (see 13:10)? How real were *all* the threats of 13:11: "They will deliver you up to councils; and you will be beaten in synagogues; and you will stand before governors and kings for my sake" (13:9)?[59] The Gospel of Mark never creates the impression that the storyteller and the community receiving the Gospel had a special interest in

---

Strong Man, 39–87) dates the Gospel between 68–70. He determines this date through a number of sociocultural reflections that depend, on the one hand, on speculations about the situation of Palestine during those turbulent years, and on the other, through a reconstruction of ideological and social strategies that appear to have been established with one eye on the Gospel of Mark and the other on the relevance of the Gospel for the post-Reagan era in the United States. For an alternative reading of the pre-70 period in Palestine, see J. McLaren, *Turbulent Times? Josephus and Scholarship on Judea in the First Century C.E.* (JSPSup 29; Sheffield: Sheffield Academic Press, 1998). As Myers confesses: "This discussion has been intended to make the notion of socio-symbolic codes, so crucial to a political understanding of the Gospel, more meaningful to the reader" (p. 72). I suspect that the evangelist's agenda may be playing second fiddle to Myers's sociopolitical commitment.

[56] W. Kelber, *The Kingdom in Mark: A New Place and a New Time* (Philadelphia: Fortress, 1974), 110.

[57] Myers's claim for a pre-70 dating, in his commentary on Mark 13 (see *Binding the Strong Man,* 324–53), is not supported by a satisfactory explanation of such crucial texts as 13:14 ("the desolating sacrilege where it ought not to be"). Interestingly, Myers's radical reading of Mark turns at this point to the conservative work of J. A. T. Robinson (*Redating the New Testament* [London: SCM, 1976], 16) to speak vaguely of the siege of Jerusalem (see p. 335). On the importance of 13:14, see D. Lührmann, *Das Markusevangelium* (HNT 3; Tübingen: J. C. B. Mohr [Paul Siebeck], 1987), 5–6, and the full-scale study of W. A. Such, *The Abomination of Desolation in the Gospel of Mark: Its Historical Reference in Mark 13:14 and Its Impact in the Gospel* (Lanham: University Press of America, 1999).

[58] See Marcus, *Mark,* 28–29.

[59] Ernst (*Markus,* 21–22) hesitatingly opts for Rome as the place of its origin, but on pp. 22–23 correctly points to Mark 13 as the key to the issue of when it was written, some time shortly after 70. The time (after the destruction of Jerusalem) and the place (Rome?) need to be held together.

Rome or the Romans. Roman characters, even in the passion narrative, where they could have been drawn more deeply into the story, remain peripheral. They are there only when they have to be there. Matters Roman, whether they be Latin loanwords or Roman characters, remain extrinsic to the Markan story. Without the long-standing *tradition* concerning the Roman origins of the Gospel of Mark, there is little that would force a reader to think that this is a gospel concerned with "matters Roman."[60]

I find it impossible to determine an exact location, region, or city where the Gospel might have first seen the light of day. I can only speculate and suggest a possible scenario. The might of Rome was felt in many parts of the Mediterranean world, and powerfully so in the recalcitrant states of Syria and Palestine. I suspect that the traditional location of the birth of Mark in the city of Rome leaves too many questions unresolved. Thus I would agree with Morna Hooker: "All we can say with certainty, therefore, is that the gospel was composed somewhere in the Roman Empire—a conclusion that scarcely narrows the field at all!"[61] I would, however, "narrow the field" to the extent that the place in the Roman Empire that produced the Gospel of Mark must have been reasonably close to Jerusalem. Reports of "wars and rumors of wars" (see 13:7) are reaching the ears of the Markan Christians. They know what the author means when he writes of "the desolating sacrilege set up where he ought not to be" (v. 14). They are wondering: is this the moment for the return of the Son of Man (vv. 7, 10, 13)? They are told: not yet, but that day will come. Be ready, and watch (vv. 24–37). For these reasons, I would hypothesize that the Markan community was somewhere in a broad area that might be called "southern Syria."[62] The dating of the Gospel also plays a part in determining its likely place of origin. A date after 70 C.E. but probably before 75 C.E. is called for.[63] The latter date presupposes that the Gospel of Mark was available to both Matthew and Luke, who wrote some time between 80 and 90 C.E. Given the almost thirty years since the death of Jesus, wherever the precise location, these early Christians were involved in a mission to the Gentiles. A number of places in the Gospel provide evidence of this mission (see, for example, 5:1–20; 7:24–8:10; 13:10). This aspect of the Markan narrative may tip the balance in favor of southern Syria,[64] but we cannot be sure of the ethnic mix of Palestine in the 70s of the first Christian century. Northern Palestine may also have provided a missionary setting, but it makes Mark's vagueness about Palestinian geography difficult to explain.[65]

---

[60] Gnilka (*Markus*, 1:34) suggests that the Gospel was written in Rome, but is puzzled by this issue. He resolves it by claiming that Mark was written in Rome, but not for the Roman Christians.

[61] Hooker, *St. Mark*, 8. See also Lührmann (*Markusevangelium*, 7): "Mark and his reader may have lived anywhere in a region close to or distant from Palestine, perhaps in Syria. However, this cannot be proved. It may have been anywhere from the Mediterranean as far into the East as the Iran and Iraq of today."

[62] See also Marcus, *Mark*, 33–37. See also, R. I. Rohrbach, "The Social Location of the Markan Audience," *BTB* 23 (1993): 114–27.

[63] See also Marcus (*Mark*, 37–39), who suggests a time not earlier than 69 C.E. and not later than 74 C.E.

[64] Marcus ("The Jewish War," 460–62) suggests "one of the Hellenistic cities" (perhaps even Pella) on the basis of the Gentile mission. As he says elsewhere, "A provenance close to Palestine, but not in it, is thus an attractive possibility" (idem, *The Mystery of the Kingdom of God* [SBLDS 90; Atlanta: Scholars Press, 1986], 10). On literary grounds (reader-response), M. A. Beavis, *Mark's Audience: The Literary and Social Setting of Mark 4:11–12* (JSNTSup 33; Sheffield: Sheffield Academic Press, 1989) suggests a Greco-Roman missionary context for the Markan community. See especially pp. 157–76.

[65] See Marcus, *The Mystery*, 10.

The Plot of the Gospel of Mark

Unlike the readers of most "stories," the original Christian readers and hearers of the Gospel of Mark knew the ending: Jesus was crucified and, they believed, raised from the dead. The following suggested plot of the Gospel of Mark traces the larger blocks of material and the smaller episodes that unfold within them according to a logic that leads inevitably toward the cross. The reader is led further into a story whose ending is known, yet is surprised along the way—and at the end. The plot as a whole is shot through with hints that look forward to the end of the story. The Gospel of Mark is unique among the gospels and unlike most other narratives in that the crises which emerge during its course are not resolved through a *dénouement* at the end of the story (Mark 16:1–8). Much is resolved, but a further crisis emerges that cannot be resolved by the story itself.[66] If I might anticipate one of the major conclusions of this commentary, this suggests that it might be resolved in the lives of the people reading the story. We should recall that in a good story the reader is told enough to be made curious without ever being given all the answers. Narrative texts keep promising the great prize of understanding—later.[67] The "later" of the Gospel of Mark, I will suggest, is the "now" of the Christian reader.

These principles provide us with a tool for understanding the emerging plot of a narrative. If we are to follow the strategies of the author as the plot unfolds, we must focus our attention upon elements in the narrative indicating major turning points in the story. These so-called textual markers indicate to the reader that the author is "up to something." Initially one notices four significant turning points in the story. The Gospel begins (1:1), Jesus begins his ministry in Galilee (1:14–15), he announces his journey to Jerusalem and his forthcoming death and resurrection for the first time (8:31), and women discover an empty tomb (16:1–4). We have domesticated the gospel story to such an extent that we are not sufficiently aware of the dramatic nature of these turning points. As has been obvious since the days of Wrede, Schweitzer, and Schmidt, this "framework" was devised by the evangelist Mark, and its appearance in the first early Christian "gospel" was intentionally a theological statement. *Whatever the first readers knew of the life-story of Jesus of Nazareth was subverted by the Markan story. They were not familiar with this plot: Jesus' presence in Galilee, his single journey to Jerusalem to be rejected, tried, and crucified, the resurrection, and the surprising silence of the women.* It saw the light of day for the first time when Mark invented it. It is this radical newness of the Markan story which must be kept in mind.[68] It is

---

[66] A strong case for the influence of Greco-Roman tragedies upon the Markan plot has been argued by G. Bilezikian, *The Liberated Gospel: A Comparison between the Gospel of Mark and Greek Tragedy* (Grand Rapids: Baker, 1977), and B. Standaert, *L'Evangile selon Marc: Composition et genre littéraire* (Brugge: Sint-Andriesabdij, 1978). For a summary, see M. A. Beavis, *Mark's Audience,* 31–35. See also the survey of studies of Mark's genre, finally suggesting that the Gospel may have been written as a dramatic reading for a Christian liturgy, in Marcus, *Mark,* 64–69.

[67] See S. Rimmon-Kenan, *Narrative Fiction: Contemporary Poetics* (New Accents; London: Methuen, 1983), 125.

[68] See the important essay by E. Schweizer, "Mark's Theological Achievement," in *The Interpretation of Mark* (ed. W. Telford; IRT 7; Philadelphia: Fortress, 1985), 42–63. W. H. Kelber (*The Oral and Written Gospel: The Hermeneutics of Speaking and Writing in the Synoptic Tradition, Mark, Paul, and Q* [Philadelphia: Fortress, 1983]) pushes this to the limit. He rightly argues that Mark took a vivacious and living oral tradition and created something quite different with his "writing" (see pp. 44–139). But he argues that the movement from oral tradition to written gospel created a writ-

an original way of telling the story of Jesus, and its author must be credited with an equally original rationale for plotting the story in this way.

On the basis of the textual markers just mentioned, one can begin to trace the author's literary design:[69]

1. Mark 1:1–13 serves as a prologue, providing the reader with a great deal of information about God's beloved Son.

2. Through Mark 1:14–8:30 the words and deeds of Jesus' ministry increasingly force the question: who is this man (see 1:27, 45; 2:12; 3:22; 4:41; 5:20; 6:2–3, 48–50; 7:37)? Some accept him, some are indifferent, and many oppose him, but the question behind the story is: can he be the Messiah? In 8:29 Peter, in the name of the disciples, resolves the problem by confessing: "You are the Messiah." The guessing has come to an end. This section of the Gospel can be framed as a question: "Who is Jesus?" It closes with an initial response to the question with Jesus' warning Peter not to tell anyone of his being the expected Messiah (8:30). This may not be the whole truth about Jesus.

3. Mark 8:31–15:47 tells of Jesus' journey to Jerusalem and his crucifixion in that city. One can sense that this part of the story forms a "second half" of Mark's literary and theological presentation of the story of Jesus. Mark 1:14–8:30 made it clear that Jesus is the Messiah (8:29), but suggested that this designation may not be adequate by itself (8:30). The second half of the story shows that Jesus is the Messiah who will be revealed as Son of God on the cross, the suffering and vindicated Son of Man (8:31; 9:31; 10:32–33; 13:26; 14:61–62). In 15:39 a Roman centurion confesses: "Truly this man was God's Son!" The suffering Christ is truly the Son of God. The mystery has come to an end. Mark 8:31–15:57 can be called "The suffering and vindicated Son of Man: Christ and Son of God."

4. Many questions raised by the story remain unresolved. The disciples have fled (see 14:50) and Jesus has cried out: "My God, my God, why have you forsaken me?" (15:34). Jesus' question is resolved in the concluding story of women visiting an empty tomb. In 16:1–8 the reader learns that God has not forsaken his Son. He has been raised (see 16:6). But the problem of the failing disciples is yet to be resolved. They are to go into Galilee, there they will see him (v. 7). The women, frightened by all that they have seen and heard, flee and say nothing to anyone (v. 8).

The identification of these major sections in the narrative rests upon the obvious textual markers at 1:1, 1:14–15, 8:31, and 16:1–4.[70] Other markers indicate that the two larger blocks of material, 1:14–8:30 and 8:31–15:47, can be further subdivided. The first half of the Gospel establishes relationships as well as raises questions concerning the person of Jesus. The Gospel of Mark is not only about Jesus, Christ and Son of God (see 1:1, 11). It is

---

ten text which was a contradiction of what went before. The thesis is overstated, but does underscore the radical newness of the Gospel of Mark. For a sympathetic use of Kelber's insights, see Myers, *Binding the Strong Man*, 91–109. For a critique, see E. S. Malbon, "Text and Contexts: Interpreting the Disciples in Mark," *Sem* 62 (1993): 81–102. This essay is now available in Malbon, *In the Company of Jesus*, 100–30.

[69] For a similar focus on "textual markers" (which he calls "text signals"), see van Iersel, *Reading Mark*, 18–30. Van Iersel follows the earlier work of Standaert (*L'Evangile selon Marc: Composition et genre littéraire*), which uses textual markers to trace a chiastic structure across the Gospel of Mark and within its single sections. See also A. Stock, *Call to Discipleship*, 47–53.

[70] Beavis (*Mark's Audience*, 163–65; see also 126–29) ignores the textual markers to produce a structure based upon an interplay between alternating blocks of "narrative" and "teaching" material that would have appealed to a Greco-Roman readership.

equally about the challenge of "following" a suffering Son of Man to Jerusalem—and beyond, as he promises resurrection and life to those who lose their lives for his sake (see 8:38–9:1). It is as much about how others, especially the disciples, respond to Jesus as it is about Jesus himself. There are indications that the first half of the Gospel has been shaped as three units, each one focusing upon a response to Jesus.[71]

On three occasions across 1:14–8:30 the narrator makes a general statement (called a "summary") about Jesus' ministry that introduces a series of events illustrating that activity (see 1:14–15; 3:7–12; 6:6a). While the Gospel of Mark contains a number of such summaries of Jesus' ministry (see, for example, 1:39, 45b; 4:33–34; 6:53–56; 9:30–31; 10:1),[72] these three are unique in that each is immediately followed by material that deals with disciples and discipleship (1:16–20; 3:13–19; 6:6b–13). Further episodes follow until, serving as a climax, three different audiences respond to the words and deeds of Jesus. Two of the responses are negative: 3:6 (the Pharisees and the Herodians) and 6:1–6a (people from "his own country"). The third is a misunderstanding: 8:29 (Peter, responding on behalf of the disciples). Each of the three summaries begins a narrative block. Each leads directly into passages that deal with disciples, and each of the three responses concludes that section of the story. These three sections unfold as follows:

1. In 1:14–15 we read a summary of the ministry of Jesus: "Now after John was arrested, Jesus came to Galilee proclaiming the good news of God and saying, 'The time is fulfilled and the kingdom of God has come near; repent and believe in the good news.'" This summary is immediately followed by the account of the vocation of the first disciples (1:16–20). Jesus then exercises his ministry in Galilee, chiefly at Capernaum (1:21–3:6), until representatives of the Jewish people, the political leaders and the religious authorities, respond to him: "The Pharisees went out and immediately conspired with the Herodians against him, how to destroy him" (3:6). This narrative unit (1:14–3:6) can be entitled: *Jesus and the Jews*.[73]

2. In 3:7–12 we find a lengthy general statement about Jesus' Galilean ministry. It concludes with the following summary: "He had cured many so that all who had diseases pressed upon him to touch him. Whenever the unclean spirits saw him, they fell down before him and shouted, 'You are the Son of God!' But he sternly ordered them not to make him known" (3:10–12). This summary leads into the account of Jesus' institution of the twelve (3:13–19). But Jesus' ministry meets opposition from his family and from Israel (3:20–30). He institutes new principles for belonging to his family (3:31–35) and teaches through parables (4:1–34) and a stunning series of miracles (4:35–5:43). When he returns to his home-

---

[71] For this proposal, which many have followed, see Schweizer, "Mark's Theological Achievement," 46–54. For a more detailed analysis, resulting in the overall structure followed by this study, see A. George and P. Grelot, eds., *Introduction à la Bible*, tome 3, *Nouveau Testament* (7 vols.; Paris: Desclée, 1976–1986), 2:48–51.

[72] The study of the summaries has played an important part in recent Markan scholarship. See, for example, C. W. Hedrick, "The Role of 'Summary Statements' in the Composition of the Gospel of Mark: A Dialog with Karl Schmidt and Norman Perrin," *NovT* 26 (1984): 289–311 (now available in *The Composition of Mark's Gospel: Selected Studies from* Novum Testamentum [ed. D. E. Orton; Brill's Readers in Biblical Studies 3; Leiden: Brill, 1999], 121–43). See also E. Best, *The Temptation and the Passion: The Markan Soteriology* (2d ed.; SNTSMS 2; Cambridge: Cambridge University Press, 1990), 63–102. Redactional studies of Mark have concentrated on these "summaries" because here, claim the redaction critics, Mark's hand is most obvious.

[73] Care must be taken with the use of the expression "the Jews." For Mark, the first part of his story of Jesus' ministry in Galilee is entirely focused upon a Jewish region and the Jewish leadership. This will be broadened in 5:1–21 and also in later episodes (see 7:24–8:10). It is in this sense that the expression "the Jews" is used.

town, his own people reject him: " 'Is not this the carpenter, the son of Mary and brother of James and Joses and Judas and Simon, and are not his sisters here with us?' And they took offense at him" (6:3). Jesus was "amazed at their unbelief" (6:6a). This narrative unit (3:7–6:6a) can be entitled: *Jesus and his own.*

3. Following Jesus' rejection in his hometown, we find another brief general summary about his ministry in Galilee: "Then he went about among the villages teaching" (6:6b). Jesus' sending out the Twelve on a mission that parallels his own follows immediately (6:6b–13). The narrative is now marked by increasing hostility between Jesus and the Jews (see 7:1–23), and a deeper involvement of his disciples, his new family, with his ministry (see 6:7–13, 30–44; 8:1–10). It draws to a close as the question that has been lurking behind the narrative from 1:14 is broached by Jesus himself: "Who do people say that I am?" (8:27) . . . "Who do you say that I am" (v. 28). Peter responds: "You are the Messiah" (v. 29). The reader, informed by the narrator at 1:1, has known from the outset that Jesus is the Messiah. However, the characters in the story, and especially the disciples, have had to stumble to this point on the basis of Jesus' words and actions. The question "Who is Jesus?" has been answered. There is a sense in which Peter is correct, but Jesus' response to the disciples ("them") sounds a warning bell and opens the door to the second part of the Gospel: "He charged them to tell no one about him" (8:30). This narrative unit (6:6b–8:30) can be entitled: *Jesus and the disciples.*

The second half of the Gospel (8:31–15:47) is provocatively introduced by Jesus' commanding his disciples to silence in 8:30 and predicting his future death and resurrection in Jerusalem in 8:31. Textual markers across 8:31–15:47 point to a further threefold articulation of the suffering and finally vindicated Son of Man, the Messiah and Son of God. There are obvious changes of place, characters, and situations across this second half of the story.

1. Mark 8:31–10:52 reports Jesus' journey to Jerusalem (8:22–52), largely focused upon Jesus' teaching of his oncoming death and resurrection (8:31; 9:31; 10:32–33) and his instruction of increasingly recalcitrant disciples. In this section *Jesus and the disciples journey to Jerusalem.*

2. He enters Jerusalem (11:1–11), brings all temple practice to an end (11:12–24), encounters and silences Israel's religious authorities (11:27–12:44), and prophesies the end of the Holy City and the world (13:1–37). This description of Jesus' ministry in Jerusalem and its temple can be entitled: *Endings in Jerusalem.*

3. The ministry is over as Jesus accepts his passion and death (14:1–15:47). The classical description of these episodes retains its cogency: *The Passion of Jesus.*

But there is more to the architecture of the Markan narrative. The evangelist designed the first half of his gospel asking the question, "Who is Jesus?" The second half responds: "the suffering and vindicated Son of Man, the Christ and Son of God." However, these two "halves" of the plot overlap. Narrative units are not separated by brick walls. One flows into the other, looks back to issues already mentioned, and hints at themes yet to come.[74] Peter's confession of faith in Mark 8:29 might mark the closure of "The Mystery of the

---

[74] For extensive consideration of this phenomenon in the Gospel of Mark, see J. Dewey, "Mark as Interwoven Tapestry: Forecasts and Echoes for a Listening Audience," *CBQ* 53 (1991): 225–36; E. S. Malbon, "Echoes and Foreshadowings in Mark 4–8: Reading and Rereading," *JBL* 112 (1993): 211–30. S. Kuthirakkattel (*The Beginning of Jesus' Ministry according to Mark's Gospel (1,14–3,6): A Redaction Critical Study* [AnBib 123; Rome: Biblical Institute Press, 1990]) offers detailed support for the structure adopted above (see pp. 26–60). However, there is little allowance for "echoing and foreshadowing" in his analysis.

Messiah," but a theme of "blindness" has emerged in 8:22–26 in the strange story of a blind man at Bethsaida who has his sight restored in stages. This theme will be resumed in 10:46–52 where a further story of a man coming to sight is reported: the story of blind Bartimaeus. Between these two stories of the miraculous cure of blind men, Jesus speaks of the upcoming death and resurrection of the Son of Man (see 8:31; 9:31; 10:32–35), an issue that has also lurked behind the events reported in 1:14–8:30 (see 3:6; 7:14–29; 8:11–15). Surrounding the passion predictions, Jesus instructs his increasingly obtuse disciples, who will not or cannot understand what it means to follow him (see 8:32–33; 9:33–37; 10:36–45). An earlier accusation of blindness also comes into play. After the second multiplication of the loaves and fishes (8:1–10) Jesus asks his dull disciples: "Do you not yet perceive or understand? Are your hearts hardened? *Having eyes do you not see,* and having ears do you not hear?" (8:18).[75] These few examples of the overlapping themes of Jesus' destiny and the failure of the disciples—equally significant textual markers for the reader—although not as important *structurally* as 1:1, 1:14–15, 8:31, 11:1–11; 14:1–2, and 16:1–4—are further indications of Mark's artistic skill. The following reading of the Gospel will highlight the regular appearance of these simple but effective literary techniques.

The Literary Shape of the Gospel of Mark

We are now in a position to suggest an overall literary shape for the Gospel of Mark. This structure, based upon the above considerations of the plot of the narrative, will determine the basis of the following interpretation. It will also allow us to see, before we begin our detailed reading, the guiding hand of a good, although uncomplicated storyteller, leading readers who know the ending of the story through a new telling of the story that transforms that well-known ending. Mark has faced a problem stated some twenty years before the Gospel appeared: "For Jews demand signs and Greeks seek wisdom, but we preach Christ crucified, a stumbling block to Jews and folly to Gentiles, but to those who are called, both Jews and Greeks, Christ the power of God and the wisdom of God. For the foolishness of God is wiser than human wisdom, and the weakness of God is stronger than any human strength" (1 Cor 1:22–25). Mark attempts to solve the scandal of the cross by means of a story which begins as "the good news" that Jesus is the Christ, the Son of God (1:1, 11), and ends with a scream from a cross and an agonizing death, an empty tomb, and an Easter message that is not delivered (15:33–16:8).

Many object to attempts to find "divisions" and "sections" in the Gospel of Mark. One of our best commentators, Morna Hooker, remarks as she makes her own first division at 3:7: "Most commentators make a major break at this point, but such divisions are largely arbitrary. There are plenty of links with previous sections."[76] There are certainly links with

---

[75] See Myers, *Binding the Strong Man,* 110–11. For a comprehensive study of the two "halves" of the Gospel, showing that the break comes between 8:30 and 8:31, see Q. Quesnell, *The Mind of Mark: Interpretation and Method through the Exegesis of Mark 6,52* (AnBib 38; Rome: Pontifical Biblical Institute, 1969), 126–76. R. E. Watts (*Isaiah's New Exodus and Mark* [WUNT 2. Reihe 88; Tübingen: J. C. B. Mohr (Paul Siebeck), 1997], 124–32) also suggests that 8:22–26 serves as a "hinge" in a section he identifies as 8:22/27–10:45/11:1, on the basis of its parallels with the new exodus theme of a journey.

[76] Hooker, *St. Mark,* 109. Similar remarks recur throughout her commentary. Dennis Nineham is even more skeptical: "Scholars are looking for something that is not there and attributing

what went before, and there are also pointers to what is yet to come.[77] But that is one of the many skills of a good storyteller. Nothing is compartmentalized, but a steady and carefully articulated argument unfolds in story form as follows:[78]

1. Prologue: The beginning (1:1–13)

2. Who is Jesus? (1:14–8:30)
   (a) Jesus and the Jews (1:14–3:6)
   (b) Jesus and his own (3:7–6:6a)
   (c) Jesus and the disciples (6:6b–8:30)

3. The suffering and vindicated Son of Man: Christ and Son of God (8:31–15:47)
   (a) On the way from blindness to sight (8:31–10:52)
   (b) The symbolic end of Israel and the world (11:1–13:37)
   (c) The crucifixion of the Son of Man, the Christ and Son of God (14:1–15:47)

4. Epilogue: A new beginning (16:1–8)

At several places in the Gospel the logic of movement from one pericope to the next is somewhat hard to follow—evidence that pre-Markan sources have been put together in a way that leaves an uneven final product. My reading of the Gospel of Mark will note these difficulties, and even some of the attempts to resolve them, but will also involve two further principles. First, whoever was responsible for the final form of the Gospel (and I will call him "Mark") attempted to write a coherent story. Second, every reader strives "even if unconsciously, to fit everything together in a consistent pattern."[79] I will trace literary and theological connections across the Gospel that may be judged as the striving of this reader to impose his *own* consistent pattern. However, it is respect and admiration for a

---

to the Evangelist a higher degree of self-conscious purpose that he in fact possessed"; *The Gospel of St. Mark* (PNTC; Harmondsworth: Penguin Books, 1963), 29. For a survey of the multiplicity of conflicting opinions on the structure of the Gospel, see Dewey, "Mark as Interwoven Tapestry," 221–25.

[77] The number and variety of "structures" proposed for the Gospel of Mark warn against rigid division into self-contained units. For a helpful survey, see H. Baarlink, *Anfängliches Evangelium: Ein Beitrag zur näheren Bestimmung der theologischen Motive im Markusevangelium* (Kampen: Kok, 1977), 73–83. For a useful, but overcomplicated, attempt to show the interplay of themes across the two halves of the Gospel, see Myers, *Binding the Strong Man*, 111–17.

[78] There is widespread agreement that the scene at Caesarea Philippi (8:27–30) is something of a watershed at the center of the narrative, and that this event divides the Gospel into two even halves. Many, however, influenced by the "inclusion" between 8:22–26 and 10:46–52 (two cures of blind men), end the first half of the Gospel at 8:21. See, for example, Marcus, *Mark*, 63–64. The above literary shape understands 1:1–13 as a prologue (widely accepted) and 16:1–8 as a conclusion, reading 16:7, "there you will see him as he said" (see 14:28), as a resumption of the theme of "beginning" from the prologue (see 1:1). See also Bilezikian, *Liberated Gospel*, 131–34, and Beavis, *Mark's Audience*, 128–29. Standaert (*Marc*, 82–108), followed by Stock *(Call to Discipleship)* and van Iersel *(Mark)*, reads 1:1 as a title, 1:2–13 as a prologue, and 15:42–16:8 as a matching epilogue. Besides the literary features that Bilezikian, Standaert, and Beavis have highlighted (influenced by Greco-Roman drama), theological considerations have informed my analysis. Baarlink (*Anfängliches Evangelium*, 83–107) has developed a literary structure similar at many points to the one proposed, but devoting more attention to how one section leads to another. He denies that 16:1–8 is an epilogue (p. 107), as it is part of a fully integrated message. I agree, but suggest that this integration is its theological relationship with 1:1–13. In this sense, 16:1–8 is an epilogue that takes the reader back to the prologue.

[79] W. Iser, *The Implied Reader: Patterns of Communication in Prose Fiction from Bunyan to Beckett* (Baltimore: Johns Hopkins University Press, 1978), 283.

"responsible Mark" that inspires this striving.[80] "Every element in the story is there for a reason, which we will discover only by combing back and forth through the text until it yields its own narrative coherence."[81]

A Theology of Jesus and His Followers

The story of Jesus, as it is told throughout the Gospel of Mark, is a story of human failure: the apparent failure of Jesus, the failure of the disciples, and the failure of Israel. But it closes with a loud, clear message; in his journey away from the absolutes of a human success story, Jesus of Nazareth has led the way into the only enduring success story: resurrection. The Christology of the Gospel of Mark is clear: Jesus, the Son, wins through to life by his willingness to lay himself open to the ways of God, no matter how much these ways may question the absolutes of history and culture. In his acceptance of God's will, through death on the cross, Jesus is Messiah and Son of God. The Roman centurion admits this as he gazes upon the crucified Jesus (see 15:39).

Much of this gospel's story is about Jesus' attempts to draw other people into a following of this way—a loss of self in the cross, a service and a receptivity that produces life (see 8:22–10:52). What of these disciples? What of the women? The disciples, whose following of Jesus had been marked by fear once Jesus set his face toward Jerusalem (see 9:30–32; 10:32; 14:51–52) has ended in flight: "And they all forsook him and fled" (14:50). It appears, however, that this will be resolved as the women are commanded to take the Easter message to the failed disciples: "But go, tell his disciples and Peter that he is going before you to Galilee; there you will see him, as he told you" (16:7). But the last word belongs to the storyteller: "And they went out and fled from the tomb; for trembling and astonishment had come upon them and they said nothing to anyone, for they were afraid" (16:8).

As we look back from our comfortable position of many centuries of Christian life and practice, it appears extraordinary that the women responded with terror, flight, and silence. This, we might claim, is a most unsatisfactory conclusion to a gospel that claims that Jesus is the Christ, the Son of God (see 1:1, 11; 9:7; 15:39). From our knowledge of the gospel tradition as a whole, we recall that Matthew, Luke, and John have the women report the events of the empty tomb, and the disciples, seeing the risen Lord, are restored to discipleship (see Matt 28:5–10, 16–20; Luke 24:8–12, 36–49; John 20:17–29). The Pauline record of these events is similar (see 1 Cor 15:3–8). None of this is found in the Gospel of Mark. At points the Matthean and Lukan narratives, although *written* after the Gospel of Mark, are probably closer to what actually took place: the account of the women's report to the disciples is one such instance (see also John 20:2).[82] It is the Markan theological agenda that has created the startling silence of the women, not the events surrounding "the third day."[83] Although later scribes added more comfortable

---

[80] For some hermeneutical reflections on this process, see F. J. Moloney, "To Teach the Text: The New Testament in a New Age," *Pacifica* 11 (1998): 159–80.

[81] Myers, *Binding the Strong Man,* 109.

[82] See H. von Campenhausen, "The Events of Easter and the Empty Tomb," in *Tradition and Life in the Church: Essays and Lectures in Church History* (London: Collins, 1968), 42–89, esp. 54–77.

[83] The bold originality and uniqueness of the Gospel of Mark as a literary initiative needs to be affirmed. The "manipulation" of the tradition in 16:8 is but one outstanding example of this originality.

endings,[84] Mark ended his gospel with an account of an empty tomb (16:1–4), and a resurrection proclamation (vv. 5–7) in the midst of terror and flight (v. 8). It appears that the story of the failure of the disciples is maintained to the last line of the Gospel. The women had not joined the disciples' flight in 14:50. They were present at the cross (15:40) and saw where he was buried (15:47). But in the end they share the fear (see 10:32) and the flight (see 14:50) of the disciples (16:8).

Throughout the Gospel of Mark it has been the disciples who, in a "this-worldly" way of judging events, had the good sense to oppose Jesus' suicidal journey to Jerusalem and to death (see especially 8:32–33). They were wise to make a few plans about how things should be organized when Jesus finally made his coup and reestablished the Davidic kingdom (see especially 9:34 and 10:35–37). Even their eventual flight (14:50), Peter's denials (14:66–72), and the flight of the women from an empty tomb (16:8) are sensible approaches to very uncomfortable and unpromising situations. Yet Mark writes "good news" (1:1, 15; 8:35): the death and resurrection of Jesus reverse the common sense of this world. The suffering Son of Man has been vindicated. The crucified Jesus is the Messiah, the Son of God, while the sensible approaches of the disciples and the women lead to failure, fear, and flight. The Markan resurrection story proclaims that the way of Jesus is the way to victory, while the way of the worldly-wise leads into terror and flight (see 14:50 and 16:8).

But problems still remain for the reader, for the disciples of later generations who take this text in hand as a word of life proclaimed in the church. The terrible question of the crucified Jesus (15:34) is resolved by the action of God in his resurrection (16:6). But what of the terror of the disciples and the women? The Gospel ends with flight and terror—yet it also ends with a promise. Even to the worldly-wise there is a word of hope in the midst of their failure and terror: "But go, tell his disciples and Peter that he is going before you into Galilee; there you will see him as he told you" (16:7). Do the terror and flight of the women thwart the promise of an eventual encounter with the risen Lord in Galilee? Is it possible that the story of the disciples, women and men, characters in the story, has been told in this way to issue a challenge to the story of the disciples, women and men, who are the readers of the story?

Conclusion

Only a more detailed analysis of the Gospel will answer that question. Today, almost two thousand years after the events reported in the story, there are still readers of the story of Jesus as it is found in the Gospel of Mark. This must say something as we go on struggling to be followers of Jesus and celebrating Easter. However complete the failure of the women reported at the end of the Gospel (16:8), the promise of 16:7 took place. There was a Galilee encounter for the failed disciples, and the church rose from the first disciples' failure and flight. There would be no Gospel of Mark unless the original writer and addressees of this particular life story of Jesus believed that such was the case. The Gospel of Mark proclaims this message to frightened and fleeing disciples of all times.

The interpretation that follows attempts to describe how the story of Jesus, as it is told in the Gospel of Mark, is not a dusty page from the past reflecting the experience of a

---

[84] Our present 16:9–20 is only one of several such endings found in the ancient manuscripts. See chapter 10, pp. 355–62.

remote Christian community. Much less is it a gospel proclaiming the "absence of Jesus" to fearful disciples struggling in the midst of a heresy that avoided the implications of following a crucified Son of Man, waiting for the Parousia.[85] While Mark has no illusions about the ambiguity of the human condition, and ultimately about the ambiguity of a church made up of failing and terrified men and women, the Markan Jesus nevertheless proclaims, in the midst of that terror: "I will go before you into Galilee. There you will see me" (14:28; see 16:7). A reading of this mysterious gospel challenges us to hope in the midst of ambiguity and failure.

---

[85] This is a caricature of the position taken by important American redaction critics who, under the leadership of the late Norman Perrin in Chicago, carry Marxsen's suggestions further. See N. Perrin, *The Resurrection Narratives: A New Approach* (London: SPCK, 1977); Weeden, *Traditions in Conflict*; J. R. Donahue, *Are You the Christ? The Trial Narrative in the Gospel of Mark* (SBLDS 10; Missoula: Society of Biblical Literature, 1973); W. H. Kelber, *The Kingdom in Mark*; W. H. Kelber, ed., *The Passion in Mark* (Philadelphia: Fortress, 1976). For detailed examinations and critiques of this perspective, see J. D. Kingsbury, *The Christology of Mark's Gospel* (Philadelphia: Fortress, 1983) and E. Best, *Following Jesus: Discipleship in the Gospel of Mark* (JSNTSup 4; Sheffield: JSOT Press, 1981).

SECTION 1

PROLOGUE

MARK 1:1–13

THE PROLOGUE (MARK 1:1–13)

Already in antiquity, certain conventions were established for beginning a story.[1] It has therefore long been recognized that "placing an item at the beginning or at the end may radically change the process of reading as well as the final product."[2] This is clearly the case for the Gospels of Matthew, Luke, and John. Each has a "beginning" that stands apart from the body of the Gospel because of its form and content: a birth narrative (Matt 1–2; Luke 1–2) or a hymn summarizing the christological proclamation of the Gospel that follows (John 1:1–18). The Gospel of Mark's account of the activity of John the Baptist also serves as a genuine prologue to the narrative that will follow.[3] Before reading the Markan prologue we need first to be aware of the debate over where the section ends (v. 13 or v. 15) and how the argument of the first page unfolds.

The Limits and the Shape of the Markan Prologue

The verbal links between 1:1 and 1:14–15, especially the presence of the expression εὐαγγέλιον in both v. 1 and v. 15, have led some scholars to claim that the Markan prologue runs from vv. 1–15. Jesus' words in vv. 14–15 contain a summary of the Gospel that will serve as a program for Jesus' ministry, a bridge into the story that follows. But they also look back to the first words of the narrator in v. 1.[4] There are good reasons for the association of vv. 14–15 with vv. 1–13 to form a prologue. But the rhetoric and literary structure of the first half of the Gospel of Mark (1:1–8:30) depend upon vv. 14–15 as the summary

---

[1] See the survey in D. E. Smith, "Narrative Beginnings in Ancient Literature and Theory," *Sem* 52 (1991): 1–9. See also R. E. Watts, *Isaiah's New Exodus and Mark* (WUNT 2. Reihe 88; Tübingen: J. C. B. Mohr [Paul Siebeck], 1997), 54–55.

[2] S. Rimmon-Kenan, *Narrative Fiction: Contemporary Poetics* (New Accents; London: Methuen, 1983), 120.

[3] On this, see F. J. Moloney, *Beginning the Good News: A Narrative Approach* (Collegeville: The Liturgical Press, 1995), 43–71; M. D. Hooker, *Beginnings: Keys That Open the Gospels* (Valley Forge: Trinity Press International, 1998), 1–21; M. E. Boring, "Mark 1:1–15 and the Beginning of the Gospel," *Sem* 52 (1991): 43–81; F. Matera, "The Prologue as the Interpretative Key to Mark's Gospel," *JSNT* 34 (1988): 3–20.

[4] The most influential figure in this debate has been L. Keck, "The Introduction to Mark's Gospel," *NTS* 12 (1965–1966): 352–70. Since then see, among many, R. Pesch, *Das Markusevangelium* (2d ed.; HTKNT 2.1–2; 2 vols.; Freiburg: Herder, 1976–1977), 1:71–74; J. Ernst, *Das Evangelium nach Markus* (RNT; Regensburg: Pustet-Verlag, 1981), 31; D. Lührmann, *Das Markusevangelium* (HNT 3; Tübingen: J. C. B. Mohr [Paul Siebeck], 1987), 32–33; Boring, "Mark 1:1–15," 55–59; J. Marcus, *Mark 1–8* (AB 27; New York: Doubleday, 2000) 137–39; Watts, *New Exodus,* 91–95. For a comprehensive list of studies of the Markan Prologue, see J. P. Meier, *A Marginal Jew: Rethinking the Historical Jesus* (3 vols.; ABRL; New York: Doubleday, 1991–2001), 2:85–86 n. 112.

introducing 1:14–3:6. In my discussion of the plot of the Gospel of Mark I suggested that, after the prologue (1:1–13), a section that asks the question "Who is Jesus?" follows (1:14–8:30), composed of three major subsections, all structured in the same fashion. They begin with a summary statement (see 1:14–15; 3:7–12; 6:6a) immediately followed by material dealing with the disciples (see 1:16–20; 3:13–19; 6:6b–30). After the identical opening of each subsection there is an extended narrative of Jesus' words and deeds during his Galilean ministry. Each subsection concludes with a decision for or against Jesus (3:6: the Herodians and Pharisees combine to eliminate him; 6:1–6a: his townsfolk will not believe in him; 8:29: Peter confesses that Jesus is "the Christ").

Against this broader pattern of summary, disciples, narrative, and decision, I would claim 1:14–3:6 as a deliberately contrived literary unit. A closer look at the cohesion of vv. 1–13 strengthens this view. Typical Markan *links* exists across vv. 1–13. After the ἀρχή of v. 1 follow ἐγένετο (v. 4), καί (v. 6), καί (v. 7), καὶ ἐγένετο (v. 9), καὶ εὐθύς (v. 10), καί (v. 11), καὶ εὐθύς (v. 12), and καί (v. 13). This steady rhythm of Markan parataxis is *broken* in v. 14 with an expression that leads the reader to another time and place: μετὰ δέ.[5] It is true that Jesus begins his ministry without reference to a *specific* time and place, but there is a shift of interest as his first words proclaim the coming of the kingdom and call for repentance and belief (1:14–15). He immediately associates disciples with this mission, calling them to follow him into a ministry of their own, fishing for people (1:16–20). A series of incidents follow in Capernaum and throughout Galilee, leading to questions about his authority and his person (see 1:27; 2:7, 12, 24). His saving and healing activity among the people (1:21–28, 29–31, 32–34, 41–45; 2:1–12; 3:1–6) prompt the leaders of two otherwise irreconcilable groups, the Pharisees and the Herodians, to "conspire . . . how to destroy him." (3:6). However much 1:14–15 restate in narrative form what was said in v. 1—and I am not denying that this is the case[6]—these programmatic words of Jesus serve to introduce the narrative proper of the Gospel. The same literary feature is found in 3:7–12 and 6:6b. Thus 1:1–13 (and not 1:1–15) is to be taken as the prologue to the Gospel of Mark.[7]

Most commentators see 1:1–13 as made up of a superscription from the hand of the author (v. 1), a description of the person and activity of John the Baptist (vv. 2–8), the baptism of Jesus (vv. 9–11), and his temptation (vv. 12–13).[8] This division of the text respects

---

[5] On the Markan use of parataxis, see R. M. Fowler, *Let the Reader Understand: Reader-Response Criticism and the Gospel of Mark* (Minneapolis: Fortress, 1991), 134–40. On 1:14–15 is the beginning of the ministry of Jesus, see Hooker, *Beginnings*, 8, C. D. Marshall, *Faith as a Theme in Mark's Narrative* (SNTSMS 64; Cambridge: Cambridge University Press, 1989), 36–43; J. B. Gibson, *The Temptations of Jesus in Early Christianity* (JSNTSup 112; Sheffield: Sheffield Academic Press, 1995), 26–29. On the unity of vv. 9–13, see pp. 26–32. For further remarks on the use of ἔρημος across the prologue (vv. 3, 4, 12, 13) as an indication of the unity of vv. 1–13, see below, note 24.

[6] See the succinct statement of the place of vv. 14–15 (and vv. 16–20) in J. Painter, *Mark's Gospel: Worlds in Conflict* (New Testament Readings; London: Routledge, 1997), 23. Among others, J. Dewey ("Mark as Interwoven Tapestry: Forecasts and Echoes for a Listening Audience," *CBQ* 53 [1991]: 225–26) points out that vv. 14–15 form a bridge, closing the prologue and opening the ministry. See also Matera, "The Prologue," 4–6. In a rather singular study, W. Feneberg (*Der Markusprolog: Studien zur Formbestimmung des Evangeliums* [SANT 36; Munich: Kösel-Verlag, 1974]) argues that 1:1–11 forms a prologue presenting baptism as the entry of the Gentile world into a Jewish Christian community.

[7] See the detailed study, supporting this position, of S. Kuthirakkattel, *The Beginnings of Jesus' Ministry according to Mark's Gospel (1,14–3,6): A Redaction Critical Study* (AnBib 123; Rome: Biblical Institute Press, 1990), 3–22.

[8] See, for example, V. Taylor, *The Gospel according to St. Mark* (2d ed.; London: Macmillan, 1966), 151–64; W. Grundmann, *Das Evangelium nach Markus* (6th ed.; THKNT 2; Berlin: Evan-

the intense presentation of both Jesus and the Baptist. It is determined by the characters in the narrative, but other criteria could be used. If one pays attention to changes in character and action, time and place, and especially to the "focalization" of the narrative,[9] five elements emerge.

1:1–3   The voice of the narrator opens the story, but what he announces reflects an omniscience that associates his words with the design of God. The narrator speaks with a "godly authority" which the reader cannot question.[10] With the exception of Mark 13:14, the narrator does not enter the story actively, and God speaks only rarely (see 1:2–3, 11; 9:7), but God determines it and the narrator shapes it. A story of "good news" is at its "beginning" (ἀρχή), and the news is that a man called Jesus is Christ, Son *of God*.[11] Only a narrator at one with God's omniscience can tell the story of the "Son of God." The words that follow (vv. 2–3) are "Words of God." They are taken from Mal 3:1 and Isa 40:3, with some help from Exod 23:20, and God speaks in the first person. The narrator and the voice of God utter a divine message, announcing the beginning of the good news that Jesus is the Christ, the Son of God, and that God is sending a messenger to prepare the way of "the Lord." The divine message is the focus of the opening verses, announcing that the good news that follows will have to do with Jesus, Christ, Son of God, Lord.

1:4–6   The narrator takes over and tells of the partial fulfillment of God's promise. Although he performs no actions, the one who will prepare the way (vv. 2–3) appears and is described.

---

gelische Verlagsanstalt, 1973), 25–35; H. Anderson, *The Gospel of Mark* (NCB; London: Oliphants, 1976), 65–83; Ernst, *Markus,* 31–54 (vv. 1–8, 9–11, 12–13, 14–15); Lührmann, *Markusevangelium,* 32–33; M. D. Hooker, *The Message of Mark* (London: Epworth Press, 1983), 7–8; Matera, "The Prologue," 6–9.

[9] Focalization pays attention to the eyes through which the reported events are seen. On this, see G. Genette, *Narrative Discourse: An Essay in Method* (Ithaca: Cornell University Press, 1980), 189–221, and idem, *Narrative Discourse Revisited* (Ithaca: Cornell University Press, 1988), 72–78. See also Rimmon-Kenan, *Narrative Fiction,* 71–85.

[10] On this feature of biblical narrative, see M. Sternberg, *The Poetics of Biblical Narrative: Ideological Literature and the Drama of Reading* (Indiana Literary Biblical Series; Bloomington: Indiana University Press, 1985), 23–35, 176–79.

[11] Many ancient manuscripts do not contain the words "son of God" (υἱοῦ θεοῦ). I am tentatively accepting it. For a full discussion, coming to the same conclusion, see C. R. Kazmierski, *Jesus, the Son of God: A Study of the Marcan Tradition and Its Redaction by the Evangelist* (FB 33; Würzburg: Echter Verlag, 1979), 1–9. See, among others, Marcus (*Mark,* 141) and Painter (*Mark's Gospel,* 25), who suggest that it must be a scribal addition; it is so appropriate that it would never have been omitted. In the light of the use of "Son" and "Son of God" through the Gospel, Painter, along with most who regard it as secondary, admits, "The title is entirely appropriate" (p. 25). Whether or not "Son of God" should be read as authentic in 1:1 is not crucial. The use of the expression "my beloved Son" in the description of Jesus in the prologue (v. 11) leaves the reader with no doubt that Jesus is "the Christ" (v. 1) and "the Son of God" (v. 1?; v. 11). C. A. Evans ("Mark's Incipit and the Priene Calendar Inscription: From Jewish Gospel to Greco-Roman Gospel," *Journal of Greco-Roman Christianity and Judaism* 1 [2000]: 67–81) argues that the anarthrous υἱοῦ θεοῦ is original, setting the theme of Jesus as "the Son of God" across the Gospel, climaxing in the anarthrous υἱὸς θεοῦ in 15:39. This theme places Jesus above all the claims for divine emperors in a time of dramatic disturbance in the Rome of 68–69 C.E. A number of contemporary scholars (e.g., A. Y. Collins, W. Cotter, T. H. Kim [see bibliography]) suggest that an originally Jewish text appeals in this way to a Greco-Roman readership, especially converts to Christianity, who are familiar with the concept of the emperor as *divi filius.*

1:7–8   The focalization shifts to the Baptist. He is no longer described but speaks in the first person, announcing the coming of "the stronger one," one before whom he is unworthy, who "will baptize with the Holy Spirit." The Baptist is preparing the way for "the Lord."

1:9–11   As with the introduction to the Baptist, the narrator again takes over and presents Jesus. Jesus does nothing, but things happen to him. He is baptized by John, the Spirit descends upon him, and a voice from heaven describes him. What Jesus might think of this is not told. God makes things happen to Jesus.

1:12–13 This final section, described by an omniscient narrator, is dominated by Jesus. Although as God's design continues to unfold things still happen to him (the Spirit drives him into the desert, Satan tempts him, angels minister to him), for the first time in the narrative, Jesus becomes the active agent: "He was with the wild beasts" (v. 13).[12]

God dominates this prologue, mentioned by name in 1:1 and present in direct speech in vv. 2–3. In vv. 4–5 and 6–8 the Baptist is the subject of most of the verbs, but his activity fulfills what God had promised in vv. 2–3. The Baptist points away from himself and eventually fades from the scene as Jesus of Nazareth is introduced as a third-person figure. God and the Spirit are the main actors in Jesus' initial experiences until, at the close of vv. 1–13, Jesus is *with* the wild beasts and served by the angels. This prologue establishes an important truth for the reader: *the chief agent in the action that follows is God.* The Gospel of Mark may read like the story of "Jesus of Nazareth" (see 1:24; 10:47; 14:67; 16:6), but its prologue suggests that an omniscient narrator tells the story of how God acts among us through the death and resurrection of the Messiah and Son.[13] This is a strange way for a God to deal with his Son, but the reader is made aware from the first page of the story that the events of the life and death of Jesus of Nazareth are determined by the pleasure of God (v. 11: "You are my beloved Son; with you I am pleased").[14]

The Prologue (1:1–13)

The authority of God (1:1–3)

The first word echoes the opening of Genesis—"the beginning" (ἀρχή)—but it also simply indicates the beginning of a long story. Both meanings are involved. The Gospel of

---

[12] Gibson (*Temptations*, 9–13) makes a strong case for the unity of vv. 9–13 as the Markan presentation of the nature of Jesus' temptation. However, Jesus as receiver (vv. 9–11) and Jesus as agent (vv. 12–13) keep them separate.

[13] On the centrality of God in the Gospel of Mark, see J. R. Donahue, "A Neglected Factor in the Theology of Mark," *JBL* 101 (1982): 563–94, and K. Scholtissek, " 'Er ist nicht ein Gott der Toten, sondern der Lebenden' (Mk 12,27): Grundzüge der markanische Theo-logie," in *Der lebendige Gott: Studien zur Theologie des Neuen Testaments. Festschrift für Wilhelm Thüsing zum 75. Geburtstag* (ed. T. Södig; NTAbh. NF 31; Münster: Aschendorff, 1996), 71–100.

[14] Marcus (*Mark*, 139–40) draws a close relationship between the prologue and Deutero-Isaiah. He associates this background with the apocalyptic expectations of the Markan community, expectations to be finally resolved by a king "who leads God's people to victory against the foe" (p. 140). That king is the beloved Son. Along similar lines, see Watts, *New Exodus*, 96–121.

Mark "begins" with an echo of God's original creative design.[15] But here "the gospel" (τοῦ εὐαγγελίου) begins, not the creation. The link with creation is left on hold as the person of Jesus is introduced. The expression "the good news" was used in the Septuagint and the Greco-Roman world. Second Isaiah used it to proclaim the "good news" of God's rule, salvation or vindication (see LXX Isa 40:9; 41:27; 52:7; 60:6; 61:1). The Greek writers used it to announce a military victory, a royal birth, or a political triumph.[16] What is new in Mark 1:1 is the use of the noun to describe the story of a human being. The good news is: Jesus is the Christ, the Son of God. The evangelist Mark introduced a new literary form into world literature: a narrative of the life, death, and resurrection of Jesus that did not pretend to recount the brute facts of history. It was written to proclaim that Jesus was the Christ, the Son of God. He called this narrative form "the good news" (τὸ εὐαγγέλιον).

The two expressions "Jesus" and "Christ" had become the proper name "Jesus Christ" before Mark wrote his gospel,[17] but the rapid succession of the human name "Jesus" and the further descriptions "Christ, the Son of God" constitutes proclamation. The good news is that Jesus of Nazareth is the Christ, the Son of God—provisionally accepting the reading "Son of God."[18] Jesus' being the Son of God will become increasingly important as the narrative unfolds (see 1:11; 3:11; 5:7; 9:7; 14:61; 15:39). The notion will develop a character of its own that will stretch the traditional understanding of the expression. However, as the Gospel opens the reader is informed that, like the ideal king of Israel (see 2 Sam 7:14; Pss 2:7; 89:26–29) and the chosen people of Israel (see Exod 4:22; Isa 63:16; Hos 11:1), Jesus can be regarded as son of God, and thus as Messiah because of his relationship with God. This relationship will have some strange twists as the story unfolds, and much still lies ahead of the reader before the full significance of "Christ, Son of God" is finally unveiled.[19]

---

[15] See Anderson, *Mark*, 66. M. D. Hooker (*St. Mark*, 33) also points to the parallel between Mark 1:1 and Hos 1:2, which reads, "The beginning (LXX: ἀρχή) of the word of the Lord through Hosea." Instead of the word of God through a prophet, however, we have the Gospel of Jesus Christ. On the importance of the ἀρχή as the beginning of the whole utterance, see Boring, "Mark 1:1–15," 47–53; Marcus, *Mark*, 145–46.

[16] Both in the LXX and in the Greco-Roman documents, the verbal form εὐαγγελίζομαι is most frequent. Paul uses the noun εὐαγγέλιον to announce his "gospel" message of God's victory won in the death and resurrection of Jesus. For summaries, see C. E. B. Cranfield, *The Gospel according to St. Mark* (CGTC; Cambridge: Cambridge University Press, 1959), 35–36; Guelich, *Mark*, 13–14. For C. Myers (*Binding the Strong Man: A Political Reading of Mark's Story of Jesus* [Maryknoll: Orbis, 1990], 122–24) the association of "Jesus" with the imperial εὐαγγέλιον subverts the Roman cultural code, but this pays too little attention to the LXX and even the Pauline use of the expression.

[17] Already in Paul "Jesus Christ" is used as a proper name. See W. Kramer, *Christ, Lord, Son of God* (trans. B. Hardy; SBT 50; London: SCM, 1966), 203–14.

[18] See note 11 above.

[19] Against, for example, E. Lohmeyer (*Das Evangelium des Markus* [17th ed.; Meyers Kommentar 1/2; Göttingen: Vandenhoeck & Ruprecht, 1967], 4) and W. L. Lane (*Mark*, 44–45), who see "son of God" already in v. 1 as "altogether supernatural" (Lane, *Mark*, 44 n. 23). See the use of 2 Sam 7 in 4QFlor 1:10–13, and the association of Ps 2 with the end time in the same fragment (1:18–2:4). See the excellent comments of E. Schweizer, *The Good News according to Mark* (trans. D. H. Madvig; London: SPCK, 1971), 40–41 (on v. 11), B. Blackburn, *Theios Anêr and the Markan Miracle Traditions: A Critique of the Theios Anêr Concept as an Interpretative Background to the Miracle Traditions Used by Mark* (WUNT 2. Reihe 40; Tübingen: J. C. B. Mohr [Paul Siebeck], 1991), 98–109, and especially the full-scale study of the question in B. J. Byrne, *'Sons of God—Seed of Abraham': A Study of the Idea of the Sonship of God of All Christians in Paul against the Jewish Background* (AnBib 83;

God enters the narrative, by means of the words of his prophet,[20] and two further elements are added to the story: there will be a God-appointed forerunner, and the one who is to come is called "the Lord" (1:2–3). In v. 1 the narrator spoke with divine omniscience, but in vv. 2–3 God speaks directly. This is made clear by the use of the passive: "as it has been written" and the voice of God speaking in the first person through the words of the prophet. The author is God and the voice is God's. God speaks as "I" to "you": "*I* send *my* messenger before *your* face." God announces that a messenger will precede the coming of the one addressed. The conflation of prophetic passages reports words of God to someone who is addressed. The one addressed is to make a journey down his "way." The theme of "the way" will have its place later in the story, but for the moment it is introduced as part of God's design for the coming one.[21] The one addressed as "you" ("before *your* face") in v. 2b becomes "the Lord" in v. 3b. A messenger will cry out in the wilderness: "prepare the way of the Lord (τοῦ κυρίου)." The "you" addressed by God in v. 2 is "the Lord" in v. 3. The prophecies from Malachi, Exodus, and Isaiah, combined to provide the words of God that begin the narrative, witness to the coming one as ὁ κύριος. This expression is used systematically in the Septuagint to translate YHWH, the sacred name for God.[22] God names a figure, yet to appear actively in the story, *by God's own name.* But a third person is involved in these words of God: a messenger who will prepare the way of the Lord. God has set the agenda. Jesus Christ, Son of God has not only been announced in v. 1, but the word of God has described him as "the Lord" who must go down a God-directed way, prepared by another character yet to appear.[23]

Rome: Biblical Institute Press, 1979), 9–78. On the recent discussion of the further "Son of God" text from Qumran, see J. A. Fitzmyer, "4Q246: The 'Son of God' Document in Qumran," *Bib* 74 (1993): 153–74. Fitzmyer denies that the expression has messianic connotations. For a messianic interpretation of the text, see J. J. Collins, *The Scepter and the Star: The Messiahs of the Dead Sea Scrolls and Other Ancient Literature* (ABRL; New York: Doubleday, 1995), 154–69.

[20] The narrator only mentions Isaiah, but the text of vv. 2–3 is a conflation of Exod 23:20 and Mal 3:1 (v. 2), and Isa 40:3 (v. 3). As Hooker (*Message*, 4) comments: "This is the only place in the Gospel where Mark himself (as distinct from the characters in the story) appeals to the Old Testament, and he manages to get his reference wrong." This has led to copyists changing "in Isaiah the prophet" (v. 2), to "in the prophets." The reference to Isaiah, for both internal and external reasons (*lectio difficilior*) is original. See B. M. Metzger, *A Textual Commentary on the Greek New Testament* (Stuttgart: Deutsche Bibelgesellschaft, 1994), 62. For a detailed study of the citations, see Watts, *New Exodus,* 57–84.

[21] For a rich understanding of "the way" in the Gospel, and the possible allusion to this meaning for the Markan community in 1:3, see J. Marcus, *The Way of the Lord: Christological Exegesis of the Old Testament in the Gospel of Mark* (Louisville: Westminster John Knox, 1992), 29–47.

[22] See G. Quell, "κύριος κτλ" *TDNT* 3:1058–81; Cranfield, *St. Mark,* 39–40. Marcus (*Mark,* 147–48) rightly warns against identification between God and Jesus. He correctly suggests: "where Jesus is acting, there God is acting" (p. 148). See further idem, *The Way of the Lord,* 37–41. For a balanced assessment of the Markan presentation of Jesus as "Lord," see E. K. Broadhead, *Naming Jesus: Titular Christology in the Gospel of Mark* (JSNTSup 175; Sheffield: Sheffield Academic Press, 1999), 134–44. However, Broadhead does not consider 1:7.

[23] On the possible prehistory of the combination of these Old Testament texts, see Watts, *New Exodus,* 85–87; Marcus, *Mark,* 143–45. Marcus (148–49) suggests, probably correctly, that the attribution of the text to Isaiah in v. 2a is not a mistake. It reflects Mark's desire to focus upon Isaiah. However, when Marcus links the use of Isa 40 as paradoxical rereading of that passage's message on a holy war with the setting of the Jewish revolt, he reads too much into the passage. Watts (*New Exodus,* 86–90) also insists upon the centrality of the Isaian citation, acting as a deliberate Markan frame (v. 1a and v. 3) around the Exodus/Malachi texts (vv. 1b, 2).

The coming of the forerunner (1:4–6)

The first figure announced by the voice of God is described in vv. 4–6. What had been promised in v. 3a, "a voice crying *in the wilderness*," happens in v. 4a: John the Baptist "appeared *in the wilderness*."[24] This is the messenger God sends before the face of the one addressed in v. 2b, whose divinely ordered task was to prepare the way of "the Lord" (v. 3b). What God says will happen does happen. Thus it will be throughout the entire story. The Baptist's preaching of repentance has its roots in the prophetic call for a wholehearted return to YHWH (see, for example, Jer 18:11; Isa 55:7; Zech 1:4) through a "turning back" toward Israel's unique God.[25] The brief description of the Baptist's appearance and diet enhance his association with similar prophetic figures. Jesus will later identify John with Elijah (see 9:11–13) and there is a similarity in dress and lifestyle between Elijah and the Baptist (see 2 Kgs 1:8). Yet the description of his dress is nothing more than "the nomadic attire of the wilderness in general and . . . the prophetic dress in particular."[26] He lives as an ascetic, neither eating meat nor drinking wine. Such behavior is typical of late Jewish prophets.[27] Whether or not John the Baptist is the expected Elijah *redivivus* (see Mal 4:5–6) is a matter that will be determined later in the story. For the moment, John the Baptist appears as one sent by God to announce a message of God.

The practice of a baptism for the forgiveness of sins is more difficult to locate within the religious culture and practice of the time. In historical terms, John's name, "the Baptizer" (βαπτιστής; "the plunger," or "the immerser") reflected a memorable aspect of his ministry,[28] and Mark describes him as ὁ βαπτίζων.[29] However familiar the Christian tradition is with this practice, it was rare in the pre-Christian period. There is a newness about the baptismal activity of John, linked with the Baptist's preparing for the eschatological event of the one who is to come.[30] Evidence exists for a use of baptism for proselytes by the

---

[24] The expression "wilderness" (ἔρημος) appears four times in the prologue, twice at the beginning (vv. 3 and 4) and twice at the end (vv. 12–13). It is another indication that the prologue is limited to vv. 1–13, between the inclusion generated by the "wilderness" of vv. 3–4 and the further use of the expression in vv. 12–13. After the omniscient and all-determining words of the narrator and God which close with God's words on the voice "in the wilderness" (vv. 1–3; see v. 3), the action is circumscribed by events that take place "in the wilderness" (v. 4 [the Baptist] and v. 13 [Jesus]). Many who argue for vv. 1–15 as the prologue point to the inclusion created by the use of εὐαγγέλιον in v. 1 and v. 14. It is better to understand the repeated use of this important expression as marking the beginnings of two discrete literary sections: vv. 1–13 (the prologue—with εὐαγγέλιον in v. 1) and 1:14–3:6 (Jesus and Israel—with εὐαγγέλιον in v. 14).

[25] The Greek μετανοεῖν translates the Hebrew *shûb*, which means to "turn back" or to "return." It implies a complete turning back from one's present direction. See Cranfield, *St. Mark,* 43–46; Schweizer, *Mark,* 32–33; Marcus, *Mark,* 150.

[26] Guelich, *Mark,* 21. Marcus (*Mark,* 157) links the Baptist's clothing and food with "a certain primal back-to-the-earth quality, reminiscent of the Garden of Eden narrative and the Jewish elaborations thereof." He cites LXX Gen 3:21, *Joseph and Asenath* 16:14, and claims that it looks forward to the Edenic nature of Jesus' being with the wild beasts in v. 13.

[27] See, for example, Dan 1:18; *The Lives of the Prophets* 4:14; *Martyrdom of Isaiah* 2:10–11. For the nonbiblical texts, see *OTP* 2:390, 158. This description finds its parallel in other synoptic descriptions of the Baptist as one who comes neither eating nor drinking (see Matt 11:18//Luke 7:33). See the survey of Meier, *A Marginal Jew,* 2:46–49.

[28] See Meier, *A Marginal Jew,* 2:50–51.

[29] This is the title given to him in v. 4 (see also 6:14), although some manuscripts omit the definite article. See the discussion in Hooker, *St. Mark,* 36–37.

[30] See the extensive treatment of Meier, *A Marginal Jew,* 2:49–56.

Pharisees, and it was part of the rituals performed at Qumran.[31] Both groups regarded it as an external sign of a serious commitment to "turning back" to God (βάπτισμα μετανοίας), but the Baptist's activity appears closer to proselyte baptism than to the rites practiced at Qumran.[32] The effectiveness of John's preaching is enhanced by the rhetorical statement that "all the country of Judea and all the country of Jerusalem" went out to him at the Jordan river.[33] This is hardly likely, but the author makes his point: John the Baptist made a great impression,[34] and "the fact that everything was astir indicated that the special salvation-time had begun in which the gospel would reach out to the whole world (13:10)."[35] Many submit themselves to John's baptism to acknowledge their sins and turn back to God, but the reader is aware that this is not the main event. God's words have pointed forward to the coming of "the Lord" (v. 3), but someone would prepare this "coming" (vv. 2–3). The storyteller is ultimately interested in the action of God. The Baptist belongs to a long line of God's prophets. Although only the one sent before the face . . . to prepare the way of the Lord (vv. 2–3), his person (v. 6) and activities (vv. 4–5) are determined by God and look forward to the coming of "the Stronger One" (see v. 7).

The voice of the Baptist (1:7–8)

The direct speech of John the Baptist's proclamation changes the focus of the prologue at v. 7. While vv. 4–6 reported a description of the Baptist, he announces his message in vv. 7–8. A prophet of Israel traditionally recalled YHWH's *past* saving intervention, but the Baptist fulfills God's *future* promise of v. 3. He points *forward* to the future coming of ὁ ἰσχυρότερος. This expression may not summon up directly messianic claims, but God has regularly been called "the Mighty One" in the Septuagint (see Deut 10:17; Judg 6:12; 2 Sam 2:32–33, 48; Jer 27:24; 32:18; Dan 9:4; Neh 1:15; 9:31–32; 2 Sam 22:31; 23:5; Ps 7:12; see also Isa 9:6). In the book of Job, the term ὁ ἰσχυρός must regularly be translated by "God" (see Job 22:13; 33:29; 36:22, 26; 37:5). The words of the Baptist shift the focus from himself (see vv. 4–6) to the mightier one who will come after him (vv. 7–8).[36] As in v. 3b, where God spoke of the coming one as ὁ κύριος, the forerunner uses another expression associated in the Septuagint with God. Before Jesus has appeared in the narrative, the reader has already been told of Jesus, the Christ, the Son of God (v. 1), the Lord (v. 3), the mightier one (v. 7).

---

[31] See W. Michaelis, "Zum jüdischen Hintergrund der Johannestaufe," *Jud* 7 (1951): 81–120; J. Gnilka, "Die essenischen Tauchbäder und die Johannestaufe," *RevQ* 3 (1961): 185–207; Meier, *A Marginal Jew*, 2:49–56.

[32] See Hooker, *St. Mark*, 39–43; Meier, *A Marginal Jew*, 2:50–52.

[33] For more detailed study of the ministry of the Baptist, see Meier, *A Marginal Jew*, 2:19–233. See also J. Murphy-O'Connor, "John the Baptist and Jesus: History and Hypotheses," *NTS* 36 (1990): 359–74; J. Ernst; "Johannes der Täufer und Jesus von Nazareth in historischer Sicht," *NTS* 43 (1997): 161–83; F. J. Moloney, "The Fourth Gospel and the Jesus of History," *NTS* 46 (2000): 45–49.

[34] The rhetorical nature of the description of huge crowds is made clear by v. 9, where a solitary Galilean receives John's baptism. See Lohmeyer, *Markus*, 20.

[35] Schweizer, *Mark*, 33.

[36] The Baptist's assertion that "the Mightier One" is coming ὀπίσω μου could have a local or a temporal sense. See BDAG, 716, s.v. ὀπίσω. If the former, it could indicate that Jesus came from among his disciples (which was probably the case, historically). See Lane, *Mark*, 52; Pesch, *Markusevangelium*, 1:82. While not discounting this more diachronic reading of the expression, vv. 7–8 form an important prolepsis, making promises to the reader that are yet to be fulfilled (see 3:27). The temporal meaning of "after me" is therefore the more important. See S. Seesemann, "ὀπίσω κτλ" *TDNT* 5:290.

bronyer

The use of κύριος and ἰσχυρότερος even suggest to the reader that claims made only for the God of Israel—Lord and Mighty One—are being shifted to the one who is to come.[37]

For all the greatness of the Baptist,[38] the messenger of God sent to prepare the way of "the Lord," a gulf lies between the messenger and the one he announces. Untying the master's sandals was the one demeaning task never required of a Hebrew servant (*Mek.* 21:1; *b. Ketub.* 96a). "To be unworthy of such a task would be to lower oneself below the status of a slave."[39] The Baptist's final words in the Gospel of Mark look back to his baptism: "I have baptized (ἐβάπτισα: aorist tense) you with water," and forward to the future activity of Jesus: "He will baptize (βαπτίσει: future tense) you with the Holy Spirit" (v. 8). The narrator has already described John's baptism in vv. 4–5, and the idea of a baptism with the spirit is not entirely new. The prophet Ezekiel had promised, in the name of YHWH:

> I will sprinkle clean water upon you, and you shall be clean from all your uncleannesses, and from all your idols I will cleanse you. A new heart I will give you, and a new spirit I will put within you; and I will take out of your flesh the heart of stone and give you a heart of flesh. And I will put my spirit within you, and cause you to walk in my statutes and be careful to observe my ordinances. (Ezek 36:25–27)

The Qumran sectarians and later Judaism spoke of a spirit baptism in which the Spirit was a gift of God to the faithful, and his promises for them would be realized through this gift.[40] It is not so much the idea of a gift of a "holy spirit" that is new but the proclamation that the coming one would dispense this gift. Not only are the names of God ("Lord" and "Mighty One") taken over by the coming one, but also one of God's functions as the giver of the Spirit.

The baptism of Jesus (1:9–11)

To this point in the prologue, Jesus the Christ, the Son of God (1:1) has not appeared in the narrative. God has been the main actor, through his word (vv. 1–3) and the partial fulfillment of that word (vv. 4–8). Jesus' entry is solemnly announced in a Greek version of a heavily Semitic introduction (see Exod 2:11; Judg 19:1; 1 Sam 28:1) of an important

---

[37] See Lohmeyer, *Markus,* 18 n. 1. Meier (*A Marginal Jew,* 2:32–42) regards the Baptist's words on "the stronger one" as ambiguous, and probably coming from the historical John the Baptist. John used the expression not of a replacement for YHWH but of an imminent eschatological figure whom he expected but did not fully understand. The shift from the Baptist's use of the expression to its present role in the presentation of Jesus in the Markan prologue allows our author to suggest a man who acts as God acts. For Marcus (*Mark,* 157–58) there are no such links. It is an indication of the relative "powers" of the Baptist and Jesus. Jesus is "stronger" than the Baptist. See, along the same lines, Broadhead, *Naming Jesus,* 61–62.

[38] It is often claimed that the Baptist material in the Gospels arose within a conflict in the early church. There was a need to place John the Baptist in a subordinate position, and to stress his inferiority to Jesus. The figure of John the Baptist was obviously important in those days (see especially Acts 18:24–19:7), but a problem with the catechesis of the ex-disciples of the Baptist rather than a polemic between Jesus' followers and the Baptist's followers may have generated the present form of the Baptist material in the Gospels. See Moloney, "The Fourth Gospel," 49.

[39] Guelich, *Mark,* 24.

[40] See 1QS 3:7–9; 4:20–21; 1 QH 16:11–12; *T. Levi* 18:6–7 (*OTP* 1:795). See Guelich, *Mark,* 24–26. For Meier (*A Marginal Jew,* 2:53–56), Mark distinguishes between the baptism "for the forgiveness of sins," which is preparatory, and the baptism in the Holy Spirit, which marks the arrival of the eschatological age.

character into a story: Καὶ ἐγένετο ἐν ἐκείναις ταῖς ἡμέραις ἦλθεν Ἰησοῦς ἀπὸ Ναζαρὲτ τῆς Γαλιλαίας. John the Baptist had been introduced with the simple ἐγένετο, but Jesus' active involvement has a more solemn biblical introduction: Καὶ ἐγένετο ἐν ἐκείναις ταῖς ἡμέραις. The formula "in those days" also highlights the eschatological nature of Jesus' "coming" (see Jer 31:33; Joel 3:1; Zech 8:23).[41] The significant claims made for Jesus earlier in the prologue are coming to resolution but are momentarily left aside as the reader is told that he comes from a little-known village, Nazareth, which calls for further identification: "of Galilee."[42] John the Baptist baptizes Jesus by immersing him in the river Jordan.[43] But as Jesus *comes up* (v. 10a: ἀναβαίνων) from the water, divine signs *come down* (v. 10b: καταβαῖνον). Jesus has a vision: "He saw heaven opened and the Spirit descending upon him like a dove."[44] The tearing open of the heavens marks the beginning of a new era. "God has ripped the heavens apart irrevocably at Jesus' baptism, never to shut them again. Through this gracious gash in the universe, he has poured forth his Spirit into the earthly realm."[45]

In a world where God abides above the firmament and the human story takes place below, the opening of the heavens promises a communication from above to below (see Gen 7:11; Isa 24:18; 64:1; Ezek 1:1; Rev 4:1; 11:19).[46] The messenger has performed his God-given task: going before the face and preparing the way for the Lord. We read of Jesus' experiences in 1:9–11, but God's action is reported. The Spirit descends upon Jesus, a hint of the older promise of the gift of the Spirit in the new creation, especially as it had been announced by the prophet Isaiah (see especially Isa 42:1–5, but also 11:1–3; 61:1; 63:10–14). It is as one gifted with the Spirit (v. 10) that Jesus will baptize with the Spirit (v. 8). The appearance of creation themes recalls the adumbration of the creation story by means of the word ἀρχή in v. 1 (see Gen 1:1). In Gen 1:3 the Spirit of God was hovering over the face of the waters, and in Mark 1:10 the Spirit of God descends upon Jesus "like a dove."[47] Despite the widespread use of the symbol of the dove in ancient literature,[48] there is no precedent for the Markan link between the Spirit and the dove.[49] The use of the symbol is to be taken at its face value. The Spirit of God, who cannot be *seen*, gently descends upon Jesus like a

---

[41] See Marcus, *Mark*, 163.

[42] Myers (*Binding the Strong Man*, 128) comments: "tantamount to announcing him as 'Jesus from Nowheresville.'"

[43] Modern scholars sometimes ask how Jesus could need John's baptism and argue whether or not it marks Jesus' conversion or his seeking forgiveness of sin. Mark's brief report of an event that no doubt took place in the life of the historical Jesus cannot bear the weight of such speculation. See, for example, Myers·(*Binding the Strong Man*, 127–30), who sees it as a genuine act of repentance, a symbolic renunciation of the old order—too much is "read into" the text.

[44] The absence of proper names in v. 10 makes it difficult to be sure who "saw." Grammatically, however, it must be the subject of v. 9 (Jesus came from Nazareth and was baptized) and the one addressed in v. 11 ("You are my beloved Son"). It is Jesus who saw the heavens opened and the Spirit descending. For "John" as the subject (with reference to John 1:31–34) see Painter, *Mark's Gospel*, 30.

[45] Marcus, *Mark*, 165.

[46] See Cranfield, *St. Mark*, 53; Hooker, *Message*, 11.

[47] For this, and further links with creation ideas and symbolism, see Marcus, *Mark*, 165–66.

[48] See especially F.-L. Lentzen-Deis, *Die Taufe Jesu nach den Synoptikern: Literarkritische und Gattungsgeschichtliche Untersuchungen* (FTS 4; Frankfurt: Josef Knecht, 1970), 170–83.

[49] Because of my suspicion that a number of creation and new creation themes are developed toward the end of the prologue, I am tempted by the suggestions of Lane (*Mark*, 56–57) and Hooker (*Message*, 11–12), who trace a link between the Spirit of God in Gen 1:3 and a dove in Jewish literature (especially *b. Ḥag* 15a). See also Marcus, *Mark*, 159–60. The evidence, however, is slight and

dove, which he can see.[50] Jesus, Christ and Son of God (v. 1), the Lord (v. 3), and the Stronger One (v. 7) who will dispense the Holy Spirit (v. 8), has now been gifted with the Spirit (v. 10).[51]

Jesus' vision of the gift of the Holy Spirit, through the medium of the gently descending dove, is paired with an aural experience: he *hears* a voice from heaven. The rabbis often spoke about a voice from above that indicated God's mind (the *bat qol*), but this was merely a sound, and it was sometimes little more than a shadowy hint. What Jesus hears is a voice (φωνή) coming from heaven. What has already been made clear in the prologue is authoritatively restated by the voice of God: "You are my Son, the Beloved, with you I am well pleased." The claim made by the omniscient narrator (1:1) is confirmed by the voice of God (v. 11). The words from heaven are close to words of God reported in Ps 2:7: "You are my Son" (LXX: υἱός μου εἶ σύ). But the Markan voice of God insists further on the uniqueness of the Son. The voice from heaven places the pronoun first (σὺ εἶ ὁ υἱός μου) and further enhances the dignity of the Son by describing him as "the beloved" (ὁ ἀγαπητός). The same expression was used to describe the special relationship that existed between Abraham and Isaac, his "beloved son" (see LXX Gen 22:2, 12, 16; *T. Levi* 18).[52] Perhaps this suggestion of the love between Abraham and Isaac, whom he was asked to sacrifice as a sign of his unconditional allegiance to YHWH, is a first subtle hint of Jesus' destiny.[53] The final words of God indicate the quality of the relationship between the Father and the Son: "with you I am well pleased." The Gospel will show, as the Son encounters the forces that oppose God and God's original design for humankind, that God's pleasure works itself out in surprising ways.

The subsequent actions of Jesus (1:12–13)

Thus far Jesus has come from Nazareth (v. 9), risen from the water (v. 10a), and seen the dove (v. 10b). These actions, however, have put him in the right place so that others (the Baptist and God) might do things *to* him and *for* him. The final section of the prologue continues Jesus' fundamentally passive role: "The Spirit immediately drove him out into the wilderness" (v. 12). The prolepses of earlier parts of the prologue continue to be fulfilled. The Baptist promised that Jesus would baptize with a holy spirit (v. 8), the heavens have opened and the Spirit has descended upon him (v. 10). The Spirit has taken

---

perhaps too late to be useful. There may be a more general link with the use of a dove by Noah in Gen 8:8–12. See H. C. Waetjen, *A Reordering of Power: A Socio-Political Reading of Mark's Gospel* (Minneapolis: Fortress, 1989), 70.

[50] Even this approach has its difficulties. For some (e.g., L. E. Keck, "The Spirit and the Dove," *NTS* 17 [1970–1971]: 41–67), ὡς περιστερὰν καταβαῖνον is to be read adverbially: "The Spirit, coming down, as a dove does." Others (e.g., Taylor, *St. Mark*, 160–61; Grundmann, *Markus*, 42; Pesch, *Markusevangelium*, 19) read it as an adjectival phrase: "like a dove." In the end, there is little between these positions. They both rightly claim that the dove is not important in itself. It is used to describe the gentle descent of the Spirit of God.

[51] On the possibility that the descent of the Spirit upon Jesus marks the moment of his becoming Messiah and Son of God, see Marcus, *Mark*, 160.

[52] See Kazmierski, *Son of God*, 54–55; Pesch, *Markusevangelium*, 93. Marcus (*Mark*, 166) suggests that "the good pleasure" of God, hints at the theme of "and it was good" in Genesis (see Gen 1:31), and is a further hint of the new creation. For Watts (*New Exodus*, 108–18) as well as Ps 2, the Isaianic Servant of Isa 42:1 also forms part of the background. See also Kazmierski, *Son of God*, 37–61; Marcus, *The Way of the Lord*, 48–56.

[53] See Hooker, *Beginnings*, 15–16; Marcus, *Mark*, 162. For Gibson (*Temptations*, 70–78), vv. 10–11 designate Jesus as the king of Israel, the Suffering Servant and sacrificial victim.

possession of Jesus, and is now the driving force of his actions. A strong verb (ἐκβάλλει) associated with the famous Markan use of "immediately" (εὐθύς) illustrates the divine urgency which determines the actions of Jesus.[54] Jesus is still the subject of the actions of God, driven out into the desert as God's words had earlier predicted (vv. 2–3). The desert wilderness has a number of meanings in the Old Testament, Judaism, and early Christianity. Above all, however, it is a place of ambiguity. This ambivalence has its origins in the experience of the Hebrew people after their liberation from Egypt and their crossing of the Reed Sea. The desert was for Israel a place of refuge against aggression, a place of privileged encounter with God, but also a place of physical and moral trials, of temptation and sin. The theme continues into the experiences of many Old Testament personalities (for example, Abraham, Elijah, and David).[55] Against this background the authors of Genesis present the fallen state of humankind divided against itself, expelled from a garden where creation was in harmony, into a place where the land and its animal inhabitants rebel against a man and a woman, who are themselves in conflict (see Gen 2:15–25; 3:14–21).[56]

Moses was forty days and forty nights on Mount Sinai without bread or water (see Exod 34:28; Deut 9:9, 18), and Elijah fled through the desert for forty days without food (1 Kgs 19:4–8). Jesus is in the wilderness for forty days (1:13a). Like Moses and Elijah, he experiences the ambiguity of the desert, and in this ambiguity he is exposed to the experience of the man and woman in Eden, tempted by Satan (v. 13b).[57] But here the parallel falters. Adam was tempted by Satan, fell, and was driven out of the garden (LXX Gen 3:24: "He [YHWH] drove out [ἐξέβαλεν] Adam"). Jesus, filled with the Spirit (v. 10), is driven (ἐκβάλλει) by that Spirit into the wilderness (v. 12). We are not told explicitly of Jesus' fall or victory (unlike Matt 4:1–11 // Luke 4:1–13). Jesus is tempted by Satan, and "he was with

---

[54] Mark uses this adverb more times in his 664 verses (forty-seven times) than the rest of the New Testament put together. The count depends upon one's acceptance or refusal of the later scribal tendency to change the Markan εὐθύς to the more elegant εὐθέως. It is often omitted in translation, but the rhythmic appearance of this word is deliberate. It indicates the urgency of what God is doing in and through Jesus.

[55] On this theme, see Meier, *A Marginal Jew*, 2:43–46; E. Corsini, *The Apocalypse: The Perennial Revelation of Jesus Christ* (trans. and ed. F. J. Moloney; GNS 5; Wilmington: Michael Glazier, 1983), 216–18; Cranfield, *St. Mark*, 41–42. The ambiguous nature of the desert wilderness continues into the early church. See Athanasius, *Life of Anthony* (trans. R. C. Gregg; Classics of Western Spirituality; London: SPCK, 1980), 33–65; P. Brown, *The Body and Society: Men, Women, and Sexual Renunciation in Early Christianity* (London: Faber & Faber, 1988), 213–40.

[56] With this paragraph I am suggesting that the use of "the desert" in Mark 1:12–13 (prepared in 1:2–3) is linked with the fall in Genesis rather than with the exodus. This does not exclude the possibility of the presence of exodus themes here. For that position, see U. Mauser, *Christ in the Wilderness* (SBT 39; London: SCM, 1963), 77–102. See especially Gibson (*Temptations*, 60–64), who insists that "*the* desert" is the place of Israel's post-exodus wandering; the place where Jesus must prove his devotion to God. Recently Watts (*New Exodus*, 96–121) has argued against both suggestions, claiming that major themes of the new exodus in Isa 40–55 emerge across the prologue, and set the agenda for the whole of the Gospel. For Painter (*Mark's Gospel*, 32), the situation in the desert introduces the reader to the Gospel's apocalyptic theme of goodness triumphing over satanic power. It was, of course, the ambiguity of the exodus that provided Israel with the hermeneutical key for the interpretation of the biblical narrative, including Gen 1–11. On the primacy of the story of Adam (and Jewish reflection upon Adam) in vv. 12–13, see Marcus, *Mark*, 169–70.

[57] For Gibson (*Temptations*, 58–60), Satan is the agent who tests Jesus' faithfulness to God. Marcus (*Mark*, 169) looks to *L.A.E.* 6 for the theme of forty years in traditions surrounding the Fall. For an overview of the development of the notion of "Satan," and his role in Jewish traditions, see S. R. Garrett, *The Temptations of Jesus in Mark's Gospel* (Grand Rapids: Eerdmans, 1998), 32–35.

the wild beasts; and the angels waited on him" (v. 13b). For the first time in the narrative Jesus is alone, and takes the initiative: "he was with the wild beasts." This may appear irrelevant, or something that one expects if one spends too much time in the wilderness (!), or even a note linking this gospel to the experience of the Roman Christians thrown to the wild beasts during the Neronic persecution.[58] Yet, "[t]his phrase, distinctive to Mark's account, holds the key to his temptation narrative."[59] In the Genesis story Satan's victory over Adam led to hostility and fear in creation (see Gen 3:14–21; Ps 91:11–13). In the Markan story that situation is reversed: he is *with* the wild beasts (ἦν μετὰ τῶν θηρίων). Prophetic tradition surrounding the new creation has been fulfilled (see Isa 11:6–9; see also 35:3–10; Ezek 34:23–31; *T. Benj.* 5:2; *T. Iss.* 7:7). One of the dreams of first-century Judaism has been realized in the coming of Jesus: what was in the beginning has been restored.[60] This link with the creation myths is further enhanced by the final remark of the narrator: "and the angels waited on him" (διηκόνουν αὐτῷ). Once again exodus, Elijah, and creation motifs are present in this lapidary statement. Repeatedly throughout the desert experience of Israel angels help and guide the wandering people (see Exod 14:19; 23:20, 23; 32:34; 33:2). During Elijah's experience of despair and hunger in the wilderness, he is served by the angels (1 Kgs 19:5–7). Although not present in the biblical account, Jewish documents speculate that Adam and Eve were fed by the angels in the Garden of Eden (see *T. Naph.* 8:3–4; *b. Sanh.* 59b).[61]

Only toward the end of the prologue does a hint of the link with the original creation, provided by the ἀρχή of 1:1, return. Jesus is "with the wild beasts" and "waited on" by the angels. His coming has repeated the experience of the original people of God in the desert, but above all, it has restored the original order of God's creation. The promise of "the beginning" in v. 1 (see Gen 1:1) and the coming of the creating presence of the Spirit of God in v. 10 (see Gen 1:3) indicate that the prologue to the Gospel of Mark is linked to the prologue to the human story, as it was told in Gen 1–11. God has been the most active figure in vv. 1–13. Although present toward the end of the prologue, Jesus has been *presented* to the

---

58 See, for example, Lane, *St. Mark*, 38. For Myers (*Binding the Strong Man*, 130), the "wild beasts" recall the animal representations of human kingdoms in Dan 7:3, 7.

59 Guelich, *Mark*, 38.

60 See also Waetjen, *Reordering*, 74–77. On Jewish hopes for the restoration of the Adamic situation, see R. Scroggs, *The Last Adam: A Study in Pauline Anthropology* (Oxford: Blackwell, 1966); W. D. Davies and D. C. Allison, *A Critical and Exegetical Commentary on the Gospel according to Saint Matthew* (3 vols.; ICC; Edinburgh: T&T Clark, 1988–1998), 1:356–57. In his major study of Mark 1:12–13, E. Best (*The Temptation and the Passion: The Markan Soteriology* [2d ed.; SNTSMS 2; Cambridge: Cambridge University Press, 1990], xv–xxiii, 3–60) makes little of creation themes (see pp. xvi–xviii, 6–7). He claims that Satan is definitively defeated in 1:12–13. For the opposite argument, see J. M. Robinson, *The Problem of History in Mark* (SBT 21; London: SCM, 1957), 21–53. See the summary of this discussion in Hooker, *St. Mark*, 51. J. W. van Henten ("The First Testing of Jesus. A Rereading of Mark 1:12–13," *NTS* 45 [1999]: 349–66) questions this interpretation. He points to the loose links with Genesis, to the need to look elsewhere for the forty days, and suggests that the background is "an allusion to Israel's period in the wilderness, with the focus upon Jesus as the people's leader" (p. 361). See also Gibson (*Temptations*, 65–69) for the rejection of any link with the Adam story. Via texts from *T. 12 Patr.*, Gibson claims that the image of being with the wild beasts indicated the testing of Jesus' faithfulness to God's covenanted obligations. Gibson's study of vv. 9–13 can also be found in idem, "Jesus' Wilderness Temptation according to Mark," *JSNT* 53 (1994): 3–34. Garrett (*The Temptations*, 55–60) also explains vv. 12–13 as a Markan indication that Jesus is not victorious over Satan, but must go on making decisions as the righteous servant of God.

61 See J. Jeremias, "Ἀδάμ," *TDNT* 1:141. For the *L.A.E.*, see *OTP* 2:258. For extensive further documentation in support of this position, see Davies and Allison, *Saint Matthew*, 1:356–57.

reader. He is the Christ, the Son of God (v. 1), the Lord (v. 3), the Stronger One (v. 7), one who will baptize with the Holy Spirit (v. 8).[62] God's voice has assured the reader that he is the beloved Son of God, and that God is well pleased with him (v. 11). He is filled with the Spirit (v. 10), and driven into the desert to reverse the tragedy of the Adam and Eve story, to reestablish God's original design (vv. 12–13).[63]

Conclusion

The storyteller has provided a dense prologue for the reader/listener. There should be no doubt in the reader's mind about *who Jesus is.* However, there have been hints throughout the prologue that pointed to a ministry, if he is to baptize with a holy spirit (1:8). There is perhaps even a hint that as God's "beloved" (v. 11) he will accept total and unconditional self-sacrifice. The reader comes to the end of the prologue well informed about *who* Jesus is, but as yet unaware of *how* Jesus is the Christ, the Son of God, the Lord, the Stronger One who baptizes with the Holy Spirit, and *how* in his person God's original creative design has been restored. The readers of this gospel know that Jesus of Nazareth was crucified, and they may well wonder how such an end could be pleasing to God (see v. 11).[64] The prologue to the Gospel lays down this challenge. Now the reader knows *who Jesus is* and must be prepared to read through a story which will show *how Jesus pleases his Father.*

Only the reader or listener is aware of what has been said in the prologue. The various characters in the story—the Pharisees, the crowds, the Romans, and *especially* the disciples—have not read the prologue. This gospel was not written to provide information about Jesus' story or the foundation of the Christian community, to which its original and most subsequent readers belong. By informing the reader—on the very first page of the story—of *who* Jesus is, the author issues a challenge. The readers know that his story ended on a cross. They therefore ask: *in what way* does Jesus, the Son, respond to God's understanding of him? *How* does he live a life, preach a message, and die a death which restore God's original design and make the Father delight in him (1:11)?[65] Answers to these questions can be found only by reading or listening to what Jesus does, what he says, what others do to him, and how he responds to the things done to him in the story that follows.[66]

---

[62] Waetjen (*Reordering*, 22) speaks of Jesus in the prologue as "God's surrogate."

[63] See also Ernst, *Markus*, 46–47; Lührmann, *Markusevangelium*, 39.

[64] It is sometimes claimed that Mark 1:1–13 tells the reader everything that needs to be known. See, for example, Hooker, *Message*, 5–7; idem, *St. Mark*, 52; idem, *Beginnings*, 16–22. This is not the case, as the reader still has a great deal to learn and experience via the story of Jesus. On this, see Matera, "The Prologue," 9–15, and idem, *New Testament Christology* (Louisville: Westminster John Knox, 1999), 6–10. On the role of "telling" and "showing" in narrative, see W. C. Booth, *The Rhetoric of Fiction* (2d ed.; Chicago: University of Chicago Press, 1983), 3–20; Rimmon-Kenan, *Narrative Fiction*, 106–8. See the good description of "the initiated reader" in B. M. F. van Iersel, *Reading Mark* (Collegeville: The Liturgical Press, 1988), 42.

[65] See Marcus, *The Way of the Lord*, 75–77.

[66] J. Drury ("Mark," in *The Literary Guide to the Bible* [ed. R. Alter and F. Kermode; London: Collins, 1987], 405) puts it well: "Between the understanding given us in its first verse and the radical insecurity and incomprehension of the subsequent tale, Mark's book gets its energy." See also Boring, "Mark 1:1–15," 63–67. For Watts (*New Exodus*, 53–136), it is the citation in vv. 2–3 which determines the shape and message of the Gospel as a whole. Watts's study is most helpful on a number of issues, especially the highlighting of the widespread presence of Second Isaiah in Mark, but the overall project is something of a *tour de force.*

For most of the narrative of the Gospel of Mark little attention will be explicitly directed to the reader (see, however, 13:14),[67] who has been the unique focus of the words of 1:1–13. However, at the end of the story (16:1–8) the author will return to the readers. They will be asked where they stand as they hear: "And they went out and fled from the tomb; for trembling and astonishment had come upon them; and they said nothing to anyone, for they were afraid" (16:8). The Gospel of Mark has both a prologue and an epilogue during which the author focuses intensely upon the reader of the intervening narrative of 1:14–15:47.

---

[67] This rare but important comment from the narrator, "Let the reader understand" (Mark 13:14), is an indication that, despite the fact that the narrator does not regularly address the reader through the narrative, the reader is the focus of the narrator's storytelling.

SECTION 2

THE MYSTERY OF JESUS

MARK 1:14–8:30

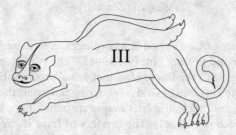

JESUS AND ISRAEL (MARK 1:14–3:6)

The reader, armed by the prologue of 1:1–13 with the knowledge of *who Jesus is,* is led into the story of Jesus' public ministry by means of the first, and perhaps major, summary statement of the Gospel (1:14–15). What follows, down to 15:47, tells *how Jesus is* all that has been claimed for him by God and the omniscient narrator in 1:1–13. The section of the Gospel which runs from 1:14 to 3:6 contains textual markers indicating that it forms a discrete literary unit. Mark 1:14–3:6 opens with a summary (1:14–15) and is immediately followed by discipleship material (1:16–20). After various events from Jesus' ministry in Galilee, representative leaders of Israel (the Pharisees and the Herodians; 3:6) make a decision. From opposite ends of Jewish leadership, the coming together of Pharisees and Herodians to plan a unified agenda indicates Israel's initial response to Jesus' words and actions: they plan to destroy him.

The Shape of Mark 1:14–3:6

The overall outline of 1:14–3:6 is clear. It is our first indication that the Gospel of Mark is the product of careful planning and writing.[1] The same care, however, can be found in the internal articulation of 1:14–3:6. Jesus bursts upon the scene in Galilee, proclaiming the gospel and demanding conversion (1:14–15). Immediately he calls others to follow, and they respond without hesitation, following him down his way (vv. 16–20). Together they go forth. From this point on there are always disciples, the Twelve, or some named members of the Twelve "with" Jesus, until they separate themselves from him, fleeing in fear in 14:50. Representative powers of evil—an unclean spirit (vv. 21–28), sickness, and taboo—are overcome as Jesus touches Simon's mother-in-law, heals her, and is served by her (vv. 29–31). The narrative pauses as the narrator summarizes Jesus' healing activity and his power over demons (vv. 32–34), but Simon and some of the disciples disturb Jesus in his prayer, and he journeys on throughout all Galilee, preaching and casting out demons

---

[1] Mark's Greek is regularly charged with being "rudimentary" (see, for example, J. Painter, *Mark's Gospel: Worlds in Conflict* [New Testament Readings; London: Routledge, 1997], 8). For an analysis of the Markan language and style, see V. Taylor, *The Gospel according to St. Mark* (2d ed.; London: Macmillan, 1966), 44–54. Taylor remarks: "Mark's Gospel is written in a relatively simple and popular form of Greek which has striking affinities with the spoken language of everyday life as it is revealed to us in the papyri and inscriptions" (p. 52). But simple language can be used skillfully. See especially M. A. Beavis, *Mark's Audience: The Literary and Social Setting of Mark 4:11–12* (JSNTSup 33; Sheffield: JSOT Press, 1989), 13–44. These pages show that "Mark is not an artless jumble of transcribed oral stories, but the result of conscious artifice" (p. 21).

(vv. 35–39). The presence of God's goodness continues as Jesus again cuts through ritual taboo, touching a leper and healing him (vv. 39–45). The reader comes away from these first pages of the Gospel with the impression that Jesus' proclamation in v. 15 is bearing fruit. The presence of the kingdom of God is rendering powerless the signs of the kingdom of evil; sickness, taboo, and unclean spirits evaporate before him, his authoritative word (vv. 25, 39, 41), and touch (vv. 31, 41). The mystery of Jesus is already present: "What is this? A new teaching! With authority he commands even the unclean spirits and they obey him" (v. 27). This authority is also seen in the vocation of the first disciples. Without a murmur, they show all the signs of conversion (μετάνοια), leave their worldly success, and walk after Jesus (vv. 16–20). The time is fulfilled, there is repentance, and the powerful presence of the kingdom of God is at hand. The initial proclamation of the gospel by word and deed brooks no opposition (v. 15).[2]

But this situation does not last. The first moments of Jesus' ministry are directed against *the powers of evil,* and such powers are unable to withstand his word and presence. This is not the case in the encounter between the word, works, and person of Jesus and *the leaders of Israel.* As the story proceeds, Jesus continues to work wonders. He cures a paralytic (2:1–12) and a man with a withered hand (3:1–6). He gathers further disciples from the peripheries of Jewish society (2:13–17), and his words and deeds arouse wonder: "We never saw anything like this!" (2:12). But opposition increases. The five episodes in 2:1–3:6 report not only the spread of Jesus' ongoing authority but also a mounting rejection of this authority. The overall argument of this section of 1:14–3:6 can be seen in the following scheme.[3]

[A] Jesus *enters* Capernaum *again* (καὶ εἰσελθὼν πάλιν εἰς), and forgives the sins of a paralytic, but some of the scribes in their *hearts* question Jesus' authority to forgive sins (see also vv. 9, 10). He affirms this authority by *raising* (v. 11; see also vv. 9, 13) the paralytic. (2:1–12)

[B] Jesus calls Levi from his tax office and shares his table and *eats* (v. 16a; see also v. 16b) with a number of similarly situated characters: sinners and tax collectors, along with his disciples. The scribes of the Pharisees complain about such behavior to his disciples. (2:13–17)

[C] At a time when the disciples of the Baptist and the Pharisees were *fasting* (v. 18a; see vv. 18b, 19, 20), people came to him and asked why he did not fast like other religious people. They will fast when the bridegroom is *taken away* (v. 20) from them. (2:18–22)

[B′] As Jesus and his disciples pluck grain and *eat* on a Sabbath, the Pharisees question Jesus on the right observance of the law, only to be instructed on Abiathar's eating the bread of the Presence (v. 26a; see also v. 26b). (2:23–28)

---

[2] The theme of the overwhelming power of the kingdom over against other powers of evil is lost in J. Marcus's title for 1:16–45: "The honeymoon period" (*Mark,* 177).

[3] This understanding of Mark 2:1–3:6 depends upon the work of J. Dewey (*Markan Public Debate: Literary Technique, Concentric Structure, and Theology in Mark 2:1–3:6* [SBLDS 48; Chico: Scholars Press, 1980]). An earlier summary can be found in "The Literary Structure of the Controversy Stories in Mark 2:1–3:6," *JBL* 92 (1973): 394–401. It is now available in *The Interpretation of Mark* (ed. W. R. Telford; IRT 7; Philadelphia: Fortress, 1985), 109–18. See also E. S. Malbon, "The Major Importance of the Minor Characters in Mark," in *In the Company of Jesus: Characters in Mark's Gospel* (Louisville: Westminster John Knox, 2000), 213–14, 217–20, and Marcus (*Mark,* 212–15), with reservations about the relationship between 2:13–17 and 2:23–28.

[A'] On a Sabbath, a man with a withered hand is present as Jesus *enters* the synagogue *again* (καὶ εἰσῆλθεν πάλιν εἰς). But "they" were watching to see what he would do on the holy day so that they might accuse him. He reduces them to silence, grieves over the hardness of their *hearts* (v. 5), *raises* the maimed man (v. 3), and performs the miracle (v. 5). The Pharisees and the Herodians hold counsel—to destroy him. (3:1–6)

Jesus enters a town and a synagogue for the two miracle stories found at the beginning (2:1–12) and at the end (3:1–6) of the collection. They both refer to raising. The theme of eating is found in the second and fourth episode (2:13–17, 23–28), while fasting lies at the heart of the central passage (2:18–22). Jesus' statement in 2:20 on his being taken away is the central message of the passage and contrasts with the references to raising in the first and last episodes. These details, italicized above, indicate that 2:1–3:6 is a "chiastic" use of traditional material, or better, an instance of ring composition.[4]

Ongoing themes develop further with each new episode. Jesus' opponents initially object "in their hearts" (2:6). They speak to the disciples (v. 16), then to Jesus (v. 18). They next dispute with him over Sabbath law (v. 24). Finally, in silence they watch so that they might accuse him (3:2) and plot his destruction (v. 6). Representatives of Israel are found in descriptions of the opponents: scribes (2:8), scribes of the Pharisees (v. 16), people (v. 18), the Pharisees (v. 24), "they" (3:2), and the Pharisees and the Herodians (v. 6). The first two episodes deal with sin and sinners (2:1–12, 13–17), and in the final two episodes Jesus performs actions that question a traditional understanding of the Sabbath (2:23–28; 3:1–6). The unveiling of Jesus' role and authority also develops, from the first miracle, where the Son of Man is shown to have authority to forgive sins (2:10), to the two final scenes, which show that the Son of Man is lord of the Sabbath (2:28). This development, however, takes place under the shadow of the cross: "The days will come when the bridegroom is taken away from them" (2:20), and that day is already being plotted as Pharisees and Herodians plan his destruction (3:6). The presence of a chiastic structure becomes obvious only at the end of the reading process. Only when the reader reaches the second miracle story does a sense of repetition generate a looking back across the passage. Meanwhile, the linear development of the story continues as Jesus announces the gospel of the kingdom only to meet increasing opposition, which will lead to his death (see 2:20; 3:6).

The overall structure of 1:14–3:6 can be presented in the following fashion:

1:14–15   Summary: Jesus announces the advent of the kingdom and calls for repentance and belief in the gospel.

1:16–45   The kingdom comes with power.
    1:16–20   Disciples are called and respond.
    1:21–28   An unclean spirit is vanquished.
    1:29–31   Sickness and taboo are vanquished.
    1:32–34   Jesus' healing and exorcizing authority is summarized.

---

[4] Some New Testament scholars trace chiasms in the text and interpret the passage in the light of the chiasm. See, most recently, J. Breck, *The Shape of Biblical Language: Chiasmus in the Scriptures and Beyond* (New York: St. Vladimir's Seminary Press, 1994). No doubt ancient authors wrote in this way, but readers do not read in chiasms. A printed page and a scholar's desk are needed to "lay out" a chiasm. Readers come to the end of a passage and are aware of a *reprise* of an earlier passage, its thought and its language. It may be better to call these literary patterns "ring compositions." The reader becomes aware of having come full circle. The temporal and linear development of the story must be allowed to proceed. See the remarks of R. M. Fowler, *Let the Reader Understand: Reader-Response Criticism and the Gospel of Mark* (Minneapolis: Fortress, 1991), 151–52.

1:35–39   Jesus is led away from prayer to preach and cast out demons throughout Galilee.

1:40–45   Sickness and taboo are vanquished.

2:1–3:6   The kingdom is opposed.

2:1–12   Jesus cures and is questioned.

2:13–17   Jesus calls disciples and is questioned.

2:18–22   Jesus is questioned over fasting.

2:23–28   Jesus is questioned over Sabbath law.

3:1–6   Jesus is watched that he might be accused, and his death is plotted.

This "list of events," however well articulated, does not indicate the richness of Mark 1:14–3:6.[5] As Jesus' words and deeds demonstrate the power of the kingdom, yet raise opposition, there is a subtle interweaving of an increasing interest and wonder in Jesus' person. Characters in the story, who have not read the prologue, encounter Jesus and raise questions: "What is this? A new teaching!" (1:27); "Everyone is searching for you" (1:37); "We never saw anything like this!" (2:12). The narrator informs the reader who has read the prologue: "They were astonished at his teaching" (1:22); "His fame spread everywhere" (1:28); "And the whole city was gathered together about the door" (1:33); "People came to him from every quarter" (1:45); "They were all amazed and glorified God" (2:12). Yet Jesus forbids the demons, who know who he is, to speak (1:34) and insists that his deeds not become the focus of attention (1:44). Mark 1:14–3:6 vigorously addresses the question of Jesus' identity.

Summary (1:14–15)

There is progression as Jesus actively preaches the gospel. Throughout 1:1–13 the storyteller speaks directly to readers, telling them who Jesus is. The first major section of the Gospel begins with a summary, followed by material on the disciples (vv. 16–20). It also begins with a geographical reference to Jesus' coming into Galilee, where he will remain until 10:1. There is a decisive break in vv. 14–15 with the period of John the Baptist, and the place of his ministry. John announced the coming of Jesus (vv. 2–8) and baptized him (vv. 9–11), but as Jesus begins his ministry, that period is closed. John has been violently swept from the scene. The verb used to speak of John's arrest (παραδοθῆναι) means both arrest and imprisonment, and it will be used later in the Gospel to speak of Jesus' being "delivered up" to authorities, and to scourging and crucifixion (9:31; 14:10; 15:1, 15).[6] The relationship between John and Jesus is maintained across the Gospel (see especially 6:14–29; 9:13), but in the Markan telling of Jesus' story, the former has already fallen into

---

[5] Some commentators regard any attempt to trace a literary structure in Mark as a lost cause. See, for example, Anderson, *Mark,* 32–40. M. D. Hooker (*St. Mark,* 109, and elsewhere) regards divisions as "arbitrary." However, although differing in detail, a number of commentators follow the above general division. For a sampling, see Taylor, *St. Mark,* 107; Lohmeyer, *Markusevangelium,* 29–70 (see also p. 7*); Schweizer, *Mark,* 44–77; Lane, *Mark,* 29; Pesch, *Markusevangelium,* 33–34; Gnilka, *Markus,* 1:71; Waetjen, *Reordering,* 77–95. For a different approach, see B. M. F. van Iersel, *Reading Mark* (Collegeville: The Liturgical Press, 1988), 43–68; Guelich, *Mark,* xxxv–xxxvii; Myers, *Binding the Strong Man,* viii–ix; Painter, *Mark's Gospel,* ix–x.

[6] See Lührmann, *Markusevangelium,* 39. On the development and use of this verb to speak of a saving death of Jesus, see N. Perrin, "The Use of *(Para)didonai* in Connection with the Passion of Jesus in the New Testament," in *A Modern Pilgrim in New Testament Christology* (Philadelphia: Fortress, 1974), 94–103.

violent hands as Jesus begins a ministry that will end in the same fashion.[7] The report of the death of John the Baptist in 6:14–29 is the Markan use of a long analeptic flashback, set between the sending out (6:6b–13) and the return (6:30) of the Twelve. Not only is John off the scene because of his "handing over," but his ministry to all Judea and many from Jerusalem (see v. 5) is left behind as Jesus goes to Galilee (v. 14). There he will exercise the major part of his ministry (1:14–9:50).

John proclaimed a baptism of repentance (v. 4) and the coming of "the stronger one" (v. 7). Jesus also proclaims (v. 14), but he points away from himself to announce the gospel of God (v. 14). In v. 1 the narrator stated that the book that follows is "the good news" about Jesus, and the content of that good news is that he is the Christ, the Son of God.[8] What eventually emerged in the prologue is restated in the words of Jesus. The "good news," however, is not primarily about what Jesus did but about what God did in and through his Son, Jesus, in whom he is well pleased (see v. 11).[9] "The content of this 'gospel' is set forth in the message of 1:15 that is epexegetic to 1:14."[10] The long-standing Jewish understanding of God as king, vindicator, and champion, so often thwarted by the events of history and the frailty of the people and their leaders, is proclaimed as "at hand" (ἤγγικεν ἡ βασιλεία τοῦ θεοῦ). Jesus' announcement creates a sense of urgency. The reigning presence of God is "at the door"—there, but not fully present, and this summons forth a response,[11] indicating an unresolved tension between the present and yet to come kingdom. The rest of the Gospel will tell a tale of different responses to this tension as various characters in the story encounter the reigning presence of God in the person and teaching of Jesus.[12] The long wait has come to an end: "the time is fulfilled." The expression ὁ καιρός is used to speak of "the time." In prophetic-apocalyptic language this word points to a time measured by God's design (see Dan 7:22; Ezek 7:12; 9:1; 1 Pet 1:11; Rev 1:3). There is ordinary time (ὁ χρόνος), which measures human events, and a God-directed opportune time (ὁ καιρός). It is the latter that is fulfilled as Jesus begins his ministry in Galilee.

Jesus' presence, however, demands a twofold response: repentance and belief.[13] The reigning presence of God, found in the person and teaching of Jesus, his Son (see 1:1–13),

---

[7] It is likely that there was a period when the ministries of John and Jesus overlapped (see John 3:22–30). The decisive separation of the two ministries serves Mark's purposes. Gnilka (*Markus,* 1:65) describes it as "a salvation-history scheme." See also Lane, *Mark,* 63.

[8] See Gnilka, *Markus,* 1:42–43.

[9] This interpretation understands the genitive τοῦ θεοῦ as a subjective genitive. It is good news "from God" rather than good news "about God" (objective genitive). See Hooker, *St. Mark,* 54; Marcus, *Mark,* 172.

[10] Guelich, *Mark,* 43.

[11] C. H. Dodd (*The Parables of the Kingdom* [London: Collins, 1936], 34–80) argued from an examination of the LXX use of the verb ἐγγίζειν that it could mean "to arrive." His suggestion has not been widely accepted. See a summary of the discussion in Guelich, *Mark,* 43–44. On the position taken above, see Gnilka, *Markus,* 1:68–69. Lane (*Mark,* 65) puts it well: "The coming of the Kingdom remains future, but it is certainly present because God has begun to bring it to pass in the coming of his Son." See also Marcus, *Mark,* 172–73.

[12] My words "the reigning presence of God" are an attempt to translate the active meaning of the Aramaic behind Jesus' expression ἡ βασιλεία τοῦ θεοῦ. The "kingdom" must not be understood as a "place where God rules," but a new situation in the lives of men and women unconditionally open to God, made possible by Jesus' teaching and person. See Ernst, *Markus,* 51–54.

[13] See C. D. Marshall, *Faith as a Theme in Mark's Narrative* (SNTSMS 64; Cambridge: Cambridge University Press, 1989), 44–56.

has been proclaimed as the "good news" (1:1, 14). The basic meaning of "repent" (μετανοεῖτε) is a radical turning back.[14] The history of God's people, long believers in God as their lord and king, is eloquent proof that false directions can be taken. The "good news" of the reigning presence of God is lived (1:11) and proclaimed (1:14) by Jesus Christ (1:1). Despite the brevity of the summary an almost physical image is conjured up, disclosing an urgent need to stop in one's tracks, turn from all that leads away from the kingdom, and become part of that kingdom by believing in the good news. It "thus properly represents the structural uniqueness of Jesus' concept of repentance . . . the sense of the beginning of a turn toward Christian faith."[15] In many ways 1:14–15 is a summary of the Gospel of Mark.[16] The rest of the narrative tells of Jesus' unfailing proclamation, in both word and deed, of the reigning presence of God.[17] It also tells, however, of the ambiguity of the response of the other characters in the narrative, especially the disciples.

The Kingdom Comes with Power (1:16–45)

Disciples are called and they respond (1:16–20)

There is widespread agreement that the bulk of 1:16–20 has come to Mark from earlier tradition.[18] Among the few Markan additions, the use of "the sea" (τὴν θάλασσαν) to describe what was generally known as "the lake" (λίμνη [Luke 5:1, 2; 8:22, 23, 33]) introduces this symbolic "sea" from the beginning of the narrative.[19] The form of the passage is highly stylized, based on the model of the prophetic vocation of Elisha in 1 Kgs 19:19–21.[20] In fact, there are two, not one, vocation stories here. A structured presentation of the text will make this clear.

---

[14] In Greek the basic idea is a change of attitude affecting one's inner self, but the Hebrew notion of repentance *(shuv)* means to turn around in one's tracks and to resume the right path, from which one has strayed. In Judaism it was understood as a return to the law. See H. Merklein, "μετάνοια," *EDNT* 2:416.

[15] Merklein, *EDNT* 2:417. The non-Markan expression πιστεύετε ἐν τῷ εὐαγγελίῳ indicates the primitive (pre-Markan) nature of this call to repentance and belief (see Gnilka, *Markus,* 1:65; Guelich, *Mark,* 44–45). Marcus (*Mark,* 174) suggests that it may come from a pre-Markan baptismal formula.

[16] "A sort of manifesto which sums up the substance and the essential meaning of the whole public ministry" (Nineham, *St. Mark,* 68).

[17] This summary serves an important Markan literary and theological purpose. Gnilka (*Markus,* 1:65) soundly remarks: "What we find here is hardly an *ipsissimum verbum* of Jesus but rather, surely, a significant new formulation of his preaching of the kingdom." See also Pesch, *Markusevangelium,* 1:107.

[18] R. Pesch, "Berufung und Sendung, Nachfolge und Mission: Eine Studie zu Mk 1,16–20," *ZKT* 91 (1969): 7–8. See also his *Markusevangelium,* 1:108–16; Nineham, *St. Mark,* 70; Lührmann, *Markusevangelium,* 46–47.

[19] The "sea" of Galilee will play an important role in subsequent episodes. See E. S. Malbon, "The Jesus of Mark and the Sea of Galilee," *JBL* 103 (1984): 363–77; idem, *Narrative Space and Mythic Meaning in Mark* (New Voices in Biblical Studies; San Francisco: Harper & Row, 1986), 76–79. On the Markan use of θάλασσα rather than λίμνη, see "The Jesus," 363–64, *Narrative Space,* 76. For a summary, see E. LaVerdiere, *The Beginning of the Gospel: Introducing the Gospel according to Mark* (2 vols.; Collegeville: The Liturgical Press, 1999), 1:41–42.

[20] See Pesch ("Berufung und Sendung," 9–12) for a detailed comparison of the two passages. See also M. Hengel, *The Charismatic Leader and His Followers* (trans. J. Grieg; Studies of the New Tes-

And *passing along* by the sea of Galilee
he saw
    Simon and Andrew the brother of Simon
    casting a net into the sea; *and Jesus said* to them,
"*Follow* me and *I will make you* fishers of men."
    And immediately *they left* their nets
    and *followed him.*
And going on a little farther,
he saw
    James the son of Zebedee and John his brother
    who were in their boat mending their nets.
And immediately *he called* them
    and *they left* their father Zebedee in the boat with the hired servants
    and *followed him.*

Jesus never rests. A glance at the first chapters of Mark's Gospel indicates almost continual motion: Jesus came from Nazareth (1:9); the Spirit drove him out (1:12); Jesus came into Galilee (1:14); and passing along (1:16); and going along a little farther (1:19); and they went into Capernaum (1:21); and immediately he left the synagogue (1:29); he rose and went out (1:35); and he went throughout all Galilee (1:39); he returned to Capernaum (2:1); he went out again (2:13). These indications of movement come from the hand of the evangelist, and show the Markan Jesus endlessly on the move, urged on by a sense of mission.[21] Within this context, carefully constructed by the evangelist, the first disciples are asked to "walk behind him."

The use of δεῦτε ὀπίσω μου (1:17) and ἠκολούθησαν (1:18), followed by a combination of the movement and the place behind Jesus in 1:20 (ἀπῆλθον ὀπίσω αὐτοῦ), shows that the disciple is involved in a physical "walking behind" Jesus. The itinerant Jesus calls disciples to go his way. However, the physical "walking behind" also involves a certain spiritual attitude, a belief in the guide who leads.[22] Jesus is not a rabbi, gathering disciples in a school.[23] The disciples of Jesus share the way and the destiny of the one calling them to come behind him. Thus the plural verb in 1:21 is very important: "And *they* went into Capernaum." Mark has joined a series of originally independent passages by means of a deliberate and continual repetition of καί. A close link exists between:

1:14–15	Jesus' bursting onto the scene, announcing the proximity and the urgency of the kingdom
1:16–20	His immediate calling of "followers"
1:21–28	The going forth of Jesus and these followers *together* to initiate the active presence of the kingdom

---

tament and Its World; New York: Crossroad, 1981), 16–18; A. Schulz, *Nachfolgen und Nachahmen: Studien über das Verhältnis der Neutestamentlichen Jüngershaft zur Urchristlichen Vorbildethik* (SANT 6; Munich: Kösel, 1962), 100–103; G. Minette de Tillesse, *Le secret messianique dans l'Evangile de Marc* (LD 47; Paris: Cerf, 1968), 258–61; Lührmann, *Markusevangelium,* 47; Marcus, *Mark,* 181–83.

[21] See van Iersel, *Reading Mark,* 45–46.

[22] See J. Donaldson, " 'Called to Follow': A Twofold Experience of Discipleship," *BTB* 5 (1975): 67–77. For a thorough study of the growth and understanding of the use of ἀκολουθεῖν in the New Testament and the early church, see Schulz, *Nachfolge und Nachahmen.*

[23] See Hengel, *The Charismatic Leader,* 42–63.

The second common feature that appears to be central to both accounts is Jesus' taking the initiative. In the first story we find: *he* saw (1:14), *Jesus* said to them (1:17), *I* will make you (1:17). In the second account we find: *he* saw (1:19), *he* called them (1:20). This feature will grow as Mark's narrative unfolds (see 3:14; 5:19–21; 10:21). The use of the strong expression "I will make" (ποιήσω) has sometimes been understood as coming from the Septuagint version of the creation story (see LXX Gen 1:1, 7, 16, 21, 25, 26, 27, 31; 2:2, 3, 4), with the implication that there is something of a new creation taking place. This is perhaps too subtle at this stage of the narrative. A strong verb with Jesus as its subject excellently conveys Mark's idea: all that will become of the disciples will take place because of the initiative of Jesus, what he will do for them and make of them, and their association with him. Old Testament background may be found in such passages as LXX 1 Sam 12:6, where Moses and Aaron are described as "appointed" (ποιήσας) by YHWH, and 1 Kgs 13:33 or 2 Chron 2:18 where the same strong verb is used for the intervention of YHWH for the appointment or institution of priests.[24] The powerful intervention and presence of Jesus is shaping their lives.

The vocation to mission is given in terms of the disciples' being made into "fishers of men." This indication of the nature of the mission of the first followers of Jesus goes back to an original, pre-Easter vocation to mission.[25] Most commentators claim that there is little Old Testament background for the metaphor, although some contact can be found with Jer 16:16 and Prov 6:26. Vincent Taylor suggests the most likely reason for the expression is that they were, in fact, fishermen.[26] W. L. Lane has pointed to the fact that several Old Testament passages use the image of fishermen and fishing to speak of God's use of human instruments to seek out the evil doers and to punish them (especially Jer 16:16–17; see also the use of fishing language to convey the same idea in Amos 4:2; Ezek 19:4–5; and 1QH 5:7–8). When one reads Mark 1:16–20 in close proximity with the message in 1:14–15 of the urgently decisive presence of the kingdom and the need for conversion, the use of such language to speak of the followers of Jesus may be significant.

> The immediate function of those called to be fishers of men is to accompany Jesus as witnesses to the proclamation of the nearness of the kingdom and the necessity for men to turn to God through radical repentance. Their ultimate function will be to confront men with God's decisive action.[27]

As the story of Jesus begins, disciples are called not only to follow Jesus along his way, but also to repeat in their lives and teaching the urgent presence of the kingdom of God.

---

[24] See B. Rigaux, "Die Zwölf in Geschichte und Kerygma," in *Der historische Jesus und der kerygmatische Christus: Beiträge zum Christusverständnis in Forschung und Verkündigung* (ed. H. Ristow and K. Matthiae; Berlin: Evangelische Verlagsanstalt, 1962), 474–75. He also looks to Old Testament background: 1 Kgs 13:33; 2 Chron 2:18, as well as 1 Sam 12:6.

[25] M. Dibelius (*From Tradition to Gospel* [trans. B. L. Woolf; Library of Theological Translations; Cambridge & London: James Clarke, 1971], 112–13) regards it as traditional, while R. Bultmann (*The History of the Synoptic Tradition* [trans. J. Marsh; Oxford: Basil Blackwell, 1968], 64) gives it no place in pre-Markan tradition.

[26] Taylor, *St. Mark,* 169. See also Guelich, *Mark,* 51. J. Manek ("Fishers of Men," *NovT* 2 [1957–1958]: 138–41) attempts to link the fishing image with the practice of baptism. It is certainly linked in early Christian art, but there is little support for this speculation in the New Testament.

[27] Lane, *Mark,* 68. See also Pesch, *Markusevangelium,* 1:111; Marcus, *Mark,* 184–85. Pesch (*Markusevangelium,* 1:112) points out that the use of καί in v. 19 to open the second vocation story (vv. 19–20) shows that the sons of Zebedee are also called to be fishers of men.

The vocation stories report a spontaneous leaving of nets, boats, father, and hired servants, to walk behind Jesus (vv. 18, 20). The response is "immediate." Although the word εὐθύς is a favorite Markan word, its insertion here is not merely stylistic or a Markan eccentricity. It has been inserted into a pre-Markan tradition deliberately, to stress the spontaneity and the immediate nature of the response. The passage may be more about the Master who calls than the disciple who follows,[28] but attention is also given to the unconditional response of the disciples. The possessions "left behind" are explicitly listed: nets, boats, hired servants, and father.[29] Their peer group's criteria of success in life are abandoned: tools of trade (nets and boats) and servants. Servants were a major sign of their success, as they control a work force.[30] For first-century Galilean fishermen it would have been madness to abandon the tools of trade that they had learned to use from long experience, to relinquish all authority over a set of dependent servants, and to give up their trade and their commercial skill. But the most radical break would be abandoning what was probably the source of all that they knew: their connections to a family and a family tradition.

Mark reports the calling of the first disciples along the lines of a traditional prophetic vocation account, to which an all-important new element has been added: the person of Jesus of Nazareth. In doing this he announced that

> [t]he call of God in Christ comes with a divine power which does not need to wait upon accidental circumstances; it can create the response it demands. And that response must be one of unconditional obedience, even to the point of sacrificing livelihood and the closest natural ties, as many of St. Mark's contemporaries must have known from experience.[31]

Mark 1:16–20 presents the basic structure of the vocation to discipleship that will remain important for all the subsequent activities of the disciples in the story.[32] Jesus calls people to follow him; they are to be associated in the critical, eschatological inbreaking of the kingdom of God. There is no place for a conditioned response. It will cost no less than everything. Here we have a deliberately designed narrative that establishes a paradigm for a disciple's vocation. These first vocation stories are not primarily about disciples and their virtue. They are about Jesus of Nazareth, the Christ and the Son of God, full of the Spirit, urgently pressing on to his assigned task (1:1–13, 16, 19). Only insofar as *he* has the initiative (1:17, 20), and the response of discipleship is in accordance with *his* world-questioning criteria (1:18, 20), can discipleship possibly succeed. Jesus' ministry in Galilee begins (1:14–15), he calls others to follow him (vv. 16–20), and together they go forth (v. 21).

Jesus vanquishes an unclean spirit (1:21–28)

At Capernaum, on a Sabbath, Jesus and the disciples enter the synagogue. Mark indicates that Jesus taught (1:21) and that his teaching generated astonishment because his au-

---

28 Bultmann, *History,* 56–57, 61.

29 The deliberate repetition of the verb ἀφίημι in vv. 18 and 20 shows that Mark wants his readers to see the importance of this action. The use of this strong verb may well have had its origins in the radical preaching of the early missionaries. See, for this suggestion, Cranfield, *St. Mark,* 69.

30 It has been suggested that the hired servants are mentioned to contrast the generosity of the disciples with the mercenary concerns of others. It is better to see them as part of the "power structure" that the disciples abandon. See Nineham, *St. Mark,* 73. This element in Markan theology has recently been strongly developed by Myers, *Binding the Strong Man;* on 1:16–20, see pp. 132–33.

31 Nineham, *St. Mark,* 71.

32 See Lane, *St. Mark,* 69–70; Guelich, *Mark,* 53.

thority was different from that of the scribes (1:22). The man with an unclean spirit, also in the synagogue (1:23), cries out in recognition of Jesus. The subtle indications of Jesus' superior authority vis-à-vis the scribes becomes a public recognition on the part of the evil spirit in the question τί ἡμῖν καὶ σοί. It is a formulaic question with Old Testament background (see 2 Sam 16:10; 19:23; 1 Kgs 17:18; 2 Kgs 3:13; Judg 11:12; 2 Chron 35:21):

> The question has the defensive function of placing the one questioned in the position of responsibility for what follows and thereby creates an irreconcilable distance between the two parties. . . . The question betrays the unclean spirit's recognition of his own status, particularly in the light of Jesus' authority.[33]

Jesus of Nazareth is called by name (1:24a), and the spirit's further question, "Have you come to destroy us?" recognizes Jesus' authority (1:24b). But the evil spirit attempts to control that authority by correctly identifying Jesus as the Holy One of God (1:24c). The reader recognizes that the evil spirit's naming of Jesus matches the presentation of Jesus in the prologue (1:1–13). In the ancient world, to call a person by name gave the one summoning a certain authority over the one summoned.[34] The evil spirit possessing the man in the synagogue has put two names together: Jesus of Nazareth (his public name) and the Holy One of God (his true identity).[35] In the cultural and religious world of the time, the evil spirit should have won the day, and the reader recognizes that truth. However, such cultural and religious absolutes do not apply to Jesus. "The Kingdom of God is absolutely incompatible with the tyranny of enslaving demonic powers."[36] He breaks through all such barriers and rebukes (ἐπετίμησεν) the spirit, reducing it to silence, thus nullifying the attempt to control Jesus by calling his name, and commanding it to come out of the man (v. 25).[37] Jesus' command has immediate effect, and the agonizing experience of the vanquished spirit is dramatically portrayed by the convulsions and the cries of the possessed man as the spirit departs (v. 26).

The exorcism, however, is not an end in itself. It serves to reinforce the issue raised at the beginning of the episode, where Jesus' authority and teaching generated astonishment (ἐξεπλήσσοντο, 1:22). A further, but parallel, experience has been generated by the exorcism. All are amazed (ἐθαμβήθησαν), and again they wonder among themselves over his new and authoritative teaching (v. 26a; see v. 22). An exorcism is regarded as teaching, as is made obvious by the description of the teaching in v. 27b: "With authority he commands even the unclean spirits and they obey him." The major elements of this exorcism came to Mark in his tradition,[38] but it is the evangelist who insists upon the unity between what Jesus says (vv. 21–22) and what he does (v. 27). The coming of the reigning presence of God in the person of Jesus is discernible in the authority of his teaching, in word and deed.

---

[33] Guelich, *Mark,* 57. Lohmeyer (*Markus,* 36) suggests that the demon's use of these "holy words" is an attempt to control Jesus. See also Marcus, *Mark,* 187.

[34] See Lane, *St. Mark,* 74, esp. n. 118.

[35] On these names, see Marcus, *Mark,* 187–89, 192–93.

[36] Van Iersel, *Reading Mark,* 57.

[37] The use of the verb ἐπιτιμάω indicates a very strong rebuke, a stern warning "in order to prevent an action or to bring one to an end" (BDAG, 384, s.v. ἐπιτιμάω). A further strong verb used for the command to silence has the aggressive meaning of the English "shut up!" (φιμώθητι). These verbs were used in the ancient world for exorcism. See Nineham, *St. Mark,* 75–76; H. C. Kee, "The Terminology of Mark's Exorcism Stories," *NTS* 14 (1968): 232–46; Guelich, *Mark,* 57–58; Marcus, *Mark,* 189, 193–94.

[38] See Gnilka, *Markus,* 1:76–78.

The evil spirit cannot hope to survive in the presence of God's kingship. Yet the crowd is astonished (v. 22) and amazed (v. 27). They are left questioning: "What is this?" (v. 27). For all his authority over the evil spirit, the human beings in the story are left amazed and wondering. This cannot be regarded as an unqualified acceptance of Jesus' presence.[39] Ironically, however, his fame spreads throughout the surrounding region of Galilee (v. 28).

Jesus vanquishes sickness and taboo (1:29–31)

There is no change in time as Jesus goes to the house of Simon on the Sabbath (1:29; see v. 21). He heals a man (vv. 21–28) and then a woman (vv. 29–31) in immediate succession. Jesus' ministry opens with evidence of his rejection of any taboo that might inhibit his ability to help those in need. As Simon's mother-in-law lay sick with a fever (v. 30), Jesus went to her and *touched* her (v. 31a). The fever departed, and she *served* them (v. 31b). The miracle unfolds as a classical healing narrative: problem, request, touch, miracle, demonstration.[40] But there is more to this miracle story than its form. A respected religious leader would not take any woman by the hand. Though there were precedents for rabbis taking the hand of another man and miraculously healing him, there are no examples of rabbis doing so for a woman, and certainly not on the Sabbath when the act could wait until after sundown. Jesus could well be accused of contracting uncleanness and violating the Sabbath.[41] Consequently, he opens himself to further accusation by allowing himself to be served by this woman. This may appear normal enough to us, but no self-respecting rabbi would allow such a thing. As Rabbi Samuel (d. ca. 254 C.E.) had said: "One must under no circumstances be served by a woman, be she adult or child."[42]

It is often suggested that Mark 1:21–34 is presented as a day in the life of Jesus.[43] If this is the case, the curing of Simon's mother-in-law forms the center of the day's activities: he cures the possessed man in the synagogue (1:21–28), raises the fever stricken woman

---

[39] See Lane, *Mark*, 76.

[40] See Bultmann, *History*, 221–26; Marcus, *Mark*, 199.

[41] B. Witherington, *Women in the Ministry of Jesus: A Study of Jesus' Attitudes to Women and Their Roles as Reflected in His Earthly Life* (SNTSMS 51; Cambridge: Cambridge University Press, 1984), 67. For the overtones such a meal might have had in a Greco-Roman context, see K. E. Corley, *Private Women, Public Meals: Social Conflict in the Synoptic Tradition* (Peabody: Hendrickson, 1993), 87–88. This is contrary to majority opinion. See Ernst, *Markus*, 68: "The story is meant to report . . . the normal service of a housewife."

[42] For detail and further Jewish texts, St-B, 1:480. The texts given in Strack-Billerbeck are late, but the ritual purity issue surrounding a woman's monthly period, the unstated problem in all "touching" (the "serving"), deserves further investigation. See Lev 15:19–24; 18:19; 20:18; Isa 30:22; Ezek 7:19–20; 18:6; 22:10; 36:17, and the tractate *Niddah* in the Mishnah and the Talmudim. On this, see T. Ilan, *Jewish Women in Greco-Roman Palestine* (Peabody: Hendrickson, 1996), 100–105. Guelich (*Mark*, 63) rejects this interpretation. J. J. Pilch (*Healing in the New Testament: Insights from Medical and Mediterranean Anthropology* [Minneapolis: Fortress, 2000], 49–51) focuses upon Mary Douglas's work on excretions from bodily orifices but does not raise this problem in his brief reference to Mark 1:29–31. Indeed, he claims that her healing has restored her to "the female status in the household" (p. 66).

[43] Commentators often point to this section of the opening "day" of Mark's Gospel as a literary construction around a typical day in which God's power breaks into the lives of the afflicted through the presence and the power of Jesus. See, for example, Taylor, *St. Mark*, 170–85; Pesch, *Markusevangelium*, 1:116–36; Lohmeyer, *Markus*, 34–40; Nineham, *St. Mark*, 73–83; Lane, *Mark*, 70–71; Guelich, *Mark*, 55. On a possible pre-Markan source for these opening events, and the Markan redaction of it, see Marcus, *Mark*, 177–79.

(vv. 29–31), and then cures all who come to him (vv. 32–34).[44] Only in v. 35 does Mark indicate the beginning of another day. Mark places the woman-episode at the center of the day's activities.[45] He thus highlights Jesus' attitude and approach to a woman as an indication of the reigning presence of God (see vv. 14–15), vanquishing the reign of evil, symbolized by devil possession, taboo, and physical illness.[46]

Jesus' ministry is summarized (1:32–34)

Closing this first day is a summary of Jesus' healing and exorcising activity, although the reference to the time after sundown links this passage with 1:21–31. Only after sunset could the sick be brought to Jesus (v. 32). As is often the case with summaries, it is marked by hyperbole: "all who were sick and possessed with demons" are brought to him; the "whole city" gathers at his door (vv. 32–34). Jesus heals and delivers many, forbidding the demons to speak, because they knew who he was, as did the evil spirit in v. 24.[47] The hyperbole provides an effective conclusion to the day. The reader also knows who Jesus is (see vv. 1–13) and has now seen the good news of the kingdom in action, present in the word and person of Jesus (vv. 16–34). He commands obedience, and followers become part of his world (vv. 16–20). Evil cannot resist the reigning presence of God as Jesus sweeps away evil spirits, sickness, and taboo (vv. 21–34).[48] But not everyone accepts that presence. Despite some who follow, and the invincible presence of a new authority for good in the midst of evil, the people still wonder and question (vv. 21–28). As yet there are mere hints that the proclamation of who Jesus is may prove unfruitful.

Jesus is led away from prayer to minister throughout Galilee (1:35–39)

The prologue has already asserted that God is acting in and through the Son in whom he is well pleased (1:1–13; see v. 11). Jesus' early rising, going to the traditional setting for personal prayer (a lonely place; ἔρημον),[49] and his prayer (v. 35a) indicate that the events of vv. 16–34 have their origins in God. Jesus is not a free agent. After the first day of restless

---

[44] Marcus (*Mark*, 200–201) makes much of the detail that the episodes of vv. 29–34 follow Jesus' presence in the synagogue for the Sabbath. It is the time of the *Havdalah* service, a period marked ("in some rabbinic and Jewish magical texts and formulae") by the fight against demonic powers. The connection is not as clear as Marcus would like to make it.

[45] See Ernst, *Markus*, 67: "The centerpiece of the day of Capernaum."

[46] It is sometimes suggested that this episode is directed to the disciples, and that the theme is one of a discipleship of service. See, for example, Schweizer, *Mark*, 53; G. T. Montague, *Mark: Good News for Hard Times* (Ann Arbor: Servant Books, 1981), 26–27; LaVerdiere, *The Beginning*, 1:72–73. This suggestion is sometimes based on a textual tradition in 1:29 that has the plural verb—"they" entered the house—and focuses upon the presence of four disciples: Simon, Andrew, James, and John (v. 29). The above interpretation, however, reads the singular: "he" entered (ἦλθεν). The detail of the four disciples comes from a Markan attempt to tell an ongoing story and looks back to 1:16–20 (see Gnilka, *Markus*, 1:83).

[47] As Gnilka (*Markus*, 1:87) points out (against Nineham, *St. Mark*, 82; Lohmeyer, *Markus*; Guelich, *Mark*, 66; Hooker, *St. Mark*, 71; and Marcus, *Mark*, 197), the distinction between the "all" who came and the "many" who were healed must be respected. It reflects what also happened in the Christian mission. It is not enough to come to Jesus for healing. More is required (see v. 15).

[48] Pilch (*Healing in the New Testament*, 70–72) helpfully sees the link between Jesus' teaching and healing as an indication that the folk section of his world saw him as a "teacher as healer."

[49] This word can also mean "desert" or "wilderness." However, its use here is probably in contrast with the busy activity of the house and the crowds at the door in the immediately preceding

activity and total success over a variety of evils, he turns to God (v. 35). But "Simon and those who were with him," a reference to the followers called in vv. 16–20, do not appreciate Jesus' orientation toward God. They were called "to follow" (ἀκολουθέω) Jesus (vv. 17–18, 20), but in this episode they "track him down" (κατεδίωξεν).[50] They have accompanied Jesus in his expulsion of the evil spirit (vv. 21–28), the healing of human sickness (vv. 29–31), and his curing of the sick and the expulsion of evil spirits (vv. 32–34). They are at one with the many who are searching for Jesus (v. 37). In v. 28 the reader is told that Jesus' fame spread throughout the whole region, and in v. 33 that "the whole city" was gathered at the door. There is wonder over the person of Jesus, and this is a moment not to be lost, in the understanding of the disciples. But Jesus' experience of prayer (v. 35) tells him otherwise. He must go on to proclaim the coming of the reigning presence of God in the next towns (v. 38a). His restless journey is a response to an authority beyond his plans and desires. A sense of God-directed mission lies behind his words "for that is why I came out" (v. 38b), and he asks his disciples to come with him.[51] The passage closes with a summary indicating that Jesus responds without reservation to God's design: "and he went through all Galilee, preaching in their synagogues and casting out demons" (v. 39). As in the earlier pericopes gathered here to form the opening of Jesus' ministry in Galilee, his coming upon the scene (vv. 14–15) brings in the reigning presence of God in both word and deed: the kingdom is proclaimed and evil spirits are overcome. "These words continue the theme of the overthrow of Satan found in the prologue"[52] and already acted out in the first events of the narrative (vv. 16–34).[53]

Jesus vanquishes sickness and taboo (1:40–45)

The account of the curing of the leper corresponds with a traditional miracle story: a problem is posed to Jesus (1:40), Jesus responds, and through the gesture of both touch and word (v. 41) cures a man with leprosy (v. 42). Wonder follows (v. 45b). The account comes from the pre-Markan tradition about Jesus' miracle-working activity, but it has been modified for its present context.[54] A Markan literary and theological technique

---

episode (v. 33). Jesus goes to a place where he can be alone. There is an interesting link between 1:35 (πρωὶ ἔννυκα λίαν) and the time of day given for the women's visit to the empty tomb in 16:1 (λίαν πρωΐ), but this may be coincidence: how else does one say "early in the morning"?

[50] The verb is almost always used in a negative sense: "to hunt down." See Marcus, *Mark,* 202–3. The formal expression "the disciples" (οἱ μαθηταί) is not used until Mark 2:18, but Nineham (*St. Mark,* 84) also suggests that it is not used here because those called to follow Jesus are not behaving like disciples. It is interesting to note that on the three other occasions when Jesus prays (see 6:46; 9:29; 14:32–42) the disciples fail: terrified by a storm, not praying for exorcism, sleeping.

[51] There is no need to see in this expression the Johannine understanding of Jesus as the preexistent "sent one." See Gnilka, *Markus,* 1:89. Nor is it necessary to limit it to a geographical "coming out" from his home to preach throughout Galilee (as in Hooker, *St. Mark,* 79). It is the Markan (earlier?) version of Luke 4:43: "I was sent for this purpose." See Guelich, *Mark,* 70; Ernst, *Markus,* 74, and Marcus, *Mark,* 203–4. Marcus further suggests that there is a military background. Jesus and his opponents are "coming out" from their respective positions (p. 204).

[52] Hooker, *St. Mark,* 77.

[53] On these grounds, and on the basis of syntax and style, vv. 35–38 should be regarded in its entirety as a Markan passage despite smatterings of pre-Markan traditions. See Gnilka, *Markus,* 1:87–88.

[54] See Gnilka, *Markus,* 1:90–92. It is not the concern of this study to investigate pre-Markan traditions. However, it must be recognized that an imaginative author has taken already existing

emerges as Jesus warns the man not to report what has happened to him, except to the priest, "as a witness to them."[55] He is permitted to make the offering required so that he may rejoin the holy people from which his disease has separated him (vv. 43–44). The man disobeys this command and talks freely. Jesus can no longer enter the towns of Galilee, which he planned to do in response to his God-given agenda (see v. 38). He must remain outside the occupied areas, but this does not stop people coming to him "from everywhere."

A traditional account has been radically remodeled for its present Markan context. There is an indication of faith as the leper states: "If you will, you can make me clean" (1:40). Jesus' complex response uttered in anger, "I will; be clean" (v. 41), responds to that faith, but goes further.[56] Quite unnecessarily, he touches the leper (v. 41). This gesture repeats his touching of a woman in v. 31. He responds to the incipient faith of the leper, overcoming the evil power of leprosy. But this sickness not only afflicted the body; it also thwarted the deepest longings of this man, who was expelled from his people (see Lev 13–14).[57] Jesus' touch both grants the man reentry into Israel (v. 44) and cuts through taboos arising from criteria "outside" the person.[58] Jesus will later attack these traditions (see 7:1–23). For the moment, as in his touching of Simon's mother-in-law (vv. 29–31), he proleptically shows his lack of concern for them. He restores the leper to health and also to his place among God's people by means of word and touch.[59] But the passion that motivated his cure ("anger") continues. His stern warning to the man to go the priest is expressed in a rare New Testament word whose basic basic meaning is "to snort angrily" (ἐμβριμησάμενος, v. 43a), and his sending him on his way is equally forceful: he thrust him away (ἐξέβαλεν, v. 43b). Possibly the account has its origins in a miracle story that reported Jesus' angry encounter with the evil spirit of leprosy,[60] but expressions of passion are retained in the reediting of the miracle for the Markan context because of their power. In this

---

narratives, shaped them for his own purposes, and placed them strategically in the unfolding story. This is the work of a creative storyteller.

[55] Often called the messianic secret. However, as we will see, very little "secrecy" is generated by Jesus' commands to silence after miracles. Mark uses the technique to direct the reader to a correct understanding of Jesus, not to "hide" his messianic status. See H. Baarlink, *Anfängliches Evangelium: Ein Beitrag zur näheren Bestimmung der theologischen Motive im Markusevangelium* (Kampen: J. H. Kok, 1977), 139–47. The meaning of εἰς μαρτύριον αὐτοῖς is debated. I have translated "as a witness to them," indicating that the plural αὐτοῖς refers clumsily to the singular "priest" in the same verse. The RSV translates "for a proof to the people." In defense of my reading, based on the fact that one priest represented them all, see Hooker, *St. Mark*, 82. Lane (*Mark*, 87–88) argues for a negative understanding of the passage: "as a testimony *against* them" (i.e., the priests), "to provide the evidence of the new thing God was doing." It is better to read the passage as evidence of Jesus' conformity to the law rather than a polemic against the priests. See Guelich, *Mark*, 76–77.

[56] The complexity of the response is reflected in the textual tradition. The best reading has ὀργισθείς ("moved with anger") but the majority of modern translations read (with the *lectio facilior*) σπλαγχνισθείς ("moved with pity"). See the discussion in Lane (*Mark*, 86), and note the contrary view of Painter (*Mark's Gospel*, 49). The following interpretation will indicate an internal reason why Jesus is motivated by anger. He rejects the exclusion of the leper on the basis of external criteria for purity. See also Gnilka (*Markus*, 1:92–93), who suggests that his anger is aroused by the disorder of leprosy within God's creative design. See also Marcus, *Mark*, 209.

[57] See Marcus, *Mark*, 208–9.

[58] See Pilch, *Healing in the New Testament*, 51–52. On the social and religious situation of a so-called "leper," see Lane, *Mark*, 84–85.

[59] In the Old Testament, only God heals a leper (see Num 12:10–16; 2 Kgs 5:1–19).

[60] See Nineham, *St. Mark*, 87.

climactic episode in a series of encounters between Jesus and the powers of evil, Jesus shows his passionate commitment to the wholeness and holiness of those who are called to enter the kingdom of God.

Why the command to silence (1:44a)? As has often been said in response to the many theories that attempt to make the Markan messianic secret a key to the interpretation of Mark:[61] this is the worst-kept secret in the history of secrecy (see v. 45)! Mark has received the tradition of Jesus' miracles, and he reports it faithfully. It is quite possible that the commands to secrecy came from the historical Jesus. They express his concern that a public image as a miracle worker might have led to a false understanding of who he was. Be that as it may, and it is probably beyond our scientific control to be certain, the reader has now seen that Jesus' miracles must not be understood as the reason for Jesus' presence. They are meant to show that the reigning presence of God is found in Jesus as he sweeps away the evils of sickness, demon possession, and taboo. The miracles are a means to an end, not an end in themselves. To understand Jesus *only* as a miracle worker is to misunderstand him.[62]

All is not well, even in the story of the cure of the leper. The restored man tells everyone of his cure, and consequently Jesus is unable to move freely about Galilee.[63] He cannot go into the towns, but he continues his ministry of curing and driving out demons in the countryside, to people who come to him "from every quarter" (1:45). While the powers of evil (demons, sickness, and taboo) collapse before him, *human beings* are yet to be convinced that the reigning presence of God is at hand (see v. 15). Between the lines lies the hint that authorities (in the towns?) are unhappy with Jesus' activities.[64] The reader, who knows how this story ends, is aware that the storyteller must make sense out of the nonsense of a crucified Messiah. The definitive public acclamation of Jesus on the basis of his

---

[61] For a good summary, see U. Schnelle, *The History and Theology of the New Testament Writings* (trans. M. E. Boring; Minneapolis: Fortress, 1998), 210–17.

[62] See Marshall, *Faith as a Theme*, 57–74. It has been suggested that the Gospel of Mark was written to reject an early Christian identification of Jesus as a "divine man" (θεῖος ἀνήρ). The outstanding supporter of this thesis is T. J. Weeden, *Mark: Traditions in Conflict* (Philadelphia: Fortress, 1971). For internal and external reasons this suggestion cannot be accepted. Externally, the case against the presence of a θεῖος ἀνήρ Christology as early as the Gospel of Mark has been convincingly argued by a number of scholars. See especially C. H. Holladay, *THEIOS ANER in Hellenistic Judaism: A Critique of the Use of This Category in Christology* (SBLDS 40; Missoula: Scholars Press, 1977). He concludes: "Its usefulness, therefore, is extremely questionable, for using it in christological discussions merely introduces into an already confused field of study yet another ill-defined, if not undefinable, category" (p. 237). See also D. L. Tiede, *The Charismatic Figure as Miracle Worker* (SBLDS 1; Missoula: Society of Biblical Literature, 1972); B. Blackburn, *Theios Anêr and the Markan Miracle Traditions: A Critique of the Theios Anêr Concept as an Interpretative Background of the Miracle Traditions Used by Mark* (WUNT 2. Reihe 40; Tübingen: J. C. B. Mohr [Paul Siebeck], 1991), 13–96.

[63] The element of danger that will become the feature of 2:1–3:6 lurks behind v. 45. But there has been a significant shift from Jesus' first appearance, alone, on the scene in vv. 14–15. He is now surrounded by disciples. He is well known and attracting many as a result of his singular manifestation of the power of the kingdom. See Lührmann, *Markusevangelium*, 55.

[64] C. R. Kazmierski ("Evangelist and Leper: A Socio-Cultural Study of Mark 1.40–45," *NTS* 38 [1992]: 37–50) highlights the boundary breaking and "deviant" nature of Jesus' activity. However, he suggests that the account is primarily about the leper who is no better off at the end of the story, still rejected by official Israel, but now spreading the word of what has happened. However, v. 45 indicates that he (and not Jesus) is no longer able to go openly in the cities. Thus 1:40–45 is already part of the conflicts that become more explicit in 2:1–3:6.

miracles does nothing to resolve the Christian problem so well stated by Paul: a crucified Christ, "a stumbling block to Jews and folly to Greeks" (1 Cor 1:23). Mark's narrator respects the tradition of Jesus as a worker of miracles but remains always aware that the ultimate explanation of Jesus' life and teaching is found in his death and resurrection. The so-called "messianic secret" is a Markan literary and theological feature that reserves the answer to the mystery of the person of Jesus, Christ and Son of God (1:1, 11), until the story comes to its climax. Jesus is not primarily a miracle worker or the expected Messiah. The reader, informed in the prologue (1:1–13) of who Jesus is, must read through to the end of the Gospel to find out how he is the Messiah and the Son of God—as the crucified one. Commands to silence during the story will direct the reader toward that conclusion.

The Kingdom Is Opposed (2:1–3:6)

Jesus cures and is questioned (2:1–12)

The series of five conflict stories (2:1–3:6) opens with Jesus' return to Capernaum and the spreading of the word that he was in a home (v. 1). It is not clear whose home is meant, but the close proximity with the home of Simon and Andrew in Capernaum (see 1:29) suggests that it was theirs.[65] Jesus' being in a home and preaching the word (v. 2) also suggests that the Markan community may identify itself with this "house" or "home." There is a close link between this miracle and the cure of the leper. "In both cases Jesus deals with the root of the complaint, and thus shows an authority superior to that of the priests, who could pronounce a man clean or forgiven only when the cure had been effected and the proper sacrifices had been made."[66] They are further linked by the use of so-called "hook words." In 1:45 the words τὸν λόγον, ὥστε μηκέτι . . . εἰσελθεῖν appear in that order, and the same words are repeated, in the reverse order in 2:1–2: εἰσελθὼν . . . ὥστε μηκέτι . . . τὸν λόγον.[67] But there are logical and chronological tensions between the two scenes. In 1:39 Jesus set out through all the villages in that region of Galilee. After a very brief time he is again back in Capernaum. In 1:45 the narrator said that Jesus could not go about openly in the towns, but that is exactly what he does in 2:1. These tensions indicate that the juxtaposition of 1:14–45 and 2:1–3:6 is determined by criteria other than chronological sequence.[68]

---

[65] See Marcus, *Mark,* 215.

[66] Hooker, *St. Mark,* 83–84. See also Gnilka, *Markus,* 1:99–100.

[67] See Dewey, *Markan Public Debate,* 67. These are signs of Markan redaction.

[68] Many scholars claim that the conflict stories in 2:1–3:6 were already gathered in a pre-Markan collection. See, for example, M. Albertz, *Die synoptischen Streitgespräche* (Berlin: Trowitsch & Sohn, 1919), 5–16; H.-W. Kuhn, *Ältere Sammlungen im Markusevangelium* (SUNT 8; Göttingen: Vandenhoeck & Ruprecht, 1971), 53–98; W. Thissen, *Erzählung der Befreiung: Eine exegetische Untersuchung zu Mk 2,1–3,6* (FB 21; Würzburg: Echter Verlag, 1974); Dewey, *Markan Public Debate,* 181–93; J. D. G. Dunn, "Mark 2:1–3:6: A Bridge between Jesus and Paul in the Question of the Law" *NTS* 30 (1984): 395–415. In their present Markan context they are not only conflict stories; they are used to continue the story of Jesus' authority and the Jewish leaders rejection of it. For a summary of the discussion, see Gnilka, *Markus,* 1:131–32. Gnilka accepts that 2:13–28 formed a pre-Markan collection of conflict stories but holds that Mark added the two miracle stories of 2:1–12 and 3:1–6, thereby changing the character of the original collection. See also Guelich, *Mark,* 81–84, 131–33; Marcus, *Mark,* 213.

The scene for the action that follows is set with considerable detail (2:2–4). The earlier situation in Capernaum (see 1:33) repeats itself as the throng gathers around Jesus, so that it is impossible even to enter the room. It is to this large crowd, overflowing the house itself, that Jesus "was announcing the word" (v. 2). An unidentified "they" arrive on the scene, four men carrying a paralyzed man upon a mobile bed (κράβαττον, v. 4).[69] The crowd, however, is so tightly packed that the four are unable to approach Jesus. The scene becomes somewhat ridiculous as Mark blandly reports the removal of the roof to create an opening directly above Jesus and the lowering of the man through the roof.[70] The paralyzed person needs four men to carry him, but they successfully clamber onto the roof, remove the simple ceiling, knowing exactly where Jesus must have been standing, and lower this fully-grown but immobile person into the room.

This is precisely the effect the narrative should have as it prepares the reader for Jesus' words highlighting the faith of the man's associates ("Jesus, seeing their faith"; 2:5a). The unnamed people responsible for bringing the man before Jesus have gone to extraordinary lengths to make him present to Jesus, and in this have shown their faith. Surprisingly, Jesus does not address the man's illness but declares that his sins are forgiven (ἀφίενταί σου αἱ ἁμαρτίαι, v. 5b). In the light of the subsequent objection from the scribes, the passive mood indicates that it is by the action of God that the sins are forgiven. Jesus' authoritative word communicates God's forgiveness (see 2 Sam 12:13). In Jewish thought, sin and illness are closely linked,[71] and Jesus' authoritatively declaring the man's sins forgiven provides the grounds for the conflict.[72] There have been hints earlier in the narrative that the scribes who witnessed Jesus' miraculous activity were not entirely convinced by such activity (see 1:21–28). Their opposition now becomes explicit. From this point on in the narrative, the relationship between Jesus and the scribes is hostile. In this first moment of conflict, however, it is not uttered. The scribes question "in their hearts" (v. 6), and their disrespect for Jesus is indicated by their designation for him: "this man" (v. 7). The reason for their opposition to Jesus is given in v. 7: he has no authority to speak in this way. The forgiveness of sin is the prerogative of God alone (see Exod 34:7; Isa 43:25; 44:22).[73] To declare the man's sins forgiven is to utter a blasphemy. Attention is given to Jesus' words: he was preaching the word (v. 2), he speaks to the paralyzed man (v. 5), and it is his "speaking" that generates the conflict (v. 7).

---

[69] A κράβαττον is the pallet of the poor, while the rich lie on a κλίνη.

[70] See J. P. Meier, *A Marginal Jew: Rethinking the Historical Jesus* (3 vols.; ABRL; New York: Doubleday, 1991–2001), 2:680. On the practice of removing the roof for entry, see D. Daube, *The New Testament and Rabbinic Judaism* (London: Athlone, 1956; repr. Peabody: Hendrickson, 1994), 385–87.

[71] See Lane, *Mark*, 94; Marcus, *Mark*, 221–22. For later Jewish material, see Str-B, 1:495.

[72] It is possible that behind this conflict story lies an original miracle story (see vv. 1–5a, 11–12) into which the conflict (vv. 5b–10) has been inserted; see Hooker, *St. Mark*, 84; Marcus, *Mark*, 219–20. Gnilka (*Markus*, 1:95–98) agrees but further points out that both the miracle and the conflict stories are pre-Markan, though knit together by Mark. There are other Markan touches, but for Gnilka the passage has been constructed as a mixed form to produce a pronouncement story highlighted by the Son of Man saying in 2:10.

[73] Marcus (*Mark*, 222–23) suggests that "but God alone" (εἰ μὴ εἷς ὁ θεός) reflects the *Shema*, the Jewish confession of the one true God in Deut 6:4. He thus traces in Mark the conflict that took place between Judaism and Christianity over "two powers in heaven." That debate does appear to be present behind John 10:30–33; see J. Ashton, *Understanding the Fourth Gospel* (Oxford: Clarendon Press, 1991), 141–47. Marcus asserts that the Markan Christology does not draw back "from the implication of near divinity that gives rise to this objection" (p. 222).

In response to the scribes' murmuring in their hearts, Jesus perceives in his spirit and asks why they raise such questions in their hearts (2:8).[74] What follows is a little clumsy.[75] It appears that Jesus has deliberately generated a situation that will require him to provide a validating miracle in support of his authoritative word. At the level of "words" it is much easier to say to a person, "Your sins are forgiven." Who knows how effective those words might be in reality? A greater test for an authoritative word would be to command, "Rise, take up your pallet, and walk" (v. 9), and then allow everyone to see whether this command bears fruit. But the theological significance of the former command remains the more important. The scribes have rightly claimed that only God has authority to forgive sins (v. 7). But the reader knows from the prologue (vv. 1–13) that prerogatives of God have been passed on to the one who was announced by the Baptist, was driven by the Spirit, and is reestablishing God's original creative order by establishing the reigning presence of God. If the prologue is not true, then Jesus' words of forgiveness are indeed blasphemy (v. 7).

Jesus thus returns to the issue of the forgiveness of sins. The miracle he is about to perform is not an end in itself. It is that the scribes "may know that the Son of Man has authority on earth to forgive sins" (2:10). Jesus' reference to himself as "the Son of Man" is unexpected. Much ink has been spilled over the origin and meaning of this expression on the lips of Jesus and in the developing theology of the early church.[76] In terms of its present place in the narrative, it can only generate a question for the reader. The first half of the Gospel (1:14–8:30) will tell of increasing interest in the identity of Jesus until Simon Peter confesses that Jesus is the Christ (8:29) and is warned to silence (8:30). Yet, very early in the narrative Jesus refers to himself as "the Son of Man" (2:10). What can it mean? That question cannot be answered at this point in the story. Only one thing is clear: Jesus calls himself "the Son of Man" and claims authority on earth to forgive sin. A divine prerogative has been given to Jesus—the forgiveness of sin—and he exercises this authority on earth as the Son of Man (ἐξουσία ἔχει ὁ υἱὸς τοῦ ἀνθρώπου . . .). By what "authority" does the Son of Man (Jesus) forgive sin?[77] A christological prolepsis has been introduced, a "gap," a spot of indeterminacy in the narrative that will be filled as the reader proceeds.[78] Only later in the

---

[74] Jesus' knowledge of their inner thoughts is sometimes taken as an indication of a θεῖος ἀνήρ Christology. There is ample Old Testament background for God's looking into the hearts of human beings (see, for example, 1 Sam 16:7; Ps 7:10; Jer 11:20; Sir 43:18–19. See also *Ps Sol* 14:6). See Gnilka, *Markus*, 1:100.

[75] The sentence is awkward and is open to a variety of translations, e.g.: "This has happened that . . ."; "Know that . . . ." The sentence is best left in its clumsy state: "But so that you may know that. . . ." See Hooker, *St. Mark*, 87.

[76] For a survey of the discussion, see M. D. Hooker, "Is the Son of Man Problem Really Insoluble?" in *Text and Interpretation: Studies in the New Testament Presented to Matthew Black* (ed. E. Best and R. McL. Wilson; Cambridge: Cambridge University Press, 1979), 155–68; J. Donahue, "Recent Studies on the Origin of 'Son of Man' in the Gospels," *CBQ* 48 (1986): 484–98; D. R. Burkett, *The Son of Man Debate: A History and Evaluation* (SNTSMS 107; Cambridge: Cambridge University Press, 2000). See the excursus "The Son of Man Discussion," pp. 212–13 below, for a more detailed presentation of the debate.

[77] Still a puzzle to the reader, the close association of "authority" and "Son of Man" summons up the language of Dan 7:14, where authority is given to one like a son of man. See Marcus, *Mark*, 222–23. For the importance of authority in 2:10, see the discussion in Guelich, *Mark*, 88–94. He rightly concludes, "Mark's primary interest here lies in the resultant conflict occasioned by Jesus' claim to authority" (p. 94; see also p. 96).

[78] Against Lührmann (*Markusevangelium*, 58), who claims that the reader is already aware of the authority of the Danielic Son of Man. On narrative "gaps" that need to be filled by the ongoing

story will the full significance of Jesus' being "the Son of Man" become clear, and only then will the reader be made aware why this Son of Man has authority on earth. For the moment, the reader accepts that Jesus is "the Son of Man," whatever that may come to mean as the story unfolds.

The miracle is rapidly reported. Jesus speaks to the man (2:10b), repeating the words used to issue a challenge to the scribes in v. 9: "Rise, take up your pallet, and go home" (v. 11). New life is granted to the man (see 16:6). The cure is immediately (εὐθύς) effected. He rises, takes up his pallet, and publicly leaves the scene "before them all" (v. 11a). The public nature of the miracle and the departure look back to v. 9, where Jesus pointed to the difficulty of commanding a physical cure that could be seen by all. The scribes have not addressed one word to Jesus throughout the account. They murmured in their hearts (v. 6), and Jesus' response came from his spiritual perception of their murmuring (v. 8a). From that point on Jesus directs the discussion. He asks questions (vv. 8b, 9), issues a challenge (v. 10), and works a miracle by issuing a command (v. 11). The scribes disappear as the miracle generates universal amazement.[79] What is most significant is that those who marvel also correctly identify as an action of God the miracle they have seen produced by Jesus' word. They render honor not to Jesus but to God, recognizing that something hitherto never seen is taking place among them (v. 12). The wonders of 1:14–45 do not cease even though some will not accept that God should be glorified for what he is doing in and through the person of Jesus, Son of God and Son of Man—whatever that last expression might mean.[80]

Jesus calls disciples and is questioned (2:13–17)

The link between earlier parts of the story continues as Jesus calls Levi (2:13–14). The literary form of a vocation story, outlined in the analysis of 1:16–20, is again found here. Jesus is on the move (vv. 13a, 14a). He sees a person who is named and whose trade is described (v. 14b). He calls Levi to follow him (v. 14c), and the summons is met with wordless obedience (v. 14d).[81] Here, unlike the stories in 1:16–18, 19–20, it is not explicitly said that Levi leaves all, nor is he commissioned as a fisher of people. But the former is implied

---

reading process, see W. Iser, *The Act of Reading: A Theory of Aesthetic Response* (London: Routledge & Kegan Paul, 1978), 182–87.

[79] Excluding the scribes from the "all" in 2:12. See the discussion of this issue in Marcus, *Mark,* 219. For a study of the passage that highlights the contrast between the faith of the powerless man and his friends and the "contentious unbelief of the religious authorities," see Marshall, *Faith as a Theme,* 78–90 (the quotation is from p. 90). On the unfaith of the leaders, see also pp. 183–88.

[80] Gnilka (*Markus,* 1:100–102) argues that the main focus of the passage is its use of the Son of Man passage. For the Markan community, this saying not only legitimizes one of Jesus' deeds but also gives to the community a newly won eschatological existence. This diachronic reading of 2:10 (locating the saying in the theology of the early church) presupposes too much of the reader meeting the Son of Man title for the first time in a synchronic reading of the Gospel of Mark. Mark 2:1–12 is primarily about conflict and the rejection of Jesus' claim to authority, as its place within 2:1–3:6 demonstrates. Its christological potential will be realized only in Jesus' predictions concerning the ultimate authority (13:26–27) and vindication (14:62) of the coming Son of Man, and at the cross.

[81] Christian tradition and early textual variations indicate difficulty with the calling of the otherwise unknown "Levi the Son of Alphaeus." This figure is not mentioned in the list of the Twelve in 3:16–19. Some manuscripts change Levi to James, as in 3:18 James son of Alphaeus is listed. Matt 9:9 gives this character the name "Matthew," and subsequent Christian speculation has suggested that he may have had two names: Matthew and Levi. The need to have all the disciples explicitly

in Levi's rising from his place in the tax office and following Jesus. The passage came to Mark as a traditional story on the vocation to discipleship. With this disciple, however, something new is added: Levi is outside the community of Judaism. He is a Jew who has worked, probably for his own ill-gotten gain, for a foreign power occupying God's holy land.[82] Levi is a sinner, and Jesus calls him to be his follower.

Mark takes this vocation story from his tradition and uses it to introduce 2:15–17, a traditional pronouncement passage leading to Jesus' words found in v. 17.[83] Verses 15–17 present a second conflict between Jesus and the scribes (see v. 6), but it is notoriously without setting. Linking the two traditions by means of his familiar paratactic καί, the narrator reports that Jesus sat at table in "his house" (v. 15).[84] This could mean either Jesus' house or the house of Levi. Grammatically, it is best identified as the house of Jesus, as the last word in the previous sentence (v. 14: αὐτῷ, "he followed him") refers to Jesus.[85] However, the linking of the two passages is not original. In 2:1 there was ambiguity surrounding the use of οἰκία.[86] As in 2:1, Mark probably does not wish to associate Jesus with a dwelling of his own. He is presented as forever on the move, and the use of "house" in Mark has two levels of meaning. In the story of Jesus, he is found in the house of others, while in the story of the Markan community, the οἰκία suggests the physical reality of the gathering of Christian believers. This is true in 2:15, where Jesus is at table with tax collectors, sinners, and disciples, as in 2:1, where Jesus preaches the word "in a home." In addition to the reference to tax collectors, sinners, and the disciples, Mark adds: "there were many who followed him" (v. 15c). This addition probably indicates that by now Jesus' followers number more than the five who have been named: Simon, Andrew, James, John (1:16–20), and Levi (2:13–14).

The disciples are present, as they have been since 1:16–20, but they are joined by a group of "sinners" (ἁμαρτωλοί).[87] As Jesus forgave sin (ἁμαρτία) in the previous episode,

---

called by Jesus in the list of the Twelve does not seem to have been a concern for Mark, however important it became for later Christianity. For a study of this issue, see R. Pesch, "Levi-Matthäus (Mk 2,14/Mt 9,9; 10,3): Ein Beitrag zur Lösung eines alten Problems," *ZNW* 59 (1968): 40–56.

[82] For some indications of first-century Jewish opinion of tax collectors, see Taylor (*St. Mark*, 202–3) and Lane (*Mark*, 100–102). On the issue of eating with them, see Hooker (*St. Mark*, 96). See also Myers, *Binding the Strong Man*, 157; J. R. Donahue, "Tax Collectors and Sinners: An Attempt at Identification," *CBQ* 33 (1971): 49–61.

[83] As with 2:1–12, in vv. 13–17 we are dealing with a mixed form: a vocation story, a meal with sinners, and a pronouncement of Jesus stitched together to form a conflict story. See Gnilka, *Markus*, 1:103–5; Guelich, *Mark*, 98–99; Marcus, *Mark*, 228–29.

[84] The Greek for sitting at table (κατακεῖσθαι) indicates intimate reclining at table, supported by one's left elbow. See Taylor, *St. Mark*, 204.

[85] See Marcus, *Mark*, 225.

[86] We do not know the setting of the independent pronouncement passage of vv. 15–17, and Mark's juxtaposition of vv. 13–14 and 15–17 creates the grammatical possibility that they were in the house of Jesus. As maintained above, this may be neither the intent of the author (Hooker, *St. Mark*, 95) nor the original setting of the pericope (see Gnilka, *Markus*, 1:104).

[87] It is sometimes suggested that ἁμαρτωλοί may refer to those people regarded by the Pharisees as sinners, the so-called "people of the land" who did not perform all required ritual obligations and were thus to some extent impure. See, for example, Myers, *Binding the Strong Man*, 156. For a further extension of this to "lewd women," see Corley, *Private Women*, 89–93. The link with the forgiveness of sin (ἁμαρτία) in vv. 5–10 indicates that people of ill repute are intended; see Guelich, *Mark* 101–2, Marcus, *Mark*, 226, and especially E. P. Sanders, *Jesus and Judaism* (Phildelphia: Fortress, 1985), 174–211. Mark wants to show that Jesus forgave sin (vv. 5–10) and shared with sinners (vv. 15–17).

drawing the charge of blasphemy from the scribes (2:5–10), he now associates himself with sinners (ἁμαρτωλοί) and again generates difficulties for the scribes of the Pharisees (2:16).[88] The conflict is becoming more public; the scribes of the Pharisees speak to the disciples of Jesus. Jesus' eating with sinners is unacceptable because it renders him impure.[89] Jesus hears of the complaint—from the disciples, one would suppose—and responds, transcending the position represented by the scribes. The narrator's presentation of the scribes is part of the larger scheme of 2:1–3:6. "The scribes" objected to Jesus' words in 2:5–10, and "the scribes of the Pharisees" object to his actions in 2:16. In the two following conflict stories (2:18–22, 23–28) "the Pharisees" emerge. In 2:18–22 a question of fasting generates the problem, and in 2:23–28 the Pharisees object to Jesus' Sabbath practice. They have already been introduced in 2:16: "The scribes *of the Pharisees*." The Pharisees will collude with the Herodians in the climax of 3:6.[90]

Jesus' words in 2:17 articulate what he has done with Levi in vv. 13–15. He has come to call not the righteous but sinners (v. 17b). In light of the reason given for this "call" in v. 17a ("Those who are well have no need of a physician, but those who are sick"), "the righteous" must be read ironically.[91] The scribes misunderstand Jesus' relationship with God: they believe he is blaspheming against God by claiming to forgive sin (vv. 5–10). The irony continues as "the righteous" claim that Jesus should not share a meal with sinners. Implicit in the response of Jesus is the introduction of a new understanding of the relationship between God and the human situation. Those who believe that they fully understand what right relationship with God entails are not the ones who need Jesus' call. Indeed, such a call would be wasted on them. The closed religious system of the scribes needs no inbreaking of the kingdom. Many, like Levi, called in their sinfulness and aware of their sickness, can be filled with the blessing of the reigning presence of God, now available in the word and person of Jesus (see 1:14–15). This is indeed good news.[92]

---

[88] Reading "the scribes of the Pharisees" (the *lectio difficilior*: γραμματεῖς τῶν Φαρισαίων) and not the common expression, found in several manuscripts, "the scribes and the Pharisees." Scribes belonged to different religious (and subsequently political) persuasions. The "scribes of the Pharisees" were an identifiable group. See Gnilka, *Markus,* 1:107–8; Marcus, *Mark,* 523–24; R. E. Brown, *The Death of the Messiah: From Gethsemane to the Grave: A Commentary on the Passion Narratives in the Four Gospels* (2 vols; ABRL; New York: Doubleday, 1994), 2:1426–28.

[89] A number of manuscripts have "eat and drink." However, major witnesses (e.g., Vaticanus, Bezae, and Washingtonensis) have only ἐσθίει. The words καὶ πίνει have probably been assimilated from Luke 5:30. For background to this complaint, see Nineham, *St. Mark,* 95–96.

[90] On the historical Pharisees and their role in the Gospel of Mark, see Lührmann, *Markusevangelium,* 60–61.

[91] On the importance of v. 17a, see Gnilka, *Markus,* 1:109. On the irony, see Lane, *Mark,* 105, and Ernst, *Markus,* 95–97. Hooker (*St. Mark,* 97) speculates (against an ironic interpretation): "Might Jesus himself have believed that there were some who were in fact obeying God's will and who did not need his help?" That is an impossible question to answer and should not be allowed to detract from the Markan irony. Gnilka (*Markus,* 1:109) also rejects irony here, suggesting that the expressions "righteous" and "sinners" simply comes from an oppositional thought-structure. His claim that the righteous are not excluded (at least in this context) is hard to accept. Guelich (*Mark,* 104–5) regards the expression as a literary pattern of statement and counterstatement.

[92] See Marcus (*Mark,* 232): "This blurring of the distinction between God and humanity is of a piece with the fundamental blurring of the structuring distinction between the realm of the pure and that of the impure; and both are related to the conviction that now, at the world's end, the grace of the heavenly world is beginning to break through into the earthly sphere."

Jesus is questioned over fasting (2:18–22)

Without any introduction or setting, the narrator announces that John's disciples and the Pharisees are fasting. An unidentified group of people approaches Jesus and speaks to him. Their question presupposes that Jesus and his disciples are not fasting (2:18).[93] The rest of the passage (vv. 19–22) is taken up entirely by words of Jesus, the product of the author's careful assembling of various pre-Markan elements.[94] He opens his words by asking a question that must receive a negative answer (v. 19a).[95] Wedding guests cannot fast while the bridegroom is with them (v. 19b). From this general and universally acceptable statement, Jesus focuses upon a forthcoming event: "The days will come" (v. 20a). There is an eschatological ring about these words, which look ominously forward to some future critical time.[96] The generic description of a wedding feast at which the guests cannot fast is rendered personal, as a specific "bridegroom" is spoken of in v. 20. When "the bridegroom" is taken away from them (ἀπαρθῇ ἀπ' αὐτῶν), then they will fast "on that day" (ἐν ἐκείνῃ τῇ ἡμέρᾳ). The eschatological hint of "the days will come" will be realized "on that day," when the bridgroom will be taken from the guests.[97] The Septuagint regularly renders the prophetic description of "that day" of final coming of YHWH as ἐν ἐκείνῃ τῇ ἡμέρᾳ.

For the first (and all subsequent) readers of this passage, the reference to the violent death of Jesus is clear.[98] However, there is more to it. The shift from the generic use of "the bridegroom" (2:19) to the specific reference to Jesus as "the bridegroom" (v. 20) has links with the Old Testament's reference to God as the bridegroom (see Isa 54:4–8; 62:5; Ezek 16:7–34). Some suggest that Judaism had developed these links into the idea of a messianic bridegroom.[99] The early church identified Jesus as the bridegroom (see Matt 25:1–2; John 3:29; 2 Cor 11:2; Eph 5:22–23; Rev 19:7–8). A messianic understanding of the bridegroom may have been part of the identification process, but this is not necessarily part of the back-

---

[93] Originally the reference may have been only to either John the Baptist's disciples or the Pharisees (see the following note). Both are mentioned in v. 18, as both belong to the old order (see vv. 21–22). The *Sitz im Leben* for this pericope may have been discussions over fasting traditions in the Markan community. For most (e.g., Gnilka, *Markus,* 1:111–12), the reference to the disciples of the Baptist was original, and it reflected the debates over fasting between followers of the Baptist and followers of Jesus (see Matt 11:18–19; Luke 7:33–34). See the discussion in Guelich, *Mark,* 108–10, 115–16.

[94] The introductory statement from the unidentified questioners (v. 18) may have originally referred to either John's disciples or the Pharisees, whose fasting regulations are well known (see J. Behm, "νῆστις κτλ," *TDNT* 4:925–35). The Pharisees do not have disciples; "disciples of the Pharisees" appear so that the behavior of the disciples of Jesus can be questioned. The parable leading to the pronouncement in v. 20 may have originally been a simple statement on the joyful presence of the bridegroom (see *Gos. Thom.* 104), to which the allegorical reference to the death of Jesus in vv. 19b–20 has been added. The parable on the old and the new (vv. 21–22) is also a traditional saying and has been transmitted in a number of ways; see the Matthean and Lukan parallels, and *Gos. Thom.* 47b.

[95] A question beginning with μή (as here) calls for a negative response.

[96] See Marcus, *Mark,* 234.

[97] See Gnilka, *Markus,* 1:114–15, and Guelich, *Mark,* 111–14.

[98] At Jewish weddings the guests left before the bridegroom. The "taking away" of the bridegroom "comes as a jarring surprise" (Guelich, *Mark,* 112).

[99] The evidence is slight and from a sixth- or seventh-century document (see *Pesiq. Rab.* 149a). For a discussion, see J. Jeremias, *The Parables of Jesus* (trans. S. H. Hooke; London: SCM, 1963), 52, n. 13; J. Gnilka, "Bräutigam—spätjüdisches Messiasprädikat?" *TTZ* 69 (1960): 298–301; Nineham, *St. Mark,* 103–4; Marcus, *Mark,* 236–37.

ground for the Markan text. The disciples cannot fast while Jesus is with them. This is the time of the messianic wedding feast (see also Isa 25:6–8; Jer 2:2, 24–26; Hos 2:19–20; Amos 4:13–15; John 2:1–11; Rev 21:2, 9), and they enjoy the presence of the bridegroom. However, Jesus' being violently taken away from them will mark an eschatological turning point (ἐν ἐκείνῃ τῇ ἡμέρᾳ). From that time on everything will be transformed and there will be fasting. The situation of the members of the Markan community becomes evident. Living in the post-Jesus era, they have developed their own fasting practices that do not originate in Jewish practice but stem from the eschatological event of the death and resurrection of Jesus.[100]

The following parable on the use of new and old cloth and new and old wineskins (2:21–22) existed independently in the pre-Markan tradition, but the association with Jesus' words in the eschatological event of the bridegroom's death (v. 20) is effective.[101] A gradual progression occurs in the parable. The image of unshrunk cloth being used to patch an old garment focuses upon the subsequent damage done to the old garment if the newer cloth is sewn to it. The patch tears away, and the old garment is left in an even more damaged state (v. 21). The destruction of the older garment is the point. The image of the new wine, however, focuses upon the need to preserve the new wine (v. 22). As with the old garment, new wine in old wineskins will destroy the wineskins. But it is not only the wineskins that are lost. "The wine is lost" (v. 22b). The point of vv. 21–22 is found in Jesus' final statement: "New wine is for fresh skins" (v. 22c).

The Markan version of this saying (see the concern for "the old" in Matt 9:17; Luke 5:37), in close association with Jesus' earlier words upon the violent taking away of the bridegroom, is radical.[102] The eschatological event of Jesus' death cannot be contained within the closed religious system of Israel. The new wine, a symbol of the time of salvation,[103] must be preserved, and this calls for new wineskins. The coming of the kingdom introduces a new time into the relationship between God and the human condition. Any attempt to contain this newness within the old ways of Israel will lead only to the destruction of both Israel and the eschatological newness. These words do not reject Israel but place God's ways in Israel within the proper history-of-salvation perspective.[104] Israel's tradition is the "old garment," the "old wineskins." That tradition has done its task as garment and wineskin, but something radically new is present and cannot be contained in the old. "Both sayings show concern lest the old be lost; yet both point to the truth that something new and fresh cannot be contained within the limits of the old and indeed must inevitably destroy the old."[105]

At the center of five conflict stories (2:1–3:6), Mark 2:18–22 has a number of unique features. Most of the passage is made up of Jesus' words. The conflict, while present in the

---

[100] See Nineham, *St. Mark*, 102; Lührmann, *Markusevangelium*, 63. We have very little information about early Christian fasting practices. For some suggestions, see Gnilka, *Markus*, 1:115, 116–18.

[101] For the history of the tradition, see Gnilka, *Markus*, 1:111–13. *Gos. Thom.* 47 has the parables in reverse order, independent of the wedding imagery (see *Gos. Thom.* 75, 104).

[102] "These brief parables directly answer the challenge implied in the question, Why do your disciples not fast?" (Lane, *Mark*, 112–13).

[103] Jeremias, *Parables*, 118–19.

[104] Marcus, *Mark*, 238–39.

[105] Hooker, *St. Mark*, 100. Hooker (pp. 100–101) draws attention to the tearing of Caiaphas's clothes (14:63) and the tearing of the temple veil (15:38), both in some way signifying the end of the old and the birth of the new.

question raised in v. 18, is not as intense as in the other pericopes. The reader encounters the word of Jesus. At the center of vv. 18–22 are Jesus' words on the eschatological event that will determine his destiny and the destiny of the disciples, and will initiate an entirely new situation (v. 20). There will be fasting, but not the fasting of the disciples of John the Baptist or the Pharisees (vv. 18–19), and the old will no longer be able to contain the newness unleashed by that eschatological moment (vv. 21–22). The death of Jesus (v. 20) will generate that new situation. No doubt the result of Mark's reworking of a number of traditions, this central passage features the cross as the turning point in God's presence to the human story (v. 20). It also features the new situation that will result from the event (vv. 18–19, 21–22). The Markan community lives that new situation. Its fasting and life-style cannot be contained within the traditions of Israel because of the eschatological event of Jesus Christ, Son of God (see 1:1, 11).[106]

Jesus is questioned over Sabbath law (2:23–28)

The Sabbath is the temporal setting for the conflict, generated by the disciples' plucking grain from the ears of corn and rubbing them in their hands[107] as they accompany Jesus through grainfields.[108] The Torah does not forbid such activity, although Deut 23:35 expressly forbids the reaping of grain with a sickle on the Sabbath. It appears, however, the scribal tradition had come to take a conservative stance, interpreting all actions resembling reaping as a breach of Sabbath rest (see *m. Šabb.* 7:2; Philo, *Mos.* 2:22; CD 10:14–11:18).[109] The presence of the Pharisees in the field, complaining to Jesus about the behavior of his disciples, indicates the artificial nature of the pericope (v. 24). They claim that the action of the disciples is forbidden on the Sabbath (οὐκ ἔξεστιν). This is the first time the Pharisees have been actively present or have spoken to Jesus. Previously Jesus' opponents have been the scribes (2:6), the scribes of the Pharisees (v. 16), an unnamed group pointing to the fasting of the disciples of the Baptist, and the disciples of the Pharisees (v. 18). The stage is now set for the direct involvement of the Pharisees, leading to their decision, taken with the Herodians in 3:6.

Jesus responds to his interrogators by recalling an episode from the life of David, where he and his companions also performed an action that was forbidden (οὐκ ἔξεστιν, 2:25–26). The event is described in 1 Sam 21:1–6, but Ahimelech, the father of Abiathar, was the high priest. The latter, however, was better known and thus the mistake is understandable.[110] The relationship between the two episodes is weak. Although both episodes

---

[106] On the centrality of the Markan Christology (rather than the church's practice of fasting), see Guelich, *Mark*, 114–16.

[107] This is all that can be implied by the description of the action. They are not harvesting in any way or tearing the heads off the stalks. See Hooker, *St. Mark*, 102.

[108] The introduction in v. 23 is clumsy, reflecting a Semitic background. Much has been made of the description of the disciples' action as ὁδὸν ποιεῖν. It may mean that they were clearing a way through the field by tearing up the crop, and there may even be links with the Baptist's mission to prepare the way of the Lord (see 1:2), or the destiny of the disciples, to go down the way of Jesus (see 10:32, 52). The more likely interpretation of this odd expression is that they are simply passing through the field. For a survey of the discussion, see Hooker, *St. Mark*, 102.

[109] See Marcus, *Mark*, 240.

[110] For a discussion of the problems generated by this error (including textual variations at this point), see Lane, *Mark*, 115–16; Marcus, *Mark*, 241–42. To Marcus, whose interpretation of the Gospel of Mark is strongly influenced by his decision that it is a Christian response to the Jewish War, the larger background of 2 Sam 15 may be invoked. Wicked authorities take control of Jerusalem, and David and his associates must live among the Gentiles.

may take place on the Sabbath,[111] the disciples are not driven by extreme hunger, they are not taking the shewbread, nor are they accused because they eat. They break the Sabbath practice by plucking the grain, not by eating it. The focus of the comparison, therefore, is not what one might or might not do on a Sabbath, on the basis of the actions of David and his companions, but upon the parallel drawn between David and Jesus. The issue is christological.[112] If such practices on a Sabbath were condoned for David and his companions, how much more should actions done on the Sabbath be condoned in light of the uniqueness of Jesus.

The christological interpretation is hammered home by means of the two pronouncements in 2:27–28, originally separate in the tradition.[113] Verse 27 affirms the superiority of the human being to Sabbath practices, a line of thought already present within Judaism, but never so succinctly—or perhaps universally—stated as here (see *Mek.* 23:12).[114] The twofold use of the word ἄνθρωπος in v. 27 (for the Sabbath was made for *the human being*, not *the human being* for the Sabbath) opens the door to the second pronouncement in v. 28: "So the Son of Man (υἱὸς τοῦ ἀνθρώπου) is lord even of the Sabbath." The christological affirmation of v. 28 adds further mystery to the gradual revelation of the person of Jesus in these initial episodes of a story that asks the question, "Who is Jesus?" (1:14–8:30). The reader has already been informed that the Son of Man has authority to forgive sin (2:10) and is now further told that the Son of Man is Lord of the Sabbath. After the prologue (1:1–13) there is no surprise that authority unique to YHWH (see Lev 23:3) has been passed on to the Son in whom God is well pleased (1:11). However, why is the expression "the Son of Man" used?[115] What might it mean? Daniel 7:14 may have come to the mind of the original readers, but that presentation of the Holy One of the Most High coming to ultimate victory and vindication, despite their persecution, rejection, and martyrdom (see Dan 7:1–27), hardly matches the contexts of Mark 2:10 and 2:28, although questions of authority lurk behind both Son of Man sayings.[116] The puzzle, the narrative

---

[111] This can be guessed for the fact that the shewbread was put before the Lord each Sabbath (Lev 24:5–9) and consumed only by the priests on the following Sabbath, according to *Lev. Rab.* 32:3. See Marcus, *Mark,* 242.

[112] See also Gnilka, *Markus,* 1:122; Guelich, *Mark,* 122–23, 128–29. It may be (as many have argued) that 2:23–26 had its origins in early Christian discussions about the Sabbath. However, the present Markan context has lessened that issue in favor of the Christology of vv. 27–28. This development of the passage in the Markan redaction shifts the focus in vv. 23–26 from the Sabbath to the comparison between David and Jesus. For an excellent survey of this discussion, and a suggestion that the final product is an example of the rhetoric of a "verbal joust," rather than a conflict, see R. Parrott, "Conflict and Rhetoric in Mark 2:23–28," *Sem* 64 (1993): 117–37.

[113] For a summary of the discussion, and a case for the original unity of 2:23–26 and the addition of both v. 27 and v. 28, see Lane, *Mark,* 117–20; Guelich, *Mark,* 119–20.

[114] See Nineham, *St. Mark,* 105–6. Hooker (*St. Mark,* 104) comments on Jewish interpretation of the Sabbath: "It consistently understands the sabbath to be God's gift to Israel, instituted for the sake of the chosen people, not to mankind in general." See Exod 20:8–11; Deut 5:12–15; CD 10:14–12:6; *Jub.* 2:19, 21; 50:9–13.

[115] In the light of the link with ἄνθρωπος in v. 27, the expression "the Son of Man" is often explained here as "man," reflecting a wordplay in an Aramaic original. See for the discussion, and the adoption of this position, Guelich (*Mark,* 125–27, 129–30). As Marcus (*Mark,* 245–46) rightly points out, while this may have been the original meaning of the passage, "it is unlikely that *Mark* understands it merely as a statement about a prerogative of humanity in general" (p. 246).

[116] Marcus makes a link between Jesus and David in vv. 25–26 (see above n. 110), and Jesus and the Danielic Son of Man in vv. 27–28, concluding that "for Mark the Davidic Messiah and the Danielic Son of Man are one and the same, and their name is Jesus" (*Mark,* 246). This interpretation

"gap" opened in 2:10, is further opened in 2:28. No explanation is offered for Jesus' use of "the Son of Man" in reference to himself. The reader must wait till the author unfolds the second major section of the narrative (8:31–15:47). Only then will the reader recognize not only *that* Jesus has authority to forgive sins and is lord of the Sabbath, but also *how* he arrives at such authority as the vindicated Son of Man (see 14:62).[117] As in all good narratives, the story promises that all questions will be answered . . . later.

Jesus is watched that he might be eliminated (3:1–6)

The briefest of settings is provided: Jesus entered the synagogue and a man with a withered hand was there (3:1; see 2:1). We are not told which synagogue, as Mark moves immediately to the unnamed "they" who watch Jesus that they might accuse him (παρετήρουν αὐτὸν . . . ἵνα κατηγορήσωσιν αὐτοῦ, 3:2).[118] Here, however, the "they" must refer to the Pharisees. They were the protagonists in the immediately preceding episode (2:24) and were addressed throughout (see 2:25, 27). At the end of the present encounter the narrator reports: "The Pharisees went out . . ." (3:6a). The potential for conflict is strong, as Jesus is carefully watched.[119] A miracle story opened 2:1–3:6; the reader senses that another miracle story is about to be told. Jesus aggressively sets the miracle in motion by calling the man with the withered hand: "Rise up" (ἔγειρε, 3:3). The reader recalls the use of the same verb in the miracle story that opened 2:1–3:6 (see 2:9, 11–12). With the deformed man by his side, Jesus turns to his potential accusers and raises a point of law. There does not appear to be any urgency about the man's condition. It could have been put off till the following day. Another element from the earlier miracle story returns, as Jesus questions his potential accusers, exactly as he did in 2:9 ("Which is easier, to say . . . or to say . . . ?"). Situating himself on one side of a long debate, Jesus asks, "Is it lawful on the Sabbath to do good or to do harm, to save life or to kill?" (3:4a). The reader senses closure in these obvious repetitions from the earlier miracle story.[120]

The Pharisees recognize that he has placed them in an impossible situation. "To delay healing for a day is to deny the Torah's true intention, which is the glory of God and the benefit of man."[121] They cannot take the option of harming or killing on the Sabbath,

---

does not give sufficient weight to the later difficulty Jesus has with his identification as "Son of David" (see 11:9–10; 12:35–37). For Lührmann (*Markusevangelium*, 65), the readers understood the passage in the light of the authority of the Son of Man in Dan 7:14. The interpretation adopted in this commentary leaves the question open. It will be resolved only as the narrative comes to its conclusion.

117 Along these lines, see the summary of Gnilka (*Markus*, 1:124).

118 "Watching" (παρετήρουν) can have the malicious meaning of "to lie in wait for." See BDAG, 771, s.v. παρατηρέω. For this meaning here, see Marcus, *Mark*, 252.

119 Both 2:23–28 and 3:1–6 may have been used in Sabbath discussions in a pre-Markan setting (see Gnilka, *Markus*, 1:129–31). These debates have no role in the Markan use of the passages within 2:1–3:6 where conflict and Christology dominate.

120 The historical Jesus did not flout Torah but certainly objected to its legalistic interpretation. His coming to the synagogue in 3:1 and other Markan passages indicate this attitude to Torah (see 1:44; 7:8–13; 10:5–9; 12:29–31). Much has been written on this. For a good survey, see A. E. Harvey, *Jesus and the Constraints of History* (London: Duckworth, 1982), 36–65.

121 Hooker, *St. Mark,* 107. Rabbinic debate over this question is intense, but generally too late to be considered relevant to this passage. See, however, *m. Yoma* 8:6 and *b. Šabb.* 12a, which may reflect discussions from the time of Hillel and Shammai. See Nineham, *St. Mark,* 109–10; Meier, *A Marginal Jew,* 2:682–83, 731–32; Marcus, *Mark,* 248.

and thus they remain silent (3:4b). Yet they could have made a case, pointing out that the man was not in danger of death. His cure could have waited till the end of the Sabbath. The silence hints at more than Jesus' superiority in legal debate.[122] "Ultimately, Jesus' confrontation with his critics lay in the claim of his ministry and not in a different interpretation of the Sabbath law."[123] Jesus acts out of the authority he claimed for himself as "the Son of Man" in 2:28. The passage is about not the Sabbath law but the Markan Christology. Jesus looked around at them in anger, saddened by their hardness of heart (ἐπὶ τῇ πωρώσει τῆς καρδίας αὐτῶν, 3:5a) recalling 2:6 (διαλογιζόμενοι ἐν ταῖς καρδίαις αὐτῶν) and 2:8 (διαλογίζεσθε ἐν ταῖς καρδίαις ὑμῶν). The "closure" process intensifies.[124] Having posed the rhetorical question (see also 2:9) and received no answer, Jesus works the miracle (3:5b; see also 2:11–12). Jesus commands in direct speech, the man does exactly as he is told, and the miracle takes place. The word of Jesus effects the cure.[125]

The cycle of conflict stories closes with the coming together of the Pharisees and the Herodians to form a common plan (συμβούλιον ἐδίδουν, 3:6a).[126] The aim of the project, joining most unlikely partners from opposite ends of the Jewish leadership—the Pharisees (leaders with pretensions to a high level of religious purity[127]) and the Herodians (political leaders who collaborated with a foreign secular power)—is to destroy Jesus (ὅπως αὐτὸν ἀπολέσωσιν, 3:6b).[128] The first miracle was greeted with amazement, the glorification of God and acclamation: "We never saw anything like this!" (2:12b). The closing miracle reverses that acclamation with an unseemly collusion between enemies aimed at destroying Jesus. It will be repeated in the passion story as the leaders of the Jews and the Romans join in bringing about Jesus' death by crucifixion (see 15:1, 15).[129]

---

[122] See Guelich, *Mark*, 134–37.

[123] Guelich, *Mark*, 140. On the difference between the positions of Jesus and of the Pharisees, see Painter (*Mark's Gospel*, 64). On the Pharisees' commitment to Jesus' death (3:6), see van Iersel (*Reading Mark*, 52).

[124] Gnilka (*Markus*, 1:126) points out that v. 5 is a Markan addition to a story that goes back to the time of Jesus. The prophet Jeremiah often laments Israel's "hardness of heart." See Jer 3:17; 7:24; 9:13; 11:18; 13:10; 16:12; 18:12; 23:17. The same lament is found at Qumran. See 1QS 1:6; 2:14; 3:3; 5:4; 7:19, 24; 9:10.

[125] G. Vermes (*Jesus the Jew: A Historian's Reading of the Gospels* [London: Collins, 1973], 25) claims that curing by word alone, and not touching the ailing man in any way, is not contrary to Torah.

[126] The expression συμβούλιον ἐδίδουν is most unusual, reflecting the Latin *consilium facere*. Yet it appears again in 15:1, an obvious Markan link between 3:6 and Jesus' passion. On who "the Herodians" may have been, see the summary of Lane, *Mark*, 124–25; Guelich, *Mark*, 138–39; Lührmann, *Markusevangelium*, 67; Marcus, *Mark*, 249–50. The Markan point, however, is that religious leaders and political powers collude.

[127] Marcus (*Mark*, 253) suggests a "tremendous ironic linkage" between the hardness of heart of the Pharisees and the hardness of heart of Pharaoh at the time of the Exodus. On the basis of a similarity of the Greek Φαραώ and Φαρισαῖος, he asserts that both were guilty for their hardness of heart, yet part of God's design. The link is tenuous.

[128] Mark is responsible for the addition of the dramatic conclusion of v. 6, closing both 3:1–6 and 1:14–3:6. See Gnilka (*Markus*, 1:126). LaVerdiere (*The Beginning*, 1:91) comments: "The next verse could very well be the opening verse of the passion," and he cites 14:1a. Ernst (*Markus*, 107) rightly points out that Mark has not begun to develop his theology of the cross, but the negative presentation of Jesus' opponents.

[129] See Hooker, *St. Mark*, 106.

Conclusion

Jesus has begun his proclamation of the gospel in Galilee (1:14–15) and called others to follow (1:16–20), and together they have gone forth. Jesus' words and deeds show the presence of the kingdom. Demons (1:21–28, 32–34), sickness and taboo (1:29–31, 32–34), and leprosy (1:40–45) cannot resist the power of the kingdom present in Jesus, responding to God as he goes throughout all Galilee (1:35–39). However, there are signs that all is not well (see 1:22, 27, 45). Jesus conquers the powers of evil, but human beings remain puzzled, and he is unable to move freely in the towns. This puzzlement becomes conflict in 2:1–3:6. In a carefully constructed series of passages, Mark has taken traditions that came to him and elaborated the theme of Israel's rejection of Jesus by means of a ring construction that is chiastic in form but continues the linear development of the opposition.[130] The parallels between 2:1–12 and 3:1–6, and between 2:18–22 and 2:23–28, are obvious. This literary structure also allows Mark to place two crucial themes at the center of 2:1–3:6: the eschatological significance of the death of Jesus, and the radical newness that this event will introduce into salvation history (2:18–22). But the gradual progression and intensification of the opposition to Jesus, from the scribes (2:1–12, 13–17), the people (2:18–22), and the Pharisees (2:23–28; 3:1–6) leads inexorably to collusion between the Pharisees and the Herodians in the destruction of Jesus.

Yet the kingdom is proclaimed by Jesus' words and deeds. People are "raised" (2:1–12; 3:1–6), disciples are called, and Jesus offers healing to sinners (2:13–17). The presence of the Son of Man (2:10, 28) and the bridegroom (2:18–20) shows that the coming of the kingdom *of God* is marked by a new authority over sin, fasting, and Sabbath, an authority previously allowed only to YHWH. A radically new era has come which cannot be contained by former traditions and ways of life (2:21–22). A further literary feature, the frame around 2:1–3:6 created by 1:45 and 3:7–8, alerts the reader to this truth. In 1:45 the narrator reports: "People came to him from every quarter," and 3:7–8 develops the same theme further: "A great multitude from Galilee followed; also from Judea and Jerusalem and Idumea and from beyond the Jordan and from Tyre and Sidon a great multitude, hearing all that he did, came to him." However intense the opposition to Jesus has become across 2:1–3:6, Jesus continues to proclaim the kingdom, and people stream to him from every corner (3:7–8; see 1:45). Jesus' presence to Israel has not been fruitless, despite the leaders' decision that he must be destroyed. It has been rightly suggested that among the many themes in 1:16–45 "the note of 'authority' rings out louder than the others."[131] However strongly contested in 2:1–3:6, the authority of Jesus, highlighted by the authority of the Son of Man to forgive sins and his authority over the Sabbath, cannot be denied. In all five conflict stories Jesus "has the last word." The "gospel" of the coming kingdom continues as the ministry of Jesus proceeds.[132] Its focus shifts from Jesus and the leaders of Israel (1:14–3:6) to Jesus and his new family (3:7–6:6a).

---

[130] See Dewey, *Marcan Public Debate,* 109–30; van Iersel, *Reading Mark,* 59–60.

[131] Guelich, *Mark,* 47.

[132] It is thus imprecise to claim, "It is clear that St. Mark envisaged a sharp break between 1:45 and 2:1" (Nineham, *St. Mark,* 89).

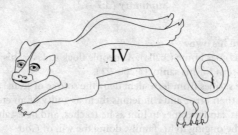

JESUS AND HIS NEW FAMILY (MARK 3:7–6:6A)

The section dedicated to Jesus and the leaders of Israel (1:14–3:6) opened with a summary of Jesus' ministry (1:14–15) and discipleship material (1:16–20). So does this new stage in the narrative (3:7–12, Jesus' ministry; 3:13–19, discipleship material). At the end of 1:14–3:6, the Pharisees and the Herodians planned together how they could best eliminate Jesus (3:6). In 6:1–6a, having established and instructed a new family, Jesus returns to his hometown. His own people refuse to accept that Jesus is anything more than the son of Mary, and he is amazed at their lack of faith. This rebuff marks the close of 3:7–6:6a, a section of the narrative devoted to Jesus and his new family.

The Shape of Mark 3:7–6:6a

The so-called summary of 3:7–12 is a mixed form, made up of some narrative associated with events from the life of Jesus (3:7, 9–10) and more obvious summary material (3:8, 11–12). There are snatches of pre-Markan material here, but the summary introduces the second major section of the first half of the Gospel. The choosing and naming of the Twelve follows (3:13–19). A long passage, which opens and closes with items dealing with Jesus and his blood family (3:20–21, 31–35), begins as Jesus enters the house. Conventional family and religious ties are questioned, and a criterion for belonging to the new family of God is provided (3:20–35). After a lengthy introduction, Jesus adopts the position of a teacher, using a boat as his "pulpit" (4:1–2), and proclaims a series of "parables," broken only by words to his new family in 4:10–11. The parables are formally concluded in 4:33–34. The parables are followed by a series of miracles that are reported without interruption from 4:35–5:43. Jesus returns to his hometown (6:1). There his townsfolk ask the right question concerning the source of Jesus' wisdom and mighty works (see 6:2) but give the wrong answer (6:3–5). Jesus is amazed (6:6a). Mark 3:7–6:6a unfolds as follows:

3:7–12   Summary
        3:7–8   As Jesus' ministry continues, people from every quarter enthusiastically receive him.
        3:9–12   He effects cures and drives out evil spirits (who know who he is). He commands them to be silent.
3:13–19   Disciples
        3:13–15   Jesus calls more disciples and from them appoints the Twelve.
        3:16–19   The Twelve are named.

3:20–35   Jesus and his own
       3:20–21   Jesus goes home (3:20a). As people flock to Jesus, his family expresses concern for his sanity (3:20b–21).
       3:22–30   The scribes from Jerusalem deny the source of Jesus' authority. Jesus points out their error and condemns them as guilty of an eternal sin.
       3:31–35   Jesus' family comes to him as he teaches, and he establishes a new criterion for belonging to his family: doing the will of God.

4:1–34   Jesus' instruction through wise parables
       4:1–2   The setting is established.
       4:1–9   Jesus tells the parable of the sown seed.
       4:10–12   Jesus addresses the disciples on the privilege of the new family of Jesus.
       4:13–20   Jesus explains the parable of the sown seed.
       4:21–25   Jesus tells the parable of the light under a bushel.
       4:26–29   Jesus tells the parable of the growing seed.
       4:30–32   Jesus tells the parable of the mustard seed.
       4:33–34   The parable section concludes.

4:35–5:43   Jesus' instruction through mighty deeds[1]
       4:35–41   Jesus calms the sea.
       5:1–20   Jesus cures the Gerasene demoniac.
       5:21–24a   Jairus approaches Jesus.
       5:24b–34   Jesus cures the woman with a flow of blood.
       5:35–43   Jesus raises Jairus's daughter.

6:1–6a   Jesus' rejection in his hometown
       6:1   Jesus goes to his hometown, followed by his disciples.
       6:2   The people from his hometown ask about his wisdom and his mighty deeds (see 4:1–5:43).
       6:3–5   They limit his origins to his mother, and they know his brothers and sisters.
       6:6a   Jesus is amazed.

The ministry of Jesus in Galilee continues along the lines of 1:14–3:6. He calls disciples to follow him (3:13–19), he teaches with authority and works miracles (4:1–5:43), amid perplexity and rejection (3:20–34). As his own blood family and national, religious, and cultural compatriots misunderstand and reject him, he sets up a new family (3:14–15, 31–35) and instructs them (4:1–5:53; see also 4:10–12, 33–34; 5:18–20). The section closes with rejection from the people of his hometown (6:1–6a).

Summary (3:7–12)

The summary in Mark 3:7–12 is an elaboration on the earlier summaries of 1:32–34 and 1:45, but in reverse order. In looking back to 1:45, 3:7–8 marks a *reprise* of the

---

[1] It has been pointed out that the miracles are associated with Jesus in a boat, and some have suggested that they belong to a pre-Markan "boat-cycle." See L. Keck, "Mark 3,7–12 and Mark's Christology," *JBL* 84 (1965): 341–58; Pesch, *Markusevangelium*, 1:277–81. For a summary and critique, see Marcus (*Mark*, 255–56). For R. E. Watts (*Isaiah's New Exodus and Mark* [WUNT 2. Reihe 88; Tübingen: J. C. B. Mohr (Paul Siebeck), 1997], 137–82), the miracles reported across 1:16–8:26 reflect a deutero-Isaian background with YHWH as warrior, healer, and provider. This helpful diachronic study, strongly stressing the Gospel's Christology, misses other elements in the unfolding plot, especially the role of the disciples.

summary which immediately preceded the five conflict stories of 2:1–3:6, showing, as the next major section of the narrative opens, that opposition to Jesus (2:1–3:6) has not diminished the effectiveness of his presence. Then 3:10–12 looks further back in the narrative, to the first day of Jesus' powerful presence in 1:32–34. The use of this leapfrog effect links the narrative as a whole. The scenario and events may change, at times disconcertingly, but fundamental themes continue. The kingdom's power was narrated in 1:14–45, and the reader is made aware that this power is not diminished by human opposition (2:1–3:6). "Jesus' ministry as depicted in 1:16–3:12 reaches its zenith in the graphic portrait of 3:7–12 when set against the backdrop of 1:21–3:6."[2]

Two elements in 3:7–12 differ from other Markan summaries. Verse 7 indicates a change of scene. Jesus withdraws with his disciples to the sea, but one of the themes of the summary is introduced as the passage concludes in v. 7b: "and a great multitude from Galilee followed." The reference to the large crowd of followers introduces a list of places of origin of those who came to Jesus: not only Galilee (v. 7b), but also Judea (v. 7c), Jerusalem, Idumea, beyond the Jordan, and the region of Tyre and Sidon (v. 8). The reason for this widespread movement toward Jesus is given: they heard what he did (v. 8; see 1:45a). This list, containing five regions (Galilee, Judea, Idumea, beyond the Jordan, and the region of Tyre and Sidon) and a city (Jerusalem), spells out the πάντοθεν ("from every quarter") of 1:45b. Thus far the region of Galilee has circumscribed the ministry of Jesus. This circumscription continues but people come to him from Judea, and explicitly from the seat of religious and political power located within that region but dominant over all Israel: Jerusalem. All other regions mentioned are outside Israel and are systematically listed: south (Idumea), east (beyond the Jordan), and north (the region of Tyre and Sidon). It is often remarked that Samaria and the Decapolis are not mentioned,[3] but the Decapolis is included in the region πέραν τοῦ Ἰορδάνου.[4] The geographical location of each place mentioned, in its relationship to Galilee, and the explicit mention of lands outside Israel have generated the list. The movement of large crowds of Gentiles *toward Jesus* is the main issue. Hearing of Jesus' deeds (see 1:45a), there is a movement from all Israel and from surrounding Gentile lands toward him (see 1:45b). Beside the sea, a symbol of untamed turmoil, Jesus continues to overcome the evils of sickness and demons. His power reaches all Israel, and transcends its boundaries to touch Gentiles.[5]

---

[2] R. A. Guelich, *Mark*, 144. See also Keck, "Mark 3,7–12," 344–45; Marcus, *Mark*, 259–60. Taylor (*St. Mark*, 225) mistakenly claims that this summary only looks forward and "there are no links back."

[3] See, for example, Lohmeyer, *Markus*, 71; Marxsen, *Mark the Evangelist*, 64; W. Grundmann, *Das Evangelium nach Markus* (6th ed.; THKNT 2; Berlin: Evangelische Verlagsanstalt, 1973), 99. There is reluctance among commentators to accept that the Gentile mission could be mentioned so early in the narrative. For the missionary interpretation adopted above, see Gnilka, *Markus*, 1:134–35; LaVerdiere, *The Beginning*, 1:99–100, 106–7; Lane, *Mark*, 129–30.

[4] As Lührmann (*Markusevangelium*, 68) remarks: "This question is posed only by those who attempt to match Mark's details with a modern 'map of Palestine at the time of Jesus.' "

[5] Thus, for example, Schweizer, *Mark*, 79; Pesch, *Markusevangelium*, 1:198–99; Taylor, *St. Mark*, 227; Ernst, *Markus*, 110; Marcus, *Mark*, 260. Not all would agree. For example, Guelich (*Mark*, 146) regards the regions as areas which "were either Jewish or had large Jewish populations." The omission of Samaria and the Decapolis (but see above on "beyond the Jordan") is taken as evidence of this. Keck ("Mark 3, 7–12," 348–51) and Weeden (*Traditions in Conflict*, 57) see curing by touch as evidence for the Markan θεῖος ἀνήρ Christology. This is reading too much into the evidence. See Guelich (*Mark*, 147–48).

A further element of the summary is introduced by an introductory passage that may be pre-Markan, linking the summary to an event. Jesus' command to his disciples to have the boat ready, because of the immensity of the crowd and to protect him from being crushed (3:9; see 4:1, where a similar scenario occurs), heightens the impression of the huge crowd and enables the author to introduce the second theme of the summary. The summary of 3:7–12 is a "mixed form" composed of summary material (vv. 8, 11–12) and two indications from the narrator which are not typical of that form (vv. 7, 9–10).[6] If 3:7–8 developed the πάντοθεν of 1:45, 3:10–12 repeats the summary of 1:32–34. As 3:7–8 developed 1:45 by describing the regions from which the crowds flocked, so also 3:10–12 develops further 1:32–34 in describing Jesus' ministry of healing and driving out unclean spirits.[7] In the earlier summary the narrator simply reported that Jesus silenced the demons because they knew who he was (1:34). In 3:11–12 their behavior on encountering him and their calling out his true name, "You are the Son of God" (v. 11), is reported in detail. In a further development of 1:34, the reason for Jesus' command to silence is given. It is not the demons who are to make known the true identity of Jesus (v. 12).

[handwritten margin note: It is our Lord's cross & resurr.]

Disciples (3:13–19)

In Mark 3:13 the form of 1:16–20 and 2:13–14 is repeated:

And *he went up* on the mountain
and *called* to him
    those whom
he desired
    and *they came* to him.

Jesus is on the move. There is an added solemnity to this vocation story, located on "the mountain." No specific mountain is mentioned, but mountains are significant places in the biblical tradition.[8] The use of the verb θέλειν indicates that he called only those whom he wanted. An immediate and wordless response follows. Certain elements from the earlier accounts are missing: the names of the people called (developed in 3:16–19), their occupation, and the abandoning of that occupation. But Jesus wrests all initiative from them.[9] It is not entirely clear whether a larger group of unnamed disciples is intended in 3:13, from

---

6 On this, see Keck, "Mark 3,7–12," 346–47, Schweizer, *Mark,* 79. Gnilka (*Markus,* 1:133) regards the passage as entirely Markan. See the summaries of discussion in Guelich, *Mark,* 144–46; Marcus, *Mark,* 258–59.

7 The word used for disease is μάστιξ, which means "a scourge." This reflects the association that existed between sickness and punishment for sin. See Cranfield, *St. Mark,* 125. C. R. Kazmierski (*Jesus, the Son of God: A Study of the Marcan Tradition and Its Redaction by the Evangelist* [FB 33; Würzburg: Echter, 1979], 73–103) traces a Gentile Christian confession of Jesus' divine sonship behind vv. 7–12.

8 This association must not be pressed too hard, as nothing is made of it in the text. See Gnilka, *Markus,* 1:139. Nevertheless, the call and commissioning of the Twelve (vv. 14–15) is a significant event, and the setting "on the mountain" heightens that (see Exod 19:20; 1 Kgs 19:8). See E. S. Malbon, *Narrative Space and Mythic Meaning in Mark* (New Voices in Biblical Studies; San Francisco: Harper & Row, 1986), 84–89. For an exodus and Mosaic background, see Marcus, *Mark,* 266.

9 See Pesch (*Markusevangelium,* 203) for the link with 1:16–20. K. Stock (*Boten aus dem Mit-Ihm-Sein: Das Verhältnis zwischen Jesus und den Zwölf nach Markus* [AnBib 70; Rome: Biblical Institute Press, 1975], 47–49) analyzes the parallel, but notes serious differences. Stock's work is weakened by his determination to force a separation between the disciples and the Twelve.

whom the Twelve are appointed, but this is probably the case (see Luke 6:13).[10] The appointment of the Twelve continues the literary form of a vocation story:

> And *he appointed twelve*[11]
>> *to be with him*
>> and *to be sent out to preach*
>> and *to have authority to cast out demons.*
> And *he appointed* the Twelve.[12]
> And *he surnamed* Simon, Peter
>> and James the son of Zebedee
>> and John the brother of James
> whom *he surnamed* Boanerges, that is, sons of thunder
>> and Andrew and Philip and Bartholomew
>> and Matthew and Thomas and James the son of Alphaeus
>> and Thaddeus and Simon the Cananaean
>> and Judas Iscariot *who betrayed him.*

There is great emphasis upon the initiative of Jesus. Of the eleven main verbs, nine report actions of Jesus, while only two refer to actions of disciples: in 3:13 "they came to him" and in v. 19 the opposite happens: Judas Iscariot is described as the one "who betrayed him." All the subordinate verbs in the ἵνα phrases, describing the future mission of the Twelve, depend upon the action of Jesus "appointing" them (ποιεῖν is again used; see 3:14, 16; see 1:17)[13] and upon their "being with him" (3:14).

It is universally accepted that 3:13–19 forms a literary unit. Verses 7–12 provide an introductory summary. In the passage following the vocation narrative (vv. 20–35) Mark has reworked earlier traditions into a synthesis of key elements: the new family of Jesus, his power as Son of God over evil, and the refusal to accept his authority.[14] In this context, the vocation and the commissioning of the Twelve look backward to vv. 7–12 and forward to vv. 20–35. The disciples have authority and power to continue Jesus' spreading of the kingdom, but only insofar as they *receive* that power and belong to the new family of Jesus, associated closely with him, in their "being with him" (v. 14).[15] Mark links the disciples

---

[10] See J. P. Meier, "The Circle of the Twelve: Did it Exist During Jesus' Public Ministry?" *JBL* 116 (1997): 638 n. 8.

[11] Many good witnesses (e.g., Sinaiticus and Vaticanus) add "whom he also named apostles," but this reading has crept into the text from Luke 6:13. See Taylor, *St. Mark,* 230; Meier, "The Circle of the Twelve," 639 n. 11; Marcus, *Mark,* 263. For a contrary view, see Guelich, *Mark,* 154, note a; Lührmann, *Markusevangelium,* 71.

[12] Mark 3:16a is also textually difficult. Many good witnesses have "and he appointed the twelve," but these are similar to the textual traditions which inserted Luke 6:13 into v. 14. I am including it because of the use of the definite article in connection with *the* Twelve. It picks up v. 14, but carries further the argument interrupted by the parenthesis created by the series of the ἵνα phrases. The accusative case of the following names (vv. 16–19) also calls for this clause. See, for this position, M.-J. Lagrange, *Evangile selon Saint Marc* (EBib; Paris: Gabalda, 1920), 80–81; Guelich, *Mark,* 160.

[13] As in 1:16–20, the use of this verb does not link Jesus' actions with Genesis and God's creation (see, for example, Lohmeyer, *Markusevangelium,* 74; Pesch, *Markusevangelium,* 1:204; LaVerdiere, *The Beginning,* 1:101), but with the appointment of kings and prophets. See Gnilka, *Markus,* 1:139.

[14] This is widely recognized. See Nineham, *St. Mark,* 120; Pesch, *Markusevangelium,* 2:198–99; Taylor, *St. Mark,* 235, 237–38, 240–41.

[15] See Stock, *Boten aus dem Mit-Ihm-Sein,* 53–70.

intimately with Jesus' task; the Markan insertion of "and have authority to cast out demons" (v. 15) into his source makes this clear.[16] By passing this authority on to the disciples he links them with his actions in vv. 11–12, preceding the call story, and the discussion in vv. 22–24 which follows. The Twelve are commissioned to be sent out, to preach, and to have authority to cast out demons (vv. 14–15). To this point in the narrative Jesus' activities have been his incessant motion as one "sent" (see 1:38), his preaching (1:14, 39, 45), and his casting out of demons (1:21–28, 32–34; 3:7–12). Involvement with Jesus' ministry was foreshadowed in 1:16–20 but becomes the central issue in 3:13–19. Despite the fact that the number "twelve" is symbolic, as the twelve tribes represent the nation Israel, the Twelve are not a "new Israel" but the basis of an eschatological people of God.[17] They are commissioned to be "with Jesus" so that they might do what Jesus does. As such they are the bearers of Jesus' mission to preach the good news of the kingdom of God.[18]

A further christological feature emerges in the commissioning of the Twelve "to be with him." Some scholars make little of this aspect of the vocation of the Twelve,[19] but it provides the christological motivation for the disciples' mission. Physical presence "with" Jesus, even though not always expressed in terms of εἶναι μετ' αὐτοῦ, seems to be characteristic of all disciples of Jesus, not just the Twelve (see especially the use of κατ' ἰδίαν in 4:34; 6:31–32; 9:2, 28; 13:3).[20] Until the dramatic flight of 14:50, disciples (and not only the Twelve) are with Jesus, except briefly during the mission of the Twelve in 6:6b–30. Although applied only to the Twelve in 3:14, all disciples will succeed or fail insofar as they are or are not "with Jesus."[21] The grammatical structure of the passage is clumsy, and it

---

[16] Pesch, *Markusevangelium*, 1:203, esp. n. 1. Mark only retouched his tradition here by adding the setting of the scene in v. 13, the reference to exorcism in v. 15, the giving of the extra names in vv. 16–17, and the additional comment to the name of Judas in v. 19 (although this also may be pre-Markan). See Pesch, *Markusevangelium*, 1:202–3.

[17] For a strong development of the eschatological theme, see Marcus, *Mark*, 267.

[18] See Gnilka, *Markus*, 1:139–40. "The sending lies in the future, not simply in the earthly story of Jesus, but in the story of the church" (p. 139).

[19] See, for example, E. Best, "The Role of the Disciples in Mark," *NTS* 23 (1976–1977): 380–81.

[20] See S. Freyne, *The Twelve: Disciples and Apostles. A Study in the Theology of the First Three Gospels* (London: Sheed & Ward, 1969), 107–19. This expression, used only of the Twelve in a positive sense (see 5:18 for its other use), is one of the keys to Stock's claim that Mark separates the role of the Twelve from that of the disciples. See Stock, *Boten aus dem Mit-Ihm-Sein*, 199–203.

[21] G. Theissen (*The First Followers of Jesus: A Sociological Analysis of Earliest Christianity* [London: SCM, 1978], 8–27) has pointed helpfully to two types of "disciples" in the earliest church: (a) wandering charismatics, and (b) sympathizers in the local communities, a group of "disciples" who do not "walk behind" Jesus (pp. 17–27). Among those wandering charismatics was a *historical* group of twelve, chosen by Jesus, following an itinerant leader (see Meier, "The Circle of the Twelve," 635–72). Yet many "disciples" were not itinerant. Here I agree in part with Meier ("The Circle of the Twelve," 636–42), who may err in regarding those who stayed in their homes as "not in the strict sense disciples" (pp. 636–37). I suspect that *historically* this is impossible to prove. It was Mark, not history, who applied the itinerant motif to discipleship as such. He may have been influenced by sources originating from that group (Simon Peter?). In this way all discipleship teaching in the Gospel of Mark presupposes itinerant followers. The role of nonitinerant disciples became marginal in a Markan theology of "following." Yet the use of εἶναι μετ' αὐτοῦ in two places (3:14 and 5:18) hints that *some* were called to follow behind the itinerant Jesus (3:14) while others were sent to home and friends (5:18–19). Associated with this discussion, and crucial for my understanding of the Gospel of Mark, is that the criteria for the Twelve, established in 3:14–15, apply to disciples ("followers") as such throughout the Gospel. For J. Painter (*Mark's Gospel*, 57–58), "disciples" were "the Twelve." I suggest that rhetorically the argument runs the other way. What is said of "the Twelve" applies to all "disciples," including the Markan community and all subsequent readers/listeners. See E. S. Malbon,

hints that the use of ποιεῖν in v. 14 applies strictly to the first of the ἵνα phrases: "He appointed twelve *to be with him.*" The remaining phrases, which attend to *what* they are *to do* rather than *where* they are *to be,* are separated from the expression in v. 14 by καί.[22] What they are to do, therefore, does not depend directly upon the ποιεῖν, but upon their "being with him." The passage would then run:

> He appointed twelve *to be* (ἵνα ὦσιν) *with him*
>   and so that (καὶ ἵνα) he might send them out to preach
>   and (καὶ) have authority to cast out demons.

The missionary character of the call of the Twelve depends upon Jesus' appointing them to be closely associated with his person.[23] In the Markan view, applied here to the Twelve, but subsequently shown as important for all disciples, the relationship of *"being with Jesus"* (v. 14ab) is crucial for all they are called to do (vv. 14c–15).[24]

This passage, set within a context of mission, shows that Jesus calls some to a physical closeness to his person so that they might do as he has done. Twelve names are given.[25] Jesus gives three of them further names: Simon is named Peter, and James and John are named Boanerges.[26] This further act of Jesus creates a smaller group within the Twelve: those named by Jesus. In time they will be called to further intimacy with Jesus (see 5:37; 9:2; 14:33).[27] As throughout the vocation stories (1:16–20; 2:15–17), the initiative of Jesus shows that the destiny of the disciple depends upon association with him. They do not make themselves disciples (3:13) or commission themselves to be members of the Twelve (3:14).

After the final name, Judas Iscariot, a note is added: "who betrayed him." Mark shows the possibility of betrayal, failure, and sin even among the closest followers of Jesus.[28] The appointment of the Twelve to the mission of sharing in the task of Jesus is determined by a vocation to "be with him." At the close of the list of people who were called to this mission the narrator tells of one who will fail, and *why* he failed. The expression ὃς καὶ παρέδωκεν

"Disciples/Crowds/ Whoever: Markan Characters and Readers," in *In the Company of Jesus: Characters in Mark's Gospel* (Louisville: Westminster John Knox, 2000), 70–99 (originally published in *NovT* 28 [1986]: 104–30).

[22] It would be impossible to have ἐποίησεν ἵνα ἀποστέλλῃ. See Lohmeyer, *Markusevangelium,* 74; Pesch, *Markusevangelium,* 1:203.

[23] See Cranfield, *St. Mark,* 127–28.

[24] Reading vv. 14c–15 as a subordinate to v. 14ab, and thus not a "statement of the *twofold* purpose of the appointment of the twelve" (Painter, *Mark's Gospel,* 67; stress in original).

[25] There are minor differences with the names and the order of the names given elsewhere in the New Testament (see Matt 10:2–4; Luke 6:14–16; Acts 1:13). On the whole the names correspond. The only variation is Thaddeus (here and in Matt 10:3), replaced by Judas the son of James in Luke 6:16 and Acts 1:13. The oddities of each tradition need not detain us here. For more detail, see the commentaries, especially Taylor, *St. Mark,* 231–34; Pesch, "Levi–Matthäus," 40–56; Meier, "The Circle of the Twelve," 643–53. On the names themselves, see Marcus, *Mark,* 263–65.

[26] In contrast to the name Πέτρος, given to Peter (see Cranfield, *St. Mark,* 129–30), the significance of Boanerges as "sons of thunder" is hard to establish, both etymologically and in regard to its applicability to the sons of Zebedee. See Guelich, *Mark,* 162–63; Marcus, *Mark,* 264.

[27] Schweizer (*Mark,* 81–82) comments: "The conferring of new names by Jesus manifests his sovereign ability to create something new." For Marcus (*Mark,* 268–69), the naming of "three" has further Jewish background. They are to be the leaders of an eschatological army, despite their fragility (already indicated here).

[28] See, for example, Taylor, *St. Mark,* 234; Pesch, *Markusevangelium,* 207–8; Lagrange, *Saint Marc,* 61. The name "Iscariot" is open to a number of meanings. See the comprehensive survey in R. E. Brown, *The Death of the Messiah: From Gethsemane to the Grave: A Commentary on the Passion Narratives in the Four Gospels* (2 vols.; ABRL; New York: Doubleday, 1994), 2:1410–16.

αὐτόν is generally rendered "who betrayed him," but given the programmatic importance of ἵνα ὦσιν μετ᾽ αὐτοῦ in v. 14, the use of παραδίδωμι in v. 19 reflects not only the fact of the betrayal but also the theological tragedy of a disciple who "gave Jesus away."[29] The account of the vocation to share in the mission of Jesus begins with the *sine qua non* of belonging to Jesus (v. 14) and closes with the ultimate explanation for the failure of one of those whom Jesus had chosen (v. 19). The negative example of Judas is Mark's first indication of the possibility of failure, even among those appointed by Jesus, and thus also in the life of any disciple.[30] Verse 19 "points forward again to Jesus' coming death,"[31] but also looks back to v. 14: one called to be "with Jesus" (v. 14) cast him off (v. 19).

Jesus and His Own (3:20–35)

Mark 3:20–35 is the first occurrence of the so-called "sandwich constructions" in this gospel.[32] A theme or a narrative begins in vv. 20–21, is apparently interrupted by the words and events of vv. 22–30, only to return in vv. 31–35. The theme of belonging to Jesus, or the family of Jesus, runs across all three sections of the sandwich. There is a long and unresolved debate over the mixture of pre-Markan elements and Markan redaction in vv. 20–35.[33] For our purposes, it is sufficient to accept that there are three distinct blocks of material: vv. 20–21, vv. 22–30, and vv. 31–35. The material in vv. 22–30 has its own history,

---

[29] The verb παραδίδωμι has a wide range of meanings, but one of its primary senses is the giving away of a possession. See LSJ, 1308, where this is the first meaning given. See also Cranfield, *St. Mark,* 306; Marcus, *Mark,* 265. There are only two "actions" of disciples in this passage. One is positive: "they came to him" (v. 13), while the other is negative: "who gave him away" (v. 19). This is missed by Marcus (*Mark,* 269), whose exaggerated focus upon the background of the Jewish War leads him to associate "Iscariot" with the "Sicarii." As Brown points out (*Death,* 2:1410–16), this identification is far from sure. On the association of this verb with Jesus' passion in early Christian tradition, see N. Perrin, "The Use of *(Para)didonai* in Connection with the Passion of Jesus in the New Testament," in *A Modern Pilgrimage in New Testament Christology* (Philadelphia: Fortress, 1974), 94–103.

[30] See above, note 21. This passage focuses upon the Twelve, but the criteria established in vv. 13–19 apply to all disciples, from among whom (v. 13) the Twelve are appointed (vv. 14–19).

[31] Hooker, *St. Mark,* 113.

[32] See E. Best, "Mark iii.20, 21, 31–35," NTS 22 (1975–76): 309–19; Lührmann, *Markusevangelium,* 74–75. Sandwich constructions or intercalations in Mark were first highlighted by E. von Dobschütz, "Zur Erzählerkunst des Markus," ZNW 27 (1928): 193–98. They have continued to attract attention. See J. R. Donahue, *Are You the Christ? The Trial Narrative in the Gospel of Mark* (SBLDS 10; Missoula: Society of Biblical Literature, 1973), 58–63; H. C. Kee, *The Community of the New Age: Studies in Mark's Gospel* (London: SCM, 1977), 54–56; F. Kermode, *The Genesis of Secrecy: On the Interpretation of Narrative* (Cambridge: Harvard University Press, 1979), 128–34; J. R. Edwards, "Markan Sandwiches: The Significance of Interpolations in Markan Narratives," NovT 31 (1989): 193–216; R. M. Fowler, *Loaves and Fishes: The Function of the Feeding Stories in the Gospel of Mark* (SBLDS 54; Chico: Scholars Press, 1981), 114–16; idem, *Let the Reader Understand: Reader-Response Criticism and the Gospel of Mark* (Minneapolis: Fortress, 1991), 147–54; T. Shepherd, "The Narrative Function of Markan Intercalation," NTS 41 (1995): 522–40; D. Rhoads, J. Dewey, and D. Michie, *Mark as Story: An Introduction to the Narrative of a Gospel* (2d ed.; Minneapolis: Fortress, 1999): 51–52. It is also possible to trace a chiastic structure in 3:20–35. See J. Lambrecht, "The Relatives of Jesus in Mark," in *The Composition of Mark's Gospel: Selected Studies from Novum Testamentum* (ed. D. E. Orton; Brill's Readers in Biblical Studies 3; Leiden: Brill, 1999), 85–102; Marcus, *Mark,* 278–79.

[33] Very well summarized by Guelich, *St. Mark,* 168–72.

and there are some minor Markan touches (especially in v. 20).[34] What must be noticed is that our present vv. 20–35 are the result of redactional activity from Mark. The "sandwich" which begins (vv. 20–21) and closes (vv. 31–35) with Jesus' blood family, and focuses on an angry encounter between Jesus and some official representatives of his culture and religious heritage (the scribes), is constructed by the storyteller for his purposes.[35]

In 3:20 the scene and the characters change as Jesus goes into a home and the crowd gathers again (πάλιν).[36] The large gathering of people from the summary of vv. 7–12 is recalled by means of the πάλιν. The crowds are so intense that "they" could not even eat.[37] Who are the "they"? Hardly the crowd, as the gathering is creating the problem. It must refer to Jesus and his associates in the house. An atmosphere of broken intimacy is created by the reference to the meal as sharing bread (ἄρτον φαγεῖν). A further group, οἱ παρ' αὐτοῦ, heard of the situation and moved to remedy it (v. 21). Three parties are involved: Jesus and his associates (disciples?) in the house, a large crowd which is preventing their meal, and οἱ παρ' αὐτοῦ, who decide that this must stop and initiate a vigorous action to attain their ends: they came out to seize him (ἐξῆλθον κρατῆσαι αὐτόν). The verb κρατέω is a violent one and reappears in 6:17 and 12:12 to describe an arrest. They move *against* Jesus, alleging that he is out of his mind (ἐξέστη).[38]

A few dissenting voices notwithstanding,[39] it is widely accepted that in light of Jesus' being at a house and sharing a meal, the οἱ παρ' αὐτοῦ refers to his blood family.[40] A "new

---

[34] Much of the material in vv. 22–30 has parallels in Q (see Matt 12:22–32; Luke 11:14–23; 12:10). But Mark is not using Q; Mark and Q reflect independent traditions. See Gnilka, *Markus*, 1:145–47.

[35] As Schweizer (*Mark*, 83) puts it: "There is scarcely any other passage where Mark's pen is as evident as it is here." For a very different assessment, see J. Painter, "When Is a House Not a Home? Mark 3:13–35," *NTS* 45 (1999): 498–513.

[36] As in 2:15, it is impossible to be certain which house is indicated. See Pesch, *Markusevangelium*, 1:211. I have translated the expression "home" to convey the familiarity of the situation. On "the home" in Mark, see G. Minette de Tillesse, *Le secret messianique dans l'Evangile de Marc* (LD 47; Paris: Cerf, 1968), 242–48; Malbon, *Narrative Space*, 117–20; F. Manns, "Le thème de la maison dans l'évangile de Marc," *RSR* 66 (1992): 1–17.

[37] The expression is clumsy: ὥστε μὴ δύναθαι αὐτοὺς μηδὲ ἄρτον φαγεῖν. Literally: "so that it was rendered impossible to them even to eat bread." The expression can simply mean to have a meal, but sharing bread is a further indication of the familiarity of the situation in the home.

[38] H. Wansbrough ("Mark 3,21: Was Jesus Out of His Mind?" *NTS* 18 [1971–1972]: 234–35) rejects this meaning, claiming that it denotes astonishment as in Mark 2:12; 5:42; 6:51. But the verb's best attested meaning is to be "out of one's mind" (literally: "to be outside oneself"), and there is no surrounding event which arouses astonishment, as in Mark 2, 5, and 6. Insanity is also often regarded as demon possession. For Painter ("When Is a House Not a Home?" 504–6), "those around him" are the disciples, and the crowd says that Jesus is beside himself. The judgment of Jesus' family may be close to that of the scribes in v. 22. See Hooker, *St. Mark*, 115. Copyists have attempted to smooth out this hard description of Jesus: see Gnilka, *Markus*, 148 n. 22.

[39] Wansbrough ("Mark 3,21," 234–35) and D. Wenham ("The Meaning of Mark iii.21," *NTS* 21 [1974–1975]: 296–97) claim that it refers to the disciples. More recently, Painter (*Mark's Gospel*, 69–71) argues that it is the disciples who restrain him, hearing the crowd say "He is beside himself." See also idem, "When Is a House Not a Home?" 501, 504–8. It is an indication that the disciples do not understand Jesus and his mission. The case argued above, that vv. 20–21 form an inclusion with the family mentioned in vv. 31–35, is firmly but unconvincingly rejected in J. Painter, *Just James: The Brother of Jesus in History and Tradition* (Studies on Personalities of the New Testament; Columbia: University of South Carolina, 1997), 20–31. See also idem, *Mark's Gospel*, 73–76, and idem, "When Is a House Not a Home?" 503–4.

[40] The expression οἱ παρ' αὐτοῦ generally means "envoys" or "adherents," but it can also mean "relatives" (see LXX Prov 31:21). For a fuller discussion, with further examples, see Taylor, *St. Mark*,

family" has been established in 3:14 as the Twelve were commissioned "to be with him." The members of his blood family are unable to understand the urgency that drives Jesus in his task of proclaiming the kingdom, and the powerful attraction which this exercises upon those who are sick, and in need of the physician (see 2:17). They are "outside" the kingdom preached by Jesus.

The scribes who came to Galilee from Jerusalem have a negative assessment of Jesus' power over evil spirits. His family regards him as insane, but the scribes go one step further, claiming that the prince of all evil spirits, Beelzebul, has taken possession of Jesus. Jesus is thus only able to drive out evil spirits as one possessed by the prince of all evil spirits (3:22).[41] This is a logical suggestion from those who refuse to accept Jesus' connection to the kingdom *of God*. His authority must come from somewhere, but the suggestion of the scribes is a fatal error, and merits a stinging reply from Jesus. Jesus asks how Satan can drive out Satan, turning to a universal principle to show the impossibility of the accusation.[42] A kingdom divided, a house divided, cannot stand. Any ordinarily unified authority, when divided, is "coming to an end" (vv. 23–26). However long internecine strife may go on, it leads all involved to destruction. On the basis of this general principle, in vv. 24–25 Jesus answers the question he posed in v. 23b. As with a kingdom or a house, Satan, when pitted against Satan—as would be the case in the situation suggested by the scribes as the explanation of Jesus' authority (v. 22)—would come to an end. There is irony here. The reader has encountered Jesus' authority over the forces of evil in 1:16–45, 2:1–12 and 3:1–6. His victories were not the result of internal strife among the demons. The house of the strong man (τὴν οἰκίαν τοῦ ἰσχυροῦ), has been invaded and the possessions taken from the house of Beelzebul (see v. 22: "the Lord of the house"). For this to have happened, the owner of the house must have been rendered powerless. He has been bound. There is a situation of conflict and opposition between the one who has possession and the one who takes these possessions from him; the strong man is overcome by the stronger one.[43] John the Baptist's description of Jesus as "the stronger one" (ὁ ἰσχυρότερος) in the prologue (1:7) comes to mind. Jesus is in conflict with the strong man; not possessed by him. However, as "the stronger one" (ὁ ἰσχυρότερος) his

---

236. Taylor insists: "The disciples are in no way suggested." See also Hooker, *St. Mark*, 114; Marcus, *Mark*, 279–71, 279–80.

[41] The derivation of the word Beelzebul is not clear. It may come from a Hebrew word meaning "Lord of the dwelling," and this would be appropriate for Jesus' words in v. 27 (see also Matt 10:25). The Syriac and Latin Vulgate translations have "Beelzebub" ("Lord of the flies"), the false god of Ekron in 1 Kgs 1:2. See Lane, *Mark*, 140 n. 82; Lührmann, *Markusevangelium*, 75–76; Marcus, *Mark*, 272.

[42] The narrator describes Jesus' response as a "parable" (v. 23). Unlike the material generally understood by Christian readers as "parables" (see 4:1–34), this appeal to general principle responds to the Hebrew *mashal*, translated regularly in the LXX as παραβολή: short pithy sayings, riddles, proverbs, etc. In the light of 4:11–12, there is little chance that the scribes will understand the parable. See Gnilka, *Markus*, 1:149.

[43] On the idea of Satan as head of the household in apocalyptic thought, see Marcus, *Mark*, 274: "God's sovereignty has been deeply disturbed, and only a violent divine invasion can restore it by ejecting the cause of the disruption." E. Best (*The Temptation and the Passion: The Markan Soteriology* [2d ed; SNTSMS 2; Cambridge: Cambridge University Press, 1990], 1–15) argues that Jesus is victorious over Satan in 1:12–13, and the proof of the victory of Jesus "the stronger one," is found in 3:27 (see p. 15). But Jesus does not win a definitive victory in 1:12–13. The text is too sparse to make such a claim. His victorious presence over evil, as the one who brings in the kingdom of God (see 1:15), is found in the episodes which open the narrative in 1:14–45.

victory over the power of "the strong man" (ὁ ἰσχυρός), already initiated in 1:12–13, is guaranteed (v. 27).[44]

Jesus continues his response to the charge by moving beyond the *logical* response of 3:23–27 into a devastating *christological* criticism of the scribes in vv. 28–30.[45] The seriousness of his words are highlighted by the opening, "Amen, I say to you." The use of "amen" at the beginning of words (rather than at the end, as in the Jewish liturgy) is unique to the Gospels, and their reporting of the words of Jesus. It is an indication of the authority with which he spoke. Jesus' opening affirmation is stunning: "All sins will be forgiven the sons of men, and whatever blasphemies they utter" (v. 28). There is a sense of freedom and a recognition of the gracious forgiveness meted out by the God of Jesus, but the affirmation accentuates the condemnation that follows in v. 29.[46] Despite God's gracious willingness to forgive human beings every possible sin and blasphemy, there is one sin that cannot be forgiven: blasphemy against the Holy Spirit. The prologue (1:1–13) is crucial to a proper understanding of these words. John the Baptist indicated that the mightier one would baptize with the Holy Spirit (1:8). At his baptism the Spirit descended upon Jesus (v. 10), and took possession of him, driving him into the wilderness (v. 12). From this point on, the reader is aware that the Holy Spirit of God is present in Jesus' words and actions, driving out demons and healing the sick (see 1:21–28, 29–31, 32–34, 39, 40–45; 2:1–12; 3:1–6, 7–12). To suggest that Jesus' authority over demons comes from the prince of all evil spirits is to deny the presence of the Holy Spirit of God. This is the eternal sin. When the presence of the Spirit of God in Jesus is denied, how can God forgive? It is unforgivable to claim that the Holy Spirit of God is an unclean spirit (v. 30) because those making such a claim place themselves outside the domain of the all-forgiving God described in v. 28.[47] They manifest "an attitude of mind . . . so fixed and obstinate that it forms a permanent obstacle between God and man."[48]

New characters enter the narrative in 3:31: his mother and his brothers. The setting of v. 20 has been maintained across vv. 20–30, albeit somewhat artificially.[49] Jesus is now "inside" and his mother and his brothers are standing "outside." They have no direct access to Jesus, and are forced to send messengers to call him (v. 31). This information is most important for the meaning of vv. 31–35, and for the understanding of its place within the broader context of vv. 20–35. A crowd is seated around Jesus. The "crowds" are neutral, neither followers of Jesus nor hostile to him. They could go either way. In this situation "they"

---

[44] For Old Testament and Jewish background to the dominion of God supplanting the dominion of Satan, see Marcus, *Markus*, 282–83.

[45] See Gnilka, *Markus*, 1:151–52.

[46] See Guelich, *Mark*, 178–79: "One could not imagine a more universal or comprehensive expression of forgiveness."

[47] For a study of Mark 3:28–30; Matt 12:31–32; Luke 12:10, see J. D. G. Dunn, *Jesus and the Spirit: A Study of the Religious and Charismatic Experience of Jesus and the First Christians As Reflected in the New Testament* (London: SCM, 1975), 49–53. Dunn claims that the Markan setting is most likely original and concludes: "His power to cast out demons was the Spirit of God. . . . To slander and reject the manifest power of God in overcoming illness and evil was to commit the unpardonable sin" (p. 52). See also Gnilka, *Markus*, 1:151; Marcus, *Mark*, 284.

[48] Hooker, *St. Mark*, 117.

[49] The composite nature of the text generates this artificiality, but the house of v. 20 provides the necessary "outside/inside" setting required for vv. 31–35. Lane (*Mark*, 147) sees vv. 31–35 as a continuation of the narrative of vv. 20–21: "When the family were unable to penetrate the crowd they sent for him and stood outside calling." The link with vv. 20–21 indicates that the mother and the brothers are not doers of the word. See Marcus, *Mark*, 285–86.

report to Jesus that his family (mother and brothers) are "outside" seeking him.[50] The family's being "outside" is repeated to maintain the reader's focus upon the crowd "inside," seated around Jesus listening to him, in contrast to his family "outside," looking for him (vv. 31–32). Jesus responds to this information with words that establish a new criterion for membership in his family.

He opens his remarks with a question: "Who is my mother and who are my brothers?" (3:33). He gazes around at the people seated "inside," around him (περὶ αὐτόν). He thus excludes those who are "outside" as he responds to his own question.[51] "Behold my mother and my brothers" (v. 34). The people upon whom he fixes his gaze, *those around him* (περὶ αὐτόν) listening to Jesus' words, are to be his new family, replacing his blood family, described in v. 21 as *those beside him* (οἱ παρ' αὐτοῦ). But there is more to achieve before this family will be in place. It is not enough simply to listen to the word of Jesus. All members of the new family, women and men, must do the will of God (v. 35). Doing the will of God is a long-standing and central requirement of Judaism. Mark's Jesus, however, has another slant on what it means to do the will of God. What is heard from Jesus and seen in Jesus must be accepted as the revelation of the kingdom of God.[52] Jesus' presence is never an end in itself. He both proclaims and is the good news of the kingdom *of God* (1:1, 15). The true family of Jesus must recognize in his word and person the revelation of the will of God to establish the kingdom of God. Jesus is the beloved Son of God, in whom God is well pleased (1:11). A positive response to Jesus' preaching is to do the will of God: accept that the kingdom of God is at hand and, through conversion, believe in the good news (see 1:15). Anyone who does the will of God, therefore, becomes the brother and the sister and the mother of Jesus (3:35). Matching the criticism of Jesus' blood family in vv. 20–21, where they thought that he was insane, his blood family here stands "outside" as Jesus sets up a new family. Like the scribes of vv. 22–30, the blood family has no claim to Jesus on the basis of who they are. Members of the new family are not tied to him through the links of blood (vv. 20–21, 31–35) or tradition (vv. 22–30), but by doing the will of God. The appointment of the Twelve in vv. 13–19 "to be with him," and Jesus' gazing upon the crowd "gathered in a circle" around him in v. 34, indicate the founding core of the new family.[53] The Markan community which first read this story, and all subsequent readers, are challenged to become members of the family of Jesus by doing the will of God.

Jesus Instructs by Wise Parables (4:1–34)

With the foundations of his new family in place (3:13–35), Jesus turns to further teaching (4:1–3). He tells the parable of the sown seed (4:4–9), and explains it to "those who were around him" (4:14–20). Between the parable and its explanation Jesus tells the new family of the Twelve (3:13–19) and "those around him" (3:34–35) of their privileged access

---

[50] Some manuscripts add "and sisters" into the report from the crowd in v. 32. It had probably been added to the original because of Jesus reference to his sister in v. 35. See Guelich, *Mark,* 168.

[51] The verb "to gaze around" (περιβλεψάμενος) indicates a deliberate running of the eyes across the assembly circled around him (κύκλῳ καθημένους). It is much more than a glance, and focuses strong attention upon the crowd, potential members of the new family of Jesus.

[52] In "will of God" the genitive is primarily subjective: doing that which God wishes to be done. See Marcus, *Mark,* 277.

[53] For Old Testament and Jewish imagery of the "family gathered around the patriarch," see Marcus, *Mark,* 286.

to the secret of the kingdom of God. Many others, to whom Jesus will speak only in parables, are "outside" (4:10–13). Jesus continues his teaching by means of aphorisms (vv. 21–25) and two similitudes on the kingdom of God (vv. 26–29, 30–32). As the collection of Jesus' wise teaching on the kingdom of God closes, the narrator again points to the privileged situation of those "inside." He speaks in parables to all who are able to hear it, but "inside," to his own disciples (κατ' ἰδίαν δὲ τοῖς ἰδίοις μαθηταῖς), he explains everything (vv. 33–34).[54]

Mark may be drawing upon an earlier collection of parables. The original parable of the sown seed (4:4–9) has all the signs of a pre-Markan passage, and the same may be the case for its interpretation (vv. 13–20). The two similitudes in vv. 26–29 and vv. 30–32 came to Mark in the tradition. They may have already been joined to the parable of the sown seed and its explanation because all four passages focus upon a sower, sowing, and seed. As such, they suited Mark's purposes very well. The collection of sayings in vv. 21–25 is possibly Markan redaction, although this is debated.[55] The present shape of the narrative is the work of the Markan redaction. The introduction to the crowd, the sea, and the boat has all the signs of a Markan introduction (see 3:7–12, 31–35; see also 4:36). The Markan interest in the new family "inside" and those "outside" dominates vv. 10–13 and 33–34.[56]

An intimate Markan link, both narrative and theological, connects Jesus' establishment of his new family in 3:7–35 and his teaching on the kingdom (4:1–34), along with further hints of the future failure of the disciples. The collection of parables looks back to the difficulty Jesus has already encountered, and instructs the new family on the inevitable eschatological victory of God (the parable of the sower and its interpretation: vv. 3–9, 14–20). It also addresses the larger crowd, and looks forward to the growth and spread of the kingdom into the Gentile world (the parables of growth: vv. 26–32), which will follow in 4:35–5:20.[57] The material can be shaped in the following fashion:[58]

---

[54] The circle of Jesus' followers has grown to include the first disciples (1:16–20), Levi, who is not mentioned in the list of the Twelve (2:13–14; see 3:15–19), those "inside" in 3:31–35, those around him "with the Twelve" in 4:10, and his own disciples in 4:34; clearly there is a large group of disciples, from which the Twelve have been chosen. The Markan theology of discipleship must be gleaned from these passages. Some (e.g., Stock, Painter) focus strongly on the Twelve, missing the importance of a more broadly based theology of discipleship for Mark's original readers, and all subsequent readers who are attempting to be "followers" of Jesus.

[55] The formal structure of these added sayings: *And he said to them,* "Is a lamp . . . . *For* there is nothing hid . . ." (vv. 21–22); *And he said to them,* "Take heed what you hear . . . *For* to him who has . . ." (vv. 24–25), separated by v. 23: "If anyone has ears to hear let him hear" (see Lohmeyer, *Markus,* 85–86), may be entirely the work of Mark. Yet, it is also argued that this aphoristic form is the reason why it existed in the pre-Markan tradition. See J. Lambrecht, *Once More Astonished: The Parables of Jesus* (New York: Crossroad, 1983), 85–96.

[56] The deliberate repetition of οἱ περὶ αὐτόν from 3:31, 34 (Markan redaction) in 4:10 is the most obvious indication of Mark's hand, although there are others.

[57] See Marcus, *Mark,* 288–89.

[58] G. Fay ("Introduction to Incomprehension: The Literary Structure of Mark 4:1–34," *CBQ* 51 [1989]: 65–72) proposes this seven-step literary structure. For the purposes of my interpretation, I have changed his headings (especially C and C'). The article also offers a survey of literary approaches to Mark 4:1–34. See, among many, Lambrecht, *Once More Astonished,* 86–87; J. Dewey, *Markan Public Debate: Literary Technique, Concentric Structure, and Theology in Mark 2:1–3:6* (SBLDS 48; Chico: Scholars Press, 1980), 147–52; B. B. Scott, *Hear Then the Parable: A Commentary on the Parables of Jesus* (Minneapolis: Fortress, 1989), 345–46; and J. Marcus, *The Mystery of the Kingdom of God* (SBLDS 90; Atlanta: Scholars Press, 1986), 221–23. The main feature of Fay's proposal is the attachment of v. 13 to vv. 10–12, and his placement of vv. 14–20 at the center, already anticipating the failure of the disciples. For a more detailed outline of the seven-step structure, see the chart

[A] Introduction (4:1–2)

    [B] Parable of seed sown (4:3–9)

       [C] A challenge to those "inside" (4:10–13)

          [D] Interpretation of the parable (4:14–20)

       [C']A challenge to those "inside" (4:21–25)

    [B'] Parables of seed growing (4:26–32)

[A']Conclusion (4:33–34)

The chiastic nature of the above presentation indicates the careful work of the evangelist. Mark blends material from his tradition with his own contributions to produce a narrative portrait of Jesus' wise teaching (see 6:2), never losing his focus upon the overarching theme of the new family of Jesus (see 3:13–19, 31–35).

[A] Introduction (4:1–2)

    A Markan introduction ("again"; see 2:1, 13; 3:1, 20) moves Jesus to the side of "the sea" (see 1:16; 2:13; 3:7). The massive movement of crowds, another regular Markan theme (2:2; 3:9, 20), allows the author to create a scene in which Jesus gets into a boat, sits down, and teaches the crowd assembled on the shore (4:1). The boat serves as a pulpit from which Jesus teaches "many things in parables," and the teaching of 4:3–34 is introduced (v. 2).[59] The introduction is balanced by a Markan conclusion to the teaching (vv. 33–34).[60] This lengthy introduction is the most formal setting for Jesus' teaching in the Gospel, a Markan equivalent to Matt 5:1–2.[61]

    Literary studies properly distinguish the literary form of "parable" from other elements in Jesus' teaching, such as the allegorical explanation of 4:13–20, the aphorisms of vv. 21–25, and the similitudes of vv. 26–32.[62] In form-critical terms, only the story of the sown seed (vv. 3–9) is a "parable."[63] However, as is already clear in 3:23, for Mark the word παραβολή, like the Hebrew mashal, describes any parable, wisdom saying, similitude, or

---

in Fay ("Introduction," 81). These approaches have been rejected by M. A. Beavis, Mark's Audience: The Literary and Social Setting of Mark 4:11–12 (JSNTSup 33; Sheffield: Sheffield Academic Press, 1989), 131–36, 151–54. She argues that 4:11–12 is "the glue that holds the parables in ch. 4 together" (p. 154) in a prophetic/apocalyptic pattern that would have made an impact in both a Jewish and a Greco-Roman social setting.

[59] On the boat as a pulpit or a podium for preaching, see Guelich (Mark, 191).

[60] For Marcus (The Mystery, 87–89), vv. 33–34a is pre-Markan, transformed by the addition of v. 34b, linking vv. 33–34 with vv. 11–12. In the end, the present function of vv. 33–34 is determined by Mark's narrative and theological agenda.

[61] As Hooker (St. Mark, 119) remarks: "Although Mark has several times referred to the fact that Jesus taught, he has so far told us nothing about the content of that teaching, apart from the brief summary in 1:15 and the sayings in the various conflict stories." On the Markan nature of vv. 1–2, see Marcus (The Mystery, 13–14). On the setting as an appeal to the reader to recognize the solemn importance of the teaching that follows, see ibid., 14–17.

[62] See, for example, J. D. Crossan, The Dark Interval: Towards a Theology of Story (Niles: Argus Communications, 1975), 47–87; idem, In Parables: The Challenge of the Historical Jesus (New York: Harper & Row, 1973), 1–36; Lambrecht, Once More Astonished, 1–23; Scott, Hear Then the Parable, 7–62.

[63] This is sometimes questioned on form-critical grounds. See, for example, Marcus (The Mystery, 41–43). For the above position, see Gnilka (Markus, 1:157).

other indirect or symbolic use of language which "hides" the immediate truth from those who are "outside." It is in this Markan sense that 4:3–34 is entirely made up of "parables."[64]

[B] Parable of seed sown (4:3–9)

The opening parable begins with a striking appeal, echoing the *Shema* of Deut 6:4: "Listen!" As listening also meant obeying, this opening command calls for an active response to what is heard.[65] Jesus then tells of a sower who went out to sow (4:3). A connection between the sower and Jesus is made obvious by the verb "went out" (ἐξῆλθεν), the same expression used to describe Jesus' mission in 1:35, 38; 2:13.[66] Despite the traditional name of this parable as the parable of the sower, what follows is not so much about the sower, who appears only once (4:3), as about the fate of the seed sown. The first century Palestinian practice of sowing is accurately described: the indiscriminate casting of seed across the field, which will be reploughed once the seed is sown. Some seed falls haphazardly on the path, allowing birds to pick it up (4:4).[67] Some falls on rocky ground, and eventually withers, rootless in the shallow ground (vv. 5–6). Some falls in the briars and is choked as it attempts to grow toward the light (v. 7). None of this seed bears fruit. Some does not even germinate (v. 4), some withers away (vv. 5–6), and some grows, but produces nothing (v. 6). Other seed falls on the good ground (εἰς τὴν γῆν τὴν καλὴν), grows, and bears fruit, multiplying itself thirtyfold, sixtyfold, and a hundredfold (v. 8). As there was a threefold failure in vv. 4–6, there is a threefold increase in the productivity of the seed that falls on good ground in v. 8.[68] Although Jesus had gotten into a boat (v. 1), the crowd was "on the land" (ἐπὶ τῆς γῆς). As the sower cast his seed in the earth (εἰς τὴν γῆν), so also Jesus utters his word to the assembled crowd (ἐπὶ τῆς γῆς).[69] How will they respond to the imperative to "listen" (v. 3)?[70] Jesus repeats the summons to listen by means of a hortatory subjunctive as the parable closes: "Let anyone with ears to hear listen!" (v. 9).

This parable reaches back to Jesus, but has been used by Mark for his own purposes.[71] A pre-Markan hand can be traced in the introduction (4:3a) and the conclusion (v. 9), and

---

[64] See Minette de Tillesse, *Le secret messianique,* 201–12; Hooker, *St. Mark,* 120–22; Guelich, *Mark,* 190–91.

[65] B. Gerhardsson ("The Parable of the Sower and Its Interpretation," *NTS* 14 [1967–68]: 165–93) bases his interpretation of the parable and its explanation (vv. 3–20) on the command of the *Shema* to love God with heart and mind and might. On the importance of this summons to the reader, and possible allusion to the *Shema,* see Marcus, *The Mystery,* 58–59.

[66] See Marcus, *The Mystery,* 37–38.

[67] This reading rejects the suggestion of Jeremias (*The Parables of Jesus,* 11–12) that the path (and the thorns and the shallow ground) would eventually be ploughed, and thus there is a brief period when the birds could take it. The path around the field is permanent. See K. W. White, "The Parable of the Sower," *JTS* 15 (1964): 300–307. Despite the importance of ἡ ὁδός in Mark (see 8:27; 9:33; 10:32, 52), nothing more than the hard-beaten path is intended here. See Hooker, *St. Mark,* 123.

[68] See Marcus, *The Mystery,* 21–23; J. P. Heil, "Reader-Response and the Narrative Context of the Parables about Growing Seed in Mark 4:1–34," *CBQ* 54 (1992): 273–76. Heil rightly stresses the theme of gradual and inevitable "increase" across the parable. It is sometimes suggested that the different levels of fruitfulness point to different qualities of Christian response (e.g., Lane, *Mark,* 154). Two factors influence this three-fold crop: first, the literary repetition of the pattern of three positive responses, after the three negative, and second, the simple fact that seed sown by casting abroad will produce in this way. As Gnilka (*Markus,* 1:159) comments: ". . . they remain in the realm of the realistic and the possible." See also Marcus, *The Mystery,* 42–43.

[69] Marcus, *The Mystery,* 38–39; Heil, "Mark 4:1–34," 275–76.

[70] Marcus, *The Mystery,* 37–39.

[71] See Gnilka, *Markus,* 1:157–58; Marcus (*The Mystery,* 29–37) provides an excellent study of the composition history of the parable and its interpretation.

on three occasions throughout the parable when the theme of growth is introduced (vv. 5b, 6b, 8b). The redactional touches serve to establish it as the first and key parable in a series of parables (see v. 13), all of which are related to the theme of growth (see vv. 14–20, 26–29, 30–32, 33).[72] It is difficult to be certain of the exact meaning of the original parable. Was it about the coming of the kingdom?—the proclamation of the word?—Jesus' teaching as the continuation of the *Shema*?—encouragement in a time of apparent failure?[73] It is impossible to be certain, but for Mark, hearers of the word are challenged to make their response to the teaching of Jesus. As always, the referent of the parable is not mentioned. The reader or the hearer must provide it, and what is supplied is usually determined by the setting of the listener or the reader. The Markan context is thus a major factor for the interpretation of the parable, which must be understood in the light of what has already been read in Mark 1:1–3:35. The parable has an eschatological ring, an urgent demand that the moment of Jesus' presence, preaching the kingdom of God and calling for conversion (1:14–15), be not lost.[74] This eschatological tone reaches back to Jesus' original use of the parable, and retains its importance within the Markan literary and theological context. As Jesus' words to the disciples (4:10–12) and the subsequent allegorical explanation of the parable (vv. 13–20) make clear, the parable is about possible responses to the coming of the kingdom. Jesus proclaims and makes God present as king.[75]

To this point in the story the response to Jesus' words and deeds has varied, but recently has become increasingly negative (2:1–3:6; 3:20–35). In the midst of rejection, Jesus has established a new family (3:13–19, 35). He momentarily turns to the larger world of "the crowd" and instructs them about the importance of their response by means of a parable that sets out a number of options. As they stand "on the land" (ἐπὶ τῆς γῆς), Jesus tells of the fruitless response of 4:4–8 and the varied but fruitful response of "the good soil" (τὴν γῆν τὴν καλὴν) in v. 8. As the twofold command to listen makes clear (vv. 3, 9), the choice is theirs. However, the parable is not only a call to decision. It is also a promise that, despite the opposition and rejection of Jesus' person and teaching, the seed sown will bear abundant fruit. Those "inside" (see 3:31–35) should not lose hope or confidence in the ultimate victory of the kingdom of God over evil and opposition.[76]

[C] A challenge to those "inside" (4:10–13)

The setting changes: "those around Jesus" (3:31–35), along with the Twelve (3:13–19), are alone with Jesus.[77] They ask him for an explanation of the parables (4:10). The

---

[72] Along with the majority of scholars, I am suggesting that the parables in Mark 4 were already collected before Mark. Thus I speak of pre-Markan redaction, although a minority would claim that the evangelist was responsible for the gathering and present arrangement of the parables. See Lambrecht, *Once More Astonished*, 89–96; Guelich, *Mark*, 196–97.

[73] See Pesch, *Markusevangelium*, 1:234–35; Gnilka, *Markus*, 1:159–60.

[74] See Gnilka (*Markus*, 1:160–61) and especially Scott (*Hear Then the Parable*, 350–62) for a reconstruction of the possible original shape and message of the parable.

[75] See Lambrecht, *Once More Astonished*, 102–4, and especially Marcus, *The Mystery*, 43–59.

[76] For this christological interpretation of the parable, see Pesch, *Markusevangelium*, 1:234–35; Gnilka, *Markus*, 1:161. On the transformation of the field into a rich harvest as a message about the eschatological victory of God that does not destroy the original field, see Marcus, *Mark*, 294–98.

[77] This setting creates problems. He was in a boat with disciples, speaking to a crowd on the shore (vv. 1–2). Where does he go to be alone with his disciples (vv. 10–13)? The problem is accentuated in 4:33–34 where it is taken for granted that the crowd has heard the parables of (at least) vv. 26–32. They are not reintroduced after Jesus explains the parable of the seed sown to the

question asks for more than an explanation of 4:3–9, as they ask for the meaning of more than one parable. It also looks back to 3:23–27, where Jesus spoke to his opponents in parables. The reader is aware that those around Jesus and the Twelve belong to the new family of Jesus (3:31–35; 13–19),[78] and thus is not surprised by the first part of Jesus' response. He draws a distinction between those asking the question, privileged "insiders" to whom the mystery of the kingdom has been given, and those "outside," to whom everything remains a "parable," an enigma that still requires involvement and response (4:11).[79] A long-hidden secret is now revealed to privileged witnesses,[80] but others remain in ignorance. This distinction makes good sense after 3:13–35. It is also an initial link between the parable just told and the listeners: there are some bearing rich fruit (4:11a: those "inside") and others who bear no fruit (v. 11b: those "outside"). But Jesus' use of Isa 6:9–10 to explain why they remain caught in the enigma of the parables is puzzling: "So that they may indeed see but not perceive, and may indeed hear but not understand; lest they should turn again and be forgiven" (4:12).[81]

The Markan understanding of παραβολή, a word he found in this pre-Markan comment on the parable of the sown seed,[82] goes part of the way in explaining the application of Isa 6:9–10 to those "outside." For Mark, whose overall message reshapes the meaning of this comment, the parable is an enigmatic form of communication that partly uncovers and partly hides the truth contained within it. The mystery of the kingdom is partly uncovered for those "outside" as they both hear and see Jesus in and through parable. However, they do not perceive, nor do they understand. But there is no immediate reason to think that all is lost. The Gospel is only at its beginning, and the reader knows of its ending: the death and resurrection of Jesus. There the mystery will be resolved. It may be that those

---

disciples in vv. 13–20, nor (probably) are they present for the wise sayings of vv. 21–25. Mark found the material in this form, and accentuated the problem by adding his introduction of the great crowd in vv. 1–2 and the conclusion in vv. 33–34.

[78] On this larger "inside" group, see Marcus, *The Mystery,* 89–93.

[79] On the "outsiders" who reject the gift of the Kingdom and persecute the Markan Christians, see Marcus, *The Mystery,* 93–96.

[80] The background to "mystery" now revealed (the passive "has been given") by God is apocalyptic-eschatological thought. See J. Marcus, "Mark 4:10–12 and Markan Epistemology," *JBL* 103 (1984): 563–67; Gnilka, *Markus,* 1:165. Some (see Nineham, *St. Mark,* 138, and especially Beavis, *Mark's Audience,* 143–46) resort to Hellenistic ideas of mystery to explain Mark's use of μυστήριον. For Beavis, the language "is a religious/philosophical term with both Greek and Jewish overtones" (*Mark's Audience,* 146). For a Jewish interpretation, see Guelich, *Mark,* 205–6; Marcus, *Mark,* 298–99.

[81] Here critical problems emerge. For surveys, see Beavis, *Mark's Audience,* 69–86; Marcus, *Mark,* 299–300. There have been numerous attempts to lessen the impact of these words. Some have suggested that they are a mistranslation of a less antagonistic Aramaic (e.g., T. W. Manson, *The Teaching of Jesus* [Cambridge: Cambridge University Press, 1967], 77–78; Jeremias, *Parables,* 15–17). Others have resorted to the non-Markan nature of the passage to conclude that it is either out of place, and incoherent with the Markan message, or that the ἵνα . . . μήποτε does not have its usual exclusive meaning in the Markan context. See Guelich (*Mark,* 210–22) who suggests a translation: "Had it been otherwise, they would have repented and been forgiven" (p. 213). Unacceptable also is the claim by Jeremias (*Parables,* 13–18) that Mark, misled by the use of παραβολή in vv. 10–11, erroneously inserted an authentic word of Jesus into the parable chapter.

[82] On the history of vv. 10–12, see Guelich, *Mark,* 199–203; Marcus, *The Mystery,* 80–87. The passage probably came to Mark already attached to vv. 3–9. His only addition is οἱ περὶ αὐτόν in v. 10. See E. Best, *Disciples and Discipleship: Studies in the Gospel according to Mark* (Edinburgh: T&T Clark, 1986), 137–40.

"outside" remain caught within the enigma of parable, neither perceiving nor understanding, in order that the full truth about Jesus the Messiah might be finally revealed in his death and resurrection.[83] This could be said of Jesus' use of Isa 6:9, but what of 6:10? It sounds as if parables are used as punishment. They are kept in parable so that they not "turn again" and be forgiven. Jesus' proclamation of the kingdom in 1:15 called for "conversion" (μετάνοια), a turning back from one's sinful ways, to enter into the kingdom. Are those "outside" spoken to in parable so that this might never happen? Are they to remain in their sin?

For Mark and the Markan community, the answer to that question must be "yes." However difficult contemporary Christians may find such a notion, the early church was puzzled by the fact that initially Israel, and then the larger world, did not accept that the kingdom of God had definitively broken into the human story in the person and message of Jesus. An eschatological characteristic of Jesus' message and person, both of which proclaim the kingdom of God, is that some decided against it, and are subsequently excluded. "Basic to this distinction is the fact that the revelation of God itself has its history of acceptance and rejection whenever it enters the human scene."[84] The same text from Isaiah is used by other New Testament authors when they face this anguished questions (see John 12:40; Acts 28:26–27; and allusions to this passage in Luke 19:42; Rom 11:8, 10). While some accepted, many did not. This had to be explained, and the Scriptures indicated why there were many who did not "turn again," and enter the kingdom.[85] The Markan text does not accurately reflect the Hebrew text or the Septuagint, and probably came from an Aramaic version. Jesus himself may have used something approximating Isaiah's words as he looked back upon his own ministry.[86] Yet, in terms of the Markan story to this point, 4:11–12 simply affirms that "the outsiders are people who do not want to listen to the word of Jesus or are unwilling to live up to it, while the insiders are those who ask Jesus for an explanation."[87]

An interesting puzzle remains. According to 4:11–12, the secret of the kingdom of God has been given to the privileged "insiders," while there are so many who will forever be unable to understand and accept this mystery. However, the rest of the story sees the disciples moving more deeply into misunderstanding and failure. Shortly, after Jesus shows his mastery over the storm, they will ask: "Who then is this?" (4:41). The failure will inten-

---

[83] See Gnilka, *Markus*, 1:165–66.

[84] Lane, *Mark*, 157–58. See also Lambrecht, *Once More Astonished*, 92–94; Painter, *Mark's Gospel*, 80–81.

[85] See B. Lindars, *New Testament Apologetic: The Doctrinal Significance of the Old Testament Quotations* (London: SCM, 1961), 159–67.

[86] For a thorough study of the question, see C. A. Evans, *To See and Not Perceive: Isaiah 6.9–10 in Early Jewish and Christian Interpretation* (JSOTSup 64; Sheffield: Sheffield Academic Press, 1989), 91–106. See also Jeremias, *Parables*, 15; Guelich, *Mark*, 200; Hooker, *St. Mark*, 127; Beavis, *Mark's Audience*, 148–51. For the way the Markan use of the Old Testament passage is determined by Mark's context and theology, see Marcus, *Mark*, 300–301.

[87] B. van Iersel, *Reading Mark* (Collegeville: The Liturgical Press, 1988), 82. Watts (*New Exodus*, 184–210), in a fine study of the passage, comes to a similar conclusion, and proposes, on the basis of a parallel with Isaiah's rejection of Israel's leaders (Isa 29; see pp. 213–18), that 3:22–30 is still in mind. Within the Markan narrative, the leaders of Israel are "blinded." Lindars (*New Testament Apologetic*, 163) remarks: "In the pre-Marcan unit of 4:11f . . . we have the kind of questioning liable to happen in Palestine, where memories of the impact of the personality of Jesus are still fairly clear, and the claims of the Church about him may be checked by enquiry on the spot." See also C. D. Marshall, *Faith as a Theme in Mark's Narrative* (SNTSMS 64; Cambridge: Cambridge University Press, 1989), 72–74; Marcus, "Mark 4:10–12," 557–74; idem, *The Mystery*, 117–23; idem, *Mark*, 306–7.

sify across the journey to Jerusalem (8:22–10:52) until Judas betrays him (14:1–2, 10–11), they all abandon him in Gethsemane (14:50), and Peter denies him (14:66–71). A Gentile will announce at the cross, "Truly this man was a Son of God" (15:39). Despite their being "insiders" do they also remain in their sins?[88] On the other hand, does the confession of the centurion indicate that "outsiders" come to perceive and understand at the cross? Ambiguity surrounds the privileged recipients of the mystery of the kingdom of God. Those "inside" are challenged in this ambiguity.

This issue is raised in the conclusion to 4:10–13. In vv. 10–11a Jesus spoke to the Twelve and those who were about him (καὶ ἔλεγεν αὐτοῖς). He again addresses them, this time using the historic present, in v. 13 (καὶ λέγει αὐτοῖς). Despite their being recipients of the mystery of the kingdom of God (v. 11a), they have sought a clarification of the parable of the sown seed (v. 10). They do not understand the urgent, eschatological nature of Jesus' proclamation of the kingdom of God. They are like those "outside" in their lack of perception and understanding (v. 12). The parable of vv. 3–9 and its explanation in vv. 14–20 must be seen as the key to all the parables. If they have not been able to understand the parable of the sown seed, how will they ever understand all the other parables?[89] A tension has entered the narrative. The disciples are at the same time "insiders," the privileged recipients of God's gift (v. 11a), yet like the "outsiders" (vv. 11b–12), unable to understand the mystery that has been made known to them (vv. 10, 13).[90] The tension will remain seemingly unresolved down to the final verse of the Gospel, where the residual "followers" of Jesus, the women who witnessed the crucifixion and were at the empty tomb, flee in fear and consternation (16:8). Within that context, a character one would initially regard as an "outsider," the Roman centurion, has confessed that Jesus was truly a Son of God (15:39).

[D] Interpretation of the parable (4:14–20)

Despite Jesus' hard words in 4:13, the explanation requested in v. 10 is provided in vv. 14–20. A different, no doubt pre-Markan literary form is used.[91] Unlike the "parable" it explains (vv. 3–9), the following words of Jesus can be called "allegory." A parable leaves it to the reader to make the connection between the story and life. As has sometimes been said, it takes two to parable. But allegory allows the teacher to make the application: the sower sows the word (v. 14; see *4 Ezra* 9:31). This parable is the key to understanding all the parables (4:13) because it describes the proclamation and reception of the gospel. Each response to the seed in the parable (vv. 3–9) is explained as a response to the word of the gospel (vv. 15–20; see 4 Ezra 8:41–44; 9:31).[92] Unlike the parable of 4:3–9, and crucial for the interpretation of 4:14–20, is the statement that in every interpretation the sown word is

---

[88] See Schweizer (*Mark*, 93–95), who points out that the disciples are described in terms of v. 12 in 8:17–21. For a fuller development of this theme, see Beavis, *Mark's Audience*, 89–114.

[89] See Hooker, *St. Mark*, 130–31.

[90] This unusual association of v. 13 with vv. 10–12 creates an interesting literary pattern. The ignorance of the disciples (vv. 10, 13) frames the description of the giftedness of those "inside" and the blindness of those who reject Jesus' preaching (vv. 11–12). Lührmann (*Markusevangelium*, 88) suggests that originally vv. 10 and 13 followed one another. See further, Lambrecht, *Once More Astonished*, 92–93; Fay, "Introduction," 71; Marcus, *The Mystery*, 99–103. On the danger of "insiders" becoming "outsiders," see Ernst, *Markus*, 131–32; Marcus, *Mark*, 310–11.

[91] See Jeremias, *Parables*, 77–79. *Gos. Thom.* 9 has a version of the parable, without the application.

[92] On "the word" as "the vital OT concept of God's word," see Marcus, *Mark*, 308. On "the word" as synonymous with the Christian Gospel, see Guelich, *Mark*, 221.

"heard" (vv. 15, 16, 18, 20), and the seed becomes different kinds of people, bearing or not bearing fruit. Followers of Jesus who have heard the word, the Twelve and those around Jesus already blessed but also threatened (vv. 11a, 13), are forced to ask, "What kind of soil am I? What kind of seed am I? Am I obdurate, hearing yet incapable of giving life to the word, thus allowing the word to be snatched away by Satan (v. 16; see v. 4)? Am I shallow, initially hearing the word, but in the face of tribulation and persecution on account of the word, falling away (v. 17; see v. 5–6)? Am I a hearer of the word, but ultimately unfruitful because of the cares of the world and the delight of riches (v. 18–19; see v. 7)? Or am I good soil, hearing the word and accepting it, producing fruit, thirtyfold, sixtyfold, and one hundredfold (v. 20; see v. 8)?"[93]

These words, addressed by Jesus to the Twelve and those around him (see 4:10), serve as a warning, coming hard on the heels of the question of v. 13. No doubt the issues raised were real in the life of the early church, as they are in the lives of disciples of all times.[94] Several of the situations described in 4:14–20 return in 13:9–13, a passage that also reflects the situation of the Markan community, and Jesus will later threaten rejection for all who are ashamed of his word (8:38).[95] It is often claimed that 4:14–20 offers encouragement in the face of opposition,[96] but the opposite is more likely the case. Coming at the center of Jesus' teaching through parable (see v. 2), a variety of possible responses to the word are indicated. This interpretation of the parable of vv. 3–9 has accommodated an original parable of Jesus in order to address the Markan community.[97] Within the Markan literary and theological context, the original parable is also a call to listeners to hear the challenge of Jesus' word and to decide accordingly. The direct application of that parable to the Twelve and those around Jesus (see v. 10) accentuates their inability to understand vv. 3–9 (v. 13a). How are they to understand all the other parables (v. 13b)? Experiences of tribulation, persecution, cares, riches, and desire threaten those to whom the word is given (see v. 11). Jesus' word must be received if it is to bear fruit. At the heart (vv. 14–20) of Jesus' teaching by word (vv. 3–34) those "inside" are told of the possibility of failure (vv. 15–19). "The new age has broken in, but in a mysterious way that does not eradicate every trace of the old age."[98] But ultimate victory and rich fruitfulness lies ahead in the

---

[93] As in the parable (see v. 8), the different yields do not represent different qualities of Christian response, but "the interpretation uses this triad to characterize the harvest in general" (Guelich, *Mark*, 223).

[94] The "timelessness" of the applications is generated by the fact that the reader is never told who the sower is: God? Jesus? Preachers of the Gospel? See Marcus, *Mark*, 311, and especially J. Marcus, "Blanks and Gaps in the Parable of the Sower," *BibInt* 5 (1997): 1–16.

[95] See Scott, *Hear Then the Parable*, 346–47.

[96] For example, Guelich (*Mark*, 223–25) attempts to show that the explanation is "more descriptive than prescriptive" (p. 224).

[97] This process has often been assessed negatively by commentators. The original *Sitz im Leben Jesu* of the parable and its original meaning have been lost. Mark's use of a tradition to apply it to a Christian community in vv. 14–20 gives the parable a new life within its present literary context. See Marcus, *Mark*, 310. It is not correct to claim that vv. 14–20 are a moralizing or psychologizing application (see Jeremias, *Parables*, 78–79; Nineham, *St. Mark*, 140; LaVerdiere, *The Beginning*, 1:121–22). Within the context of 4:1–34, the eschatological urgency to accept the word of Jesus and bear fruit accordingly in a hostile society retains its relevance. See the remarks of Guelich, *Mark*, 217–19, 221; Marcus, *The Mystery*, 59–71.

[98] Marcus, *Mark*, 313. Marcus interprets vv. 14–19 against the background of defections of Markan Christians, unable to survive the attacks of "the age-old powers that hold humanity captive" (pp. 312–13).

seemingly impossible hundredfold harvest (v. 20). The story thus far has shown both powers in action: Jesus' bringing in the kingdom (1:14–45) and obdurate resistance to it (2:1–3:6). It is not otiose for the author to ask the question: what kind of soil are you? "Though the interpretation may come from the Church, rather than from Jesus, it has perhaps not distorted the original parable as much as is sometimes suggested: rather, as in the account of Nathan's parable in 2 Sam 12, we detect at each point the warning of an early preacher—'this could mean you.' "[99]

[C'] A challenge to those "inside" (4:21–25)

Jesus continues to speak to those "inside."[100] The attention given to the privilege, yet ambiguity, of the Twelve and those around Jesus in 4:10–13 returns in vv. 21–25, in a collection of wisdom sayings which came to Mark in the tradition.[101] The words of Jesus on the correct place and function of the lamp are a warning. It is common sense that a lamp comes to be placed on a stand,[102] so that its light can illuminate the surroundings. One does not provide the possibility of illumination, and then hide it under a container normally used to measure,[103] nor does one place it in obscurity, under a bed (v. 21). Recalling the privilege given to those "inside" in v. 11a, the *function* of that secret is developed in v. 22: it is not to be hidden nor kept in secret. The expression ἵνα appears four times in vv. 21–22. The coming of the light is for a purpose. The word of Jesus must be heard.[104] The secret of the kingdom of God is given *so that* it will be made manifest and come to light. Jesus' words are directed to the disciples.[105] They are privileged, but they also have a serious responsibility: to manifest the light. In v. 23 Jesus repeats the warning he uttered in v. 9. There is a hearing of Jesus' revelation that hears, and there is a hearing that is deaf. Those who have right hearing will hear, but implicit is the truth that some will not hear. The kingdom is present, despite its rejection by many.[106] Nevertheless, the proclamation of the kingdom must be heard, and this is what the disciples are to hear.[107]

---

[99] Hooker, *St. Mark*, 130.

[100] See Fay, "Introduction," 73–79; Marcus, *The Mystery*, 140–41.

[101] Luke includes these sayings in their Markan context (see Luke 8:16–18), and they are also found scattered throughout Matthew and Luke (see Matt 5:15; 10:15; 7:2; 13:12; 12:29; Luke 11:33; 12:2; 16:38; 19:26; *Gos. Thom.* 5, 33, also has a parable about a lamp, and sayings similar to Mark 4:22, 23, and 25). For a helpful synoptic chart, see Marcus, *Mark*, 316–17. For an attempt to establish a history of the composition, see idem, *The Mystery*, 129–40. It is impossible to recover the original context of these sayings. For Mark, the sayings on the lamp (vv. 21–22) and the measure (vv. 24–25) are regarded as "parables" (see 4:2). See Jeremias, *Parables*, 90; Pesch, *Markusevangelium*, 1:252.

[102] Most translations render μήτι ἔρχεται ὁ λύχνος in the passive: "Is a lamp brought in . . . ," but the active sense of a light coming should be retained. It gives the text a christological hint. See Marcus, *The Mystery*, 141–43; Heil, "Mark 4:1–34," 274–75; Hooker, *St. Mark*, 133. Gnilka (*Markus*, 1:179) suggests that it is a Semitism, but on p. 180 also makes the christological application. See also Lane, *Mark*, 165–66. The christological sense is rejected by Guelich, *Mark*, 228–29.

[103] The word μόδιος refers to a container used to measure grain, in this case empty, that can be placed over a lamp, thus closing out its light.

[104] On the lamp as a symbol for the word of God, see Marcus, *Mark*, 318.

[105] This is not explicitly stated. See the discussion in Guelich, *Mark*, 228.

[106] Marcus (*Mark*, 318–19) interprets vv. 21–22 as symbolic of Jesus' revelation present in darkness. The darkness will lead to Good Friday, but Easter Sunday reveals Jesus as Messiah and Son of God. In the Markan community, therefore, the kingdom is still partially hidden, and persecution continues.

[107] See Guelich, *Mark*, 230–32.

On the basis of the statement of 4:21–22 and the warning of 4:23, Jesus addresses his second saying to the disciples (vv. 24–25). True disciples must have right hearing, recognizing that much has been given to them (see v. 11a). Yet more will be given to those "inside," while those "outside," who have closed their ears definitively to the word of Jesus, lose every privilege. The *Sitz im Leben* for the present redaction of these words is again the Markan community. There are many contacts between 4:10–13 and 4:21–25, as Jesus instructs disciples on their privilege and responsibility.[108] The disciples of Jesus are urged to recognize the responsibilities that are theirs (v. 11a: given the mystery of the kingdom; v. 24: given a measure, and promised even greater gifts) in a society that rejects them (vv. 11–12: "those outside"; v. 25: "the one who does not have").[109] In a Palestinian setting, where these words may have had their origin, the Jewish people were God's chosen people, but in rejecting Jesus lost all they once had (see v. 25b; see also 2:22). In the broader setting of the Gospel of Mark, Jesus continues to urge ambiguous disciples to bear fruit in a hostile environment. It may appear that the light they bear is being snuffed out, but they must hear Jesus' promise and not lose heart in the midst of difficulties. The use of the passive in v. 25 indicates that God gives and takes away. In the kingdom of God, despite present experience, the apparent victory of those opposed to Jesus is reversed.[110] It must be so, as it is impossible to oppose the ways of God.

[B′] Parables of seed growing (4:26–32)

The collection of parables that follows looks back to the theme of "growing," present in the parable of the seed sown (4:3–9). Although they are not explicitly mentioned, the hearers of these Markan parables are the people in the crowd, as in the former parable of growth. Their return to the scene is demanded by 4:33–34, where it is explicitly stated that he spoke to everyone in parables, and explained them to the disciples.[111] But this little collection in 4:26–32 also continues the theme of Jesus' words in 4:21–25: however difficult growth may appear, the seed grows silently and relentlessly (vv. 26–29), and the insignificant becomes great (vv. 30–32).[112] In contemporary form-critical terms, the two "parables" are "similitudes" which probably had their origins in Jesus' teaching. The relationship between the themes of seed and growth in the original parable of 4:3–9 and the similitudes in 4:26–32 has led many scholars to suggest that these "parables" were

---

[108] See Hooker, *St. Mark,* 134–35. It is widely agreed that vv. 21–22 and vv. 24–25 came to Mark in the tradition, and that v. 23 is Markan. See, for example, Schweizer, *Mark,* 99–100; Pesch, *Markusevangelium,* 1:247, 252–53; Marcus, *The Mystery,* 136–37.

[109] Thus, Guelich (*Mark,* 228): "The motive of special privilege and accountability in 4:24–25 connects with the thrust of 4:11a and the hard questions in 4:13. This contextual setting in Mark 4 greatly influences how one then reads these generalized sayings." On p. 234, Guelich suggests that not only the loss of those "outside" is described here. It is also a warning for the privileged: "haves" can become "have nots."

[110] See Pesch, *Markusevangelium,* 1:251. See also Marcus, *The Mystery,* 160–62, and idem, *Mark,* 319–21, for an extensive treatment of vv. 24–25 in the light of Jewish background.

[111] The conclusion in vv. 33–34 indicates that Jesus has resumed addressing the crowd. It is not entirely clear when this happens, but see Marcus (*The Mystery,* 140–41) for the case that they are present from v. 26. For the improbable view that they return at v. 21, see Lane (*Mark,* 164).

[112] See Guelich, *Mark,* 235. As always in chiastic readings of the text, one also must pay attention to the linear development of the argument. There are obvious links between vv. 3–9 and vv. 26–32, but the argument of vv. 21–25 is extended by means of the parables in vv. 26–32.

already joined before Mark took them over.[113] There is a close literary symmetry between the two similitudes. Both begin with "and he said" (vv. 26, 30: καὶ ἔλεγεν) and both make an immediate reference to the kingdom of God (v. 26: οὕτως ἐστὶν ἡ βασιλεία τοῦ θεοῦ; v. 30: πῶς ὁμοιώσωμεν τὴν βασιλείαν τοῦ θεοῦ).

The kingdom is like the seed cast into the ground (4:26).[114] The sower lives through his sleeping and waking hours. The human being, the ἄνθρωπος of v. 26, has nothing to do with the seed's growing into the blade that cuts through the soil, then the green ear, and finally the ripe grain (vv. 27–28).[115] He returns to the action only when he puts in the sickle for the reaping of a harvest that owes nothing to his efforts. The image of the harvest and the putting in of the sickle recalls the prophetic description of the harvest of the end time and God's final judgment in Joel 3:13.[116] The kingdom of God is like the mystery of growth, beyond human control. The earth produces fruit, independent of human effort. Continuing Jesus' teaching on the ambiguity of the response of those who hear the word (vv. 21–25), the people are told that the word will be sown, and its growth is the result of the action of God. There will be a harvest at the end of time.[117] The ultimate outcome of Jesus' presence in word and deed is without question (see vv. 3–9, 14–20). The kingdom of God will grow and bear fruit, but it will not be the result of the successful labor of the disciples. The harvest is the outcome of the gracious gift of God, despite the ambiguity of those who sow the seed (see vv. 10–13, 21–25).[118]

The kingdom is like a seed, the mustard seed, tiny when sown in the ground (4:30–31).[119] Something of the preceding parable continues into the parable of the Mustard Seed, as the tiny seed grows into the healthy shrub without the intervention or control of a human agent. Its growth is part of God's gracious action. So it is also with the kingdom of God.[120] However tiny and insignificant the mustard seed may be, its ultimate

---

[113] There is considerable scholarly discussion of this issue, but the position taken above has wide support. See Pesch, *Markusevangelium,* 1:254–55, and the surveys in Guelich, *Mark,* 238–39; Marcus, *Mark,* 325–26.

[114] On the importance of a focus upon the seed and not the farmer, see Guelich, *Mark,* 240. This is the only parable of Jesus unique to Mark. There is a remote contact with Matt 24:30, and some see the suggestion of an exhortation to carefree living, as found in Matt 6:25–34. See Schweizer, *Mark,* 102.

[115] Guelich (*Mark,* 241–42) helpfully translates αὐτομάτη as "without visible cause," further interpreted as "without human efforts." See also Gnilka, *Markus,* 1:184–85; Marcus, *Mark,* 328. Marcus reads this as a criticism of Jewish revolutionaries who are trying to "force the end" (p. 326).

[116] See Guelich, *Mark,* 242. The growth of the kingdom depends upon God.

[117] The eschatological reaping leads Marcus (*The Mystery,* 171–85) to conclude that the man in the story is Jesus (and not God or the Christian disciple).

[118] See Guelich, *Mark* 245. For similarities in Jewish apocalyptic writings, see Marcus, *Mark,* 328. See also Marcus, *The Mystery,* 185–99, for the parable of vv. 26–29 as an indication of a Markan periodization of time: the ministry of Jesus, the period of the church, and the Parousia.

[119] There should be no quibble with the poetic license used in the description of the mustard seed as "the smallest of all the seeds on earth" and the shrub as "the greatest of all shrubs" (see also Matt 17:20; Luke 17:6). This may not be true, but it is a tiny seed that produces a healthy bush. The suggestion of J. D. Crossan ("The Seed Parables of Jesus," *JBL* 92 [1973]: 256–57), that the description of the seed creates a Markan "sandwich" flanked by the affirmations of vv. 31a and 32bc, highlights the rhetorical nature of the smallness of the seed. However, in Jewish folklore, the mustard seed was regarded as the smallest of all seeds. See J. Hunzinger, "σίναπι," *TDNT* 7:287–91. On the seed's smallness, see p. 288. See also Pesch, *Markusevangelium,* 1:261–62.

[120] See Schweizer, *Mark,* 104–5.

growth into a shrub which can even shelter the birds of the air is assured.[121] Possible allusions to such passages as Ezek 17:23 and Dan 4:12, 21, both of which refer to the gathering of all sorts of beasts in the branches and the shade of a great tree, suggest "an implicit meaning of an immense kingdom . . . which encompasses the nations."[122] The apparently tiny and insignificant—Jesus, his word, and the adhesion of the disciples—will eventually achieve its due stature. "For the dominion of God is like the word: paltry in appearance, but hiding a tremendous divine potency behind its apparent insignificance."[123] The growth of the kingdom, already present in the word and person of Jesus (see 1:14–15), is assured.[124] This parable adds a note of encouragement and hope in the midst of so many indications of misunderstanding, lack of hearing, and ambiguity. The contrasting themes of the presence of the kingdom (1:14–45) and its rejection (2:1–3:6) continue to intertwine as the narrative tells of Jesus' establishment of a new family of God in spite of misunderstanding and rejection by his family and nation (3:13–35). But the fragility of the new family has already been highlighted in Jesus' wise teaching (4:10–13, 14–20, 21–25). A fundamental element in the Markan theology of discipleship is stated in the parables that close this section (vv. 26–32). The ultimate fruitfulness of the word of God and the definitive presence of the kingdom of God are assured. There is no cause for discouragement, despite apparent failure and insignificance. God will have the last word.[125]

[A′] Conclusion (4:33–34)

Two earlier passages combine as Mark draws his description of Jesus' teaching in parables to a conclusion. He looks back to Jesus' teaching both the crowds and the disciples with "parables" beside the sea in 4:1–2 (vv. 33–34a), and returns to the theme of the privileged situation of the disciples, first mentioned in 4:10–13 (v. 34b).[126] The Markan use of parable calls for ears that are prepared to hear (vv. 9, 13, 23). As with the Hebrew *mashal*, there is a level of obscurity in the parable, and only the attentive ear of the believer can resolve that obscurity. Jesus' teaching to the crowds is summarized in v. 33. A collection of Markan parables has been offered to the reader in 4:1–32, but it should not be thought that this was the only occasion when Jesus practiced such teaching. He spoke "with many such parables."[127] The crowd's ability to hear (v. 33b) measures the effectiveness of Jesus' teaching. Some became lost in the obscurity and could bear no more, while others persevered.[128] Unlike v. 12,

---

[121] The contrast between the seed and the shrub emerges as the basic point of the parable, despite logical and syntactic problems present in vv. 30–32. See Jeremias, *Parables*, 147–49; Pesch, *Markusevangelium*, 1:260.

[122] Guelich, *Mark*, 251; Marcus, *The Mystery*, 214–15.

[123] Marcus, *Mark*, 323.

[124] See Hooker, *St. Mark*, 136–37. The parables of vv. 26–32 speak about the ultimate victory of the kingdom, thanks to the action of God, but they also presuppose that the kingdom is already present in the person and word of Jesus. See Pesch, *Markusevangelium*, 1:258–59, 262–63; Marcus, *The Mystery*, 215–17.

[125] See Marcus, *The Mystery*, 217–20.

[126] It is regularly claimed that v. 33 was the original conclusion to the parable collection, and that Mark added v. 34 as his own conclusion, developing his theme of those "outside" and "inside." See, for example, Pesch, *Markusevangelium*, 1:264–64. For a study of the composition history of vv. 32–34, see Marcus, *The Mystery*, 87–89.

[127] See Lane, *Mark*, 172.

[128] As Painter (*Mark's Gospel*, 85) remarks: "Right hearing is attentive, committed, determined, obedient hearing which bears fruit."

where the situation of those who had definitively closed their ears to Jesus' proclamation was described, in v. 33 the "possibility" of hearing and understanding the parabolic speech of Jesus remains open.[129] Nevertheless, to those "outside" Jesus reveals himself only in parable (v. 34a). They are not excluded, but must have ears to hear (see v. 9).[130] But the disciples, those "inside" (see v. 12), continue to receive an explanation of everything, just as *alone* the parable of the sower (vv. 3–9) had been explained to them "in private" (v. 34b: κατ' ἰδίαν; see v. 10: κατὰ μόνας, and vv. 14–20). As can be seen from Jesus' further demands that those who have ears should hear (vv. 13 and 23, both found in passages directed exclusively to the disciples), being "inside" does not lessen the challenge to listen to the word of Jesus with faith. "Only through revelation does the enigma become partially resolved; not until the consummation . . . will it become resolved for all."[131]

The careful selection of material from pre-Markan tradition and its presentation *come* *probabl* across 4:1–34 serve as a paradigm for the Gospel's presentation of Jesus the teacher.[132] He reveals the kingdom by means of parabolic speech, demanding that those who have ears hear (see vv. 9, 13, 23). It can be understood, for all its obscurity, but only by those who lay themselves open to the word of God as it is revealed in the word and person of Jesus. There is, however, a chosen group, a collection of people who now form the new family of Jesus (3:13–19, 31–35). As "insiders," Jesus communicates to them privately, explaining fully the mystery of the kingdom. Yet, through 4:1–34 they have been warned that they may not always live up to the privilege that they have been given (vv. 10–13, 14–20, 21–25).[133] They too must have ears to hear.[134]

Jesus Instructs by Mighty Deeds (4:35–5:43)

A link is established between Jesus' teaching in parables in 4:1–34 and the series of miracles that follows from 4:45–5:43. The narrator tells the reader that what is about to follow was "on that day," but later, at the onset of the evening (4:35a). Within this temporal setting, linked with the teaching in parables, Jesus' words to his disciples introduce a change of place: "Let us go across to the other side" (4:35b).[135] This "going across" to the other side presupposes the setting of 4:1–2 beside the Sea of Galilee. They are now about to cross it, and during that crossing of a hostile sea, the miracle cycle will begin. It is widely accepted that Mark is using a pre-Markan collection of miracles,[136] but the steady growth

---

[129] Schweizer (*Mark,* 106) makes the important theological point that, when speaking about the action of God (the kingdom *of God*), one must speak metaphorically.

[130] On the movement from "outside" to "inside," especially for the reader, see the remarks of Painter (*Mark's Story,* 85–86): (a) it is possible in the story; (b) it is a reality for the reader of the story, who also hears the explanation; and (c) the rejection of Jesus is explained in a way which nevertheless maintains his authority and credibility.

[131] Lane, *Mark,* 173.

[132] See Pesch, *Markusevangelium,* 1:266–67.

[133] Structurally, these warnings come at the center of 4:1–34, flanked by the introduction (vv. 1–2), the parable of the seed sown (vv. 3–9), and the parables of the seeds growing (vv. 26–32), and the conclusion (vv. 33–34).

[134] See Fay, "Introduction," 79–80; Heil, "Mark 4:1–34," 271–86.

[135] The pronoun in λέγει αὐτοῖς in 4:35 refers back to the τοῖς ἰδίοις μαθηταῖς of 4:34.

[136] For a survey of that discussion, and full bibliographical indications, see J. P. Meier, *A Marginal Jew: Rethinking the Historical Jesus* (3 vols.; ABRL; New York: Doubleday, 1991–2001), 2:924–25, 1003–4.

in the significance of the evils overcome by Jesus' powerful presence reflects a Markan insistence:

4:35–41	Jesus calms the stormy sea, overcoming the force of *nature*.
5:1–20	Jesus drives out a legion of demons, overcoming the force of the *demonic*.
5:21–24	Jairus makes his request and Jesus goes with him.
5:25–34	Jesus heals the woman with a flow of blood, overcoming the force of *incurable human illness*.
5:35–43	Jesus raises Jairus's daughter, overcoming the force of *death*.

No power—whether nature, demons, human illness, or death itself—can withstand the kingdom.[137]

Jesus overcomes the stormy sea (4:35–41)

As already noted, the introduction to the miracle story in 4:35 looks back to the setting of Jesus' teaching in parables (4:1–2). The link continues into 4:36. The crowd (see v. 1) is left behind as the disciples respond to Jesus' command that they set out for the other side of the sea by taking him with them in the boat, "just as he was" (ὡς ἦν ἐν τῷ πλοίῳ, v. 36). He has asked that a boat be kept in readiness because of the large crowds (3:9) and then has used the boat as a pulpit to teach in parables (4:2). Without any alteration to Jesus' situation, Jesus and his disciples (those "inside") head off across the sea in that same boat (4:35–36). In a seemingly superfluous remark the narrator adds, "and other boats were with him" (ἦν μετ' αὐτοῦ).[138] But the reader recalls the use of this expression in the association of the Twelve with Jesus in 3:14. It will appear again in the request of the Gerasene demoniac in the very next pericope (5:18). The additional boats indicate that Jesus' entourage is increasing. Although the narrative which follows only focuses upon those in the boat with Jesus, the judgment of Jesus and the ongoing failure of the disciples, described at the end of the pericope, embrace this larger gathering of people.[139] All have experienced the storm, the miracle, the misunderstanding, and none of them have yet come to faith (see 4:39–41). Despite the variety of sources and shifting narrative perspectives across 3:7–4:41, the theme of the boat holds the narrative together. Indeed, the boat is in some ways at the center of the story: will it sink or not?

The description of the fierce storm is brief: strong winds, large waves beating into and over the sides of the boat, and the gradual filling of the boat (4:37).[140] Mark, in line with

---

[137] See Grundmann, *Markus*, 102; Ernst, *Markus*, 148; Lührmann, *Markusevangelium*, 105.

[138] Lane (*Mark*, 174–75) suggests that this is one of several elements which indicate that the account "bears the marks of a personal reminiscence." See, however, the warnings of Taylor (*St. Mark*, 272).

[139] See also LaVerdiere, *The Beginning*, 1:126; Marcus, *Mark*, 336. This possibility is missed entirely by Painter (*Mark's Gospel*, 86) in his determination to limit "the disciples" to "the Twelve." Most commentators would agree that the other boats have no further part to play in the story. Nineham (*St. Mark*, 149) suggests that it might be to indicate the fulfillment of Ps 107:23: "They went down to the sea in ships." See the summary of opinions in Pesch, *Markusevangelium*, 1:270 n. 7.

[140] Such sudden storms, created by the winds that sweep through the steep valleys which run down to the Sea of Galilee, especially on its southern and eastern coast, are well known. They create turbulent waters, still difficult for modern small boats. See G. Dalman, *Sacred Sites and Ways: Studies in the Topography of the Gospels* (London, SPCK, 1935), 182–83; Lane, *Mark*, 175.

much mythological thought, presents the stormy sea as a place of potential chaos, caused by demonic powers. In a way that parallels Jonah's sleeping in a boat during a storm (see Jonah 1:1–17),[141] Jesus is in the stern, comfortably asleep on a cushion and indifferent to the storm raging about them, and the dangers that threaten to sink the boat (4:38a). The impossibility of such sleep in the midst of a storm indicates that it is there for a purpose. Jesus' peaceful sleep already indicates his lordship over a seemingly chaotic situation.[142] How will the disciples respond? The disciples arouse him and ask him a question which itself indicates that, while they may be "insiders," their ears have not yet properly heard (see vv. 9, 23, 33b). In their first address to Jesus in the Gospel, they call him "teacher" (διδάσκαλε), a respectful term, but a long way from the author's agenda, to present Jesus as Christ and Son of God (1:1, 11).[143] They doubt his desire to save them: "Do you not care if we perish?" (4:38b). Since 1:16, all Jesus' words and actions have been said and done in the presence of disciples. Yet they are unmoved by what they have experienced and doubt his desire to save them. It is only a doubt, however. Their question is framed in a construction (beginning with the negative particle οὐ and not μή) that hopes for a positive answer: yes, Jesus is concerned about their safety.[144] The question nevertheless indicates that they have little awareness of the reigning presence of God in the person and activity of Jesus (see 1:14–15; 4:1–34). They have ears, but they cannot hear.

His response is to show mastery over the storm, and his use of the imperative mood to address the wind and the sea reinforces the idea that the storm is generated by demonic and chaotic powers. In a terse sentence, the reader is told that Jesus woke, rebuked the sea, commanding the wind to silence and the sea to stillness.[145] The result is immediate as the wind ceased, and great calm came over the waters. The great storm (λαῖλαψ μεγάλη) of v. 37 has been subdued, to become the "great calm" (γαλήνη μεγάλη) of v. 39. The disciples have shown their inability to understand Jesus, and he indicates to them that he is the Lord of creation.[146] But there is more to come. The praise of YHWH as Lord of land and sea is recalled (see Pss 29:1–11; 65:7–8; 89:9; 104:3–4; 107:24–32) as Jesus rightly speaks harshly to his disciples. This appeal to the lordship of Jesus may also have made an impact upon converts to Christianity, already familiar with the lordship of ancient gods, heroes, and Roman emperors over the stormy seas.[147] There was no cause for fear, but they have not yet

---

[141] See Lane, *Mark,* 175–76 n. 91; Gnilka, *Markus,* 1:194. Meier (*A Marginal Jew,* 2:930–32) and Marcus (*Mark,* 337–39) offer critical evaluations of possible Old Testament and other Jewish background to the account. In an unpublished paper ("The Stilling of the Storm [Mk 4:35–41]: Context and Claims") delivered at the Annual Meeting of the Catholic Biblical Association of America at Loyola Marymount University, Los Angeles, in August 2000, Wendy Cotter argues strongly for a literary contact with the Jonah story (pp. 11–15). See also Ernst, *Markus,* 150.

[142] Gnilka, *Markus,* 1:195. Some link reference to "evening" (v. 35) with Jesus' sleep. It has been a long, hard day!

[143] See Painter, *Mark's Gospel,* 87.

[144] See Meier, *A Marginal Jew,* 2:926.

[145] The language reflects an exorcism. See Meier, *A Marginal Jew,* 2:926–27. For the parallels with 1:21–28, see Marcus, *Mark,* 340.

[146] A number of Markan miracles that are not healings present Jesus as the Lord of creation: see 6:30–44, 45–52; 8:1–10; 11:12–13, 20–23. It is possible that these miracles formed part of a collection used in the early church to teach that Jesus Christ is Lord. There are connections with YHWH's dominance of creation in the Old Testament, particularly present in the exodus account (see especially Exod 14:21–31), but see also Pss 33:7; 65:7; 77:16; 107:25–30; 147:18; Prov 30:4; Job 12:15; 28:25; Amos 4:13; Nah 1:3–4.

[147] For Cotter ("The Stilling," 3–11, 19–30), Greco-Roman literature also helps the reader to grasp the possibilities of the Markan story. See also W. Cotter (*Miracles in Greco-Roman Antiquity: A*

come to faith, as Jesus' question shows (v. 40b). The question is rhetorical, as they are failing to understand who Jesus is, but the use of "not yet" leaves open the possibility that they
might be on the way to true faith.[148]

For the moment, they answer the question themselves. They have been warned against
fear (4:40a), but they respond to Jesus' question concerning their present lack of faith by
further emotional confusion. They are filled with a mighty fear (v. 41). Jesus' authoritative
transformation of a "great storm" (v. 37) into a "great calm" (v. 39) only serves to produce
a "great fear" (φόβον μέγαν) among the disciples (v. 41). This is the first time the verb
φοβέω has been used to describe the response of the disciples. As the reader will discover, it
is not the last. It will return regularly to describe the disciples' self-concern as they move
further from the one who called them "to be with him" (3:14). The crucial importance of
the use of this verb in association with disciples is strongly indicated by its being the last
verb used in the Gospel. The women will flee from the empty tomb ἐφοβοῦντο γάρ ("for
they were afraid," 16:8). The emotional reaction of the disciples already indicates failure to
understand, but they articulate their unbelief in the telling question of 4:41. They have
seen Jesus' authority of the wind and the sea (v. 41b). He has commanded one to silence
and the other to stillness, and they have obeyed (v. 39). There can be no questioning the
events, but the disciples are unable to make the connection between Jesus and the presence
of God's kingdom among them. They cannot and will not understand who Jesus is: "Who,
then, is this man?" (v. 41a). He has saved them from peril, but they cannot recognize the
one who saved them (vv. 38, 41).[149]

Sourcebook for the Study of the New Testament Miracle Stories [London: Routledge, 1999], 131–48)
for a collection of impressive texts from the Greco-Roman world which would have been familiar to
Markan converts. The question of Greco-Roman influence is complex, with most scholarly opinion
against it. For recent support for such influence upon the Markan readers, see A. Y. Collins, "Mark
and His Readers: The Son of God among Greeks and Romans," *HTR* 93 (2000): 85–100. One must
be aware of what Cotter and Collins are arguing. They are not claiming that the Greco-Roman
world formed the pre-Markan or Markan tradition. Rather, they argue for a multiplicity of possible
interpretations among the Markan readers. Cotter especially is anxious to point to the ready awareness among converts of the claims for the Markan Jesus: he, and not the traditional gods, miracle
workers, or the emperor, is Lord. See her full study, W. Cotter, "The Markan Sea Miracles: Their History, Formation, and Function in the Literary Context of Greco-Roman Antiquity" (Ph.D. dissertation; University of St. Michael's College; Toronto School of Theology, 1991). See also A. Y. Collins,
"Mark and His Readers: The Son of God among Jews," *HTR* 92 (1999): 393–408; T. H. Kim, "The
Anarthrous υἱὸς θεοῦ in Mark 15,39," *Bib* 79 (1998): 221–41; C. A. Evans, "Mark's Incipit and the
Priene Calendar Inscription: From Jewish Gospel to Greco-Roman Gospel," *Journal of Greco-Roman
Christianity and Judaism* 1 (2000): 67–81. For a rejection of any influence on this particular miracle
story, see B. Blackburn, *Theios Anēr and the Markan Miracle Traditions: A Critique of the Theios Anēr
Concept as an Interpretative Background of the Miracle Traditions Used by Mark* (WUNT 2. Reihe 40;
Tübingen: J. C. B. Mohr [Paul Siebeck], 1991), 141–45. However, Blackburn's study is concerned
with the historical development of the story. Cotter, Collins, Kim, and Evans do not debate the Jewish *origins* or the account, but point to its impact upon a Greco-Roman *readership*. On the wider
issue, P. L. Danove (*The End of Mark's Gospel: A Methodological Study* [BibIntS 3; Leiden: Brill,
1993], 229) asserts: "The analysis . . . reveals no necessary presuppositions of direct ties to the
Greco-Roman narrative or rhetorical traditions." See also T. Dwyer, *The Motif of Wonder in the Gospel of Mark* (JSNTSup 128; Sheffield: Sheffield Academic Press, 1996), 26–91. It is this position that
the above-mentioned scholars would question.

148 See Meier, *A Marginal Jew,* 2:927.

149 For Cotter ("The Stilling," 30–36), the Greco-Roman and Jewish (especially Jonah) background provides the unspoken answer to the disciples' question. Jesus is "the one who commands
the forces of earth as 'God's Son'" (p. 36).

On the whole, the traditional form of a miracle story is found in 4:35–41. There is a setting that ties the story to its present context (vv. 35–36), a problem emerges (vv. 37–38), a miraculous resolution of the problem (v. 39a), evidence that the miracle has taken place (v. 39b), and a final response of wonder (v. 41).[150] But there is one element that does not fit the pattern, Jesus' question in v. 40: "Why are you afraid? Have you no faith?" On form-critical grounds alone, it is clear that Mark used this miracle story, which came to him in his tradition, to develop his presentation of the mystery of Jesus, and also to portray the disciples' steady movement toward misunderstanding and failure.[151] Despite their being the privileged "insiders" of 4:1–34, they remain "outside" the mystery of Jesus. Nevertheless, the failing disciples, those in the boat with Jesus and also those in the other boats, as Jesus' entourage increases (v. 36), have been invited to "cross over" the terrors of the sea which he conquers. They witness Jesus perform his mighty works for the first time in a Gentile land. As hitherto, the disciples will continue to be "with him" across the sea, in Gerasa (5:1–20).

Jesus drives out a legion of demons (5:1–20)

The narrative flows naturally into the following episode, one of the most odd events reported in the Gospel of Mark: the healing of the Gerasene demoniac. Having calmed the storm (4:35–41), Jesus and the disciples arrive at the other side of the sea, the land of the Gerasenes, the region surrounding a Gentile city in the Decapolis.[152] Having climbed out of the boat, Jesus is met by a man from the tombs, a man with an unclean spirit (5:1–2), and his plight is described in great detail. The account bears the marks of a popular folktale. His abode among the tombs is repeated (v. 3; see also v. 2),[153] and particular attention is given to the inability of anyone to restrain his raging, even with chains around his body and fetters on his feet (vv. 3–4).[154] His miserable situation, an outcast from the sophisticated Hellenistic world of the Decapolis region, is summed up in the description of his calling out and gashing himself with rocks, day and night (v. 5).[155] In 5:1–5 the scene has

---

[150] See Meier, *A Marginal Jew*, 2:925–28.

[151] See Gnilka, *Markus*, 1:193–94. See Marshall, *Faith as a Theme*, 213–20.

[152] Difficulty in locating Gerasa (a town about thirty-three miles southeast of the Sea of Galilee) beside the sea has led to a number of scribal attempts to amend the text of 5:20. The most popular alteration is to replace "Gerasenes" with "Gadarenes" although "Gergesenes," "Gergisenes," and "Gergastenes" are also found. For the discussion, see Metzger, *Textual Commentary*, 72; Guelich, *Mark*, 275–76. Gerasa (modern Jerash) is a long way from the sea, and it is probable that an original exorcism story, without the introductory arrival in the boat (vv. 1–2) and report of the pigs drowning (vv. 11–13), had no association with the sea. See Meier, *A Marginal Jew*, 640–42 n. 32, 651; J. F. Craghan, "The Gerasene Demoniac," *CBQ* 30 (1968): 522–36; Schweizer, *Mark* 112. See Anderson (*Mark*, 147–48) for the importance of the Decapolis.

[153] The repetition of the man's presence in the tombs locates him in a favored dwelling place for demons in the ancient world. See Guelich, *Mark*, 278.

[154] It is often pointed out that there are a number of terms in vv. 3–4 that are peculiar to these two verses, or very rare in the rest of the New Testament. As there is no story which matches Mark 5:1–20 elsewhere, this is not surprising.

[155] There is ample evidence from the ancient world of these practices (crying out and slashing the body) among those possessed or insane. There was often no distinction made between the two conditions. This is already indicated in the performance of the prophets of Baal in 1 Kgs 18:20. See Lane, *Mark*, 182 n. 9. A number of scholars draw parallels from Isa 65, and even suggest that vv. 3–5 are something of a midrash on that text. See the summary in Guelich (*Mark*, 277).

been set: the location, the characters, and the situation are established. With vv. 1–5 as an introduction and vv. 19–20 as a conclusion, the account can be divided into five moments in chiastic form:[156]

[A] Introduction: The possessed man's approach to Jesus. (5:1–5)

  [B] Jesus' encounter with the possessed man (5:6–10)

    [C] The episode involving the herd of swine (5:11–14a)

  [B'] Jesus' encounter with the townspeople (5:14b–17)

[A'] Conclusion: the cleansed man's approach to Jesus (5:18–20)

Formally, the account follows the pattern of an exorcism: (a) Jesus meets one possessed (5:1–5); (b) the demon(s) utter an exclamation (v. 7a); (c) an identification of Jesus (v. 7b); (d) Jesus' expulsion of the demon(s) by means of a standard formula (v. 8); (e) a complete transformation of the one formerly possessed (v. 15). The only element missing is a command from Jesus silencing the demon(s). This elaborate episode, however, renders such a command unnecessary as the demons are silenced by being engulfed by the sea. An originally simpler exorcism has been greatly developed in the tradition, and then further developed by Mark for the purposes of the Gospel narrative. Despite the elaborate nature of the account, it plays an important role in the Markan narrative design, continuing the report of Jesus' mighty works (see 6:2), and establishing a beachhead for the coming of the kingdom among the Gentiles (5:19–20).[157]

The possessed man was said to meet Jesus (5:2), and is then reported as seeing Jesus from afar (v. 6a). This unevenness may reflect stages in the development of the story,[158] but it also allows the action of the man, running up and prostrating himself before Jesus (v. 6b), to be highlighted. On the one hand there is an inevitable attraction toward the man whom he recognizes and confesses as "Jesus, Son of the Most High God" (v. 7b), and on the other a recognition that conflict between the force of good, found in Jesus, and the force of evil, dwelling in the man, is inevitable. No one is strong enough to subdue him (οὐδεὶς ἴσχυεν, v. 4), but the reader is aware that Jesus is "the mightier one" (ὁ ἰσχυρότερος, 1:7), and that the outcome of the encounter is already obvious. The man asks, in a formula, "What have you to do with me?" and requests that Jesus not torment him (5:7a, c). The demonic powers recognize Jesus' superiority from the beginning of the encounter.[159] Both detailed descriptions of encounters between Jesus and the possessed

---

[156] Careful writing marks the final version of the story. It has an introduction and a conclusion (vv. 1–5 and vv. 18–20), two encounters—between Jesus and the demoniac (vv. 6–10), and between Jesus and the townspeople (vv. 14b–17)—with the episode of the swine at the center (vv. 11–14b). Thus, it is the Markan insertion of the episode with the swine that is a point of focus. As Ernst (*Markus,* 154) comments, "Today the reader will see the text as a whole and must understand it from the perspective of the final redactor." This is not to deny that there are many tensions in the narrative. For an indication of these tensions and reference to the complex discussion of the development of the present story, see Meier, *A Marginal Jew,* 2:650–53, 664–65 n. 15. See also Gnilka, *Markus,* 1:200–203; Guelich, *Mark,* 272–75; Ernst, *Markus,* 153–54; Marcus, *Mark,* 347.

[157] For this reason alone, I find Meier's description of Mark 5:1–20 as a "rambling, sometimes incoherent, yet concrete and bizarre narrative" (*A Marginal Jew,* 2:650) too harsh. For a more positive assessment of the story, see Lührmann, *Markusevangelium,* 98–99.

[158] See, for example, Hooker, *St. Mark,* 143.

[159] Lane (*Mark,* 183) suggests that the crying out in a loud voice indicates the extent of the demoniac's fear as he encounters Jesus.

(cf. 1:21–28) are marked by the demonic recognition of Jesus' relationship with God. The demonic is not limited to this world, and thus has access to truths that the *characters in the story* do not know. The *reader of the story,* however, has been well prepared by the prologue (1:1–13). In a very real sense, for Mark (and the rest of the ancient world) demons belong to the sphere of the supernatural.[160] In Capernaum the demon recognized Jesus as "the Holy One of God" (1:24), and here he is identified as "son of the Most High God" (5:7).[161] This use of a correct name for Jesus should empower the evil spirits,[162] but such is not the case in the story of Jesus. In a brief analepsis, the narrator explains the demonic outburst by recalling Jesus' formal command to the demon: "Come out of the man, you unclean spirit!" (v. 8).[163] Jesus does not address the man, but the demon that had taken possession of the man. This is most effective. By creating an analepsis, holding back the direct speech of Jesus' formal command until v. 8, the storyteller is able to run directly into Jesus' further authoritative intervention. As the demon has named Jesus, but failed to control him, Jesus now shows himself master of the situation by demanding the name of the demon, as part of the process of freeing the suffering man. Unable to resist, the demon(s) must reply: "My name is Legion; for we are many" (v. 9).[164] At face value, the use of the name λεγιών, pos- ~~Legion~~ sibly a loanword from Latin, could simply mean that the man is possessed by an entourage of demons.[165] However, in a world where the Roman legions ruled, sometimes brutally, the word probably indicates a large number of demons (as the text states) and also describes them in a pejorative fashion.[166]

The encounter between Jesus and the possessed man began with the initiative of the man, and closes with a final initiative from Legion. In a very strong request, the demon "begged him eagerly" not to send them out of the χώρα (5:10).[167] This is an admission of defeat, but an attempt to make the most of it. They may be driven out of the individual from Gerasa, but they wish to maintain their position in the countryside, where other human beings might be found. Their possession of the Gerasene has led to his being expelled from the city to the demonic place of the graveyard (vv. 1–5). Legion pleads to be allowed to lurk outside the cities and villages, ready to bring destruction and suffering to

---

160 See Lane, *Mark,* 183–84; Anderson, *Mark,* 148.

161 "The Most High God" is an expression found in the Old Testament on the lips of non-Israelites, speaking of Israel's God. See, for example, Gen 14:18–20; Num 24:16; Isa 14:14; Dan 3:26, 42. See also Acts 16:17. It is appropriate on the lips of the demon in this Gentile land. See Marcus, *Mark,* 343–44.

162 See Gnilka, *Markus,* 1:204.

163 The location of 5:8, following the words of the demon in v. 7 which were generated by Jesus' command in v. 8, has been the subject of much debate. Some suggest that it was originally before v. 7, some that its present position comes from pre-Markan tradition, some that it is editorial, and others (including myself) that it is an elegant analepsis, added by Mark. For a summary of the discussion, see Lane, *Mark,* 184 n. 16; Guelich, *Mark,* 280.

164 As in English, so also in Greek, this is a clumsy expression, moving from the singular to the plural, "my name (ὄνομά μοι) . . . we are many (πολλοί ἐσμεν)."

165 See, for example, Lane, *Mark,* 184–85. Lane suggests that it is not necessarily a loanword from Latin. He points out that it is a military word found in Hellenistic Greek and Aramaic. It simply indicates the presence of many demons "in common possession of the same victim."

166 See, among many, Gnilka, *Markus,* 1:205; Marcus, *Mark,* 351–52.

167 The word χώρα is generally taken to mean "the region" in 5:10. This is the first meaning for the word given in BDAG, 1093, s.v. χώρα, par. 2. The word, however, also indicates the notion of "space." See LSJ, 2015, s.v. χώρα, par. I. See also BDAG, 1094, par. 5. Using this meaning, Legion accepts dismissal from the man, but asks for freedom to wander.

further victims. This is a bold request, presupposing a bargaining position with Jesus. They are not to have their way, and as the story proceeds, the presence of Jesus will purify not just the man, but the whole χώρα.   region

The focus of the story shifts as the narrator describes the presence of many swine, feeding on the nearby hillside (5:11). A new theme has been broached, but the issue of cleanliness continues. Unclean spirits inhabit the possessed man, and unclean animals graze on the hillside of this Gentile land. From a Jewish perspective, only Gentiles would maintain a large herd of animals that could be compared to the unclean spirits possessing the Gerasene (see Deut 14:8; Lev 11:1–8).[168] In a further request, the Legion of demons asks that they be allowed to enter creatures that are unclean like themselves (v. 12). The single voice of Legion now becomes plural, as a multitude of demons asks to be sent into a multitude of unclean animals (πέμψον ἡμᾶς; εἰσέλθωμεν, v. 12). The granting of their wish, and the subsequent destruction of both the demons and the roughly two thousand swine as they rush headlong over the cliff to be drowned in the sea (v. 13), have generated much discussion.[169] Two issues are fundamental to the story. In the first place, both the Legion and the two thousand swine are totally destroyed.[170] Jesus has just tamed the chaotic and demonic powers of the sea (see v. 39, where he "exorcises" the sea). It is into that demonic depth that he now plunges both the unclean spirits and the unclean swine.[171] Legion asked to be allowed to take possession of the unclean swine, but Jesus responds by destroying both unclean elements within the depths of the demonic sea.[172] The second issue of importance is linked to the original request from Legion to be allowed to roam about in the χώρα (see v. 10). The opposite situation has resulted from Jesus' encounter with Legion. He has purified the man of the Legion of demons, and he has purified the "countryside" (χώρα) of the unclean animals. The kingdom of God continues to overpower all forces of evil, rendering clean both people and place. The episode closes with the not surprising flight of the swineherds (mentioned for the first time in v. 14a) announcing in both city and country what Jesus had done. No judgment is made upon the swineherds. They simply serve the storyteller as a means to have *the facts* of the encounter between Jesus and the Gerasene demoniac reported far and wide.

The final episode of the body of the miracle story is reported in 5:14b–17. Jesus' actions call for a response. There is a subtle development of the response in vv. 14b–15. Initially, curiosity draws people to see what had happened (v. 14a), but the sight of the totally

---

168 See also *m. B. Qam.*, 7:7: "None may rear swine anywhere."

169 For a sampling of these discussions, see H. van der Loos, *The Miracles of Jesus* (NovTSupp 9; Leiden: Brill, 1965), 390–91. Jesus does not grant the wish of Legion (cf., for example, Guelich, *Mark*, 282). He uses their request to destroy both demons and swine. Marcus (*Mark*, 345, 352) traces sexual innuendo here, and suggests that the idea of rape is behind the entering and destruction of the swine.

170 Only Mark mentions the number of swine. There may be a link between the numbers in a Roman legion (between five and six thousand troops) and the "about two thousand" swine. A link is also sometimes suggested between the insignia of the Tenth Roman Legion, a boar's head, and the swine. There is little in the text, however, which supports this "Roman" interpretation of the event.

171 This interpretation is already represented in the Lukan rewrite of the episode. The demons ask not to be plunged into the "abyss" (Luke 8:31). See Nineham, *St. Mark*, 154. The expression refers to the primal ocean, the realm of the dead. For the LXX it also denotes the original flood and (in the plural) the realm of the dead, "a prison for the powers opposed to God" (O. Böcher, "ἄβυσσος," *EDNT* 1:4). See also J. Jeremias, "ἄβυσσος," *TDNT* 1:9–10.

172 The twofold mention of "the sea" ("into the sea," "in the sea") in v. 15 accentuates the place. See LaVerdiere, *The Beginning*, 131.

transformed ex-demoniac leads to fear (v. 15). The fierce description of the man's desperate situation in vv. 2–5 is reversed in v. 15a: seated, clothed, and in his right mind.[173] This was the one who had the Legion (v. 15b). This awkward insertion reminds the reader of the raving demoniac at the beginning of the story (vv. 2–5). An important, but negative, Markan phrase is used for the response of the people: they were afraid (καὶ ἐφοβήθησαν). The response of the disciples in the immediately previous miracle was great fear (καὶ ἐφοβήθησαν φόβον μέγαν, 4:41). As the disciples failed to understand and accept the presence of the kingdom of God in the person of Jesus, so also do the people who came to Jesus after his purification of both the man and the countryside.[174] Fear is the rejection of the presence of the kingdom of God, and an inability to recognize Jesus as the one in whom God is pleased (see 1:11). Hitherto inactive characters appear in v. 16a: "those who had seen it." The only people present with Jesus during the encounter with the demoniac and the Legion were the disciples (see v. 1). Are they the ones who tell the details of what happened to both the Legion and to the swine (v. 16b)? It is possible that such was the intention of the storyteller, further indicating that Jesus' disciples are unable to penetrate the deeper mystery of the person of Jesus. Whoever "those who had seen it" might have been (and the disciples are good candidates),[175] their report leads to the request that Jesus leave the countryside (v. 17). The fear of v. 15 becomes the rejection of Jesus in v. 17. As Jesus had driven the unclean from their land in v. 13, they now ask the "Son of the most high God" to leave their land.[176] There is deep irony in this request.

This well-crafted narrative closes with a final encounter between Jesus and the ex-demoniac (5:18–20). Jesus has journeyed across the sea to arrive at the Gentile region of Gerasa (v. 1), and now he prepares to leave, responding to the demand of those who cannot or will not accept his presence (v. 18a). But the ex-demoniac begs Jesus (παρακάλει αὐτόν) "that he might be with him" (ἵνα μετ' αὐτοῦ ᾖ). But this is impossible. The reader is aware that discipleship results from the initiative of Jesus (1:16–20; 2:13–14; 3:13–19; 4:10, 36).[177] It was Jesus who had established the Twelve "to be with him" (3:14: ἵνα ὦσιν μετ' αὐτοῦ). The initiative must be taken from the ex-demoniac, and this is what happens in 5:19. He desired to "be with Jesus," but Jesus must determine the agenda. As he had determined the destiny of both the unclean elements in the land of Gerasa, and sent them to their destruction, he now issues a further set of commands, and offers the possibility of the kingdom in the land of Gerasa. The ex-demoniac is not to be "with Jesus," but he is commanded to go back to his own home and his own people. There he is to announce (ἀπάγγειλον) the action of the Lord: all that God (ὁ κύριος) had done for him and how God had been merciful to him.[178]

---

[173] Whatever one makes of the possible tradition history of vv. 2–5, there is a deliberate counterbalance between vv. 2–5 and v. 15.

[174] On the theme of fear, its link with the previous miracle, and some suggestions (somewhat forced) for the background of this theme in the Markan community, see Marcus, *Mark,* 352–53.

[175] Gnilka (*Markus,* 1:206) and Ernst (*Markus,* 157) reject this possibility.

[176] It is not clear who makes this request. "They" could refer to "those who had seen it," and grammatically this is the better option. However, it is more likely that those who came out from the city and heard what had happened make the request.

[177] Schweizer (*Mark,* 114) aptly comments: "Discipleship is not a way of salvation by which the individual can secure his own happiness."

[178] The verb ἀπαγγέλλειν is closely associated with the idea of preaching the good news (see 1:4, 7, 14, 38, 39; 3:14; 6:12; 13:10; 14:9; see also Acts 17:30; 26:20; 1 Cor 14:25). See Gnilka, *Markus,* 1:206–7.

The man does exactly as he is told. The direct speech of Jesus is repeated almost verbatim in the description of the response of the man. He returns to his home and people, and announces in the Decapolis all that has been done to him (5:20). However, there is one important difference. He does not attribute the merciful action to ὁ κύριος, but to ὁ Ἰησοῦς (v. 20). For Mark, both the command of Jesus and the response of the ex-demoniac are correct. It is the authority of God that lies behind all that Jesus did for the possessed man. However, the authority of God lies in the person of Jesus, and the ex-demoniac rightly recognized that "Jesus" was "the Lord." Legion's description of Jesus as "Son of the Most High God" (v. 7) is correct, but here the association of the name of God with the name of Jesus is to spread the good news, not to overcome it. In this proclamation of the deeds of God, made present in the deeds of Jesus, the good news is preached in a Gentile land for the first time in the Gospel of Mark.[179] The response of those who hear the proclamation is muted. There is no wholesale conversion. Mark carefully reports that everyone was "amazed" (v. 20). No doubt the experience of the Markan community, involved in a Gentile mission, leads Mark to this carefully determined description of the first response of the Gentile world to the preaching of all that Jesus had done in a Gentile land.[180] The fear of those who had asked Jesus to leave their land (vv. 15–17) is transformed into wonder (v. 20). The door has been opened to faith, but more will be required before anyone in the story— disciples, crowd, Gentiles, or Jews—will recognize Jesus as the Son of God. Such faith will only be possible after the death and resurrection of the Christ, the Son of God.

Jairus, the curing of woman with the flow of blood, and the raising of Jairus's daughter (5:21–43)

The Markan narrative framework is continued as 5:18a is resumed: Jesus crosses back to the Jewish side of the sea and remains beside the sea as a great crowd gathers about him (v. 21). The stark encounter between Jesus and the demoniac among the tombs has been replaced by the usual bustle of Jesus' ministry. Jairus, otherwise unknown but described as a leader of the synagogue (εἷς τῶν ἀρχισυναγώγων),[181] comes to Jesus, sees him, and wordlessly demonstrates his belief in Jesus: he falls at his feet (v. 22). The theme of faith has been broached, and it will persist across the passage. His request of Jesus, that he come and perform the gesture of laying his hands upon his daughter who is very near death, is not simply a request for medical assistance. He demonstrates his belief in Jesus' power and authority: "she will be made well (ἵνα σωθῇ) and live" (v. 23).[182] Thus far, Jesus has not said anything to Jairus, but merely responds to the request and sets out with the leader of the synagogue (v. 24a). This is important for the overall interpretation of 5:21–43. The episode that follows, the curing of the woman with the flow of blood (vv. 24b–34), takes

---

[179] See Guelich, *Mark*, 286; Marcus, *Mark*, 353–54.

[180] See, among many, Schweizer, *Mark*, 113; Ernst, *Markus*, 181. For some, 5:1–20 prepares the way for Jesus' Gentile ministry, reported in 7:24–8:10. See especially, R. H. Lightfoot, *History and Interpretation in the Gospels* (London: Hodder & Stoughton, 1935), 89–90. See also Painter, *Mark's Gospel*, 89.

[181] Just what this title means is difficult to determine. The "ruler of the synagogue" probably led worship services, but is presented here as an important figure in the Jewish community. See E. Schürer, *The History of the Jewish People in the Age of Jesus Christ (175 B.C.–A.D. 135)* (ed. G. Vermes, F. Millar, and M. Black; 3 vols.; Edinburgh: T&T Clark, 1973–1987), 2:432–46; Meier, *A Marginal Jew*, 2:845 n. 30.

[182] On the faith demonstrated in Jairus's actions (coming, falling) and words (especially the use of σῴζειν), see Markus, *Mark*, 365–66.

place *while Jesus is on his way.* These two miracles must be read together, as it is not until v. 43 that the issues raised by the encounter with Jairus in vv. 21–24a are resolved.

The story of the daughter of Jairus frames the account of the woman with the flow of blood. It is another example of the Markan practice of "framing" stories, or of a "sandwich construction." The technique of "sandwiching" or "framing" calls for an interpretation that takes account of the unification of the two episodes. They have been put together by Mark, or the tradition before Mark, precisely because each episode throws light upon the other.[183] But the reader encounters two "woman stories," forming the conclusion of a section of the Gospel that has been dedicated to a systematic gathering of Jesus' miraculous activity. From Mark 4:35 onward there has been a crescendo of increasingly significant miracles as Jesus overcomes nature (4:35–41) and then the demonic world (5:1–20). The episodes reported in the sandwich of 5:21–43 tell of his victory over sickness (5:25–35) and death (5:21–24, 36–43). But it is also significant that the major characters in both of the final miracles are women.[184] The theme of faith has already been introduced by the approach of Jairus, and the same theme will be stated, negatively, in the response of the disciples to Jesus' question in the story of the woman with the flow of blood. Resumed from 5:21, the scene is set with the description of the great crowd pressing about him. The woman with the flow of blood is introduced. The two major characters, apart from Jesus, are at opposite ends of the social and religious scale. Jairus is an important male synagogue leader, while she is a marginalized woman.[185] She has been suffering from uncontrolled menstrual bleeding for twelve years (v. 25). This ailment renders her ritually impure at all times, unable to play an active life in the community of Israel (see Lev 15:25; *m. Zabim* 5:1, 6). Her impurity places her "outside" the chosen people of God.[186] The severity of the ailment, and the inability of *human agents* to resolve her suffering, both physical and religious, is accentuated by the narrator's report that she had "suffered" under many physicians. This is an eloquent description of the humiliation and increasing rejection of the woman. Her ailments, both physical and spiritual, "grow worse."

Her faith has been aroused because she has heard about Jesus (5:27). This theme, initiated in the prostration and the request of Jairus, continues into this central segment of the sandwich construction. There is a startling element of self-abandon in the ruler of the synagogue, who lowers himself from his dignified position to fall at the feet of Jesus (v. 22). The woman with the hemorrhage also takes a risk in reaching out to touch Jesus, despite her lowly state as a person suffering from impurity (v. 28).[187] The response to Jairus's

---

[183] This point is missed by B. Witherington (*Women in the Ministry of Jesus: A Study of Jesus' Attitudes to Women and Their Roles as Reflected in His Earthly Life* [SNTSMS 51; Cambridge: Cambridge University Press, 1984], 71–72) because of an overambitious attempt to show the "historicity" of the sequence of events as we have them reported in Mark 5:21–43. For a documented survey of the discussion over the pre-Markan or Markan redaction of vv. 21–43, see Meier, *A Marginal Jew,* 2:841–42 n. 19. Meier reconstructs the pre-Markan tradition and takes it back to the historical Jesus (see 2:780–88).

[184] It is possible to overemphasize the womanly side of these accounts. See, for example, LaVerdiere, *The Beginning,* 1:133. No doubt these accounts pointed to Jesus' radical "crossing of traditional boundaries" and challenged the Markan community to question cultural attitudes to women. However, the point of the stories is primarily christological.

[185] See Marcus, *Mark,* 366.

[186] See the excellent documentation in Marcus, *Mark,* 357–58.

[187] As J. J. Pilch (*Healing in the New Testament: Insights from Medical and Mediterranean Anthropology* [Minneapolis: Fortress, 2000], 67) points out: "it is out of the ordinary for a woman to plead her own cause."

demonstration of faith and trust is pending, but the woman gets immediate results: she is healed of her disease (v. 29). There are two levels of discourse going on in the narrative. Jesus, in the midst of the throng, senses that God has acted through him, and he turns to discover who had touched him to receive the power that has gone out from him (v. 30). On the other hand, there is the "good sense" of the disciples who almost mock Jesus' question: "You see the crowd pressing round you, and yet you say: 'Who touched me?'" (v. 31).[188] A similar response returns in the mockery and laughter surrounding Jesus' later statement that the daughter of Jairus is only asleep (vv. 39–40). The discourse of "good sense," however, is ignored by Jesus as he accepts the bold faith of the woman who, like Jairus, falls at his feet (see v. 22) but goes further, confessing her act in fear and trembling (v. 33). There is a sense of "holy awe" in the fear and trembling (see 1 Cor 2:3; 2 Cor 7:15; Phil 2:12; Eph 6:5), a recognition that she has been touched by the power of the kingdom of God in her touching of the clothing of Jesus.[189] Jesus' words confirm the miracle (5:34c), but more importantly, grant her access to peace (v. 34b). He calls her his daughter, bringing her into a chosen people of God, and informs her that her faith in what God could do in and through Jesus has made her whole (σέσωκέν σε). The promise to the believing Jairus of the future health of his daughter (see v. 23: ἵνα σωθῇ) has been anticipated by the restoration of the woman to wholeness because of her faith. Her wholeness, however, is not only physical.

The raising of the daughter of Jairus repeats a number of elements from the miracle of the woman with the flow of blood. Widespread "good sense" is represented by minor characters in the narrative: those from the ruler's house who announce that she is dead and thus that Jesus should not be furthered bothered (5:35), and the professional mourners who mock him (vv. 38, 40a). But Jesus is more aggressive. In literary terms, the strong presence of Jesus is extremely effective. In 5:21–24a he acquiesced to the request of Jairus without comment. In 5:24b–34 the woman took the initiative, and it was only as a consequence of her actions that Jesus responded and admitted her to wholeness and holiness. In 5:36–37, 39, 40b, Jesus lays aside all objections and "practical" understandings of the situation.[190] He insists that faith must replace all fear (v. 36), claims that she is only asleep (v. 39), and takes a chosen group of people, his more intimate disciples and the child's parents, into the place where the child is (v. 40b). This more aggressive approach of Jesus continues into the account of the raising. Jesus' role in the narrative develops from silence (vv. 21–24a), to question (v. 30), to affirmation (v. 34), and finally to a series of aggressive actions (vv. 35–43).

Nevertheless, the key to the interpretation of the raising of the daughter of Jairus may be found by tracing its close association with Jesus' cure of the woman with the flow of blood. Why did Mark, or the tradition before Mark,[191] join the story of the woman with the hemorrhage and the raising of the daughter of Jairus? The message about faith was certainly one of the reasons. The link between faith and the miracles of Jesus is important for Mark. The two miracles just reported show that his miraculous activity can reveal unfaith (see 4:35–41) or produce faith (see 5:1–20). In 5:21–43, Jesus responds to the faith of Jairus and the woman. Then there are the lesser characters in the narrative, the disciples, the

---

[188] See Marcus, *Mark*, 359.

[189] On the "holy awe" of the woman's reaction, see Marcus, *Mark*, 359–60.

[190] Scholars debate whether Jesus "overheard" or "ignored" (παρακούσας, v. 36) what was said. See the discussion in Meier, *A Marginal Jew*, 2:846 n. 32. My reading accepts that he hears, and responds in vv. 37ff.

[191] Whether it was Mark or an earlier tradition which linked these miracles is not crucial. Whatever the origin of this juxtapositioning, they serve the Markan agenda admirably.

crowds, and the official mourners at the home of Jairus. They all demonstrate "good sense," treat Jesus' words or actions as irrelevant (vv. 31, 38, 40a), and provide a narrative foil to the woman who is cured and Jairus who believes.[192] The daughter of Jairus is a major character also, even though she appears only in the narrative in vv. 40–43. She is present to the reader from vv. 22–23 on. Jesus moves toward the home of Jairus throughout.

Some commentators have pointed to the appearance of the number "twelve" in both stories: the illness had lasted twelve years (5:25), and Jairus's daughter was twelve years old (v. 42).[193] However, they do not make enough of the repetition. For example, Taylor, followed by many others, regards the reference to the twelve years in the case of the flow of blood as a "round number to describe an affliction of long standing."[194] The age of the twelve-year-old girl was "added to explain the walking." Thus, when Jesus commands her to arise, the reader knows that she will be old enough to walk.[195] Although the number twelve may have played a role in linking the two originally independent miracle stories, its function was merely formal. Lagrange dismisses the issue of the appearance of the twelve years in both episodes as simple coincidence.[196] Our reading of the Gospel of Mark to this point would suggest that such details are not coincidental.

As well as the unifying theme of faith, outlined above, two additional elements in the stories link them and point to a further, more christological theme. In the account of healing of Simon's mother-in-law, Mark highlighted Jesus' touching of the sick woman and her serving of the group, once restored to health (1:29–31). No women have played an active part in the story since then, but in 5:21–43 two women are at center stage, and the theme of touching reappears. It occurs four times in the account of the woman with the flow of blood:

5:27	"She had heard about Jesus, and came up to him in the crowd and *touched* (ἥψατο) his cloak."
5:28	"If I *touch* (ἅψωμαι) even his garments I shall be made well."
5:30	"Who *touched* (ἥψατο) my garments?"
5:31	"You see the crowd pressing around you, and yet you say, 'Who *touched* (ἥψσατο) me?'"

Once we see the centrality of the theme of "touching" in the miracle of the woman with the flow of blood, that same theme emerges in the raising of Jairus's daughter. The verb "to touch" is not found, but Jesus is described as taking her by the hand (κρατήσας τῆς χειρὸς τοῦ παιδίου, v. 41a). Following Jesus' words to the girl, its translation into Greek (v. 41b), and the girl's response (v. 42a), the narrator provides the unexpected indication that the girl was twelve years old (v. 42b): "Taking her by the hand, he said to her 'talitha cum,' which means, 'little girl, I say to you, arise.' And immediately the girl got up and walked; for she was twelve years old." (vv. 41–42)[197]

---

[192] For a thorough study of the theme of faith of Jairus and the woman, see Marshall, *Faith as a Theme*, 90–100 (Jairus), and 101–10 (the woman).

[193] For a survey of the suggestions that have been made, as well as his own hypothesis, regarding the "pairing" of these originally independent accounts, see Pesch, *Markusevangelium*, 1:312–14, and the literature cited there. See further, Meier, *A Marginal Jew*, 866 n. 33.

[194] Taylor, *St. Mark*, 290.

[195] Ibid., 294.

[196] Lagrange, *Saint Marc*, 135. See also Meier, *A Marginal Jew*, 2:736 n. 142.

[197] Many manuscripts read κουμι, which would be the proper Aramaic form of the feminine imperative. The best reading, however, retains the more difficult masculine form (*lectio difficilior*). See Metzger, *Textual Commentary*, 74–75.

Perhaps it is not only the miracle that generates the great amazement (v. 42b), even though such a reaction from the bystanders is a proper ending to a miracle story. Given Mark's reporting of Jesus' easy preparedness to touch women of any state or condition (1:29–31; 5:28–31), the precise indication that the young girl was, in fact, a young woman of twelve years of age may have been intended to increase the shock created by Jesus' action. She was of marriageable age. As Brown explains, in reference to Jewish marriage practices:

> The consent, usually entered into when the girl was between twelve and thirteen years old, would constitute a legally ratified marriage in our times, since it gave the young man rights over the girl. She was henceforth his wife.[198]

In such a situation, Jesus' "taking her by the hand" is an ambiguous gesture for a religious leader. There is a hint in the text that she may not have been dead (v. 39),[199] and this would excuse Jesus from the impurity which he would incur by touching a dead body (according to Num 19:11–13), but her being "twelve years old" makes her a woman. The Markan Jesus is portrayed as unconcerned about the possibility of incurring ritual impurity.[200] He is prepared to take a twelve-year-old girl by the hand. Along with the teaching on the relationship between faith and miracles, Mark makes the christological point that Jesus ignores issues of ritual impurity or taboo when it is a case of giving life (see 7:1–23).

The affectionate gesture of touching is further enriched by the transliterated Aramaic expression ταλιθα κουμ (5:41).[201] It has been retained in the Greek version of Mark because of its eloquence and its importance.[202] The encounter between Jesus and this young woman takes on a special significance, and a link between the two miracle stories, so entwined in the Gospel tradition (see also Matt 9:18–26; Luke 8:40–56), becomes more obvious. In both miracles Jesus touches the unclean. He touches a woman in a pathological condition which renders her permanently ritually unclean (see Lev 15:25; *m. Zabim* 5:1.6), and he touches the dead body (see Num 19:11–13) of a young woman (see *b. Ber.* 5b).[203] In both touchings Jesus brings wholeness and holiness. The power of the reigning presence of

---

[198] R. E. Brown, *The Birth of the Messiah: A Commentary on the Infancy Narratives of Matthew and Luke* (New York: Doubleday, 1977), 123. See further, J. Jeremias, *Jerusalem in the Time of Jesus: An Investigation into Economic and Social Conditions during the New Testament Period* (trans. F. H. and C. H. Cave; London: SCM, 1969), 364–68. See, however, the modification of this widely held position in T. Ilan, *Jewish Women in Greco-Roman Palestine* (Peabody: Hendrickson, 1996), 65–69.

[199] It is difficult to be sure whether "sleep" is a euphemism for death in this case, as it was for Lazarus in John 11:11, or a statement of fact. The former option is the more likely. In either case, Jesus behaves improperly. See LaVerdiere, *The Beginning*, 1:139–40; Meier, *A Marginal Jew*, 2:843–44 n. 26.

[200] Pilch (*Healing in the New Testament*, 66) rightly sees the woman with the flow of blood as restored to society, but does not mention the issue of impurity, despite his earlier support for Mary Douglas's work on human excretions (see pp. 49–51). In strong support of the above interpretation, see M. J. Selvidge, "Mark 5:25–34 and Leviticus 15:19–20: A Reaction to Restrictive Purity Regulations," *JBL* 103 (1984): 619–23.

[201] There is a level of affection in the word ταλιθα, a word indicating smallness and youth.

[202] It is not analogous to the tradition of using foreign terms in magical formulae, as some would claim. See the survey in Marcus, *Mark*, 363.

[203] This is often disregarded. For example, Lührmann (*Markusevangelium*, 104–5) notes the repetition of "twelve," but claims that the woman's being unclean is never mentioned, and that the girl is clearly a *Mädchen* (young girl). Ernst (*Markus*, 161–66) rejects any importance in the "touching," insisting on the centrality of the theme of faith in the saving word of Jesus.

God, which Mark insists was at hand in the gospel and in Jesus' person (see 1:14–15), overcomes the barriers of cultic and ritual observance.[204]

The girl of twelve years of age—now marriageable—gets up and walks (5:42a). She rises to womanhood. The young woman, who now begins to pour forth her life in menstruation, and the older woman, who experiences menstruation as a pathological condition, are both restored. They are "given" new life. Here we find that the life-giving powers of women, manifested in the flow of blood, are not "bad" or "impure" (the older woman). Nor are they the cause of problems for Jesus as he touches the younger woman. They are not to be cut off in death (the younger woman). They are "restored" so that the women can go and live in *shalom* (see v. 34: ὕπαγε εἰς εἰρήνην), in the well-being of God's reigning presence, which has "touched" their lives in Jesus of Nazareth.[205]

The account closes with the strange juxtaposition of a Markan command not to make the miracle known (5:43a) and a further command, probably coming from earlier tradition, that the young woman be given something to eat (v. 43b). The Markan secrecy theme continues. It is crucial that Jesus not be understood as Messiah or Savior on the basis of his wonderful miracles (v. 43a). It is not as a wonder-worker that Jesus will respond to the design of God (see 1:11), but as a crucified and risen Christ and Son of God. Although odd, as it is hardly likely that any such command could be obeyed, its place at the end of a series of miracles (4:35–5:43) explains why the warning has been inserted. "The miracle of the resurrection can only be understood by those who believe in the one who has himself been raised from the dead."[206] For someone who has been raised from the dead, life must proceed, and thus Jairus's daughter must be nourished (5:43b). Part of the earlier stage of this story, the insistence that the girl be cared for stresses that she has returned to everyday life.[207]

Jesus Is Rejected in His Hometown (6:1–6a)

Jesus leaves the place where he has performed his miracles, to come to his own hometown (εἰς τὴν πατρίδα αὐτοῦ).[208] He does not go alone. He is followed (ἀκολουθοῦσιν) by his disciples (6:1). Themes from the beginning of 3:7–6:6a return: Jesus is among his own (see 3:20–21, 30–35), and disciples are with him (see 3:13–19). Much has happened since

---

[204] Marcus (*Mark*, 364–65, 366–67) notes that Jesus boldly ignores the issue of uncleanness and the related problem of the "touching." He does not, however, draw conclusions from these details.

[205] See, for this suggestion, E. Schüssler-Fiorenza, *In Memory of Her: A Feminist Theological Reconstruction of Christian Origins* (London: SCM, 1983), 122–24. See also R. C. Wahlberg, *Jesus according to a Woman* (New York: Paulist Press, 1975), 31–41.

[206] Hooker, *St. Mark,* 151. See also Minette de Tillesse, *Le secret messianique,* 52–57; Ernst, *Markus,* 165–66.

[207] One should not read too much into the complex association of vv. 43a and 43b. The Markan command to silence here, by far the most incongruous of the commands to silence, points forward to the death and resurrection of Jesus (see Meier, *A Marginal Jew,* 2:779–80). Commands to silence alert the reader that the full truth will only be made known in the climactic revelation of Jesus as Messiah and Son of God in his death and resurrection. The request that the girl be fed does make sense, even though it had its origins in an earlier stage of the story. See Meier, *A Marginal Jew,* 2:780–81.

[208] The Greek πατρίς means "fatherland" but has come to mean "hometown" in the New Testament. See Marcus, *Mark,* 374.

he established a new family (3:31–35) in the face of misunderstanding and rejection from his blood family and his fellow Jews (3:21–30). He has taught wisely in parables (4:1–34) and devoted special attention to those around him—his new family, specially privileged with the gift of the kingdom of God (4:10–11). He has demonstrated his authority over nature, demons, sickness, and death (4:35–5:43). The disciples have experienced difficulty in understanding Jesus during these miraculous events. After the calming of the stormy seas they ask who he might be (4:41). They perhaps report what they have seen to those who eventually ask Jesus to leave Gerasa (5:16), and they demonstrate a level of "common sense" that does not accept Jesus' awareness of his power when someone touched him in the pressing crowd (5:31). Despite their shortcomings, however, they are still "following him" as he returns to his hometown (6:1).

Preceding events determine the response of Jesus' townsfolk, reported in 6:2–3. Following custom, he has the opportunity to teach in the synagogue on the Sabbath, but those who heard him are not drawn to his teaching.[209] They are perplexed (ἐξεπλήσσοντο, v. 2)[210] and they ask a series of questions, all of which presuppose the reader's knowledge of the earlier part of the Gospel.[211] They want to know the source (πόθεν) of Jesus' words and deeds (v. 2c). They wonder about the wisdom that has been given to him (v. 2d), and the mighty works that are done by his hands. The narrative has already answered these questions. The reader knows the source of all that Jesus is and does from the prologue (see 1:1–2, 7–8, 9–11), and has recently encountered the wisdom of Jesus (4:1–34) and his mighty works (4:35–5:43). The kingdom of God is at hand. It is time to repent, and to believe in the gospel (1:14–15). Even the demons (see 1:24; 5:7) have announced that Jesus is the Son of God. For Mark, it is Jesus' relationship with God that authorizes him to speak wisely and to work such wonders. But his own people, who have not read the prologue and who do not have access to the spiritual realm, do not recognize this. They are not prepared to go beyond the limitations of their own domestic experience: they know his mother, his brothers, and his sisters.[212] They live in the same town! Rejecting any possibility that such wise words and wonderful works could have come "from God," they reject Jesus, whose family they meet every day.[213] They thus find it impossible to accept Jesus, and they stumble and

---

209 On the Sabbath practice, see Lane, *Mark,* 200–201.

210 On the negative use of this verb in this context, see Guelich, *Mark,* 308.

211 See Pesch, *Das Markusevangelium,* 1:317–18.

212 See Ernst, *Markus,* 169–70. Important witnesses read "the son of the carpenter" rather than "the carpenter, the son of . . ." For the discussion, see Taylor, *St. Mark,* 300; Guelich, *Mark,* 309–10. The textual problems have been created by the long debate over the "brothers and sisters" of Jesus. This is a sensitive area of debate, as Roman Catholics have developed a tradition that insists that the mother of Jesus remained a virgin after the birth of Jesus. For a good summary, see Ernst, *Markus,* 123–25. Suffice it to say that, although the New Testament evidence most likely points to sibling brothers and sisters (see Hooker, *St. Mark,* 153), this is not the only possible solution. The words used *could* refer to the wider family. For a recent study from a Roman Catholic scholar, see J. P. Meier, "The Brothers and Sisters of Jesus in Ecumenical Perspective," *CBQ* 54 (1992): 1–28. Meier surveys the debate and concludes that Jesus had blood brothers and sisters. Another Catholic scholar, L. Oberlinner (*Historische Überlieferung und christologische Aussage: Zur Frage der "Brüder Jesu" in der Synopse* [FB 19; Stuttgart: Katholisches Bibelwerk, 1975], 149–361), argues that Mark is using pre-Markan traditions that took it for granted that Jesus had siblings. It is not necessary to resolve the problem here in order to understand the Markan theological agenda. But it is important that the various Christian traditions be respected. On the identification of Jesus by a matronymic, see Marcus, *Mark,* 375.

213 See LaVerdiere, *The Beginning,* 1:142.

fall (καὶ ἐσκανδαλίζοντο ἐν αὐτῷ).[214] Jesus' presence to Israel in 1:16–3:6 led to rejection from the leaders of Israel (3:6). In a parallel fashion, his establishment of a new family and his instruction of them by word and deed also meet rejection from his own people.[215]

Jesus' comment upon this rejection, "a prophet is not without honor, except in his hometown, among his own family and in his own home" (6:4), reaches back to a saying of Jesus himself. It is a proverbial saying that may have had its parallels in popular speech (see John 4:44 and the *Gos. Thom.* 31, as well as the parallel in Matt 13:57 and Luke 4:24, which may have come to Luke independently).[216] The original form of the saying may be better rendered in Luke 4:24: "No prophet is acceptable in his own country." Jesus' comment at the end of a section devoted to his new family, nonplussed by the final response of his hometown, has been determined by the Markan agenda. For Mark, Jesus is not only rejected by his own country (see Luke 4:24), but also by his blood family and in his own house.[217] These Markan developments of a traditional proverb round off the earlier treatments of Jesus' rejection by his family in a house (3:20–21), and support his decision to create a new family, not dependent upon the ties of blood or nation (3:31–35).

This rejection leads to Jesus' powerlessness. As Mark has made clear in the miracle stories which formed 4:35–5:43, his wonders are done within a context of faith, even if only incipient or failing.[218] There is no context of faith in his hometown, and he is reduced to performing some healing by means of a laying on of hands. The healing which resulted from his laying on of hands is not necessarily regarded as miraculous. Mark may simply indicate that Jesus had a wholeness of touch that brought peace and healing into the lives of some (6:5b).[219] This interpretation makes sense of v. 5a: "He could do no mighty work there." Jesus has met unfaith among "his own," just as he met rejection and a decision by the leaders of Israel that he must die in 3:6. Mark rounds off this second major section of the mystery of the Messiah (1:14–8:30) with the explicit comment insisting that: "He marveled because of their unbelief" (6:6a).[220] However, "the opposition that God's dominion is suffering does not cancel belief in it but rather testifies to its provocative power."[221]

Conclusion

Jesus' Galilean ministry continues in 3:7–6:6a, but the focus upon the new family of Jesus is unmistakable. After the introductory summary (3:7–12) Jesus has generated a new

---

[214] For this interpretation of ἐσκανδαλίζοντο, see Hooker, *St. Mark*, 153; Marcus, *Mark*, 376; Marshall, *Faith as a Theme*, 192–93.

[215] Lührmann (*Markusevangelium*, 107) draws a parallel with the similar question asked in 1:27, but rightly points out that in 1:27 he was met with lack of understanding, while in 6:2–3 he is rejected. See also Marshall, *Faith as a Theme*, 188–95.

[216] Guelich (*Mark*, 310) calls it "an aphoristic rule of thumb." There are also numerous Greek parallels. See Pesch, *Markusevangelium*, 1:320; Marcus, *Mark*, 376.

[217] See, for example, Gnilka, *Markus*, 1:232; Guelich, *Mark*, 311.

[218] See Gnilka, *Markus*, 1:233; Guelich, *Mark*, 312–13.

[219] This interpretation is not crucial. Some would suggest that the rejection was not total, and thus a few healing miracles were possible. See, for example, Grundmann, *Markus*, 158; Guelich, *Mark*, 312.

[220] Only here in the Gospel of Mark is the verb θαυμάζειν used of Jesus. It highlights the evangelist's concern to show the negative response Jesus receives in his hometown. See Gnilka, *Markus*, 1:233.

[221] Marcus, *Mark*, 380.

family (3:13–19), and provided a new criterion for belonging to that family (3:31–35). He has continued his powerful proclamation of the kingdom in both word (4:1–34) and deed (4:35–5:43). Nature, demons, sickness, and death succumb, but human beings remain ambiguous or hostile. Those most likely to accept him, his blood family and his fellow Jews, either consider him insane (3:20–21), driven by the prince of evil spirits (3:22–30), or of no consequence, because they know his mother, brothers, and sisters (6:1–6a). Faced by this opposition and rejection, Jesus teaches enigmatically, by means of parables, but explains their deeper meaning to his new family, the disciples (4:10–13; 14–20, 33–34), "insiders" specially gifted with the mystery of the kingdom of God (4:11).

Yet the first signs of the disciples' inability to accept Jesus emerge as he tells the parables of the kingdom. He questions their ability to understand the parable of the seed sown (4:13) and he issues a warning, across the collection of parables, that those with ears must hear (see vv. 9, 23, 33). After the miracle of the calming of the sea, where they show that they do not yet understand who Jesus is (4:41), they are present with Jesus at Gerasa (5:1). They may be the ones who make an unfavorable report on his actions to the Gerasenes who ask Jesus to leave their land (5:16).[222] They join with those at the house of Jairus and the professional mourners who regard Jesus' presence as a waste of time (see 5:35) and laugh at him (see 5:40a). Similarly, the disciples mock Jesus when he asks who touched his garment in the milling crowd (5:31).

Like 1:14–3:6, the section devoted to Jesus and his new family (3:7–6:6a) opens with a summary (3:7–12), followed immediately by discipleship material (3:13–19). The narrative episodes that develop the theme of Jesus' new family conclude when the people of Jesus' hometown dismiss him as a person without authority. They know his mother, brothers, and sisters (6:1–6a). Israel has decided against him (3:6), and so have his own people (6:1–6a). Nevertheless, his disciples are still with him, following him, despite their shortcomings (6:1). The question "Who is Jesus?" will come to a climax in the following section. The question will be raised more urgently, and eventually answered, as Jesus challenges his disciples to tell him: "Who do you say that I am?" (6:6b–8:30; see 8:29).

---

[222] This is but a possible interpretation of οἱ ἰδόντες in 5:16.

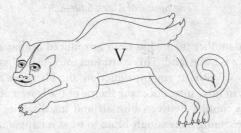

JESUS AND THE DISCIPLES (MARK 6:6B–8:30)

The final section of that part of the Gospel of Mark dedicated to the question of Jesus' identity (1:14–8:30) runs from 6:6b–8:30. As with the earlier sections, it opens with a summary (6:6b; see 1:14–15; 3:7–12), immediately followed by discipleship material (6:7–30; see 1:16–20; 3:13–19). In the ensuing narrative, the disciples play an increasingly important role (see 6:31–32, 35–37, 41; 52, 7:17–23; 8:1–7, 14–21, 27–30), and it is to the disciples that Jesus will direct the question: "Who do you say that I am?" (8:29a). The section closes, as did the earlier sections (see 3:6; 6:1–6a), with a decision: "You are the Christ" (8:29b). But unlike 3:6 and 6:1–6a, a comment from the narrator rounds off the first half of the Gospel: "And he commanded them severely not to speak about him to anyone" (8:30). Peter's confession that Jesus is the Christ, uttered in the name of the disciples, may not be the complete answer and thus is not to be publicly proclaimed. There is a sense of "not yet" about the confession at Caesarea Philippi. There is more to the messiahship of Jesus of Nazareth than the disciples' confession, and it is unveiled in 8:31. Jesus will tell of the oncoming suffering, death, and resurrection of the Son of Man. Jesus may be the Messiah (see 1:1), but he is also the Son of Man (8:31). What that means will be the major theme of 8:31–15:47. As 6:6b–8:30 closes, the reader is prepared for many of the themes and events of the second half of the Gospel. Crucial to the closing section of the first half (1:14–8:30), and increasingly important across the second half of the Gospel of Mark (8:31–15:47), is the fragile relationship between Jesus and the disciples.

The Shape of Mark 6:6b–8:30

The brief summary of 6:6b leads into the mission of the disciples and their return, framing the account of 6:7–30. The highlight of the material which follows is the presence of two bread miracles (6:31–44; 8:1–10) and an apparent series of repeated events which follow the miracles: boat trips (6:45–56; 8:10),[1] conflicts (7:1–23; 8:11–21), and healing miracles (7:24–37; 8:22–26). Food and eating dominate the angry debate between Jesus and Israel in 7:1–23 and the subsequent encounter between Jesus and the Syrophoenician

---

[1] In current literature, much is made of the sea, and the various crossings. See, for example, E. S. Malbon, "The Jesus of Mark and the Sea of Galilee," *JBL* 103 (1984): 363–77, and especially the figures on pp. 365 and 369. See also E. S. Malbon, *Narrative Space and Mythic Meaning in Mark* (New Voices in Biblical Studies; San Francisco: Harper & Row, 1986), 76–79; B. M. F. van Iersel, *Reading Mark* (Collegeville: The Liturgical Press, 1988), 86–92. Many of these suggestions are enlightening (especially the links between 4:35–41; 6:45–52 and 8:14–21; see Malbon, *Narrative Space*, 77–78; van Iersel, *Reading Mark*, 95–98). For Pesch (*Markusevangelium*, 1:349), this linking of the miracles by means of a boat trip belongs to the pre-Markan redaction. On this pre-Markan miracle cycle, see 1:277–81, but see Malbon, "The Jesus of Mark," 370–73.

woman (7:24–30). Yet another theme has been introduced in that sequence: Jesus' movement from Israel into a Gentile land. This continues into 7:31–37 and leads into the feeding of Gentiles in 8:1–9. Without any introduction, the Pharisees return to dispute with Jesus (8:11–13). Jesus, in turn, introduces the theme of the leaven of the Pharisees and the Herodians, leading to conflict between himself and his disciples as he crosses the sea (8:14–21). They are becoming increasingly blind to what is happening around them. They are unable to understand the miracles of the multiplication of the bread, despite their being Jesus' agents in both events (see 6:41; 8:6–7). The theme of blindness is continued into the story of the curing of the blind man at Bethsaida, in stages (8:22–26), leading directly into the questions concerning Jesus' identity, Peter's reply, and Jesus' warning (8:27–30).

But the theme of blindness, first raised in Jesus' accusation of the disciples in 8:18, also opens the door to the first major section of 8:31–15:47. We are able to trace breaks and divisions in the narrative, and the confession at Caesarea Philippi is surely a moment of climax. However, these divisions do not separate one part of the story from another.[2] As the first half of the story comes to a close, the second half is already under way. The curing of the blind man at Bethsaida in 8:22–26 is reprised in the curing of blind Bartimaeus in 10:46–52. Between these two stories of blind men (closely associated with the blindness of the disciples) Jesus will three times tell of the forthcoming passion, death, and resurrection of the Son of Man (8:31; 9:31; 10:32–34). In a deliberate literary "overlap," 8:22–30 concludes 1:14–8:30 and introduces 8:31–15:47.[3] Mark 6:6b–8:30 unfolds as follows:

6:6b   Summary: The ongoing itinerant teaching mission

6:7–30   Disciples
    6:7–13   Jesus associates the Twelve with his mission.
    6:14–29 While they are on their mission, the death of John the Baptist is reported.
    6:30   The Twelve return.

6:31–44   The first multiplication of the loaves and fish—in Israel (the feeding of the five thousand through the ministry of the disciples)

6:45–56   The first sea journey: Contrasting responses to Jesus
    6:45–52 The disciples do not recognize Jesus, who comes to them across the stormy seas, because their hearts are hardened and they have not understood about the loaves.
    6:53–56 On arrival at Gennesaret, the opposite reaction takes place. Unlike the disciples, the people recognize him and he works many miracles.

7:1–23   The first conflict: Jesus and the traditions of Israel
    7:1–13   In a bitter encounter, the Pharisees and the scribes attack Jesus on his lack of observance of purity traditions. He accuses them of rejecting the commandments of God and replacing them with human traditions.

---

[2] This is true of all the so-called "divisions" of the Gospel. For example, H. C. Waetjen (*A Reordering of Power: A Socio-Political Reading of Mark's Gospel* [Minneapolis: Fortress, 1989], 123–31) offers a brief but attractive reading, linking 6:1–6a with 6:6b–56 under the title, "Rejection in Nazareth and the rising need to prepare the disciples for their own ministry in the future." The link between the rejection of Jesus in 6:1–6a and the turn toward the disciples in 6:6b–8:30 is surely intended. On this feature across the Gospel, see J. Dewey, "Mark as Interwoven Tapestry: Forecasts and Echoes for a Listening Audience," *CBQ* 53 (1991): 221–36; E. S. Malbon, "Echoes and Foreshadowings in Mark 4–8: Reading and Rereading," *JBL* 112 (1993): 211–30.

[3] Despite the obvious importance of the confession at Caesarea Philippi, there is little agreement on its role in the unfolding narrative. For some it serves as a climax to the first half of the Gospel, and for others it is already part of a second section, beginning in 8:22. Once one recognizes that 8:22–26 serves to conclude the first half and introduce the second, some of these difficulties are eased.

7:14–15   He instructs "the people" on the importance of what comes out of a person, rather than that which is outside and superficial.

7:17–23   He further instructs his disciples on why this is so.

7:24–37   The first miraculous healing—in Gentile lands

    7:24–30   Jesus grants the request of the Syrophoenician woman in the region of Tyre and Sidon.

    7:31–37   Jesus cures the deaf mute in the land of the Decapolis, and the <u>people respond by suggesting that Jesus might be the Messiah</u> (using Isa 35:5–6).[4]

8:1–9   The second multiplication of the loaves and fish—among the Gentiles (the feeding of the four thousand through the ministry of the disciples)

8:10   The second sea journey—to Dalmanutha

8:11–21   The second conflict: Jesus debates with the Pharisees and the disciples

    8:11–13   The Pharisees appear from nowhere, asking a convalidating sign, but Jesus rejects their pretensions.

    8:14–21   On another boat trip across the sea, the disciples are unable to recognize "the bread" they have with them and have not understood the two bread miracles. They are accused of blindness.

8:22–26   The second miraculous healing: A blind man cured in stages at Bethsaida

8:27–30   Climax: The confession at Caesarea Philippi. The people are totally blind to Jesus' identity, and the disciples have partial sight. They are to say nothing about their partial understanding of Jesus. The rest of the story must be told for fullness of vision.

After the summary (6:6b) and the discipleship material (6:7–30), a cycle of bread miracle, sea journey, conflict stories, and curing miracles is told and retold.[5]

Although the same literary pattern has been followed in 1:14–3:6, 3:7–6:6a, and 6:6b–8:30, the argument develops as the protagonists central to the Gospel of Mark, Jesus

---

[4] In this combination of miracle stories, the word "healing" is used to cover the expulsion of a demon from a distance (7:24–30) and the cure of a deaf-mute (7:31–37).

[5] Following the suggestion of R. H. Lightfoot (*History and Interpretation in the Gospels* [London: Hodder and Stoughton, 1935], 114–17), a number of scholars have traced literary and theological patterns around the repetition of: bread miracles (6:31–34; 8:1–9), sea journeys (6:45–52; 8:10), conflict stories (7:1–23; 8:11–12), and curing miracles (7:32–37; 8:22–26). See also Lane, *Mark,* 269. For a survey, see R. M. Fowler, *Loaves and Fishes* (SBLDS 54; Chico: Scholars Press, 1981), 7–11. Lightfoot's insight continues to influence my reading of 6:31–8:21, but I have modified it somewhat, as his sequence is more governed by form than content. See Grundmann, *Markus,* 138. As Fowler (*Loaves and Fishes,* 10–11) and others have pointed out, one encounters more a sense of repetition than a series of closely related parallels. The boat trip in 8:13–21 is particularly "out of order," but there can be no denying the close link between vv. 11–13 and 14–21, both of which can be regarded as a conflict over the signs which Jesus has performed. P. J. Achtemeier ("Toward the Isolation of Pre-Markan Miracle Catenae," *JBL* 89 [1970]: 265–91, and idem, "The Origin and Function of the Pre-Markan Miracle Catenae," *JBL* 91 [1972]: 198–221) suggests that Mark incorporated a pre-Markan cycle of miracles made up of two catenae (see the summary in Fowler, *Loaves and Fishes,* 24–31). Also, following much contemporary scholarship, I extend the sequence to make a close link between 8:22–26 and the climactic 8:27–30. For a survey, see M. A. Beavis, *Mark's Audience* (JSNTSup 33; Sheffield: Sheffield Academic Press, 1989), 120–22. Attempts to trace "cycles" across this section of the Gospel did not begin with Lightfoot. See the survey covering 1864–1982 (omitting Lightfoot) in G. van Oyen, *The Interpretation of the Feeding Miracles in the Gospel of Mark* (Collectanea biblica et religiosa antiqua 4; Brussels: Wetenschappelijk Comité voor Godsdienstwetenschappen Koninklijke Vlaamse Academie van België voor Wetenschappen en Kunsten, 1999), 1–19.

and the disciples, emerge more clearly. Each section has also led into the next, and this is particularly obvious in 6:6b–8:30, where 8:22–26 is to be linked with 10:46–52, framing the three passion predictions in a section which will be dedicated to the instruction of the disciples as they follow Jesus down his "way" to Jerusalem.

Summary (6:6b)

The reader has already encountered major summary statements in 1:14–15 and 3:7–12, which opened subsections of the first half of the Gospel (1:1–8:30). The summary statement of 6:6b opens a further subsection. It succinctly describes Jesus' commitment to the ongoing task of teaching, moving from village to village. A passage from earlier in the story comes to mind: "Let us go on to the next towns, that I may preach there also; for that is why I came out" (1:38). For all its brevity, the statement of 6:6b indicates that Jesus remains committed to the purpose for his "coming out." Besides serving as a textual marker (a summary statement followed immediately by discipleship material), 6:6b functions within its own immediate context: it associates Jesus' mission with his sending out the Twelve on a parallel mission (6:7–13).[6]

Disciples (6:7–30)

The majority of commentators do not see Mark 6:6b–30 as a Markan sandwich construction. Many link v. 30 with the bread miracle that follows in vv. 31–44.[7] Others see it as a part of a bridge passage from the account of the death of the Baptist into the bread miracle.[8] Some who link v. 30 with vv. 6b–13 understand οἱ ἀπόστολοι as a title of honor, a rare use of this expression outside Luke-Acts and the Pauline Letters.[9] A closer analysis of the link between vv. 6b–13 and v. 30 indicates that this description of the disciples as "apostles," the only place outside Luke-Acts and the Pauline literature where such a description is to be found, is primarily an indication of the intercalation created by vv. 6b–16 and v. 30.

After the summary statement of 6:6b, the narrator reports: "And he called to him the Twelve, and began to send them out two by two" (v. 7a). The remainder of v. 7 recalls the earlier association of the Twelve with Jesus in 3:13–14. In vv. 8–9 the narrator continues to report explicit instructions on what they are to take on the mission. Verses 10–11 are

---

[6] Most would accept that v. 6b leads into the association of the disciples with the mission of Jesus. But Lagrange (*Saint Marc*, 143–44), K. Stock (*Boten aus dem Mit-Ihm-Sein: Das Verhältnis zwischen Jesus und den Zwölf nach Markus* [AnBib 70; Rome: Biblical Institute Press, 1975], 83), and Guelich (*Mark*, 313–14) associate 6a and 6b as the final verse in the unit of 6:1–6.

[7] See, for example, Lagrange, *Saint Marc*, 158–59; B. H. Branscomb, *The Gospel of Mark* (MNTC; London: Hodder & Stoughton, 1937), 111–12; Nineham, *St. Mark*, 182; Lohmeyer, *Markus*, 122–23; Anderson, *Mark*, 170–71; Pesch, *Markusevangelium*, 1:345; Gnilka, *Markus*, 1:254–55; Guelich, *Mark*, 336. The awkwardness of this decision can be seen in the comment of Lührmann (*Markusevangelium*, 118): "With v. 30 Mark himself picks up the pen of the narrator of 6b–13 and carries on with his story."

[8] See, for example, Taylor, *St. Mark*, 318–20; Schweizer, *Mark*, 131–32; Lane, *Mark*, 223–36; Hooker, *St. Mark*, 162; Stock, *Boten aus dem Mit-Ihm-Sein*, 97.

[9] See Stock, *Boten aus dem Mit-Ihm-Sein*, 98–99; Ernst, *Markus*, 186–88; Painter, *Mark's Gospel*, 103–4; Hooker, *St. Mark*, 162. LaVerdiere (*The Beginning*, 1:169) comments: "It has already become traditional among early Christians." This is hardly the evidence of Mark, Matthew, and John.

marked by a change from the narrator's report to the direct speech of Jesus. He gives instructions on how they are to behave in a concrete missionary situation.[10] In vv. 12–13 the narrator's voice returns to report the success of those who were sent out in v. 7. These remarks open with, "So they went out" (v. 12a). No longer "with Jesus" (see 3:14), they scatter to do the things that Jesus has done (6:12b–13). The section on the death of the Baptist is then inserted (vv. 14–29). In v. 30, themes from the beginning and the end of vv. 7–13 return. Both passages are from the narrator and, most likely, indicate Markan redaction. The "going out" is reversed as the narrator tells the reader that they "returned." Indeed, they do not simply return, but come back to gather around Jesus again (see 3:14). Jesus' action of "sending out" (ἀποστέλλειν, v. 7a) is recalled as those who return are described as the "sent ones" (οἱ ἀπόστολοι, v. 30). There is no need to associate the use of οἱ ἀπόστολοι here with its widespread occurrence as an honorific title in Luke-Acts and Paul. In the light of the rest of the Gospel of Mark, the word cannot bear the weight of such dignity.[11] The Twelve are called ἀπόστολοι (v. 30) simply because they were the ones whom Jesus began to send out (ἤρξαντο ἀποστέλλειν, v. 7a). It is an appropriate noun to use as the storyteller refers back, in v. 30, to recall the beginning of his "sandwich" in vv. 7–13.[12]

An initial suggestion concerning the literary structure of Mark 6:6b–30 can now be proposed:

6:6a–13   The disciples are associated with the mission of Jesus as they are "sent out." They are scattered as they go, two by two, to their successful missionary activity.

6:14–29   John the Baptist dies.

6:30   Those "sent out" return to make their report to Jesus. They "gather" and tell Jesus what they have said and done.[13]

Key words state Jesus' initiative in sending out disciples (v. 7a) so that they might do what he has done thus far in the story, and their scattering (v. 12a) to perform this mission (v. 7a: sending out; v. 12a: they went out). The sending out and the scattering frame vv. 7–13. The "coming back" of "those sent out" opens v. 30, a deliberate reprise of vv. 7–13.

But how does 6:30 relate to 6:31? My suggestion—that v. 30 concludes vv. 6b–29 as the final statement in a sandwich construction—does not mean that v. 30 is entirely unrelated to v. 31. In a good narrative one episode is not rigidly separated from another. Clearly,

---

[10] This change of literary form, from a narrator's report to Jesus' direct speech, is a hint that vv. 6a–13 is composite, formed by pre-Markan traditions (vv. 8–9), material from the earliest missionary experiences (vv. 10–11), and the redactional hand of the evangelist (vv. 6a, 7, 12–13).

[11] See the succinct but accurate survey by J.-A. Bühner in his two articles, "ἀποστέλλω" and "ἀπόστολος," *EDNT*, 1:141–46.

[12] See also Schweizer, *Mark,* 125; Taylor, *St. Mark,* 319; Anderson, *Mark,* 171; Marcus, *Mark,* 385.

[13] Although not common in the commentaries, scholars who have focused attention upon Markan intercalations regularly see 6:6b–30 as an example of this technique. See, for example, J. R. Donahue, *Are You the Christ? The Trial Narrative in the Gospel of Mark* (SBLDS 10; Missoula: Society of Biblical Literature, 1973), 59; H. C. Kee, *Community of the New Age: Studies in Mark's Gospel* (Philadelphia: Westminster, 1977), 54; F. Kermode, *The Genesis of Secrecy: On the Interpretation of Narrative* (Cambridge: Harvard University Press, 1969), 128–31; Fowler, *Loaves and Fishes,* 114–32; J. R. Edwards, "Markan Sandwiches: The Significance of Interpolations in Markan Narratives," *NovT* 31 (1989): 198, 205–6; T. Shepherd, "The Narrative Function of Markan Intercalation," *NTS* 41 (1995): 530–31, 534–35, 539. See also F. J. Moloney, "Mark 6:6b–30: Mission, the Baptist, and Failure," *CBQ* 63 (2001): 663–79. In a most unlikely division of the material, Cranfield (*St. Mark,* 123, 204) makes a major division between 6:13 (closing a section running from 3:7–6:13: "Later Stages of the Galilean Ministry") and 6:14 (opening a section running from 6:14–8:26: "Jesus goes outside Galilee").

there is a relationship between v. 30 and v. 31. It is to "the Twelve" of v. 30 (see v. 7) that Jesus addresses the words of v. 31. As we shall see, a new theme is introduced in v. 31. The storyteller prepares for a new moment in the story by Jesus' request that the disciples come away so that they might be alone (v. 31a). It is a brief calm before the storm, but the trigger for what follows in the narrative is found in 6:31b: "For many were coming and going, and they had no leisure even to eat." There is very little resting in a lonely place (v. 31a) in the Gospel of Mark! The "coming and going" of great crowds (see 6:33–34, 44, 54–56; 8:1–4) and the theme of "eating" (see 6: 36–44; 7:2–5, 14–15, 18–20, 26–28; 8:1–10, 14–21), intro-duced in 6:31b, will dominate 6:33–8:21.[14]

Jesus associates the Twelve with his mission (6:7–13)

The summary statement in 6:6b may have been in the pre-Markan tradition, but its present setting comes directly from Mark's hand.[15] It indicates his careful insertion of this part of the narrative into a larger literary design. His hand is also present in the close asso-ciation of what follows (vv. 7–13) with v. 6b by means of the regular use of καί. Each state-ment, either from the narrator or from Jesus himself, is linked to what went before by means of "and." The Markan "paratactic καί"[16] appears no less than seven times in seven verses. However inelegant, it makes clear that what is said and done to the disciples in 6:7–13 associates them with Jesus' own ongoing mission, succinctly described in 6:6b. We are dealing with a deliberate Markan literary construction, elements of which may have had different origins before they were placed side by side in the Gospel of Mark.[17] There are three constituent elements in 6:7–13:

6:7–9	The giving of authority and the external signs of the missionary are reported. Much of v. 7 could be from the hand of Mark, but the rest of the passage came to Mark from earlier traditions.
6:10–11	Jesus instructs the Twelve on the behavior of the missionary in a concrete situa-tion. The experience of early Christian missionaries is reflected in this passage.
6:12–13	A report from the narrator, largely composed by the evangelist, closes the passage, telling of the success of the mission of the Twelve.

Each of these sections has its importance, and their connection by the Markan paratactic καί indicates that they are to be understood as a unified message on the mission of the disciples.

---

[14] It is widely recognized that the reports of the feeding of the milling crowds in the two bread miracles (6:31–44 and 8:1–10, with its aftermath in 8:11–21) serve as "bookends" around disputes which have much to do with the theme of "eating" in 7:1–23. The miracle of 7:24–30 continues the theme of "eating" but introduces a new theme, further developed in 7:31–37. The first half of the Gospel (1:14–8:30) asks, "Who is Jesus?" and 7:24–37 serves to introduce the Gentile world into this discussion. See the suggestions of Fowler, *Loaves and Fishes,* 91–147, especially pp. 116–19.

[15] See Pesch, *Markusevangelium,* 1:325–26. For a survey of possible relationships between tradi-tion and Markan activity in 6:6b–13, 30, see E. Best, *Following Jesus: Discipleship in the Gospel of Mark* (JSNTSup 4; Sheffield: JSOT Press, 1981), 190–93; idem, *The Temptation and the Passion: The Markan Soteriology* (2d ed.; SNTSMS 2; Cambridge: Cambridge University Press, 1990), 75–76; Lohmeyer, *Markus,* 113. I regard vv. 6b, 7, and 12 as Markan, with redactional touches in other verses. See Gnilka, *Markus,* 1:236–38. For a summary and critique of attempts to reconstruct a pre-Markan source, see Fowler, *Loaves and Fishes,* 1–42.

[16] BDF, 239, par. 458. On Mark's use of parataxis, see R. M. Fowler, *Let the Reader Understand: Reader-Response Criticism and the Gospel of Mark* (Minneapolis: Fortress, 1991), 134–40.

[17] See Ernst, *Markus,* 174.

Instructions for missionaries parallel to those of Mark 6:8–9 are found in Q (see Matt 10:8–10; Luke 10:4).[18] Such instructions were already a part of Christian tradition, reproduced in different contexts by Mark, on the one hand, and by Matthew and Luke (Q) on the other. Scholars regularly point to the instructions—no bread, no bag, no money, and only one tunic[19]—as a deliberate attempt on the part of the early Christian missionaries to separate themselves from the wandering Cynic preachers who were allowed such trappings.[20] But crucial for the Markan context is Jesus' giving authority to the Twelve over the unclean spirits (v. 7).[21] Such authority, up to this point of the narrative, belonged only to Jesus (see 1:27). It was earlier promised to the Twelve, appointed to be with him (3:14) "to have authority to cast out demons" (3:15). Promise becomes reality as the disciples are formally given a share in the authority of Jesus over the demons.

What Mark contributes to the tradition of the sending out of the missionaries is the indication of their sharing in the mission of Jesus. This becomes clear when one looks back to the establishment of the Twelve in 3:14–15. The intimate association of the Twelve "with Jesus" is what authorizes them to do what, up to this point in the story, only Jesus has done. Jesus is the one who was sent out to preach (see 1:14–15, 27, 38–39; 2:2, 13) and to have authority over demons (see 1:21–28, 32–34, 39; 3:11–12). The Twelve are promised a share in this mission in 3:14–15, and in 6:7–9 they are authoritatively commissioned to begin this activity.[22] The fundamental element, however, in the Twelve's sharing in the mission of Jesus is that they "be with him . . . so that they might . . ." (3:14–15). Grammatically (and theologically), their being sent out to preach and their having authority over demons in 3:14b–15 depends upon the ὦσιν μετ' αὐτοῦ of 3:14a.[23]

The reader of Mark 6:7–9 recalls the crucial relationship between the "being with" Jesus and the participation in the mission of Jesus, programmatically spelled out in the appointment of the Twelve in 3:14–15. One could state the Markan affirmation as follows: associated with Jesus the Twelve have authority to preach and cast out demons, but separated from Jesus all such authority will cease. It no longer has its source in the relationship initiated and established by Jesus. The sense of Mark 3:14–15 has been accurately translated into the Johannine Jesus' remark to the disciples in John 15:5: "Without me you can do nothing." *He* appointed the Twelve (3:14), *he* calls them (6:7a), *he* began to send them out (v. 7b), and *he* charged them (v. 8a). The initiative of Jesus can be traced even in his sending them out two by two (v. 7b). This command recalls the familiar Old Testament legislation concerning witness (see Deut 17:6; 19:15) and reflects early Christian practice (see, for example, Paul and Barnabas, Peter and John, in Acts). It also looks back to Mark 1:16–20 where Jesus called the first disciples in pairs (v. 16: Simon and Andrew; v. 19:

---

[18] See the discussion in Lührmann, *Markusevangelium,* 108–9, and the helpful synoptic chart in Marcus, *Mark,* 386–87.

[19] Lagrange (*Saint Marc,* 146–47) insists that two tunics were a sure sign of excessive wealth. One tunic was all that was necessary, given the urgency of the situation. A second tunic may also have served as a temporary shelter for the wandering preacher. See Lührmann, *Markusevangelium,* 111.

[20] See Pesch, *Markusevangelium,* 2:326–28; Guelich, *Mark,* 324; Marcus, *Mark,* 383–84.

[21] A Matthean version of this passage is found in Matt 10:1, where it is used as the opening of Jesus' missionary discourse (10:1–11:1). It picks up on earlier uses of this passage in Matthew (see 4:23–24; 9:35). In Matthew it is not immediately connected with the sending of the Twelve in 10:5–10. There is no parallel in Luke.

[22] The importance of the link is seen by Lührmann, *Markusevangelium,* 110.

[23] On this, see the important study of Stock, *Boten aus dem Mit-Ihm-Sein.* On 3:14–15, see pp. 15–27.

[handwritten: Curly by two's. Sent out by two's.]

James and John), and indicates the authoritative nature of the missionaries' representation of Jesus.[24]

In the light of this background, the traditional sayings commanding the missionary to go without bread, bag, money, and a second tunic may insinuate a further Markan message. This becomes even more likely when one considers that only in the Markan version of this saying are the Twelve *permitted* to take a staff and to wear sandals (6:8–9; contrast Matt 10:10; Luke 10:4). One of the features of the Markan narrative is the presentation of Jesus as a preacher and a miracle worker who is forever on a journey. Until such time as Jesus arrives in Jerusalem, almost every pericope begins with a verb of motion (see 1:12, 14, 16, 19, 21, 29, 35; 2:1, 13, etc.). When these verbs of motion are read in conjunction with the regular Markan use of the breathless adverb εὐθύς, the reader receives the impression of an unconditional response to a divine urgency which marks a charismatic wanderer. The staff and the sandals are symbols of this lifestyle, and the disciples, devoid of all other necessities, are permitted to join Jesus in his missionary journey.[25] This is a creative use of tradition that also gives theological weight to the command that the disciples take no necessities. The resource of their commission is their dependence upon Jesus (3:13–14), their being "followers" of Jesus (1:16–20), joining him in a journey in response to God. There may have been an attempt to differentiate Christian missionaries from wandering Cynics in pre-Markan tradition. But in 6:7–9 Jesus authorizes the Twelve to join his missionary journey, and thus they have the signs of a person on such a journey. Their taking nothing else is a further sign: they depend totally upon him. "Messengers are not to be believed if they rely upon their own resources (material or spiritual) rather than on the One whom they proclaim."[26]

The Twelve are commissioned to associate themselves with the mission of Jesus. A further essential component to the mission of the Twelve is apparent to the reader in the light of earlier parts of the narrative. Disciples have been chosen by Jesus (see 1:16–20; 2:13–14; 3:13) and from among them, Jesus has further "instituted" the Twelve (ἐποίησεν δώδεκα, 3:14). The disciples, and thus also the Twelve, are to be followers of Jesus (1:16–20; 2:13–14). They are intimately associated with him (3:14) and it is from this intimate association that their mission flows (3:14b–15). Thus, the Twelve are missionaries of Jesus only insofar as they respond to the initiative of Jesus, remain with him, recognize that their authority to preach and cast out demons is from him. They remain at all times "followers" of Jesus.

---

[24] See J. Jeremias, "Paarweise Sendung im Neuen Testament," in *New Testament Essays: Studies in Memory of Thomas Walter Manson 1893–1958* (ed. A. J. B. Higgins; Manchester: Manchester University Press, 1959), 136–38. For a detailed collection of this and further material on the need for two or three witnesses, see Stock, *Boten aus dem Mit-Ihm-Sein,* 86–87. Lohmeyer (*Markus,* 113) suggests that it might come from Eccl 4:9: "Two are better than one, because they have a good reward for their toil."

[25] For Pesch (*Markusevangelium,* 1:328–29), the exception in Mark is explained by the antiquity of the tradition. It takes into account the rough and dusty nature of Palestine, the original setting of the Christian mission. See the similar remark in Hooker, *St. Mark,* 156. I would regard the Q tradition as more original, and thus see a Markan theological point of view emerging here. LaVerdiere (*The Beginning,* 1:154–56) associates the staff and the sandals with Exod 12:11, and comments: "Their Christian journey would be a new exodus, a personal passage from slavery to freedom" (p. 155). See also Marcus, *Mark,* 388–90.

[26] Schweizer, *Mark,* 130. See also Lagrange, *Saint Marc,* 145. Lohmeyer (*Markus,* 114) rightly comments: "It is a question of the Twelve with God's authority and in God's place."

The instructions on the behavior of the missionaries in any given situation reflect the experience of the earliest missionary activity of the Christian communities.[27] The literary form changes from report (vv. 7–9) to direct speech (vv. 10–11).[28] There are parallel instructions in Matt 10:11–15 and Luke 10:5–12, which may each reflect an independent tradition (M and L).[29] Mark is using a tradition that came to him from the setting of early Christian missionary practice. All three Synoptic Gospels, when they come to deal with the question of mission, place these instructions in the mouth of Jesus to establish principles to guide wandering missioners. Two basic points are made, one a warning and the other a recognition of the importance of the task of the missioner, associated with the spreading of the kingdom of God.

There may have been difficulties in the early missionary activity of the Christian communities. As well as the evidence in the three synoptic passages just mentioned, there are clear warnings in *Didache* 11:1–12. Missioners were to stay in the first house that offered them accommodation. To arrive in a village, begin preaching the gospel, but then be seen to move from house to house—perhaps in pursuit of better lodgings or more congenial company—would make a lie of the gospel the missionary was preaching.[30] Thus, Jesus warns: "When you enter a house, stay there until you leave the place" (v. 10; see also *Did.* 11:3–6). It is on Jesus' authority that missioners are now warned that they must live the gospel they claim to preach. This is an early Christian recommendation to put one's life where one's words are.

Jesus' second recommendation is linked to a practice reported in later Jewish literature. The Lukan redaction of this instruction shows that there was need for further explanation for this practice to make sense in a Gentile setting, once it was removed from an audience familiar with Jewish practices (see Luke 10:10–11).[31] The shaking off the dust from the feet comes from the belief that Israel was God's "holy land." Returning from the impure lands that surrounded Israel, travelers would shake the dust from their feet. This gesture indicated the impurity and godlessness of the land they had just left, and the holiness of the land they were entering (see *m. 'Ohal.* 2:3; *m. Tehar.* 4:5; *b. Šabb.* 15b). Within the early Christian mission this gesture takes on an eschatological significance. That place which did not receive the missioner, or would not hear the proclamation of the gospel, was to be judged as "godless" by means of a symbolic shaking of the dust from the feet of the missionary.[32] In a symbolic sense, they no longer belong to God's chosen people. This was to be a sign, a witness (v. 11) against all who rejected the opportunity offered by the Christian message.[33]

---

[27] This should be said for the whole of vv. 7–13 (see Pesch, *Markusevangelium,* 1:325–26), but it is particularly clear in vv. 10–11. The commentary of Marcus (*Mark,* 385–91) devotes particular attention to vv. 7–13 as instructions for a post-Easter community. See also Lührmann, *Markusevangelium,* 110–12.

[28] See Pesch, *Markusevangelium,* 1:326.

[29] On the difficulty of being certain over the nature of the history and the relationships of the traditions in vv. 7–13, see Stock, *Boten aus dem Mit-Ihm-Sein,* 95–96; Pesch, *Markusevangelium,* 1:325–26.

[30] See Schweizer, *Mark,* 130.

[31] See Pesch, *Markusevangelium,* 1:330.

[32] The verb δέχομαι (to receive) is a technical term, used to indicate the reception of the missionary and her or his message (see 9:37; 10:15). Marcus (*Mark,* 384) claims that the Jewish evidence (and he adds Neh 5:13 and Acts 18:6) of shaking the dust from one's person is a symbolic indication of desire to break communion.

[33] There is a possible link between the sending out "two by two" in v. 7 and the need for two witnesses to act appropriately in v. 11.

The missionaries were to put their lives where their words were, and proclaim the gospel in both word and deed (v. 10). Thus they had authority to indicate to that place which rejected the missionaries and their message the judgment they brought upon themselves (v. 11).[34] As with vv. 7–9, however, it is not the missioner who is rejected. They are only "witnesses" to the message.[35] Although not as obviously linked to the earlier Markan passages on the choosing of disciples (1:16–20; 2:13–17; 3:13) and the sending of the Twelve (3:14–15), it is as *emissaries of Jesus* that the missioners have authority to proclaim judgment. Despite its origins in the missionary practice of the early church, the Markan paratactic καί links 6:10–11 with 6:7–9 and the more obvious connections found there with 3:14–15. The missionaries have authority because of their "being with him" (3:14).

The concluding report of the immediate and apparently universal success of the mission does not present great exegetical difficulties. What Jesus said *would* happen *does* happen (6:12–13). This is not surprising. But in v. 7 they were given authority over the unclean spirits. In vv. 12–13a, as well as casting out demons they also preach conversion. Again 3:14–15 is formative of this passage. As the Twelve were appointed they were promised authority to preach and to cast out demons (3:14b–15), flowing from their "being with him" (3:14a). However, the nature of their preaching is further specified in 6:12. They "preach that people should convert." This preaching of conversion reaches even more deeply into an association with the mission of Jesus. His entire ministry was placed under the rubric of preaching conversion in the opening summary of 1:14–15.

The healing of the sick is a further association of the missionary activity of the Twelve with the ministry of Jesus up to this point in the narrative (see 1:29–31, 34, 40–45; 2:1–12; 3:1–6, 10; 5:25–34; 6:5). The link between the successful mission of the disciples and their healing many of the sick (v. 13), reported in such close literary proximity to Jesus' failed mission in his own town (6:1–6a), where all he could do was heal a few of the sick (6:5), is ironic. In terms of the unfolding argument of the narrative, the new family of Jesus (see 3:34–35) takes over and expands the mission of Jesus beyond the boundaries imposed upon him by those who could not transcend the limitations of his human origins (see 6:2). The practice of anointing with oil was widespread in the Hellenistic world, and by the time of the writing of the Gospel of Mark had probably become part of Christian practice (see especially Luke 10:34; James 5:14).[36]

Much of what was said in conclusion to the analysis of 6:7–9 returns here. The Twelve are commissioned to associate themselves with the mission of Jesus. That was already very apparent in vv. 7–9, but it has been further reinforced by means of the instruction on the authority of the missioners in v. 11, and especially in the deepening of the relationship between the mission of the Twelve and that of Jesus in vv. 12–13. Indeed, they are more successful than Jesus had been in the immediately previous scene: Jesus in his hometown (6:1–6a). Earlier parts of the narrative continue to act as intertext to the reading experience. Disciples have been chosen by Jesus (see 1:16–20; 2:13–14; 3:13) and from among them Jesus has further "instituted" the Twelve (3:14). The disciples, and thus also the Twelve, are to be followers of Jesus (1:16–20; 2:13–14). They are intimately associated with

---

[34] Hooker (*St. Mark*, 157) makes an interesting link with the rejection of Jesus by his townsfolk in 6:1–6a: "These words indicate the urgency of the situation. Jesus' words read ominously, coming so soon after the story of his own rejection in his home town."

[35] See Gnilka (*Markus*, 1:240): "The rejection of the messengers is the rejection of the message."

[36] For a full discussion of this issue, see L. T. Johnson, *The Letter of James* (AB 37a; New York: Doubleday, 1995), 330–32.

him (3:14) and it is from this intimate association that their mission flows (3:14b–15). Like Jesus, they go out, preach conversion (6:12; 1:14–15), drive out demons, and heal the sick (6:13; 6:5). The conclusion to 6:7–9 can be restated: the Twelve are missionaries of Jesus only insofar as they respond to the initiative of Jesus, remain with him, recognize that their authority to preach conversion, to cast out demons, and to heal the sick is from him. They remain at all times "followers" of Jesus. Without him, they can do nothing (see 3:14–15; see also John 15:5).[37]

The death of John the Baptist (6:14–29)

Morna Hooker has accurately described majority opinion about the location of this passage in the Gospel of Mark:

> Between the account of the sending out of the Twelve and that of their return, Mark inserts an account of Herod's reaction to the rumours about Jesus, together with the story of his beheading of John the Baptist.[38] There seems no logical connection between the two themes, but the somewhat artificial insertion provides an interlude for the disciples to complete their mission.[39]

But the framing of 6:14–29 with vv. 6b–13 and v. 30 provides a very "logical" sequence to the two themes. Indeed, the death of John the Baptist (vv. 17–29), prefaced by a brief discussion over Jesus (vv. 14–16), serves as the central section of the "sandwich," providing meaning to the flanking passages on the sending out and the return of the Twelve.

There are two parts to the report on the death of the Baptist.[40] Herod's concerns over Jesus are reported in 6:14–16. This passage is christological, but the figure of John the Baptist is entwined with Herod's assessment of Jesus at every turn. The first reason given for the increasing fame of Jesus is the suggestion on the part of "some" that John the Baptist has been raised from the dead (v. 14).[41] The resurrection of John the Baptist may point to an expected eschatological prophet, and Jesus, John the Baptist *redivivus,* would thus be

---

[37] See especially Stock, *Boten aus dem Mit-Ihm-Sein,* 82–97.

[38] The Herod in question is Herod Antipas, who was the tetrarch over Galilee and Perea (east of the Jordan) from 4 B.C.E. until 39 C.E. It is not correct to call him a "king," but that may be Markan irony, as Marcus (*Mark,* 392, 398–99) suggests.

[39] Hooker, *St. Mark,* 158. Compare Pesch (*Markusevangelium,* 1:344): "The position between the sending of the Twelve (6:7–13) and their return (6:30) recommended itself as a more favorable location." The theological and literary questions are well summed up by LaVerdiere (*The Beginning,* 1:153): "Our biggest challenge is to see how Jesus' identity and John's death and burial are related to the mission of the twelve." Edwards ("Markan Sandwiches," 206 n. 37) rightly points to the further need to relate "the Baptist's martyrdom to the twelve as well as to Jesus' impending crucifixion."

[40] Pesch (*Markusevangelium,* 1:332, 338–40) suggests that 6:14–16 had been added to the non-Christian folkloric tale of vv. 17–29 prior to Mark. This accounts for the presence of the passage in the Gospel. The link between vv. 14–15 and 8:28 is clear. See Gnilka, *Markus,* 1:244–45. Pesch further claims that vv. 17–29 is a mixture of traditions of Jewish martyrdom and oriental dinner-parties, influenced by the Book of Esther. See also J. P. Meier (*A Marginal Jew: Rethinking the Historical Jesus* [3 vols.; ABRL; New York: Doubleday, 1991–2001], 2:173–74) and Marcus (*Mark,* 401–2) for further biblical and nonbiblical background. On the possible history of the tradition, see Gnilka, *Markus,* 1:244–47.

[41] There is strong textual support for the singular form of the verb here: "and he (Herod) said" (ἔλεγεν). However, the plural (ἔλεγον) is to be retained. The singular was probably transferred from the report of Herod's opinion in v. 16. See Painter, *Mark's Gospel,* 100. In support of the singular, but translating it as "Und man sagte," see Pesch, *Markusevangelium,* 1:333. See also Lagrange, *Saint Marc,* 149 ("on disait").

the prophet of the end time, possessing great powers (v. 14).[42] Perhaps there is no need to make such a dramatic link between John the Baptist and Jesus. As Hooker remarks, "It is not clear what is meant by the suggestion that John the Baptizer has been raised from the dead; if such a rumor ever circulated, then the idea of an individual being raised was not incredible in popular imagination."[43] The opinion expressed in v. 14 may be as simple as that. Thus it may not be very different from the opinion of "others" who suggest that Jesus is one or another of the several expected prophetic forerunners to the messianic era: Elijah (see Mal 4:5–6), or one of the prophets from of old (with possible links to Deut 18:18?),[44] found in v. 15. The reader, instructed by the prologue (1:1–13) and the narrative to this point, knows that all suggestions miss the point, but the question "Who is Jesus?" continues to be raised by the characters in the story.

Herod decides that Jesus must be the risen John the Baptist, whom he beheaded (6:16). These words from Herod ("John, whom I beheaded") allow Mark to pick up the tale of John's martyrdom, reporting it in a lengthy flashback in vv. 17–29. For the reader, the issue has been raised of the relationship between John the Baptist and Jesus, and with it the awareness that as the Baptist went to death, so also must Jesus.[45] There are important differences between the reports we have of John the Baptist's death in the Gospels (basically Mark 6:17–29, repeated in an abbreviated form by Matt 14:3–12 and pared down to a brief statement in Luke 3:19–20) and in Josephus (*Ant.* 18.116–119): This is not the place to discuss the differences,[46] and Mark has made some glaring errors of fact.[47] It is helpful

---

[42] The reference to resurrection and the possession of great powers (v. 14) has led K. Berger and R. Pesch to identify Jesus as the expected eschatological prophet who would rise from the dead and be a miracle worker. See K. Berger, *Die Auferstehung des Propheten und die Erhöhung des Menschensohnes: Traditionsgeschichtliche Untersuchungen zur Deutung des Geschickes Jesu in frühchristlichen Texten* (SUNT; Göttingen: Vandenhoeck & Ruprecht, 1976). For its application to this context, see Pesch, *Markusevangelium*, 1:333–37. But see Meier's bald assessment: "There seems to have been no idea in pre-Christian Judaism about Elijah returning to prepare the way for a messiah" (*A Marginal Jew*, 2:226).

[43] Hooker, *St. Mark*, 159. In 9:11–13, however, Jesus is again linked with John the Baptist. In an interesting suggestion, L. T. Johnson (*Religious Experience in Earliest Christianity* [Minneapolis: Fortress, 1998], 77–78) suggests that v. 14 reflects beliefs associated with necromancy: "Was it possible that the beheaded John the Baptist was more powerfully at work in this man whom he had baptized?" (p. 78). See also Marcus (*Mark*, 393) with reference to Morton Smith.

[44] There may be no contact between Deut 18:18, where YHWH promises to raise up a prophet like Moses, and "the prophets of old" in v. 6. The simplest interpretation is that many regard Jesus as belonging to the line of Israel's great prophets. See Lohmeyer, *Markus*, 116–17; Gnilka, *Markus*, 1:249.

[45] See LaVerdiere (*The Beginning*, 1:156–68) for a stimulating presentation of the narrative as a "historical parable." Drawing upon R. Aus (*Water into Wine and the Beheading of John the Baptist: Early Jewish-Christian Interpretation of Esther 1 in John 2:1–11 and Mark 6:17–29* [BJS 150; Atlanta: Scholars Press, 1988], 39–74), LaVerdiere concludes, "With a brilliant interplay between history and literature, between the death of John the Baptist and the book of Esther together with its ancient rabbinical traditions and commentaries, the story pointed repeatedly to the passion of Jesus."

[46] For discussions, see Meier, *A Marginal Jew*, 2:56–62; Marcus, *Mark*, 394–96, 399–400. See further, H. W. Hoehner, *Herod Antipas: A Contemporary of Jesus Christ* (Grand Rapids: Zondervan, 1980), 110–72.

[47] It was incorrect to call Herod Antipas a "king," and Philip was not married to Herodias, but to her daughter, Salome. Herodias had previously been married to a half-brother of Antipas, known simply as Herod. See the simplified Herodian family tree in Marcus (*Mark*, 394). Herod was in no position to be offering half his kingdom, and it was most improbable that a royal daughter would dance at a celebratory meal. Women were often introduced after such feasts, but not royal daughters. See Meier, *A Marginal Jew*, 2:172. Marcus (*Mark*, 402–3) highlights the evil nature of the two women, and further points to the strategic location of these two "daringly evil female figures," set

to be aware that, for Josephus, Herod killed the Baptist because he was afraid of a rebellion by the people. This enables us to see the Markan theological focus more clearly.[48] The christological issues raised in vv. 14–16 lie hidden underneath the folkloric narrative of vv. 17–29.[49] For Mark, John the Baptist is put to death by a ruler who recognized that he was "a righteous and holy man" (v. 20; see also v. 26), but who succumbed to public pressure (see vv. 22–26). The Baptist would not give in weakly to pressure, even from one who recognized his virtues. He stood by his God-given task, preaching repentance and forgiveness of sins (see 1:4). For Mark, John's judgment of Herod's marriage is a public call that sinfulness be recognized (see 6:17–19).[50]

There is much in this Markan version of the story, the only episode in the Gospel that does not have Jesus at its center, which points forward to Jesus' death. He too is put to death by a ruler who recognizes his goodness (see 15:9–10, 12, 14) but who succumbs to public pressure (see 15:10. 14–15). Herod's venal lifestyle and self-indulgence leads to the slaying of a prophet who proclaims the truth.[51] Jesus does not give in to public pressure, not even to save his life, but boldly announces the present and future coming of God as king (see 14:58, 60–62), which would flow from his self-gift unto death (see 8:31; 9:31; 10:33–34). Yet there is a difference between John and Jesus. After the slaying and the ghoulish presentation of the head upon a dish (6:27–28), Mark's account of John the Baptist's death closes as his body is taken by his disciples and laid in a tomb (v. 29). According to vv. 14–16, rumors of the resurrection of the Baptist are in the air, but they are only rumors. The Christian community reading this story is told that the Baptist was buried (v. 29), but believes that Jesus has been slain, buried, and has been raised from the dead (see 16:1–8).[52] A further difference emerges. John the Baptist is buried by his loyal disciples, but Jesus, abandoned by his disciples (see 14:50), is buried by a member of the council, Joseph of Arimathea, who should have been his enemy (see 15:43–46).[53]

Mark uses his traditions concerning the death of John the Baptist for at least two reasons. John the Baptist is the messenger of God (see 1:2–3), the one who announces Jesus (1:7–8). He has an unswerving commitment to his God-given mission: to preach a baptism of repentance for the forgiveness of sins (1:4). It has cost him his life (6:17–29).

---

between the two "daringly positive female figures," the woman with the flow of blood (5:24–34) and the Syrophoenician woman (7:24–30). The word "daughter" appears in all three stories.

[48] See Meier, *A Marginal Jew,* 2:171–76. Meier argues against any attempt to harmonize Mark and Josephus, insisting that "Josephus is to be preferred for history; Mark is to be mined for tradition history and theological intent" (p. 175).

[49] On the "foreign" nature of vv. 17–29 within the Markan text, see Lohmeyer, *Markus,* 117–21.

[50] For background on the Jewish martyr as an advocate of the law before the authorities, see 2 Macc 6:18–31; 4 Macc 5:1–6:3. See also Guelich, *Mark,* 331.

[51] Marcus (*Mark,* 396, 401) stresses the sexual and self-indulgent nature of Herod's response to the dance of the daughter. On Herod as an antitype of Jesus within the context of the feeding accounts, see Fowler, *Loaves and Fishes,* 85–86, 119–27; K. E. Corley, *Private Women, Public Meals: Social Conflict in the Synoptic Tradition* (Peabody: Hendrickson, 1993), 93–95.

[52] For a good summary of the links between Jesus and John the Baptist, see F. J. Matera, *The Kingship of Jesus: Composition and Theology in Mark 15* (SBLDS 66; Chico: Scholars Press, 1982), 97–100, although Matera strains the data when he associates the two destinies with Jesus' royal status. See also LaVerdiere, *The Beginning,* 1:161–63; C. Myers, *Binding the Strong Man: A Political Reading of Mark's Story of Jesus* (Maryknoll: Orbis, 1990), 214–17; and especially P. L. Danove, *The End of Mark's Story: A Methodological Study* (BibIntS 3; Leiden: Brill, 1993), 110–15.

[53] See E. S. Malbon, "The Jewish Leaders in the Gospel of Mark: A Literary Study of Markan Characterization," in *In the Company of Jesus: Characters in Mark's Gospel* (Louisville: Westminster John Knox, 2000), 157–58 (originally published in *JBL* 108 [1989]: 259–81).

Second, his life and death have close parallels with the life and death of Jesus. Much information about discipleship has been provided for the reader in the narrative thus far (1:16–20; 2:13–14; 3:13–19, 20–35; 4:10–11, 33–34). The disciples have had a moment of weakness on the stormy sea (4:35–41), and there are hints of their inability to "hear" in 4:13, 24–25. The reader is aware that *unconditional commitment to God's design and being a follower of Jesus* should mark the life of the Twelve, at present out on their mission (6:7–13). It is also made clear for the first time, by means of this interlude, that discipleship will cost no less than everything.[54] As followers of Jesus, the disciples are called to share in the destiny of Jesus,[55] proleptically acted out in the martyrdom of John the Baptist.[56] "John's martyrdom not only prefigured Jesus' death, it also prefigures the death of anyone who would come after him!"[57]

The return of those sent out (6:30)

Those who were sent out in 6:7 return in 6:30 and gather around Jesus. The use of the verb συνάγειν indicates more than a simple return. The returning Twelve adopt a physical position around Jesus (πρὸς τὸν Ἰησοῦν) which is reminiscent of the εἶναι μετ' αὐτοῦ of 3:14.[58] That context (3:14–15) was very present in Jesus' commissioning and sending out the Twelve in 6:7–9. It returns in the first seven words of 6:30a. But the final nine words indicate that they have not understood what has happened to them, and what they have done. They "announce" (ἀπήγγειλαν) their achievements to Jesus. This is a strong verb, generally used in contexts of public revelation (see, for its only other uses in Mark, 5:14, 19).[59] They are the masters of the situation, as they come back to proclaim to Jesus πάντα ὅσα ἐποίησαν καὶ ὅσα ἐδίδαξαν (v. 30b). What must be noticed is the transferal to the Twelve of the authority for what they have done and said. Despite the focus upon Jesus as the one who authorizes and sends in 6:7–13, they report in 6:30 "everything" that *they* did and everything that *they* said.[60] This is to miss the point of their being *sent by Jesus* on a mission (3:14b–15; 6:7–13), which will only be an effective proclamation of the kingdom (however "successful" it might appear) if they are "with Jesus" (3:14a).

They were authorized by Jesus to act and speak. Separated from him, acting as their own agents, they are no longer behaving as disciples of Jesus. There is deep irony in the fact that the returning missionaries report to the one who authorized them, who gave them ἐξουσία (see 3:15; 6:7), telling him all the things that "they" have done and said (6:30). The reader knows that their missionary activity depends entirely upon the one to whom they are announcing their success! The essential qualities of a true disciple have been made clear by means of the episode of the death of the Baptist (the middle of the sandwich). Not only are they authorized by Jesus, but, also like the Baptist, they are to accept the destiny which the following of Jesus necessarily brings. "The intercalation of the story of the Baptist probably . . . points to the paradox that the miraculous successes of Christian missionaries

---

54 A theme unequivocally developed in 8:31–9:1, and echoing across 8:31–15:47.

55 Explicitly stated by Jesus in 8:34–35.

56 See Gnilka, *Markus,* 1:252; Ernst, *Markus,* 186.

57 Edwards, "Markan Sandwiches," 206.

58 See Stock, *Boten aus dem Mit-Ihm-Sein,* 99.

59 It is also used in the longer ending of Mark (see 16:10, 13). The solemnity associated with the verb is obvious there.

60 Stock, *Boten aus dem Mit-Ihm-Sein,* 100, comments, "The πάντα ὅσα indicates a totality (cf. Mark 11:24; 12:44) and means 'they reported everything without looking back.'"

are made possible by the suffering death of Jesus, to which the death of the Baptist points."[61] There is nothing of this in the report of the Twelve as they come back from their mission. They are unable to recognize that they have associated themselves with Jesus in a mission that has to do with the reigning presence *of God* (6:6b), cost what it may (vv. 14–29). They come back flushed with their success, yet show that they have failed as disciples of Jesus.[62] Mark has already portrayed the disciples' inability to understand *who Jesus is* in 4:35–41 (see 4:41). In 6:7–30, he further shows that they have difficulty in grasping *who they are.*

[handwritten: Disciples of Christ — — are they separating themselves from this reality??]

The First Multiplication of the Loaves and Fish: In Israel (6:31–44)

In 6:31 Jesus addresses his disciples. Despite early promise (see 1:16–20; 2:13–14; 3:13–19), they have difficulty in understanding Jesus, his message, and their role in his mission (4:13, 23, 40–41; 5:31; 6:7–30), but he does not turn away from them. His presence to faltering disciples is highlighted by the use of the historic present: καὶ λέγει αὐτοῖς.[63] There is a genuine transition in Jesus' command to the disciples to leave their present location, to go to another place to rest. It looks forward to 6:31b for motivation: "many were coming and going, and they had no leisure even to eat." Important *new* themes enter the narrative in v. 31: the attention of Jesus to his failing disciples (v. 31a), the hustle and bustle of "many" (v. 31b), and the theme of eating (v. 31c). These themes return in the sequence of the miracle story of 6:31–44, the boat trip in vv. 45–52, and the conflict and the healing which follow in 7:1–37. They continue in the second miraculous feeding story in 8:1–9, the boat trip in 8:10, the conflict and its aftermath in 8:11–21, and the healing of 8:22–26.[64] This sequence will lead to the dénouement of the first half of the Gospel of Mark in 8:27–30.

Jesus and the disciples physically leave one place and go to another, described as εἰς *[handwritten: desert place]* ἔρημον τόπον (a desert, or lonely place) by means of a sea crossing (6:32), but to no avail, as their destination is known and many gather, running on foot "from all the towns." They are waiting for Jesus and the disciples on their arrival (v. 33). Wide-reaching themes have been adumbrated in 6:31, and the scene for the narrative that now follows (6:34–44) has been set in 6:32–33.[65] But additional rich themes have been introduced in the setting: the theme of "desert" recalls Israel's experience of the exodus, and the flocking of many people, running from all the towns, indicates the enthusiasm of the people. Such enthusiasm further highlights the increasing obtuseness of the disciples (see vv. 7–30).[66] Jesus'

---

[61] Marcus, *Mark,* 397. See also Lührmann, *Markusevangelium,* 117, and especially Malbon, "The Major Importance of Minor Characters in Mark," in *In the Company of Jesus,* 206–7.

[62] A disturbed textual tradition (the uncials of Alexandrinus, Leningrad, and Oxford, and the Gothic translation) suggests that the Twelve tell Jesus about the death of the Baptist ("and they reported everything to him and what they had said and taught"). See Gnilka, *Markus,* 1:258. Perhaps the earliest interpreters (the copyists) tried to avoid the problem of further failure from the disciples.

[63] A number of witnesses (Bezae, Tbilisi, Family 13, etc.), perhaps sensing the break between v. 30 and v. 31, read, "And Jesus said to them."

[64] Pesch (*Markusevangelium,* 1:346) remarks: "With the catchword φαγεῖν he unfolds the whole section 6:30–8:26."

[65] It is widely accepted that vv. 31–33 are Markan (see Gnilka, *Markus,* 1:254–55), and thus set the scene for a Markan interpretation of what follows.

[66] See LaVerdiere, *The Beginning,* 1:170–71.

sight of the large crowd, running from all quarters, arouses his compassion (v. 34a), and Mark uses the image of "sheep without a shepherd" to describe Jesus' sentiments (v. 34b). Mark again recalls the exodus. The image has its origins in words of YHWH to Moses: "the Lord's community may not be like sheep without a shepherd" (Num 27:17; see also Ezek 34:5–6). In the light of the Markan use of the passage from Torah, the reader suspects that the lostness of the people is about to be remedied.[67] But the shepherd image does not cease there. As the account of the miracle proceeds, Jesus becomes the Lord and shepherd of the people (see vv. 39, 42, and Ps 23:1), and he will command his disciples that they too must care for the flock (see vv. 37–41, and Ezek 34:1–31). Guelich comments on the shepherd motif in v. 34: "This perspective may well hold the Christological key to this miracle story."[68] Against this background the narrator reports that Jesus taught the crowd "many things" (πολλά). Although briefly recorded, Jesus is likened to Moses, who both taught and provided nourishment in the desert (v. 34c).[69]

The rest of the story depends upon the relationship between Jesus and the disciples. In contrast to Jesus' compassion for the crowd (6:34), the disciples remind Jesus of the lateness of the hour and the loneliness of the place. They ask that the crowd be sent into the surrounding countryside and villages, to buy themselves something to eat (vv. 35–36). Replying to this suggestion, Jesus commands them: "You give them something to eat!" (v. 37a). There is a sharpness in this reponse that must not be missed. The disciples' right-headed reply, telling Jesus of the large amount of money required to purchase bread to feed the crowd, indicates that the disciples continue to misunderstand Jesus.[70] The theme of the need to feed the people is clearly articulated. It is mentioned three times in 6:36–37 (τί φάγωσιν [v. 36]; δότε αὐτοῖς ὑμεῖς φαγεῖν; δώσομεν αὐτοῖς φαγεῖν [v. 37]). The sheep without a shepherd must be cared for, and Jesus instructs his disciples to do so. The narrative presents Jesus as lord of the situation, but there is irony in this instruction. The disciples respond to the command of Jesus in terms of money and bread (v. 37b).[71] He now asks how much bread they have in their possession, and they respond that they have five loaves and two fish (v. 38). The reader recalls that the disciples, in the immediately preceding passage, were sent on a mission, commanded to carry "no bread, no bag, no money in their belts" (6:8). They return to Jesus and confess that they have five loaves and two fish (v. 38). The disciples, who announced their success in 6:30, continue to misunderstand their mission and its relationship with the mission of Jesus.[72] It is what *they possess*, in this case its paucity, that disturbs them.

The exodus has already been alluded to by the use of "a desert place" in 6:32, and in the description of the people as sheep without a shepherd in 6:34. In this desert place, Jesus arranges the crowd as if for a sumptuous feast. He commands them to sit down in

---

[67] See Marcus, *Mark,* 406.

[68] Guelich, *Mark,* 340. See also, Lane, *Mark,* 226.

[69] See Hooker, *St. Mark,* 165. This link with Moses continues the close contact with the exodus, but does not present Jesus as a second Moses. This theme is foreign to Mark (see Gnilka, *Markus,* 1:259).

[70] Lane (*Mark,* 228) describes this reply as "disrespectful in tone, but points unmistakably to the impossibility of complying with Jesus' order." Pesch (*Markusevangelium,* 1:351) describes it as a "skeptical question" reflecting the misunderstanding motif.

[71] As the denarius was regarded as a day's wage, the sum mentioned (two hundred denarii) is considerable. Marcus (*Mark,* 407) approves its being the value of half a year's wages.

[72] See especially Fowler, *Loaves and Fishes,* 116–19. See also Schweizer, *Mark,* 138–39; Painter, *Mark,* 105–6; Marcus, *Mark,* 418. Contrary to Hooker (*St. Mark,* 166): "Perhaps Mark has forgotten that earlier command."

companies (συμπόσια συμπόσια). This language recalls the Greek symposion that influenced early Christian eucharistic practice, and the command that the people recline for the meal further heightens the allusion to such practices.[73] The starkness of Mark's storytelling seems to waver for a moment as he indicates that these companies are to sit "upon the green grass" (v. 39). This detail is not added for color; it recalls Ps 23:1: "The Lord is my shepherd, and nothing I shall want. In green fields he leads me."[74] Jesus had compassion upon the crowd, regarding them as sheep without a shepherd (6:34, with its reference to Num 27:17 and Ezek 34:5–6), and now acts as shepherd to them. Exodus themes continue as Jesus has the crowd sit down in companies of hundreds and fifties (v. 40). The numbers reflect the companies on the march in the desert, described in Exod 18:21–25, Num 31:14, and Deut 1:15. This tradition continued among the sectarians at Qumran. They idealized an assembly of the true people of God, into groups of one thousand, one hundred, fifty, and ten (1QS 2:21–23; 1QSa 1:14–15, 28–29; 2:1; 1QM 4:1–5, 16–17; CD 13:1).[75]

Taking from the little that the disciples had by them, despite 6:8 (see v. 38), Jesus performs a number of actions: "taking," "he looked up to heaven," "blessed," "broke the loaves and gave," "set before" (v. 41). These actions have their origins in the early liturgical practices of a Christian community (see Mark 14:22).[76] "Mark's words remind his readers of their own eucharistic celebrations."[77] But Jesus gives the blessed and broken bread to the disciples to set before the people. His command that they must feed the sheep without a shepherd (see v. 37a) has been acted upon, despite their failure to understand their shepherding role (see Ezek 34:1–31). The two fish are also divided, but the fish are not crucial to the eucharistic reading of the passage.[78] They are omitted in 8:18–21, a Markan passage recalling the miracles of 6:31–44 and 8:1–9.[79] The narrator's comment: "And they all ate

---

[73] See LaVerdiere, *The Beginning*, 1:174.

[74] This link is seldom noticed by commentators, but see Guelich (*Mark*, 341), Lane (*Mark*, 229), Pesch (*Markusevangelium*, 1:350), Ernst (*Markus*, 192), and especially D. C. Allison ("Psalm 23 [22] in Early Christianity: A Suggestion," *IBS* 5 [1983]: 132–37). For a survey of opinions, see Gnilka, *Markus*, 1:260. He suggests that it reflects a Jewish (rabbinic?) idea of an eschatological festive garden celebration. See also Schweizer, *Mark*, 139.

[75] Gnilka (*Markus*, 1:260–61) makes little of the exodus connection, and interprets the gathering as an indication of the establishment of God's eschatological people. So also Grundmann, *Markus*, 134–38; Guelich, *Mark*, 341.

[76] See, among many who have shown these links, B. van Iersel, "Die wunderbare Speisung und das Abendmahl in der synoptischen Tradition (Mk VI 35–44, par.; VIII 1–10, par.)," *NovT* 7 (1964): 167–94; J.-M. van Cangh, *La multiplication des pains et l'eucharistie* (LD 86; Paris: Cerf, 1975), 67–109; S. Masuda, "The Good News of the Miracle of the Bread: The Tradition and Its Markan Redaction," *NTS* 28 (1982): 191–219, especially pp. 201–3; Meier, *A Marginal Jew*, 2:959–66; Marcus, *Mark*, 410; 418–20.

[77] Hooker, *St. Mark*, 167. This is rejected by a number of scholars. There is no wine at the multiplication, and no fish at the last supper. See, for example, Guelich, *Mark*, 342–43, and the bibliography there. Gnilka (*Markus*, 1:261–62) regards the scene as a presentation of Jesus as the "Hausvater" in a typical Jewish meal. For a comprehensive rejection of this view, see Meier, *A Marginal Jew*, 2:963–64.

[78] There is no agreement on the history of the text. For example, van Iersel ("Die wunderbare Speisung," 169–82) and others claim that the fish belong to a pre-Markan non-eucharistic tradition, while the opposite position is adopted by, among others, Gnilka (*Markus*, 1:257), who asserts that the reference to fish is a pedantic addition to an already eucharistic narrative. Grundmann (*Markus*, 136) argues that the fish are essential for the meal (see *b. Ber.* 44a: "A meal without fish is not a meal").

[79] It is tempting to see in the Markan use of the word ἰχθύς a hint of the later widespread christological use of both the word and the symbol (the Greek letters provide the first letters for the confession: "Jesus Christ Son of God Savior" ['Ιησοῦς Χριστὸς θεοῦ υἱὸς σωτήρ]). However, this use

and were satisfied" (v. 42), returns to the shepherd theme of Ps 23:1. The linguistic links are not close, as what is stated negatively in the MT and the Septuagint (LXX 22:1: καὶ οὐδέν με ὑστερήσει) is rendered positively in Mark (ἐχορτάσθησαν, v. 42). Contacts with the exodus also emerge, as after the daily gift of the manna in the desert, the people could eat their fill (see Exod 16:8, 12, 16, 18, 21). The links are strong between this first bread miracle, the exodus, and the Jewish traditions of the people and their shepherd.[80]

Further indications of a close link between the feeding of the five thousand, early eucharistic celebrations, and the world of Israel appear in 6:43–44. The disciples gather κλάσματα (broken pieces of bread) and remains of the fish, and fill twelve baskets. Eucharistic traditions possibly lie behind the use of the expression κλάσματα, used in the early church to speak of the eucharistic bread (see John 6:12; *Did.* 9:4; *1 Clem.* 34:7, and Ignatius, *Pol.* 4:2).[81] The most important theological link with Israel is the collection of the twelve baskets of remaining food. The meal shared with the crowds, which ran from all the towns of Israel (see v. 33), is still open. The nourishment generated by Jesus is still available in the twelve baskets. At this stage, the number "twelve" may not strike the reader as important, but it is a foundational number for Israelite history, the number of Israel's tribes, and (since 3:14–19) also the number of those men called to be with Jesus in a special way.[82] On arrival at the parallel gathering of the fragments in 8:8, only seven baskets will be filled, and the significance of the "twelve" will become more obvious to the reader.[83] In addition to the Jewish link with the number "twelve," the Roman satirist Juvenal (*Satirae,* 3:14; 6:542) regards the Greek word κόφινος as a distinctively Jewish word for "basket," characteristic of the poorer classes in Rome.[84] This detail, however will not strike the reader until another word (σπυρίς) appears in the second account of the gathering of the remnants into "baskets."

The episode closes with a note that five thousand "men" (ἄνδρες) had eaten the loaves. The focus upon the male participants reflects the patriarchy of the ancient world. They are the ones who count and are thus numbered. No malice is intended, and the figure indicates the immensity of the crowd and thus the greatness of the miracle.[85]

---

of the word, with its accompanying iconography, is probably too late for such an application. See Schweizer, *Mark,* 140.

[80] See the remarks of Marcus (*Mark,* 421), who sees the eucharistic background as a continuity of the exodus and the Mosaic traditions, yet adding much that is new: "If Jesus, then, fulfills the Mosaic model, he also transcends it."

[81] The eucharistic link is only "possible" because the parallels, beginning with John and into the second century, may be too late to draw conclusions about Mark. Indeed, Mark 6:43 may lie behind the later use of τὰ κλάσαματα to refer to eucharistic bread.

[82] Some New Testament texts explicitly link "the Twelve" with the twelve tribes of Israel (Matt 19:28; Luke 22:30; Rev 21:12–14), but the link is implied in much New Testament use of "the Twelve." For a full discussion, see J. P. Meier, "The Circle of the Twelve: Did It Exist During Jesus' Public Ministry?" *JBL* 116 (1997): 635–72.

[83] The tradition history of the two multiplication miracles (6:31–44; 8:1–9) is debated. Some regard 6:31–44 as the more primitive (e.g., M. Dibelius, *From Tradition to Gospel* [trans. B. L. Woolf; Library of Theological Translations; Cambridge & London: James Clark, 1971], 78 n. 1), while others regard 8:1–9 as the original tradition, elaborated by Mark to form 6:31–44 (e.g., Fowler, *Loaves and Fishes,* 43–90). Both suggestions run into serious difficulty, and it is more likely that independent traditions (see also John 6:1–15) were used by Mark (and John). For the discussion, and this conclusion, see Meier, *A Marginal Jew,* 2:951–58. See also Guelich, *Mark,* 337.

[84] See the discussion in BDAG, 563, s.v. κόφινος. See also Marcus, *Mark,* 411–12. Lane (*Mark,* 231), on the evidence provided by Juvenal, describes the κόφινοι as "small wicker baskets which every Jew carried with him as a part of his daily attire."

[85] See Lohmeyer, *Markus,* 125. Gnilka (*Markus,* 1:262) rightly warns against giving symbolic significance to the numbers, but grants that there may be something behind the use of "twelve." The

In a Jewish world, a narrative shot through with references to the exodus and Israelite shepherd imagery tells of disciples who are called to continue Jesus' presence (see 3:14–19; 6:7–13). They administer the gift of the loaves and fish to a crowd that has run to Jesus from every town (6:33). The gift of food in a desert place recalls the gift of the manna to Israel.[86] But unlike the exodus manna stories, where the manna could not be kept from one day to another (see Exod 16:19–20), the bread given by Jesus is collected into twelve baskets so that it will remain available (6:43). Yet another biblical passage lies behind this miracle story. In 2 Kgs 4:42–44 Elisha commands his servant to give barley loaves and new grain to the people to eat. His servant objects that he does not have enough to feed "one hundred men." Elisha repeats his command, concluding, "For thus says the Lord, 'They shall eat and there shall be some left over' " (2 Kgs 4:43). And so it happens (6:44).[87] Some refuse to accept that there is a link between this first multiplication of the loaves and fish and Jesus' nourishment of Israel through the ministry of the disciples.[88] Careful attention to the narrative as a whole shows that the "Jewishness" of Mark 6:31–44 is unmistakable.

The First Sea Journey: Contrasting Responses to Jesus (6:45–56)

The account of the walking on the water (6:45–52) and the summary of the response of the multitudes who throng about Jesus (vv. 53–56) existed in the pre-Markan tradition, and they are to be read together for a proper appreciation of the Markan story. Jesus' walking on the seas, following hard on the heels of the feeding of the multitudes (vv. 31–44), in which the disciples were key figures, only leads them to further lack of understanding (vv. 51–52).[89] Yet the crowds who assemble around Jesus at Gennesaret, who have witnessed neither the miracle of the feeding nor Jesus' authority over the stormy sea, believe that even the touch of the fringe of his cloak can make people well. And they are correct (v. 56). The Markan redaction, even if a little clumsily, links the two accounts by means of

---

focus on the men only is explicitly stated in Matt 14:21. Marcus (*Mark,* 414) points to Exod 12:37 and Num 1 and 26. Only males bearing arms are numbered, even though women and children are present.

[86] As LaVerdiere (*The Beginning,* 1:171–72) comments: "Mark never mentioned the word manna, but the story of how the hungry people of God was tested and wondrously nourished in the desert fills the atmosphere."

[87] On the contacts with 2 Kgs 4:42–44, see Marcus, *Mark,* 415–16.

[88] See, for example, M. D. Hooker (*The Message of Mark* [London: Epworth Press, 1983], 44–50). She describes this focus on the Jewishness of the first story as reflecting "an imagination which has been allowed to run riot" (p. 47). Similarly, Gnilka (*Markus,* 1:262) simply comments, "There is no indication here that the Jews were guests at table (and in 8:1 ff. the Gentiles)." Ernst (*Markus,* 192–93) also rejects this symbolic reading. He makes an odd major break in his structure after 6:56, ending the report of Jesus' activity in Galilee and among the Gentiles, reading 7:1–8:26 as Jesus on the way outside Galilee (but what of 7:31, 8:11–12, and 8:22?): see pp. 198–99. This forces a wedge between the two "cycles" identified above.

[89] It is probable that the pre-Markan tradition already had the miracle of the multiplication and the story of Jesus' walking on the water as a unified narrative. This tradition is found independently in John 6:1–21. As the more detailed reading of the passage will indicate, however, a simpler story of Jesus' sending away the disciples, dismissing the crowd, and coming across the water to help the disciples, eventually bringing them to land, has been heavily reworked to further the evolving Markan description of failing disciples, and perhaps to develop allusions to Old Testament traditions. Along these lines see Meier's fully documented treatment (*A Marginal Jew,* 2:905–14). For an exhaustive study of the tradition history, the way in which each evangelist's theological perspective has shaped its telling, and the historicity of the episode of Jesus' walking on the sea, see Meier, *A Marginal Jew,* 2:905–24.

their setting. Jesus firmly sends the disciples away to Bethsaida in the boat while he dismisses the crowd (v. 45). He joins them by coming across the stormy sea (vv. 48–51), "and when they had crossed over, they came to the land at Gennesaret, and moored to the shore" (v. 53). The people recognize him and run to him, bringing their sick (vv. 53–55).

The walking on the sea (6:45–52)

Jesus remains the master of the situation as he "made" (ἠνάγκασεν, "forced," 6:45) his disciples set out to the other side of the lake, to Bethsaida, while he dismissed the crowd.[90] This happens "immediately" (εὐθύς), and a scenario is established for the following two scenes. Jesus remains on the shore, and goes up on the mountain to pray (v. 46), having dismissed the crowd that was fed in the preceding episode. There is no identification of "the mountain," and the exodus hints of 6:31–44 continue into this moment of prayer (see also 1:35–38; 3:13–19). Moses had conversed with God on a mountain, and mountains subsequently become important places for prophets and holy people to establish contact with YHWH (see Deut 33:2; Hab 3:3).[91] As evening falls, the disciples are alone on the sea, and he is alone on the land (v. 47). There is no need to suppose miraculous vision in Jesus' seeing that the disciples were struggling against the heavy wind, but it is not until a time between three and six o'clock in the morning, in the darkness of "about the fourth watch," that he comes to them across the sea, intending to pass them by (v. 48). The exodus, and biblical reflection upon the Reed Sea crossing, continues to influence the Markan text (see Exod 33:19–23; 34:6; Job 9:8; Ps 77:16–20; Isa 43:16–17; 51:10). The disciples, who have witnessed much to this point of the narrative, including the calming of the stormy sea in 4:35–41, are to be challenged. Jesus is deliberately not coming to their aid.[92] The intention to pass them by heightens the epiphanic nature of Jesus' coming across the waters.[93] But they continue to show their inability to grasp *who it is* that they are following. They take the figure on the sea for a ghost (φάντασμα) and cry out in fear. The reader recognizes the disciples' terror as a further sign of unbelief (see 4:41). Mark reinforces this by insisting that every person in the boat saw him but was nevertheless terrified (6:50a). In a formula of self-revelation, which has its parallels in Old Testament theophanies (see Exod 3:14; 33:19–23; Num 11:17; Judg 6:11–24; 1 Kgs 19:11), Jesus "immediately" commands the disciples to take heart and not fear. He is not a φάντασμα but Jesus: ἐγώ εἰμι (v. 50b). This could be a simple self-identification ("Do not worry. Pull yourselves together, it's only me!"). But the earlier reference to Jesus' prayer on the mountain (v. 46), and the scenario of the early hours of the morning and a stormy sea, indicate that Jesus' self-identification approximates a revelation of his oneness with YHWH (see Exod 3:14; Deut 32:39; Isa 41:4; 43:10).[94]

---

[90] LaVerdiere (*The Beginning*, 1:178) suggests that the use of the strong verb "to force" (a *hapax legomenon* in Mark) is a further hint of the disciples' resistance to Jesus' design for them.

[91] See Marcus, *Mark*, 422–23; Malbon, *Narrative Space*, 84–89.

[92] Gnilka (*Markus*, 1:267–69) makes much of a "storm" and Jesus' going to help the disciples in need. Thus he claims that an original epiphany story has been transformed into a rescue story. But this is not evident in the text. See the sound remarks of Schweizer (*Mark*, 141), Ernst (*Markus*, 196), and Pesch (*Markusevangelium*, 1:358, 360–61), who rightly claim that it is an epiphany story. Marcus (*Mark*, 423–26) rightly associates the "passing by" with YHWH's "passing by" in Exod 33:17–34:8, and related traditions.

[93] See Lohmeyer, *Markus*, 133–34; Pesch, *Markusevangelium*, 1:361–63.

[94] See C. H. Williams, *I Am He: The Interpretation of 'Anî Hû' in Jewish and Early Christian Literature* (WUNT 2. Reihe 113; Tübingen: J. C. B. Mohr [Paul Siebeck], 2000), 215–28. See also Marcus,

Jesus' lordship over the elements, already evidenced in 4:39–41, causes the wind to cease, but the response of the disciples—despite all that they have seen, experienced, and done (and despite Jesus' earlier challenge in the parallel situation described in 4:40)—do not demonstrate faith. They are "utterly astounded" (6:51). In one of his crucial comments upon the disciples, Mark tells his readers why this was the case: "for they did not understand about the loaves, but their hearts were hardened" (v. 52). The author provides an initial explanation for the developing portrait of failing disciples. The disciples, drawn into the circle of Jesus (3:13–19) and sent out to continue his mission (6:7–13), have experienced a significant sharing in Jesus' ministry in the first story of the miraculous feeding (6:31–44). But they are unable to understand that the kingdom *of God* is manifesting itself in the words and deeds of Jesus.[95] To this point in the narrative, only the Pharisees have been described as suffering from hardness of heart (ἐπὶ τῇ πωρώσει τῆς καρδίας αὐτῶν, 3:15). In both miracles on the sea (4:40–41; 6:51–52) the disciples have shown their unbelief.[96] The use of the passive mood to indicate that their hearts were hardened (πεπωρωμένη) raises an important question: who is responsible for this hardening? Is this the result of the influence of Satan, or part of God's design? There is nothing in the text to indicate the former, and thus the possibility of the latter remains. Why that should be the case leads the reader further into the narrative, searching for an explanation of such hardening of hearts.[97]

Jesus' healing ministry and the faith of the people (6:53–56)

This passage is an extended summary, and has all the characteristics of Markan redaction.[98] After the description of the arrival of Jesus and the disciples at Gennesaret,[99] it links

---

Mark, 427, 430–32. Marcus (pp. 432–33) links Jesus' coming to the distressed disciples closely with the experience of the Markan community in the eschatological excitement and suffering accompanying the Jewish War. See the warning against those who falsely claim ἐγώ εἰμι in 13:6. One must be careful not to claim too much for this expression in Mark. It is not to be compared to the widespread use of ἐγώ εἰμι in the Fourth Gospel, although it may indicate the beginnings of a theological tradition which reached its New Testament zenith in the Fourth Gospel. See Lührmann, *Markusevangelium,* 122; Gnilka, *Markus,* 1:269–70; Hooker, *St. Mark,* 170. For a detailed study of the Old Testament background to the passage, see Meier, *A Marginal Jew,* 2:914–19.

[95] As Hooker (*St. Mark,* 169) rightly remarks, "his concern here . . . seems to be with the question 'Who is Jesus?' " Marcus (*Mark,* 434–35) connects both the eucharistic passage (vv. 31–44) and the walking on the water (vv. 45–52) with exodus background. Eucharistic allusions also link the passages. Along with Quesnell (see below, n. 97), he claims that the presence of Jesus in the eucharistic section should instruct Markan disciples of his symbolic presence to the distressed community in the distribution of the eucharistic bread.

[96] See Gnilka, *Markus,* 270: "This extremely sharp criticism is ultimately aimed at their unbelief." See also Guelich (*Mark,* 352–53), where a close link with 4:41 is also made. On the narrative links between 4:35–41 and 6:45–52, see van Iersel, *Reading Mark,* 95–98.

[97] For a study of 6:52 and its function within the first half of the Gospel, see Q. Quesnell, *The Mind of Mark: Interpretation and Method through the Exegesis of Mark 6,52* (AnBib 38: Rome: Pontifical Biblical Institute, 1969). Although at times overstating a sacramental interpretation, this study provides a rich analysis of Markan scholarship up to the late 1960s.

[98] See Gnilka, *Markus,* 1:272–72. However, not all agree. See the discussion of possible sources for 6:53–56 in Guelich, *Mark,* 1:355. Guelich regards the passage as stemming from pre-Markan tradition, part of the redactional activity which developed the pre-Markan miracle collection behind 4:35–6:53. See also Pesch, *Markusevangelium,* 1:364. A feature of the so-called pre-Markan miracle cycle is the framing of the miracles between the summaries of 3:7–12 and 5:53–56.

[99] The boat trip has lost its way. The disciples set out for Bethsaida on the northeast side of the Sea of Galilee. They arrive at Gennesaret on the western shore. For some this is the result of the

this summary with the previous episode (v. 53; see also 5:21). Common Markan events are reported. Jesus is recognized by the people (v. 54), and they run about the district, bringing sick people to him (see 2:1–12) wherever he might be (v. 55; see 5:2, 6; 6:31–33). As Jesus journeys on, through villages, cities, or countryside (see 1:33, 45; 5:14, 6:6, 33, 36), the sick are brought to him (see 3:7–12). The people recognize that Jesus is the bearer of a unique authority and power (see 1:32–34). With an unconditional trust, which contrasts sharply from the disciples' terror, crying out in fear, astonishment, lack of understanding, and hardness of heart (see vv. 50–52), they believe that the touch of his garment will heal the sick (v. 56; see 3:10; 5:27–28).[100]

Mark constructs this account of Jesus' healing ministry by gathering material from episodes already narrated. It is linked to the story of Jesus' walking on the water to close the first sea journey (see vv. 53–54a). Having read thus far, the reader is not surprised by Jesus' healing ministry, but the increasing fragility of the disciples has been thrown into sharp relief.[101]

The First Conflict: Jesus and the Traditions of Israel (7:1–23)

The link between the preceding episodes and the introduction of the debate with the Pharisees and its consequences that now follow (7:1–23) is loose, determined by the Markan literary and theological agenda. However, the arrival of the boat in Gennesaret and Jesus' subsequent journeying through the countryside locates Jesus in Jewish territory. The coming of the Pharisees with some of their scribes from Jerusalem is geographically possible (v. 1). At first glance, it appears that 7:1–23 is one of the few episodes in 6:6b–8:30 where the disciples are not the author's main focus. Jesus enters into conflict with the Pharisees and some of the scribes over food laws and ritual purity (vv. 1–13), and then addresses the crowd, explaining the position he has taken with the Pharisees and scribes (vv. 14–15). Only at the end of the passage does he enter the house to discuss the issue with the disciples (vv. 17–23). This "first glance" is deceptive. The disciples, their behavior, and their understanding are crucial to the passage.[102] The Pharisees and scribes question Jesus over the behavior of *some of the disciples* (vv. 2–4). They are to be regarded as present as Jesus replies to his accusers (vv. 6–13) and explains his attack to the people (vv. 14–15). In the end, in a discussion with the disciples (vv. 16–23), Jesus asks the question, "Then you are also without understanding?" (v. 18). Their lack of understanding and, by association, their hardness of heart continue (vv. 6, 19, 21; see 6:52).

---

storm, for others a change of direction from a Gentile to a Jewish destination, or the result of secondary redactional activity. See Gnilka, *Markus,* 1:266; Guelich, *Mark,* 348, 356–57; and Marcus, *Mark,* 436. Pesch (*Markusevangelium,* 1:359) claims that these geographical difficulties reflect Mark's poor knowledge of the area, and are of no consequence for the author.

[100] See Pesch, *Markusevangelium,* 1:366–67. Contrary to Schweizer (*Mark,* 142), who sees the account as critical of "the blindness of those whose only interest is the miraculous." See also Lane, *Mark,* 240–41; Painter, *Mark,* 108. For Marcus (*Mark,* 437, 439) the "fringe of the garment" looks to Num 15:39. The fringe is a reminder to Jews to observe all the commandments of God. Jesus is presented as an observant Jew. It introduces the following section (7:1–23) where he will do battle with those who have reduced the commandments of God to commandments of human beings.

[101] Guelich, *Mark,* 358. Contrary to, for example, Nineham (*St. Mark,* 186), who reads the faith of the people in vv. 53–56 as a foil to the Jewish leaders in 7:1–13. Lührmann (*Markusevangelium,* 123) claims that the passage serves primarily as a summarizing bridge.

[102] See LaVerdiere, *The Beginning,* 1:185.

Mark returns to the conflict between Jesus and the representatives of the traditions of Israel, parallel to the episodes reported in 2:1–3:6. Here, however, it is not a single point of the law that is at stake, but a difference of opinion between Jesus and Israel on the question of ritual purity. Located strategically between the two feeding miracles (6:31–44; 8:1–9), the debate and the subsequent discussions with the people and the disciples focus upon the issue of eating (see 7:2, 3, 4, 15, 18–19). The reader follows the steady progress of a narrative that challenges the disciples to follow the shepherd in feeding the hungry (see 6:31–44), as Jesus pushes beyond the boundaries of the closed religious system represented by the Pharisees and the scribes in 7:1–5. In the episodes that follow (7:24–30, 31–37) those boundaries will reach further, into the Gentile world, and will lead to Jesus' next challenge to the disciples, that they feed the hungry Gentiles, who "have come a very long way" (8:1–9, esp. v. 3).

The location of the event is not given, but 7:1–23 forms a literary unit.[103] The themes of eating and purity run across the passage, and a change of place in 7:24 indicates the beginning of another pericope. The argument of the present passage can be outlined as follows:

1. Introduction
   a. The Pharisees and scribes observe the disciples eating with unclean hands (vv. 1–2).
   b. The tradition of the elders is explained by the narrator (vv. 3–5).
   c. Two questions are put to Jesus.
      (1) Why do the disciples not follow the tradition of the elders (v. 5a)?
      (2) Why do the disciples eat with unclean hands (v. 5b)?

2. Jesus defends the disciples through a response that focuses upon the tradition of the elders (Question 1 [v. 5a]).
   a. Jesus attacks "this people," using Isa 29:13 (vv. 6–8).
   b. Jesus attacks the tradition of the elders, using Exod 20:12 (see Deut 5:16) and Exod 21:17 (vv. 9–13).

3. To "the people" he states the new law of purity, transcending the issue of the washing of hands. Alone with the disciples he explains why the new law is true. The issue of unclean hands (Question 2 [v. 5b]) is irrelevant.
   a. To the people, Jesus states the new law in a parabolic form (vv. 14–15).
   b. Alone with the disciples, he laments their misunderstanding, but openly teaches them the principle that determines the new law (vv. 17–23).[104]

---

103 See J. Lambrecht, "Jesus and the Law: An Investigation of Mk 7,1–23," *ETL* 53 (1977): 24–82, for a detailed study of this passage, which traces its various redactional stages from the historical Jesus to the Markan redaction, presents the internal structure of the passage (which I have largely used in what follows), and offers an interpretation of the text. Did Mark combine a conflict story (vv. 1–13; see Pesch, *Markusevangelium*, 1:369–70) with a teaching narrative (vv. 14–23; see Pesch, *Markusevangelium*, 1:378), or did vv. 1–23 come to Mark already united? For surveys of this discussion, see Guelich, *Mark*, 360–62; Gnilka, *Markus*, 1:276–79; and Marcus, *Mark*, 447–48. While opinions vary concerning the pre-Markan history of vv. 1–13 and 14–23, all agree that the present form of 7:1–23 is a literary unit.

104 Verse 16, "If anyone has ears to hear, let him hear," is widely attested in the manuscripts, but is omitted by Sinaiticus and Vaticanus, among others. The addition recognizes the parallel between Mark 4 and Jesus' teaching the people enigmatically in vv. 14–15, and then explaining further to the disciples in vv. 17–23. Verse 16 thus parallels 4:3–9. It is also a fitting sequel to v. 14. See Metzger, *Textual Commentary*, 81. All modern critical texts and most translations omit it.

They will gather for themselves

Introduction (7:1–5)

The passage begins abruptly, linked loosely with the preceding summary with a paratactic καί. That Jesus is in Israel is indicated by the reference to Gennesaret and surrounding regions; thus the Pharisees' and the scribes' arrival from Jerusalem makes sense (7:1). There is an air of aggression and threat in their "gathering" (συνάγονται πρὸς αὐτόν). *Because* Conflict looms—and breaks out when the Pharisees observe the activity of some of the disciples. The themes of "eating" and "bread" are continued from 6:31–44, as the Pharisees and scribes judge "unclean" the eating practices of some of the disciples (ὅτι κοιναῖς χερσίν, τοῦτ' ἔστιν ἀνίπτοις, ἐσθίουσιν τοὺς ἄρτους). It is crucial for the overall literary structure and theological argument of this "feeding" section of the story (6:31–8:21) that only "some" of the disciples (τινὰς τῶν μαθητῶν) were behaving in this fashion.[105] If *some* were eating in a manner that could be judged as defiled, *some* were not! There is division among the disciples.[106] It is to the group of divided disciples, and thus to the Markan readership, that the pronouncements of Jesus which are to follow are addressed. Once this is recognized, then division among the disciples is the issue when Jesus finally speaks to them alone in 7:17–23.

The event generating the conflict has been stated, but further explanation is required. Thus 7:3–4 describes "the tradition of the elders" (τὴν παράδοσιν τῶν πρεσβυτέρων). A succinct summary of certain laws regarding the proper preparation before eating follows. None of them are, in themselves, remarkable, and while the author's insistence that "all the Jews" practiced these lustrations is not precise, it can hardly be called "incorrect."[107] Judging from the slim evidence available (Num 18:8–13; *b. Hul.* 105a, 106a–b; *b. Šabb.* 13b–14), such practices may have been evolving in early postwar Judaism. Such evidence is late, but Mark's text itself indicates the emergence of such practices. Returning from the dirt, hustle, and bustle of a first-century marketplace, one required purification,[108] but there is no indication that a tradition of the elders was involved (v. 4a).[109] Other practices are briefly mentioned. The washing of various vessels made of bronze (v. 4b) probably emerged from the interpretation of Leviticus 11–15, which deals with cleansing articles

---

[105] The presence of the disciples across this section is clear. The heavy-handed addition ἐσθίουσιν τοὺς ἄρτους in v. 2 has all the characteristics of a Markan redactional touch to link this passage with the feeding of the five thousand (6:31–44), the misunderstanding of the disciples (6:52), the play on feeding in the encounter with the Syrophoenician woman (7:24–30), the feeding of the four thousand (8:1–9), and the leaven of the Pharisees (8:11–21). See Marcus, *Mark*, 440.

[106] See LaVerdiere, *The Beginning*, 1:190–91. This interpretation (important for what follows) is regarded by Pesch (*Markusevangelium,* 1:370 n. 1) as "hardly thinkable."

[107] Contra Lohmeyer (*Markus,* 139–40). For a discussion of the issue, see Marcus, *Mark,* 441.

[108] Some manuscripts have βαπτίσωνται, indicating a more complete bathing, while others have ῥαντίσωνται, suggesting a less complete sprinkling with water. Despite the presence of the latter verb in both Sinaiticus and Vaticanus, the widespread occurrence of the former across the majority of textual families indicates its superiority. See, for example, Lane, *Mark,* 243 n. 6.

[109] There is an untranslatable word associated with the washing of hands after returning from the marketplace: πυγμῇ. From the earliest stages of the transmission of the Gospel the difficulty of the word was noted. Sinaiticus and others replace it with πυκνά (often, thoroughly), while others omit it. As the *lectio difficilior* it is surely original. Almost every commentator has a different interpretation of it (see the survey in Guelich, *Mark,* 364–65), and most modern translators simply omit it. It obviously has an adverbial meaning, lost to us, describing the process of the hand-washing. Among many, see M. Hengel ("Mk 7,3 πυγμῇ: Die Geschichte einer exegetischen Aporie und der Versuch ihrer Lösung," *ZNW* 60 [1969]: 182–98), and the summary of the discussion in Marcus, *Mark,* 441.

which may have been in contact with unclean objects.[110] Verses 3–4 set out Mark's view of things, however much they may or may not reflect first-century Jewish practice.[111] There is no criticism of the practices in themselves; they are listed to exemplify the practices that the Pharisees, and the Jews, *including some of the disciples,* followed before eating. With that background in place, the question posed to Jesus by the Pharisees and scribes is provided. It has two parts. He is first asked: "Why do your disciples not live according to the tradition of the elders?" (v. 5a).[112] A closely related question follows: "Why do your disciples eat with hands defiled?" (see 5b). The rest of the passage is formed by Jesus' responses to each question in turn. First Jesus addresses the Pharisees and scribes, and attacks certain so-called "traditions of the elders" (vv. 6–13). Then he speaks to the people and the disciples about eating (vv. 14–23).

The tradition of the elders (7:6–13)

The response of Jesus to the Pharisees and the scribes is confrontational. He accuses his interrogators of hypocrisy, turning to Isaiah as proof for his claim.[113] Isaiah, he asserts, wrote of their approach to religious practice: "This people honors me with their lips, but their heart is far from me. In vain do they worship me, teaching as doctrines the precepts of men" (Isa 29:13). A faint hint of the disciples is present in the prophet's words against those whose hearts are far from God (see 6:52). But the accusation is against a religiosity (and honoring with the lips) that makes "human precepts" into doctrines (7:7). Mark's use of Isa 29:13 is closer to the Septuagint than to the Masoretic Text, but he has reworked the closing words to make Jesus' intention clear. The Septuagint accuses the people of Jerusalem of vain worship, "teaching human precepts and doctrines" (διδάσκοντες ἐντάλματα ἀνθρώπων καὶ διδασκαλίας). Mark heightens the distinction between divine teachings and human commandments: "teaching as doctrines human precepts" (διδάσκοντες διδασκαλίας ἐντάλματα ἀνθρώπων). The words of Jesus render the accusation of Isaiah specific. He charges "this people" with changing the divine doctrines of Torah into human precepts. The words of the prophet provide Jesus' response to the question in v. 5a concerning the tradition of the elders. His comment on the citation from the prophet restates his concern: they hold fast "the traditions of men" (παράδοσιν τῶν ἀνθρώπων) and abandon (ἀφέντες) the commandment of God (τὴν ἐντολὴν τοῦ θεοῦ, v. 8).

---

[110] On these practices, see Hooker, *St. Mark,* 175–76; Gnilka, *Markus,* 1:279–80; Marcus, *Mark,* 441–43. For further discussion, see the specialized studies of R. Banks, *Jesus and the Law in the Synoptic Tradition* (SNTSMS 28; Cambridge: Cambridge University Press, 1975), 132–46; R. Booth, *Jesus and the Laws of Purity: Tradition History and Legal History in Mark 7* (JSNTSup 13; Sheffield: JSOT Press, 1986), 117–216.

[111] For a full discussion, see Booth, *Jesus and the Laws of Purity,* 23–114. For Guelich (*Mark,* 364): "The phrase 'the Jews' does indicate that the writer and implied reader/hearer viewed 'the Jews' as different and strongly suggests a Gentile setting for this generalization." In defense of Mark's use of "all the Jews," see Lane, *Mark,* 245. He makes reference to the same expression in *Let. Aris.* 305, and argues that "Mark was following accepted Jewish practice in describing Jewish customs to a Gentile audience." See also, Grundmann, *Markus,* 147–49.

[112] The Greek word rendered "live" is περιπατοῦσιν ("walk"). It is the only place in the synoptic tradition where the Jewish technical notion of *halakah* ("to live by") appears. See Lohmeyer, *Markus,* 140–41.

[113] On Jewish and early Christian understanding of "hypocrite" as "a person whose interpretation of the law differs from one's own," see Marcus, *Mark,* 444.

This attack upon the Pharisees and the scribes needs substantiation. What Jesus must show is that what he has described as "human precepts" (7:7) and the "human tradition" (v. 8) is a rejection of the commandment of God (v. 8).[114] The discussion has moved steadily from a debate over "the traditions of the elders" (vv. 3, 5) to what Jesus terms "human precepts" (v. 7) and "human tradition" (v. 8). In the second part of his response to his accusers, he shows that living according to the traditions of Pharisees and the scribes (τὴν παράδοσιν ὑμῶν, "*your* tradition," v. 9) can lead to the rejection of the commandment of God. He opens his attack with biting sarcasm, speaking of the "fine" (καλῶς) way they keep their tradition. There has been a subtle shift from "the tradition of the elders," via the "human commandment" and the "human traditions," to "your traditions." Jesus affirms that the traditions of the Pharisees and the scribes are no less than a rendering null (ἀθετεῖτε) the commandment of God (v. 9; see vv. 7–8).[115] Jesus turns to a citation of Torah ("For Moses said," v. 10): "Honor your father and your mother" (Exod 20:12; Deut 5:16) and "Whoever speaks evil of father or mother must surely die" (Exod 21:17; see Lev 20:9). In rabbinic debate there can be no quibble with the word of Moses; this is ἡ ἐντολὴ τοῦ θεοῦ (see vv. 8, 9). Jesus then critiques a tradition that permits a person to dishonor rather than honor parents. The adversarial nature of Jesus' description of the tradition of the elders is clear: "But you say . . ." (v. 11) set over against "For Moses said" (v. 10). What follows is not a critique of Torah as such (v. 10) but of another "saying" that comes from the Pharisees and the scribes (v. 11).

Jesus brings the difficult issue of corban into the discussion. This is a technical term referring to an offering made to God with an oath.[116] Light has been thrown upon the first-century significance of the expression from a Jewish ossuary inscription found by J. T. Milik at Jebel Ḥallet eṭ-Ṭûri. J. A. Fitzmyer translates the inscription: "All that a man may find to his profit in this ossuary (is) an offering to God from him who is in it."[117] The presence of the word on this ossuary "indicates that Jesus was referring to a dedicatory-formula which was commonly used by Jews in the last centuries B.C. and well into the Christian era."[118] But establishing this fact is only the beginning of the interpretative problem. Jesus' words against the Pharisees and the scribes could be addressing either of two possible scenarios: (1) The son is denying support to his parents because the corban is really going to the temple. (2) The son makes a rash oath to his parents—along the lines of, "This money is corban as far as you are concerned"—which (7:12 implies) Jesus' interrogators, the Pharisees and the scribes, do not later permit him to annul.[119] If the former is the case, Jesus is not pitting the traditions of the elders against the law of God, but raising the question to these strict enforcers of the letter of the law of the relative importance of God and parents. Would it be worthier to give your material possessions to your parents, or to conse-

---

114 Marcus (*Mark*, 449–50) detects an irony here that would not be lost on the Markan readers. For the Pharisees, it was Jesus who has turned to human traditions, while they follow the tradition handed down. Jesus insists that the opposite is the case.

115 There is an increasing intensity in Jesus' critique. In v. 8 he charges his opponents that they "leave" (ἀφέντες) the commandment of God. In v. 9 he accuses them of "rendering null" (ἀθετεῖτε) the commandment of God. The latter is more aggressive than the former. See H. B. Swete, *The Gospel according to St. Mark* (London: Macmillan, 1909), 147–48.

116 It appears eighty times in the Old Testament, but only in Leviticus, Numbers, and Ezekiel.

117 See J. A. Fitzmyer, "The Aramaic Qorbān Inscription from Jebel Ḥallet eṭ-Ṭûri and Mark 7:11/Matt 15:5," *JBL* 78 (1959): 60–65. For the translation, see p. 62.

118 Lane, *Mark*, 251.

119 See Gnilka, *Markus*, 1:283–84. See also Marcus, *Mark*, 445–46, 452.

crate them to God by an oath? Jesus has already addressed this question in the establishment of his new family in 3:31–35. If doing the will of God transcends all family obligations, the latter scenario must be the issue at stake in Jesus' accusation.[120] A person who makes a hasty oath and later wishes to have it annulled is not permitted to do so. This situation does not oppose the traditions of the elders to the law of God. Torah supports the inviolability of an oath (see Num 30:2; 23:21–23), and thus the issue at stake is a classic case of pitting one part of Torah against another.

In 7:10–12 Jesus presupposes that the Pharisees and the scribes upheld the strict letter of the law: oaths cannot be nullified (Num 30:2). But in doing so they allowed a person to dishonor his parents. This is a case of following the letter of Torah rather than the spirit of Torah. "Since the honoring of oaths is scriptural, the tradition which is described as revoking the word of God must be understood as the decision that the oath must be kept at whatever cost."[121] Jesus is attacking the interpretative tradition of the Pharisees and the scribes, rather than claiming their traditions are opposed to the Law.[122] Jesus cannot accept that a tradition of interpretation of Torah could deny a person the right to take back a rash oath toward parents when he has had a change of heart, and wishes to give them due honor and respect. Looking back to v. 6, the appropriateness of the citation of Isaiah becomes clear: "You honor me with your lips, but your hearts are far from me" (Isa 29:13). Such an interpretative tradition "makes void" the word of God, rendering it empty and senseless. Jesus leaves his questioners with a final stinging remark: "And many such things you do" (v. 13). Despite the suggestion (vv. 7–8, v. 9) that Jesus might reject "the traditions of the elders," such has not proved to be the case. He rejects human interpretations of that tradition that place the letter of Torah against its spirit.

The new law of purity (7:14–23)

The more positive teaching concerning Jesus' own understanding of what makes pure and impure is divided into two sections, marked by different literary forms. In 7:14–15 Jesus addresses the people in a way which is reminiscent of the beginning of his parabolic teaching in 4:2–3. His summons to listen to him (ἀκούσατέ μου πάντες καὶ σύνετε) echoes Deut 6:4 and introduces an authoritative saying (see 4:3).[123] However, what follows is stated awkwardly, lacking introduction or explanation. At one level Jesus is answering the second part of the question asked by the Pharisees and the scribes in v. 5b: why do some disciples eat with hands defiled? But there is an important twist in Jesus' answer. The Pharisees ask questions about *how* one should eat, and Jesus' answer describes *what* determines uncleanliness. In the light of the treatment of "the traditions," these parabolic words of Jesus to the people continue his theme of the proper living of Torah. There is

---

[120] This is the position of most commentators. See, for example, Nineham (*St. Mark*, 195–96), Hooker (*St. Mark*, 177–78), Cranfield (*St. Mark*, 238), Lane (*Mark*, 251), and Gnilka (*Markus*, 1:282–84).

[121] Hooker, *St. Mark*, 178.

[122] A. E. J. Rawlinson made an interesting, but unprovable comment in this regard (cited in Nineham, *St. Mark*, 190–91): "The case need not have been purely hypothetical; there may have been some contemporary *cause célèbre* of this description which formed a subject of current talk in the bazaars of Galilee."

[123] Taylor (*St. Mark*, 342) regards the introduction as a phrase intended to stress Jesus' authority to make pronouncements on Old Testament subjects.

every likelihood that this saying reaches back to the historical Jesus. But is he really canceling all the food laws of Torah in Lev 11?[124] In the Markan context, the debate with the Pharisees and the scribes continues to color Jesus' teaching. He is not pitting himself against Torah, but asking a further question: what is more important, ritual cleanliness or moral cleanliness? Both moral cleanliness and ritual cleanliness are supported by Torah. Indeed, the major part of the vices listed by Jesus in 7:20–23 are condemned there. Therefore, both answers given by Jesus thus far (vv. 6–13, vv. 14–15) raise the question concerning which part of Torah should be observed. The Markan Jesus ate with sinners (2:16–17), permitted his disciples to ignore traditional fasting practices (2:18–22), and allowed them to pluck grain on the Sabbath to satisfy their hunger (2:23–28) and to eat without proper ritual purifications (7:5). The unexplained principle of 7:15, to be further clarified to the disciples in vv. 17–23, states the principle which determined Jesus' actions in this respect: that which defiles a person is moral impurity and not ritual impurity.[125]

The situation of Mark 4 is again recalled as Jesus enters into "the house" (v. 17), leaving the people, allowing the disciples to ask for a fuller explanation of his enigmatic public pronouncements (for Mark, παραβολή; see v. 17) in vv. 14–15 (see 4:10–13, 33–34).[126] There is no indication which house is implied, but as often with Mark, the use of ὁ οἶκος indicates the gathering of the community at two levels. It reflects the world of the story, where Jesus instructs his disciples, but it also reflects the situation of the readers, privileged recipients of the mystery of the kingdom of God (see 4:11).[127] Coming at the end of the pericope, Jesus' response to the disciples shows that they have never been far from the author's focus. *Some of them* were the cause of the problem for the Pharisees and the scribes (see v. 5), suggesting that *others* were sympathetic to the stance taken by Jesus' interrogators. The citation from Isaiah aimed at the Pharisees and the scribes made reference to their hardness of heart (v. 6). Jesus has already had reason to grieve over the hardness of the hearts of the Pharisees (3:5), but the disciples have also shown hardness of heart (6:52). Thus Jesus' first words to them, once he is alone with them, indicate that he is addressing division and misunderstanding within the group. Some were able to live according to the spirit of Torah, and others were not, and thus wished to live according to the Pharisaic interpretation of the traditions of the elders (see 7:5, 7, 8, 9). Strongly reminiscent of much that has been said of the disciples to this point in the narrative (see 4:40–41; 5:16, 31; 6:30, 52), he chides them for their misunderstanding (7:18a). The disciples in Mark need further instruction on the primacy of moral cleanliness over ritual cleanliness, and no doubt this form of instruction—set at the center of a long section dealing with feeding and eating (6:31–8:21)—spoke to the situation of the Markan readers. There is subtlety in Jesus' question, "Are you *also* without understanding?" (7:18a). Many do not understand Jesus' teaching on these matters, but it is disappointing that Markan disciples are among them!

---

[124] It is likely that Jesus' attitude toward Torah reflected in v. 15 is close to that of the historical Jesus. For this conclusion, see Gnilka, *Markus,* 1:286–87; Guelich, *Mark,* 375–76. For a contrary opinion, see H. Räisänen, "Jesus and the Food Laws: Reflections on Mark 7,15," *JSNT* 16 (1982): 79–100. On the proverbial form of v. 15, see Pesch, *Markusevangelium,* 1:379. The saying exists independently in *Gos. Thom.,* 14.

[125] See Lane, *Mark,* 253–54; Gnilka, *Markus,* 1:287; Marcus, *Mark,* 452–54.

[126] On the parabolic nature of v. 15, see Painter, *Mark,* 111–12. Lane (*Mark,* 244) suggests that 7:1–23 plays the same function at the center of 6:7–8:26 as 4:1–34 played at the center of 3:7–6:6. See also Lohmeyer, *Markus,* 137.

[127] See Guelich, *Mark,* 377.

To clarify to *all* the disciples what he meant by the principle expressed in 7:15, Jesus explains the parable in two steps. In 7:18–19 he explains what cannot defile (see v. 15a). He begins with a rhetorical question of the disciples, to which they can only answer "yes" (οὐ νοεῖτε).[128] They must agree that what goes into a person only enters the stomach, while that which comes out of a person comes from the heart (see v. 6 and the use of "heart" in Isa 29:13). What enters the stomach goes through the usual bodily processes, and these processes cannot defile anyone (vv. 19–20a). The narrator then adds: "Thus he declared all foods clean" (v. 19b). The text reflects the widespread, and certainly pre-Markan, debate concerning the superiority of moral cleanliness over ritual cleanliness. It was perhaps part of a debate between the Markan community and Judaism. The earlier indication that only "some of the disciples" were disregarding laws of purity (see v. 2) makes it clear that "Jesus' response to the Pharisees was intended to move the disciples out of their shadow."[129] However, in the redactional comment of v. 19b the debate is closed! The Markan reader is told that "For him (Mark), Jesus . . . has swept away the Mosaic regulations about what is clean and unclean."[130]

Jesus then explains the second part of the parable (7:15b): what does defile (vv. 20–23). Interestingly the list of "evil things" which defile (see v. 23), coming out of the heart of a person, is traditional (see also Rom 1:29–31; Gal 5:19–21; 1 Pet 4:3).[131] The word "heart" again appears, challenging the disciples to distance themselves from the accusations made against the Pharisees and the scribes in 7:6 through the citation of Isa 29:13 and its use of the word "heart." The danger of their <u>hardness of heart (see 6:52)</u>, paralleled only by the hardness of the hearts of the Pharisees in 3:5, is recalled.[132] The list, which opens with "evil thoughts" (οἱ διαλογισμοὶ οἱ κακοί), is made up of six nouns in the plural and six in the singular.[133] It draws heavily on moral practices widely regarded as sinful: evil thoughts, fornication, theft, murder, adultery, coveting, wickedness, deceit, licentiousness, envy, slander, pride, foolishness (vv. 21b–22). Certain tensions within early Christianity can also be sensed: not all of Torah has been abrogated, but the food laws have. Not surprisingly, as Christianity emerged from its Jewish matrix, such problems surfaced in Pauline circles (e.g., 1 Cor 8:1–12; 10:14–11:1), and are reflected in the Acts of the Apostles (Acts 10:1–11:18; 15:1–35).[134] But there is another detail in the list of Mark 7:21–22 that deserves attention. Most elements in the list have their origin either directly in Torah, or are

---

[128] An interrogation beginning with οὐ normally expects a positive answer. See BDF, 226, par. 440.

[129] LaVerdiere, *The Beginning,* 1:189.

[130] Hooker, *St. Mark,* 179; see also Marcus, *Mark,* 457–58. There has been much discussion over Jesus' inconsistency in 7:1–23. The argument with the Pharisees and the scribes defends Torah (vv. 6–13) while the parable and its explanation rejects it (vv. 14–23). A certain inconsistency is present, but generated more by the Markan situation than Jesus' attitudes to the law. See Hooker (*St. Mark,* 173): "We have here a tension found repeatedly in the New Testament: the strict adherents of the Torah are accused of failing to keep it, and their Christian accusers claim on the one hand to be fulfilling it, on the other to be free from its restrictions." See also Schweizer, *Mark,* 145–47.

[131] For a fuller list of similar traditions, both pagan and Christian, see Pesch, *Markusevangelium,* 1:381–83.

[132] See also Lane, *Mark,* 255.

[133] Taylor (*St. Mark,* 345) helpfully suggests that οἱ διαλογισμοὶ οἱ κακοί serves as an introduction: "not merely evil thoughts, but evil devisings which issue in degraded acts now mentioned."

[134] See Lane, *Mark,* 256–57. As LaVerdiere (*The Beginning,* 1:187) comments: "It (7:1–23) provides a bridge from the community's earliest days to the days of Mark and the new challenges confronting the community." See Lambrecht, "Jesus and the Law," 28–39, 66–67.

related to its legislation. However, this is not so immediately obvious in the final three "evil things." Is it possible that the evilness of slander, pride, and foolishness, seemingly small things compared to fornication, theft, murder, and adultery, are in this list because they were problems faced within the Markan situation?[135]

There is sufficient indication in the text that division existed among the disciples (7:5, 18), no doubt a division reflected in the community of Markan readers. Perhaps the author regarded the presence of slander, pride, and foolishness as part of the cause for the division in the community. All such things—those found in Jewish traditions concerning food laws and those emerging from within the hearts of some members of the Christian community—come from within and therefore defile (v. 23). This critical assessment of the performance of the disciples, in their relationship to the newness of the message of Jesus over against the traditions of Israel, is subtly related to a parallel critical assessment of the performance of the Markan readers regarding their relationship to Jesus and their tendency to fall back into the more secure practices of Israel. Tensions within the Markan community, challenged by the Gentile world, will be further laid bare when Jesus journeys out of Israel, into the region of Tyre and Sidon and the Decapolis (7:24–30, 31–37), to feed a crowd on the Gentile side of the lake (8:1–9).

The First Miraculous Healing: In Gentile Lands (7:24–37)

Following the conflict with the Pharisees and the scribes, and the subsequent parable on what defiles with its private explanation to the disciples (7:1–23), Jesus works two healing miracles: he heals the daughter of the Syrophoenician woman (vv. 24–30), and the deaf and dumb man (vv. 31–37). These two accounts existed independently in the tradition, but Mark gives explicit indications of geographical locations to generate a Markan association of two miracles worked by Jesus for Gentiles in Gentile lands. In 7:24 Jesus is described as taking his leave of the Jewish region around Gennesaret, where he has been since 6:53–56, and going away (v. 24) to the region of Tyre. The following miracle takes place in that Gentile region (vv. 25–30). From there, he makes a long, circular journey back to the Sea of Galilee "through the region of the Decapolis" (v. 31). In the region of the Decapolis they bring him a deaf and dumb man, whom he cures (vv. 32–37). The superimposed geographical locations indicate that, whatever might have been the original placement of these miracle stories, Mark has given both of them Gentile settings. Thus they form a single moment in the Markan narrative: Jesus turns away from Israel and works miracles for Gentiles in Gentile lands (7:24–37).

The Syrophoenician woman (7:24–30)

Jesus' departure from the Jewish region in which his previous activities have taken place is very deliberate: Ἐκεῖθεν δὲ ἀναστὰς ἀπῆλθεν εἰς τὰ ὅρια Τύρου (v. 24a).[136] Markan themes continue as the narrator describes Jesus' entry into a house so that it would not be

---

[135] Ernst (*Markus,* 206–7) also raises this issue.

[136] The words καὶ Σιδῶνος (and Sidon) may be original, but they are missing from a number of manuscripts, and might be there as the result of an assimilation from Matt 15:21. For their exclusion, see Guelich (*Mark,* 382 n. b.), Gnilka (*Markus,* 1:291), and Metzger (*Textual Commentary,* 82). For their inclusion, see Schweizer, *Mark,* 152.

known he is in the region, but such matters could not be kept secret (v. 24b).[137] This redactional introduction to the encounter with the Syrophoenician woman (v. 25) sets the Gentile scene, and indicates for the critic that the story as a whole, while certainly containing many pre-Markan elements, comes largely from the hand of Mark.[138] It is in this place in the Gospel because it serves the Markan literary and theological agenda to locate it here.[139] Jesus is in a Gentile region, having deliberately "risen" from his earlier Jewish location and "gone away" from there.[140] Despite hopes that his presence in the region of Tyre would not become public knowledge, it was impossible for him to hide (see also vv. 36–37). The rest of the account, with a notable (and infamous) exception, follows the regular form of a miracle story:

a. A problem is identified (7:25).
b. A request is made (7:26).
c. Jesus responds by word, touch, or gesture (7:29).
d. The cure takes place (7:30).

The verses not present in this classification (7:27–28) record Jesus' apparently shocking rebuff of the woman's request, and her response.[141] Along with other accounts in the synoptic tradition (see Matt 8:5–13 // Luke 7:1–10) and the Fourth Gospel (see John 4:46–54), this miracle is an example of a miracle worked from a distance. All New Testament examples of this genre lack the marveling that generally concludes most miracle stories (see, for example, vv. 31–37). Mark 7:24–30 has been further complicated by the exchange of words between Jesus and the woman.[142]

The public awareness of Jesus' presence (7:24c) prepares the stage for the approach of the Syrophoenician woman. Two matters are mentioned: the fact that she has a daughter possessed by an unclean spirit, and that she responds "immediately" to the word that he is present. She came and fell at his feet (v. 25). The marks of a believing response to Jesus are found here: she hears of his presence and prostrates herself before him. There is

---

137 On the Markan nature of v. 24, see Guelich, *Mark*, 383–84. It has nothing to do with the possible shame of being in a Gentile household, but part of the Markan attempt to present Jesus as someone who, in the end, cannot be hidden. See Gnilka, *Markus*, 1:291. See also below, on vv. 36–37.

138 Mark did not create this story of the Gentile woman. It came to him in his sources. However, Mark is responsible for its present location in the narrative theology of the unfolding Gospel story. See Meier, *A Marginal Jew*, 2:660.

139 See Marcus, *Mark*, 446. For a summary of discussions of the history of the tradition, and suggestions concerning the place of the story in the Markan redaction, see Meier, *A Marginal Jew*, 2:659–61, 674–77.

140 Against this suggestion, claiming that there is nothing particularly "Gentile" about the region of Tyre, see Hooker, *St. Mark*, 181. Most commentators agree that in 7:24 Jesus moves into Gentile territory. See, for example, Guelich (*Mark*, 383); Gnilka (*Markus*, 1:291); Nineham (*St. Mark*, 197), with reservations; Lührmann (*Markusevangelium*, 130–31); LaVerdiere (*The Beginning*, 1:200); Lane (*Mark*, 259–60).

141 The present text combines a number of form-critical elements, and there is little agreement about its "form": see Guelich, *Mark*, 383–83; Gnilka, *Markus* 1:289–91. On the classification of a distance miracle, see Grundmann, *Markus*, 153; Pesch, *Markusevangelium*, 1:385–86. The Matthean version of the Markan original (see Matt 15:21–28) is not included in this list, although it is distinctive. See W. D. Davies and D. C. Allison (*A Critical and Exegetical Commentary on the Gospel according to Saint Matthew* [ICC; 3 vols.; Edinburgh: T&T Clark, 1988–1997], 2:542–43) for a clear defense of the Markan originality of the pericope.

142 On the basis of this exchange of words a number of scholars (e.g., Gnilka, *Markus*, 1:291) regard it as a teaching story, while others (e.g., Taylor, *St. Mark*, 347) classify it as a pronouncement story.

recognition of who he is, in a prostration that parallels the actions of Jairus and the woman with the flow of blood (see 5:22, 33). She appears to be confident of his ability to remedy the ailment of her daughter. But before the communication between the only characters in the narrative begins, the author must return to the matter which has determined his arrangement of the material: "Now the woman was a Greek, a Syrophoenician by birth" (7:26a). To the generic word "Greek" (Ἑλληνίς) is added a more local ethnic (and geographical) specification: Syrophoenician; i.e., she is Phoenician, born in Syria. This information is important for Mark's ongoing narrative and theological argument, and also for the detail of this particular story. Once the Gentile character of the woman is established, the traditional pattern of a miracle story can follow: she asks that Jesus cast the demon out of her daughter (v. 26).

While Jesus' response continues themes which have been building since 6:31–44, it introduces the Gentile theme with an unexpected sharpness. In 6:31–44 Jesus fed the Jewish multitudes in a Jewish region. As we have seen, that narrative was heavily marked by Jewish themes: the desert location (vv. 31, 35), the shepherd (v. 34), the sitting in companies (vv. 39–40), connections with Ps 23 (vv. 34, 39, 42), bread in the desert (v. 41), and the collection of the fragments into twelve baskets (v. 43). However, in 7:1–23 the representatives of Israel (the Pharisees and the scribes) demonstrated that they had their own understanding of what and how one should eat (see 7:2, 5). They are not prepared to accept the newness that Jesus, the shepherd, brings to Israel with his gift of bread. The parable which he speaks to the people (7:14–15) and its private explanation to the disciples (7:17–23) comments further upon the closed religious system of Israel, and exhorts Jesus' "new family" (see 3:7–6:6a) to transcend such limitations. The representatives of Israel claim to preserve the traditions of the elders, but in fact impose "human commandments" (7:7), "human tradition" (v. 8), "your tradition" (v. 9), thus annulling the commandments of God (v. 9). Consequently the sharp remarks that Jesus addressed to the Syrophoenician woman in 7:27 seem at odds with the narrative to this point. In the face of a negative reception, Jesus has risen from his place in Israel and walked away (v. 24). Yet Israel remains the privileged recipient of Jesus' gift of bread (ἄρτος).[143] Despite the encounter recorded in 7:1–23, he insists: "Let the children first be fed, for it is not fitting to take the children's bread (ἄρτον) and throw it to the dogs" (v. 27).

Several remarks must be made. In the first place, this saying is certainly pre-Markan, and has the ring of a traditional proverbial saying.[144] The region of Tyre (see v. 24a) was regarded as Gentile, but also contained many Jews.[145] Within a setting of a mixed population of Gentiles and Jews, Jesus' words sound very like the proverbial response of the Jewish population which regards itself as God's people, and thus superior to the surrounding "lesser" groups of Gentile origin.[146] The description of the Gentiles as "dogs" (κυνάρια) is not surprising when some such setting for the saying is recognized.[147] We must appreciate

---

[143] See Waetjen, *Reordering*, 134–35.

[144] See Pesch, *Markusevangelium*, 1:389.

[145] See Hooker (*St. Mark*, 181): "the population was as mixed as in Galilee."

[146] See Taylor, *St. Mark*, 350. Using the criteria for historicity, a good case can also be made that these are *ipsissima verba Jesu*: Meier, *A Marginal Jew*, 2:659–71. Even if this were the case, the original setting for these words has been lost in what is now an important Markan story in the "bread" cycle of 6:31–8:21. Schweizer (*Mark*, 151) is surely correct in claiming that "the story must have been directed from the very beginning to the problem of the relation of the Gentiles to the Jews."

[147] As Pesch (*Markusevengelium*, 1:389) remarks: "The regular presence of diminutive forms in the passage indicates the common folk-language." See also Ernst, *Markus*, 212–13.

the subtlety and strength of the Markan rhetoric in this encounter. Having walked away from an arrogant Israel (v. 24; see vv. 1–23), Jesus initially perseveres with the theme of 6:31–44: he gives bread to Israel. He insists that "the children," Israel, be fed first, claiming that it is improper to take that bread and cast it to the Gentiles ("the dogs"). But the reader is aware that Israel has been fed "first." The same verb for feeding (χορτάζω, 7:27) was used in the narrator's remark in 6:42 that all ate and were satisfied. But the response of "the children" has been an arrogant rejection of Jesus' new law of freedom (vv. 1–23). Verses 24–30 cannot be understood without placing them within this context. Jesus is not initiating the move to feed the Gentiles. This woman has heard of him, has come to him, and has fallen at his feet (v. 25).[148] This response to the presence of Jesus is the paradigm for a Gentile world recognizing Jesus and coming to faith in him. But Jesus' initial reaction is to maintain the priority of the mission to Israel (v. 27).[149] This resistance on the part of Jesus matches the resistance of the early Christian church.[150] There may have been some in the Markan community who shared sentiments similar to those expressed by Jesus in v. 27. However, they probably stopped there. They may have been unmoved by the worshiping response of Gentiles to Jesus, coming to him once they have heard of him (see v. 25).

But the encounter between Jesus and the Syrophoenician woman does not stop there! The rhetoric of the passage, read in a community where many were uncertain about the presence of Gentiles at the Christian table, would have been powerful. Coming hard upon the heels of Israel's rejection of Jesus' offer of bread, the woman *accepts* that she is a "dog," and that she must place herself second, after the prior (πρῶτον, v. 27) feeding of Israel (v. 28).[151] In her nothingness, she comes with a complete openness to Jesus. She recognizes that she brings nothing to the meal, but addresses Jesus as "Lord" (κύριε) and asks to sit under the table to be fed the crumbs which fall from the meal Jesus has prepared for the nourishment of Israel (see 6:31–44).[152]

The contrast between Israel's response to Jesus (7:1–23) and the response of the Gentile Syrophoenician woman (7:24–30) could not be more stark. The impact of this se-

---

148 The woman's actions are described with the strong verb προσπίπτω, rather than simply πίπτω. The former verb does not necessarily indicate "worship," but it involves a placing of oneself at the mercy of others. See BDAG, 884, s.v. προσπίπτω. The same verb is used to describe the action of Jairus in 5:22. Guelich (*Mark,* 385) comments: "The contrast in types between a Gentile woman and a president of the synagogue could not be more exaggerated."

149 See, among many, Pesch (*Markusevangelium,* 1:388). The four Gospels and even Paul (see Rom 15:8) attest that Jesus had no missionary program to the Gentiles. See the fundamental study on this question by J. Jeremias, *Jesus' Promise to the Nations* (trans. S. H. Hooke; London: SCM, 1967).

150 There is hardly need to document this. The Pauline literature (especially Galatians, Philippians, and Romans) and early chapters of Acts are eloquent proof that such was the case. For the Lukan paradigm of the tension and its solution, see Acts 15:1–29. The Markan community was not free of this tension. See Lührmann, *Markusevangelium,* 131.

151 The power of the rhetoric is lost by those who attempt to soften the expression, or direct the word "dog" away from the Gentile woman. See, for example, Lohmeyer (*Markus,* 147), Lane (*Mark,* 262), Cranfield (*St. Mark,* 248), and Schweizer (*Mark,* 152), who, on the basis of the diminutive form of κυνάριον (see BDAG, 575, s.v. κυνάριον), suggest it is an affectionate term, and LaVerdiere (*The Beginning,* 1:201–2), who appeals to the phrase's proverbial nature to claim that it does not apply to this specific woman. See the survey in Corley (*Private Women,* 99–100). Against this, see Nineham (*St. Mark,* 201); Guelich (*Mark,* 586–87); Pesch (*Markusevangelium,* 1:389); Marcus (*Mark,* 463–64).

152 The expression κύριε may simply indicate a respectful and formal manner of address ("Sir"), but in this context (see especially v. 25) "it is possible that Mark sees a deeper significance in it" (Hooker, *St. Mark,* 183). See also Gnilka, *Markus,* 1:293.

quence of words and events upon a readership that was comfortable with Jesus' words in 7:26, words which reflected both a traditional proverb and their own mind-set, must be recognized. Jesus grants her request. He tells her that she may leave, as the demon has left her daughter (v. 29b). The motivation for the granting of the miracle is also specified: διά τοῦτον τὸ λόγον ("because of what you have just said," v. 29a).[153] The boundaries between Jew and Gentile are important.[154] Nevertheless, they are transcended by those who come to Jesus in their nothingness, recognize that only in Jesus can God's design be discovered, and seek it from him alone.[155] This is what the woman has done. Even the well-established and much respected boundaries between Jew and Greek must fall when such faith is shown. The miracle has been worked at a distance. All New Testament accounts of miracles worked at a distance (Matt 8:5–13; Luke 7:1–10; John 4:46–54) are performed as the result of a Gentile request.[156] This "is perhaps to be understood as symbolic of the salvation which comes to the Gentiles, hitherto far away."[157]

The sharp response of Jesus in 7:27 serves a number of purposes. It links this narrative with the ongoing discussions over bread and feeding which are very present from 6:31 to 7:23 and will continue until 8:21. It articulates the position of some in the Markan community who would prefer to limit the Christian community, *and its table*, to Jews.[158] It establishes a rhetorical effect that throws into sharp relief the Gentile woman's recognition of her nothingness. The passage concludes rapidly. Her recognition of *who she is* in v. 28 further enhances her earlier recognition of *who Jesus is* in v. 24. Jesus shares himself (and thus his table: vv. 27–28) with a Gentile woman who returns home and finds that his "word," in response to her "word" (v. 29), is effective: what he said would happen has happened. The child is lying in bed and the demon has left her (v. 30). The astonishment of those readers who, like the disciples in v. 18, were still "without understanding" is still with us, as even the contemporary reader finds this passage, when read outside its Markan context, so difficult. A skillful storyteller is leading a puzzled readership toward an unexpected conclusion as Jesus walks deeper into Gentile territory in v. 31.

---

[153] On this understanding of διά in v. 29, see Cranfield, *St. Mark*, 249.

[154] Many commentators see behind the πρῶτον ("first") an early reflection of salvation history: first the Jews and then the Gentiles (see Rom 1:16; 2:9–10; Acts 13:46). See, for example, Gnilka (*Markus*, 1:294); Marcus (*Mark*, 469). But Lane (*Mark*, 263), on the basis of the food falling from the table and consumed by the dogs, suggests that the woman is subtly arguing that "they are fed *at the same time* as the children" (stress in original). This is unlikely. See Pesch, *Markusevangelium*, 1:388.

[155] As Hooker (*St. Mark*, 183–84) comments: "Her words are an indication of her faith that the power of God is at work in Jesus, and the healing is therefore linked with the same kind of faith-response that characterizes the other miracles. She has no claims to assistance but depends wholly on grace." See the similar remarks in Schweizer, *Mark*, 153.

[156] In defense of the βασιλικός in John 4:46–54 as a Gentile, see F. J. Moloney, *Belief in the Word: Reading John 1–4* (Minneapolis: Fortress, 1993), 182–83.

[157] Hooker, *St. Mark*, 184. Corley (*Private Women*, 95–102) points out that the account has all the possibilities of an encounter between Jesus and a public, promiscuous woman, but that Mark shows no interest in this. His concern is Jesus' encounter with a Gentile.

[158] On the relevance of the passage in the Markan community, see Marcus, *Mark*, 470–71. Many commentators correctly link this passage with the mission to the Gentiles (see, for example, Nineham, *St. Mark*, 197–98). However, the positioning of the passage in the "bread section" of the Gospel (6:31–8:21) indicates that the question of a mission to the Gentiles may no longer be the *major* problem (see Guelich, *Mark*, 387). A further issue emerges: are these Gentiles to be part of the shared table? On this, see the suggestion of Taylor (*St. Mark*, 350), and the groundbreaking (although overstated) work of Quesnell (*The Mind of Mark*, 224–28). The suggestion that this might mean the eucharistic table is rejected by, among others, Gnilka (*Markus*, 1:293).

The healing of the deaf and dumb man (7:31–37)

A "returning" from the region of Tyre, first to the north, via Sidon, and then east and south to the Sea of Galilee by means of a journey through the region of the Decapolis (7:31) is a very odd journey.[159] In a Markan strategy, Jesus is led deep into a Gentile region. The region of Tyre was occupied by a mixed population of Gentiles and Jews, but the region of the Decapolis was predominantly Gentile. The miracle which follows is a perfect example of a miracle story:[160]

    a. A problem is identified (7:32a).
    b. A request is made (7:32b).
    c. Jesus responds by word, touch, and gesture (7:33–34).
    d. The cure takes place (7:35).
    e. The miracle is greeted by wonder (7:37).

There are three major insertions into the traditional miracle story: the Gentile setting (7:31), the typically Markan command to secrecy which is enthusiastically ignored (v. 36), and the allusion to Isa 35:5–6 when the people who brought the man to Jesus express their astonishment (v. 37b). These additions to the tradition suggest the literary and theological reasons for the author's placing the account at this stage of his narrative.[161]

A deaf and dumb man is led to Jesus by unidentified people.[162] Mark has devoted much attention to the introduction of this episode into the narrative (7:31), and has placed it immediately after Jesus' encounter with a Syrophoenician woman (see also v. 24). The man and his companions must be regarded as Gentile (v. 32a).[163] The man's associates ask that Jesus lay his hand upon him (v. 32b). The request is typical of a miracle story. There is no explicit request that Jesus cure the man of his ailments, but it is implied in the request for a gesture regularly associated with miracle-working.[164] Jesus takes the man

---

159 Hooker (*St. Mark*, 185) continues to strain against any reference to Jesus' presence to Gentiles in Gentile regions. She admits that the journey is strange, but claims that "there is no reason why we should suppose, either that Jesus necessarily went from one place to another by the quickest route, or that Mark believed that he always did so." For detailed and documented discussions of this odd Markan journey, see Taylor (*St. Mark*, 352–53); Guelich (*Mark*, 391–93). Painter (*Mark's Gospel*, 116) rightly remarks: "The overall journey inclines the reader to conclude that Jesus continued to deal with Gentiles." See also Lührmann, *Markusevangelium*, 132–33.

160 Taylor, *St. Mark*, 352; Gnilka, *Markus*, 1:296; Guelich, *Mark*, 390. On the rhythmic nature of the pre-Markan story, see Lohmeyer (*Markus*, 149); Grundmann (*Markus*, 155).

161 On account of the numerous structural and thematic parallels between 7:31–37 and 8:22–26, it is generally agreed that these two stories were transmitted together, perhaps with the acclamation now found in 7:37 common to both. See, for example, Cranfield, *St. Mark*, 253–55; Gnilka, *Markus*, 1:296; Guelich, *Mark*, 398; Meier, *A Marginal Jew*, 2:691; Marcus, *Mark*, 476–77.

162 The English term "dumb" is not precise. The rare word μογιλάλον literally indicates that he was able to make noises, but not able to speak coherently. Mark chooses this rare word because it points toward v. 37 and the allusion there to Isa 35:6, where this word also appears in the LXX. See Nineham (*St. Mark*, 202); Cranfield (*St. Mark*, 251).

163 A number of commentators regard this as unimportant, claiming that Mark never indicates that either the deaf and dumb man or his colleagues are Gentiles. See, for example, Gnilka, *Markus*, 1:296; Guelich, *Mark*, 391; Hooker, *St. Mark*, 185. The context *demands* that they be regarded as Gentile, whether or not Mark explicitly says so. Text without context is pretext. See Guelich, *Mark*, 394.

164 Against Lane (*Mark*, 266), who suggests that the reason for their surprise in v. 37 stems from the fact that in v. 32 they only requested a blessing, not a cure.

aside so that they might be alone (see also 8:23),[165] and a series of gestures are described. There is evidence that such gestures were widespread among miracle-workers: touching the place of the ailment (fingers in the ears and touching the tongue), and spitting (see John 9:6; Pliny, *Nat.*, 28:4.7; Tacitus, *Hist.*, 4:81; 6:18; Suetonius, *Vesp.*, 7).[166] As well as the gestures, however, Jesus speaks what may have been regarded in the original tradition as something of a magic word: "*ephphatha*." This Aramaic word is translated by the author as "be opened."[167] The need to translate the expression indicates that it was obscure to the Gentile man and his companions as well as to the readers of the Gospel and would sound like the gibberish found in non-Christian magic texts.[168]

The miracle follows immediately: the man's ears are opened and his tongue loosened. He hears and speaks coherently (7:35).[169] The Markan theme of the need for secrecy follows. Jesus commands them strongly not to tell anyone. However, as has become increasingly the case in the unfolding story, the more he commands, the more his deeds are proclaimed (v. 36). A secret that can no longer be kept secret leads toward the first public recognition of Jesus in 7:37.[170] Coming as it does toward the end of 6:6b–8:30, this unfolding command to secrecy in 7:36, repeated in 8:26, points toward the climax of the first half of the story (8:27–30) and the beginnings of the second half (8:31). The unidentified companions of the deaf and dumb man, and possibly the multitudes mentioned passingly in v. 33, are "absolutely overwhelmed" (ὑπερπερισσῶς ἐξεπλήσσοντο).[171] This hyperbolic statement of their astonishment leads to a report, in direct speech, of their understanding

---

[165] It is too much to claim on the basis of the expression κατ᾽ ἰδίαν in v. 33 and the use of the same expression in 4:10 and 7:17 that the man is being called to discipleship. For this position, see LaVerdiere, *The Beginning*, 1:204.

[166] Str-B, 2:15–17; Dibelius, *From Tradition to Gospel*, 84–86; Taylor, *St. Mark*, 354–55; Gnilka, *Markus*, 1:297; Guelich, *Mark*, 395; Marcus, *Mark*, 473–74; B. Blackburn, *Theios Anêr and the Markan Miracle Tradition: A Critique of the Theois Anêr Concept as an Interpretive Background to the Miracle Traditions Used by Mark* (WUNT 2. Reihe 40; Tübingen: J. C. B. Mohr [Paul Siebeck], 1991), 218–19.

[167] There has been a long dispute whether the word is Hebrew and Aramaic. See the summary in Guelich, *Mark*, 395–96. It is now generally agreed that it is Aramaic, and many regard the presence of an Aramaic word in the tradition as indication of the antiquity of the pre-Markan tradition. See the detailed and fully documented study of this issue in Meier, *A Marginal Jew*, 2:759 n. 159. Meier (pp. 711–14) believes that the account shows that "during his ministry Jesus claimed that he empowered the deaf to hear" (p. 714).

[168] For a collection, see C. K. Barrett, *New Testament Background: Selected Documents* (London: SPCK, 1956), 29–36, esp. 31–35; also Guelich, *Mark*, 396; Painter, *Mark's Gospel*, 117. Jesus' "sighing" is also a part of these magical traditions. See Marcus, *Mark*, 474.

[169] It is sometimes suggested that the "loosening" (ἐλύθη) reflects the man's being under the thrall of Satan (see Luke 13:16). See Nineham, *St. Mark*, 204; Grundmann, *Markus*, 157 n. 7; Schweizer, *Mark*, 154; Pesch, *Markusevangelium*, 1:397. Against this, see Taylor, *St. Mark*, 355; Lane, *Mark*, 267.

[170] The question of the so-called "messianic secret," discussed above (see pp. 59–60), returns. See Lohmeyer, *Markus*, 151; Grundmann, *Markus*, 157; Schweizer, *Mark*, 154; Pesch, *Markusevangelium*, 1:398. Possibly the historical Jesus "played down" exaggerated suggestions concerning a messianic status, and this would be the origins of a literary and theological feature developed in the Gospel of Mark. The secret which is not a secret leads to potential misunderstandings of who Jesus might be. Commands to secrecy disappear after 8:27–30 (see 4:35–36; 5:37, 40; 6:31–32; 7:36; 8:23, 30). It is no longer a secret: Jesus is the Messiah (8:27–30), but also a Son of Man whose suffering will be vindicated by the action of God (see 8:31; 9:31; 10:32–34). As Hooker (*St. Mark*, 185) rightly remarks: "It is only those who believe in the risen Lord who can understand the full significance of what was taking place in Jesus' ministry. Mark presumably expected those for whom he was writing to be among those who were able to comprehend." The irony might be, given the portrait of the disciples, that they did not comprehend—and this is one of the reasons why the Gospel was written.

[171] The translation of the overstated Greek is from Guelich, *Mark*, 397.

of what Jesus' actions reveal: "He has done all things well; he even makes the deaf hear and the dumb speak" (v. 37). The allusion to Isa 35:5–6 is unmistakable.[172] This passage, already used in messianic contexts in pre-Christian times,[173] and part of the Christian use of the Old Testament to describe Jesus (see Matt 11:5 // Luke 7:22; Acts 26:18),[174] is proclaimed (ἐκήρυσσον, 7:36) by Gentiles.[175] This is the first public recognition of Jesus as a potential messiah figure and, anticipating the end of the Gospel (see 15:39), Gentiles are first to recognize this possibility.[176] However, the earlier command of Jesus to secrecy warns the reader that this identification may not represent the whole truth. It must not be thought that the mystery of the Messiah has been solved in this suggestion of the Gentiles in 7:37. That honor lies with the disciples, represented by Peter, in 8:29, but even that confession will be followed by a command to silence. Something of the mystery remains, and the rest of the story attempts to unravel it.[177]

Jesus has broken through the barrier of a table closed to the Gentiles (7:24–30), and Gentiles are the first people publicly to recognize Jesus' messianic potential (vv. 31–37). He has done all things well (v. 37). This expression of faith may be faltering and incipient, but it matches the response of the woman to the presence of Jesus in v. 25b and v. 28. The disciples have not been part of the action across these two episodes, but the last time they appeared they were described by Jesus as "without understanding" (v. 18). The Syrophoenician woman displays the signs of a true believer (vv. 25, 28–29), and the Gentiles from the region of the Decapolis have made an initial and limited suggestion that Jesus might be the Messiah (v. 37). There is a narrative contrast between the privileged disciples (see 1:16–20; 3:13–14; 6:7–13) and characters from the Gentile world (7:24–37).[178] But the reader is not unprepared for this contrast. The theme of the increasing fragility of the disciples' faith has already emerged (see 4:40–41; 5:16, 31; 6:30, 35–37, 52; 7:18).

The focus upon the Gentiles does not disappear in the episode that follows.[179] There is no change of location, and a close link is made with what has been told in 7:24–37 through the expression "in those days." This vague Markan link leads into the second multiplication of the loaves and fish, where the disciples will once again be actively associated with Jesus' ministry (8:1–9). The reader has come to the end of a cycle that reported a multiplication

---

[172] It is an allusion, not a direct citation, of LXX Isa 35:5–6. However, as pointed out above, the reader has already been prepared for it through the use of the words κωφόν and the rare μογιλάλον in v. 32 to describe the ailments of the man. Both words appear in LXX Isa 35:5–6. See the detailed analysis in Lane, *Mark*, 268 n. 81. Gnilka (*Markus*, 1:298) also sees a link between καλῶς πάντα πεποίηκεν with LXX Gen 1:31, and a hint of Jesus' actions demonstrating an eschatological new creation. See also Lohmeyer, *Markus*, 151; Cranfield, *St. Mark*, 253; Ernst, *Markus*, 217; Meier, *A Marginal Jew*, 2:711–12; Marcus, *Mark*, 480–81.

[173] See C. K. Barrett, *The Holy Spirit in the Gospel Tradition* (London: SPCK, 1970), 70–71.

[174] It is often associated with the similar sentiments expressed in Isa 61:1–2 (see also 58:6). See B. Lindars, *New Testament Apologetic: The Doctrinal Significance of the Old Testament Quotations* (London: SCM, 1961), 248. Lindars claims that these Isaianic passages are found only in Q and Luke. Mark 7:37 has been overlooked. It is also used in the rabbinic tradition. See *Gen. Rab.* 95; *Tep.* 146:8.

[175] See Nineham (*St. Mark*, 204), who cites Lightfoot favorably: "Here . . . we must suppose that the Evangelist wishes to draw attention to the messianic nature of the act of Jesus."

[176] It is insufficient to claim, as does Nineham (*St. Mark*, 202), that the Gentiles are saying: "How exactly he fulfils the prophecies!" If that is the case, the further question is posed: who is he?

[177] See Schweizer, *Mark*, 155.

[178] See also Guelich, *Mark*, 399.

[179] As Lohmeyer (*Markus*, 144) makes clear.

of loaves and fishes (6:31–44), a journey in a boat and two reactions to Jesus (6:45–56), conflict (7:1–23), and healing (7:24–37). The cycle reopens with the report of a second multiplication of loaves and fish.[180]

The Second Multiplication of the Loaves and Fish: Among the Gentiles (8:1–9)

Two indications of time open the episode which follows: "in those days" and "again." The former expression links the events which follow with the immediately previous episodes: the healing of the daughter of the Syrophoenician woman and the deaf and dumb man in a Gentile land (7:24–37).[181] The latter looks back to the earlier multiplication of loaves and fish (6:31–44). In 6:34 Jesus had looked upon a "great crowd." Large groups of people have been associated with Jesus in the intervening episodes (see 6:45; 7:14, 17, 33), but not until 8:1a are they described as a "great crowd." A deliberate reprise of 6:31–44 is initiated by the use of πάλιν in 8:1a.[182] With the earlier feeding of the great crowd in mind, enriched by the ongoing conflicts and discussions over bread and the sharing of table (see 6:52; 7:2–4, 5, 18–19, 27–28), the reader learns from the narrator in 8:1b that this second crowd had nothing to eat.[183]

Jesus' sentiments reported in 6:34 (ἐσπλαγχνίσθη ἐπ' αὐτούς) become his words to the disciples in 8:2: "I have compassion on the crowd" (σπλαγχνίζομαι ἐπὶ τὸν ὄχλον), but a new element is added to the second story with the introduction of Jesus' description in 8:2b–3 of the situation of the large crowd. Another link is made with Jesus' immediately previous presence "in the region of Tyre" (7:24) and "the region of the Decapolis" (7:31). The crowd has been with Jesus for three days. The "three days" may be the remnant of an earlier tradition, but in the present narrative it indicates that Jesus is still on the Gentile

---

[180] Lane (*Mark*, 265) remarks that v. 37 closes the first cycle "on a doxological note." There is some truth in this claim, but one must be aware of the limitations to the link between the Markan Christology and the messianic expectations of LXX Isa 35:5–6.

[181] Against those (e.g., Hooker, *St. Mark*, 188) who reject the close temporal link created by "in those days." See Taylor, *St. Mark*, 357; Cranfield, *St. Mark*, 255; Painter, *Mark's Gospel*, 118–19.

[182] See Guelich, *Mark*, 403; LaVerdiere, *The Beginning*, 1:205 n. 24.

[183] Scholarly discussion of the tradition history of the two bread miracles is inconclusive. Majority opinion suggests that Mark has used two originally independent traditions: see, e.g., Gnilka, *Markus*, 1:300–301; Ernst, *Markus*, 218–19; Hooker, *St. Mark*, 187, K. P. Donfried, "The Feeding Narratives and the Marcan Community," in *Kirche: Festschrift für Günther Bornkamm zum 75. Geburtstag* (ed. D. Lührmann and G. Strecker; Tübingen: J. C. B. Mohr [Paul Siebeck], 1980), 95–103, and Meier, *A Marginal Jew*, 2:951–58, with the noteworthy added consideration of the tradition behind John 6:1–15. Lagrange (*Saint Marc*, 193–94) and Lane (*Mark*, 271–72) claim that Mark understood that Jesus had multiplied loaves and fishes twice. See the discussion of these positions in Guelich, *Mark*, 401–2. Fowler (*Loaves and Fishes*, 43–90) has attempted to separate tradition from redaction, and claims that 8:1–9 (minus the redactional vv. 1–2) is the original tradition, reworked by Mark to form 6:31–44. The suggestion that Mark is depending upon a pre-Markan doublet of 6:35–7:37 and 8:1–26 (see the summary in Quesnell, *The Mind of Mark*, 28–38) is widely rejected. For an exhaustive survey of theories concerning the redaction history of the passages, from Wendling (1905) to a series of articles published in 1995, see van Oyen, *The Interpretation of the Feeding Miracles*, 21–171, and the briefer summary on pp. 174–86. My understanding of 6:31–8:21 as a statement and restatement (following Lightfoot) makes no presupposition about the shape of pre-Markan sources. This is effective storytelling on Mark's part (see Nineham, *St. Mark*, 206–7).

side of the Sea of Galilee, with a crowd that has accompanied him during the episodes among the Gentiles of 7:24–37.[184] The reader also recalls it was on the same eastern side of the lake that Jesus had his first encounter with the Gentile world of the Gerasene demoniac, the Legion, and the unclean swine (5:1–20).[185] The motive for Jesus' concern for the Gentile crowd is different from his earlier compassion.[186] Against a background of Ps 23 and Ezek 34, Jesus had compassion on the Jewish crowd because they were like sheep without a shepherd, and he began to teach them (6:34). In 8:2–3 no reference is made to this Jewish literary and theological background. Jesus' concern is motivated by the hunger of the Gentile crowd. He is unwilling to send them away to their homes, as they will faint on the way. There is no call for symbolic interpretation of this "fainting." It is preparation for the closing statement of Jesus' reason for concern: "some of them have come a very long way" (v. 3c). This statement may be taken on its face value. For humanitarian reasons, they must not be sent away; many of them might faint on a long journey. But set within the broader and the immediate context, it is a further indication of the Gentile origin of the crowd. The larger context has provided Jesus' ongoing presence in a Gentile land, with Gentile crowds. The immediate context, read as a reprise of 6:31–44, has already associated this crowd with Jesus' activity among the Gentiles in the immediately preceding episodes (8:2b). Also, the Jewish elements in the earlier miracle story have been eliminated. Jesus is no longer the shepherd of Israel, teaching a troubled people, but anxious to feed people who have come a very long way (see v. 3, in the light of 6:34). The background to this expression, therefore, must be found in such passages of Josh 9:6, 9, and Isa 40:4, where the Gentiles are described as "coming from afar" (see also Acts 2:39; 22:21; Eph 2:12, 17).[187]

The disciples continue to display their lack of understanding of who Jesus is and what he is able to do. This lack of understanding parallels the earlier bread miracle. They ask: "How can one feed these men with bread here in the desert?" (ὧδε χορτάσαι ἄρτων ἐπ' ἐρημίας, v. 4). They have learned nothing from their association with Jesus' earlier feeding (6:42: ἐχορτάσθησαν) the multitudes in the desert (see 6:35: ἔρημος) with bread (see 6:37, 38, 41, 44: ἄρτος).[188] He asks a question of the disciples which leads them again to indicate that they have not remained true to the command they were given as they were sent out on the mission (see 6:7–13). When asked, they admit they are carrying seven loaves (8:5), despite the fact that in 6:8 they were told to take no loaf. The disciples' behavior in this epi-

---

[184] Marcus, *Mark,* 492. As often in her interpretation of 8:1–9, Hooker (*St. Mark,* 189) struggles to deny that the "three days" associates the crowd with the immediately previous events: "*It is natural to suppose* that he thinks of Jesus teaching the crowd throughout the period" (stress mine). Such subjective arguments do not convince. However, it is too much to read the "three days" as a proleptic reference to the presence of the postresurrection Jesus to Jew and Gentile (see LaVerdiere, *The Beginning,* 1:208–9; Marcus, *Mark,* 492).

[185] See Guelich, *Mark,* 402–3; against Hooker, *St. Mark,* 188: "Mark makes no reference to his being on Gentile territory." The earlier location of the Gerasene demoniac (5:1–20) on this side of the lake is a good internal reference. The author of the Gospel of Matthew has already seen this. He relocates the second multiplication on a Galilean mountainside, near the shore of the Sea of Galilee (see Matt 15:29–39).

[186] See Taylor, *St. Mark,* 358; Lane, *Mark,* 273.

[187] Guelich, *Mark,* 404; Marcus, *Mark,* 487; against Hooker, *St. Mark,* 188: " 'have come a long distance' could well mean that we are to understand that they have come from Galilee." See also Schweizer, *Mark,* 156. Gnilka (*Markus,* 1:302), while admitting the possibility of a reference to the Gentiles, does not think that it is the case here.

[188] See Marcus, *Mark,* 495–96.

sode, as in 6:31–44, is a central concern of the storyteller.[189] In the indications that follow, the Jewish elements in the first bread miracle are consistently absent. Jesus commands the people to sit down on the ground (v. 6a). All reference to the exodus people, in companies of hundreds and fifties, and the background of Ps 23 in the earlier indication that they sat on the green grass (6:39–40), has disappeared in this reprise. Even this early in the episode the Markan reader is aware of the Gentile nature of the feeding that will follow.

As in 6:41, Jesus' actions and words in 8:6 recall the eucharistic practices of the early church.[190] Unlike the earlier account, where Jesus blessed, broke, and gave to the disciples to distribute the bread and the fish, in 8:6 only the bread is mentioned, heightening the eucharistic allusion.[191] Nevertheless, out of respect for the tradition, and also to maintain the nature of the reprise, Mark adds that there were also some small fish, which Jesus blesses and commands the disciples to set before the crowd (v. 7). As in 6:31–44, Jesus generates nourishment for the hungry from the disciples' meager (and perhaps questionable: see 6:8) possessions, and they administer the meal.[192] The fish, however, are not part of the "blessing," the "breaking," and the "giving," as they were in 6:41. A further subtle alteration has taken place. In 6:41 the word for the blessing was εὐλόγησεν, while it is rendered εὐχαριστήσας in 8:6. This may simply indicate a stylistic variation, an attempt to improve upon a pre-Markan source, but this is hard to defend in the light of the use of εὐλογεῖν in 8:7 to speak of Jesus' action over the fish. A deliberate distinction is made between the two verbs in 6:41 and 8:6. The distinction is made more obvious in 8:7 by the return to the expression used in 6:41. The Greek εὐλογεῖν renders more faithfully the Hebrew idea of *berakah*, indicating that an object is blessed, but not "thanked."[193] The word εὐχαριστεῖν means more than blessing. It has the sense of "giving thanks" and rapidly became the term used to speak of the Christian celebration of the Lord's table.[194] Both are translated with the English verb "to bless," but the former reflects a Hebrew idea of blessing, while the latter a

---

[189] See Lagrange, *Saint Marc*, 192; Lohmeyer, *Markus*, 153–54. Fowler (*Loaves and Fishes*, 91–99), in a narrative approach to Mark 6:31–8:9, shows that the failure of the disciples to understand Jesus' power in 8:1–9, after their experience recorded in 6:31–44, is the main feature of the account. As Schweizer (*Mark*, 156) remarks: "The fact that after the experience described in 6:32–44 the disciples now (vs. 4) have no idea whatever about what can be done cannot be explained psychologically." Against LaVerdiere (*The Beginning*, 1:207–8), who suggests that the disciples' role in the second multiplication "has become secondary."

[190] This is widely, but not universally (see Gnilka, *Markus*, 1:303), recognized. See, for example, Taylor, *St. Mark*, 359–60; van Iersel, "Die wunderbare Speisung," 178; H. Patsch, "Abendmahlsterminologie ausserhalb der Einsetzungsberichte," *ZNW* 62 (1971): 227; Pesch, *Markusevangelium*, 1:404; Guelich, *Mark*, 405–6; Hooker, *St. Mark*, 190; LaVerdiere, *The Beginning*, 1:205–10; van Oyen, *The Interpretation of the Feeding Miracles*, 206–12.

[191] See LaVerdiere, *The Beginning*, 1:209–10; Marcus, *Mark*, 496–97. Marcus also points to the Jewish background of the eschatological renewal of the feeding with manna in the desert. Exodus, Eucharist, and eschatology combine.

[192] So Marcus, *Mark*, 497: "Despite their foibles, they will be used by Jesus to transmit the gift of God to the multitudes."

[193] See Marcus, *Mark*, 488.

[194] One of the main objections to a eucharistic hint in 6:31–44 and 8:1–9 is the absence of reference to the cup. See, for example, Gnilka, *Markus*, 1:262–63, 303. But the tradition has been rendered eucharistic by Mark (or even before Mark), all the while respecting the elements of loaves and fish. For a rejection of eucharistic hints on narrative grounds, see Fowler, *Loaves and Fishes*, 132–47. Fowler argues that one must not read 6:31–44 and 8:1–9 in the light of 14:22–25, claiming that eucharistic hints are "scholarly concerns" (p. 135) and would not be noticed by the reader at this stage of the narrative. Such a suggestion shows how early (1991) narrative critics regarded "the reader" as virginal. The original Christian reader (implied and intended) and all subsequent "real

more Greek-Christian idea of blessing and giving thanks. Although one must be careful not to push these hints too hard, Mark 8:1–9 may be written in a way more closely reflecting the words used at the eucharistic celebrations of a Greek-speaking, Gentile world.[195]

In 8:8–9 the account, paralleling 6:42–43, is rapidly concluded. Everyone ate and was satisfied (ἐχορτάσθησαν) and the κλάσαματα are gathered (8:8; see 6:42). Jesus' feeding of the Gentile crowd has not come to an end. It is still open, as the fragments have been gathered into seven baskets. Perhaps further indications of the Gentile nature of this second feeding can be found in the change from δώδεκα κοφίνων ("twelve baskets") of 6:43 to the ἑπτὰ σπυρίδας ("seven baskets") in 8:8. It is possible that "twelve," closely associated with the foundational tribes of Israel and its continuation in Jesus' establishment of "the Twelve" to be with him (see 3:13–19), has been changed to "seven." The fundamental reason for the use of the number in this context is its association with completion and fulfillment. It is sometimes claimed that it also points to the Gentiles. According to the list provided in Gen 10:2–31 there are seventy nations in the world. When the Hebrew Bible was translated for the Greek-speaking world, it became the Septuagint, through the mythical account of its miraculous composition by seventy-two scholars in seventy-two days, reported in the *Letter of Aristeas* (28–51, 301–321). Similarly, there is a hint in Acts 6:1–6 that the basic group around which the early Hellenistic Christian community formed itself was based upon "seven men of good repute" (v. 3).[196] The word κόφινος, as already mentioned, is widely used to describe a small basket used as a regular part of the apparel of Jewish people in the diaspora. The term σπύρις has no such connotation; it is the regular Greek word for a large mat basket used for provisions.[197] It cannot be mere chance that such careful rewriting occurs in 8:8, which so closely parallels 6:42–43.[198] The episode closes, paralleling 6:44, with the indication that a large number of people have been nourished. Here the number is four thousand, while in 6:44 a crowd of five thousand had been fed. One should not read too much into the different numbers.[199] The importance of the distinction will emerge shortly, as Jesus recalls *both bread miracles* with his ignorant disciples (see 8:19–20).

---

readers" recognize eucharistic language when they see it or hear it. On the fallacy of the "virginal reader" in biblical narrative criticism, see F. J. Moloney, *The Gospel of John* (SP 4; Collegeville: The Liturgical Press, 1998), 13–20.

[195] Gnilka (*Markus*, 1:303) accepts these links, but thinks that they do not apply in its present Markan context ("unsicher"), as the terms are interchangeable. See also Cranfield, *St. Mark*, 256; Patsch, "Abendmahlsterminologie," 218–19. Guelich (*Mark*, 405–6) agrees, but then rightly adds: "Taken in the context of this story as a whole, however, the change in expressions may indeed reflect a eucharistic influence on the tradition" (p. 406).

[196] The links between the number "seven" and the Gentile world, however, are less convincing than other Gentile indications in the text; see Marcus, *Mark*, 488–89. See, however, Grundmann, *Markus*, 159; Painter, *Mark's Gospel*, 118–19. A symbolic sense of the number seven is not needed for the interpretation of this feeding as Gentile in context. After reviewing the discussion, Guelich (*Mark*, 407–8) suggests that it may be as simple as the number of loaves (v. 5) producing the number of baskets (v. 8): "seven" in each case. But if this were so, why do five loaves produce twelve baskets in 6:38, 43?

[197] See Marcus, *Mark*, 489.

[198] Hooker's attempt (*St. Mark*, 188) to minimize these points of Gentile reference is strained. She rightly insists, however, that too much symbolism should not be read into the use of numbers. Cf. Lane, *Mark*, 274. See also the surveys of some suggestions in Guelich, *Mark*, 405, 408. Hooker and Gnilka (*Markus* 1:304) are prominent among those who reject the interpretation of 6:31–44 and 8:1–9 as of Jewish and Gentile provenance (see also Lohmeyer, *Markus*, 153 n. 6).

[199] See Marcus, *Mark*, 490.

In 8:1–9 the closely related themes of the disciples, bread, feeding, and participation at the table have reached an important moment in a development which began in 6:31. A deliberate reprise of 6:31–44, where Jesus fed a *Jewish crowd*, 8:1–9 is a carefully located story of Jesus' feeding a *Gentile crowd*. After his angry encounter with the Pharisees and the scribes in 7:1–13, and the ongoing difficulty with his disciples' imperfect understanding (7:14–23), Jesus has extended his healing activity into the Gentile world. There it is suggested for the first time in the narrative that he might be the messianic figure announced by Isa 35:5–6 (7:24–37; see v. 37). Jesus has fed the children in 6:31–44 (see 7:27), and in 8:1–9 he has acted out his acceptance of the principle articulated by the Syrophoenician woman: "Even the dogs under the table eat the children's crumbs" (see 7:28). He has fed the Gentiles.[200] But the theme of bread, the disciples, and the feeding of both Jew and Gentile continues until Jesus further reveals the hardness of heart, the blindness, and the deafness of disciples whose understanding of Jesus is running dangerously close to that of the Pharisees and the Herodians (8:11–21).[201]

The Second Sea Journey: To Dalmanutha (and Beyond) (8:10 [8:13c–21])

Throughout the Gospel, sea journeys are used to connect episodes (see 4:35–41; 5:21; 6:45–52; 8:10). Jesus' getting into the boat with his disciples and sailing to the district (τὰ μέρη) of Dalmanutha marks a movement from one episode to another.[202] The reader is familiar with this narrative technique, but it also continues the Markan construction of two parallel cycles; the miraculous multiplication of loaves and fish is followed immediately (εὐθύς, 8:10; see 6:45) by a boat journey (8:10; see 6:45–52). There are two important issues—one obvious and the other beyond scientific control—in this brief passage. The former is the insistence of the author on the presence of the disciples with Jesus. They have been the consistent point of reference from 6:6b until this moment. Their presence is crucial to the closing episodes of the first half of the story (8:11–30). Second, one must accept that the region "Dalmanutha" is unrecoverable. The problem posed by this unknown location was already attested by the textual traditions that replaced Dalmanutha with either Magadan or Magdala, variant names for a single location regarded as "the most important town on the west shore prior to the founding of Tiberias."[203] But "Dalmanutha" must be retained as original.[204] An attempt has been made to suggest that "Tiberiadaamathous," a

---

[200] See Guelich, *Mark*, 409. As Grundmann (*Markus*, 159) comments: "The feeding of the children follows that of the dog; now they too should be filled."

[201] Accepting that 8:1–9 is a symbol of Jesus' feeding Gentiles (see p. 497), Marcus (*Mark*, 483–85) has nevertheless shown some parallels with Jewish exodus traditions (especially Exod 16–17; Num 14; Pss 78, 95) and Mark 8:1–21. Ernst (*Markus*, 220–21), despite his lack of enthusiasm for a "Jewish" reading of 6:32–44, accepts that 8:1–9 points to Jesus' eschatological nourishment of everyone, including Gentiles. Lührmann (*Markusevangelium*, 118–20, 134–35) disregards the Jewish-Gentile question. However, he correctly insists that central to the bread miracles is the question: "Who is this man?" See also van Oyen, *The Interpretation of the Feeding Miracles*, 213–18.

[202] The expression τὰ μέρη localizes the reference. It is not a large "region," but a "division" of a larger area.

[203] Guelich (*Mark*, 412–13). Mark usually refers to well-known places, and thus most assume that this name comes from the pre-Markan tradition. See Pesch, *Markusevangelium*, 1:405–6; Gnilka, *Markus*, 1:305; Fowler, *Loaves and Fishes*, 51–53.

[204] Tbilisi (among others) witnesses to "Magdala" and Bezae and Sinaitic Syriac (among others) have "Magada" (see Matt 15:39). There are a number of other, less significant variations (for a

popular corruption of "Tiberias" and "Ammathous," the ancient town replaced by the Roman Tiberias, lies behind "Dalmanutha."[205] Others suggest that the textual tradition's tendency to insert Magada or Magdala indicates an awareness that Dalmanutha was to be identified with these well-established regions on the western side of the lake.[206] Whatever one makes of these <u>unresolvable problems,</u> it is widely accepted that Jesus' boat journey takes him and his disciples away from the Gentile side of the lake toward which he headed, via the Decapolis, in 7:31. In 8:10 he crosses to the land of Israel, where he will again enter into conflict with the Pharisees (vv. 11–13).[207] However, this brief encounter breaks awkwardly into a sea journey, which Jesus resumes in 8:13c: "and getting into the boat again he departed to the other side."

The Second Conflict:
Jesus Debates with the Pharisees and the Disciples (8:11–21)

Critics discuss the origin and the function of 8:11–13.[208] The Pharisees appear without introduction to test Jesus by asking for a sign (v. 11). They elicit a powerful negative response from him (v. 12) and he leaves them, continuing his boat journey "to the other side" (v. 13c). The narrative flows naturally without vv. 11–13b: "And immediately he got into the boat with his disciples, and went to the district of Dalmanutha (v. 10) . . . on the other side (v. 13c). . . . Now they had forgotten to bring bread; and they had only one loaf with them in the boat" (v. 14). The encounter with the Pharisees (vv. 11–13ab) was an independent piece of pre-Markan tradition, inserted into a boat trip (vv. 10 + 13c–21).[209] This Markan insertion corresponds to a similar Markan insertion, the words of Jesus to the disciples in v. 15: "Beware of the leaven of the Pharisees and the leaven of Herod." Thus, 8:11–13b renders more precise for the reader what Jesus means when he warns the disciples of "the leaven of the Pharisees" in 8:15. The storyteller has provided an example of what the "leaven" might be, in the encounter between Jesus and the Pharisees in 8:11–13.[210]

The juxtaposition of 8:11–13 and 8:14–21 is the work of the storyteller. As Mark nears the end of this final section of the first half of the Gospel, during which much of the focus has been upon the disciples (6:6b–8:30), the author's purposes are well served by this sharp-edged juxtaposition.[211] Mark wishes the reader to sense the disciples' gradual assimilation of certain characteristics of those who oppose Jesus (see 3:6). Whatever one makes of the history

---

list, see Gnilka, *Markus,* 1:306 n. 2). Apart from the principle of *lectio difficilior,* the external evidence of Sinaiticus, Vaticanus, Alexandrinus, and the Ephraem Rescript make the reading "Dalmanutha" unassailable.

[205] Taylor, *St. Mark,* 360–61 (following Burkitt). See the survey of other suggestions in Lohmeyer, *Markus,* 154–55.

[206] See, for example, G. Dalman, *Sacred Sites and Ways: Studies in the Topography of the Gospels* (London: SPCK, 1935), 128; Lane, *Mark,* 275.

[207] See Marcus, *Mark,* 501.

[208] See the summary in Guelich, *Mark,* 410–12.

[209] See, for suggestions of the state of the pre-Markan material and its Markan reworking, Pesch, *Markusevangelium,* 1:405, 411; Gnilka, *Markus,* 1:305; Guelich, *Mark,* 411. The present form of the boat trip, of course, is also the result of Markan rewriting for literary and theological purposes. See Marcus, *Mark,* 502–3.

[210] As we will see, the "leaven" passage is entirely Markan, and creates difficulties for the flow of the narrative. Yet, it is crucial for the interpretation of the Markan narrative of 6:31–8:21.

[211] See Guelich, *Mark,* 412.

of the traditions that lie behind the present text, 8:11–21 report conflicts between Jesus and the Pharisees, and between Jesus and the disciples, who continue to misunderstand: they run the risk of seduction by "the leaven" of the Pharisees and "the leaven" of the Herodians.

Jesus and the Pharisees (8:11–13)

The Pharisees and their intentions are introduced sharply: they came, and began to argue, to trap him (πειράζοντες αὐτόν). Jesus has not been in Jewish territory since his last angry encounter with the Pharisees and the scribes, with its aftermath, in 7:1–23. That setting is required to understand their demand that Jesus provide a sign for them. This is not a simple fact-finding encounter, but an argument that might lead to Jesus' entrapment.[212] He has spoken with authority against what they regarded as the traditions of the elders, describing their use of the traditions as an annulment of God's command (see 7:6–9). It is in the light of his apparent claim to an authority that outstrips their tradition that they seek a validating sign from him (see Deut 13:1–2; 1 Sam 2:30–33; 10:1–8; Isa 7:1–14; *Sipre* 18:19; *b. Sanh.* 98a).[213] As earlier in the story, the authority of Jesus is at stake when he meets the Pharisees or their representatives (see 1:27; 2:6–9, 16, 24; 3:2, 20–30; 7:1–13).[214] "They were asking that God step in and confirm Jesus' credibility."[215] As the request of the Pharisees constitutes a threat (v. 11), Jesus responds with equal power. A deep sigh announces his forthcoming prophetic utterance.[216] He turns upon "this generation" and asks why they seek a sign. No such validating miracle will be offered to them (v. 12). The expression "this generation" focuses attention on *these particular characters in the story.*[217] Jesus has

---

[212] The use of the verb πειράζω in this context makes this clear. It has the basic meaning of "to attempt" or "to put to the test," but also, as here, carries the possible undercurrent of "enticement to sin." See BDAG, 792–93, s.v. πειράζω. See also Marcus, *Mark,* 500–501. The sense of the verb, from the standpoint of the Pharisees, has been caught by Taylor (*St. Mark,* 362): "If he tries to give a sign he will fail; if he refuses he will lose popular support."

[213] On convalidating signs, see K. Rengstorf, *TDNT* 7:234–36. A similar request for a sign from Jesus can be found in Q (Luke 11:29 // Matt 12:39), Matt 16:1, John 6:30; see Hooker, *St. Mark,* 191. Marcus (*Mark,* 498–99) provides Jewish background for the ambiguity of the request for a sign. As C. K. Barrett (*The Gospel according to St. John* [2d ed.; London: SPCK, 1978], 288) comments on the Johannine passage: "He who makes greater claims than Moses must provide a more striking attestation of his right." See F. J. Moloney, *Signs and Shadows: Reading John 5–13* (Minneapolis: Fortress, 1996), 46–47.

[214] On the adversarial nature of the Pharisees' relationship to Jesus in the narrative to this point, see Guelich, *Mark,* 413; Lührmann, *Markusevangelium,* 136–37.

[215] Guelich, *Mark,* 414. Some would claim that the sign requested is a cosmic, apocalyptic miracle (e.g., Lohmeyer, *Markus,* 155; Grundmann, *Markus,* 161; Schweizer, *Mark,* 159), others read "from heaven" as an indication of the eschatological nature of Jesus' ministry (e.g., Pesch, *Markusevangelium,* 1:407; Gnilka, *Markus,* 1:307). The above interpretation takes the latter position.

[216] See Pesch, *Markusevangelium,* 1:408. This interpretation relates more closely to the eschatological authority of his response (see LXX Ezek 21:11–12; LXX Isa 21:2) than that he had reached a point of painful frustration with the Pharisees. For the latter interpretation, see Taylor, *St. Mark,* 362; Grundmann, *Markus,* 208; Lane, *Mark,* 277. Marcus (*Mark,* 501), with reference to 7:34, helpfully links both suggestions (eschatological and frustration) by claiming that the sigh "seems to suggest a struggle with a demonic obstacle." This raises the conflict with the Pharisees above mere frustration.

[217] The expression "this generation" can also have a pejorative tone (see Gen 7:1; Ps 95:10–11; Deut 32:5, 20). Later in the narrative it will certainly have a negative meaning as negative adjectives are added to it (see 8:38; 9:19). This may be present here (see Nineham, *St. Mark,* 210), but the focus of the author is upon Jesus' interrogators as witnesses to his words and deeds. The stress is more on the "this" than "generation": see Cranfield, *St. Mark,* 259. LaVerdiere (*The Beginning,* 1:212)

said and done much before the leaders of Israel (see 2:1–12; 3:1–6; 7:1–13), and Israel has been miraculously fed in 6:31–44. Now the Pharisees seek a sign! The story thus far has made amply clear that they refuse to accept that the reigning presence of God has broken into the human story in the person, words, and deeds of Jesus. By contrast to others who come to him in faith, anticipating God's offer of help and healing (see 7:24–37), the Pharisees fail to see God's sign and do not believe in Jesus or his ministry.[218] In fact, the only recognition of Jesus' authority has been to suggest that it comes from Satan (see 3:22–20).[219] Along with the Herodians, they are already plotting Jesus' death (see 3:6). No sign can be given to them.[220] The attempt to have Jesus conform to their criteria is a further attempt to trap him (πειράζοντες αὐτόν, v. 1).[221]

This insertion into a boat trip that began in 8:10, and is resumed in 8:13, serves the author's purposes very well. Jesus separates himself from the hostile audience (v. 13a), rejoins the disciples in the boat (see v. 10), and departs "to the other side." The movements of Jesus and his disciples, although somewhat haphazard, are clear enough. After leaving the Gentile side of the lake (v. 10), Jesus journeys with his disciples into Jewish territory for his encounter with the Pharisees (vv. 11–12). He now leaves that unknown location ("Dalmanutha") and sets out for a place further along the coast of the lake. There has been a criss-crossing: from the eastern (v. 10) to the western side of the lake (vv. 10–11), finally to come to an area slightly east of the entry of the Jordan into the Sea of Galilee (v. 22), reasonably close for the forthcoming journey to Caesarea Philippi (see vv. 27–30).[222] But having exposed the Pharisees' inability to see and accept what God is doing in Jesus (vv. 11–13), the stage is set for the following encounter between Jesus and the disciples (vv. 14–21).

Jesus and the disciples (8:14–21)

Several issues emerging in 8:14–15 indicate that the discussion that follows serves to conclude certain themes that have been running through the narrative for some time. The narrative also addresses the question of Jesus' destiny, and the associated destiny of

---

suggests (via Ps 95:7–11) that it may be reference to a new exodus and a new people of God which is failing. See also Marcus (*Mark*, 501), who accepts the argument of E. Lövestam (*Jesus and "This Generation": A New Testament Study* [ConBNT 25; Stockholm: Almqvist & Wiksell, 1995]) that Jewish traditions about the evil generations of the flood and of the wilderness form the primary background to this phrase in the New Testament. I would still insist that Jesus' words to "this generation" must be understood primarily in terms of the Pharisees in the narrative.

218 Guelich, *Mark*, 416; Marcus, *Mark*, 503.

219 Lane, *Mark*, 277.

220 As has often been pointed out, Jesus' words have the form of an oath formula (see Gen 14:23; Num 32:11; Deut 1:35; 1 Kgs 3:14; LXX Ps 94:11) in which the apodosis is missing. It is a severe negation of the request. For further detail, see Cranfield, *St. Mark*, 259; Guelich, *Mark*, 415.

221 Nineham, *St. Mark*, 212; Hooker, *St. Mark*, 192. For impressive links with the performance of the wilderness generation, who demanded signs from Moses, see Marcus, *Mark*, 503–4; Lövestam, *This Generation*, 24–26. For its applicability to the period of the Jewish War, with its false "sign prophets" (13:22), see Marcus, *Mark*, 505–6. For J. B. Gibson (*The Temptations of Jesus in Early Christianity* [JSNTSup 112; Sheffield; Sheffield Academic Press, 1995], 158–95), the temptation of 1:9–13 returns. Jesus is put in a situation where he must choose between rejection of the will of God, or submission. His faithfulness is being questioned. See also idem, "Jesus' Refusal to Produce a 'Sign' (Mk 8.11–13)," *JSNT* 38 (1990): 37–66.

222 See J. F. Strange, "Beth-Saida," *ABD* 1:692–93. Some have suggested that Jesus returns to the Gentiles; see Lane, *Mark*, 279. This is not the case, as the context demands; see Guelich, *Mark*, 415–16. The geography is, however, hard to follow. See Nineham, *St. Mark*, 211.

disciples, which will dominate 8:31–16:8. The narrator reports that, once in the boat on the lake, the disciples had forgotten to bring bread (ἄρτους), and then seems to contradict that statement by immediately affirming that they had one loaf/bread (ἕνα ἄρτον) with them (v. 14).[223] But the backward-looking link with the accounts of the multiplication of the loaves is obvious (6:31–44; 8:1–9). On both occasions there was insufficient food to feed the multitudes: five loaves (ἄρτους, 6:38) and seven loaves (ἄρτους, 8:5). The theme of "bread," present across this section of the narrative (see 6:31–44; 7:1–23, 24–30; 8:1–9), continues into 8:15. Jesus warns the disciples against the "leaven" of the Pharisees and the "leaven" of the Herodians (v. 15).[224] The warning is very severe (διεστέλλετο . . . ὁρᾶτε, βλέπετε ἀπό, v. 15), and recalls Jesus' immediately previous encounter with the Pharisees (vv. 11–13). That encounter looks back, in turn, to 7:1–23.[225] The reader is made aware of what Jesus intends by the warning. But the association of the Herodians adds a note of violence. The Pharisees and the Herodians had already decided that Jesus must be slain (3:6), and it was the weak Herod who had bowed to peer pressure to give Herodias the head of the slain John the Baptist (6:14–29). The disciples, who have been with Jesus (see 3:14) throughout all that has been told from 6:6b to this point in the narrative, are warned against the superficiality of the Pharisees, who will not accept who Jesus is and what he is able to do. They are also warned that such an approach to Jesus leads to an association with the deeper agenda of the Pharisees and the Herodians: Jesus' death. It is a challenge for any reader to be told that the disciples, who responded so positively in 1:16–20, 2:13–14, and 3:13–19, might need the warnings of 8:15. But they had already begun to stumble when Jesus told the parables (4:1–34), and their superficiality and lack of understanding have increased since then (see 4:35–41; 5:16, 31; 6:7–30, 35–36, 45–52; 7:17–18; 8:4). The disciples have witnessed Jesus' gift of "bread" (6:31–8:9) but they are to beware of the "leaven" of the Pharisees and the Herodians (8:15). Such warnings are called for at this turning point of Jesus' story.[226]

The disciples, with no recollection of Jesus' deeds in 6:31–44 and 8:1–9, discuss among themselves Jesus' saying on the leaven. They are unable to make any link with leaven and, focusing on their lack of bread (ὅτι ἄρτους οὐκ ἔχουσιν, v. 16), they ignore Jesus' warnings about the leaven of the Pharisees and the leaven of the Herodians.[227] Jesus, aware of the discussion, asks why they show such concern. They should know better, but they do not. Thus he accuses them of lack of perception and understanding, and hardness of heart

---

[223] The oddness of the affirmation from the narrator is very clear in the Greek: καὶ ἐπελάθοντο λαβεῖν ἄρτους καὶ εἰ μὴ ἕνα ἄρτον οὐκ εἶχον μεθ᾽ ἑαυτῶν. See Guelich, *Mark*, 420–21.

[224] As well as its link with the "bread" theme, there is evidence that the ancients regarded "leaven" as an element of corruption. See, for example, Lane, *Mark*, 280. For Lohmeyer (*Markus*, 157–58), it points to political corruption and abuse of power. However, Marcus (*Mark*, 506) rightly stresses the use of the expression here as a contrast to Jesus' miraculous provision of bread.

[225] LaVerdiere, *The Beginning*, 1:215.

[226] Many critics point to the awkwardness of v. 15 within the context. It is Markan, and has no doubt been deliberately (however clumsily) added to this pericope to enable the reader to make such connections across the earlier parts of the narrative, so marked by the theme of "bread." For the discussion, see Taylor, *St. Mark*, 365–66; Guelich, *Mark*, 419–20, 422–24; Nineham, *St. Mark*, 215–16. The link between "leaven" and "bread" is seldom noticed by the commentators, but see Lohmeyer, *Markus*, 157 n. 3; Quesnell, *The Mind of Mark*, 116; Painter, *Mark's Gospel*, 122.

[227] This is indicated by the use of the imperfect διελογίζοντο. They go on discussing the fact that they are short of bread: Taylor, *St. Mark*, 366; Grundmann, *Markus*, 208; Hooker, *St. Mark*, 195. Taylor (*St. Mark*, 366) renders this even sharper by reading the expression as a discussion of "why they have no bread."

(v. 17). None of this is new for the reader, as the disciples have already shown lack of perception (see 7:18) and understanding (see 4:12; 6:52; 7:14). In their hardness of heart they have joined the Pharisees (3:5; 6:52). The allusions to the prophets is more subtle, but also recalls an earlier episode in the narrative: Jesus accuses them in the words of Jeremiah (5:21) and Ezekiel (12:2), "Having eyes do you not see, and having ears do you not hear?" (v. 18ab). This allusion to the disciples' blindness and deafness looks back to Jesus' restoration of hearing and speech to the Gentile man in 7:31–37. Gentiles greeted that healing by means of an allusion to the Old Testament, in 7:35: "He has done all things well; he even makes the deaf hear and the dumb speak" (see Isa 35:5–6). None of this seems to have made an impression on the disciples, and no such acclamation has accompanied their constant presence with Jesus.[228] They are even unable to remember the actions of God, done in and through Jesus (v. 18). Two elements in Jesus' accusation are new: blindness and the need to remember. The need to overcome blindness will play a major theological and literary function in the section of the Gospel which follows (8:22–10:52), and the storyteller is writing so that his readership, and disciples of all times and places, might "remember."

The fragility of the disciples is laid bare as they are interrogated about immediate past events in the narrative: the multiplication of five loaves of bread (πέντε ἄρτους) for the five thousand and the twelve baskets that remained (8:19; see 6:31–44), and the multiplication of seven loaves of bread (ἑπτὰ ἄρτους) for the four thousand and the seven baskets that remained (8:20).[229] This is what they should remember instead of worrying about the lack of bread in the boat.[230] They are dangerously close to the agenda of the Pharisees who argued and tested Jesus (vv. 11–12), unable to see the signs of the kingdom of God in the presence of Jesus. God's reigning presence has been liberally manifested to them in the two bread miracles, and the κλάσματα from those feedings are still available to Jew and Gentile. But they seem to have no recollection as they worry over the lack of bread.[231]

Jesus' stinging question to them, "Do you not yet (οὔπω) understand?" closes the episode (8:21). It also closes a long section in the narrative that has never been far from the theme of bread (6:31–8:21). The use of οὔπω offers hope that a time will come when they will understand.[232] But read together with the narrator's harsh words to these same dis-

---

228 Together with the subtle link back to 7:37, Jesus' use of words from Jeremiah and Ezekiel elevate his words to the form of a prophetic accusation; Guelich, *Mark,* 424–25.

229 Reading ἑπτὰ ἄρτους, along with P[45], Sinaiticus, Ephraem Rescript, Washington, Family 13, and others. Excellent witnesses (Alexandrinus, Vaticanus, Bezae, and others) omit ἄρτους. It is stylistically better to drop it, and thus I would claim that its inclusion is a *lectio difficilior.* The author repeated the expression to ensure that the reader would not miss all the "bread" connections that are now coming to a close. For an uncharacteristic symbolic reading of the numbers 7 and 12 as eschatological, see Marcus, *Mark,* 514.

230 This interpretation relates vv. 14–21 and the "one bread" of v. 14 with the fact that Jesus has already made much out of very little, and thus provided nourishment in 6:31–44 and 8:1–9. See, for example, Guelich, *Mark,* 421–23. It is not necessary to argue that the "one bread" is the eucharistic bread for all the nations (e.g., Quesnell, *The Mind of Mark,* 242–43; Ernst, *Markus,* 226; Marcus, *Mark,* 509–11), or even to interpret the "one bread" christologically: Jesus is sufficient for all their needs (e.g., Grundmann, *Markus,* 162; Pesch, *Markusevangelium,* 1:414; Gnilka, *Markus* 1:312; LaVerdiere, *The Beginning,* 1:214–15). As Guelich rightly remarks, with reference to 6:31–44 and 8:1–9: "We have then in 8:14 the ingredients (need, limited resources) for another Feeding miracle" (p. 422). See also Hooker, *St. Mark,* 193–94.

231 On the christological importance of 6:31–44, 8:1–9, and 8:14–21, see Lührmann, *Markusevangelium,* 137–39.

232 Guelich, *Mark,* 426; Marcus, *Mark,* 508. On the narrative role of the failure of the disciples within the story to this point, see Marcus, *Mark,* 512–14.

ciples after the first bread miracle (see 6:52: "for they did not understand about the loaves but their hearts were hardened"), the question of 8:21 reflects a problem behind the narrative.[233] The bread miracles have contacts with the eucharistic practice of the Markan community (see 6:41; 8:6). The disciples have been commanded to feed the hungry from their table (6:37) and they were responsible for the distribution in both accounts (6:41; 8:6). The feeding of the multitudes, both Jewish and Gentile, is a task the disciples must perform. The two bread miracles (6:31–44; 8:1–9), each with its subsequent critical encounter between Jesus and the disciples (6:45–52; 8:14–21), are set within Jesus' sending out of the disciples on their mission (6:13–30), Jesus' angry rejection of Israel's ritual table practices (7:1–23), and his subsequent presence among the Gentiles (7:25–37). Feeding and bread were recurrent themes (see 7:2, 3, 4, 5, 15, 18, 19, 27, 28). But the disciples' hearts are hardened (6:52; 8:17), and they do not understand about the bread (6:52; 8:17–18). They would prefer the people look after themselves (6:35–36; 8:3–4).

The difficulties of members of the Markan community, necessarily involved in their Gentile mission, lie behind this carefully composed narrative. The Markan story of Jesus instructs them that they are to "remember" (8:18c). They must share in the universal mission of Jesus, cost what it may (see 6:14–19). An important part of that mission was table fellowship, and the closely related eucharistic fellowship.[234] The community was to provide bread for many different people, Jews and Gentiles, as the bread provided by Jesus was still available in the κλάσματα gathered after his feeding of Jews (6:31–44) and Gentiles (8:1–9).[235] A story has been told of an original group of disciples who would have preferred to exclude some people from the table. Such an approach to the sharing of the bread provided by Jesus reflects lack of understanding and hardness of heart (6:52; 8:17–18). The problem of table fellowship in the early church was understandably widespread (see Acts 10–11; Gal 2:11–21), and the members of the Markan community, who originally read or listened to this story, were not free from such problems. The increasing focus upon the fragile relationship between Jesus and his disciples *in the narrative* (6:6b–8:30), addresses disciples *hearing or reading the narrative*. The members of the Markan audience are asked: "Do you not remember? . . . Do you not yet understand?" (vv. 18c, 21).

The Second Miraculous Healing: A Blind Man (8:22–26)

The boat trip concludes as Jesus and the disciples come to Bethsaida, where "some people" lead a blind man to Jesus and beg him to touch him (8:22).[236] A terse but effective

---

[233] For what follows, see my fuller treatment in F. J. Moloney, *A Body Broken for a Broken People: Eucharist in the New Testament* (rev. ed.; Peabody: Hendrickson, 1997), 37–44. See also D. Senior, "The Eucharist in Mark: Mission, Reconciliation, Hope," *BTB* 12 (1982): 67–72.

[234] Even if (as some maintain) there are no eucharistic hints in 6:31–44 and 8:1–9, the issue of table fellowship lies behind the composition of 6:31–8:21. The problem intensifies once eucharistic contacts are accepted.

[235] Gnilka (*Markus*, 1:309 n. 1) overstates his case when, in the light of vv. 18 and 19, he claims that a focus upon the different terms used for "baskets" 6:42 and 8:8 (repeated in vv. 18–19) is "pedantic." His own rejection of any comparison between these terms is somewhat high-handed. Once he has accepted that 6:31–44 and 8:1–9 depend upon a basic source developed into two pre-Markan narratives (1:255–56), *some explanation* for the change of expression, still respected in vv. 18–19, must be given.

[236] Typical Markan inaccuracy is traced in the description of Bethsaida as a "village" (κώμη) in vv. 23 and 26. Bethsaida was a large and prosperous town (πόλις). See Matt 11:20; John 1:44;

introduction sets the location for what follows, and prepares the reader for a miracle story. A totally blind man, who cannot walk by himself or speak for himself, is presented to Jesus. Much in this account parallels the miracle that closed the first bread cycle, reported in 7:31–37.[237] This is part of the Markan technique, but there are important differences between the two miracles. On the whole, the healing is told in a traditional miracle story form. Jesus responds to the request of 8:22 by gesture and word, *but the cure is not effected* (vv. 23–24) and Jesus must again touch the man, who only then sees clearly (v. 25). The usual Markan command to secrecy closes the episode (v. 26). It could be claimed that this "failed first attempt" is historical, as it provides an otherwise unseen glimpse of Jesus' limitations as a miracle worker.[238] Both Matthew and Luke, who follow the Markan narrative closely at this point, omit this episode (see Matt 15:1–16:20; Luke 9:10–36).

Such a judgment, however, undervalues Markan theological and literary strategies. The brief miracle story of 8:22–26 plays an important literary role in at least two ways:

1. Following an episode during which Jesus accused his disciples of blindness (see v. 18a), the miracle tells of a man who moves from no sight (v. 22), to a limited vision (vv. 23–24), to full sight (v. 25), before being dismissed from the scene (v. 26). The passage looks back to the blindness of the disciples (v. 18), and forward to the episode which follows, closing the first half of the Gospel, where two of these stages of "sight" will be realized (8:27–30). It also opens the door upon the second half of the Gospel (8:31–15:47), during which the nature of "full sight" will be explained by the teaching and the death of Jesus.

2. The "overlap" between the first and second major sections of the Gospel begins with 8:22–26. As the first half of the story draws to a close, the destiny of both Jesus and the disciples has become central. For the first time the disciples have been described as blind (8:18a), and the three-staged cure of a blind man follows. On arrival at 10:46–52—after a section of narrative devoted to Jesus' journey to Jerusalem, speaking of his oncoming death (8:31; 9:31; 10:32–34), and instructing his disciples on the destiny of anyone who wishes to "follow" Jesus—another blind man is cured. Thus, as the literary and theological agenda of 1:14–8:30 draws to a close, to be concluded in Peter's confession and Jesus' warning in 8:29–30, the second half of the Gospel has already begun in 8:22–26. There is a deliberate "framing" of a series of episodes and Jesus' teaching between 8:22–26 and 10:46–52.[239]

With one exception, the actions of a traditional thaumaturge are provided in considerable detail in 8:23abc. Initially, Jesus takes the man by the hand and leads him out of the village. This movement sets the scene for Jesus' final command to the man in v. 26 not to go back into the village. Once outside, however, the spitting and laying on of hands are *what*

Josephus, *Ant.*, 18.28. Some textual traditions read "Bethany" rather than "Bethsaida," and scholars suggest that the tradition was not originally associated with Bethsaida. For a full discussion, see Lane, *Mark*, 283 n. 42.

[237] See the discussion in Taylor, *St. Mark*, 368–69; G. Minette de Tillesse, *Le secret messianique dans l'Evangile de Marc* (LD 47; Paris: Cerf, 1968), 57–62; Lane, *Mark*, 286–87. Against the suggestion of the two cycles, on tradition-historical grounds, see Gnilka, *Markus*, 1:315. Gnilka is rightly critical of some suggestions concerning pre-Markan traditions, but devotes too little attention to the possibility of Markan literary creativity. Hooker (*St. Mark*, 197) also rejects the theory that 7:32–37 and 8:22–26 stem from the same tradition, but rightly suggests "that Mark has deliberately used the two stories as parallels, and the similarities between them may well be the result of his editing."

[238] See, for example, Taylor, *St. Mark*, 369.

[239] See, among many, Best, *Following Jesus*, 134–45; van Iersel, *Reading Mark*, 122–41. Meier (*A Marginal Jew,* 2:691) rightly observes that Mark has endowed this story with "a Janus-like quality." It looks both backward and forward for its full meaning within the Markan narrative.

one would expect in the cure of a blind man. There is ample evidence of parallel activities from the ancient world.[240] In answer to Jesus' question concerning his sight (v. 23d), we are told that the man regained sight (ἀναβλέψας), and reported that he saw human beings, but they looked like walking trees (v. 24).[241] The point of this report is that the man sees, but he does not see properly, an initial response to a curing activity also found in the Hellenistic world.[242] Jesus' initial intervention, using expected thaumaturgic practices, has produced only partial sight. Thus, Jesus again lays his hands upon the man's eyes. The spitting ritual has been omitted. This action results in an intense gaze from the man (διέβλεψεν), total cure, and fullness of vision (ἐνέβλεπεν τηλαυγῶς ἅπαντα, v. 25).[243] The man has made a journey from "no sight" (v. 22) to "partial sight" (v. 24) to "full sight" (v. 25).[244] He can be dismissed from the story, but is prohibited from going back into the town, lest false messianic expectations be aroused.[245] The Markan defense of Jesus' messianic identity is now urgent as this section that consistently raises the question of Jesus' identity draws to a close. That mystery will shortly be partially resolved in Peter's confession in 8:29 and finally resolved on the cross.[246] The climax must not be anticipated, and thus the man disappears from the scene entirely (v. 26).[247]

Jesus' accusation of the disciples in 8:18a leads into this miracle story. The reader has followed the increasing blindness of the disciples. They have moved from their initial unconditional response to Jesus' call (see 1:16–20; 3:13–19) into lack of understanding (4:10, 13, 23; 5:16, 31; 6:7–30, 37; 8:4), unbelief (4:40–41), hardness of heart (6:52), and a dangerous proximity to the leaven of the Pharisees and the Herodians (8:11–21). Jesus' accusations in 8:17–21 are well-grounded! But in 8:21 he asks whether they did "not yet" understand. There is hope that they may still move from the blindness of their unfaith into true sight. The miracle story of 8:22–26 is a paradigm of that possibility, and plays an important literary function in setting the agenda for the rest of the Gospel.[248]

---

[240] For example, Tacitus, *Hist.*, 4.81, Suetonius, *Vesp.*, 7.2–3, and Dio Cassius 66.8 all report Vespasian's healing of a blind man in Alexandria in this way. For further information and sources for Greco-Roman parallels, see Pesch, *Markusevangelium*, 1:418 nn. 9–12. As Pesch comments: "Jesus *proclaims himself as a physician*" (p. 418; stress in original). Guelich (*Mark*, 345) describes the scene as "loaded with thaumaturgical traits familiar to the hellenistic world." See also Lührmann, *Markusevangelium*, 139–40.

[241] The verb ἀναβλέπειν can mean either "to look up" (see 7:34) or "to regain sight." For the latter meaning here, see Lagrange, *Saint Marc*, 202; Guelich, *Mark*, 433.

[242] In an inscription recording a cure at Epidaurus, a certain Alcetus of Halice first saw trees in the temple precincts. For the reference, see Nineham, *St. Mark*, 219; Pesch, *Markusevangelium*, 1:419.

[243] It is possible that the progressive use of different -βλέπειν verbs moves toward a climax (so Cranfield, *St. Mark*, 264–65; Lane, *Mark*, 285–86 n. 51), but it may be a stylistic attempt to avoid the use of the same verb throughout. See Pesch, *Markusevangelium*, 1:419.

[244] The use of the rare word τηλαυγῶς, "clearly from afar," indicates the complete nature of the cure and accentuates the effectiveness of Jesus' second intervention; see Gnilka, *Markus*, 1:314; Guelich, *Mark*, 434.

[245] This theme has been further developed in a complex conflation of the text. There are some longer versions, developing especially a command that he say nothing to anyone. For a summary, see Metzger, *Textual Commentary*, 84, and Taylor, *St. Mark*, 372–73, who accepts a longer reading.

[246] Gnilka, *Markus*, 1:314.

[247] The literary feature of the so-called messianic secret continues to point the reader further into the narrative, toward the final revelation of Jesus as the crucified Christ and Son of God. He is not to be understood as a messianic miracle worker.

[248] Guelich, *Mark*, 430.

Climax: The Confession at Caesarea Philippi (8:27–30)

Jesus' journey with his disciples from Bethsaida to the region of Caesarea Philippi is geographically plausible (8:27a).[249] But Mark's point is that "on the way" (ἐν τῇ ὁδῷ, v. 27b) Jesus interrogates his disciples.[250] Jesus and his disciples are still in the northern reaches of Palestine. But a theme of "the way" has been introduced. A journey has begun. It leads from Caesarea Philippi, via the mount of transfiguration, back to Galilee (9:30). From Capernaum (9:33) he will travel through Judea and the Transjordan (10:1), to Jericho, and from there to Jerusalem. Mention that Jesus and his disciples are on "the way" will be frequent in the second half of the Gospel (see 10:17, 46, 52; 11:8; 12:14), especially in association with the three passion predictions (see 8:27; 9:33, 34; 10:32).[251] As he begins this journey Jesus asks the question which has been lurking behind the narrative since 1:14. The reader, having read 1:1–13, knows who Jesus is, but characters in the story do not. To them Jesus poses the question: "Who do people say that I am?" (v. 27c).[252]

The stepwise movement from blindness to sight, recorded in the miracle story of 8:22–26 (which immediately followed Jesus' accusation that the disciples were blind: v. 18), is partially repeated in the responses first of the disciples (v. 28) and then of Peter (v. 29).[253] The disciples' description of the opinion of many highlights Jesus' prophetic charism, with possible hints of his being the expected precursor of the messianic era. Some say that he is John the Baptist, others Elijah, and yet others one of the prophets (v. 28). Herod has already suggested that Jesus was John the Baptist *redivivus* (6:16), and the reader is aware of the accuracy of the disciples' report of what has already been said about Jesus in 6:15: "It is Elijah. . . . It is a prophet, like one of the prophets of old."[254] For Christian readers, John the Baptist was also Jesus' precursor (1:2–3, 7–8). There was Jewish speculation that Elijah would return to bring in the messianic era (see Mal 4:5) and also that Isaiah and Jeremiah (see 2 Esd 2:18) or an eschatological Mosaic prophet might usher in

---

[249] See the discussion of the various movements that have led to this point in Guelich, *Mark*, 431–32.

[250] Jesus' questioning his disciples comes as a surprise. It is unusual for the master to interrogate followers; see Lohmeyer, *Markus*, 162; Cranfield, *St. Mark*, 268.

[251] Lührmann, *Markusevangelium*, 141; LaVerdiere, *The Beginning*, 2:8–9.

[252] Lane (*Mark*, 288) observes that between 1:1 and 8:29 there has been no recognition of the fact that Jesus is the Messiah. This is only true of 1:14–8:29, and even so, there has been a glimmer of recognition in the use of Isa 35 to describe his deeds in 7:37.

[253] The parallels between vv. 22–26 and vv. 27–30 were highlighted by Lightfoot (*History and Interpretation*, 90–91) and have been accepted, with variations, by many scholars since then. See, for example, Nineham, *St. Mark*, 218–19; Grundmann, *Markus*, 164–65; Lane, *Mark*, 286–87 n. 54; Best, *Following Jesus*, 134–39; Pesch, *Markusevangelium*, 1:420–21; Guelich, *Mark*, 436; Hooker, *St. Mark*, 198; and LaVerdiere, *The Beginning*, 2:16–18. See especially F. J. Matera, "The Incomprehension of the Disciples and Peter's Confession (Mark 16,14–8,30)," *Bib* 70 (1989): 153–72. Matera traces the disciples' failure across 6:37, 52; 7:8; 8:4, 14–21, and shows how vv. 22–26 forms a "bridge" into a confession that Jesus is the Shepherd Messiah (vv. 27–30). Not unexpectedly, Gnilka (*Markus*, 1:315) remarks: "A detailed correspondence between the step-by-step healing on the one hand and the step-by-step introduction to the understanding of the person of Jesus on the other goes too far and is to be rejected." This outstanding commentary on the Gospel of Mark sometimes falters when it comes to the question of accepting the Markan literary and theological design. See also Ernst, *Markus*, 228–31 (on 8:22–26) and 312–16 (on 10:46–52). No literary connection is made between the two miracles. Ernst separates the two episodes: 8:22–26 closes a major section (pp. 228–31), and 8:27–33 forms unified literary piece, opening the second major section of the Gospel (p. 232).

[254] Gnilka, *Markus*, 2:14–15.

the eschatological age (see Deut 18:18).[255] Whether people are suggesting that Jesus is another prophetic figure, or even giving him the dignity of the expected messianic precursor, the reader knows that, in the light of 1:1–13, they are wrong.[256] This understanding of Jesus matches the complete blindness of the man in 8:22.

Jesus turns to the disciples, and asks his fragile followers who they think he might be. Despite their failures, they are the ones to whom the secret of the kingdom has been given (4:11), and it is as specially privileged "insiders" that Jesus asks them the question.[257] Peter, speaking in their name, replies: "You are the Christ" (σὺ εἶ ὁ χριστός, v. 29).[258] There is a sense in which this confession of faith is correct. Jesus was called "the Christ" in 1:1, but more was said of Jesus in the prologue. Especially important were the words from heaven: "This is my beloved Son, in whom I am well pleased." The story has already indicated that the mystery of Jesus' messiahship will involve suffering and death (see 2:20; 3:6), and for that reason the narrator closes the first half of the Gospel by reporting that Jesus "warned them severely (ἐπετίμησεν αὐτοῖς) to tell no one about him" (v. 30).[259] Jesus' warning to the disciples, who have come to a partial understanding of who Jesus is, does not negate their confession. It is a warning that it is not the whole truth, and thus must not become the basis of their proclamation.[260] It thus matches the second stage of the blind man's journey, when he saw once again, but did not see properly (see vv. 23–24). As Jesus' initial laying on of hands and spitting applied traditional healing medical methods (Pesch: "like a physician"), but only produced partial sight, so also Peter's confession of Jesus as "the Messiah" is an acceptance of a culturally, religiously, and historically conditioned meaning of that expression.[261] The disciples' confession, subsequent to Jesus' accusing them of blind-

---

[255] For the possibility that Jesus was the forerunner to the eschatological era, see Lohmeyer, *Markus*, 162; Pesch, *Markusevangelium*, 2:31–32.

[256] Lane, *Mark*, 290.

[257] Lohmeyer, *Markus*, 162.

[258] Pesch (*Markusevangelium*, 2:28, 32) regards Peter as an important figure in the pre-Markan passion source, which, he claims, begins with 8:27–30 (see 2:1–27).

[259] The verb ἐπιτιμάω carries the sense of "rebuke," and is very strong in this context. It has been used in 1:25 and 3:12 to silence unclean spirits. See BDAG, 384, s.v. ἐπιτιμάω. See also Nineham, *St. Mark*, 224–25.

[260] Lohmeyer, *Markus*, 163–64; Lührmann, *Markusevangelium*, 146–47.

[261] There is little agreement on what first century messianic hopes might have been, and some even doubt that there were such hopes. There is almost universal agreement that there was no *uniform* messianic expectation. See J. H. Charlesworth, ed., with J. Brownson, M. T. David, S. J. Kraftchick, and A. F. Segal, *The Messiah: Developments in Early Judaism and Christianity* (The First Princeton Symposium on Judaism and Christian Origins; Minneapolis: Fortress, 1992). Minimally, the idea of a royal figure anointed to God's service and enjoying divine protection can be found in Exod 29:7, 21; 1 Sam 10:1, 6; 16:13; 1 Kgs 19:16; Ps 105:15; Isa 61:1–4. This is applied to a figure from the Davidic line in 2 Sam 7:14–16; Isa 55:3–5; Jer 23:5–6; 4QpGenᵃ 5:1–5. Gnilka (*Markus*, 2:15) states baldly that 8:29 is a Christian confession, but the early church and the Markan tradition received the idea from somewhere. For helpful assessments of where they found it, and how it was applied to Jesus in the Markan tradition, see the following studies in the above volume: N. A. Dahl, "Messianic Ideas and the Crucifixion of Jesus" (pp. 382–403); M. Hengel, "Christological Titles in Early Christianity" (pp. 425–48); D. H. Juel, "The Origin of Mark's Christology" (pp. 449–60). The messianic figure indicated by the Markan disciples' later expectations of Jesus (see Mark 9:34; 10:37) seems to be reflected in the Pharisaic *Pss. Sol.* 17:23–25; 18:1–10 (contrary to Gnilka, *Markus*, 2:15). On the Qumran material, see J. Zimmermann, *Messianische Texte aus Qumran: Königliche, priesterliche und prophetische Messiasvorstellungen in der Schriftfunden von Qumran* (WUNT 2. Reihe 104; Tübingen: J. C. B. Mohr [Paul Siebeck], 1998), and G. Xeravits, "The Early History of Qumran's Messianic Expectations," *ETL* 76 (2000): 113–21.

ness (v. 18), indicates that they are capable of arriving at a stage of partial sight: partial and imperfect belief. We may not be sure of the precise contours of messianic expectation in the first century.[262] Later the narrative will make it clear that the disciples wish to follow a figure who will go to Jerusalem in glory, surrounded by powerful people on his right and his left (see 9:34; 10:37).

Peter is correct when he confesses, in the name of the disciples, that Jesus is the Christ (see 1:1). But, like the blind man (see 8:23–24), he is only partially correct, his eyes are not fully open to the truth about Jesus. There is a deeper mystery to the messianic status of Jesus of Nazareth, whom the disciples are following. They are yet to come to full sight, matching the final experience of the blind man, seeing everything clearly (v. 25). After commanding them to silence, he immediately broaches that deeper mystery, announcing in the first prediction of his forthcoming passion that the Messiah is the Son of Man who must go up to Jerusalem to be slain and to rise from the dead (v. 31). These words open the second major section of the Gospel of Mark, dedicated to the story of the crucified Christ and Son of God, the suffering and finally vindicated Son of Man.

Conclusion

The disciples have been at the center of much of the action through 6:6b–8:30. Part of the new family of Jesus established in 3:7–6a, after rejection by the leaders of Israel in 1:14–3:6, they have been sent on a mission which matches Jesus' own. But they failed to recognize all that it entails (6:7–30). They faltered as Jesus involved them in the first multiplication of loaves and fish to feed a Jewish crowd (6:31–44). In the subsequent boat trip, they show lack of trust and belief, in contrast to the faith of the many at Gennesaret who flocked to Jesus (6:45–56). Jesus' conflict with the leaders of Israel and its aftermath (7:1–23) is marked by his concern over the disciples' lack of understanding (v. 18). Episodes in which they are present, but not as major players, follow as Jesus makes his healing presence felt among the Gentiles. But Jesus' ministry there addresses the problem of a ministry to the Gentiles (7:24–37). The healings in Gentile lands lead to the second bread miracle, and a further cycle unfolds. The disciples misunderstand as Jesus feeds the Gentile crowd (8:1–9), journeys in a boat with them to Dalmanutha (8:10), enters into conflict with the Pharisees, and speaks sharply to the disciples during the boat trip (8:11–21). The second cycle concludes as Jesus heals the blind man at Bethsaida (8:22–26). As in the healing miracles in Gentile lands, the disciples are again present, but not active. Yet their future relationship with Jesus, their ability to see with the eyes of faith, is addressed in this brief but paradigmatic miracle story. There is a sense of climax as the first half of the Gospel, which puzzled over Jesus' identity (1:14–8:30), closes with Peter's confession and Jesus' warning at Caesarea Philippi (8:27–30). As earlier in the first half of the Gospel, the major characters in the section come to a decision: Peter, in the name of the disciples, confesses that Jesus is the Christ (8:27–30).

The pattern of summary (1:14–15; 3:7–12; 6:6a), disciples (1:16–20; 3:13–19; 6:7–30), narrative, and final decision (3:6; 6:1–6a; 8:27–30) has determined the literary design of 1:14–3:6, 3:7–6:6a, and 6:6b–30. But the dramatic presentation of the life of Jesus and the

---

[262] These issues complicate efforts to reconstruct the possible pre-Markan traditions for this episode. See the survey in Lührmann, *Markusevangelium,* 143–45.

increasing fragility of the disciples has developed as each section unfolded. The first signs of the disciples' lack of faith, evident in 3:7–6:6a, have become a major theme in 6:6b–8:30. Yet they are still Jesus' disciples, associated with him in his mission (6:7–13) and in his compassionate service (6:31–44; 8:1–9). It is Peter, in the name of the disciples, who has confessed that Jesus is the Messiah, thus resolving the mystery which drove much of the first half of the Gospel narrative. In their blindness (see 8:18) they obviously still have much to learn, and the three-staged miracle of the blind man at Bethsaida is paradigmatic. The disciples have certainly gone beyond total blindness as they follow Jesus "on the way" (see 8:27). The confession at Caesarea Philippi begins the disciples' further response to the paradigm of a movement from blindness to full sight. Peter's confession, followed by Jesus' warning (vv. 29–30), shows that they have achieved partial sight.

Their difficulty is understandable. They have not read the prologue (1:1–13), and have witnessed the ominous increase of tension between Jesus and the leaders of Israel (see 2:1–3:6; 7:1–23; 8:11–13, 15). The slaying of John the Baptist (6:14–29) adds to the atmosphere of impending violence, and Jesus has warned that the day will come when he will no longer be with them (2:20). The remaining half of the Gospel will indicate that true faith and fullness of sight result when one accepts that Jesus is Messiah and Son of God (see 1:1, 11; 9:7; 8:29), the Son of Man who must suffer, die, and rise in Jerusalem (see 8:31; 9:31; 10:32–34). The stage is set for the reading of 8:31–15:47, where this presentation of Jesus unfolds, along with the story of the disciples' struggles to come to fullness of sight.

SECTION 3

JESUS, THE SON OF MAN AND SON OF GOD

MARK 8:31–15:47

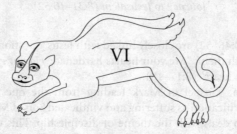

JESUS AND THE DISCIPLES JOURNEY TO JERUSALEM
(MARK 8:31–10:52)

The first of two cures of blind men found in the Gospel of Mark (8:22–26 and 10:46–52) has already been discussed. There we saw that the storyteller not only uses the three-step cure to lead into the confession at Caesarea Philippi (8:27–30), but also creates a literary "overlap" with the following section of the Gospel. Between the two miracles where Jesus heals blindness, he also predicts his passion three times (8:31; 9:31; 10:32–34).[1] There are developments and differences between the predictions, but all are based on the same elements: Jesus, with the disciples "on the way" to Jerusalem, predicts a violent death and a resurrection. The passion predictions may have their origins in Jesus' own words about his fate, and Mark 9:31 may be reminiscent of what he said perhaps on a number of occasions (see also Luke 9:44).[2] Necessarily, they have been further developed in the tradition, using the events from the passion narrative to prophesy Jesus' death and resurrection (see 10:32–33 and 14:53–16:8). The hand of a careful storyteller can be seen in this threefold prediction of the passion. All three, framed by two stories of blindness transformed into sight, are directed to the disciples as they journey toward Jerusalem.[3] The two miracles of

---

[1] E. S. Malbon ("The Major Importance of the Minor Characters in Mark," in *In the Company of Jesus: Characters in Mark's Gospel* [Louisville: Westminster John Knox, 2000], 199–201, 210–13) has shown the importance of the "framing" of the two miracles which touch the lives of "minor characters," and also the important role of other such characters within this section of the narrative: the father of the epileptic boy, and the rich man.

[2] The question of Jesus' speaking of his oncoming death does not necessarily raise the thorny issues of his so-called "messianic self-consciousness"; see the summary of this issue in Ernst, *Markus*, 245–47. His continual difficulties with Jewish leadership, and the heavy-handed dealing of Roman authorities with local troublemakers, would give Jesus ample reason to anticipate a bleak future. It is beyond this study to delve further into the question. The words of Jesus in Mark 9:31, without the reference to the resurrection (see Luke 9:44, where they are absent), may reflect something like his actual words. See the discussion in Ernst, *Markus*, 272. In my opinion, however, he also spoke of his ultimate vindication by God. How, we do not know. Christians believed that the resurrection was that vindication, and thus words foretelling the resurrection are found in all three Markan passion predictions. Similar conclusions are reached by the comprehensive survey of R. E. Brown (*The Death of the Messiah: From Gethsemane to the Grave: A Commentary on the Passion Narratives in the Four Gospels* [ABRL; 2 vols.; New York: Doubleday, 1994], 2:1468–91). See also C. F. D. Moule, "From Defendant to Judge—and Deliverer," in *The Phenomenon of the New Testament* (SBT 2/1; London: SCM, 1967), 82–99; F. J. Moloney, "The End of the Son of Man?" *DRev* 98 (1980): 280–90; Hooker, *St. Mark*, 204–5.

[3] For R. E. Watts (*Isaiah's New Exodus and Mark* [WUNT 2. Reihe 88; J. C. B. Mohr (Paul Siebeck), 1997], 221–57), the "way" section has been shaped, on the basis of the citation of Isa 40:3 in the prologue (see 1:3), on the Isaianic theme of the "way" of YHWH's new exodus coming. The same theme may have also informed the widely used theme of "the way" to describe the Christian life in the early church.

blind men (8:22–26; 10:46–52) are closely linked with Jesus' question of the disciples in his earlier harsh words with them: "Are your hearts hardened? *Having eyes do you not see*, and having ears do you not hear?" (8:17–18).

The section of the Gospel of Mark leading from the question "Who is Jesus?" (1:14–8:30) to his identification as suffering and vindicated Son of Man, Christ, and Son of God (8:22–10:52), also deals with the theme of discipleship. This was an important element in 1:14–8:31, but the literary indications briefly outlined above show that further themes gather around the disciples as the story unfolds, and chief among them are blindness and suffering. More than anywhere else in the Gospel of Mark, Jesus directs his attention and his teaching toward the disciples, and there is a subtle shift in the form of Jesus' instruction. Until now, Jesus has largely "taught" in parables and miracles. Across 8:22–10:52 the reader regularly encounters formulae which reflect a teaching situation: "whoever . . . then" (see 8:34, 35, 38; 9:35, 37, 41, 42; 10:11–12, 15, 29–30, 44), "and if . . . then" (9:43–47). The story continues to unfold as Jesus and the disciples make their way to Jerusalem, interrupted by other characters on only three occasions (see 9:14–27; 10:2–9, 17–22). Each of these episodes is used for the instruction of the disciples (see 9:28–29; 10:10–12, 23–31). The following literary structure emerges.[4]

8:22–26   The cure of a *blind man* at Bethsaida
  8:27–33   The *first passion prediction* and the failure of Peter
    8:34–9:29   The *first instruction* of the disciples:
        8:34–9:1   *The cross* and the disciples
        9:2–13   The instruction of the transfiguration
        9:14–29   The lesson of the boy the disciples could not heal
  9:30–34   The *second passion prediction* and the failure of the disciples
    9:35–10:31   The *second instruction* of the disciples:
        9:35–50   *Service and receptivity* as marks of a disciple
        10:1–31   The practice of discipleship
            10:1–12   In marriage
            10:13–16   Through *receptivity*
            10:17–31   In attitude to riches and possessions
  10:32–35   The *third passion prediction*
    10:36–40   The *failure* of James and John. Their *instruction* on the *cross*
    10:41–44   The *failure* of "the other ten." Their *instruction* on *service*
    10:45   The christological motivation for the teaching on cross, service, and receptivity
10:46–52   The cure of a *blind man:* Bartimaeus

The careful arrangement of the material suggests a reading of Mark 8:22–10:45 as an instruction of the disciples on the way of the Son of Man, under three headings: (1) the cross; (2) service and receptivity; and finally (3) the cross and service. The instruction closes as it began, with the cure of a blind man (10:46–52; see 8:22–26).

---

[4] This structure, and subsequent reading, of Mark 8:22–10:52 owes much to N. Perrin, "The Christology of Mark: A Study in Methodology," *JR* 51 (1971): 173–87. A slightly revised version of this article is also available in W. Telford, ed., *The Interpretation of Mark* (IRT 7; Philadelphia: Fortress, 1985), 95–108. As will become apparent, my understanding of the motif of the failure of the disciples differs from that of Perrin and his students. For earlier suggestions along the lines eventually developed by Perrin, see R. H. Lightfoot, *History and Interpretation in the Gospels* (London: Hodder and Stoughton, 1935), 117–20, and E. Haenchen, "Die Komposition von Mk vii 27—ix 1 und par.," in *The Composition of Mark's Gospel: Selected Studies from* Novum Testamentum (ed. D. E. Orton; Brill's Readers in Biblical Studies 3; Leiden: Brill, 1999), 1–29.

The Way of the Son of Man: The Cross (8:27–9:29)

The paradigm of the three-staged journey from blindness to full sight (8:22–26) has led to a presentation of the blindness of "the people." They saw Jesus as a prophet and perhaps the one who was to usher in the messianic era (vv. 27–28). Better than this, but still demonstrating only a partial sight, the disciples confessed that Jesus was "the Christ" (v. 29). The limited nature of this confession leads Jesus to charge them to tell no one about him (v. 30). With this warning the "overlap" comes to an end.[5] It links the conclusion of the first part of a narrative (1:14–8:30) with the second (8:31–15:47). Mark 8:22–30 has both provided a response to the question of the identity of Jesus (v. 29) and introduced the second half of the story: if Jesus' warning about Peter's messianic confession indicates that it reflects only partial sight, what more is required?[6]

The passion prediction (8:31)

In 8:31–15:47 Jesus, the Christ, Son of God and vindicated Son of Man, will be made known to the reader, by word and deed. Mark immediately introduces the first passion prediction: "And he began to teach them that the Son of man must suffer many things, and be rejected by the elders and the chief priests and the scribes, and be killed, and after three days rise again. *And he said this plainly*" (8:31–32a). For the first time in the Gospel, Jesus speaks clearly of who he is, the Son of Man, and he describes the destiny of the Son of Man: suffering, rejection, killed, and risen.[7] Phrased to point forward to the death and resurrection of Jesus, these words also build upon the traditions behind Mark 14–16.[8] The use of δεῖ indicates that the future suffering, dying, and rising of the Son of Man will not fall upon him as some inevitable and unavoidable tragedy; it forms part of God's design for Jesus, the Christ, the Son of Man.[9] In a deliberate contrast to 8:30, where the disciples were severely warned against speaking about Jesus as "the Christ," Jesus openly proclaims his message of the Son of Man for the first time: καὶ παρρησίᾳ τὸν λόγον ἐλάλει (v. 32a).[10] The use of the imperfect tense indicates that Jesus went on saying this word publicly and boldly (παρρησίᾳ). He is not a powerful, royal Messiah (v. 29). Such an understanding of Jesus is not to be spread abroad (v. 30). His messiahship is to be found in his future as the Son of Man. That future will involve rejection, suffering, death, and resurrection after three days

---

[5] The function and meaning of 8:22–30 were dealt with above: see pp. 162–67.

[6] Lane (*Mark*, 292) rightly remarks: "With verse 31 an entirely new orientation is given to the Gospel" (see pp. 292–94). See also Lagrange, *Saint Marc*, 205–6.

[7] See Excursus 1, "The Son of Man Discussion" below, pp. 212–13.

[8] Much has been written of the suffering and rising motifs. See especially Pesch (*Markusevangelium*, 2:48–56), who sees the saying as a blending of the wisdom traditions of the righteous sufferer and the Jewish notion of the eschatological prophet. What actually happened to Jesus must be seen as playing an important part in this *vaticinium ex eventu*. The mention of the elders and the chief priests and the scribes in v. 30 is an indication that this prophecy is built upon the Markan passion traditions. One might expect the Pharisees or the Herodians (see 3:6; 8:15), but the elders, the chief priests, and the scribes are active in the passion account (see 14:1, 43, 53, 55; 15:1, 3). The Pharisees do not appear.

[9] See W. Grundmann, "δεῖ κτλ," *TDNT* 2:21–25, especially pp. 23–24.

[10] The use of "the word" (ὁ λόγος) may hint, paradoxically, that the message of 8:31 is gospel. See Painter, *Mark's Gospel*, 125.

(v. 31).[11] This is true sight, a fullness of vision. This truth must not be hidden; it must be openly proclaimed.[12] This is the first appearance of the expression "the Son of Man" since Jesus' earlier claim of authority to forgive sin (2:10) and over the Sabbath (2:28). The reader is led further into the enigma as Jesus tells of his forthcoming death, and ultimate victory through resurrection, and speaks of himself, slain and raised, as the Son of Man.

The disciples' failure (8:32–33)

Peter, again in the name of the disciples, vigorously opposes Jesus' first self-revelation. Peter was ready to confess that Jesus was the Messiah (v. 29), but talk of death and resurrection was not a part of his scheme. Thus Peter "took hold" of Jesus and began to rebuke him (ἤρξατο ἐπιτιμᾶν αὐτῷ, v. 32bc). The roles of master and disciple, clearly established in 1:16–20, 2:13–14, and 3:13–19, have been reversed. Peter, the disciple, rather than accept the warning of Jesus (see v. 30: ἐπετίμησεν), attempts to impose upon Jesus a messianic expectation that has no place for suffering and death. The physical "taking hold" and the reversal of who should warn whom (see vv. 30, 32) indicate that Peter fails to accept Jesus' self-revelation as the Son of Man (v. 31).

Jesus' reaction does not focus only upon Peter: "Turning and *seeing his disciples . . .*" (8:33a). Peter has spoken in 8:29, and acted in 8:32 in the name of the disciples. Jesus' words to Peter are directed to all the disciples. Right order is restored as Jesus rebukes Peter (ἐπετίμησεν, v. 33), addressing him as "Satan," a Greek word with Aramaic origins. The master is once again determining the narrative, and the expression "Satan," while primarily linking Peter with the designs of the Satan, briefly described in 1:12–13, also carries with it the meaning of "stumbling block."[13] Jesus and the disciples are "on the way" (v. 27), but Peter is blocking that way, holding Jesus back, and rejecting Jesus' acceptance of God's plan. The vocation of the disciples is recalled as Peter and all the disciples are told that they must take their correct place: "get behind me" (ὕπαγε ὀπίσω μου, v. 33b; see 1:16–20; 2:13–14).[14] There is a blend of angry reproof in the use of "Satan" and a command that disciples keep their place "behind" Jesus, and not block his path to Jerusalem with their all-too-human understanding.[15] The spatial and the theological are involved in Jesus' indication to Peter (and the disciples) that they are not on the side of God, but on the side of

---

[11] On the variations in this "third day" language, see Taylor, *St. Mark*, 378; Gnilka, *Markus*, 2:16. There is no call for the suggestion that the Markan "after three days" may go back to Jesus' use of Hos 6:2 and Jonah 1:17, simply to mean "after a short while." See Nineham, *St. Mark*, 229–30. On the use of "three days" in Jewish tradition, see the summary in Pesch, *Markusevangelium*, 2:52–53. The possibility that "third day" language began when an empty tomb was found three days (in a Jewish reckoning of "days") should not be discounted. See H. von Campenhausen, "The Events of Easter and the Early Tomb," in *Tradition and Life in the Church: Essays and Lectures in Church History* (trans. A. V. Littledale; London: Collins, 1968), 42–89.

[12] Contrary to Lohmeyer (*Markus*, 167), who regards the interpretation of a public proclamation as "hardly understandable."

[13] See the references in M. Jastrow, *A Dictionary of the Targumim, the Talmud Babli and Yerushalmi, and the Midrashic Literature* (2 vols.; New York: Pardes, 1950), 2:973, s.vv. *seṭan, sāṭān, sāṭānāʾ, siṭnāʾ*. This is made explicit in Matt 16:18, 23, where Peter is called "rock" (v. 18: Πέτρος . . . πέτρα) upon which the Church will be founded, and also "stumbling block" (v. 23: Σατανᾶ . . . σκάνδαλον) to Jesus, the stone along the road that could cause a fall. See B. A. E. Osborne, "Peter: Stumbling-Block and Satan," *NovT* 15 (1973): 187–90.

[14] See LaVerdiere, *The Beginning*, 2:31–32.

[15] Lagrange (*Saint Marc*, 207) catches the sense: "Get behind me! —not in a kind sense . . . but to say: get back into your proper place!"

human beings (v. 33c). Standing in Jesus' way, blocking his journey, continues the idea of Peter being a "stumbling block," out of his correct place "behind" Jesus. However, Jesus' journey is not mere geography. It is a response to the design of God. Thus, their being "out of place" also means that they are opposing God's design. The rejection of Jesus' prophecy of his oncoming suffering and death as Son of Man is a rejection of God's plan (v. 31) for the Messiah (v. 29).[16]

Jesus instructs the failing disciples: the cross (8:34–9:1)

The discourse that follows in 8:34–9:1 is made up of formal instruction.[17] The author opens the possibility of discipleship to others, beyond the group that has come to be identified as such in the narrative thus far. Jesus' calling the multitude as well as the disciples (v. 34a) addresses readers and listeners. *Anyone* who wishes to be a follower of Jesus (v. 34b) is addressed by the words that follow. The disciples *in* the story and the readers *of* the story hear the words of Jesus.[18] Typical didactic forms pile on top of one another: "anyone who . . ." (v. 34), "whoever . . ." (v. 35a), "whoever . . ." (v. 35b), rhetorical questions (vv. 36–37), "whoever . . ." (v. 38). In 9:1 the teaching comes to a climax.

Based upon the predicted experience of the Son of Man (8:31), a disciple is called to renounce himself, take up his cross,[19] lose his life for Jesus and the gospel (vv. 34b–35) and never to be ashamed of Jesus and his words (v. 38). As Jesus rejects the expected messianic glory and embraces the destiny of the suffering Son of Man, so must the disciple.[20] Jesus'

---

[16] Taylor, *St. Mark*, 380; Lane, *Mark*, 304. The use of the passive voice to speak of the Son of Man's being rejected and killed and raised indicates to the reader that it is God (the so-called "divine passive") who determines the destiny of the Son of Man. For the close relationship between Jesus' temptation by Satan in 1:9–13 and Peter's Satanic role at Caesarea Philippi, see J. B. Gibson, *The Temptations of Jesus in Early Christianity* (JSNTSup 112; Sheffield: Sheffield Academic Press, 1995), 212–23. For Gibson, Jesus is being tempted to wage wars of deliverance, a temptation he resists in order to fulfill his mandate as king of Israel, Suffering Servant, and sacrificial victim (see 1:9–13). See also S. R. Garrett, *The Temptations of Jesus in Mark's Gospel* (Grand Rapids: Eerdmans, 1998), 76–82.

[17] With the exception of 9:1 which has a different character, these sayings are very traditional; see Hooker, *St. Mark*, 207–8. They may go back to sayings from the historical Jesus, gathered and reworked in the tradition and by Mark. See Gnilka, *Markus*, 2:22–23, 27; Pesch, *Markusevangelium*, 2:58–59, 62. On the didactic form, see Ernst, *Markus*, 247–48.

[18] This passage alone indicates that the Markan story of disciples reaches beyond the limitations of the story itself. Jesus "calls" and describes them as those who "come after him," Markan expressions associated with discipleship. Sinaiticus, Alexandrinus, and Vaticanus, among others, read ἐλθεῖν, "to come," rather than ἀκολουθεῖν "to follow." This is, however, due to assimilation to Matt 16:24, and the Markan verb for a disciples' following must be retained (see 1:17, 20; 2:14–15). The portrait of the disciples in the Gospel of Mark is written for "anyone who wishes to come after" Jesus. On this, see R. C. Tannehill, "The Disciples in Mark: The Function of a Narrative Role," in *The Interpretation of Mark* (ed. W. Telford; IRT 7; Philadelphia: Fortress, 1985), 134–57; E. S. Malbon, "Disciples/Crowds/Whoever: Markan Characters and the Readers," in *In the Company of Jesus: Characters in Mark's Gospel* (Louisville: Westminster John Knox, 2000), 70–99, originally published in *NovT* 28 (1986): 104–30.

[19] Given the practice of crucifixion at the time of Jesus, it is not impossible that Jesus used this expression to speak of the shame a disgraced discipleship might bring. See M. Hengel, *Crucifixion in the Ancient World and the Folly of the Message of the Cross* (trans. J. Bowden; London: SCM, 1977). However, it certainly gained its Markan meaning in the light of Jesus' death on a cross. See Gnilka, *Markus*, 2:23–24; Ernst, *Markus*, 249; Lührmann, *Markusevangelium*, 151–52.

[20] See Lührmann, *Markusevangelium*, 152: "V. 38 is the definitive basis for v. 34b, or rather for the whole context of vv. 34b–37."

coming and the gospel are closely associated (see 1:14–15). The disciple must be prepared to give all for Jesus and the gospel. Life itself is at stake. One can have all the glory of this world (see v. 29) but lose one's life (v. 36), for which there is no substitute (v. 37).[21] Jesus' call to discipleship is paradoxically both a call to self-gift unto death and a summons to life. Crucial to this paradox is the identity between Jesus and the suffering Son of Man vindicated in resurrection (v. 31). The vindicated suffering and dying Son of Man will come "in the glory of his Father with the holy angels" at the end of time (v. 38).[22] Rejection of the way of the Son of Man, of Jesus and his words by "this adulterous and wicked generation," will lead to rejection when the same Son of Man comes in glory (v. 38).[23] The Son of Man will exercise his authority. For the first time in the narrative, some light is shed upon the puzzle of Jesus' use of "the Son of Man" in 2:10 to declare his authority to forgive sin, and his use of the same term to declare his authority over the Sabbath in 2:28. The appearance of the expression "the Son of Man," which Jesus used to affirm his authority twice in conflicts with those who reject him and ultimately seek his death (see 3:6), has created "a gap" in the narrative.[24] It cannot be explained within its immediate context, but the reader waits until the author provides further information—later in the story—which may explain why Jesus, the Son of Man, has authority over sin and over the Sabbath. The promise of his future coming in power, with the angels, in the glory of his Father, to exercise his authority against the rejection of those who were ashamed of Jesus and the gospel, goes a large part of the way. Yet the promise of 8:38 still requires fulfillment. The reader looks to the remaining parts of the narrative for further information on the authority of the Son of Man.

This first, more formally didactic, section dedicated to Jesus' instruction of his failing disciples closes with an enigmatic saying that may have had a long and complicated history in the tradition. It is open to a number of interpretations but must be understood in the light of 8:31d: καὶ μετὰ τρεῖς ἡμέρας ἀναστῆναι. There is solemnity in Jesus' opening words, ἀμὴν λέγω ὑμῖν, indicating to the reader that something climactic is about to be said, after having asked for commitment to the cross, self-loss, the word of Jesus, and the gospel (vv. 34–38).[25] He promises the gathered disciples and the crowd that some of them

---

[21] On the meaning of ψυχή as that which is essential to human life, experience, and existence, in the sense of the Hebrew *nefesh*, see Lagrange, *Saint Marc*, 211; Gnilka, *Markus*, 24–25.

[22] Mark, the tradition before him, or Jesus, may have made this identification. Many scholars claim that the Son of Man is *only* an eschatological term (see the excursus "The Son of Man Discussion," pp. 212–13 below). If the pre-Markan tradition or Mark, and not the historical Jesus, made this identification in v. 38 (as is most likely), it is also probable that Mark added the eschatological connection (coming in the glory of the father with the angels). However, this need not be debated here. For Mark, the issue is clear. An ashamed rejection of the suffering Son of Man *now* leads to final rejection by the Son of Man *then*. This negative statement, which may have its origins in a situation of martyrdom (see Pesch, *Markusevangelium*, 2:65), is rendered positive in Luke 12:8–9.

[23] Grundmann, *Markus*, 177–78. The reference to "this generation" (ἐν τῇ γενεᾷ ταύτῃ), further described with the adjectives "adulterous and sinful," looks back to Jesus' angry encounter with the Pharisees in 8:12. There the author used the expression "this generation" to link Jesus' interlocutors with the narrative. After all they had witnessed they were still seeking signs. The same literary link with the "world within the text" is happening here, but the "generation" is further described as wicked, aided by language which comes from Israel's prophetic tradition (see Isa 1:4; 2:1; Ezek 16:32; Hos 2:4). See Lane, *Mark*, 310.

[24] On this feature of narrative (also called "blanks" or "places of indeterminacy"), see W. Iser, *The Act of Reading: A Theory of Aesthetic Response* (London: Routledge & Kegan Paul, 1978), 182–87.

[25] The use of "amen" acts as a separation between Jesus' promise in 8:38, which will take place at the Parousia, and the further promise in 9:1, which will take place at the resurrection. It is not necessarily eschatological, as per Gnilka, *Markus* 2:26, following K. Berger, *Die Amen-Worte Jesu: Eine*

will not die before they see the kingdom of God come with power (9:1). The pre-Easter Jesus may have expected that the time between his apparent human failure and his return in power would be brief. It is difficult to be sure about that, but there was certainly a time in the early church when confusion reigned over Jesus' final return, which may have had its origins in the memory of Jesus' own words about the urgency of the times (see 1 Thess 4:13–5:11). The saying may also have originated in the Markan community when Jesus' return with power as the eschatological Son of Man was expected at any time.[26] In its present Markan context, however, its meaning must be determined by that context.

The future of Jesus, Messiah and Son of Man (8:29, 31), is fundamental to the future of the disciple who takes up the cross, lays down his life, and is not ashamed of Jesus. In words influenced by early credal statements concerning the resurrection (see 1 Cor 15:4), Jesus has told the disciples that he will be slain, "and after three days rise again" (v. 31). This is what the "some who are standing here" will experience. The crucified yet risen Christ will be the guarantee of the truth of Jesus' teaching. The Son of Man will be slain, but his loss of self in death will be vindicated in resurrection. There are some standing there hearing Jesus' words who will experience the apparent failure of the crucifixion, overcome by God's power in the resurrection. The resurrection of Jesus will be the kingdom of God coming in power. This will be true sight: an acceptance of a discipleship which responds to the teaching of Jesus in 8:34–38 (cross, loss of self, and ultimate vindication), empowered by the presence of the risen Jesus, the kingdom of God come in power. As the storyteller looks back upon the world within the text, he singles out this privilege for "some who are standing here" in the time of the narrative. However long past it may have been, the Markan community and its Gospel exist because of the experience of some who were standing there. They experienced the transformation of suffering into power, and their witness lies behind the Markan narrative.[27]

The instruction of the transfiguration (9:2–13)

Six days separate the initial teaching of all who would be disciples of Jesus (8:34–9:1) and Jesus' taking the "inner circle" of the Twelve, Peter, James, and John (see 3:16–17), on to a high mountain where they could be by themselves. "After six days" may indicate that the event took place on the seventh day, and would thus have a sense of fulfillment. It also recalls Exod 24:16, where Moses, accompanied by Joshua, spent six days on the mountain

---

Untersuchung der Legitimation in apokalyptischen Rede (BZNW 39; Berlin: de Gruyter, 1970), 62–67. Context must be allowed to determine the meaning of text. Nor is it liturgical, used to introduce the transfiguration story, as claimed by LaVerdiere (*The Beginning*, 2:39–41). For Pesch (*Markusevangelium*, 2:67), LaVerdiere (*The Beginning*, 2:41–45), and Lane (*Mark*, 313–14), Peter, James, and John are those "standing there" (v. 1) who see the Son of Man coming with power in vv. 2–8, a proleptic experience of the Parousia. Against this suggestion, see Lagrange, *Saint Marc*, 215; Nineham, *St. Mark*, 236.

[26] These possibilities (and variations upon them) are not to be dismissed out of hand. For a survey of opinions, see Cranfield, *St. Mark*, 285–89. On the history of the interpretation of 9:1 see also Taylor, *St. Mark*, 384–86.

[27] This interpretation separates the two "times" of the coming of the Son of Man in 8:38 (the Parousia) and the coming of the kingdom with power in 9:1 (the resurrection). The formal "amen" saying (9:1a) between 8:28 and 9:1 is used to indicate this separation. Lagrange (*Saint Marc*, 214–15) is close to this interpretation. He claims that the coming of the kingdom with power (9:1) will be found in the post-resurrection preaching of the gospel. See also Lührmann, *Markusevangelium*, 153–54.

until, on the seventh day, YHWH called to him from the cloud. It also links 9:2–13 with the preceding 8:27–9:1. The location on the mountain marks what follows as akin to a theophany. In the Bible, mountains are regularly the places where the divine and the human touch.[28] Without any flourish, Mark reports "he was transfigured before them" (μετεμορφώθη ἔμπροσθεν αὐτῶν). The self-contained narrative of 9:2–8 was shaped by the storyteller and inserted into this place in the narrative to continue the double-pronged message being developed here: the significance of Jesus' relationship to God (vv. 1–4, 7), and the fragility of the disciples (vv. 6–5, 8).[29] The aftermath (vv. 9–13) continues these themes.[30] Jesus further informs the privileged disciples about his resurrection and his relationship to Elijah (vv. 9, 12–13), but they are not able to understand this information (vv. 10–11).

An important narrative strategy is at work here. The reader is aware of Jesus' relationship to God, made clear in the prologue (see especially 1:1–3, 9–11), but none of the *characters in the story* have been given this information. It is revealed to Peter, James, and John on the mountain. In a parallel fashion, the reader is also aware of Jesus' relationship to the Elijah figure of John the Baptist from the prologue (see 1:4–8), but only as Jesus and the disciples come down from the mountain is this relationship made known to *characters in the story*. The reader follows the response of the disciples, armed with the knowledge provided by the authoritative voices of God (1:2–3) and the narrator (1:1, 4–13). How will the disciples respond to this crucial information?[31]

The description of Jesus' transformation uses language associated with the appearance of heavenly beings: the impression of a bright and intense whiteness (9:3a; see Dan 7:9), beyond anything that could be generated by human hands (9:3b).[32] What is most surprising about the scene, however, is the introduction of Elijah with Moses, talking to Jesus

---

[28] Malbon, *Narrative Space,* 84–89.

[29] The narrative of the transfiguration existed before the Gospel of Mark, but it has been notoriously difficult to discover a *Sitz im Leben* for the development of the account. Schweizer (*Mark,* 180) is probably correct: "It is no longer possible to explain the history of the tradition of this passage." Is it the rewriting of an extraordinary experience that actually happened? In support, see Lagrange, *Saint Marc,* 219–21, in polemic with Loisy; Taylor, *St. Mark,* 386–88; Cranfield, *St. Mark,* 293–94; Lane, *Mark,* 316–17. See also Grundmann, *Markus,* 179, where the positions of A. von Harnack, E. Meyer, and R. A. Hoffmann are summarized. Was it originally a resurrection appearance, transported back into Jesus' life-story, as argued by R. Bultmann, *History of the Synoptic Tradition* (trans. John Marsh; Oxford: Basil Blackwell, 1968), 259–61? Perhaps the episode is a product of the symbolic writing of the early church, using motifs from the Old Testament (see Lohmeyer, *Markus,* 178–81) or a proleptic but misunderstood revelation of the risen and glorified Lord to the three disciples (Pesch, *Markusevangelium,* 2:71–77). For surveys, see Ernst, *Markus,* 255–26; J. Marcus, *The Way of the Lord: Christological Exegesis of the Old Testament in the Gospel of Mark* (Louisville: Westminster John Knox, 1992), 80–93. As Hooker (*St. Mark,* 214) remarks: "In his [Mark's] God-filled universe, a heavenly confirmation of Jesus' identity would have seemed no more out of place than the acknowledgment of his identity by the unclean spirits."

[30] Pesch (*Markusevangelium,* 2:69–84) rightly regards 9:2–13 as a unit. More problematic is his claim (p. 69) that this unit comes from the pre-Markan passion narrative, and has only been slightly reworked by Mark.

[31] Every detail of the story points to the instruction of the disciples: he was transfigured *before them* (v. 2), there appeared *to them* Elijah with Moses (v. 4), the cloud overshadowed *them* (v. 7a), *you* listen to my beloved Son (v. 7b), only Jesus was *with them* (v. 8). "The whole event, from first to last, takes place solely for the sake of the three disciples" (R. H. Lightfoot, *The Gospel Message of St. Mark* [Oxford: Clarendon Press, 1950], 44). See also Pesch, *Markusevangelium,* 2:70.

[32] For further suggestions concerning Jewish background for this description of the transfigured Jesus, see Gnilka, *Markus,* 2:33; Pesch, *Markusevangelium,* 2:73.

(v. 4), and especially the naming of Elijah before Moses. Traditionally, these two figures have been explained as representatives of the Law (Moses) and the Prophets (Elijah).[33] But the two figures are introduced in the reverse order. Also, if reference to the Law and the Prophets were intended, there was no need to go beyond Moses, regarded by Jewish tradition to be the first and the greatest of all the prophets (see Deut 18:15–18), as well as the figure who mediated God's gift of the law. There are probably two elements involved. In the first place, both Elijah and Moses were figures who had experienced theophanies on a mountain (see Exod 19:16–25; 1 Kgs 19:11–18). More importantly, both were celebrated in Jewish tradition as having been transported into heaven. This is clear for Elijah in 2 Kgs 3:9–12, and subsequent Jewish reflection (see Sir 48:9; 1 Macc 2:38; *1 En.* 89:52; 93:8; Josephus, *Ant.* 9:28). Even though Moses' death is recorded, the place of his burial is unknown (Deut 34:5–8), and subsequent tradition associated Moses with exaltation to heavenly glory (see Josephus, *Ant.* 3:5.7; 4:8.48; *L.A.B.* 19:12,16; 32;9; *As. Mos.* 11:5–8; Philo, *Mos.* 2.288, 291–292; *QG* 1.86).[34]

Once this link is made, then the conversation between Jesus, Elijah, and Moses is to be linked to Jesus' words in 8:38. Like Elijah and Moses, Jesus will be transported to heaven, and thus take his place as the Son of Man in the glory of his Father and the holy angels (8:38). The scene, therefore, is an anticipation of the glorification of Jesus that must take place by means of his suffering, death, and resurrection into glory (see 8:31).[35] Elijah, however, is named first because he has been so important in the surrounding narrative. In 8:28 the disciples reported that some people regarded Jesus as Elijah, and in the scene which immediately follows, as Jesus descends the mountain with Peter, James, and John, it is again the figure of Elijah who is discussed (9:11–13). The close association of "what is written" of Elijah, and the slaying of John the Baptist (6:14–29) as an anticipation of what will be done to the Son of Man, determines his position before Moses at the transfiguration.[36] As with the didactic 8:34–9:1, it is the Christology of the passion prediction in 8:31 which determines the meaning of Jesus' further dealings with the disciples.

But the disciples fail. Again speaking in the name of the other disciples, Peter, addressing Jesus as "rabbi,"[37] suggests that the theophanic experience be held in perpetuity (9:5). The setting up of three booths to make a permanent shrine of the transfigured Jesus, along

---

[33] See, for example, Lagrange, *Saint Marc,* 217.

[34] Contrary to Gnilka (*Markus,* 2:34), who claims that there is little evidence for this, Marcus (*The Way of the Lord,* 80–93) makes much of the Moses material. However, he summarily dismisses the important location of Elijah prior to Moses (pp. 83–84), and neglects Elijah speculations which parallel those of Moses.

[35] Grundmann, *Markus,* 182–83.

[36] M. D. Hooker, "What Doest Thou Here, Elijah?" in *The Glory of Christ in the New Testament: Studies in Christology in Memory of George Bradford Caird* (ed. L. D. Hurst and N. T. Wright; Oxford: University Press, 1987), 59–70. Also, as Lagrange (*Saint Mark,* 216–17) points out, Elijah is described as "with Moses" (Ἐλίας σὺν Μωϋσεῖ) and this expression could retain the primacy of Moses, who dignifies Elijah with his presence.

[37] It is often pointed out that this address, so soon after 8:29, is strange. For some (e.g., Taylor, *St. Mark,* 391) it indicates the primitive nature of the tradition. It may, however, serve the Markan agenda well. Despite his partially correct confession of faith in 8:29, within the context of a transfigured Jesus, he falls back to an unsatisfactory title (9:5), ignorant and full of fear (see v. 6). C. R. Kazmierski (*Jesus, the Son of God: A Study of the Markan Tradition and Its Redaction by the Evangelist* [FB 33; Würzburg: Echter Verlag, 1979], 118–26) argues that the disciples do not fail, but manifest holy awe as they are introduced to the divine mystery of Jesus.

fear

with his heavenly companions, is a further flagrant rejection of Jesus' words on his destiny as the Son of Man (8:31) and his invitation to all who would be his disciples to share in that destiny (8:34–9:1).[38] The narrator's comment for the reader makes it clear that such is the case. He was ignorant and he was frightened (v. 6). These two qualities have already been part of the disciples' response to Jesus. Their ignorance was the subject of Jesus' harsh words to them in 8:17–18, and it will not disappear as they journey with Jesus to Jerusalem. This is not the first time that the disciples have experienced φόβος. On two earlier occasions it was a prelude to the disciples' lack of faith (see 4:41; 6:50), and the expression will return regularly across the second half of the story, until its final dramatic occurrence as the Gospel's penultimate word (see 16:8). Privileged yet failing disciples are wrapped in a cloud, which recalls the experience of God's intervention into the life of Israel at Sinai, a theme which returns regularly to speak of God's presence to the people (see, for example, Exod 13:21–22; 24:16; 33:7–11; 34:5; 40:34–35; Ezek 1:28; 11:23). From the cloud comes a voice which repeats for the disciples what had previously been made known only to the reader: "This is my beloved son" (9:7b; see 1:11). While that passage looked back to Ps 2:7 and Gen 22:2, 12, 16, to speak of God's pleasure in his Son, here the words are aimed at the disciples. They are instructed: "Listen to him" (v. 7b). They must listen to the word of the beloved son. The words of God to Israel in Deut 18:15, 18 come to mind: "The Lord your God will raise up for you a prophet . . . him you shall heed."

While the disciples have confessed Jesus as the Messiah (8:29), the opening moments of the mystery of the Son of Man have been marked by Jesus' prediction of his suffering and death (8:31). He has asked all who would follow him to share this destiny (8:34–9:1). The disciples have resisted this invitation (8:29, 32–33; 9:5–6). Who has the authority to make such demands? Three of them now have the response to that question from the most authoritative voice in the Gospel: the voice of God tells them that they have gathered around the Son of God and that they must listen to him. Imperceptibly, the major christological categories of the Gospel of Mark have been introduced across the center of the Markan narrative: Messiah, Son of Man, and Son of God. It appears that Jesus' sonship is the interpretative key for understanding the messianic Son of Man. The reader has now heard the voice of God twice announce the sonship of Jesus (1:11; 9:7), but this is the first time God has spoken to characters in the story. However troublesome the words of Jesus have become, and however difficult his demands will become as he leads them to Jerusalem, the disciples must listen to him, Christ (8:29), Son of Man (8:31), and Son of God (9:7). The same collection of christological titles will appear, ironically, as Jesus goes to his death (see 14:61–62; 15:31–39). For the moment, however, there is more story to tell, and the situation is transformed as the disciples look around confusedly. The only person they now see is Jesus, without the trappings of glory (v. 8).[39] There is no sign that the disciples have overcome the partial sight expressed by Peter in 8:29, or their unwillingness to accept Jesus' agenda in 8:32–33, and God's agenda in 9:5–6. Yet, they are not abandoned. The authoritative word of God has assured them that they are followers of his beloved Son, and are to listen to him. The reader wonders: will they?

---

[38] The word used for "tents" (σκηνάς) recalls the building of tents and the Feast of Tabernacles, with its association with Israel's messianic expectation; see F. J. Moloney, *Signs and Shadows: Reading John 5–12* (Minneapolis: Fortress, 1996), 66–70. It appears forced, however, to make this link with the Markan narrative, as in Nineham, *St. Mark*, 236–37; Lane, *Mark*, 316–17; see also n. 16; Gnilka, *Markus*, 2:24–25; Ernst, *Markus*, 258.

[39] It is not explicitly said that he had returned to his "ordinary self." However, the Greek, with its negatives and the adversative ἀλλά, makes it clear: οὐκέτι οὐδένα εἶδον ἀλλὰ τὸν Ἰησοῦν μόνον.

As in earlier situations in the Gospel, Jesus instructs the chosen disciples (vv. 9–13; see 4:10–25; 7:17–23; 8:14–21).[40] They are not to speak of their proleptic experience of the Son of Man coming in the glory of his Father with the angels (9:2–4; see 8:38) until Jesus, the Son of Man, has crossed the essential threshold of the cross and the resurrection. Both elements are involved in the narrator's report of Jesus words: "until the Son of Man should have risen from the dead" (v. 9). There will be no resurrection without violent death, and the return in glory, prefigured in the transfiguration, is fundamentally dependent upon the fulfillment of the passion prediction of 8:31. For once it appears that this command is obeyed, and they keep the matter to themselves, but they wonder what rising from the dead might mean. The categories of 8:31, repeated in various ways in Jesus' teaching (8:34–9:1) and the transfiguration (9:1–8), continue to puzzle the disciples.[41] The idea that the proximate death of Jesus, the Son of Man, would be overcome by a resurrection from the dead is beyond them.[42] They will not "listen" to the voice of the beloved Son (see v. 7) as they attempt to puzzle things out in their ongoing ignorance. They do, however, have something of an answer in the tradition of the scribes that Elijah must first come (v. 11). The Jewish tradition, already reflected in the juxtaposing of Mal 3:1–2 and 4:5–6, that Elijah would return to introduce the messianic era is something they would like to investigate further. Is this the meaning of "rising from the dead"? It might be, but their puzzlement seems to be with the notion of the resurrection of the Son of Man (8:31; 9:9). What is the relationship between the Son of Man and Elijah?

They have much to learn, but Jesus does not abandon his disciples as they flail about in their ignorance. The hint of the possible identification of John the Baptist and Elijah, provided for the reader in 1:4–6, is now clarified. It is true that Elijah comes before the messianic era to restore all things, but there is a twist to the story.[43] The problem that must now be faced and resolved is that the Messiah (8:29) is also the suffering and dying Son of Man (8:31). It is widely claimed that nowhere is it "written" that the Son of Man "should suffer many things and be treated with contempt" (v. 12). This claim, however, depends upon the rejection of the possible interpretation of "the one like a son of man" in Dan 7:13 as the personification of "the holy ones of the Most High," whose experience is described in Dan 7:15–27. Jesus, in rendering personal "the one like a son of man" indicates that, like "the holy ones of the Most High" who remained faithful to the God of Israel under Antiochus IV, persecution, suffering, and death are the inevitable destiny of the Son of Man.[44] It has been written in the vision of Dan 7 that the Son of Man should suffer.[45] And

---

[40] This is a difficult passage, no doubt reflecting a complex history before it came to Mark. Some have suggested that the difficulties come from scribal interpolation. See the summary in Nineham, *St. Mark,* 240–41. Others suggest that vv. 11–13 originally followed v. 1 (Bultmann, *History,* 124–25). The interpretation that follows is strongly determined by the overall context.

[41] Hooker, *St. Mark,* 218–19.

[42] LaVerdiere, *The Beginning,* 2:46: "The disciples were asking about Jesus' resurrection because it presupposed his death."

[43] There has been considerable debate over this question, some (C. Milikowsky and D. C. Allison) affirming such a tradition, others (M. M. Faierstein and J. A. Fitzmyer) rejecting it. See the summary, accepting the Milikowsky-Allison position, in Marcus, *The Way of the Lord,* 110.

[44] Hooker, *St. Mark,* 220.

[45] It has been customary to look to Isa 52:13–53:12 and the suffering servant for this scriptural reference. See, for example, Lane, *Mark,* 325–26; Pesch, *Markusevangelium,* 2:79, who also adds the righteous sufferer and the eschatological prophet (see also pp. 80–81); LaVerdiere, *The Beginning,* 2:46. But the theological links between the Son of Man and the Suffering Servant are tenuous at best. Added to this, there are no close verbal links between Mark 9:12 and the Isaianic passage. On the

the forerunner, Elijah, who has come in the person of John the Baptist (see 1:4–6), puts everything in order (ἀποκαθιστάνει πάντα). This description of the role of John the Baptist as the Elijah *redivivus* is obscure, but its explanation is that there first had to be the Baptist and his experience, and then the Son of Man. By means of this sequence everything is "put in order." The order referred to is the order of God's design.[46] John the Baptist "has accomplished his mission successfully,"[47] even though, as the reader is aware, they have done to him whatever they pleased (see 6:14–29). The forerunner, Elijah–John the Baptist, and Jesus, the Messiah–Son of Man, must undergo suffering. The Elijah figure is a forerunner of the Son of Man in every way. What was written has already taken place in the experience of the Elijah *redivivus* (see 6:14–29), and is yet to take place in the experience of the Son of Man (9:13; see 8:31).[48] The Son of Man coming in the glory of his Father and with the holy angels (9:2–8; see 8:38) will make sense only in the light of his prior death and resurrection (vv. 9–13). Subsequent to the wonder of the transfiguration, Jesus has led the thoughts of Peter, James, and John back to the message which has begun (see 8:31–9:1) and will continue to dominate 8:31–15:47: there can be no glory without the cross.

The lesson of the boy whom the disciples could not heal (9:14–29)

A close temporal link is maintained between the transfiguration (9:2: "and after six days"), the discussion between Jesus and the three disciples (v. 9: "and as they were coming down the mountain"), and their subsequent rejoining the other disciples (v. 14: "and when they came to the disciples").[49] The account that follows was originally a miracle story, but it has been transformed into instruction for the disciples.[50] The traditional description of

question, see M. D. Hooker, *Jesus and the Servant: The Influence of the Servant Concept of Deutero-Isaiah in the New Testament* (London: SPCK, 1959), 93–97. Marcus (*The Way of the Lord*, 94–107) has creatively proposed that a Jewish exegetical practice of *middah* is at play: the seemingly contradictory biblical witness of the glorious return of Elijah and a scriptural expectation that the Son of Man would suffer have been reconciled. Thus v. 13 "is Mark's way of reinterpreting the concept of Elijah as the Messiah's forerunner in terms of the concept of a suffering Messiah" (p. 106).

[46] This explanation takes the verb ἀποκαθίστημι to mean more than simply "restore" as is often translated, but "to restore to its proper order." See BDAG, 111–12, s.v. ἀποκαθίστημι; LSJ, 200–201, s.v ἀποκαθίστημι.

[47] Hooker, *St. Mark*, 220.

[48] Gnilka, *Markus*, 2:42; Ernst, *Markus*, 262–63. There is no prophecy of suffering for the returning Elijah. Some commentators have speculated about a lost apocryphal work that may have contained such a prophecy (see J. Jeremias, "Ἡλείας," *TDNT* 2:939–41; Lohmeyer, *Markus*, 183), but that is a desperate measure. It may simply be a reference back to 1 Kgs 19:1–3: Herodias has succeeded in doing to the second Elijah what Jezebel tried to do to the first. See Lagrange, *Saint Marc*, 224; Taylor, *St. Mark*, 395; Hooker, *St. Mark*, 220–21; B. M. F. van Iersel, *Reading Mark* (Collegeville: The Liturgical Press, 1988), 128; Painter, *Mark's Gospel*, 131.

[49] Some important witnesses (e.g., Alexandrinus, Ephraim Rescript, and Bezae) read the singular ἐλθὼν . . . εἶδεν. The plural, however, also has good support (e.g., Sinaiticus, Vaticanus, Paris, Washington). Some accept the singular, certainly the *lectio difficilior* (e.g., Gnilka, *Markus*, 2:46), but most regard the textual support for the plural slightly superior and more Markan in style. See the discussion in Taylor, *St. Mark*, 396; Metzger, *Textual Commentary*, 85.

[50] The passage has a number of odd features. The crowd seems to come to Jesus twice (see vv. 15, 25) and there are two reports of the illness (vv. 17–18, 22). Some suggest that two traditions have been put together, thus causing repetitions: Bultmann, *History*, 211–12; G. Bornkamm, "Πνεῦμα ἄλαλον: Eine Studie zum Markusevangelium," in *Geschichte und Glaube* (4 vols.; BEvT 53; Munich: Kaiser, 1971), 4:21–36; Schweizer, *Mark*, 187. Most likely, however, the Markan rewriting of this traditional miracle story to insert it into his unfolding presentation of the relationship between

the ailment (vv. 17–18, 20–22a), Jesus' rebuke of the unclean spirit (v. 25), the cure (vv. 26ab–27), and the response of the crowd (v. 26c) provide the basic account. Elements directed at the disciples have been inserted into the traditional cure: the gathering of the disciples, the crowd and the questioning scribes (vv. 14–16), the inability of the disciples to effect a cure (vv. 18c–19), and Jesus' explanation of why they failed (vv. 28–29). This "mixed form" of healing and teaching provides a conclusion to a series of encounters between Jesus and his fragile disciples (8:32–9:29) after the first passion prediction (8:31). It is followed immediately by the second passion prediction and its setting in 9:30–31.

In 9:14–15 the crowd acts as intermediary. Disciples and scribes are arguing as Jesus, Peter, James, and John approach them.[51] The "great crowd" initially gathered around the argument are "greatly amazed" (ἐξεθαμβήθησαν) and they "all" run from the argument toward Jesus.[52] The highly charged language, already hinting at unresolved frustration, sets the scene for Jesus' asking what was being discussed. This allows one of the crowd to provide the initial material required for the miracle story: the description of a son's ailment (vv. 16–18ab). Addressing Jesus as "Teacher" (v. 17b), the unnamed member of the crowd describes an illness that resembles what modern society would call epilepsy: seizures, falling, foaming at the mouth, and grinding of the teeth (v. 18ab).[53] But he regards the illness as possession by a dumb spirit (v. 17c). His initial desire was to bring the sick boy to Jesus (v. 17b), but in the absence of Jesus, he asked the disciples to cast out the spirit, but they were not able to do so (v. 18c).

The reference to the disciples' inability to effect a cure leads to Jesus' harsh words, which must be read as directed at the disciples (9:19).[54] He has earlier addressed the

---

Jesus and the disciples has created the oddities. See Meier, *A Marginal Jew: Rethinking the Historical Jesus* [3 vols.; ABRL; New York: Doubleday, 1991–2001], 2:653–56. Gnilka (*Markus*, 2:44–46), however, claims that the disciples were already in the original pre-Markan story (although vv. 28–29 are Markan), and that the history of the tradition is now beyond rediscovery. He justifiably argues that the repetitions have their place in the logic of the account (see also Lohmeyer, *Markus*, 184–85). Yet there are times when Gnilka strains to explain it (e.g., the second coming of the crowd [v. 25]; see *Markus*, 2:48). For a similar position, but excluding the disciples and including the scribes in the original miracle story, see Pesch, *Markusevangelium*, 2:84–85.

[51] The scribes play no further part in the story (despite Pesch, *Markusevangelium*, 2:88), nor is there indication of the nature of the argument. From what follows, one supposes it is over the disciples' inability to cure the possessed boy. For Lohmeyer (*Markus*, 185) and Grundmann (*Markus*, 189), they are arguing over Jesus. The scribes have probably been introduced in this "argument" situation in the light of later difficulties between early Christians and Jewish scribes. It is universally accepted that v. 14 reflects Markan redaction. Mark's readers would have no difficulty in accepting that scribes were arguing with disciples (see earlier 2:6–7, 16; 3:22; 7:1–5). This scenario has led some scholars to locate the development of the present form of the story in the time of Jesus' absence, when the exorcistic practices of the early church are being put to the test. See, for example, Pesch, *Markusevangelium*, 2:95–96. Gnilka (*Markus*, 2:45–46) suggests that it comes from a missionary background, where exorcism was a problem.

[52] This is an extraordinary way to present the crowd. Miracle stories generally end with wonder, but this one begins with the use of the strong Markan verb ἐκθαμβέομαι (only found in Mark; see 14:33; 16:5, 6). Hooker (*St. Mark*, 222–23) speculates that, coming as it does after the transfiguration, this may be reminiscent of Exod 34:29–30, where Moses returns to the people and they are astounded at his appearance. See also G. Minette de Tillesse, *Le secret messianique dans l'Evangile de Marc* (LD 47; Paris: Cerf, 1968), 92; Grundmann, *Markus*, 188; Gnilka, *Markus*, 2:46. The ἀλλὰ τὸν Ἰησοῦν μόνον of 9:8, however, makes this difficult, as Hooker admits. See the discussion in Lane, *Mark*, 330 n. 48.

[53] On epilepsy in the ancient world, see Pesch, *Markusevangelium*, 2:89–90.

[54] Cranfield, *St. Mark*, 301; Lane, *Mark*, 332; Ernst, *Markus*, 267; Lührmann, *Markusevangelium*, 161; Painter, *Mark's Gospel*, 133; Marshall (*Faith as a Theme in Mark's Narrative* [SNTSMS 64; Cambridge: Cambridge University Press, 1989], 117–18), who sees the rebuke directed toward

Pharisees as "this generation" (8:12) and further described the world, hostile to him and his disciples, as an "adulterous and sinful generation" (8:38). The danger that the disciples might draw close to this generation (see 8:15) is becoming a reality. It is their lack of faith (ὦ γενεὰ ἄπιστος, v. 19) that frustrates, and leads Jesus to wonder just how much more time he must spend with them in their increasing failure. This is an important question, and it remains with the reader as the narrative proceeds. As failure increases, one might expect Jesus to declare "enough," but this is never the case.[55] Although expressed in different words, Jesus called the Twelve to be "with him" in 3:14–15, to share his life and ministry. The same idea is present here, but stated from Jesus' side of the relationship. The brief expression of anger and frustration, which prepares for Jesus' response to the disciples in 9:29, does not lead to Jesus' abandoning of the disciples. Not does it influence his decision to help the member of the crowd (v. 19c). Both the rhetorical question of 9:19 and the action that follows in 9:20–27 serve as instruction for failing disciples.

The boy is led to him and the initial conflict between Jesus and the demon takes place (9:20; see 1:24; 5:7–10). There is a brief interlude, breaking into the rhythm of the traditional miracle story, as Jesus asks how long the boy has had this condition, and is informed that he has been like this since childhood (v. 21). This interlude prompts a second description of the ailment in 9:22a. The repetition (see vv. 17, 18ab) serves as an introduction to the man's earnest initial statement of faith: "If you can do anything, have pity on us and help us" (v. 22b).[56] The theme of faith, already raised as Jesus scolded the unfaith of the disciples who could not cure the boy (vv. 14, 18, 19), returns. There can be no question of Jesus' capacity to have pity and help, as all things are possible for the one who believes (πάντα δυνατὰ τῷ πιστεύοντι). There is a double meaning to this famous expression.[57] The context demands that "the one who believes" is, in the first place, Jesus. He has been asked to help, if he can (εἴ τι δύνῃ, v. 22b), and as one who believes, Jesus responds to the man's hopes. His immediacy with God is the source of his miraculous authority. But the believing subject quickly becomes the father. The disciples, who have become increasingly arrogant in their self-understanding (see 6:7–30; 8:32–33), have not been able to work this cure, despite Jesus' earlier promises (3:14–15) and their initial successes (see 6:13, 30). In contrast, the man proclaims his belief—and his littleness of belief (πιστεύω, βοήθει μου τῇ ἀπιστίᾳ,

---

the disciples and the father (at that stage); Blackburn, *Theios Anêr and the Markan Miracle Traditions: A Critique of the Theios Anêr Concept as an Interpretative Background of the Miracle Traditions Used by Mark* (WUNT 2. Reihe 40; Tübingen: J. C. B. Mohr [Paul Siebeck], 1991), 124–26. The majority of scholars wish to direct these words to a broader audience: the nation, the crowd. See, for example, Gnilka, *Markus*, 2:47; Pesch, *Markusevangelium*, 2:19–20; Hooker, *St. Mark*, 223–24. LaVerdiere (*The Beginning*, 2:50–51) has it both ways: "all in general but the disciples in mind." See also Grundmann, *Markus*, 189–90; van Iersel, *Reading Mark*, 133.

[55] The universalization of the question in v. 19 forces interpreters to find in the prophets similar questions and threats concerning God's presence to Israel (see, for example, Gnilka, *Markus*, 2:47). This may be useful background, but should not detract from the timing of the question in a narrative that tells of increasing failure on the part of the disciples. Nor should the words be understood psychologically, i.e., Jesus is frustrated by the lack of response to his goodness (see, for example, Lagrange, *Saint Marc*, 226). Among others, Lohmeyer (*Markus*, 186–87) and Nineham (*St. Mark*, 243) claim that Jesus indicates his desire to return to the divine world.

[56] Pesch (*Markusevangelium*, 2:95–96) regards the repetition of a detailed description of the ailment as a sign of the historicity of the event. See also Taylor, *St. Mark*, 395; Cranfield, *St. Mark*, 299.

[57] See Gnilka, *Markus*, 2:48: "Jesus, not the Father, is the model of belief." See also Pesch, *Markusevangelium*, 2:92–93; Hooker, *St. Mark*, 224; Marshall, *Faith as a Theme*, 118–20. The rejection of this leads to complicated translations and theological reflection. See, for example, Cranfield, *St. Mark*, 302–3; Nineham, *St. Mark*, 247.

v. 24b).[58] The example of the Syrophoenician woman is recalled. She was prepared to admit that she brought nothing to her request of Jesus, except her belief that the dogs might be fed by the crumbs from the table (see 7:26–28). This is a fundamental issue in the Markan understanding of faith, and an explanation for the increasing failure of the disciples. They are beginning to impose their designs upon Jesus (see especially 8:32) and regard discipleship as something they can determine (see 6:7–30). For this they are regarded as a "faithless genera- tion," not prepared to admit their failure (see v. 19). The father of the possessed boy recog- nizes his lack of faith, and crying out (κράξας), asks Jesus to help him in failure.[59] The author exploits this gap between the lack of faith of the disciples (v. 19) and the faith of the man from the crowd (v. 24). There is no sign that the disciples are turning to Jesus in their need.

The man from the crowd has turned to Jesus in nothingness and, as with the Syrophoenician woman (see 7:29–30), Jesus effects the cure of his son (vv. 25–27). The re- port of the cure is largely traditional: the running together of an excited crowd (v. 25a), the rebuking of the spirit (ἐπιτίμησεν, v. 25b) by means of a firm command (ἐπιτάσσω, v. 25c).[60] As with earlier healings, the spirit leaves after convulsing the possessed boy (v. 26a; see 2:26), creating the impression that the boy is dead (v. 26b; see 5:39). But this is a false impression! Jesus takes the boy by the hand and raises him up (ἤγειρεν αὐτὸν καὶ ἀνέστη, v. 27; see 5:41–42). The Christian language of resurrection rings out as the miracle story comes to a close.[61] But the Markan purpose for telling this tale is yet to be finalized. Reflection on the failing disciples has been part of the story throughout (see vv. 18, 19, 24), and they return to the action in 9:28–29.[62]

Following a now familiar pattern in the Gospel, the disciples make use of their privi- leged association with Jesus by asking him privately ("when he had entered the house"; see 3:20; 4:10–12, 33–34; 7:17) why they had been unable to drive out the demon. Jesus' open- ing statement on their lack of faith (v. 19), the key to his ability to work the miracle be- cause of his oneness in faith with God (v. 23), and the man's openness to Jesus (v. 24), articulated at the center of the pericope, come to a climax in his reply (v. 29).[63] The dis- ciples are presented as becoming increasingly self-sufficient. They were called to "follow" Jesus (1:16–20; 2:14–15), to "be with" him in order to be able to cast out demons (3:14–15). They were sent by Jesus and succeeded in their mission of casting out demons

---

[58] Seeing the presentation of the man as a contrast to the disciples, not as paralleling their lim- ited faith, as many would claim (e.g., Grundmann, *Markus,* 190–91; Hooker, *St. Mark,* 224).

[59] Lohmeyer (*Markus,* 188) suggests that the miracle has been delayed so that the man could ar- rive at a point of a divinely inspired "crying out." However, the cry probably indicates his sense of need, rather than divine inspiration.

[60] The second running of a crowd to Jesus in v. 26 (see v. 15) is odd. Some have suggested that the original crowd were no longer present, and that the usual Markan secrecy motif (e.g., taking the ailing person out of the village: 8:23) has been omitted but probably should be understood. It is another crowd that runs toward Jesus. See, for example, Lagrange, *Saint Marc,* 228; Swete, *St. Mark,* 200. It is best explained as the rearrangement of pre-Markan tradition. The crowd wit- nesses the miracle, but their wonder has already been reported in v. 15.

[61] As Hooker (*St. Mark,* 225) observes: "The vocabulary will have reminded many of Mark's readers of the greater miracle of resurrection, and will have encouraged them with the belief that Jesus will one day raise those who appear to unbelievers to have died." See also Marshall, *Faith as a Theme,* 122–23. LaVerdiere (*The Beginning,* 2:51–52) agrees, but also claims baptismal background.

[62] Most commentators do not highlight Jesus' instruction of his disciples in 9:14–29. For many (e.g., Lohmeyer, *Markus,* 189–90; Taylor, *St. Mark,* 401), their return in vv. 28–29 simply resumes v. 14. For a strong focus on the unbelief of the disciples, see Marshall, *Faith as a Theme,* 220–24.

[63] Lührmann (*Markusevangelium,* 162) points out that Jesus' response in v. 29 addresses the situation of the Markan community.

(6:7–13), but returned to Jesus, to report all the things *they had done* (6:30). They have decided that Jesus is the Christ (8:29), but they reject that, as Son of Man, he must go to Jerusalem, to suffer, die, and rise (8:32). Their lack of faith (4:41), hardness of heart (6:52), and increasing blindness and lack of understanding (8:17–18) have brought them to a stage where they are unable to perform as disciples *of Jesus* (9:18, 28). This is why he tells them to redirect their attention to God: "This kind cannot be driven out by anything but prayer."[64] It is not *the disciples* who drive out demons, but God. All things are possible for Jesus because of his immediacy with God (v. 23); they must learn to turn to God in faith and prayer if they hope to be successful *disciples of Jesus*.[65] The correction of Peter (8:33) and the subsequent instruction on the need for all disciples to share in the cross of Jesus, and thus come to glory (8:34–9:1), has made no impact. Peter, James, and John have failed to understand the transfigured Jesus (9:5–6), and remain puzzled about what glory through death and resurrection might mean (9:10–11). Peter, James, and John are not alone; all the disciples in the story fall under the accusation of Jesus: "You are not on the side of God, but of men" (8:33b).[66] "The stress on the powerlessness of the disciples is an element not found elsewhere in the evangelical tradition, but this is closely related to their failure to understand Jesus or the power released through him."[67] Yet, importantly, even though Jesus has asked the frustrated question, "How long am I to be with you? How long am I to bear with you?" (9:19), he is still *with them*, instructing them as they journey to Jerusalem.

The Way of the Son of Man: Service and Receptivity (9:30–10:31)

The second passion prediction (9:30–31) and the material that follows (9:32–10:31) differs considerably from the prediction, teaching, transfiguration, and the healing story of 8:31–9:29. However, the overall structure and argument is repeated. Jesus will tell his disciples of his oncoming death and resurrection (9:30–31; see 8:31) and the disciples will refuse to accept his teaching and its implications for themselves as they follow Jesus (vv. 32–34; see 8:32–33). In a short teaching section, Jesus will establish the principles of service and receptivity (vv. 35–37; see 8:34–9:1). Episodes and further teaching follow, showing that the disciples still have a great deal to learn about these principles (9:38–10:31; see 9:2–29).

The passion prediction (9:30–31)

The theme of Jesus' ongoing journey returns as an introduction to the second passion prediction. The expression "on the way" (ἐν τῇ ὁδῷ; see 8:27; 10:32) is not found, but is im-

---

[64] Some important manuscripts (e.g., Vaticanus and Sinaiticus) add "and fasting." They are missing in other major witnesses of both the Alexandrian and Western families, however, and have no doubt been added because much early Christian exhortation was to "prayer and fasting." For their inclusion, see Minette de Tillesse, *Le secret messianique*, 98–99; Lane, *Mark*, 329. See the discussion in Metzger, *Textual Commentary*, 85; Cranfield, *St. Mark*, 304–5.

[65] As will become clear in due course, the theme of faith and its associated summons to prayer is proximate preparation for one of the elements of Jesus' subsequent teaching on discipleship: the call for receptivity (see especially 9:35–37).

[66] Lohmeyer, *Markus*, 190–91; Gnilka, *Markus*, 2:50; Schweizer, *Mark*, 189–90. As Grundmann (*Markus*, 192) comments: "Prayer is God-directed faith, which receives strength and fulfillment." Hooker (*St. Mark*, 225), however, regards Jesus' response as "entirely at variance with the stress in the story on the need for faith."

[67] Lane, *Mark*, 329.

plied in the passing on from the place of the cure of the epileptic boy (vv. 14–29), through Galilee, toward Jerusalem (v. 30a).[68] The focus upon the disciples is highlighted by Jesus' concern that no one know of their whereabouts, "for he was teaching his disciples" (vv. 30b–31a).[69] The content of the teaching is the briefest of the Markan passion predictions. Again referring to himself as the Son of Man (see 8:31), Jesus announces that he will be handed over to the "hands" of men. The use of the passive, παραδίδοται, indicates that the divine plan is involved in this handing over of Jesus unto death.[70] Those to whom he is handed over will put him to death. However, he will rise from death after three days (v. 31bc).[71]

The disciples' failure (9:32–34)

The description of the disciples' failure is immediate, couched in language that indicates their growing inability to accept the challenge of discipleship. They did not understand the saying (ἠγνόουν τὸ ῥῆμα; see 4:13, 33–34; 5:31; 6:30, 35–36; 7:18; 8:4, 17–18) and they were afraid (ἐφοβοῦντο; see 4:40–41; 6:49–52; 9:5–6) to ask him. The reader is aware that the earlier hesitations, fear, lack of understanding, and hardness of heart are gathered by the storyteller as he records their reaction to the second passion prediction. But there is more. On arrival in Capernaum, again in the privacy of "the house" (see 3:20; 7:17), Jesus asks what they were discussing "on the way" (ἐν τῇ ὁδῷ, v. 33).[72] This expression was not immediately associated with the passion prediction, but it tells the reader that the disciples have been called to follow Jesus down his way to Jerusalem, toward the events prophesied in 8:31 and 9:31. The disciples remain silent, for on the way they had been discussing who was the greatest (v. 34). Despite their silence in the face of Jesus' direct question, they have not progressed beyond the messianic expectations expressed by Peter's confession (8:29),

---

[68] No reference is made to Jerusalem, but it can be implied from the reentry into Galilee and the motif of the journey; see Lane, *Mark*, 336.

[69] It is sometimes argued that Jesus' desire that no one know of his whereabouts (v. 30b) is associated with a secret journey through Galilee. He will have to do only with the disciples, and not with a larger audience, as his Galilean ministry is finished; see, for example, Taylor, *St. Mark*, 402–3; Nineham, *St. Mark*, 248; LaVerdiere, *The Beginning*, 2:54. But this hardly makes sense of 10:2–9 and 10:17–22. The secrecy in v. 30b is to be limited to the passion prediction. He is intent on making his destiny (and implicitly the destiny of his "followers") known to the disciples; see Lohmeyer, *Markus*, 191–92.

[70] In 8:31 the use of δεῖ made this point, but that expression is not found in 9:30–31; see Lagrange, *Saint Marc*, 229–30; Pesch, *Markusevangelium*, 2:100–101. Hooker (*St. Mark*, 226) suggests that there may also be a hint of Judas's betrayal in the use of the word (see 3:19; 14:18–21). This is the only element in the passion narrative not mentioned in the other two passion predictions (8:31; 10:32–34). On the use of παραδίδωμι in the development of the early church's understanding of the soteriological significance of the death of Jesus, see N. Perrin, "The Use of *[Para]didonai* in Connection with the Passion of Jesus in the New Testament," in *A Modern Pilgrimage in New Testament Christology* (Philadelphia: Fortress, 1974), 94–103.

[71] The simplicity of v. 31b, with no reference to the events of the passion (trial and cross) and the possible play on words in an original Aramaic saying ("Son of Man . . . men"), may indicate that Jesus spoke of his oncoming death with words like this; see Grundmann, *Markus*, 192. While he believed that his death was not the end of God's plans for him (see Taylor, *St. Mark*, 402), his vindication is reported here in words which come from the early church's belief in Jesus' resurrection from death "after three days." For Gnilka (*Markus*, 2:53), v. 31a certainly is pre-Markan, but this is denied by Lührmann (*Markusevangelium*, 163).

[72] The naming of Capernaum, the theme of "on the way," and the failure of the disciples are widely recognized as indications of Markan authorship; see Pesch, *Markusevangelium*, 2:101–2.

nor have they accepted Jesus' teaching on the cross (8:34–9:1). Their sight is still partial (see 8:22–26), as they suspect that the Messiah they are following to Jerusalem will establish himself with power. They are concerned about their own respective places in the power structure of the messianic kingdom which Jesus will establish after his victory.

Jesus instructs the failing disciples: service and receptivity (9:35–37)

Repeating his response to their earlier failure to accept his "teaching" (see v. 31a), Jesus solemnly takes up a teaching position, summons the Twelve, and speaks to them (v. 35a; see 8:34).[73] The instruction takes the form of two didactic passages (v. 35b, beginning with εἴ τις ["if any one . . ."]; v. 37, beginning with ὃς ἄν ["whoever . . ."]), which frame the parabolic action of Jesus' taking the children in his arms (v. 36). The theme of the reversal of the expectations that surround human success, initiated with the call to the cross in 8:34–9:1, is developed further.[74] The one who would wish to be first of all in Jesus' view of greatness (see v. 34) must be last of all. This is further described as a call to be "servant of all" (πάντων διάκονος, v. 35). The call to service, however, is rendered more precise by Jesus' symbolic action (v. 36) and his explanation of it (v. 37).

Jesus places a child in the midst of the disciples. The child becomes the focus of attention as the disciples are asked to stop looking at themselves. Perhaps offering a glimmer of his own personality, Jesus takes the child in his arms.[75] But the message to the disciples, not Jesus' personality, is the point of the narrative. It is the child, held in the arms of Jesus, who best typifies what it is like to be "with him" (see 3:14), something that is becoming increasingly difficult for the disciples.[76] The teaching of Jesus that flows from the gesture further explains what it means to be last of all and servant of all (v. 35). The universal experience of a young child, eyes open and questions flowing, is the *reception* of as much as possible from the new and exciting world he or she is beginning to experience. The feature highlighted by Jesus' words to the disciples is "receptivity." The verb δέχομαι, "to receive," is found four times in 9:37. There is an intimate link between "receiving" the child, "receiving" Jesus, and "receiving" the one who sent Jesus. The service of the disciple will be found in service of those who look to them for such service. The child is not a "prop" for Jesus' teaching. The child refers to others who believe in Jesus, but who still have much to learn.[77] They

---

[73] The pattern of Jesus' formally calling an audience subsequent to the disciples' failure is repeated across this section (see 8:34; 9:35; 10:42). Its importance must not be underestimated; see LaVerdiere, *The Beginning*, 2:56. However, the audiences vary: the crowd with his disciples (8:34), the Twelve (9:35), the "other ten" (10:42). As throughout the Gospel of Mark, specific instructions to "disciples" and "the Twelve" are aimed at disciples as such, i.e., the original Christians who heard or read this story and who claimed to be followers of Jesus. See Pesch, *Markusevangelium*, 2:104, and especially Malbon, "Disciples/Crowds/Whoever," 70–99.

[74] It is often pointed out (e.g., Taylor, *St. Mark*, 404; Lohmeyer, *Markus*, 193) that of the two Markan passages dealing with children (9:36; 10:13–16), the latter would have made better sense in the present sequence. Matthew 18:1–4 uses Mark 10:13–16 at this stage in the narrative, and omits it in Matt 19:13–15. However, both probably come from a single pre-Markan tradition, and they have been appropriately used in their respective places within the unfolding narrative. See Gnilka, *Markus*, 2:50, 80.

[75] See Lane, *Mark*, 340.

[76] On the countercultural use of a child to instruct disciples, see the presentation of the negative understanding of children in antiquity in Gnilka, *Markus*, 2:57.

[77] The disciple has been described by Jesus in v. 35 as "the last of all." The use of the child as a model for disciples fits that description. In antiquity, the child was "the last of all." See Lagrange, *Saint Marc*, 232; Schweizer, *Mark*, 193.

must be "received" as Jesus received the child, and this theme will return in 9:42–50.[78] But the disciple is also called to "receive" Jesus, and thus the one who sends him. When the disciples asked why they failed to drive out the evil spirit from the possessed boy (vv. 14–29), Jesus spoke of the need for prayer (vv. 28–29). Disciples are called to be receptive to one another, and also to the design of God, to be found in prayer. They are called to service in the believing community, but also to a profound receptivity of all that Jesus asks of them, and that includes the cross (see 9:30–31), rather than the glory expected by those considered "the greatest" among them (see v. 34).

Further failure and instruction on service and receptivity (9:38–41)

One of the privileged three, John (see 3:16–17; 5:37; 9:1–8), gives arrogant witness to the disciples' ongoing failure. As Peter failed after the first passion prediction (see 8:32), John fails after the second. Like Peter, in the presence of the transfigured Jesus, John addresses Jesus as "teacher" (v. 38a; see 9:5: "Rabbi"), and tells of an action almost incomprehensible to the reader who has followed Jesus' instruction of the disciples. The disciples saw someone (εἴδομέν τινα) casting out demons *in the name of Jesus* (ἐν τῷ ὀνόματί σου) and they forbade him, because he was not following *them* (ὅτι οὐκ ἠκολούθει ἡμῖν, v. 38b).[79] As if the mark of discipleship was to be a follower of the Twelve! Just after Jesus taught the need for service and receptivity, we find a remarkable lack of both virtues. The fundamental principle of a disciple as a *follower of Jesus* (see 1:16–20; 2:14–15; 8:33) has been forgotten. The disciples are *not receptive* to anyone who does not meet their criterion, and that criterion is not whether the person is acting in Jesus' name, but whether that person is following the Twelve. Given the outrageous failure of service and receptivity witnessed to by John, Jesus' response is mild. There is correction, but the reader may have expected something more severe, especially after Jesus' condemnation of the failing disciples in v. 19.

The principle of Jesus' response is clear: whoever does things *in the name of Jesus* must be allowed to proceed. Evil words will not come from a person driving out demons in the name of Jesus, as a kingdom divided against itself cannot stand (9:39; see 3:24). There can be no half measures in the kingdom of God. People are either for or against Jesus (v. 40),[80] and those who do good to members of Jesus' community, simply because they bear the name of Christ, are "for Jesus" and will not lose their reward (v. 41).[81] These unnamed people give witness to *service,* as the called and appointed disciples of Jesus (see 1:16–20; 3:13–19) show a marked lack of *receptivity.* This passage, like the passage that follows

---

[78] The *Sitz im Leben* of this teaching may have been instruction to members of a Christian community to serve one another, and may reflect a situation where some members of the community regarded themselves as "greater" (see v. 34) than others. However, the further insistence of receiving Jesus and thus the one who sent him indicates that the passage cannot be limited to this setting.

[79] The phrase "in my name" appears across vv. 38–41 (see vv. 38, 39, 40), beginning a literary process of assembling originally independent sayings around these catchwords. On the use of "in my name" in vv. 38–41, see Lohmeyer, *Markus,* 195–96.

[80] The expression in v. 40 is most likely a popular proverb. See Gnilka, *Markus,* 2:60–61, for some examples from Rabbinic and Greco-Roman sources. It is the only statement in vv. 38–41 without reference to the "name" of Jesus.

[81] The expression "because you bear the name of Christ" (v. 41) is not too distant from the Lukan record that Jesus' followers were called Christians (see Acts 11:26); see Nineham, *St. Mark,* 254.

(vv. 42–50), reflects the situation of the post-Easter community, wondering who belongs to the community, who does not, and what are the criteria for making such a decision.[82] The criteria given by Jesus are the development of his invitation to disciples to be receptive servants (see v. 35). Those who do works in the name of Jesus and share even the simplest of goods, a cup of water, deserve the reward due to followers of Jesus. The first of all (the doer of mighty works in the name of Jesus: v. 39) is also the servant of all (sharing a cup of water: v. 41; see v. 35).

Instructions for a community of serving and receptive disciples (9:42–50)

At first glance, the following instructions appear haphazard,[83] but they form part of the logic of the ongoing narrative, and have their own internal literary and theological coherence.[84] In 9:36–37 Jesus has used the image of a child to teach the disciples the need for service and receptivity, and in 9:38–41 John has witnessed to the *lack* of service and receptivity among the Twelve, linking sayings with the catch phrase "in my name." The noun changes from "child" to "little one," but Jesus' words on receiving "one such child" (v. 37) become a threat in v. 42. Jesus warns his disciples in the words: "Whoever causes one of these little ones who believe in me to sin . . ." The argument is ongoing.[85] The storyteller's use of earlier traditions to continue his presentation of Jesus' teaching is prompted by issues raised by John's remarks and Jesus' answer concerning those who belong to Jesus and the community which "bears the name of Christ" (vv. 38–41; see v. 41). This passage is a collection of originally independent sayings from pre-Markan tradition, gathered on the basis of two principles. The first of these principles is the problem of sin within the community, the theme stated in 9:42a. People who considered themselves "great" may not concern themselves overly with "the little ones," yet such a person would be better eliminated from the community.[86] The image of such a person cast into the sea with a millstone around the neck speaks eloquently of total annihilation (v. 42b).[87] If a violent death by drowning, with a millstone attached to the neck to assure death, is *better* than giving scandal, one can only imagine how devastating would be the punishment for causing a member of the community to sin. The use of the verb σκανδαλίζειν in v. 42 brings into play the second generative principle in this passage: link words, already part of the author's technique in 9:38–41.[88]

From the "causing to sin" (σκανδαλίση, v. 42), the author moves to consider other parts of the body—the hand (v. 43), the foot (v. 45), and the eye (v. 47)—which might lead

---

[82] Gnilka, *Markus,* 2:59–60; Hooker, *St. Mark,* 229; against Cranfield (*St. Mark,* 309–10), who claims that the report of the strange exorcist is historical.

[83] Bultmann (*History,* 149–50) suggests that there was a pre-Markan collection of sayings, made up of vv. 35, 37, 41–50, which may have been used for the instruction of the community. See, however, Pesch, *Markusevangelium,* 2:101–2. Nineham (*St. Mark,* 250) correctly remarks: "Readers may well feel slightly bewildered after a first glance at these verses."

[84] Gnilka, *Markus,* 2:63–64; Lane, *Mark,* 338–39.

[85] Grundmann, *Markus,* 198; Painter, *Mark's Gospel,* 138–39.

[86] LaVerdiere, *The Beginning,* 2:59.

[87] This form of execution is taken from Roman practice, and was not unknown among the Jews; see Lagrange, *Saint Marc,* 234–35.

[88] Some commentators link v. 42 with vv. 38–41 (e.g., Lane, *Mark,* 345–46), but the link generated by σκαναλίζειν locates it firmly as the opening statement in vv. 42–50. There is also a reprise of the call for oneness in v. 50, recalling the necessary care for the "little ones" in v. 42. See Taylor, *St. Mark,* 407–8, especially the discussion of link words across vv. 37–50 on p. 409.

to sin (σκανδαλίζῃ).[89] This group of sayings was probably already a unit in the pre-Markan tradition, formed in the same fashion: if a part of the body causes sin (σκανδαλίζῃ, vv. 43, 45, 47), then it is to be cut off and cast away. One is better to enter life maimed than to go to the unquenchable fire of hell. These demands are regularly explained as Semitic hyperbole—cutting off hand and foot, plucking out the eye—but this is not the case.[90] Jesus' words mean what they say. They are not about the maiming, but the unsurpassable blessing of life! His words ring true: "God is even more important than the most important parts of our body."[91] It is better, given the richness of the life offered by the kingdom of God, to be without a hand, a foot, or an eye, than to lose the opportunity to enter that life.[92] In the end, one can do without a hand, a foot, or an eye, but one cannot do without life. To have both hands, both eyes, and both feet, but to have allowed them to lead you into sin and death, forever in the unquenchable fire of hell, is unthinkable. Rather than a threat, however, the extreme measure of cutting off and plucking out witnesses to the unparalleled richness of the life offered to those "little ones who believe in Jesus" (see v. 42).[93] Originally these sayings referred to sin as such, but in their present context they refer to sin that brings scandal and further sin into the community. This meaning is determined by the introduction (v. 42), where causing the little ones who believe in Jesus to sin is the theme, and the same message is taken up in the conclusion of 9:49–50, where living in peace with one another is stressed.

A description of gehenna closes 9:43–47, a section dominated by the alternatives of fullness of life maimed or never-ending torment (see already v. 43). Isaiah 66:24 is cited: "where the worm does not die and the fire is not quenched" (v. 48).[94] These words lead the author to attach other originally independent sayings. The word "fire" (πῦρ) in the citation of Isaiah leads to the addition of a further saying: "For everyone will be salted with fire (πυρί)" (v. 49).[95] The word "salted" in 9:49 (ἁλισθήσεται) leads to a fourfold play on "salt" in v. 50 (ἅλας, ἅλας ἄναλον, ἅλα). Salt was a widely used but precious commodity in antiquity, giving ongoing life and flavor to food.[96] The threatening image of the penetrating and destroying fire of gehenna (v. 49) has been transferred to refer to the life-giving uniqueness of the believers. The move from the destructive power of fire to salt as a source of life may run the danger of confusing metaphors, but, paradoxically, it gives unity to the message.

---

[89] Verses 44 and 46 are omitted by the best witnesses. They are identical to v. 48, and were introduced to add clarity to the passage; see Metzger, *Textual Commentary,* 86–87.

[90] See, for example, Hooker, *St. Mark,* 232; LaVerdiere, *The Beginning,* 2:61.

[91] Schweizer, *Mark,* 198.

[92] In vv. 43 and 45 Jesus speaks of entering "life," while in v. 47 he speaks of entering "the kingdom of God." For Mark, they are the same; see Grundmann, *Markus,* 199.

[93] The sayings are, therefore, a strong affirmation of the life offered by following Jesus, cost what it may. Commentators rightly see the link with 8:34–9:1. The sayings "sharpen the issue of radical obedience in the context of costly sacrifice" (Lane, *Mark,* 349).

[94] "Gehenna" was the name given to a valley to the southwest of Jerusalem where human sacrifices had been offered to the gods Moloch and Baal. After the reform of Josiah (see 1 Kgs 23:10) it became the city rubbish dump, where fires burned continually. It thus became a symbol for the place where the wicked would be destroyed. See D. F. Watson, "Gehenna," *ABD* 2:926–28. It should be noticed that the wicked are destroyed, not punished forever. It is the fire which is unquenchable, not the punishment.

[95] This enigmatic saying, which crosses from the punishing fire to the blessing of salt, has a complicated textual history. For the discussion, and the establishment of the above text, see Lane, *Mark,* 346–47 n. 76; Cranfield, *St. Mark,* 314–15.

[96] LaVerdiere, *The Beginning,* 2:63–64.

Like fire, salt is an agent of purification (Ezek 16:4; 43:24); it can also bring desolation and destruction (Judg 9:45; Zeph 2:9). But unlike fire, salt is a source of life (2 Kgs 2:19–22); it can be used to preserve food from putrefaction. However mixed the metaphor, the idea that men can be salted with fire sums up exactly the message of vv. 43, 45 and 47: the purificatory process may destroy, but it can also preserve.[97]

Having salt in themselves, believers are penetrated by belief in God and openness to God's ways (v. 50).[98] Once this salt, giving sense and flavor to the Christian's commitment to the way of Jesus, is lost, nothing can replace it. Whether or not this happens, or how it might happen, is irrelevant;[99] the image retains its power, as one cannot imagine what a salted object might be like without its saltiness.

This lengthy collection of originally independent sayings is drawn together in a conclusion that comes from Mark. Having salt, the driving force that makes sense of Christian life and gives it flavor, is described as being at peace with one another (v. 50b). The issue that opened these sayings returns—the warning against leading a little one who believes in Jesus into sin (vv. 42, 50).[100] This theme, in turn, looks back to Jesus' criticism of the divisive practices of the Twelve, described by John, that would never produce peace (vv. 38–41). This complex gathering of traditions and somewhat bewildering linking of images by means of catchwords and phrases has been used by the storyteller to expand upon Jesus' fundamental teaching to the Twelve, after their initial failure (vv. 32–34) and their continued arrogance (v. 38). Gathered from a variety of independent sources, the storyteller has generated a message directed to all disciples. No doubt he was concerned about the original readers of this story of Jesus, who wondered about authority. He cares for the more fragile members of the community. Despite the literary complexities, Jesus' teaching in 9:35–50 is clear. Disciples are to be the least of all and the servants of all, like children themselves, receptive to the least of all (vv. 35–37), never judging anyone who works in the name of Jesus (vv. 38–41), never endangering the faith of even the most fragile (vv. 42–50). They are to be at peace with one another in the kingdom (v. 50). Disciples open to this teaching receive Jesus and the one who sent him (vv. 35–37).[101]

The practice of discipleship (10:1–31)

The section of the Gospel running from 8:22–10:52 deals almost exclusively with Jesus' presence with his disciples. There are only two exceptions. In 10:1–9 he debates with the Pharisees over divorce, and then speaks to the disciples "in the house" in 10:10–12. After a passage where children are brought to Jesus (10:13–16), recalling 9:36, Jesus offers a wealthy man the possibility of eternal life (10:17–22) and subsequently speaks to his disciples (10:23–31). The storyteller has a purpose for taking these three elements from his traditions (discussion over divorce, the bringing of the children, and the encounter with the rich man) and using them in his account of Jesus' journey to Jerusalem with the

---

[97] Hooker, *St. Mark*, 233.

[98] The καί linking having salt and being at peace indicates consequence: "have salt in yourselves, *and then* you will be at peace among yourselves." See Lohmeyer, *Markus*, 197; Taylor, *St. Mark*, 414.

[99] Hooker (*St. Mark*, 233) regards the discussions about salt losing its taste as "pedantic."

[100] As Grundmann (*Markus*, 201) remarks: "And thus will lead back to the beginning." See also Pesch, *Markusevangelium*, 2:118.

[101] Gnilka, *Markus*, 2:67. Rightly does Grundmann (*Markus*, 193–201) regard vv. 33–50 as a unified "conversation with disciples."

disciples.[102] Thus far he has called the disciples to the cross (8:34–9:1), and to service and receptivity (9:35–50). These instructions have been *at the level of principle*, in secret discussions between Jesus and the disciples (see 9:30b). Before moving to the third and final passion prediction (10:32–34), Jesus will speak of marriage and wealth. The disciples, attempting to live God's design in their affective and sexual lives, and in the administration of their possessions, draw *principle* into *every day life*. In marriage and in the administration of possessions the call to the cross, service, and receptivity are most at risk. Mark 10:1–31 is concerned with the *practice*, rather than the *theory*, of discipleship.

Marriage and discipleship (10:1–12)

Jesus' journey toward Jerusalem is sketched by the narrator. He leaves Capernaum (see 9:33) and proceeds to "the region of Judea and beyond the Jordan." This geography is hardly precise, but probably reflects a journey of Jesus from Galilee into Judea by means of the other side of the Jordan (10:1a). Although longer, this was regarded as the more secure journey, given the banditry rife in Samaria (see Josephus, *Ant.* 20.118; *J. W.* 2.232).[103] Crowds gather and Jesus teaches them (v. 1b). The scene is set for the encounter with the Pharisees which follows (vv. 2–9) and Jesus' private discussion with the disciples (vv. 10–12). The nature of the encounter is indicated by the fact that the Pharisees came to test him (πειράζοντες αὐτόν, v. 2a).[104] They question him about the lawfulness of divorce (v. 2b). There was some debate about this matter among the leading rabbinic schools of Hillel and Shammai, but this debate is not reflected in the Pharisees' question.[105] They ask for a judgment from Jesus on whether divorce should be allowed.[106] It must be noted that

---

[102] The uniqueness of 10:1–45 has long been noticed. See, for example, Grundmann, *Markus,* 199–200; Schweizer, *Mark,* 201–2; Gnilka, *Markus,* 2:105. It has been extensively treated by H.-W. Kuhn (*Ältere Sammlungen im Markusevangelium* [SUNT 8; Göttingen: Vandenhoeck & Ruprecht, 1971], 146–91) and widely recognized as a Markan collection directed toward a catechetical instruction on right order in the community. See the summary of the discussion in Pesch, *Markusevangelium,* 2:128–30. Pesch argues, more conservatively than Kuhn, that the majority of the passages are pre-Markan, and that there are even traces of the pre-Markan passion narrative embedded within it. However, he agrees with the consensus that the section is used to instruct the Markan community on the right understanding of authority and honor. What follows is less interested in the pre-Markan text, and suggests that the passage is best understood within the overall Markan context of 8:22–10:52, determined by the frame of the two blind men and highlighted by the three passion predictions. See also Lohmeyer, *Markus,* 197. The message is about a discipleship determined by the Markan Christology, especially as it is articulated in the passion predictions, culminating in 10:45, and is not primarily about church order. See, on this, Lührmann, *Markusevangelium,* 171.

[103] LaVerdiere, *The Beginning,* 2:64–66.

[104] Lohmeyer, *Markus,* 199; Nineham, *St. Mark,* 264.

[105] There is some doubt about the authenticity of the words "and Pharisees came up." The original text may have simply had the impersonal ἐπηρώτων, rendering the meaning "The question was put to him." The better manuscripts have the reference to the Pharisees, but the impersonal plural is a feature of Markan style, and the reference to the Pharisees may have been imported from Matt 19:3. See Metzger, *Textual Commentary,* 88.

[106] The Matthean rendition of the question (Matt 19:3–12) asks whether the perspective of Hillel is lawful: to divorce one's wife "for any cause" (Matt 19:3). Rabbi Shammai and Rabbi Hillel interpreted the "shame of a thing" (*ᶜerwat dabar*) of Deut 24:1, but Shammai, accentuating "shame," insisted that there be some moral defect. Hillel focused upon "thing" and thus claimed that "any cause" was sufficient. See *m. Giṭ* 9:10; *b. Giṭ* 90a; *j. Soṭah* I:1.16b; *Num. Rab.* IX:30, and F. J. Moloney ("Matthew 19,3–12 and Celibacy: A Redactional and Form Critical Study," *JSNT* 2 [1979]: 43). While this debate may lie behind the discussion in Mark 10:2–9, the question appears more radical.

the Pharisees' question concerning divorce only touches upon *the rights of a man* to divorce his wife.[107]

Jesus responds to their question in the manner of rabbinic debate. He asks them about the command of Moses (v. 3). They respond that according to Moses (see Deut 24:1–4) it is lawful to write a certificate of divorce, and in this way to put a wife out of the man's house (v. 4). The "testing" (see v. 2) of Jesus by the Pharisees is not about possible interpretation of the laws of divorce. Although nothing has been said in the narrative that might hint at this aspect of Jesus' teaching, it appears to be based upon a previous knowledge of Jesus' absolute prohibition of divorce.[108] They sense that they have Moses on their side; how can Jesus take another position? Jesus concedes that Moses allowed the certificate of divorce that enabled a man to send a woman away from his home (v. 5). However, he insists that this is not God's original plan for women and men. It has crept into the Jewish tradition, via Moses, because of the hardness of the heart of the Israel the Pharisees represent (πρὸς τὴν σκληροκαρδίαν ὑμῶν, v. 5).[109] God's original creative design was to be found in his action "from the beginning of creation" (ἀπὸ δὲ ἀρχῆς κτίσεως).[110] The reader recalls the presentation of Jesus in the prologue. In 1:13 Jesus was presented as "with the wild beasts" in the desert, reestablishing God's original design of a unified creation. Like Adam and Eve, he was ministered to by the angels.[111] As Jesus breaks onto the scene proclaiming the advent of the kingdom of God (1:14–15), the restoration of God's original design is initiated.

Jesus develops this by making his own the words of Genesis describing God's creation of man and woman (v. 6b; see Gen 1:27) and God's subsequent gift of man to woman and woman to man that they might become one flesh (10:7–8a; see Gen 2:24).[112] Jesus comments upon the Genesis passages: "So they are no longer two but one flesh" (v. 8b). Two separate human beings have now been joined together in a loving and sexual union by God's design.[113] Torah has been used against Torah. For Jesus, the legislation of Deut 24:1–4, established subsequent to creation as a concession to men who were unable to live as God had planned, was provisional.[114] In Jesus' restoration of God's original created

---

[107] Although determined by the male party, the certificate of divorce was designed to ensure that the woman was protected from unscrupulous dismissal into poverty and shame; Gnilka, *Markus*, 2:71–72.

[108] Most scholars would agree that Jesus opposed divorce. It is possible that there was a strain within first-century Judaism that tended toward the prohibition of divorce (cf. Mal 2:13–16; CD 4). See J. A. Fitzmyer, "The Matthean Divorce Texts and Some New Palestinian Evidence," *TS* 39 (1976): 221–23; LaVerdiere, *The Beginning*, 2:73–75. Nevertheless, Jesus' position flies in the face of majority Jewish and universal Greco-Roman practice. As well as Mark 10:5, an absolute prohibition of divorce is found in Q (Matt 5:32; Luke 16:18), and in 1 Cor 7:10–11 Paul speaks of the prohibition of divorce as "a word of the Lord." It is preserved in the tradition, despite the difficulties such a position must have created in the early church. The exception clauses in Matt 5:32 and 19:9 are certainly the fruit of the Matthean situation. On this, see Moloney ("Matthew 19,3–12," 43–49).

[109] On the Old Testament use of σκληροκαρδία as an accusation, see LaVerdiere, *The Beginning*, 2:72–73.

[110] These words reflect both the beginning of creation and time, and the book of Genesis. See Lagrange, *Saint Marc*, 243.

[111] See above, pp. 37–40.

[112] There is a similar use of these texts from Genesis in CD 4:21.

[113] Grundmann, *Markus*, 204; Lohmeyer, *Markusevangelium*, 200–201.

[114] Hooker (*St. Mark*, 235) observes: "It is significant that Mark does not suggest here that Jesus contradicted the Torah, but rather that he pointed to its true fulfilment." See also Lohmeyer, *Markusevangelium*, 200.

order (see 1:13–15), there should be no divorce. The conclusion that Jesus draws flows logically from the rabbinic-style argument he has pursued with the Pharisees thus far.[115] To their question (v. 2), Jesus posed a further question concerning Torah (v. 3). The Pharisees responded by pointing to Torah (Deut 24:1–4; see v. 3), but Jesus rejects their argument with a further citation of Torah, which looks back to God's creation, a time before Moses (Gen 1:17; 2:24; see vv. 5–8a). He comments that the union between man and woman is of God's design (v. 8b). In 10:9 he closes his case by pitting man against God. God has established the union between a man and a woman. No man has the right or the authority to tear that union apart (ἄνθρωπος μὴ χωριζέτω).[116] The process used by Jesus has taken the Pharisees from an awareness of what was *commanded by Moses* (see v. 3) to what *God wills* (see vv. 6–9).[117]

The Pharisees disappear. The debate comes to an abrupt end, as the real interest of the storyteller does not lie with the Pharisees, but with the disciples.[118] Jesus uses the debate over divorce to further instruct his disciples on receptivity and service (see 9:35–37). As is now customary, "the house" is the place for this private teaching (3:20; 7:17; 9:33). The disciples ask for further clarification on the debate they have just witnessed (v. 10). With the Pharisees, Jesus argued in rabbinic fashion and reduced his opponents to silence. With the community of disciples he gives a Christian motivation: men and women are equal and equally responsible for their marital oneness (vv. 11–12). It is often pointed out that there is shift in the argument here. In 10:2–9 the issue was divorce, while in 10:11–12 Jesus speaks of the remarriage of the divorced as adultery.[119] Jesus' discussion takes this direction, however, to press his case further. There was no law against divorce, and Jesus has established a new interpretation of Torah. However, there was a law against adultery, and Jesus' words to his disciples show how disobedience to his interpretation of Torah leads to the breaking of Torah.[120] The practice of placing a writ of divorce in a woman's hand, sending her out of the family, and marrying another is male arrogance and, as Jesus has just shown in his debate with the Pharisees, opposed to God's design. It is a sin against the commandments of God: adultery (see Exod 20:14; Deut 5:18). But it is not only an offense against God's commandment. It is an offense of adultery against the woman, to whom the man is bound in one flesh (v. 11).[121] No disciple of Jesus, called to cross, humble service,

---

[115] Among others, Gnilka (*Markus*, 2:70) classifies vv. 2–9 as a conflict story. This is correct, but the use of Torah makes it a rabbinic form of conflict. However, Jesus' use of Genesis to give Moses' teaching its correct setting is untypical of a rabbinic debate.

[116] The reference to "man" (ἄνθρωπος) in v. 12 is not to the legal system, or to "the human being" in general (which the Greek could mean). It refers in this case to the male partner who had the power to divorce his wife. See Lagrange, *Saint Marc*, 244; Nineham, *St. Mark*, 266.

[117] Lagrange (*Saint Marc*, 242–43) argues that the Pharisees have used Moses wrongly. He did not "command" (see v. 3) divorce; he permitted it (Deut 24:1–4). Thus, Jesus does not negate the teaching of Moses.

[118] Gibson (*The Temptations of Jesus*, 256–87) focuses upon the πειράζοντες in v. 2, and regards this "temptation" an effort on the part of the Pharisees to have Jesus make a public declaration against divorce, and thus alienate Herod. Jesus thus runs the risk of losing his life in defense of God's truth in this matter. This reading of the passages misses the point of its setting, and the Markan addition of vv. 10–12 that turns the debate with the Pharisees into instruction for the disciples.

[119] See, for example, Hooker, *St. Mark*, 236.

[120] See Gnilka, *Markus*, 2:74–75, and his excursus on divorce and remarriage on pp. 76–78. See also LaVerdiere, *The Beginning*, 2:67–71.

[121] The rabbis accepted that a man could commit adultery against another man by seducing his wife (see Deut 22:13–19) and a wife could commit adultery against her husband by infidelity. However, it is never said that a man could commit adultery against his wife. See Lane, *Mark*, 357; Cranfield, *St. Mark*, 321.

and receptivity, can contemplate such action. However, there is more to it. What is said of the man must also be said of the woman (v. 12). However, nothing is said of the woman's committing adultery against the man, resulting in an imbalance in the statements about the adultery of the man (v. 11) and the adultery of the woman (v. 12). The former event was more likely than the latter.[122] Verse 12 envisages the situation in the Roman world, where women were able to divorce their husbands.[123] All disciples of Jesus, male and female, are called to recognize that they are equally part of the restoration of God's original design in the kingdom inaugurated by Jesus (see 1:14–15).[124]

The most intimate of human experiences, the union between a woman and a man, can lead to the cross. The suffering and self-denial that were Jesus' own destiny (and the destiny of all who would claim to be his followers) are shown to be more than mere words. Jesus' new law in a new situation of God-human relationships, where the original creative design of God is restored, can be costly. Being a disciple of Jesus does not remove the need for service and receptivity in the continual demand to give oneself unswervingly within the bonds of God's design for man and woman in marriage. The teaching of Jesus on this matter is as idealistic, countercultural, and difficult today as it was in the time of Jesus, but Mark has taken this element from Jesus' teaching and used it to point out to disciples that cross, service, and receptivity are not simply *theory*. They come into play in one of the fundamental structures of their day-to-day lives: in man-woman relationships.[125]

Receiving the children (10:13–16)

Jesus and the disciples are still "in the house" (see v. 10), on the other side of the Jordan (see v. 1), as unidentified people bring children to Jesus[126] that he might touch them.[127] Four parties are involved in this brief episode: the people bringing the children (parents?), the children themselves, Jesus, and the disciples. The choice of the expression παιδία (rather than τέκνα) indicates that these children are past infancy, but not yet

---

122 Hooker, *St. Mark,* 236–37.

123 On this broadening of perspective in v. 12, see, for example, Lohmeyer, *Markusevangelium,* 202; Grundmann, *Markus,* 205; LaVerdiere, *The Beginnings,* 2:76–79. This nuance is reflected in the text found in Sinaiticus, Vaticanus, Ephraim Rescript, and other important witnesses. There are, understandably, three important versions of this remarkable statement. For the textual discussion, see Gnilka, *Markus,* 2:75–76; Cranfield, *St. Mark,* 321–22. For a different opinion, see Lane, *Mark,* 352 n. 5.

124 This study cannot enter the complex pastoral issues raised by this "gospel message" in contemporary society. It must be said, however, that Mark presents Jesus' teaching as the reconstruction of God's original design. In most situations, this "ideal" is not present, but church legislation presupposes that it is, from the first moment of marriage. This is to make the "ideal" the "real," with complex consequences. See Hooker, *St. Mark,* 237; F. J. Moloney, "Biblical Reflections on Marriage," *Compass Theology Review* 28/1 (1994): 10–16.

125 The above interpretation, strongly determined by the Markan context, rejects fanciful proposals based on Israel as the bride and Jesus as the bridegroom (Lightfoot, *The Gospel Message,* 114), or the suggestion that it is here for the sake of variety (Wellhausen, as cited in Nineham, *St. Mark,* 259–60). The passage is not about adultery (so Taylor, *St. Mark,* 415–21). Nineham has claimed: "It is not clear why St. Mark has chosen this particular point in the Gospel to introduce this debate, *which seems to have little in common with what precedes or with what follows*" (*St. Mark,* 259, stress mine). The link with what precedes and what follows is very close.

126 There is no indication of a change of place or time; by juxtaposing 10:10–12 with 10:13–16, the latter is set in the same time and place as the former. In v. 17 the scene will change.

127 On the practice of bringing children to significant people for a laying on of hands, see Grundmann, *Markus,* 206.

assuming adult responsibility. They are still *dependent*.[128] The point of the narrative is found in the reaction of the disciples to the presence of the children (v. 13c), Jesus' response to the disciples (vv. 14–15), and his relationship with the children (v. 16). Strategically located between Jesus' instructions on marriage (vv. 1–12) and possessions (vv. 17–31), the passage plays the same role as 9:35–37 within the larger context of 9:32–50. As 9:35–37 established the *theoretical basis* for Jesus' teaching on service and receptivity in 9:32–50, so also does 10:13–16 within 10:1–31. While expressed in different terms, probably the result of Mark's deliberate reworking of a single pre-Markan tradition,[129] the message of 9:35–37 and 10:13–16 is identical: discipleship is to be marked by service and receptivity.

The disciples rebuke (v. 13: ἐπετίμησαν) those who led the children to Jesus, as Peter rebuked Jesus in his misunderstanding of Jesus' first passion prediction (8:32).[130] Paralleling his response to Peter in 8:32–33, Jesus was very indignant (ἠγανάκτησεν).[131] As with Peter in 8:32, the disciples in 10:13 refuse to accept or understand Jesus' teaching and his way to Jerusalem.[132] But there is more to their failure. They have no recollection of Jesus' earlier words to them about children (9:35–37).[133] Yet he does not abandon his recalcitrant disciples. He asks that the children be allowed to come to him, τῶν γὰρ τοιούτων ἐστὶν ἡ βασιλεία τοῦ θεοῦ. Arrogance (9:38–41) and sin (9:42–50) exclude people from the life of the kingdom. The gift of the kingdom *of God* calls for receptivity, paralleling the receptivity of children whose growth depends upon what they hear, smell, touch, taste, and experience. The child becomes the adult through the *reception* of all that is offered. "The Kingdom belongs to such as these because they receive it as a gift."[134] Having made this positive statement about the παιδία (v. 14), Jesus uses negative language to speak a solemn warning to the disciples, opening with the words, "Amen, I say to you" (v. 15a). The disciple whose arrogance and sin makes such receptivity impossible cannot enter the kingdom. Much is being offered to the disciples, but they are loath to accept it (v. 15).[135] The scene closes with Jesus' taking the children in his arms, blessing them, and laying his hands upon them. The scene recalls what Jesus offered the Twelve in 3:14, appointing them to be

---

[128] Lagrange, *Saint Marc*, 246.

[129] In the end, one cannot be sure whether Mark had two separate traditions or reworked a single tradition. For the position taken (tentatively) above, see Gnilka, *Markus*, 2:55, 80.

[130] It has been claimed (see, for example, O. Cullmann, *Baptism in the New Testament* [trans. J. K. S. Reid; London: SCM, 1950], 71–80) that this prohibition reflects a *Sitz im Leben* in the early church where children were banned from baptism. Against this, see Gnilka, *Markus*, 2:80–81; Schweizer, *Mark*, 207–8. For a more broadly based baptismal reading of the passage, see LaVerdiere, *The Beginning*, 2:80–89. Grundmann (*Markus*, 206) shows that the disciples' response was accepted practice, both culturally and religiously.

[131] The verb ἀγανακτέω indicates irritation which reflects itself in a physical reaction. See LSJ, 5–6, s.v. ἀγανακτέω. It may have been somewhat muted in Koiné Greek. See BDAG, 5, s.v. ἀγανακτέω.

[132] LaVerdiere, *The Beginning*, 2:83.

[133] Painter, *Mark's Story*, 143. This repeats their failure in 8:1–9, after their experience of the first bread miracle in 6:31–44.

[134] Lane, *Mark*, 360. Lohmeyer (*Markusevangelium*, 203) misses this in his suggestion that Jesus looks back to 9:1. These young children are the ones who will see the kingdom of God coming with power.

[135] Verse 15, beginning with "amen," was probably originally a separate saying. It is omitted in Matthew's parallel to Mark 10:13–16 (Matt 19:13–15), but found in Matt 18:3, the parallel to Mark 9:36–37 (see also John 3:5). The negative form of this warning is classified by Pesch (*Markusevangelium*, 2:133) as a call to conversion. See the excursus on v. 15 in Lohmeyer, *Markusevangelium*, 204–6.

"with him" (ἵνα ὦσιν μετ' αὐτοῦ). But their performance to date has shown that they are drifting away from him.[136] It is the children who are used as a model of the true disciple, with Jesus and blessed by him. Jesus' actions put into practice what he taught the disciples after their failure in Capernaum (see 9:32–34).[137] There he insisted that the one who would be first of all must be the servant of all (v. 35), receiving the children, and thus receiving Jesus and the one who sent him (v. 37). Jesus is, for Mark, the first of all (see 1:1–13), and he shows this by taking the lowliest of all into his arms, blessing them, and laying his hands upon them (10:16).[138]

The storyteller places this instruction between two passages dealing with the *practical,* day-to-day challenges of living discipleship (marriage and in the administration of one's possessions: vv. 1–12; vv. 17–31). Mark will not allow the reader to forget the *principles* that should determine the disciple's performance. "He has used a story which is linked to his basic theme of the meaning of discipleship."[139] The children are presented as receptive to the gift of the kingdom, and Jesus' taking these "little ones" (10:16; see 9:42) into his arms, blessing them, and laying his hands upon them demonstrates that the greatest of all is the servant of all, even the most lowly (see 9:35–37).

Possessions and discipleship (10:17–31)

The genitive absolute (καὶ ἐκπορευομένου αὐτοῦ) moves Jesus away from his location in the region beyond the Jordan (10:1), as he sets out on "the way" to Jerusalem (v. 17a). While on this journey he is approached by an unnamed man who asks a question which determines the following episode. The man "runs" to Jesus and takes up the unusual position of kneeling before him. These details indicate his sincere enthusiasm. Addressing Jesus as "good teacher," he asks what *he must do* to inherit eternal life (v. 17b).[140] Jesus' teaching to the disciples on the need to *receive* the gift of the kingdom and eternal life has dominated the immediately previous context (see 9:29, 35–37, 43, 45, 47; 10:13–16).[141] The reader senses the further development of a theme that has been strongly present since Jesus' second passion prediction (9:30–31). The question, "What must *I* do?" is the wrong question.[142] The dialogue between Jesus and the man has two moments. In the first place,

---

[136] The expressions are different, but the verb ἐναγκαλίζομαι (found only here and in 9:36 in the New Testament) means to place one's arms around a person. As we saw in the analysis of 3:14, the same idea of close physical relationship was implied in Jesus' appointment of the Twelve "to be with him."

[137] Many commentators remark on the fact that Jesus' actions in v. 16 go beyond what was asked of him in v. 13; see, for example, Lagrange, *Saint Marc,* 247; Taylor, *St. Mark,* 424; Nineham, *St. Mark,* 268. That is precisely what Jesus asks of his disciples by both his words and his actions.

[138] On the background to the "helpless and dependent" child, see also LaVerdiere, *The Beginning,* 2:85–87.

[139] Hooker, *St. Mark,* 238. It is not placed immediately after 10:1–12 because it is "fitting" to have a passage on children after a passage on marriage. See, for example, Taylor, *St. Mark,* 422.

[140] The running, the kneeling, and the salutation are all rarely found in parallel situations in Jewish literature; see Gnilka, *Markus,* 2:85; Lane, *Mark,* 364–65. For Nineham (*St. Mark,* 270), the man already shows his colors: "The stranger was altogether too obsequious and effusive in his approach."

[141] Hooker (*St. Mark,* 241) points to the use of both "eternal life" and "kingdom of God" in the previous context and rightly concludes, " 'Inheriting eternal life' is equivalent to 'entering the Kingdom of God,' and in this section the phrases alternate." See Lane, *Mark,* 365 n. 42, where Jewish evidence for the same equivalence is provided.

[142] On this question as a Torah-oriented way to life, see Gnilka, *Markus,* 2:85–86.

Jesus establishes that only God is good, and thus points to a selection of the Decalogue, the commandments of God, as the way to eternal life (vv. 18–19). On hearing that the man has observed these commandments all his life (v. 20), he calls him to discipleship (v. 21), but the man is not *receptive* to Jesus' word and the demands of discipleship, and departs (v. 22). Not surprisingly, Jesus begins to discuss possessions and the kingdom with his disciples (vv. 23–24a). But he passes quickly from the practical example of the rich man to some fundamental criteria for anyone who wishes to enter the kingdom (vv. 24b–31). He insists that true discipleship is made possible only by the action of God (v. 27) who, in and through Jesus, calls for a radical reversal of accepted values (v. 31).[143]

Jesus' awareness of being the one sent by God (see 9:37), and in this sense "the Son of God" (1:11; 9:7), enables him to point to the absolute goodness of God.[144] But the issue is not who is good. In affirming the goodness of God, Jesus provides the basis for his instructions to the man that he is to follow God's commandments, already known to him (v. 19).[145] Jesus makes a selection of the commandments from the Decalogue (cf. Exod 20:12–16; Deut 5:16–20). Those chosen might be called social commandments, for they deal with the man's treatment of his neighbor: adultery, theft, false witness, defrauding, and respect for parents (v. 19).[146] These are the commandments that a rich man might be prone to violate. Ritual obligations toward God may be in place (see Exod 20:2–10; Deut 5:6–15), but one's weaker neighbor is dealt with sinfully. However, this is not the case; the man replies that he has always lived according to these commandments, from his youth (v. 20). At this point Jesus' attitude to the man changes. He has shown Israel's way to God, but the man who ran up to him and knelt before him (v. 17b), who has dealt justly with his neighbor all his life (v. 20) and is yearning for eternal life (v. 17c), senses that Jesus has something more to offer for eternal life.[147] His problem lies in his belief that he can attain this "something more" by his own efforts (see v. 17b).

On hearing this reply, "Jesus looking upon him loved him" (v. 21).[148] This is the first indication of a movement from Jesus toward the rich man. Thus far all the initiative has

---

[143] Mark may be working creatively with four originally independent passages: vv. 17–22 (the rich man), vv. 23–27 (wealth and entry into the kingdom), vv. 28–30 (reward for the disciples), v. 31 (the reversal of values). The final text has a good balance between the question about eternal life in v. 17, and the promise of eternal life in v. 30. See Grundmann, *Markus*, 208–9.

[144] Christian tradition has had difficulty with 10:18 as it appears to insinuate that Jesus is not unconditionally good. Such problems are anachronistic, and would not have been raised by either Jesus or Mark. They reflect the later christological thought of the church. The difficulty, however, has already been resolved in Matt 19:16 (but not in Luke 18:18). For a full discussion, see Taylor, *St. Mark*, 426–27.

[145] Pesch, *Markusevangelium*, 2:139; Gnilka, *Markus*, 2:86.

[146] The list given does not follow the biblical order of what is commonly called the "second table." The fifth to the tenth commandment are listed, with the fifth at the end. The commandment not to covet has been replaced with a command not to defraud, not found in the Decalogue, but in Deut 24:14–15 (part of a larger group of decrees on justice; see Deut 24:6–25:4; also Sir 4:1, where the same words are found). No satisfactory explanation can be found for this change (see the survey in Hooker, *St. Mark*, 241–42), but it is probably determined by the context: a rich man is likely to defraud.

[147] The passage reflects the early Christian belief that, however valuable Torah was to find God's ways, following Jesus and his teaching went further. See Lohmeyer, *Markusevangelium*, 211; Grundmann, *Markus*, 210–11; Cranfield, *St. Mark*, 330.

[148] Some have suggested that the use of the verb ἀγαπάω ("to love") means that some gesture accompanied Jesus' loving: caressing or putting his arm around him. See, for example, M. Dibelius, *From Tradition to Gospel* (trans. B. L. Woolf; Cambridge and London: James Clark, 1971), 50 n. 1; Nineham, *St. Mark*, 275. However, see the critical remarks of Taylor, *St. Mark*, 428–29.

come from the man himself (see vv. 17a, 17b, 20). Capable of doing everything that he sets out to do, and having the means to do it, he asks Jesus' advice on *what he must do* to attain eternal life (v. 17b). Jesus, looking upon him and loving him (v. 21a), attempts to wrest the initiative from the man and to call him to discipleship. There is only one thing that he lacks.[149] He must rid himself of his possessions and his habitual determination of his own life. He must first sell everything he has and give it to the poor. Reduced to a situation of need and dependence he will have the opportunity to be *receptive* to the action of God in his life. He will not locate his treasure in this life, but it will be with the only one who is good (see v. 18), God in heaven.[150] As the reader has learned from the story of the Syrophoenician woman (7:24–30) and the father of the epileptic boy (9:14–29), these are the requirements of true faith.[151]

The invitation "Come, follow me" links this account to the earlier vocation stories (see 1:16–20; 2:13–17; 3:13–19).[152] A feature of those accounts was the initiative and authority of Jesus, and the immediate, wordless obedience of those called. So also here; Jesus attempts to take the initiative in v. 21. In the earlier vocation stories, the first disciples left their nets, boats, hired servants, and their father (1:16–20), and Levi left his tax house (2:13–15), but there was no command to sell everything and give it to the poor to become disciples of Jesus. Such a command is found *only in this story*.[153] The disciple must be *receptive* to the call of Jesus, thus manifesting trust in his person and word. "Jesus' demand is radical in character. He claims the man utterly and completely, and orders the removal of every other support which could interfere with an unconditional obedience."[154] The man fails, "for he had great possessions," and "went away" sorrowfully rejecting a vocation to discipleship (v. 22).[155] The theme of *receptivity* has been further developed by means of this story of a failed vocation to discipleship; the everyday danger of allowing possessions to determine one's life is the reason for the man's failure to become a disciple.[156] The link with the theme of discipleship, made clear in Jesus' calling him to follow in 10:21c, knits this episode into the wider context of 9:30–10:31.[157]

---

[149] The stress is not upon the lack, but upon the "one thing"; see LaVerdiere, *The Beginning*, 2:96.

[150] "Treasure in heaven" is a circumlocution, widely found in Jewish literature, avoiding the name of God, to say that the man's treasure will be with God, where it should be, rather than with himself. It has nothing to do with the joys of the afterlife. See Pesch, *Markusevangelium*, 2:140.

[151] As Lane (*Mark*, 363) comments: "Entrance into the Kingdom is defined as a gift of God bestowed upon those who acknowledge their helplessness in relationship to the Kingdom."

[152] Hooker, *St. Mark*, 242.

[153] On the misuse of Mark 10:17–22, and especially Matt 19:17–22 (with its additional "if you would be perfect" [Matt 19:21]) as the basis for so-called "evangelical poverty," see F. J. Moloney, *A Life of Promise: Poverty-Chastity-Obedience* (Wilmington: Michael Glazier, 1984), 55–65; see also Taylor, *St. Mark*, 429–80; Schweizer, *Mark*, 212–13. Lohmeyer (*Markusevangelium*, 214, 217–19) claims that 10:17–31 contains elements that show Jesus, basing himself on a Jewish practice of poverty, as the founder of an eschatological poverty movement. Gnilka (*Markus*, 2:84–85) sees an "ascetically oriented community" behind these traditions.

[154] Lane, *Mark*, 368.

[155] Rather than following (ἀκολούθει μου; see v. 21), he went away (ἀπῆλθεν). The verbs indicate opposite directions, and the man chooses the latter.

[156] Painter (*Mark's Gospel*, 145) makes an interesting point: "Jesus exposed a serious flaw in the man's response to the commandments, which had remained hidden throughout the discussion of the last six commandments. He failed to keep the first and great command expressed in the Shema (Deuteronomy 6.4–5). Riches came between him and God, between him and eternal life."

[157] The tragic nature of this failure is shown by the narrator's comment that the man went away "sorrowful." See Gnilka, *Markus*, 2:88.

As with the discussion of divorce, Jesus follows his discussion with the rich man by focusing upon the disciples (10:23–31; cf. 10:10–12). Jesus comments upon the difficulty people with many possessions will have entering the kingdom of God (v. 23). The countercultural nature of Jesus' remarks is highlighted by the amazement of the disciples (v. 24a). They are unable to accept that such teaching could be correct. Their world was a world where the wealthy determined everything, from religion to politics, and everything in between.[158] Hard on the heels of a discussion over marriage and divorce (vv. 1–12), the right use of one's possessions, a second *practical* indication of what it means to serve and be receptive, leaves the disciples stunned.

Jesus increases their amazement by drawing back from the specific case of the rich man and speaking in general about the difficulty facing *anyone* entering the kingdom of God (v. 24b).[159] The disciples, and the readers, are involved as Jesus compares the difficulties the rich have entering the kingdom with a camel passing through the eye of a needle (v. 25).[160] This statement means what it says: it is impossible.[161] From the *difficulty* (δυσκόλως) of those having possessions (v. 23), Jesus moves to an *impossibility* (v. 25).[162] Understandably, the disciples move from amazement over Jesus' words regarding people who have many possessions (v. 24a) to being overwhelmed when he speaks about the difficulties facing anyone who wishes to enter the kingdom (v. 24b). He associates their difficulties with the impossibility experienced by the rich (v. 25; see v. 26a: περισσῶς ἐξεπλήσσοντο). If for everyone it is difficult, and for the rich impossible, the disciples' question makes sense: "Then who can be saved?" (v. 26b). "The disciples understood Jesus correctly. The application of this saying is not limited to the case of this rich man but is relevant for everyone."[163] The universal nature of the question indicates that the disciples

---

[158] On this, see the very helpful study of K. C. Hanson and D. E. Oakman, *Palestine in the Time of Jesus: Social Structures and Social Conflicts* (Minneapolis: Fortress, 1998), 99–129. See also Lane, *Mark*, 369, for evidence that "In Judaism it was inconceivable that riches should be a barrier to the Kingdom."

[159] Even the copyists did not like this general statement (v. 24) and wished to apply the whole of vv. 23–27 only to the rich. A number of variations have been added; the most regular (and most important: Alexandrinus, Ephraem Rescript, Claromontanus, Koridethi) is "for those who trust in riches," after "how hard it is" in v. 24. But this insertion, not present in many important witnesses, "limited its generality and brought it into closer contact with the context" (Metzger, *Textual Commentary*, 90). Some copyists have attempted to ease the situation by reversing the order of v. 24 and v. 25. This should also be rejected; see Cranfield, *St. Mark*, 331–32. The move from the difficulties of the wealthy in v. 23 to a remark on the difficulty for anyone to enter the kingdom in v. 24b—despite Taylor, *St. Mark*, 432, Nineham, *St. Mark*, 275, and others—explains the extraordinary emotion of the disciples in v. 26a. It is difficult for everyone (v. 24) and impossible for the rich (v. 25).

[160] The saying is probably proverbial. Something akin to it is found in *b. B. Meṣiʿa* 38b. A few late manuscripts soften the saying by changing "camel" (κάμηλος) to "rope" (κάμιλος). Some interpreters have suggested that there was a narrow gate in the walls of Jerusalem, called "the eye of a needle," through which it was difficult to lead a camel. There is insufficient evidence for these suggestions. See P. Minear, "The Needle's Eye: A Study in Form Criticism," *JBL* 61 (1942): 157–69.

[161] It is misleading to regard Jesus' words as "hyperbole," as do, for example, Taylor (*St. Mark*, 431) and LaVerdiere (*The Beginning*, 2:100–101). Jesus means exactly what he says. It is impossible for anyone to enter the kingdom by his or her own means. As Nineham (*St. Mark*, 275) comments: "It would be a mistake to ignore the utterly serious truth it expresses." Rightly does Gnilka (*Markus*, 2:88) call it a "paradox."

[162] Grundmann, *Markus*, 213.

[163] Schweizer, *Mark*, 214. See also Gnilka, *Markus*, 2:88: "The evangelist prepares for his interpretation of the following scene with Peter, in which he points out that those who are not wealthy are also dependent upon God."

are shocked (v. 26a) at the association of everyone (v. 24) with the impossibility of those with possessions entering the kingdom.

The use of the passive voice in this question (τίς δύναται σωθῆναι) shows that the disciples do not completely lack understanding. They recognize that people are saved by the action of God, and this enables Jesus to answer their question. No one enters the kingdom of God. It is not something that human beings are able to do by virtue of their possessions, strength, wisdom, or authority. The practical examples of marriage (10:1–12) and possessions (vv. 17–22) teach that God's ways are unlike human ways. All human effort to enter the kingdom is like trying to get a camel through the eye of a needle. It cannot be done. For human beings, entry into the kingdom is impossible, but God sees to it that even the impossible becomes possible: all things (πάντα) are possible with God. The "all things" must be taken seriously. The rich man who has gone away sorrowful (v. 22), and the disciples who sink deeper and deeper into misunderstanding and fear, might all enter the kingdom of God. However, this will take place because God makes it possible for them.[164] What is asked of them, as shown by the example of the restoration of God's order in love and marriage (vv. 1–9), and the rich man's inability to accept a vocation to discipleship (vv. 17–22), is *receptivity* to the countercultural ways of God, made evident in the person and teaching of Jesus.

The instruction ends on a hopeful note. Peter looks back to the beginnings of the Gospel story (see 1:16–20; 2:14) and recalls that—in contrast to the man of 10:17–22—the disciples left everything, and unquestioningly followed Jesus (v. 28). The early vocation stories must not be forgotten as the disciples struggle to maintain their "following" of Jesus.[165] Jesus acknowledges this, moves from his long series of instructions and warnings to praise, and makes promises to those who have responded to the gospel, opening this pronouncement with a solemn "amen." No doubt reflecting the concerns of people reading this story, Mark has Jesus list the many possessions, regarded as essential in their contemporary culture, which they have put at risk: home, brothers and sisters, mother and father, children and lands.[166] Jesus' call to lose life for his sake and for the sake of the gospel (see 8:35) has received a response. Peter's words (10:28) recall that this has already happened to *people in the story,* but 10:29–31 indicates that it has taken place in the lives of some who are listeners, or *readers of the story* (10:29). They will be blessed abundantly even now, with the houses, the brothers and sisters, and the mothers, children, and land that come with belonging to a Christian community.[167] The community, however, also suffers persecutions,

---

[164] As Lagrange (*Saint Marc,* 254) remarks: "This very authentic word of Jesus contains the nucleus of Paul's doctrine."

[165] It is oversubtle to read Peter's question as exaggerated, and to distinguish between the tenses of ἀφήκαμεν (aorist) and ἠκολουθήκαμεν (perfect) to claim that "the decisive renunciation in Peter's mind stood out against the permanent following" (Taylor, *St. Mark,* 433). The context indicates that Jesus is not critical of Peter's question.

[166] A Roman persecution under Nero in the mid-60s C.E. corresponds well to the issues raised by Jesus' words in vv. 29–30. We cannot discount the possibility, however, that similar events, however local, may have taken place elsewhere.

[167] The list of the hundredfold blessings in this life in v. 30 almost repeats what was left behind for the sake of Jesus and the gospel in v. 29. However, "fathers" are missing, no doubt because of the Markan view that God was the father of the new family of the Christian community (see 11:25: "your Father in heaven"); Lane, *Mark,* 372. Pesch (*Markusevangelium,* 2:145) somewhat speculatively locates this focus on only God as father in the wandering missionary activity of the early church. The idea that all these blessings would be found a hundredfold (e.g., LaVerdiere, *The Beginning,* 2:103: "Their house and home is wherever the disciples gather") may be something of an ideal. See Taylor, *St. Mark,* 434–35. As such, it is not only encouragement for the Markan readers, but also exhortation.

and that must be accepted as part of "this time" (νῦν ἐν τῷ καιρῷ τούτῳ, v. 30a).[168] They will eventually be blessed with entry into the eternal life promised by the kingdom (ἐν τῷ αἰῶνι τῷ ἐρχομένῳ, v. 30b).[169] The agenda of Jesus turns the world upside down. A vocation to *service* and *receptivity,* now indicated as the *only* way to enter the kingdom (vv. 24–27), is a vocation to a reversal of values. Praise and promise are found in 10:29–30, but this praise and promise are directed toward the many whom society and culture would regard as the least. Paradoxically, they will be the first, while those regarded as the first will become the last (v. 31).[170]

Jesus has instructed failing disciples (9:32–34) on receptivity and service (9:35–50). He has provided everyday examples of what this means in marriage (10:1–12) and in the administration of power and possessions (10:17–24a).[171] The twofold use of the image of the children, the least of all, received and served as those to whom the kingdom is *given* (see 9:35–37; 10:13–16), has provided apt comment along the way. The section closes as Jesus makes a radical statement about the ultimate lordship of God and the reversal of human values (10:24b–31). The storyteller has tolled the same bell throughout 9:31–10:31: serving and receptive disciples are called to follow Jesus' way, through death, to life and the kingdom which only God can give. But as well as instruction on receptivity and service, the reader is prepared for Jesus' final prediction of the passion (10:32–34) and his description of himself as one who serves and lays down his life (10:45).[172]

The Way of the Son of Man: Cross and Service (10:31–45)

The unfailing presence of Jesus to failing disciples has been a feature of 8:22–10:30. Both elements, Jesus' presence and disciples' failure, are intensified in and around the third and final passion prediction (10:33–34). Jesus describes his coming passion in Jerusalem, but the disciples, first James and John (vv. 35–37) and then "the other ten" (v. 41), fail to understand and accept what the prediction means for Jesus and for their hopes. As in 8:31–9:29 and 9:30–10:31, Jesus does not abandon his failing disciples. He instructs them on their vocation to the cross (vv. 38–40) and to service (vv. 42–43). His teaching closes with words that provide the christological basis for all he has asked from his disciples

---

[168] See Lohmeyer, *Markus,* 217.

[169] The contrast between "this time" and "the time to come" is widespread in apocalyptic thought; Pesch, *Markusevangelium,* 2:145. On its use here, the only place where Mark contrasts "this time" and "the time to come," see Gnilka, *Markus,* 2:93.

[170] Verse 31, although not out of place in the overall argument, comes rather suddenly into the discussion. It was doubtless a "floating" saying of Jesus in the tradition (see Matt 20:16; Luke 13:30), and has been used by Mark to close both this pericope, and the unit that has been running since 9:30–31 (see the parallel between 9:35 and 10:31).

[171] The focus upon the instruction of the disciples is highlighted by 10:10–12 and 10:23–31. Form- and redactional-critical studies often identify the passages on divorce and possessions as catechesis for the post-Easter community. See, for example, Ernst, *Markus,* 285–86, 294–95. This location of the passages in the tradition is no doubt true, but Mark has used them within the context of 8:22–10:52 *primarily* as instruction for the disciples in the story.

[172] The addition of the originally independent v. 31 to vv. 17–30 (Gnilka, *Markus,* 2:93: "a surprise") closes the passage a little clumsily, but leads elegantly into the passion prediction and the Christology of 10:32–45. This verse should not be interpreted eschatologically, in terms of the surprising judgment of God at the end of time (see, for example, Cranfield, *St. Mark,* 333–34). Jesus' own story (10:45) challenges the reader to a reversal of the absolutes of worldly power and wealth in the present age.

across 8:31–10:44: the Son of Man came to serve and not to be served, and to give his life for all (v. 45).[173]

The setting for the third passion prediction is elaborate, and focuses strongly on the situation of the disciples. The theme of "the way" returns. Jesus and the disciples were "on the way," and for the first time the end of the journey is mentioned: Jerusalem (v. 32a). The attitudes of the characters mentioned in 10:32 are markedly different. Jesus strides ahead of the disciples, indicating his unconditional acceptance of all that lies ahead of him (v. 32b). That has already been made clear in 8:31 and 9:31. The disciples, however, struggle with their amazement (ἐθαμβοῦντο; see 1:27; 5:20; 6:6; 10:24) and their fear (ἐφοβοῦντο; see 4:41; 5:36; 6:50; 9:32). These emotions have highlighted their increasing inability and unwillingness to accept Jesus' agenda, for himself and for those following him.[174] But the disciples are still described as "those who followed." *Despite* their failures, they still maintain their place as those who come after Jesus (see 1:16–20; 2:13–14; 6:1; 8:33, 34; 10:21, 28). Jesus addresses amazed and frightened followers (v. 32c) as he takes the Twelve and begins to tell them what was to happen to him (v. 32d). The universal situation of disciples who follow Jesus—the Christ, the Son of God, who is also the Son of Man—is described in 10:32. They struggle with fear and amazement as they follow Jesus, who strides on ahead toward his destiny in Jerusalem.

This report of "what was going to happen to him" (v. 32d) is Mark's most detailed prediction of the passion. It reads like the summary contents page to 14:1–16:8. Every particular is mentioned: Jerusalem (11:1–13:37), betrayal of Jesus by Judas to the Jewish leaders (14:1–11, 43–50), and their subsequent condemnation of Jesus to death (14:53–72). In their turn, the leaders of the Jews will hand Jesus over to Roman authorities (15:1–15), who will mock him, spit upon him (15:16–20), and finally kill him (15:21–41). After three days he will rise (16:1–8). Constructed on the basis of the Markan passion traditions, the final prediction leaves nothing to the imagination.[175] The solemn announcement of the ascent of Jesus and the disciples to Jerusalem (ἀναβαίνοντες εἰς Ἱεροσόλυμα),[176] coupled

---

[173] On the narrative unity of this passage, formed from a variety of sources, see Lohmeyer, *Markusevangelium*, 221.

[174] The noun φόβος and the verb φοβέομαι have been used consistently to describe the increasing failure of the disciples. Amazement has been expressed, to this point, by the verb θαυμάζω, but in 9:32 the stronger θαμβέομαι was introduced to speak of the disciples' amazement over Jesus' words on the difficulties the rich would have entering the kingdom. This verb reappears in 10:32 to describe their emotions as they follow Jesus. It was also used in 1:27 to describe the unbelieving amazement of those who questioned Jesus' authority to command the unclean spirits. Lohmeyer (*Markusevangelium*, 219), Taylor (*St. Mark*, 437–38 [tentatively]), and Hooker (*St. Mark*, 244–45), on the basis of two subjects—"they" for amazed, and "those who followed" for afraid—suggest that *everyone* was amazed, including Jesus. Only those who followed were afraid. This heightens the significance of Jesus' striding ahead toward Jerusalem, on which see LaVerdiere, *The Beginning*, 2:106–8. The grammatical difficulty is very real and has produced a number of textual variations. Some (e.g., Cranfield, *St. Mark*, 335; Painter, *Mark's Story*, 147) suggest that a more general group was amazed, while only those who followed (the Twelve?) feared. For a discussion of the text and a defense of the position adopted above, that "those who followed" are amazed and frightened, see Lane, *Mark*, 373 n. 60.

[175] Lane, *Mark*, 374–75. Not all would agree. For some (e.g., Lohmeyer, *Markusevangelium*, 220), the anti-Jewish polemic and the inclusion of the Gentiles in Jesus' suffering, or the possibility that all the passion sayings go back to pre-Markan strata (e.g., Pesch, *Markusevangelium*, 2:149), point to a pre-Markan source.

[176] The language of "going up to Jerusalem" is customary for a pilgrim's journey to the Temple City for a feast or to offer sacrifice; see Grundmann, *Markus*, 215–16.

with the details of betrayal, unjust condemnation by Jew and Gentile, insult, and death, link God's design with the violence and tragedy that will happen to Jesus. For the first time, influenced by the passion account, the prediction mentions the action of the Gentiles, insulting and slaying Jesus. As always, however, the Son of Man will not only undergo suffering and death, but he will also be vindicated in resurrection (vv. 33–34). There is simply no excuse for not understanding Jesus' destiny. His prediction of what would be done to him (see v. 32d) could not be clearer (vv. 33–34).[177]

But the disciples fail. Peter failed immediately after the first passion prediction (8:32), John failed immediately after the second passion prediction (9:38), James and John fail after the third (10:35–37). Those specially named by Jesus (see 3:16–17), who have been present with Jesus at privileged moments (see 5:37; 9:2), are singled out to voice an understanding of Jesus that does not correspond to Jesus' predictions of his future. They have had privileged access when Jesus raised the dead (5:35–43) and was transfigured (9:2–8), but these experiences have only heightened their idea of Jesus' messianic authority. James and John, rejecting all suggestions that they be *receptive* to what God might have in store, demand that Jesus do for them what *they* ask of him (v. 35). Jesus asks what it is they would like him to do for them (v. 36) and is told that they wish to hold the two most important places of authority, after Jesus himself, when he comes to establish his "glory" in Jerusalem. One on the right and one on the left of the all-powerful Jesus, they would share most intimately in that power and have considerable influence upon the establishment of the messianic rule they imagine Jesus will initiate (v. 37).[178] There is no recognition of *what will happen to Jesus* in Jerusalem (see v. 32d), as they plot to be in powerful positions when Jesus *makes things happen for them* in Jerusalem (v. 37).[179]

Jesus does not abandon the failing sons of Zebedee, but instructs them (see 8:34–9:1; 9:35–50). They do not understand what the "glory" of Jesus will be in Jerusalem. Through a question he clarifies what intimate participation in Jesus' destiny means. He asks if they are able to drink the cup that Jesus drinks and be baptized with the baptism with which he is baptized. A share in Jesus' oncoming suffering and death is all he can offer these disciples, thinly disguised behind language which makes sense in a Jewish and a Christian world (v. 38). The image of emptying a cup is used by the prophets to speak of a suffering that must be endured (see Isa 51:17, 22; Jer 25:15; 49:12; 51:7; Lam 4:21; 23:31–32; Hab 2:16; see also Pss 11:6; 75:9; *Ps. Sol.* 8:14). Part of that suffering experience, however, is the acceptance of God's plan. Baptism meant the total submersion of a person within the terrors of water (see 2 Sam 22:5; Ps 42:8; 69:2–3; Isa 43:2; 1 QH 3:13–18). Jesus can only offer the two disciples a share in God's design.[180] A discipleship committed to the cross is all that Jesus can offer James and John. It will mean suffering and annihilation, but the Christian reader and listener hears echoes of eucharist and baptism in this promise of Jesus.[181]

---

[177] Gnilka, *Markus,* 2:97.

[178] They are not asking for places of honor at a messianic banquet as, for example, Lane (*Mark,* 378–79) would claim, but for power in the hoped-for messianic kingdom to be established in Jerusalem. See Lohmeyer, *Markusevangelium,* 222; Grundmann, *Markus,* 217–18; Pesch, *Markusevangelium,* 2:155–56. On the close relationship between this passage and 8:27–30 (Caesarea Philippi), see Gibson, *The Temptations of Jesus,* 225–36.

[179] Gnilka (*Markus,* 2:101) comments: "The misunderstanding of the disciples increases as he approaches Jerusalem, the place of revelation."

[180] Lane, *Markus,* 380–81; Pesch, *Markusevangelium,* 2:156–58.

[181] By this, I do not mean what could be called "a sacramental interpretation" that somehow "spiritualizes" Jesus' words. Jesus' offer to the sons of Zebedee is glory through suffering and death.

His words recall the instruction that followed the first passion prediction (8:34–9:1). As in 8:34–9:1 the question to the disciples is a further instruction for all members of a Christian community, summoned to follow Jesus through suffering and the cross to resurrection and life in their baptism and eucharist. The disciples confidently accept the challenge (v. 39a), and Jesus, in a saying which is often suggested as indicating that both James and John have suffered violent death prior to the writing of the Gospel of Mark, tells them that they will indeed experience suffering and annihilation (v. 39).[182] Jesus has no authority to offer anything more to those who follow. There will be places of honor in the company of Jesus, the Son of Man, after his vindication by the action of God. There will be a time when Jesus will be "in the glory of his Father with the holy angels" (8:38). But that situation is entirely determined by God, the Father of Jesus. There is a design for Jesus, and for all who follow him, but it is God's design. How things will be, and who will occupy what position, has nothing to do with Jesus. He responds to God by journeying to Jerusalem, and all subsequent honor, both for Jesus and his followers, will be God's doing (v. 40).

The prediction of the passion was directed to the Twelve (v. 32d), and the reader takes it for granted that the other ten have heard two of their number ask for positions of honor (v. 37). The remaining disciples have heard not only the passion prediction (vv. 33–34), but also the instruction on the necessity of the cross, delivered to James and John.[183] Yet, they join their colleagues in failure. They burst into indignation over the presumption of James and John, angry that they might find themselves jockeyed into lesser positions of authority because of the preemptive strike for power on the part of the sons of Zebedee. In the face of this further failure, Jesus calls the disciples and teaches them (10:42a; see 8:34–9:1; 9:35–50; 10:38–40). The rhythmic repetition of Jesus' calling and teaching those who have failed is a feature of 8:22–10:52 (see 8:27, 34; 9:35; 10:32).[184] Despite a brief word of anger (see 9:19), Jesus never abandons the failing disciples. In a memorable passage, Jesus establishes service as the feature of Christian discipleship. He points to the observable truth that those who are supposed to be (οἱ δοκοῦντες) the rulers and great figures in the Gentile world have a certain way of relating to their subjects. The phrase "supposed to be" is subtle irony. In the design of God, their all-powerful and self-sufficient rule is only apparent.[185] Yet they lord it (κατακυριεύουσιν) over and exercise authority (κατεξουσιάζουσιν) over

---

The early church attempted to embrace this agenda and recognized its presence in its practice of baptism and eucharist (see Mark 14:36; Luke 12:50). See Lohmeyer, *Markusevangelium,* 223; Grundmann, *Markus,* 218; Lührmann, *Markusevangelium,* 180; Gnilka, *Markus,* 2:102.

[182] For a discussion of the history of vv. 35–40, seeing v. 39 as an addition to the final redaction of a passage made up of originally independent traditions, see Gnilka, *Markus,* 2:99. However obvious it may appear that v. 39 is a *vaticinium ex eventu* (see Pesch, *Markusevangelium,* 2:159–60), it is not entirely clear when James and John died, or whether they were both martyred. It appears that James was martyred by Herod at an early date (see Acts 12:2), but the death of John, the son of Zebedee, is a matter of considerable uncertainty. See Taylor, *St. Mark,* 442, and more recently, M.-E. Boismard, *Le martyre de Jean l'apôtre* (CahRB 35; Paris: Gabalda, 1996). It may simply be instruction on suffering; see Hooker, *St. Mark,* 247. If the passage is not a *vaticinium ex eventu,* Taylor (*St. Mark,* 441), Cranfield (*St. Mark,* 339), and Schweizer (*Mark,* 218) maintain that it may be an authentic word of Jesus; the early church could not have created it.

[183] Taylor (*St. Mark,* 443), on the grounds that the other ten "heard," suggests that only the ten are instructed in vv. 42–45. This distinction is not called for.

[184] All these passages are regarded by the redaction critics as "redactional," i.e., the result of Markan "editorial" activity (see, for example, Gnilka, *Markus,* 2:11–12, 22, 55, 95). But this activity is not "editorial" or "redactional" in any negative sense. These passages are key to the understanding of the *point of view of the storyteller.*

[185] Cranfield, *St. Mark,* 340.

their subjects (v. 42b).[186] Jesus announces that it must not be so among his disciples (v. 43a). The theme of the reversal of values, clearly stated in 10:31 ("many that are first will be last, and the last first") returns, as does the theme of service, which was the feature of Jesus' instruction after the second passion prediction (9:35–50). Established patterns of lordship and authority are to be subverted in the community of disciples. Jesus' instructions on the need for the one who would be great to be the servant of all (v. 43b) explicitly recalls what he said in 9:35, and the call for the one who would be first to be the slave of all (v. 44) recalls 10:31. The juxtaposing of these two instructions renders the words of Jesus powerful, so clearly set in opposition to culturally accepted methods of exercising power and authority (v. 42). Addressed to the Twelve, these words reach beyond the limits of the text. The step-by-step logic of the argument proceeds from what disciples know (οἴδατε, v. 42b) to a series of rejections of this well-known truth, at first addressed to the "you" of the disciples (οὐκ οὕτως δέ ἐστιν ἐν ὑμῖν, v. 43a) but immediately broadening that reversal to "anyone" (ἀλλ' ὃς ἂν θέλῃ . . . , v. 43b; καὶ ὃς ἂν θέλῃ, v. 44). The steady progress of the οἴδατε . . . δέ . . . ἀλλά . . . καί establishes a fundamental principle of Markan discipleship. Over against all the culturally accepted and expected ways of showing greatness and exercising authority, the disciple is to be the servant of all and the slave of all (vv. 42–44).[187]

There is a tight narrative unity from 10:32 to 10:44: the disciples are described, struggling to follow Jesus who tells them, with the utmost clarity and detail, of his destiny (vv. 32–34). But two of them immediately fail and are instructed that to follow Jesus means to share in the experience of the cross (vv. 35–40). The other ten join them in their failure and receive unforgettable instruction on the call of disciples of Jesus to the service of all. A further καί links 10:45a with 10:32–44, and the ἀλλά opening 10:45b concludes the argument. Most likely an independent pre-Markan saying of Jesus, 10:45 is used as Jesus' final words to his disciples in this section of the Gospel. After the first passion prediction, Jesus insisted on the need for all disciples to take up their cross and give their lives for the sake of Jesus and the gospel (8:34–9:1). After the second passion prediction, he insisted on the need for disciples to serve even the least of all (9:35–50). Jesus' instruction after the third passion prediction returned to these two essential elements of discipleship: the cross (vv. 38–40) and service (vv. 42–44).

But it becomes clear in 10:45 that Jesus does not ask suffering and service from his disciples as a distant lawgiver. He, the Son of Man, leads the way: "For the Son of Man also came, not to be served, but to serve (ἀλλὰ διακονῆσαι: cf. 9:35–37; 10:43) and to give his life (δοῦναι τὴν ψυχὴν αὐτοῦ: cf. 8:34–37; 10:38) as a ransom for many" (v. 45).[188] The Son of Man in Dan 7:14, 27 comes in splendor, and one might expect that he should be served: "all dominions shall serve and obey him" (Dan 7:27). However, it is this same Son of Man who, as the personification of "the holy ones of the Most High," represents those who suffer because of their commitment to YHWH's law and nation. For the sake of the nation,

---

[186] These two verbs, both beginning with κατά, carry a strong message of forceful subordination. No doubt the Markan readers had experience of such authorities and rulers. See Lane, *Mark*, 382. Grundmann (*Markus*, 219) claims that the words indicate the abuse and misuse of authority.

[187] See Lührmann, *Markusevangelium*, 181. Some (e.g., LaVerdiere, *The Beginning*, 2:117–19) suggest that being a servant (διάκονος) and slave (δοῦλος) are not identical. The former indicates a generous response to all that needs to be done for others, and the latter giving up all personal claim on oneself for the good of all. However, it is most likely that, in this context, they are identical. This is called for by v. 45, where Jesus describes himself only in terms of service (διακονεῖν), and this implies giving his life. See Painter, *Mark's Gospel*, 149.

[188] See excursus 2, "Son of Man and Suffering Servant in Mark 10:45," pp. 213–14 below.

persecution, suffering, and martyrdom are endured (see Dan 7:7, 23–25). The same historical period produced parallel ideas about the Maccabean martyrs, giving their lives so that
the nation might have life (see 4 Macc 17:21–22). Jesus is the Son of Man, and (καί) despite
what the disciples may think (see 8:29) he is not to be served (v. 45a), but (ἀλλά) to serve.
His service will take the form of his self-giving unto death, so that others might have life
(v. 45b).[189] The disciple of Jesus, called to self-giving for the sake of Jesus and the Gospel
and to the service of even the most lowly, is called to *follow* Jesus. His life story, insists
Mark, is the paradigm for all subsequent discipleship. The glory sought by the sons of
Zebedee and the other ten (see vv. 37, 41) can be gained only through cross and service.
Those who are not ashamed to take up the cross and to serve will save their lives and share
in the glory of Jesus when he comes with his Father and the holy angels (see 8:38).

The Cure of a Blind Man (10:46–52)

The journey to Jerusalem continues as Jesus and the disciples both come to Jericho,
and then leave it along with a large crowd (v. 46a).[190] As the final stage of the journey, the
fifteen miles from Jericho to Jerusalem, begins blind Bartimaeus is introduced into the
narrative, sitting by the roadside (v. 46b).[191] His position by the roadside makes two
points. First, he is stationary (ἐκάθητο) as Jesus, the disciples, and the crowd move toward
Jerusalem. He is not part of Jesus' journey "on the way," as he is seated "by the way" (παρὰ
τὴν ὁδόν).[192] His blindness and his position, seated by the road, also indicate his smallness
in the eyes of the world at large. He is not only blind (τυφλός), but also a beggar
(προσαίτης).[193] Bartimaeus is nobody of importance and has nothing, not even his sight.
The reader recalls the earlier cure of a blind man (8:22–26). It will soon become apparent
to the reader that the disciples do not.

On hearing that Jesus of Nazareth was passing by, Bartimaeus cries out a confession of
faith: "Son of David, have mercy on me!" (10:47). There are two elements in this confession. The narrator reports that he hears that "Jesus of Nazareth" is passing by. This is Jesus'
everyday name.[194] Bartimaeus appeals to Jesus of Nazareth with the designation "Son of

---

189 For this interpretation, built upon the background of Dan 7 and the Maccabean martyrs,
see Hooker, *St. Mark,* 129–31; C. K. Barrett, "The Background of Mark 10.45," in *New Testament Essays: Studies in Memory of T. W. Manson* (ed. A. J. B. Higgins; Manchester: Manchester University
Press, 1959), 1–18. See further, M. D. Hooker, *The Son of Man in Mark: A Study of the Background of
the Term "Son of Man" and Its Use in St. Mark's Gospel* (London: SPCK, 1967), 140–47.

190 See E. Netzer, "Jericho," *ABD* 3:723–40, especially pp. 737–39.

191 A Greek translation of Bartimaeus ("son of Timaeus") is provided for those readers who do
not understand Aramaic. There is no call for symbolic meanings for the name. See Lagrange, *Saint
Marc,* 267; Gnilka, *Markus,* 2:109–10. LaVerdiere (*The Beginning,* 2:122) points out that there may
be an interplay between the introduction of Bartimaeus as the insignificant and unknown "*son of
Timaeus,*" who recognizes the greatness of Jesus, "*Son of* David." The placing of the explanation ὁ
υἱὸς Τιμαίου before "Timaeus" has led some (e.g., Bultmann, *History,* 241; Taylor, *St. Mark,* 448) to
suggest that the name may be a gloss, pointing to a well-known Timaeus of Jericho. But see Meier, *A
Marginal Jew,* 2:735 n. 39.

192 LaVerdiere, *The Beginning,* 2:122.

193 This association of being blind and having to beg for survival was regular in the ancient
world, as it remains today.

194 Lagrange, *Saint Marc,* 267. Pesch (*Markusevangelium,* 2:171) accepts this, but claims that
the use of "Jesus of Nazareth" is also an indication that 10:46–52 was part of a pre-Markan passion
narrative (see 14:67; 16:6; but see 1:9, 24).

David." It is the man Jesus who is recognized and confessed "Son of David." Bartimaeus believes that, as "Son of David," Jesus of Nazareth can bring relief to his suffering and nothingness.[195] Like the Syrophoenician woman and the man with the epileptic son, Bartimaeus cries out in faith, asking for mercy in the light of his need. Mark shows little interest in the messianic title "Son of David," and Jesus will later argue that the Messiah is not the Son of David (see 12:35–37).[196] But there is no need to have recourse to the notion of a messianic Son of David.[197] John Meier has shown that an association between a "Son of David" and a miraculous healer is present in early Jewish tradition.[198] The only reigning king to be called "Son of David" in the Old Testament is Solomon, and by the first century he had acquired a reputation as a healer (see Josephus, *Ant.* 8.46–49; *Test. Sol.* 20:1). Too much weight must not be given to the man's confession, but to his enthusiastic recognition that Jesus of Nazareth could bring mercy and healing into his nothingness. He uses "Son of David" to make that clear. The rest of the episode centers upon the man's response once Jesus calls him.[199] "A great deal of the interest centers not on Jesus but on the attitude and the action of the blind man."[200] The many who surround Jesus rebuke the blind man (ἐπετίμων αὐτῷ).[201] Among "the many" are the disciples who, along with the crowd, journey with Jesus from Jericho to Jerusalem (v. 46). The passage is not directed against the disciples, but they have been absorbed into the ὄχλος ἱκανός of 10:46, to become part of the πολλοί of 10:48. This is the second time the disciples have been with Jesus in a situation which repeats an earlier experience in the narrative (see 6:31–44 and 8:1–9; 8:22–26 and

---

[195] For background to this link between a messianic Son of David and healing, see Gnilka, *Markus,* 2:110, and especially Meier, *A Marginal Jew,* 2:689–90. Lohmeyer (*Markusevangelium,* 225) and Grundmann (*Markus,* 222) claim that "Son of David" here is to be linked with the context of Suffering Servant and Son of Man. They argue that one does not approach a worldly messianic king for mercy, but a godly lord. For Pesch (*Markusevangelium,* 2:171–72, 174), both "Son of David" and "Rabbouni" speak for the historicity of the account. Lagrange (*Saint Marc,* 268) claims that the Matthean and Lukan rendition of "Lord" (κύριε) "translates well the meaning of the Aramaic word."

[196] Grundmann (*Markus,* 220) points out that this title on the lips of the blind man prepares for the acclamation "Blessed is the coming kingdom of our father David" in 11:10; see also Nineham, *St. Mark,* 282; Meier, *A Marginal Jew,* 2:686–87. As we shall see, that acclamation reflects a false messianic expectation.

[197] Commentators are almost universally puzzled by Jesus' acceptance of the "messianic title" of Son of David in 10:46–52. This seems both out of character with the rest of the Gospel, where Jesus rejects overt messianic confessions, and in conflict with later passages in the Gospel (11:1–11; 12:35–37) where Jesus rejects identification between himself and the messianic Son of David.

[198] For what follows, see the treatment of Meier (*A Marginal Jew,* 2:689–90) and especially J. H. Charlesworth ("The Son of David: Solomon and Jesus," in *The New Testament and Hellenistic Judaism* [ed. P. Borgen and S. Giversen; Peabody: Hendrickson, 1997], 72–87). This suggestion had been raised and rejected by Ernst (*Markus,* 314). Ernst, however, also rejects the identification of Jesus and the messianic Son of David in Mark. He suggests that the use of the title "is better explained by the laws of cultic acclamation than by the psychology of a person in search of help." This does not seem to resolve the problem. Does Jesus accept the cultic acclamation "Son of David"? What does that mean for the Markan Christology?

[199] Some have suggested that he uses the title while still blind, and thus incorrectly, moving to a title of honor ("Rabbouni") once he can see; Lane, *Mark,* 387–88. For W. Kelber (*The Kingdom in Mark: A New Place and a New Time* [Philadelphia: Fortress, 1974], 94–95), the correct Markan title in the passage is "Nazarene," and thus the blind man's use of "rabbi" and "son of David" places his faith at the same level as that of the failing disciples. But the titles are not the main issue. The man's unconditional dependence upon Jesus corresponds to the Markan theology of discipleship.

[200] Nineham, *St. Mark,* 283. See also Schweizer, *Mark,* 224–25.

[201] In earlier uses of ἐπιτιμάω (see 1:25; 3:12; 4:39; 8:30; 9:25) Jesus commands silence. Here it is the crowds, acting *ultra vires.*

10:46–52). On both occasions the disciples show that they have not learned from their earlier experience. But Bartimaeus continues to cry out his profession of faith, with even greater enthusiasm and energy.

Jesus stops his journey and commands, "Call him" (φωνήσατε αὐτόν, v. 49a). The verb φωνέω ("to call") is used twice in 10:49b as those surrounding Jesus respond. They call Bartimaeus and tell him, "Take heart; rise, he is calling you" (θάρσει, ἔγειρε, φωνεῖ σε). As expressions associated with vocation and resurrection are combined, the Christian listener and reader is aware that Bartimaeus is called into the possibility of life.[202] Bartimaeus has already been described as blind, a beggar, and seated beside the road (v. 46). He now leaps to his feet and comes to Jesus (v. 50b). The immediacy of his response to Jesus' call matches that of the first disciples (see 1:16–20; 2:13–14). Those disciples left their trade, their possessions, and their fathers. Again matching that response, but perhaps surpassing them, he leaves his only vestige of dignity by the side of the road: he throws off his cloak (v. 50a).[203] It is with nothing that Bartimaeus presents himself to Jesus, who is calling him, in order to receive the mercy and healing he believes Jesus, the Son of David, can administer (see vv. 47–48).

The contrast with the disciples' increasing search for authority, power, and security is strong. This is highlighted by Jesus' words to Bartimaeus, which repeat what he asked of the son of Zebedee: "What do you want me to do for you?" (10:51a; cf. 10:36). The sons of Zebedee addressed Jesus as διδάσκαλε (10:35), and asked for positions of honor and power when Jesus came to the δόξα of his messianic kingdom in Jerusalem (10:37). Bartimaeus, addressing Jesus as ῥαββουνί, develops the earlier address of διδάσκαλε, by adding a note of dependency ("*my* master") and asks that he might see (v. 51b).[204] Within the context of 8:22–10:52, during which the disciples have never progressed from the partial sight which Peter, representing the group, attested in his confession (8:29), it appears that Bartimaeus is asking for the gift which has thus far eluded the disciples. The link between "faith" and "sight" was broached in 8:16–21, and made explicit in 8:27–30, when read in the light of 8:22–26. Jesus identifies them in 10:52b: "Your faith has made you well." Bartimaeus's unconditional commitment to Jesus as a Son of David, able to give him full sight (vv. 47–48), cost what it may (v. 50), is the reason for the miracle. The insults of the crowd (including the disciples) did not deter him. He only cried out his faith all the more insistently (vv. 47–48). His lowly position did not deter him. Indeed, before coming to Jesus he cast off his last shred of dignity (v. 50). Blind Bartimaeus joins the Syrophoenician woman

---

[202] Marshall, *Faith as a Theme*, 140–41. LaVerdiere (*The Beginning*, 2:124–25) overreads a baptismal background into the summons of Jesus.

[203] R. A. Culpepper, "Mark 10:50: Why Mention the Garment?" *JBL* 101 (1982): 131–32. It is generally pointed out that the cloak was spread on the ground to collect any offerings; see, for example, Nineham, *St. Mark*, 286; Lane, *St. Mark*, 388. This may be true but there is nothing of it in the text, and the idea seems to be that he sheds his clothing; Taylor, *St. Mark*, 449. For Ernst (*Markus*, 315) there is nothing unusual about the casting off the cloak. It would be a normal action before going to Jesus. But then why does Mark make so much of it? There is weak attestation for the reading ἐπιβαλών (minuscule 565, Sinaitic Syriac, and Ethiopic), indicating that he "put on" his cloak, which would be the proper thing to do before going to Jesus. Some commentators (e.g., Lohmeyer, *Markusevangelium*, 226 n. 2; Grundmann, *Markus*, 221) prefer this reading. On both text-critical and theological grounds, the reading ἀποβαλών is to be retained. For the link with 1:16–20, see Marshall, *Faith as a Theme*, 141–42; Painter, *Mark's Gospel*, 152.

[204] Marshall, *Faith as a Theme*, 140. Gnilka (*Markus*, 2:111) claims that for non-Jewish listeners "Rabbouni" would sound like a title of honor. Grundmann (*Markus*, 222) points to the rarity of the expression, and claims that it indicates a meeting between the human and the divine.

(7:24–30) and the father of the epileptic boy (9:14–29) in presenting himself to Jesus, bringing nothing except faith, and thus comes to full sight.

The link between the miracle of the curing of a blind man in stages in 8:22–26 and the subsequent presentation of the limited, partial sight, of the disciples from 8:27–10:45, is highlighted by Jesus' command to the now seeing man to go away (v. 52a). He is now free to go wherever he will, and is no longer limited to his place beside the road, begging. The response of the man is to become a follower of Jesus (καὶ ἠκολούθει αὐτῷ ἐν τῷ ὁδῷ, 10:52c). Earlier uses of "the way," so closely associated with the passion predictions and Jesus' journey to Jerusalem (see 8:27; 9:33; 10:32–33), are deliberately recalled, as are the uses of the quasi-technical verb ἀκολουθεῖν (see 1:18; 2:14, 15; 6:1; 8:34; 9:38; 10:21, 28, 32) to refer to the challenge of discipleship. Bartimaeus is presented to the reader as a disciple prepared to follow the way of Jesus through the cross to resurrection.[205] Tracing the "movement" in this passage is instructive: Jesus is journeying on the road to Jerusalem, while Bartimaeus is stationary, seated beside the road (v. 46). Jesus stops to associate himself with the blind man, who calls out to him in trust and faith (v. 49). By calling Bartimaeus, motion restarts for all concerned as he leaps to his feet and comes to Jesus (vv. 49–50). The journey is resumed as a crowd, the disciples (see v. 46), and Bartimaeus follow Jesus along the road to Jerusalem (v. 52).[206] "The story of Bartimaeus stands in contrast to the preceding failure of the disciples and symbolizes the ability of those who have faith in Jesus to see the truth."[207]

Conclusion

This section of the Gospel began with a miracle story which instructed on the three possible stages of sight: blindness, partial sight, and full sight (8:22–26). At Caesarea Philippi the disciples confessed their faith in Jesus as the Messiah (8:29), but they were warned not to spread this abroad; there is more to a proper understanding of Jesus (8:30). Since then they have shown they will not understand or accept that Jesus is also the Son of Man who will come to his glory only by means of a journey to a cross in Jerusalem. Three times Jesus has spoken of his oncoming suffering, death, and resurrection in Jerusalem (8:31; 9:31; 10:33–34). All three passion predictions have been accompanied by the disciples' failure to accept the challenge of "following" Jesus to Jerusalem (8:32–33; 9:32–34; 10:35–37, 41). But the failing disciples have not been abandoned. With systematic regularity, Jesus calls the disciples and instructs them further, on the cross (8:34–9:1), on service (9:35–37), and on the cross and service (10:38–40, 42–43). Jesus climaxes his instructions with the christological foundation for discipleship: the Son of Man did not come to be served, but to serve, and to give his life as a ransom for all (10:45).

Other episodes within this section are designed to further highlight the disciples' ongoing failure and to continue Jesus' never-failing instruction. Particularly significant were

---

[205] Lührmann, *Markusevangelium,* 183–84, against those who prefer to restrict the notion of "discipleship" to the Twelve. See, for example, Lane, *Mark,* 389. The present location of the narrative within the Markan story reflects the skill of the storyteller. The event itself, however, may have its roots in an event that took place in the life of Jesus. See the summary of the earlier discussion in Taylor, *St. Mark,* 447. Most recently, see Meier, *A Marginal Jew,* 2:686–90, 733–38.

[206] Lohmeyer, *Markus,* 224.

[207] Hooker, *St. Mark,* 252. See also Marshall, *Faith as a Theme,* 142–44; LaVerdiere, *The Beginning,* 132–33; van Iersel, *Reading Mark,* 140–41.

the transfiguration (9:2–8; located immediately after the first passion prediction and Jesus' teaching on the place of the cross in the life of a disciple), and the instruction on marriage and divorce (located at the center of this section, 10:2–12; 17–31, after the second passion prediction). At the transfiguration three disciples learn who this is who asks them to follow through the cross into resurrection. This is the Son of God; they must listen to him (9:7). In the discussions over divorce and riches, the call to cross and service is located in the practical experience of all disciples: their affections and their possessions. The reader wonders about the disciples' partial sight. Will they never come to see (cf. 9:19)? What is required of them? The curing of blind Bartimaeus answers the second of those questions (10:46–52).[208] Like the Syrophoenician woman, the father of the epileptic boy, and blind Bartimaeus, they are to shed their pretensions and believe. This means accepting the challenge of believing that Jesus is the Christ (8:29), the Son of Man (8:31, 38; 9:31; 10:32–34), and following him down his way to Jerusalem (10:52). It is to Jerusalem that the narrative now turns.

Excursus 1: The Son of Man Discussion

I am taking it for granted that the third-person reference to "the Son of Man" in 8:31, and throughout the rest of the Gospel, is Jesus' way of speaking of himself. It is universally accepted that such is the case within the Markan narrative. Whether this was so in the life of the pre-Easter Jesus has been long debated. It was once accepted that "the Son of Man" was an expected eschatological figure at the time of Jesus, and that he identified himself with that figure; see J. Jeremias, *New Testament Theology* (trans. J. Bowden; London: SCM, 1971), 257–76; Lane, *Mark*, 296–303; H. Baarlink, *Anfängliches Evangelium: Ein Beitrag zur näheren Bestimmung der theologischen Motive im Markusevangelium* (Kampen: J. H. Kok, 1977), 175–98.

Many interpreters claim that, under the influence of Dan 7, Jesus used the term of his future coming in an apocalyptic sense, and that the sayings referring to the present Son of Man, and to his future suffering, were added by the early church; see, for example, Grundmann, *Markus*, 171–73; J. Gnilka, *Jesus of Nazareth: Message and History* (trans. S. S. Schatzmann; Peabody: Hendrickson, 1997), 248–65.

Some scholars hold that Jesus did not use the expression, but that it came into the tradition via Christian reflection: P. Vielhauer, "Jesus und der Menschensohn: Zur Diskussion mit Heinz Edward Tödt und Eduard Schweizer," *ZNW* 60 (1963): 133–77; H. Conzelmann, *An Outline of the Theology of the New Testament* (trans. J. Bowden; London: SCM, 1969), 131–37; N. Perrin, *Rediscovering the Teaching of Jesus* (London: SCM, 1967), 164–99.

Others claim that Jesus spoke of a future eschatological figure other than himself, which the early church subsequently identified with Jesus: R. Bultmann, *Theology of the New Testament* (trans.

---

[208] The setting of the passion predictions and the instruction of the disciples between the two blind miracles is widely accepted. See, for example, N. Perrin, *What Is Redaction Criticism?* (London: SPCK, 1970), 40–63; idem, "Towards an Interpretation of the Gospel of Mark," in *Christology and a Modern Pilgrimage: A Discussion with Norman Perrin* (ed. H. D. Betz; Missoula: Scholars Press, 1974), 6–21; D.-A. Koch, "Inhaltliche Gliederung und geographischer Aufriss im Markusevangelium," *NTS* 29 (1983): 147–49; Best, *Following Jesus*, 1–16; D. Senior, *The Passion of Jesus in the Gospel of Mark* (The Passion Series 2; Wilmington: Michael Glazier, 1984), 28–36; Meier, *A Marginal Jew*, 2:686–87. Some dissent. For example, Gnilka (*Markus*, 2:107) reads 10:46–52 as the first episode in a section dedicated to Jesus' activities in Jerusalem, but he does not arrive in Jerusalem until 11:1. Gnilka ignores this "textual marker" of 11:1 because of his earlier rejection of any literary and theological relationship between the three-staged miracle in 8:22–26 and the following instruction of the disciples; see Gnilka, *Markus*, 1:315.

K. Grobel; 2 vols.; London: SCM, 1952–55), 1:28–32; F. Hahn, *The Titles of Jesus in Christology* (trans. H. Knight and G. Ogg; London: Lutterworth, 1969), 15–33; H. E. Tödt, *The Son of Man in the Synoptic Tradition* (trans. D. M. Barton; London: SCM, 1965).

Another approach has been to claim that Jesus used the Aramaic expression *bar nasha* as a modest self-reference, a circumlocution for "I," and that this was later rendered christological: G. Vermes, *Jesus the Jew: A Historian's Reading of the Gospels* (London: Collins, 1973), 160–91. Subsequent to Vermes's study, there has been a recent return (see the earlier suggestions of E. Schweizer, *Jesus* [trans. D. E. Green; London: SCM, 1971], 19–22, and idem, *The Good News according to Mark* [trans. D. H. Madvig; London: SPCK, 1971], 166–71) to a focus upon the originality of the present sayings, with different nuances: see M. Casey, *Son of Man: The Interpretation and Influence of Daniel 7* (London: SPCK, 1979), 224–40; B. Lindars, *Jesus Son of Man: A Fresh Examination of the Son of Man Sayings in the Gospels* (London: SPCK, 1983), 17–28; D. R. A. Hare, *The Son of Man Tradition* (Minneapolis: Fortress, 1990), 257–82.

A minority position, which I follow, suggests that the tradition developed in the opposite direction. On the basis of Dan 7, Jesus used the term to speak of the need to experience suffering, as did "the Son of Man" = "the Saints of the Most High" in Dan 7. However, while addressing the need for suffering (the original setting of Dan 7), the expression always indicates that God will have the last word. Ultimate authority will be given to the Son of Man. In this way, the historical Jesus took upon himself "*the* Son of *the* Man" (rendered in the Gospels as ὁ υἱὸς τοῦ ἀνθρώπου), the expression used for the suffering but vindicated "one like a son of man" (LXX: ὡς υἱὸς ἀνθρώπου) of Dan 7:13. See C. F. D. Moule, "Neglected Features in the Problem of 'the Son of Man,'" in *Neues Testament und Kirche: Festschrift für Rudolf Schnackenburg* (ed. J. Gnilka; Freiburg: Herder, 1974), 413–28; idem, *The Origin of Christology* (Cambridge: Cambridge University Press, 1977), 11–22; Hooker, *The Son of Man in Mark*, 174–98; idem, "Is the Son of Man Problem Really Insoluble?" in *Text and Interpretation: Studies in the New Testament Presented to Matthew Black* (ed. E. Best and M. McL. Wilson; Cambridge: Cambridge University Press, 1979), 155–68; Moloney, "The End of the Son of Man?" 280–90. This position is summarized in Hooker, *St. Mark*, 88–93.

For summaries of contemporary discussions, see J. R. Donahue, "Recent Studies in the Origins of 'Son of Man' in the Gospels," *CBQ* 48 (1986): 484–98; F. J. Matera, *The Kingship of Jesus: Composition and Theology in Mark 15* (SBLDS 66; Chico: Scholars Press, 1982), 100–116; D. R. Burkett, *The Son of Man Debate: A History and Evaluation* (SNTSMS 107; Cambridge: Cambridge University Press, 2000). The reduction of "the Son of Man" to *the* human being (see, for example, LaVerdiere, *The Beginning*, 2:28) does not do justice to the biblical and Jewish background for the expression. See, along these lines, Grundmann, *Markus*, 173.

Excursus 2: Son of Man and Suffering Servant in Mark 10:45

It is beyond the limitations of this study to enter into the scholarly discussions that surround the *Traditionsgeschichte*, the possible link with Old Testament themes (Dan 7 and Isa 53), and the implications of Jesus' self-gift "as a ransom for many" (λύτρον ἀντὶ πολλῶν) of 10:45. Many have attempted to trace these words to Jesus himself; see, for example, Lagrange, *Saint Marc*, 266; Taylor, *St. Mark*, 445–46; Lane, *Mark*, 377–78 n. 75; Cranfield, *Mark*, 341–44. This, however, is unlikely; see Nineham, *St. Mark*, 280–81; Pesch, *Markusevangelium*, 2:162–64.

Matthew 20:28 repeats Mark 10:45 (with some stylistic improvements), but Luke has a closely related saying with strong links with v. 45a within the context of Jesus' words to the disciples at the table on the night before he died: "For which is the greater, one who sits at table or one who serves? Is it not the one who sits at table? But I am among you as one who serves" (Luke 22:27). The words of v. 27c (ἐγὼ δὲ ἐν μέσῳ ὑμῶν εἰμι ὡς ὁ διακονῶν) probably provide the earliest version and the eucharistic setting of Jesus' words on his self-gift in service. This theme was most likely developed from this setting within the pre-Markan tradition; see Hare, *The Son of Man Tradition*, 202–4, 276–77; Gnilka, *Markus*, 2:100.

The idea of "ransom for many" (a Greek way of rendering the Semitic "all God's people"; see 1QS 6:1, 7–25; CD 13:7; 14:7) has been traced back to the Servant Song in Isa 53:10–12. The same idea is found in a more hellenized form in the confession of faith in 1 Tim 2:6 (ὁ δοὺς ἑαυτὸν ἀντίλυτρον ὑπὲρ πάντων). This suggests that the idea of "ransom for all" is the product of the early church's reflection upon the death of Jesus, rather than Jesus' identification of himself with the Suffering Servant. However, if Isa 53 lies behind Mark 10:45 (see Lagrange, *Saint Marc*, 264–65; Jeremias, *New Testament Theology*, 271–72; Lane, *Mark*, 383–85; Grundmann, *Markus*, 219–20; Gnilka, *Markus*, 2:104; Pesch, *Markusevangelium*, 2:163; Painter, *Mark's Gospel*, 150; LaVerdiere, *The Beginning*, 2:119–20), then the association of the Son of Man and the Suffering Servant is found only here in the New Testament. There are difficulties with this association. The Septuagint never renders the Hebrew ʾ*asham* with λύτρον, a Greek word otherwise widely used in Deutero-Isaiah (see Hooker, *Jesus and the Servant*, 74–79; idem, *St. Mark*, 248–49).

Alternative backgrounds have been suggested. Especially important is the suggestion of C. K. Barrett that the background of the Maccabean martyrs (see 1 Macc 2:50; 6:44; 4 Macc 17:21–22; *Mek.* 12:1) is closer to the saying than Isa 53:10–12; Barrett, "The Background of Mark 10.45," 1–18. It is also possible that behind the "ransom" saying lies the memory of a saying of Jesus that a man might risk his life for the many, further developed in the pre-Markan tradition to form v. 45b. For our purposes, a final decision on these critical issues is not called for. See the summary, reflecting much of the above, in Lindars, *Jesus Son of Man*, 76–84.

An energetic response to the above problems and a restatement of Isa 53 as background to 10:45 is found in Watts, *New Exodus*, 257–87.

It is sometimes claimed that the antithetic parallelism between v. 45a and v. 45b indicate a Semitic background (Jeremias, *Theology*, 14). But the parallelism could also be the result of careful writing in Greek. The perfect christological climax which 10:45 provides for Jesus' instruction of the disciples from 8:34–10:44 suggests strongly that, whatever the background and history of the saying, its present location originates in the theological and literary skills of a gifted storyteller. It is the christological motivation for all that Jesus has asked of the disciples. For this reason alone Taylor is correct in claiming, "This saying is one of the most important in the Gospels" (*St. Mark*, 444).

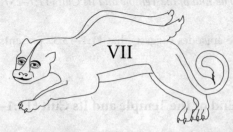

VII

ENDINGS IN JERUSALEM (MARK 11:1–13:37)

Throughout the Gospel of Mark, textual indicators have highlighted turning points in the narrative: the prologue (1:1–13; see v. 1), the three stages in the section which asks who Jesus might be (1:14–8:30; see 1:14–15; 3:7–12; 6:6b), and the beginning of the response to that question (8:31–15:47; see 8:31). This pattern continues as Jesus approaches Jerusalem (11:1) and enters the city (11:1–11). The remaining narrative (11:12–16:8) is located in Jerusalem and its environs. In general terms, one could say that 11:1–13:37 tells of what Jesus says and does in Jerusalem, with the textual markers of Jesus' approach to Jerusalem in 11:1, and his entry in 11:11 opening this section of the narrative. Mark 14:1–15:47 reports what others did to Jesus in Jerusalem, with the textual marker of the plot to kill Jesus in 14:1–2 opening that section. Useful as it is as a general indication, this distinction is far from precise. In 11:1–13:37 others interact with Jesus, and in 14:1–15:47 Jesus endures his passion. But Jesus' death and the events that lead into it provide some of the most important moments in Mark's narrative proclamation of Jesus as the Christ, the Son of God (see 1:1, 11; 9:7).

Jesus' words and deeds in 11:1–13:37 bring significant Jewish institutions to an end, and forecast the end of Jerusalem and the end of the world. "The arrangements of the material in 11:1–13:37 is such as to present Jesus' visit to the Temple as an historic occasion, the climactic events of his ministry in which he criticizes the Temple cultus, is challenged by the nations' leaders, confronts and bests in argument their chief representatives and finally pronounces the Temple's destruction."[1] These claims must be tested by a careful reading of the text of 11:1–13:37, which unfolds as follows:

11:1–25   Jesus enters Jerusalem and *brings to an end* Israel's cultic practices in the temple.

11:27–12:44   Jesus, teaching in the temple, debates with the leaders of Israel and reduces them to silence. In this way, he *brings to an end* religious leadership in Israel.

13:1–23   Jesus, coming out of and sitting opposite the temple, foretells the *end of Jerusalem*.

13:24–37   Jesus foretells the *end of the world* as we know it.

---

[1] W. R. Telford, *The Barren Temple and the Withered Tree: A Redaction-Critical Analysis of the Cursing of the Fig-Tree Pericope in Mark's Gospel and Its Relation to the Cleansing of the Temple Tradition* (JSNTSup 1; Sheffield: JSOT Press, 1980), 39. This is missed by those who, for various reasons, single out Mark 13 as a self-standing unit. See, for example, Lührmann, *Markusevangelium*, 185, 214. In a perceptive essay, E. S. Malbon ("The Jewish Leaders in the Gospel of Mark: A Literary Study of Markan Characterization," in *In the Company of Jesus: Characters in Mark's Gospel* [Louisville: Westminster John Knox, 2000], 131–65) warns against the stereotyping of the Jewish leaders. Scribes and Pharisees on the one hand, and elders, chief priests, and scribes on the other, play a negative role (see pp. 138–52). However, some emerge positively (the scribe of 12:34, Jairus, and Joseph of Arimathea; see pp. 157–65). Response to Jesus does not depend upon one's social or religious role. This study was originally published in *JBL* 108 (1989): 259–81.

This initial listing of the episodes suggests that 11:1–13:37 presents a series of *endings in Jerusalem.*[2]

The End of the Temple and Its Cult (11:1–25)

Two major events mark Jesus' arrival in Jerusalem: the entrance itself (11:11) and Jesus' presence in the temple (11:15–19). These events are circumscribed with Jesus' entry and exit from the city. From Bethany and Bethphage, Jesus prepares his entry (vv. 1–2), and after entering the temple and looking around at everything, he returns to Bethany (v. 11). He sets out from Bethany on the next day (v. 12) and, after his presence in the temple, in the evening withdraws from the city (v. 19). The following day, he journeys back to Jerusalem (v. 20). His final arrival in Jerusalem is noted in 11:27.[3] A number of encounters between Jesus and other characters take place across 11:27–12:44, but Jesus never leaves the temple. Thus, the movement to and from Jerusalem in 11:1–25 sets up an uneasy relationship. Tension is mounting in those first days of Jesus' presence in the city.[4] Observing Jesus' movement to and from Jerusalem in vv. 1–25, the description of the first days can be outlined as follows:

In 11:1–11: Jesus enters Jerusalem, with reference to Bethany in vv. 1 and 11. There is a tripartite structure to the episode:

[A] Jesus prepares to enter Jerusalem (11:1–7a).

[B] Jesus is welcomed as he approaches the city (11:7b–10).

[A'] Jesus enters the city, visits the temple, and departs (11:11).

A similar tripartite division is found in the report of Jesus' presence in the temple in 11:12–25: textual markers indicate Jesus' journey from Bethany in 11:12 and his exit from the city in 11:19. He is again on the move in 11:20 and does not arrive in Jerusalem until 11:27. This passage is designed to create a sandwich of Jesus' presence in the temple in

---

[2] On this, see W. Kelber, *The Kingdom in Mark: A New Place and a New Time* (Philadelphia: Fortress, 1974), 67–147; idem, *Mark's Story of Jesus* (Philadelphia: Fortress, 1979), 57–70. This overall theme is seldom recognized in classical commentary on the Gospel. See the very different approach to the passage, with a strong christological focus, addressing Jewish Christians in Rome in the midst of chaos, in S. H. Smith, "The Literary Structure of Mark 11:1–12:40," in *The Composition of Mark's Gospel: Selected Studies from Novum Testamentum* (ed. D. E. Orton; Brill's Readers in Biblical Studies 3; Leiden: Brill, 1999), 171–91. See, however, Lohmeyer, *Markus,* 227: "In the end this passage [11:1–13:37] has a great theme, during which on only one occasion the shadow of Jesus' forthcoming suffering is cast (12:1–12): it is the message of Jesus for or against the holy city."

[3] Most early witnesses across all text types do not have v. 26 ("But if you do not forgive, neither will your Father who is in heaven forgive your trespasses"). It is universally accepted that copyists inserted the passage, in imitation of Matt 6:15. See Metzger, *Textual Commentary,* 93; Telford, *The Barren Temple,* 50–54.

[4] On the Markan nature of these three days and the use of intercalation within them, see Telford, *The Barren Temple,* 42–49; Lührmann, *Markusevangelium,* 185–86. B. M. F. van Iersel (*Reading Mark* [Collegeville: The Liturgical Press, 1988], 144) makes the interesting suggestion that the coming and going reflects Jesus' awareness that his life is under threat. Staying in Jerusalem at night, with the gates closed, Jesus would be trapped in the city (see Acts 9:23–25). For Kelber (*Mark's Story,* 62 and elsewhere), Jesus' moving away from the city shows that Jerusalem and its temple are not "his place." He takes up his abode elsewhere, so that he can turn against the temple.

11:15–19 with his words to the fig tree in 11:12–14, and the discovery of the withered fig tree and Jesus' comment upon the events which have just taken place, in 11:20–25:

[A] The cursing of the fig tree (11:12–14)

  [B] Jesus in the temple (11:15–19)

[A′] The withered fig tree and Jesus' teaching (11:20–25)

Mark has constructed the report of these first days in Jerusalem with considerable care, highlighting Jesus' arrival in Jerusalem and especially his presence in the temple, with a narrative that brings established hopes and practices to an end.

Jesus' entry into Jerusalem and the temple (11:1–11)

The approach to Jerusalem is mentioned in association with two villages that lie in close proximity to the city, Bethphage and Bethany. Both villages lie on the way from Jericho (see 10:46) to Jerusalem, although one would arrive in Bethany before Bethphage. The geographical location of these villages, both on the slopes of the Mount of Olives, legitimates the position of Jesus and the disciples πρὸς τὸ ὄρος τῶν ἐλαιῶν (v. 1ab).[5] From that location, already within sight of the city, he sends two of the disciples into the village "opposite" (vv. 1c–2a). It is not clear which of the two villages (Bethphage or Bethany) is intended.[6] Jesus' words to the disciples set the theme for 11:2bc–6. This is the only place in the Gospel of Mark where Jesus is credited with foreknowledge other than the passion predictions and chapter 13.[7] The disciples are instructed, with considerable detail, on where they are to go (immediately entering the village), what they will find (a young ass upon which no one has ridden), and what they are to do (untie it and bring it to Jesus).[8] They are to say that the Lord (ὁ κύριος) has need of it. There is no need to read complicated speculations or an exalted Christology into this use of ὁ κύριος.[9] The strangeness of unknown disciples taking possession of a young ass, and their response to queries about their right to

---

[5] Those who wish to make every element in this story point to its messianic meaning, look to 2 Kgs 15:32; Ezek 11:23; Zech 14:4–5 and Josephus, *J.W.*, 2.261–263; *Ant.*, 20.167–172 for indications that in the first century the Messiah was expected to appear on the Mount of Olives. See, for example, Lohmeyer, *Markus*, 229. This claim is rejected by Cranfield, *St. Mark*, 348, who asserts that the sources used do not warrant the link between the Mount of Olives and the appearance of the Messiah.

[6] On the two villages, see Gnilka, *Markus*, 2:115–16. The subsequent importance of Bethany (see vv. 11, 12) suggests that Bethany may be intended, but this is not certain; see Taylor, *St. Mark*, 453. It is also possible that from Bethany the disciples are sent to the next village, Bethphage; Lane, *Mark*, 395. There is considerable textual disturbance in v. 1 generated by the elimination of Bethphage by some witnesses (Bezae and some Latin witnesses). The village is mentioned only here in Mark (and in the parallels, Matt 21:1; Luke 19:29).

[7] Unlike the Fourth Gospel, where it is one of the features of the Johannine Jesus.

[8] The noun πῶλος can refer to the colt or foal of a horse or of an ass; Taylor, *St. Mark*, 453–54. The influence of Zech 9:9 on commentators has led to the universal acceptance that it is an ass. An ass is more likely to be the case because in the villages of Palestine they were far more common domestic animals than the horse; Nineham, *St. Mark*, 295.

[9] It has been suggested that the expression indicates that the owner (one of the disciples?) of the ass needs it (Taylor, *St. Mark*, 455; Cranfield, *St. Mark*, 350), or that at this stage of the narrative Mark feels that the full christological "Lord," reflecting the LXX's use of κύριος for the divine name, can be introduced into the narrative (Anderson, *Mark*, 261). For a summary, see Hooker, *St. Mark*, 258–59. For Pesch (*Markusevangelium*, 2:180–81), Jesus is the real owner of the messianic animal.

do so as fulfilling the needs of "the Lord," indicate that they do what they are told.[10] They are obedient to the man they follow, referred to as "the master," and once this is made clear they are free to act as they were instructed. This oddness adds to the impression that something more than Jesus, the disciples, and taking possession of a young ass is involved in these preparations. They are further instructed on how they are to respond to any objections to their taking the colt (vv. 2bc–3). The description, in the third person, of what then takes place matches exactly what Jesus had said: they find the ass, untie it, resolve the objections by saying that their Lord has need of it, and bring the colt to Jesus (vv. 4–7a).

Jesus' foreknowledge, however, is not the point of the story. After early suggestions about Jesus' destiny (see 2:20; 3:6; 6:14–29; 8:11–12), he has now made it clear that he is going to Jerusalem to suffer, die, and rise again (see 8:31; 9:31; 10:32–34).[11] The instructions Jesus gives to his disciples, and the exact correspondence between his instructions and what happens, tells the reader that Jesus accepts his final crossing over from the Mount of Olives to the city of Jerusalem. But there is more to it. Jesus' awareness of the events that will bring him into the city points beyond Jesus to God. The passion predictions made it clear that Jesus was responding to God's design, and this thought is carried further in the correspondence between Jesus' orders and what, in fact, happens. Jesus' preparations for his entry into Jerusalem are a further step in the unfolding of God's plan.[12]

In 11:1–7a Jesus initiates everything that happens. In 11:7b others enter the action.[13] The disciples throw their garments on the colt (v. 7b), and "many" spread their garments and branches on the road. "Those who went before and those who followed" proclaim the coming of the one who comes in the name of the Lord, and the coming of the kingdom of David (vv. 9–10). The only action of Jesus in this passage is to sit upon the colt, fulfilling his earlier words of instruction, that the Lord had need of it (see vv. 3, 6).[14] The decorating of the colt with the disciples' garments, the laying of further garments to form a pathway for the man riding the decorated colt, and the spreading of leafy branches cut from the field, are gestures that welcome Jesus as a powerful figure.[15] They recall earlier solemn

---

[10] Lagrange (*Saint Marc*, 270–71) rightly points out that the promise to return the animal suggests that the disciples are speaking in the name of their master. That promise (αὐτὸν ἀποστέλλει πάλιν, v. 3c) is rendered variously in the manuscript tradition. For the variants and its inclusion in this form, see Taylor, *St. Mark*, 454; Metzger, *Textual Commentary*, 92. Hooker (*St. Mark*, 258) objects to the NEB's translation of "our Master." She claims that this may have been its meaning at an earlier stage of the tradition, but that more is involved in its present Markan context. Gnilka (*Markus*, 2:113–15) argues that the passage is made up of two traditions, vv. 1–7, associated with the finding of the ass, built on Old Testament motifs (especially Zech 9:9 and Gen 49:10–11), and already confessing Jesus as "Lord," and vv. 8–11, a messianic entry.

[11] The Markan literary and theological agenda must drive the interpretation here, not speculation about earlier visits, or a comparison with the Johannine location of the purification of the temple (John 2:13–25). Jesus' presence in Jerusalem has been delayed until now. On this, see F. J. Moloney, "The Fourth Gospel and the Jesus of History," *NTS* 46 (2000): 42–58.

[12] See A. E. Harvey, *Jesus and the Constraints of History* (London: Duckworth, 1982), 122–23. A close parallel to 11:2–7a is found in Jesus' sending two disciples to prepare for the final meal in 14:13–16. Both passages are used by Mark (perhaps based on a single pre-Markan tradition) to show Jesus' unfailing openness to God's design.

[13] This change in direction in v. 7b militates against Gnilka's reconstruction of two originally independent pre-Markan traditions, vv. 1–7, vv. 8–11 (*Markus*, 2:114–25).

[14] For Pesch (*Markusevangelium*, 2:182), even Jesus' action of sitting (καθίζω) on the ass is a royal gesture.

[15] The Markan setting for this event is several days before the celebration of the Passover (see 14:1). On the basis of the text, one could argue for five days (11:1, 19, 20 indicate three days, and

entries to take possession of Jerusalem. The recent freeing of Jerusalem by Simon Maccabeus (142 B.C.E.) comes to mind. "On the twenty-third day of the second month, in the one hundred and seventy-first year, the Jews entered it with praise and palm branches and with harps and cymbals and stringed instruments, and with hymns and songs, because a great enemy had been crushed and removed from Israel" (1 Macc 13:51).[16] Jesus' teaching on the purpose of his journey to Jerusalem (see 8:31; 9:31; 10:32–24) is ignored by both the disciples who decorate the ass (v. 7b), and the "many" who strew Jesus' path with garments and branches (v. 8).

The acclamation of Jesus in 11:9 makes explicit the failure of both the disciples and the crowds who prepared Jesus' way. Two groups have been involved in the welcome to this point: those who prepared the way of Jesus (v. 8), and the disciples (v. 7b). The former are called "those who went before," and the disciples are given their familiar title, "those who followed" (οἱ ἀκολουθοῦντες).[17] Both groups join in the acclamation: "Hosanna! Blessed is he who comes in the name of the Lord! Blessed is the kingdom of our Father David that is coming. Hosanna in the highest" (vv. 9–10). The initial cry of "Hosanna" has its roots in Ps 118:25, and is a petition, meaning "grant salvation." In its Markan context, however, it is an acclamation.[18] The remainder of 11:11 cites Ps 118:26a (see LXX Ps 117:26a). Given the context of the preparation of the colt and the strewing of the roadway, the reader suspects that an acclamation welcoming Jesus as the one who comes in the name of the Lord expresses a false messianic expectation. The suspicion is confirmed by the words of 11:10. The disciples and the crowd develop what is meant by the one who comes in the name of the Lord (v. 9) with a description of their expectation: he is bringing in the restoration of the kingdom of David (v. 10; see Amos 9:11; Isa 9:6–7).[19] Nothing could be further from the truth. Jesus is bringing in the kingdom of God, and he has made it clear that this kingdom will be established by means of rejection, death, and resurrection in the city of

---

14:1 says "after two days"). This chronology should not be pushed too hard, either for strict chronology or symbolism. See the careful remarks of Lane (*Mark*, 390–91). In contrast, Nineham (*St. Mark*, 289–90) sees an already established "Holy Week" behind Mark 11–16. LaVerdiere (*The Beginning*, 2:140–41) overinterprets the three days of 11:1–20 as "evoking the days of the passion and the resurrection." The use of the leafy branches in v. 8 and the proclamation of Ps 118 has led some to suggest that Jesus may have come to Jerusalem for the celebration of Tabernacles (T. W. Manson) or Dedication (F. C. Burkitt). But the context is clearly Passover; Ernst, *Markus*, 321. At the feasts of Tabernacles and Dedication the branches are not strewn on the road, but waved during the recitation of Ps 118:1 during a solemn procession from Siloam to the temple area. For details, see F. J. Moloney, *Signs and Shadows: Reading John 5–12* (Minneapolis: Fortress, 1996), 67–68.

16 See also Lohmeyer, *Markus*, 230 n. 8; Taylor, *St. Mark*, 456; Harvey, *Jesus*, 125–26. There is no direct link between Mark 11:7–10 and 1 Macc 13:51. That will be made in John 12:12–16; see Moloney, *Signs and Shadows*, 184–85. However, the same expectation—the freeing of Israel from a great enemy—is expressed, as throughout the earlier passages on the disciples' misunderstanding of Jesus' mission to Jerusalem (see 8:32–33; 9:32–34; 10:35–37, 41). It is this moment which is celebrated annually in the feast of Dedication (see 1 Macc 13:52). Hooker (*St. Mark*, 259) refers to the reception of Jehu by laying garments on the road in 1 Kgs 9:13, and helpfully suggests "it may be that that passage reflects a recognized custom." For a Roman parallel from Plutarch, see Lagrange, *Saint Marc*, 271.

17 The reference to two groups, the "many" from v. 8 and the unnamed disciples from v. 7, resumed in "those who went before and those who followed" (v. 9a) is seldom noticed by the commentators. See, however, Kelber, *Mark's Story*, 57–58. The careful distinction made in v. 9a is more than "a large crowd going in front of him and following behind him" (Painter, *Mark's Gospel*, 155).

18 Hooker, *St. Mark*, 259–60.

19 Harvey, *Jesus*, 121.

David.[20] His command to bring an ass, rather than a horse (see v. 2), had set the scene for a humble entry, but it has been transformed by the disciples and the many who have their own understanding of who Jesus is, and what he will do in Jerusalem.[21] The hopes of those who welcome him in triumph, as the one who is coming in the name of the Lord to bring in the kingdom of David, have missed the point. The praise to God (see Ps 148:1) which closes the acclamation is not enough to correct the false messianic expectation. The disciples have again failed to accept that Jesus has come to Jerusalem as the Son of Man who will suffer, die, and be vindicated in the resurrection (8:31; 9:32; 10:32–34).[22] "As far as the followers are concerned, Jesus enters Jerusalem in order to establish the Kingdom in power. That is cause for celebration. As far as Jesus is concerned, he enters into suffering and death. He will not be King until he is nailed to the cross."[23]

For Mark, however, the acclamation of the messianic Son of David takes place outside Jerusalem.[24] The entry is held back until 11:11, and even here it is mentioned only passingly. The storyteller's main concern is to report Jesus' entry into the temple. Jesus is the only active figure in 11:11. After the crowd and the acclamation of 11:7b–10, there is an ominous silence and even a note of threat as Jesus, alone, enters Jerusalem and goes into the temple. No word is spoken as Jesus looks around at everything that can be seen

---

[20] Lührmann (*Markusevangelium,* 189) makes an interesting distinction. He suggests that the acclamation is half right: he is bringing in the kingdom, but not the kingdom of David. He correctly comments, " 'King of Israel,' like 'Son of David,' does not belong to authentic Markan Christology." See also Ernst, *Markus,* 322.

[21] It remains true that Jesus' gesture of riding into Jerusalem is irregular. Pilgrims normally walked into the city. Later reflection on this scene will make use of the prophecy of Zech 9:9 to characterize Jesus' entry as humble. However, there is no trace of Zech 9 in the Markan episode, and we should not speculate that perhaps Mark had it in mind as Schweizer (*Mark,* 227), Harvey (*Jesus,* 121–22), and Hooker (*St. Mark,* 257) also insist. Jesus' entry on an ass is probably part of the pre-Markan tradition, exploited to create a misunderstood episode of humble entry on an ass rather than a warhorse; see Taylor, *St. Mark,* 452. Most commentators, however, find the use of πῶλος (in both Mark 11:2, 4, 7 and Zech 9:9) as enough to develop a formative influence of the Zechariah text upon the Markan tradition; see, for example, Lohmeyer, *Markus,* 229. It is impossible to be sure about a pre-Markan stage of the narrative. For example, Gnilka's reconstruction (*Markus,* 2:116–17) of a pre-Markan passage, on the basis of Zech 9:9 and Gen 49:10–11, is pure speculation. Pesch (*Markusevangelium,* 2:176–78) regards the whole episode as from the pre-Markan passion source. As with most who read the passage in a messianic sense, Grundmann (*Markus,* 224–26) uses Zech 9:9, Gen 49:10–11, and late rabbinic material to support his messianic interpretation of the passage. See also Lane, *Mark,* 395–96; Pesch, *Markusevangelium,* 2:178–79. For a survey of earlier scholars, see Taylor, *St. Mark,* 451.

[22] The above reading of Mark 11:1–11 is at variance with the majority of interpreters who read the passage as a correct, if veiled, confession of Jesus' messianic status; Lagrange, *Saint Marc,* 273–74; Nineham, *St. Mark,* 291–94, stressing, however, the ambiguity of the passage; Hooker, *St. Mark,* 259–60; Gnilka, *Markus* 2:120, with reference back to Bartimaeus's confession of Jesus as the Son of David (10:47–48) as immediate preparation for this messianic acclamation; Lohmeyer, *Markus,* 232–33, strongly aware of the ambiguity of the passage; LaVerdiere, *The Beginning,* 2:142–50, who makes everything, "the Lord," the ass (via Zech 9:9), the clothing, the branches on the road, and the acclamation, correct recognition of Jesus' messianic status; Lane, *Mark,* 397–98; Schweizer, *Mark,* 229, but stressing the lack of understanding; R. E. Watts, *Isaiah's New Exodus and Mark* (WUNT 2. Reihe 88; Tübingen: J. C. B. Mohr [Paul Siebeck], 1997), 296–310.

[23] Kelber, *Mark's Story,* 58. See also idem, *The Kingdom,* 92–97. For a different reading, see F. Matera (*The Kingship of Jesus: Composition and Theology in Mark 15* [SBLDS 66; Chico: Scholars Press, 1982], 70–74), who argues that there is a deliberate ambiguity in Jesus' entry. At one level Mark wishes to present Jesus as a royal figure, but the Markan readership is aware that his royalty will be exercised on the cross.

[24] Schweizer (*Mark,* 227) suggests that the entry may have taken place in Bethany, and that Jesus went on to Jerusalem and the temple the following day.

there.[25] Silence falls upon the acclamations as Jesus surveys the temple. At least two responses are generated by 11:11. The silence and the disappearance of the crowd and of the acclamations all indicate that Jesus does not accept what has been said and done.[26] Nothing is explicit, but the reader is sufficiently aware of the reasons for his first and only visit to Jerusalem to understand that this lonely entry into the city and the temple implies Jesus' rejection of the acclaim just offered him. Second, a tension is generated in the narrative. Why does Jesus go directly to the temple? Why does he look around at everything? The text records no judgment upon what he sees. He leaves the city and retires to the neighboring village of Bethany with his disciples.

Jesus' departure marks the end of the first episode in Jerusalem. It has demonstrated Jesus' acceptance of God's agenda for his presence in Jerusalem (vv. 1–7a), but it has also shown the failure of the disciples and many others to do so (vv. 7b–10). It closes, ominously, with Jesus' entry into Jerusalem and his survey of the temple (v. 11). He will return there in the next episode (vv. 12–25).

> Jesus' first entry into Jerusalem is aimed at the temple (11:11). The temple, not the city as such, is of interest to him. . . . The Twelve are made to witness his solitary inspection of the temple. What they observe is hardly a triumphal entry. Jesus is neither recognized in the streets of Jerusalem nor installed in the temple as the Davidic Messiah. . . . The temple will not be "his place," let alone the site of universal salvation.[27]

The end of temple worship (11:12–25)

[A] *The cursing of the fig tree (11:12–14)*

A journey from Bethany the next day separates the episodes which follow (11:12–19) from those surrounding Jesus' entry into Jerusalem (11:1–11). Another morning journey, apparently along the same route, will begin in 11:20. However, as we have already noted, 11:12–14 and 11:20–26 act as a frame around the account of Jesus' presence in the temple (11:15–19). In 11:12–14 a fig tree is cursed, and in 11:20–26 the consequences of that curse, and the significance of the whole episode, are reported.[28] The scene in the temple (11:15–19) is "sandwiched" between the cursing of the fig tree on one morning, and its being found withered on the next.

The reader is told that Jesus was hungry (11:12c) and saw a fig tree in leaf in the distance. He goes to the tree to find some fruit to assuage his hunger, but finds only leaves,[29] for it was not the time for figs. Jesus finds the external signs of good health, but no fruit.

---

[25] See Taylor, *St. Mark,* 457–58.

[26] Commentators who read 11:1–11 as Jesus' messianic entry into Jerusalem devote little attention to the enigmatic v. 11. Hooker (*St. Mark,* 260), for example, describes it as "something of an anticlimax," and Lane (*Mark,* 398) claims that it is "the quiet before the storm." For Taylor (*St. Mark,* 458), it is a sign of the basic historicity of the narrative: "Presumably the crowds have melted away." Nineham (*St. Mark,* 294) suggests that v. 11 "seems to have been composed by St. Mark in the interests of his time-scheme." Grundmann (*Markus,* 232) catches the mood well: "It makes the remarkable animosity between Jesus and Jerusalem." See also Lohmeyer, *Markus,* 252.

[27] Kelber, *Mark's Story,* 58–59.

[28] For a history of the interpretation of 11:12–25, see Telford, *The Barren Temple,* 1–38.

[29] Some have complained that Jesus' hunger is strange, as he is staying with friends in Bethany, and he has just set out for the day. How could he already be hungry? See, for example, Grundmann, *Markus,* 228. Mark does not concern himself with such issues, as he uses Jesus' hunger to "prepare the way for the story" (Taylor, *St. Mark,* 459). For C. D. Marshall (*Faith as a Theme in Mark's Narrative* [SNTSMS 64; Cambridge: Cambridge University Press, 1989], 160), the hunger is a

The comment from the narrator, explaining why there were only leaves and no fruit, makes Jesus' subsequent words extremely harsh. Jesus condemns the tree to fruitlessness: "May no one ever eat fruit from you again." The condemnation of the fruitless tree at a time of the year when there could not have been fruit seems unreasonable.[30] The word for "time" (καιρός) can mean "season of the year,"[31] but is also used regularly in both the Septuagint and the New Testament to speak of an opportune moment, and to speak theologically of the moment opportune for God's action.[32] It is the term used in Jesus' initial announcement: "The time is fulfilled, and the kingdom is at hand" (1:15). The reader is left wondering about this strange condemnation of a fruit tree which has all the signs of life, but no fruit, because this was not its καιρός. The cursing of the fig tree may be a symbolic condemnation of Israel (see Hos 9:10, 16–17; Mic 4:4; 7:1; Jer 8:13; 24:1–10; 29:17; Zech 3:10), but more of the story is required before the reader can be sure.[33] The episode comes to an end with a further remark from the narrator, important for the formation of the sandwich construction around Jesus' presence in the temple (vv. 15–19). The disciples heard Jesus' punishing words against the fig tree (v. 14b), and they will recall it as they pass by the tree on the following day (vv. 20–21).

[B] *Jesus ends the cultic activity of the temple (11:15–19)*

Jesus comes to Jerusalem and enters the temple, as he did on his first arrival (v. 15ab; see v. 11a). Earlier he gazed at everything that was to be seen there (v. 11b). An ominous silence surrounded his first arrival, but on this occasion he moves into action. He begins to drive out those who sold and bought, he overturns the tables of the money-changers and the stools of the sellers of pigeons (v. 15bcd).[34] This action strikes at functionaries essential to the temple cult. No other location other than the temple itself (v. 15) is given for this ac-

---

symbol of Jesus' demand for faith, while LaVerdiere (*The Beginning*, 2:151) suggests that he is hungry for the messianic kingdom of God.

[30] Lohmeyer (*Markus*, 234) tries to overcome the harshness of Jesus' words by suggesting that the reference to the time of the year might be a gloss. See also Anderson, *Mark*, 265. LaVerdiere (*The Beginning*, 2:153) attempts to deflect the problem by regarding the curse as directed at the disciples.

[31] See BDAG, 497–99, esp. paras. 2 and 3.

[32] Kelber (*Mark's Story*, 60) asserts: "It is not a botanical term indicating the season for figs but a religious term denoting the time of the Kingdom of God." Gnilka (*Markus*, 2:124) comments on attempts to calculate what season of the year is indicated: "These botanical minutiae hardly reflect his interest."

[33] Gnilka (*Markus*, 2:125), in the light of the prophetic use of the fig tree to refer to Israel, suggests that already in vv. 12–14 the message of Israel's failure to respond to the eschatological καιρός is present. See also Marshall, *Faith as a Theme*, 160–61. Many have rightly suggested that the story is a "legendary concretising" (Anderson, *Mark*, 263) of the parable in Luke 13:6–9, where the fig tree is clearly an image for Israel. Some commentators (e.g., Taylor, *St. Mark*, 458–60), defending the basic historicity of the account, regard the miracle as an illustration of the divine power of Jesus. This misses the point of the function of the fig tree episodes as a frame around Jesus' presence in the temple. For many, especially those whose concern is to defend the historicity of the narrative, this passage, the only miracle of destruction worked by Jesus, "bristles with difficulties" (Cranfield, *St. Mark*, 354). These difficulties are lessened when the literary, metaphorical, and symbolic elements of vv. 12–25 are given their full importance. Pesch (*Markusevangelium*, 2:189–202) regards vv. 11–21 as entirely from the pre-Markan passion story. He regards the relationship between the destruction of the fig tree and the end of the temple as unclear and questionable. The passage is to be understood in terms of the oncoming passion, not the temple.

[34] The expression "he began to drive out" (ἤρξατο ἐκβάλλειν), although a common construction in the Gospel of Mark (ἤρξατο + infinitive), creates the impression that Jesus' activity went on for some time.

tion. We are accustomed to supplying the entrance gate, or the open court of the Gentiles.[35] But that is not in the text. Jesus enters the temple, and within this sacred site of Israel the following actions and words take place. Money-changers were present at the temple to ensure that the coinage used to pay the half-shekel temple tax levied on Jews was acceptable within the temple precincts. Coins carrying human effigies were changed into Tyrian coinage.[36] In this way the bearer's money was safe and available for the half-shekel tax, but so was the purity of the temple area. Essential to the cultic life of the temple were the sacrifices and offerings, great and small, that the faithful Jew made while there. This necessarily generated a buying and selling of goods which could be offered and sacrificed, including pigeons, the offering of the poorest and humblest (see Lev 12:8; 14:22; 15:14, 29).[37] Jesus' actions stop all supply of material for the cultic practices of the temple, and make it impossible for people to change their coins to enter the precincts of the temple without impurity.

The brief description (v. 16) of Jesus' further action in the temple provides the key to the interpretation of his presence. Jesus has taken control of everything that goes on in the temple. He decides what will be allowed or not allowed there. He will not allow ἵνα τις διενέγκῃ σκεῦος διὰ τοῦ ἱεροῦ (v. 16). The word σκεῦος has many possible meanings. It can be a general indication of an object used for any purpose at all, thus a "thing," widely used in English translations (e.g., "he would not allow anyone to carry anything through the Temple"; RSV). It also has the meaning of a vessel, or an instrument, and on the basis of some difficult New Testament texts (see 1 Thess 4:4) has come to be interpreted as a "chosen vessel," one's own body, or the body of one's wife.[38] In 11:16 the word, set within the context of the temple cult, can be given its basic meaning of a vessel or an implement, with the nuance, "all that belongs to a complete outfit."[39] Here (11:16) the expression refers to the vessels and instruments that were used in the temple as part of its traditional cultic practices. Jesus will not allow the use of any of the vessels or implements that form part of the day-to-day practices of the temple. The movement of this variety of vessels and implements comes to a halt.[40] On his second day in Jerusalem, the Markan Jesus brings to an end practices essential for the purity of the temple area (v. 15bc) and trades essential for the provision of even the simplest victims for sacrifice (v. 15d). He prohibits the use of all vessels and implements necessary for sacrifices and offerings (v. 16).[41] The effect of Jesus'

---

[35] See, for example, Taylor, *St. Mark,* 462; Cranfield, *St. Mark,* 357; Hooker, *St. Mark,* 267; Gnilka, *Markus,* 2:128. They locate the incident in the Court of the Gentiles.

[36] See I. Abrahams, *Studies in Pharisaism and the Gospels* (First Series; Cambridge: Cambridge University Press, 1917), 82–89; Hooker, *St. Mark,* 267–68.

[37] On both the money-changing and the animals, see E. P. Sanders, *Jesus and Judaism* (Philadelphia: Fortress, 1985), 63–65. As in all commercial activity, corruption was possible, and there was already a strain within pre-Christian Judaism that attacked such corruption. For a survey, see Hooker, *St. Mark,* 263–64.

[38] On these meanings, see the discussion in BDAG, 927–28, s.v. σκεῦος.

[39] LSJ, 1607, s.v. σκεῦος.

[40] The usual explanation for v. 16 is that Jesus stops people taking short cuts through the temple area, a practice prohibited in *m. Ber.* 9:5. See, for example, Lagrange, *Saint Marc,* 277; Grundmann, *Markus,* 231; Taylor, *St. Mark,* 463; Cranfield, *St. Mark,* 358; Hooker, *St. Mark,* 268. This explanation trivializes the dominance Jesus here asserts over the temple and its cult. Nineham (*St. Mark,* 304) comments, "Our Lord here seems to be simply enforcing a recognized rule." This is hardly right, unless the scene is an authentic memory which has somehow been preserved amid all the symbolism and metaphor of vv. 12–25.

[41] Lührmann, *Markusevangelium,* 193. As Kelber (*Kingdom,* 101 n. 43) points out, over one-third of the references to σκεῦος in the LXX refer to sacred cult objects of the tabernacles, altar, or

actions, described in 11:15–16, is that all activity in the cultic center of Israel comes to a stop! The storyteller succinctly states that Jesus takes command of the temple area, deciding what is allowed and not allowed. In this symbolic narrative, Jesus is the master of the temple. To suggest that the historical Jesus was able to drive out all who served temple practice (v. 15), and then to determine what was allowed to happen or not happen within the entire temple area, strains all imagination.[42] But the Markan message is clear. On his first full day in Jerusalem, Jesus brings to an end the cultic activity of the Jewish temple.[43]

The teaching which follows, in which Jesus explains his actions, is solemnly introduced (ἐδίδασκεν καὶ ἔλεγεν αὐτοῖς, v. 17a) and particularly eloquent to the Markan readers and listeners.[44] As with the actions of Jesus, the larger literary and theological design determines the meaning of Jesus' words. Citing LXX Isa 56:7, Jesus assumes the authority of YHWH, speaking in the first person in the Psalm. The House of God, symbol-

---

temple. Ernst (*Markus*, 329) doubts the connection with the sacred vessels. He regards Jesus' actions as putting into question the Jewish temple cult. Jesus' actions are more radical than "putting into question."

[42] Grundmann, *Markus*, 230. As Sanders (*Jesus and Judaism*, 70) remarks: "Any real effort to stop the trade necessary to the temple service would have required an army, and there is no evidence of a substantial martial conflict." See also Lohmeyer, *Markus*, 237; M. Hengel, *Was Jesus a Revolutionist?* (Philadelphia: Fortress, 1971), 16–17. Taylor's attempt to overcome this difficulty is unconvincing (*St. Mark*, 463). However, the "historicity" of the incident is widely accepted. See, for example, Lane, *Mark*, 403–5; Gnilka, *Markus*, 2:130–31. It appears to me that this question should be broadened. Was Jesus' presence in Jerusalem and the temple a problem *on only one occasion* (thus accepting the Markan scheme)? Perhaps Mark 11:15–19 is a blend of pre-Markan and Markan traditions which reflect Jesus' regular presence in Jerusalem and its temple, as in the Fourth Gospel. See the following note.

[43] Kelber, *Kingdom*, 97–102. Kelber (*Mark's Story*, 60) observes: "Jesus' two actions are tantamount to the shutting down of the business and the religious functions of the temple." Kelber's assessment of "endings" in Jerusalem is correct. However, his major case—that Jerusalem is being condemned in favor of Galilee as the "place" of the kingdom (see *Kingdom*, 105–7), following the Lohmeyer-Marxsen geographical reading of Mark—goes beyond the evidence. For a more balanced assessment, see Marshall, *Faith as a Theme*, 161, and Gnilka, *Markus*, 2:129. The terse indications of vv. 15–16 are highly charged symbolic actions. What Jesus actually did in the temple and when he did it is, I believe, beyond our scientific control. A great deal of time and effort has been devoted to this question, especially in the light of Sanders (*Jesus and Judaism*, 61–76). Sanders suggests that Jesus' actions are a symbol of the temple's future destruction, and not a cleansing. Among several responses to this suggestion, see C. A. Evans, "Jesus' Action in the Temple: Cleansing or Portent of Destruction?" *CBQ* 51 (1989): 237–70, and M. D. Hooker, "Traditions about the Temple in the Sayings of Jesus," *BJRL* 70 (1988): 7–19, summarized in *St. Mark*, 263–66. I suspect that the Markan location of the temple scene, shortly before the passion, is a Markan construction, based on the memory of Jesus' troublesome presence in Jerusalem and especially in the temple, *on the numerous occasions* that he was in Jerusalem. In this respect, I suggest that the Johannine placing of the temple episode at the beginning of Jesus' ministry (see John 2:13–25) better reflects the fact that Jesus was a nuisance to the established practices *whenever he was in Jerusalem and in the temple.* See the interesting note in Taylor (*St. Mark*, 461–62), showing the difficulties inherent in deciding for either the Markan or the Johannine date. See also Moloney, "The Fourth Gospel," 52–57. Historically, his actions may have been a prophetic gesture of cleansing the temple, as Evans and Hooker argue, but for Mark, Jesus symbolically brings to a close all temple practice. For Painter (*Mark's Gospel*, 158), Jesus objects to the practices in the temple because they exclude Gentiles. For an earlier suggestion along these lines, see R. H. Lightfoot, *The Gospel Message of St. Mark* (Oxford: Clarendon, 1950), 60–63. Nineham objects to this thesis (*St. Mark*, 302). "The entire story must be interpreted symbolically whether or not it is historical" (Schweizer, *Mark*, 230).

[44] On the historical impossibility of such teaching in the midst of the chaos of vv. 14–17, see Anderson, *Mark*, 266.

ized by the temple, does not belong to the leaders of Israel. Metaphorical and symbolic language continues as Jesus insists that the temple is "my house." The scripture claiming that God's house, now Jesus' house, will become a house of prayer for all the nations must be fulfilled (v. 17b). The abominations now visible in the temple of Jerusalem must be transformed. Jesus addresses an unspecified audience (ὑμεῖς) and accuses them of having made God's temple into a σπήλαιον λῃστῶν (v. 17c).[45] The audience identifies itself in 11:18a: καὶ ἤκουσαν οἱ ἀρχιερεῖς καὶ οἱ γραμματεῖς. But the reference to the "den of thieves" must not simply be read as an attack of Jesus upon the Jewish leadership *in the world of the story.* It must be read at two levels, as it has an association with *the world of the readers.*[46]

At one level Mark records the memory of the historical Jesus' dissatisfaction with the abuses of the temple in his time. There may have been one incident in the temple, or there may have been several, of different intensity.[47] This memory, probably already existing as a pre-Markan tradition,[48] is reported in 11:15–19. However, the words that record his accusation must be linked with the violence in the temple area which marked the final period of the Jewish War in 70 C.E. The term here used for "robbers" (λῃστής) is favored by Josephus to describe (always negatively) the Zealots, whom he blamed for the disasters that fell upon Israel and Jerusalem.[49] It is not ordinarily used for those involved in sharp business practices. In the final days of the war, as the Roman armies encircled the city of Jerusalem and broke through the walls, the leaders of the revolt drew back into the temple area and used it as a fortress.[50] These events, fresh in the minds of the readers of the Gospel of Mark (who are hearing of wars and rumors of wars: 13:7), provide contemporary meaning to Jesus' accusation. In the immediate postwar period, Mark's readers and listeners are aware that the temple, reduced to a σπήλαιον λῃστῶν by the leaders of Israel in revolt, has been destroyed by the Roman armies.[51] There is need for a new way for Israel and all the nations to turn to God in prayer. Symbolically, however, before the physical

---

[45] The expression "den of robbers" is rendered as in LXX Jer 7:11. This does not exclude the possibility of a Markan reading of the expression in terms of the Jewish revolt (see below).

[46] J. L. Martyn (*History and Theology in the Fourth Gospel* [rev. and enlarged; Nashville: Abingdon, 1979], 129–51) identified a Johannine technique of presenting the Jesus story as a "two-level drama." However, this literary technique should be applied to all four Gospels.

[47] On the variety of possible causes for Jesus' concern and action against practices in the temple which made it a den of robbers, see Grundmann, *Markus*, 232.

[48] Gnilka, *Markus*, 2:127–28.

[49] See M. Hengel, *The Zealots: Investigations into the Jewish Freedom Movement in the Period from Herod I to 70 A.D.* (Edinburgh: T&T Clark, 1989), 41–46. Hengel remarks: "Josephus used the word λῃσταί to brand the Zealots as lawless rebels and criminals in the Roman sense and as men who in the end received the punishment they deserved." See also K. H. Rengstorf, "λῃστής," *TDNT* 4:257–62.

[50] Josephus, *J.W.* 6.68–80. This section of *Jewish War* is written with considerable passion and little objectivity. At one point, refugees from the temple area appeal to those inside to save the nation by surrendering the temple to the (noble) Romans. Josephus describes the response from inside the temple: "These appeals only excited fiercer opposition, and retorting by heaping abuse on the deserters, they ranged their quick-firers, catapults, and *ballistae* above the city gates, so that the surrounding temple-court from the multitude of dead resembled a common burial ground and the temple itself a fortress" (*J.W.* 6.121).

[51] G. W. Buchanan, "Mark 11:15–19: Brigands in the Temple," *HUCA* 30 (1959): 169–77; C. K. Barrett, "The House of Prayer and the Den of Thieves," in *Jesus und Paulus: Festschrift für Werner Georg Kümmel zum 70. Geburtstag* (ed. E. Ellis and E. Grässer; Göttingen: Vandenhoeck & Ruprecht, 1975), 13–20; Lührmann, *Markusevangelium*, 193.

destruction of the temple, Jesus has already brought its practices to a close (vv. 15–16), and indicated to the Jewish leadership that their administration of God's house had frustrated its purpose (v. 17). In Jesus' later discussion with the disciples he will tell them how the prophecy of Isa 56:7 will be fulfilled (see vv. 22–25). Despite the attempts of Israel to frustrate God's designs, Jesus' house will become a house of prayer for all the nations. A memory from the story of Jesus speaks eloquently to the experience of the Christian community.

The leaders of Israel, hearing Jesus' words, renew the earlier decision of the Pharisees and the Herodians to plan the death of Jesus (11:18a; see 3:6). Their plan lies dormant for the moment, due to the extreme wonder and amazement of the crowds at Jesus' teaching (11:18b).[52] It will be hatched in due course as the plot of the chief priests and the scribes, still aware that they must work carefully to avoid a revolt among the people, draws in Judas (14:1–2, 10–11). As the passion of Jesus unfolds, they manage to avoid the opinion of the people. Paradoxically, as the reader (and the disciples!) already know from the passion predictions (8:31; 9:31; 10:33–34), the success of their plan to destroy Jesus leads to his resurrection. The reader, the disciples, and the leaders of the Jews will soon be told that the rejected cornerstone will become the foundation of a new temple (see 12:10–11; 14:57–58).[53] The house of Jesus—not the temple of Jerusalem, now destroyed—will provide access to God for all the nations. The second day of Jesus' presence closes as he and the disciples leave the city in the evening.[54] Jesus has brought worship in the Jewish temple to an end, and has promised that his house would be a house of prayer for all the nations (v. 19; see v. 17b).

[A'] The withered fig tree, and a new way to God (11:20–25)

The following day Jesus and the disciples return to Jerusalem (see v. 27), passing the fig tree on their way. They all see the fig tree, now withered away to its roots. It is completely destroyed (11:20). Jesus' words have come true; no one will eat of the fruit of this tree (11:14a). The reader is aware of a reprise. The second part of the sandwich construction is under way. The link with the earlier passage continues as Peter, in the name of all the disciples, who heard what Jesus had said on the previous day, remembers and speaks (11:21a; cf. 11:14b). Addressing Jesus as "rabbi," he points out that the curse has had its effect (11:21b). The fig tree is an obvious symbol of Israel and its temple (see Hos 9:10, 16–17; Mic 4:4; 7:1; Jer 8:13; 24:1–10; 29:17; Joel 1:7, 12; Zech 14; Ezek 17; 47).[55] Traditional access to God through Israel's temple cult and worship had external splendor (see 11:13 and 11:17). But Mark's story of Jesus is now nearing its end. He has been in Israel, preaching and demonstrating the advent of the kingdom of God (see 1:14–15). He has met

---

[52] The amazement of the crowd (ὁ ὄχλος ἐξεπλήσσετο) over Jesus' teaching (ἐπὶ τῇ διδαχῇ αὐτοῦ) repeats 1:22, leading Taylor (*St. Mark,* 465) to suggest that it shows that Jesus made the same impression in Jerusalem as he did in Galilee.

[53] Gnilka, *Markus,* 2:129–30.

[54] Reading the plural ἐξεπορεύοντο in v. 19, rather than the strongly supported (e.g., Sinaiticus, Ephraim Rescript, Bezae, Koridethi) singular ἐξεπορεύετο. It is difficult to be certain, as v. 18 makes the plural in v. 19 the *lectio difficilior,* however it may have been introduced to create a smooth passage to the plural of v. 20. The weight of the external evidence (e.g., Alexandrinus, Vaticanus, Paris, Freer Gospels) tips the balance in support of the plural (Metzger, *Textual Commentary,* 92). For a contrary position, see Taylor, *St. Mark,* 465; Cranfield, *St. Mark,* 359.

[55] See Gnilka, *Markus,* 2:124 and especially Telford, *The Barren Temple,* 128–63. Telford draws upon later Jewish material that further supports this association (pp. 176–204).

only resistance and rejection (see 2:1–3:6; 3:20–35; 6:1–6a, 14–29; 7:1–23; 8:11–13; 10:2). The time of Jesus among them, the καιρός, the time of his bringing the kingdom of God to them, is drawing to an end. *Never has Israel shown receptivity to Jesus' person and words. The offer of the kingdom has been steadily rejected.* Even his chosen disciples are struggling to comprehend and accept all it involves. Jesus has begun a series of encounters with Israel's traditional ways to God, bringing them to an end. The fig tree, a symbol of Israel and its temple, which has rejected the possibility of Jesus' presence as the coming of the kingdom (see 1:14–15), will thus be forever unfruitful. The coming of Jesus is not the καιρός of Israel and its temple.[56] Jesus' deeds in 11:15–16 symbolically brought to an end the cultic practices of the Jerusalem temple. As the Markan community was aware, the house of God had become a den of thieves, and has been destroyed.

Jesus does not explain the link between the withered fig tree and the now defunct temple. He moves directly to explain how the prophecy of Isa 56:7, cited in 11:17, will be fulfilled. No longer does one look to a defunct temple and cult, destroyed both symbolically by Jesus' deeds and concretely by the actions of the Romans, but to faith (vv. 22–23), prayer (v. 24), and forgiveness (v. 25). Jesus' house will be a house of prayer for the nations (see v. 17b). A radical commitment to faith in God is called for (v. 22).[57] The hyperbolic example of the workings of such faith indicates its unconditional and profoundly internal nature. It also hints that the wonder of the fig tree's withering is the result of Jesus' faith in God.[58] Believers are to ask the impossible: a mountain is to be taken up and cast into the sea, already symbolized in Jesus' bringing to an end the cult on the temple mount.[59] Jesus' earlier words on the fundamental importance of what comes out of a person, rather than what goes in, also uttered within a context of conflict with Israel (see 7:14–15, 18–23), come to mind. The impossible becomes possible for the one who does not doubt in his heart, but believes what he says (v. 23). The issue is not whether mountains move, but

---

56 Telford, *The Barren Temple*, 237–38; Gnilka, *Markus*, 2:134. For Lührmann (*Markusevangelium*, 191), the question of the time of the year and the fruitfulness of the tree is not the issue. The reader must be made aware that what Jesus says will happen, does happen.

57 Some important witnesses (e.g., Sinaiticus, Bezae, Koridethi) make Jesus' words conditional, "If you have faith in God." This reading, however, is probably the result of an assimilation to Luke 17:6; Matt 21:21. See Marshall, *Faith as a Theme*, 164–65.

58 On the history of the tradition, and the Markan literary and theological activity in linking vv. 22–25 to the cursing of the fig tree, see Telford, *The Barren Temple*, 49–59. The expression πίστις θεοῦ is rare in the New Testament (cf. Rom 3:3; 1 Thess 1:8; Heb 6:1; John 14:1). Here the genitive is objective, i.e., "faith in God"; Gnilka, *Markus*, 2:134. Nowhere else in the Gospels are the disciples commanded to believe in God. For an attempt to include a subjective dimension in this faith (a faith that equals the faith of God), see LaVerdiere, *The Beginning*, 2:160–61.

59 Most suggest that the following sayings were collected from a variety of sources on the basis of catchwords: believe, pray. See, for example, Lohmeyer, *Markus*, 238–39; Taylor, *St. Mark*, 465; Nineham, *St. Mark*, 300; Grundmann, *Markus*, 233; Gnilka, *Markus*, 2:133; Painter, *Mark's Gospel*, 160. For Pesch (*Markusevangelium*, 2:202–8), the collection is a Markan insertion into the pre-Markan passion narrative as instruction of the disciples on the new temple. It is sometimes suggested (e.g., Grundmann, *Markus*, 234; Hooker, *St. Mark*, 269–70) that "this mountain" may refer to the temple mount (or the Mount of Olives), and thus an extension of the destruction of the fig tree as an action against the temple. An association with the temple mount is part of the Markan message. It was a traditional saying (see Matt 17:20; Luke 17:6; 1 Cor 13:2; *Gos. Thom.* 48, 106), elaborated and inserted into this context by Mark to make this point. For detailed support of this conclusion, see Telford, *The Barren Temple*, 95–119. See also Marshall, *Faith as a Theme*, 165–69; Watts, *New Exodus*, 332–37. For long-standing links between moving mountains and faith, see S. E. Dowd, *Prayer, Power and the Problem of Suffering: Mark 11:22–25 in the Context of Markan Theology* (SBLDS 105; Atlanta: Scholars Press, 1988), 69–94.

Jesus' insistence that prayers coming from the unquestioning and believing heart will, unlike the now defunct temple, bear fruit. Such teaching shifts naturally into the theme of
prayer, catching up, initially, what was said in 11:23 about faith. There the issue was asking
with unconditional faith, while in 11:24 Jesus stresses the actions of a believing supplicant.
Union with God, established by faith in God (v. 22), leads the believer into a situation
where, in faith, whatever is asked for is already granted (v. 24). None of this can be proved,
or fixed into a formula or a cult.[60] It demands an unconditional openness to the ways of
God, and establishes a oneness between the praying believer, and the God who grants the
request.[61] Jesus' instruction on prayer, however, is not only about the relationship between
the believer and God. Matching the articulation of this teaching in Q (see Matt 6:12,
14–15; Luke 11:4),[62] Jesus insists that the relationship between the believer and God will be
fruitless unless there is forgiveness between the believer and the believer's neighbor. The
first action in prayer is to forgive, so that the Father in heaven, father of both the one praying and the one forgiven, can forgive the sins of the one praying (v. 25).[63] One cannot pray
to God, the Father in heaven, with hate in one's heart.[64]

The way to God expressed in the cultic practices of the Jerusalem temple has been
brought to an end (vv. 13–14, 15–16, 20–21). There is another way to God: a way of life
marked by faith, prayer, and forgiveness (vv. 20–25).[65] Within the house of Jesus one finds
a house of prayer for all the nations (see v. 17b). The reader is being led to accept that there
will be another temple, and within that temple faith, prayer, and forgiveness, not the cultic
practices of Israel, will unite the believer with God.[66] These are not easy practices. They demand an unconditional commitment which comes from the depths of one's heart, and the
prior forgiveness of one's neighbor before one turns to address the Father in prayer
(vv. 22–25). The theme of the new temple, a new way to God hinted at in 11:12–15, will
emerge more strongly in the following conflicts between Jesus and the leaders of Israel
(11:27–12:44; see 12:10–11), and will culminate in the passion narrative (see 14:58;
15:37–39).[67]

---

[60] On the relationship between prayer and the temple, see Dowd, *Prayer*, 45–55.

[61] Dowd (*Prayer*, 95–122) shows the intimate relationship between prayer, faith, and power. The
community addressed by vv. 22–25 is called to believe that nothing is impossible for God (see 10:27).

[62] This aspect of Jesus' teaching on prayer reaches back to the teaching of the historical Jesus,
but there is no need to claim, as does Taylor (*St. Mark*, 467), that v. 25 "reflects a knowledge of the
Lord's Prayer."

[63] The universal rejection of v. 26 as original has led to the suggestion that v. 25 may also be a
gloss. It is to be retained; see Lane, *Mark*, 410–11, Marshall, *Faith as a Theme*, 172–74, and especially
Dowd, *Prayer*, 38–45.

[64] On the function of forgiveness in the newly constituted temple of the Markan community,
see Dowd, *Prayer*, 123–29. This is the only place in the Gospel of Mark where God is called "your Father in heaven." Prayer seems to be the place where disciples had to understand their relationship to
God as Father (see Matt 6:9; Luke 11:2); see Grundmann, *Markus*, 234–35.

[65] "Mark employs the material positively to give content to the new 'house of prayer' destined to
supplant the old 'den of robbers'" (Marshall, *Faith as a Theme*, 163). See also Ernst, *Markus*, 334–35.

[66] On the praying community in vv. 24–25 as the expression of the faith (see vv. 22–23) of the
eschatological community, see Marshall, *Faith as a Theme*, 170–72. For a helpful study of 11:12–25
that focuses upon the social system of the time of Jesus and up to the time of the writing of
Mark, see D. E. Oakman, "Cursing Fig-Trees and Robbers' Dens: Pronouncement Stories within
Social-Systemic Perspective: Mark 11:12–25 and Parallels," *Sem* 64 (1993): 253–72. Oakman
locates the corruption in the social system of Roman Palestine, and not just in the cult. This "old world
order" is cursed and replaced by the kingdom.

[67] Schweizer, *Mark*, 235–36.

The End of Religious Leadership in Israel (11:27–12:44)

Jesus' encounters with the leaders of Israel take place within the temporal context of a single day and a single geographical location, the temple in Jerusalem. In 11:27 the narrator announces that Jesus came again to Jerusalem and was walking in the temple (see 11:11, 15). Jesus does not move from the temple until 13:1a ("And as he came out of the Temple"). The unity created by these temporal and geographical considerations is reinforced by unvarying focus upon the leaders of Israel. Jesus debates with the chief priests, the scribes, and the elders (vv. 27–33), and tells a parable that these same interlocutors recognize is "against them" (12:1–12). Three public conflicts follow: with the Pharisees (vv. 13–17), the Sadducees (vv. 18–27), and a scribe (vv. 28–34). Jesus reduces his opponents to silence: "And after that no one dared to ask him any question" (v. 34c). The section closes with a reflection on the relationship between the Christ and the Son of David, arguing that the scribal interpretation is incorrect (vv. 35–37), followed by a denouncing of the scribes (vv. 38–40) which leads directly into the contrasting example of a poor widow, who gives her whole life (vv. 41–44). The reader moves steadily through a series of episodes that lead the leaders of Israel to silence and condemnation.

11:27–12:12 Jesus reduces the chief priests, scribes, and elders to silence.

12:13–17   Jesus reduces the Pharisees and the Herodians to silence.

12:18–27   Jesus reduces the Sadducees to silence.

12:28–34   Jesus draws a scribe toward the kingdom and reduces his opponents to silence.

12:35–37   Jesus confounds the scribes in their interpretation of the Christ as the Son of David.

12:38–44   Jesus denounces the false religion of the scribes.

Jesus has entered Jerusalem and its temple (11:1–11) and symbolically ended the traditional way to God through the cultic activity of the temple, replacing it with the promise of a new temple, a way of life marked by faith, prayer, and forgiveness (11:12–25). He now condemns and reduces the leaders of Israel to silence: chief priests, scribes, elders, Pharisees, Herodians, and Sadducees.[68] Over against these traditional "powers in the land" he points to the example of a poor widow who gave her all (11:27–12:44).

Jesus silences the chief priests, the scribes, and the elders (11:27–12:12)

The setting for all that follows, until Jesus leaves the temple in 13:1, is established in 11:27. It continues the day already begun with the discovery of the withered fig tree and its explanation in 11:20–25. This is not coincidental. The conflictual nature of Jesus' stance over against the institutions of Israel continues with further conflict with the religious leaders

---

[68] D. Daube (*The New Testament and Rabbinic Judaism* [London: Athlone, 1956; repr. Peabody: Hendrickson, 1994], 158–69) suggests that Mark was aware of the structure of the Passover liturgy. Four types of questions, in exactly the order produced in Mark 12:13–37, appear in descriptions of the Passover liturgy. See *Mek.* 13:8,4; *j. Pesah.* 10:37d; *b. Nid.* 69b–71a, also Lane, *Mark*, 421. The lateness of this material, especially from the Talmudim, makes the suggestion somewhat speculative.

of Israel.[69] In the city of Jerusalem, walking in the temple,[70] Jesus is accosted by a group who will question his authority (11:27–33), and to whom he will then address the parable of the wicked tenants (12:1–12): the chief priests, the scribes, and the elders.[71]

The chief priests, scribes, and elders ask a double-pronged question concerning Jesus' authority. This question may have been asked of Jesus often (see 1:22, 27; 3:13; 6:7), and thus may already have existed in the pre-Markan tradition.[72] They wish to know by what authority or—a variation of the same question—who is the source of Jesus' authority to do "these things" (v. 28). Within the present context, the question refers back to Jesus' actions in the temple (11:15–19; cf. John 2:18), although an echo of his entry into Jerusalem (vv. 1–11) may also be part of the question.[73] Authoritative action and teaching, within a Jewish world, must be based upon a prior authority. Authority is passed on from master to follower, from rabbi to rabbi, ultimately reaching back to Moses. For Jesus' opponents, Jesus has no such established authority.[74] The reader is aware that Jesus' authority comes from God (see 1:11; 9:7), but the chief priests, scribes, and elders question his human authority. This group will question Jesus over his God-given authority later in the narrative (see 14:60–63).[75] For the moment Jesus uses the rabbinic practice of responding with a question.[76] If they answer his question, he will answer theirs (11:29). Jesus' question lifts the discussion beyond issues of human traditions that give authority, to

---

[69] It is often pointed out that the conflicts in 11:27–12:44, as Jesus' ministry comes to a close, match those of 2:1–3:6, which marked the beginning of his ministry. Some propose that the two sets of conflict stories came from the same source. See, among many, Nineham, *St. Mark*, 306; Schweizer, *Mark*, 236. For a survey of the discussion, see J. Dewey, *Markan Public Debate: Literary Technique, Concentric Structure, and Theology in Mark 2:1–3:6* (SBLDS 48; Chico: Scholars Press, 1980), 41–63; Gnilka, *Markus*, 2:172.

[70] The text does not indicate where he was walking. It should not be supplied. See, for example, Lagrange, *Saint Marc*, 282; Lane, *Mark*, 413. There may even be a hint that his lordship over the temple, established in vv. 15–19, continues. Hooker (*St. Mark*, 271–72), investigating the relationship between John and Jesus, tentatively suggests that there may be a link between the words of 1:2 and its use of Mal 3:1 which returns at this point of the story. John was the messenger, but Jesus is the Lord who comes suddenly to his temple (Mal 3:1–4).

[71] For Mark, this group was mentioned in the first passion prediction (8:31) and later forms what comes to be identified in the passion narrative as the Sanhedrin (see 14:1; 15:1). This is widely accepted to be the case; see, for example, Lagrange, *Saint Marc*, 282; Lohmeyer, *Markus*, 240; Grundmann, *Markus*, 236; Pesch, *Markusevangelium*, 2:210. However, the composition of the Sanhedrin may have been more fluid, and the Pharisees may well have exercised influence. See, already, J. Jeremias, *Jerusalem in the Time of Jesus: An Investigation into Economic and Social Conditions during the New Testament Period* (trans. F. H. and C. H. Cave; London: SCM, 1969), 159; Taylor, *St. Mark*, 469; and recently R. E. Brown, *The Death of the Messiah: From Gethsemane to the Grave: A Commentary on the Passion Narratives in the Four Gospels* (2 vols; ABRL; New York: Doubleday, 1994), 1:350–57. For a recent attempt to trace a pre-70 portrait of the Pharisees, see R. Deines, *Die Pharisäer: Ihr Verständnis im Spiegel der christlichen und jüdischen Forschung seit Wellhausen und Graetz* (WUNT 101; Tübingen: J. C. B. Mohr [Paul Siebeck], 1997), 515–55, and esp. J. P. Meier, *A Marginal Jew: Rethinking the Historical Jesus* (3 vols.; ABRL; New York: Doubleday, 1991–2001), 3:289–388.

[72] The question may have been raised concerning his teaching and healing activity in general; Hooker, *St. Mark*, 271.

[73] Lohmeyer, *Markus*, 240. It is impossible to be sure of its reference in the pre-Markan stage of the tradition. See R. Bultmann, *History of the Synoptic Tradition* (trans. John Marsh; Oxford: Basil Blackwell, 1968), 19–20, and Taylor, *St. Mark*, 469–70.

[74] Daube, *The New Testament*, 205–23. There is nothing sinister in this first question, which opens the debate in a traditional fashion; Cranfield, *St. Mark*, 362.

[75] Pesch, *Markusevangelium*, 2:212.

[76] On vv. 28–30 as having "the form of a rabbinic school- or controversy-saying," see Lohmeyer, *Markus*, 241; see Str-B, 1:861–62.

the possibility that authority can also come "from heaven." Was the baptism of John from heaven or of human origin (v. 30)? Jesus' question already hints at the correct answer to the question posed concerning his own authority. The baptism of John was either from God,[77] and thus of lasting importance, or a human phenomenon, terminated along with the Baptist. Hidden behind this question is the awareness that Jesus' authority must also be explained as having its source either in heaven or with men,[78] and the reader recalls that it was within the context of the baptism of John that the voice from heaven announced Jesus' sonship.[79]

The chief priests, scribes, and elders fall into disarray. They are unable to resolve their dilemma once Jesus introduces the possibility that God may be part of John's activity. In the Markan story, there is no indication of an association of the Jewish leadership with the activity of John the Baptist (see 1:4–11).[80] They dare not say that his baptism was from heaven. That answer would place them in a bad light, given their lack of interest in his baptism (v. 31). But many others did go to him, and now "all" maintain that he was a prophet (v. 32). The dilemma shows that the leaders of Israel place their concern in their own reputation and status.[81] They are unable to explain why they did not accept John's baptism, and they are unwilling to be badly regarded by "the crowd" (vv. 31–32). They thus have to escape from the dilemma by claiming ignorance (v. 33a). The condition set by Jesus in 11:29 enables him to avoid answering their question concerning the source of his authority. Jesus' encounter with the chief priests, scribes, and elders comes to a close with his refusal to respond to their question.

But he moves from a defensive strategy (11:27–33) to an attack on these same religious leaders in the parable of the wicked tenants (12:1–12). The audience is the same as Jesus begins to speak to "them" in parables (καὶ ἤρξατο αὐτοῖς ἐν παραβαλαῖς λαλεῖν, 12:1).[82] The use of παραβολή in this instance does not introduce a mysterious message, open only to a few (see 4:11–12), but an allegory which is understood by the listeners and requires an appropriate response (see v. 12).[83] It is widely accepted that the parable may go back to Jesus' attack on the leaders of Israel, accusing them of betraying the God of Israel

---

[77] The use of "heaven" as a circumlocution for "God" was widespread; Lagrange, *Saint Marc,* 283; Grundmann, *Markus,* 236.

[78] Lagrange, *Saint Marc,* 284; Taylor, *St. Mark,* 470. The close association between the action of John and Jesus, present throughout the Gospel (see 1:1–13; 6:14–29; 8:9–13), continues. If Jesus is "the mightier one" (see 1:7), then the question of the heavenly origin of his authority emerges; Bultmann, *History,* 20; Lührmann, *Markusevangelium,* 197–98. Lohmeyer (*Markus,* 242 n. 3) rightly points out that the discussion is not about John and Jesus, but about *the baptism* of John, and thus about the authority of Jesus' deeds.

[79] Lohmeyer, *Markus,* 242; Grundmann, *Markus,* 236–37; van Iersel, *Reading Mark,* 148.

[80] Lagrange (*Saint Marc,* 283) comments: "It was well known that the leading class had not been docile to the preaching of John."

[81] The ἅπαντες indicates commonly accepted opinion, which the leaders do not wish to contest. Gnilka (*Markus,* 2:139–40) asserts: "This unwitting self-accusation is the kernel of the pericope." Grundmann (*Markus,* 237) calls the leaders "opportunists." See also Cranfield, *St. Mark,* 364.

[82] Grundmann (*Markus,* 238) suggests that the parable interrupts the sequence, and that the third-person plural audience may have been originally a generalized plural. See also Lohmeyer, *Markus,* 243. In its present setting, however, it is theologically and narratively linked with 11:27–33. The plural "in parables" is followed by a single parable. Lagrange (*Saint Marc,* 285) remarks: "It thus appears that the plural only indicates a genre of instruction, not the multiplicity of cases." See also Cranfield, *St. Mark,* 364.

[83] Schweizer (*Mark,* 240) asserts: "For Mark a parable is a way of speaking about God, to which a mere intellectual response is not possible. The only person who can understand a parable is one who is willing to accept or reject its message."

in their administration of what was God's vineyard.[84] The use of the vineyard, its owner, the tenants, the fruits, the messengers of God, and his Son must be understood allegorically.[85] The reader, coming from the account of the destroyed fig tree, encounters another Old Testament symbol for Israel: the vineyard (cf. Isa 5:1–2; Ps 80:8–13; Jer 2:21). But on this occasion it is not the vineyard that is rendered fruitless. Those commissioned to care for the vineyard are under attack. The vineyard is not Israel, but the larger reality of the kingdom, eventually taken from the care of the leaders of Israel and given to others (see v. 9).[86] Mark describes the construction of a typical vineyard of first-century Palestine: setting a hedge, digging a pit, and building a watchtower. The details of the digging, the watchtower, and hewing out the wine vat (12:1) are all close to LXX Isa 5:1–2.[87] There is no call for an allegorical reading of these elements in the story, nor of the man who planted the vineyard and left. These details, common enough among Palestinian landowners, are needed for the logic of the story.[88]

Another expression found in the cursing of the fig tree returns in this parable, as Jesus tells of the owner's sending of a servant to the tenants "when the time came" (τῷ καιρῷ) to gather from the fruit of the vineyard (12:2). The link is unmistakable. The inability of Israel to see that the time (ὁ καιρός) was fulfilled and that the kingdom of God was at hand (1:14–15; 11:13) continues in Jesus' description of the tenants' dealing with the servant. They took him, and beat him, and sent him away empty-handed (12:3). The process repeats itself, with increasing violence against additional servants. The second servant sent is

---

[84] See Luke 20:9–17 and *Gos. Thom.* 65, for evidence of a simpler and perhaps earlier tradition, out of which the Markan account may have grown, although this has not gone uncontested; see the summary in Lane, *Mark,* 416 n. 8, and K. R. Snodgrass, "The Parable of the Wicked Husbandmen: Is the Gospel of Thomas Version the Original?" *NTS* 21 (1974–1975): 142–44. As well as the majority of commentators, see the detailed defense of the basic historicity of the parable, in W. G. Kümmel, "Das Gleichnis von den bösen Weingärtnern (Mk. 12:1–9)," in *Heilsgeschehen und Geschichte: Gesammelte Aufsätze, 1933–1964* (ed. E. Grässer, O. Merk, and A. Fritz; 2 vols.; Marburger Theologische Studien 3; Marburg: Elwert, 1965), 1:207–17, including a good survey of the literature to that point; M. Hengel, "Das Gleichnis von den Weingärtnern Mc 12,1–12," *ZNW* 59 (1968): 1–39; J. D. Crossan, "The Parable of the Husbandmen," *JBL* 90 (1971): 451–65.

[85] Much modern parable research has rejected allegorical language in Jesus' parables. It is claimed that, as Christian tradition allegorized many famous parables, they must be de-allegorized to regain their original sense. But a blanket rejection of the possibility that Jesus spoke allegorically is unacceptable; see M. Boucher, *The Mysterious Parable: A Literary Study* (CBQMS 6; Washington: The Catholic Biblical Association of America, 1977), 1–25; Pesch, *Markusevangelium,* 2:214. For a failed attempt to remove all traces of allegory from Mark 12:1–12, see Jeremias, *The Parables of Jesus* (trans. S. H. Hooke; London: SCM Press, 1963), 70–77, and the response to Jeremias in Cranfield, *St. Mark,* 366–68. A good summary of the discussion can be found in Nineham, *St. Mark,* 308–11.

[86] See Lohmeyer, *Markus,* 245, and especially pp. 247–48. The background of Isa 5 is obvious, but the links are more verbal than theological. One glaring difference between Jesus' parable and Isa 5:1–7 is that in Isaiah the vine is at fault. In Mark it is the tenants who err. Second, as mentioned above, in Isa 5 the vineyard is a symbol for Israel, but in Jesus' parable it represents God's kingdom. However, for a strong evaluation of the impact of the Isaianic background on 11:27–12:12, see Watts, *New Exodus,* 338–49.

[87] Redaction critics agree that 12:1a and 12:12 come from Mark, and that the use of the OT in 12:10–11 has been added to the pre-Markan parable. See, for example, Gnilka, *Markus,* 2:142; Schweizer, *Mark,* 239; Pesch, *Markusevangelium,* 2:213. For an attempt to see 12:10–11 as original to Jesus, see Cranfield, *St. Mark,* 368–69.

[88] Taylor, *St. Mark,* 472. For examples of patristic allegorical readings of the passage, see Lagrange, *Saint Marc,* 286. The practice of rich landowners letting out their properties is well attested, especially in the Zenon papyri. For further details and references, see Lane, *Mark,* 416–17 nn. 6, 10.

wounded in the head and treated shamefully,[89] the next is killed,[90] and all the others either beaten or killed. Israel's history of rejecting the prophets, the servants of the Lord (see Jer 7:25; 25:4; Amos 3:7; Zech 1:6; 1QpHab 2:9; 7:5) is close to the surface.[91] God plants the vineyard and consigns it to a chosen people that they might use it well and produce fruit. When this does not happen, prophets are sent, but they are abused, insulted, injured, and slain (vv. 4–5).[92] The Markan reader immediately identifies Jesus as the one, final emissary, the owner's beloved son (υἱὸν ἀγαπητόν, v. 6a).[93] Jesus has twice been identified by the voice of God as his beloved Son (ὁ υἱός μου ὁ ἀγαπητός, 1:11; 9:7). The owner expects that the tenants will respect his beloved son (v. 6b), but the opposite happens. The tenants say to one another that this is their opportunity to take possession of the vineyard. In a way reminiscent of the plot of Jacob's sons to murder Joseph (see Gen 37:20), they regard the slaying of the beloved son as a means to acquire what should be his birthright.[94] The vineyard, which the son should inherit, will pass to them (v. 7). They act accordingly; the son is taken, killed, and cast out of the vineyard, left to rot without burial.[95] The Christian reader hears the story of the crucifixion and death of Jesus behind these words from the narrator, but again too much should not be made of the details. The slaying and the unseemly dealing with the corpse certainly applies to Jesus in this setting, but there is no call for reading the Markan passion story back into the details of 12:8.[96]

Jesus' question to his audience is telling: "What will the owner of the vineyard do?" (12:9a; see Isa 5:5). The strange logic that has led the wicked tenants to slay all those who came to call for what was due to the owner of the vineyard and finally to slay his beloved son, in the belief that his inheritance would fall to them, is laid bare.[97] The chief priests, the

---

[89] The precise meaning of ἐκεφαλίωσαν is not clear, and the textual tradition has attempted to clarify its meaning. It is widely accepted that, despite the oddness of this use of the verb, "wounded in the head" is intended; see Cranfield, *St. Mark*, 365.

[90] It is sometimes claimed that the third servant, the first to be killed, is a Markan reference to John the Baptist. See, for example, LaVerdiere, *The Beginning*, 2:173–75.

[91] Pesch, *Markusevangelium*, 2:216–17. Taylor (*St. Mark*, 474) suggests that allegorical reference to the prophets is not necessary and that "the slaves merely belong to the story."

[92] Commentators point out that Matthew (21:34–35) and Luke (20:10–12) arrange the sending of the servants in a more orderly fashion. Lagrange (*Saint Marc*, 287) regards the lack of order in Mark as indicating the primitive character of the Markan story.

[93] Lührmann, *Markusevangelium*, 199. Lohmeyer (*Markus*, 245) remarks that a theology of God's patience can be read between the lines. See also Lagrange, *Saint Marc*, 283.

[94] On the links with the Joseph story—jealousy and the desire to have his birthright—see A. Weihs, "Die Eifersucht der Winzer zur Anspielung auf LXX Gen 37,20 in der Parabel von der Tötung des Sohnes (Mk 12,1–12)," *ETL* 76 (2000): 5–29.

[95] For Jeremias (*Parables*, 72–73), Jesus is referring to himself, and there is no messianic hint in "beloved son." Grundmann (*Markus*, 240) suggests that Jesus presented himself as a son, but also as a prophet, like all those sent before him. The ἀγαπητός is a Markan addition. For Pesch (*Markusevangelium*, 2:217–19), the beloved son is the eschatological prophet. According to J. D. M. Derrett (*Law in the New Testament* [London: Darton, Longman & Todd, 1970], 286–88), the reference to a son may be original. A son could act as a father's representative in a way which servants could not. This was the owner's last attempt to establish his ownership. See also Lane, *Mark*, 418–19. Most scholars, however, would see Mark's hand behind the addition of "the beloved Son." See, for example, Gnilka, *Markus*, 2:143, 144; Ernst, *Markus*, 341. For Lohmeyer (*Markus*, 247–49), the impossibility of the events reported and the theology of the son as martyr and suffering servant indicate that the whole parable is the product of the early church. Matera (*The Kingship*, 74–79) traces the theme of royalty behind the expression.

[96] Jeremias, *Parables*, 73.

[97] For attempts to explain this logic in terms of first century Palestine, see Taylor, *St. Mark*, 475.

scribes, and the elders could answer the question, but Jesus answers it for them: the tenants are destroyed and the care of the vineyard is given to others (12:9b). The broader context of Jesus' symbolic bringing to an end of Israel's way to God through the temple (11:12–25) is recalled. The prophecy *(ex eventu?)* of 12:9b already looks beyond Israel and its leaders to a new people.[98] But Jesus makes clear the link with the end of the Jewish temple in the question he poses to listeners concerning the scripture (LXX Ps 118:22–23). The slaying of the son in 12:8 becomes christological through the application of the promise of Ps 118:22–23 to the rejected son (12:10–11). The violent slaying of Jesus, the beloved Son, is reported in 12:8, but the meaning of that event in God's design is provided in 12:10–11. In fulfillment of Ps 118, the one who has been rejected, "the stone" (Ps 118:1), has become the foundation of a new building.[99] The reader is aware that Jesus' death would lead to resurrection (see 8:31; 9:31; 10:33–34), but here the promise of 11:12–25 is further clarified.[100] The traditional way to God, by means of the temple cult, has been brought to an end (11:12–21), and faith, prayer, and forgiveness provide a new way to God (11:22–25). But there is also to be a new temple, and the cornerstone of that temple is the rejected beloved Son of God (12:8, 10).[101] The leaders of Israel have rejected and slain the Son, in the hope that they would be masters of the vineyard, but they are acting against God's design. The establishment of the slain one as the cornerstone of a new temple is the Lord's doing. As always within this gospel, the ways of God are so at variance with the expected, it is a wonder to all who behold and believe in what has happened (12:11).[102]

The chief priests, scribes, and elders make their last appearance in the public ministry of Jesus in an attempt to arrest him. The leaders of Israel are aware that Jesus is accusing them of being unfaithful and wicked tenants. For Jesus, they deal badly with God's vineyard, continuing the long and tragic history of the rejection and slaying of those sent by God to call them to conversion (cf. 1:14–15). Did they understand his claim to be the beloved Son? If so, they reject the beloved Son, unable to accept that their stewardship will come to an end and be passed on to others when they slay him. They are not prepared to make the link between the beloved Son of God, the lord of the vineyard, and Jesus who tells them the parable.[103]

Just as they were unable to respond to Jesus' question concerning the baptism of John for fear of the multitude (11:32), they are unable to move against Jesus for the same reason

---

[98] Gnilka, *Markus*, 2:147.

[99] For Matera (*The Kingship*, 79–84), the rejected stone refers to the rejected son/king of v. 6. The royal theme is continued. The expression translated "cornerstone" (κεφαλὴ γωνίας) may mean either a large cornerstone in the foundation or the keystone of an arch. The former is taken as the meaning above, but for the purposes of the image of the new temple, the difference is not great. See Lohmeyer, *Markus*, 246–47; Gnilka, *Markus*, 2:148 n. 29.

[100] For the link with the passion predictions, see Lane, *Mark*, 420. See also the reflection in Lohmeyer (*Markus*, 248–49) on the tradition of the martyrdom of the son at the hands of the Jews and its link with the Suffering Servant.

[101] Hooker, *St. Mark*, 277. Kelber (*Mark's Story*, 63) overstates the contrast between the two temples: "With this parable Jesus has set himself up as the cornerstone of the new temple, the Kingdom of God, which however is not synonymous with the old temple, but antithetical to it."

[102] See the detailed study in Marcus, *The Way of the Lord*, 111–29. As often with the work of Marcus, this valuable analysis of the Markan use of Ps 118:6 is marred by exaggerating the eschatological expectation of the suffering Markan community.

[103] Grundmann, *Markus*, 241. Hooker (*St. Mark*, 277) asks if the leaders understood Jesus' claim to be the beloved Son? "If so, then this story, with the previous one, is for Mark the real turning point of the gospel, the moment at which the Jewish authorities reject their Messiah, and when his fate—and theirs—is sealed." See also van Iersel, *Reading Mark*, 150–51.

(12:12)—as yet. They learn nothing from the multitude's attachment to the Baptist and Jesus. The brief reference to the attachment of the people at large in 11:18 and 12:12 draws a line between the leaders of Israel and the people. It is the leaders who seek to destroy Jesus in 11:18, and whom Jesus accuses of being murderers in 12:1–12. False tenants of the vineyard, they have their own agenda. They leave Jesus to depart from the scene, reduced to silence by Jesus' question concerning the baptism of John (11:27–33), their behavior condemned by Jesus' parable of the wicked tenants (12:1–12). When they reappear (14:1), the passion narrative will begin.

Jesus silences the Pharisees and the Herodians (12:13–17)

The chief priests, the scribes, and the elders, having been confounded by Jesus, send another representative group from Israel's leadership (τινας τῶν Φαρισαίων καὶ τῶν Ἡρῳδιανῶν) to challenge Jesus (12:14). Mark created the link between 12:1–12 and 12:13–17.[104] One silenced group sends an impossible representative combination, Pharisees and Herodians.[105] The two groups stood at opposite ends of first century Jewish life and practice, but have already been associated in the plot to eliminate Jesus in 3:6.[106] Toward the end of the first half of the Gospel, as Jesus instructs his disciples between the two bread miracles, he warned them to beware of the leaven of the Pharisees and the leaven of the Herodians (8:15). The encounter that follows (12:14–17), however, came to Mark in the tradition. The question they wish to raise is introduced with a lengthy and overloaded *captatio benevolentiae*. The reader is aware that the title given to Jesus, διδάσκαλε, is respectful but lacks true understanding of who Jesus is and how one should relate to him (see 4:38; 5:35; 9:17, 38; 10:17, 20, 35).[107] Jesus is true, does not allow himself to be influenced by the status of any particular individual or swayed by popular opinion,[108] and teaches the way of God, as the Pharisees and the Herodians state. Their praise is an attempt to see whether he will show such boldness when tested on a matter that may land him in trouble.[109]

A trap is set, and sprung in the question: "Is it lawful to pay taxes to Caesar or not?" (v. 14e), pressed upon Jesus with further urgency in 12:15a: "Should we pay them or should we not?" The background to the question is the payment of the infamous κῆνσος or poll tax, imposed upon Judea, Samaria, and Idumea when those regions became a Roman

---

104 Not all would regard the chief priests, the scribes, and the elders as the subject of ἀποστέλλουσιν, but suggest that it is an "impersonal plural." See, for example, Pesch, *Markusevangelium*, 2:225. But the continual use of the third person plural in vv. 12–13 makes it obvious that all verbs have the same subject. See the strong link drawn between the two pericopes by Lagrange, *Saint Marc*, 292, and Grundmann, *Markus*, 242.

105 Gnilka, *Markus*, 2:140. Lohmeyer (*Markus*, 250–51) points out that it is most unlikely that the Herodians would be testing Jesus on the payment of the tax, and suggests that they have been added by Mark, in the light of 3:6 and 8:14.

106 On the Markan nature of 12:13 and the link with 3:6, see Gnilka, *Markus*, 2:150–51. On the use of Pharisees and Herodians across the Gospel, see LaVerdiere, *The Beginning*, 2:176–78; and esp. Meier, *A Marginal Jew*, 3:289–388, for a study of the Pharisees at the time of Jesus.

107 Without exception, every prior use of this salutation shows a poor understanding of Jesus and a limited belief in him.

108 On the possible meanings of this expression and its semitic background, see Taylor, *St. Mark*, 478–79; Cranfield, *St. Mark*, 370. It can have a negative or positive sense. Here the meaning is positive.

109 Anderson, *Mark*, 274; J. B. Gibson, *The Temptations of Jesus in Early Christianity* (JSNTSup 112; Sheffield: Sheffield Academic Press, 1995), 288–317. Gibson's detailed study shows how the account presents Jesus' careful avoidance of a revolutionary stance.

province in 6 C.E. This tax, along with the commandeering and parceling out of land, created a revolt under Judas (see Acts 5:37). According to Josephus (*Ant.* 18:1–10), it gave rise to the Zealot movement. This has been debated and is generally regarded as a part of the Josephan rhetoric against the Zealots. Nevertheless, Josephus indicates the animosity generated by the demand for the payment of the κῆνσος.[110] The trap lies in the fact that the question is loaded against Jesus, no matter which answer he gives.[111] If he says that it is lawful, he will offend the Pharisees, who stood for the purity of Israel and abhorred the presence of a foreign power in God's land, symbolized by the tax. If he says that it is unlawful, he will offend the Herodians, the followers of a puppet ruling family depending entirely upon the favor and support of Caesar.

Jesus' answer is introduced by an assertion that he knew their hypocrisy (12:15b). The hypocrisy lies not in the question, which had its importance, but in the fact that these two incompatible parties from the leadership of Israel have come together to ask him to answer a question that divided them. His response plays upon that division, and reduces them to amazement and silence (v. 17). He challenges them for putting him to the test over a matter they were unable to resolve (v. 15b).[112] Jesus requests a silver denarius, the coin with which the tax was paid (v. 15c). Jesus himself does not have the coin on his person (see 6:8), and thus his questioners provide the denarius, so that he might examine it (v. 15d). "And they brought one" (v. 16a). The temple setting for this incident, as with all the other incidents from 11:27–12:44 (see also 12:35), places the Pharisees and the Herodians at a disadvantage: they should not have been carrying coins bearing effigies in the temple precincts.[113] Unlike the widely used copper coins of Palestine, the denarius bore the image and the inscription of the emperor.[114] Jesus asks them whose likeness and inscription are upon the coin. They are forced to answer, "Caesar's" (v. 15d–16). Jesus' response, widely used in debates over the relationship between church and state, possessions and holiness, and a number of other related issues, must be interpreted within its own context.[115] Jesus has taken a coin from the people who are interrogating him and examined it. He finds that the coin bears the effigy of Caesar. The Pharisees and the Herodians, bearing that effigy in the temple area, are proof of their ambiguity on the matter. There are things that belong to Caesar, and the silver denarius bearing his effigy is one of them. But there are things that belong to God, and the teaching of Jesus concerning the kingdom is focused entirely upon "the things that are God's." "By this statement early Christianity clearly set itself and Jesus apart from an apocalyptic view according to which the world was something completely

---

110 It is widely claimed that κῆνσος, being a Latin loanword from *census,* points to the evangelist's Roman background. See, however, Lagrange (*Saint Marc,* 293) for evidence of the widespread use of the term also in Greek and in an Aramaic transcription.

111 Gnilka (*Markus,* 2:152) comments: "We are dealing with one of the most tension-filled questions in the Gospel." The argument, however, is typically rabbinic. See Pesch, *Markusevangelium,* 2:225.

112 In 8:11 and 10:2 the verb πειράζειν is used by the narrator to indicate Jesus' opponents' attempts to trick him into error. Only in 12:15 does the verb appear on the lips of Jesus. Lane describes Jesus' question as containing "an understandable note of exasperation" (Lane, *Mark,* 423).

113 Gnilka, *Markus,* 2:152–53. Pesch (*Markusevangelium,* 2:227) argues that this detail shows that the tradition was not originally located in the temple area. But this misses the point of its present location in the narrative.

114 For a description of the Tiberian (14–37 C.E.) silver denarius, see Lane, *Mark,* 424.

115 For a summary of the subsequent *Wirkungsgeschichte* of this passage, see Gnilka, *Markus,* 2:154–55.

unimportant and would disappear, and from the attitude of the Zealots who believed the world was something which one must fight because it belonged to the evil one."[116]

The Pharisees and the Herodians are trapped in their own game. They recognize that the question of the payment of the tax has been resolved, and their trick question has lost its effect as more important issues have been raised.[117] They provided the coin and have shown that they bear "things that belong to Caesar." "Those who use the money clearly owe some kind of allegiance to Caesar, since the image and inscription are Caesar's, and the coin therefore belongs to him."[118] On the other hand, Jesus' life and teaching are caught up with "the things of God." The Pharisees and the Herodians have not only rejected his teaching; they are also planning to kill him (see 3:6). No further word is uttered by his opponents. They are reduced to amazement over him, but there are no indications of faith or any drawing toward the "things of God" that are at the heart of Jesus' person and presence. The Pharisees and the Herodians, who have plotted Jesus' slaying (3:6), and against whose designs Jesus has warned his disciples (8:15), disappear from the narrative. They will never be heard from again.

Jesus silences the Sadducees (12:18–27)

Without any introduction or change of place, another representative group from the leaders of Israel, the Sadducees, present themselves to Jesus (12:18a). Mark refers briefly to their rejection of the idea of a resurrection, to guide the reader through the debate that follows (v. 18b), and introduces their question (v. 18c).[119] Like the Pharisees and the Herodians, they show their lack of genuine belief in Jesus by addressing him as διδάσκαλε (v. 19a; cf. v. 14). Reflecting the Sadducean commitment to Torah only, they challenge Jesus with the levirate law, taught by Moses in Deut 25:5–10 (v. 19; see also Gen 38:8; Ruth 4:5, 10).[120] When a man died without leaving a son, his next of kin had the responsibility

---

[116] Schweizer, *Mark,* 244.

[117] Hooker (*St. Mark,* 280) observes: "Jesus' answer accepts the legitimate demands of the Roman government, but immediately switches our attention to the more important demands of God." See also Anderson, *Mark,* 275–76. Lohmeyer (*Markus,* 253) makes the point that the coin bears the image of Caesar, but every human being bears the image of God. The relative importance of Caesar over God is obvious. See also Grundmann, *Markus,* 244.

[118] Hooker, *St. Mark,* 281. Jesus' words state that the Roman authority must be accepted. The verb traditionally translated as "render" (ἀπόδοτε) means "pay the debt"; Taylor, *St. Mark,* 481–82; Cranfield, *St. Mark,* 372. For a review of attempts to show that Jesus evades the trap, see Gnilka, *Markus,* 2:153.

[119] As with the encounter between Jesus and the Pharisees and the Herodians, the introduction of v. 18 is Markan, but the debate over the resurrection from the dead would have come to Mark in the tradition. See Gnilka, *Markus,* 2:156–57. The Sadducees were members of the priestly aristocracy, conservative and distrustful of new ideas, like the resurrection from the dead and the existence of angels. Only the written law was binding, and the Torah was regarded as having greater authority than the other sacred books. There was a great gulf between the Pharisees and the Sadducees, and an even greater gulf between the Sadducees and the ordinary people; Josephus, *J.W.* 2.162–166; *Ant.* 13.293–298; 18.16–17. For further detail on the Sadducees, see E. Schürer, *The History of the Jewish People in the Age of Jesus Christ (175 B.C.–A.D. 135)* (3 vols.; rev. and ed. G. Vermes, F. Millar, and M. Black; Edinburgh: T&T Clark, 1973–1987), 2:404–14; G. G. Porton, "Sadducees," *ABD* 5:892–95; A. J. Saldarini, *Pharisees, Scribes and Sadducees in Palestinian Society* (Wilmington: Michael Glazier, 1988), especially the summary on pp. 298–308. See now the remarkable study of Meier, *A Marginal Jew,* 3:389–48.

[120] Lohmeyer (*Markus,* 255) points out that the Pharisees and the Herodians raise political issues, while the Sadducees question Jesus in the interpretation of Torah. As with the debate with the

of raising up a son by his widow, "that his name may not be blotted out of Israel" (Deut 25:6). On the basis of the Mosaic principle of the levirate law, the Sadducees develop a case that, in their understanding, shows the impossibility of a resurrection (12:20–23). All seven brothers have the same woman as a wife, and all seven die without leaving children.[121] Finally the woman also dies. If there is a resurrection, then whose wife will the woman be, as all seven brothers have had her as wife? As far as the Sadducees are concerned, the existence of the levirate law shows that Moses did not believe in the resurrection of the dead.

Jesus' response charges them of error on the basis of ignorance of the Scriptures and the power of God (12:24). This is a serious charge, attacking the Sadducees on the very issues they regarded as central to their understanding and practice of Judaism: the Torah, and the uniqueness of YHWH. Having charged them with an ignorance of the Scriptures, and then of the power of God, Jesus reverses the order as he explains himself. He first deals with the power of God (v. 25), and then uses a Jewish exegetical technique to prove to them that Torah implied resurrection from the dead (vv. 26–27).[122] They do not understand the power of God because they imagine that the life of the resurrection is simply a continuation of life on this side of death.[123] Risen from the dead means to be empowered by God to join the heavenly realm, with the angels in heaven. Jesus takes for granted the existence of the angels, rejected by the Sadducees, as beings privileged to share already in a life generated by the power of God.[124] The dead, raised by the power of God, join them. The risen one now lives because of the power of God to raise the dead, and is no longer under the sway of time, change, and the need to raise up children in Israel.[125] Therefore the

---

Pharisees and the Herodians, the debate with the Sadducees is typically rabbinic. Lohmeyer (*Markus*, 257) calls it "an outstanding example of Jesus' rabbinic style."

[121] They are said to remain entirely without issue (σπέρμα). The number "seven" is traditional, and may have distant links with Sarah, the daughter of Raguel in the Book of Tobit. Her seven husbands prior to Tobias had died (see Tob 3:8; 6:13; see also Isa 4:1). For a similar story in the Jerusalem Talmud, see Str-B, 1:887.

[122] These two "proofs" fit rather awkwardly into the flow of the argument, and it is possible that one or other of them may have been added to the passage as the tradition developed. See Schweizer, *Mark*, 246.

[123] On the Jewish idea that marriage was continued in the resurrection, see Str-B, 1:888–90; Schweizer, *Mark*, 247. The new idea of the resurrection, developed especially in Pharisaic circles, was not clear on the relationship between this life and the next. Some texts are extremely physical and portray a situation after death that is an extension of the present life (e.g., 2 Macc 14:46). Others stress a new form of spiritual existence (e.g., Dan 12:2–3; Wis 14:1–4). For Jesus, the power of God produces radical transformation, more akin to the tradition found in Wis 14:1–2. For the Christian reader, the influence of Jesus' resurrection is also indication of the power of God. This may also lie behind the present narrative, as Jesus has three times declared that he would rise from the dead (8:31; 9:31; 10:34). See Schweizer, *Mark*, 249.

[124] On Jewish discussion of angels, and the Sadducean rejection of it, see Gnilka, *Markus*, 2:159; Schürer, *The History of the Jewish People*, 2:411; Saldarini, *Pharisees, Scribes and Sadducees*, 304–5.

[125] It is sometimes suggested that this passage presents the afterlife as "a bloodless existence where the warmth of human relationships has ceased to matter" (Hooker, *St. Mark*, 284). But the point made is the radical transformation of the human condition by means of the power of God. It is not a description of the afterlife as "angelic," and in this respect is different from some of the Jewish parallels often drawn into this discussion: see *1 En.* 54:4; *2 Bar.* 51:10; *b. Ber.* 17a. See, for example, Taylor, *St. Mark*, 483; Pesch, *Markusevangelium*, 2:233. See the pertinent comment of Lagrange (*Saint Marc*, 297): "The comparison is aimed less at the nature of the angels than at their occupation."

question of the seven brothers and the one wife becomes irrelevant, as there is no need for marriage in the realm of God.

The argument from Torah is more subtle, and the resumption of this second part of the argument against the Sadducees ("as for the resurrection of the dead," v. 26) suggests that what follows may have originally been an independent saying.[126] Jesus dips into one of the fundamental Mosaic texts in Torah: the encounter between YHWH and Moses at the burning bush, where the name of God was revealed to Moses (Exod 3:1–22).[127] Prior to the revelation of the name in 3:14–15, YHWH identifies himself as Israel's traditional God, the God of Abraham, Isaac, and Jacob. Septuagint Exod 3:6 states: ἐγὼ ὁ θεὸς Ἀβραὰμ καὶ θεὸς Ἰσαὰκ καὶ θεὸς Ἰακώβ. Abraham, Isaac, and Jacob were long since dead when YHWH spoke to Moses at the burning bush. Yet, using an accepted exegetical method, Jesus points out that while speaking to Moses, YHWH identified himself as the God of the patriarchs. Jesus' case depends upon a shared belief that God would not style himself the God of dead heroes. Therefore the patriarchs must be alive—in the resurrection.[128] The closing words of the debate make that point. YHWH is not the God of dead heroes, but of the living (v. 27a). The long since dead patriarchs are alive with the God of Israel.[129] Other Jewish traditions make this claim (see 4 Macc 7:19; 16:25), but Jesus has shown that Torah "proves" that there is a resurrection from the dead.[130]

The Sadducees have been beaten at their own game. Masters of the traditional faith of Israel, and rigidly committed to the use of Torah for their understanding of that faith, they are accused of being totally mistaken (12:27b).[131] There is no reply from the Sadducees to the authoritative statement from Jesus. This is the only appearance of the Sadducees in the Markan story. Like the chief priests, scribes, and elders (11:27–12:12), Pharisees, and Herodians (12:13–17), they are reduced to silence. As with the Pharisees and Herodians, they never appear again in the narrative. The chief priests, scribes, and elders are the only leaders of Israel who reappear. They were reduced to silence in the debate over Jesus' authority (11:27–33) and through Jesus' stinging parable of the unfaithful tenants, aimed at them (12:1–12). But the parable pointed to a later moment in the narrative when they would murder the beloved son (12:6–8). They have been reduced to silence but have not disappeared from the story. Aware of Jesus' impact upon the multitude, they have left the scene (12:12), but the reader is aware they must return.

---

[126] Nineham, *St. Mark,* 319–20.

[127] Lohmeyer, *Markus,* 256.

[128] It is sometimes claimed that the use of the present tense of the verb in English "*I am* the God of . . ." indicates the presence of the patriarchs with God (e.g., Nineham, *St. Mark,* 321–22; Anderson, *Mark,* 279). However, there is no verb in the Greek, or in the Hebrew, of Exod 3:6. The text itself states the reason for the presence of the patriarchs in a risen life: God is not a God of the dead (12:27a).

[129] F. Dreyfus ("L'argument scripturaire de Jésus en faveur de la résurrection des morts [Marc XII, 26–27]," *RB* 66 [1959]: 213–24) takes this further and attempts to show that in first-century Jewish prayers the expression "God of Abraham, God of Isaac, God of Jacob" used by Jesus referred to God as the protector of the three patriarchs in their lives and in their afterlives. See also Lane, *Mark,* 429–30; Pesch, *Markusevangelium,* 2:234. The dating of some of the key texts used by Dreyfus (especially the *Shemoneh 'Esreh*), makes this suggestion somewhat speculative.

[130] If something of this debate reaches back to the time of Jesus, and there is every possibility that such is the case (see Gnilka, *Markus,* 260–61; Pesch, *Markusevangelium,* 235), Jesus sides with the Pharisees on the question of resurrection after death.

[131] The Scriptures and the power of God, experienced in the resurrection, were part of the Christian preaching. See, for example, Gal 3:1; 1 Cor 1:18–31; Acts 2:14–36. See Hooker, *St. Mark,* 284.

Jesus draws a scribe toward the kingdom and silences his opponents (12:28–34)

The following encounter between Jesus and a scribe (12:28–34), like the passages that preceded it, is introduced rather artificially. The scribe is brusquely brought into the scene (12:28a), and his presence is linked with the previous episode by the Markan note that he heard the dispute between Jesus and the Sadducees, and was impressed by Jesus' answers to them (12:28bc). The artificiality of the link is highlighted by the important question the scribe asks: "Which commandment is the first of all?" (12:28d). The debate with the Sadducees was at least partly concerned with the right interpretation of Torah, but hardly the type of discussion that would lead a bystander to pose this question, which is known to have been current in Judaism at the time of Jesus.[132] As there were said to be 365 prohibitions and 248 positive commands in Torah, discussions among the rabbis looked for a basic principle behind the detailed legislation.[133]

Jesus, asked for one commandment, gives two, both from Torah. The first (12:29–30) is from the *shema,* a traditional and fundamental expression of Jewish thought and practice, recited every morning and evening by a pious Jew. The text here is taken from LXX Deut 6:4–5. There is only one God, and this unique God must be loved unconditionally with every part of one's mind and being.[134] The second (12:31) comes from Lev 19:18: "You shall love your neighbor as yourself." It is not clear whether this combination of love of the one God and love of neighbor originated in Judaism before the time of Jesus, in Jesus, or in the early church.[135] There are numerous examples of parallel exhortations to love of God and neighbor (e.g., *Sipra* 89b; *b. Šabb.* 31a; *T. Iss.* 5:2; *T. Dan.* 5:3; *T. Zeb.* 5:1–2; *T. Benj.* 3:3; Philo, *Spec.* 2.63).[136] Jesus' response, and his further comment that there is no commandment greater than love of God and of neighbor (v. 31b), is open to at least two interpretations. It could simply be taken as providing a principle for understanding all the commandments, all of which still had to be observed, in keeping with the ongoing debate within the Judaism of the time. On the other hand, it could point more radically to the end of the need for the detailed legislation that governed the life of a practicing Jew. The narrative context of Jesus' words demands that the latter is the case. He has brought the temple practices to an end and silenced the leaders of Israel. He now points to love of God and

---

[132] It is therefore most likely that v. 28abc is the work of Mark, continuing to link a series of previously independent passages; see Gnilka, *Markus,* 2:163. Gnilka rightly points out that the passage as a whole came to Mark in the tradition, but that he has added links backward (28ab) and forward (34c). See also Lohmeyer, *Markus,* 257; Taylor, *St. Mark,* 485, 490. The question posed in v. 28d, however, was commonly asked. It would have come to Mark from his tradition, and may well reflect a question put to the historical Jesus; see Schweizer, *Mark,* 250.

[133] For the debate between R. Shammai and R. Hillel over this question, see Lohmeyer, *Markus,* 260–61; Grundmann, *Markus,* 251.

[134] Mark cites LXX Deut 6:5 freely here, replacing ψυχή ("inner being") with διάνοια ("mind"), and δύναμις ("might") with ἰσχύς ("strength"). See Lagrange, *Saint Marc,* 300.

[135] Scholars differ. In favor of its originality with Jesus, see G. Bornkamm, *Jesus of Nazareth* (trans. I. and F. McLuskey with J. Robinson; London: Hodder & Stoughton, 1963), 100; Taylor, *St. Mark,* 488. Gnilka (*Markus,* 2:167) judges the pericope to be the product of the Hellenistic Jewish Christian community. See the discussion in Nineham, *St. Mark,* 324–25.

[136] As the *Testaments of the Twelve Patriarchs* have been subjected to Christian editing, the Gospel passage may be behind the use of the double command to love. For further rabbinic texts, see Lagrange, *Saint Marc,* 301–2; Str-B, 1:907–8. Lohmeyer (*Markus,* 258) points out that love of God could be regarded as a summary of the "first table" of the Decalogue, and love of neighbor as a summary of the second table.

love of neighbor as the fulfillment of the law in the sense that detailed legislation is now transcended by the double command of love.[137]

The scribe recognized Jesus' response as "right," "in truth" a correct answer to his question. He restates Jesus' answer in a similar collage of Old Testament passages. He restates Deut 6:4, "he is one," and interprets the uniqueness of God in a paraphrase of Isa 45:21, "and there is no other but he" (12:32). From Deut 6:5 he takes, "and to love him with all the heart, and all the understanding, and with all the strength."[138] He also connects love of God with love of neighbor as oneself, using Jesus' words (12:33). But his final words, not taken directly from Jesus, or from the Scriptures, indicate that the scribe has understood Jesus' teaching, and that Mark is using this scribe to articulate his point of view. Within the temple, which Jesus has brought to a standstill (11:15–25), he accepts Jesus' two commandments as "much more than all burnt offerings and sacrifices" (12:33c). The words of the scribe, placing behavior before sacrifices, have parallels in the Old Testament (see 1 Sam 15:22; Ps 40:7; 51:20–21; Isa 1:11; Jer 7:22–23; Hos 6:6), but their literary and theological context in the Gospel of Mark make them more than a repetition of that teaching. The detailed legislation of Torah has been replaced by Jesus' double command of love, just as the new temple, with Jesus as its cornerstone (see vv. 10–11), marked by faith, prayer, and forgiveness (see 11:22–25), is to replace the holocausts and sacrifices of the now silent temple of Jerusalem (see 11:15–19).[139]

The scribe has posed a question to Jesus that was widely debated in the Judaism of his time. It is the type of question that could open an interminable rabbinic debate, as each person in the discussion aired a point of view. This does not happen in this case. He accepts the rightness and the truth of Jesus' association of love of God and love of neighbor, and repeats his words to him, almost verbatim. He adds his own comment on the superiority of the love command to the traditional cultic practices of the temple, indicating that he fully understands the consequences of Jesus' double command of love. This is the only place in the Gospel where a leader in Israel agrees with Jesus. The acceptance of Jesus' words, and his interpretation of them, show that he answered "wisely." Jesus announces to the scribe: "You are not far from the Kingdom of God" (12:34a). According to the agenda set in 1:15 ("Repent and believe in the gospel"), the scribe's acceptance of the word of Jesus (the gospel?) brings him toward the kingdom. Within the literary context of hostility between Jesus and the Jewish leaders, the movement of this scribe toward the kingdom shows that Jews, as such, are not excluded from the kingdom. They too are called to hear the word and accept it.[140] As the Gospel draws to a close, this "nearness" may also be related to the imminent coming of the kingdom with power in the death and resurrection of Jesus,

---

[137] It is possible that Jesus himself responded to this (apparently) widely discussed question by asserting the double command to love. Once the context of the discussion was shifted from the life of Jesus to the Markan literary and theological context, its intent became more radical. The two "contexts" must not be confused. Grundmann (*Markus*, 252) rightly interprets the Markan message: "Thereby a new position is established over against the whole pre-Christian concept of religious righteousness and interpersonal relations." See also Lohmeyer, *Markus*, 259; Pesch, *Markusevangelium*, 2:238; Anderson, *Mark*, 281–82.

[138] The LXX's ψυχή is again replaced, this time by σύνεσις. Cranfield (*St. Mark*, 379) is probably correct when he remarks that the change "introduces a little variety, but makes no appreciable difference to the sense."

[139] Against Taylor (*St. Mark*, 489): "He says no more than is already said in I Kgdms xv.22." See Hooker, *St. Mark*, 289; LaVerdiere, *The Beginning*, 2:189.

[140] Gnilka, *Markus*, 2:166–67.

promised to "some standing here" in 9:1. The scribe, accepting the word of Jesus, joins others as the kingdom approaches.[141]

A single scribe draws close to the kingdom preached and lived by Jesus. Chief priests, scribes, elders, Pharisees, Herodians, and Sadducees have attempted to draw Jesus into conflicts to show their superiority, and thus justify their rejection of him and his message of the kingdom (11:27–12:27). Systematically, they have been reduced to silence (see 11:33; 12:12, 17, 27). But a scribe has recognized the rightness and the truth of Jesus' teaching, and the new approach to God involved in the establishment of the kingdom (v. 34a). Not only does Jesus reduce the leaders to silence; he also draws one of their colleagues toward the kingdom by the rightness and the truth of his understanding of the greatest commandment: the love of God and the love of one's neighbor (12:28–34). This is better than holocausts and sacrifices.

The narrator closes this systematic presentation of Jesus' encounters with the leaders of Israel with a lapidary comment: "And no one (οὐδείς) asked him a question any longer (οὐκέτι)" (12:34b). The two negatives, one stating that *no person* asked a question, and the other stating *no longer*, indicate the result of Jesus' encounters with the leaders of Israel. Only silence exists between Jesus and the leaders of Israel. He has gained the upper hand in every encounter and three groups, the Pharisees, the Herodians, and the Sadducees, disappear from the story at this point. As Jesus' presence symbolically brought the temple and its practices to an end, he has now symbolically silenced the leaders of Israel. They have had their final say in Jesus' public life. In the passion story some will return, and appear to win, but the reader knows that, appearances notwithstanding, the efforts of the chief priests, scribes, and elders to put an end to Jesus will also be thwarted by resurrection (8:31; 9:31; 10:33–34).[142]

The scribes, and the question of the Messiah as David's son (12:35–37)

Jesus moves on to the final moments of the day in the temple.[143] Having reduced the leaders of Israel to silence, only the voice of Jesus is now heard as he teaches (12:35a). In the first episode his teaching (διδάσκων, 12:35) corrects the scribes' faulty understanding of Scripture and the relationship between the Messiah and the Son of David (vv. 34–37). In the second, as he teaches (ἐν τῇ διδαχῇ, 12:38) he contrasts the false religion of the scribes with the widow whose offering of her all makes her a model for disciples (12:38–44). One of the scribes has approached the kingdom, but no one dares speak any longer (12:34). Jesus condemns the scribes as such. They misunderstand the Scriptures (12:35–37) and are condemned for their false religiosity (12:38–44).[144]

---

141 Schweizer (*Mark*, 253) makes a link with the nearness of the passion story, but does not associate it with 9:1.

142 Lührmann (*Markusevangelium*, 185, 214) points out that across the three days of Jesus' encounters with his opponents, as in the passion, he is challenged but never found lacking or guilty in any way.

143 For most commentators, the encounter with the leaders closes with the silence of v. 34. See, for example, Schweizer, *Mark*, 255; Pesch, *Markusevangelium*, 2:236. Lohmeyer (*Markus*, 261) suggests that the three conflicts are now followed by three teaching passages (vv. 35–37, 38–40, 41–44). Mark's editorial work on his sources, maintaining his focus on the scribes (see vv. 35, 38), suggests that the conflict continues. Verses 35–37 came to Mark in the tradition, but he has framed it with v. 35a and v. 37b to knit it into the ongoing narrative. See Gnilka, *Markus*, 2:169.

144 Commentators, puzzled by Jesus' rejection of Davidic descent, miss the importance of the ongoing conflict with the leaders of Israel, running since 11:27. They attempt to construct a *Sitz im*

Throughout the encounters between Jesus and the leaders of Israel, the opponents have regularly posed a question to Jesus (see 11:28; 12:14, 19–23, 28). This is no longer possible, as they have been reduced to silence (12:34). However, Jesus has not concluded his systematic elimination of the leaders. He questions the scribal interpretation of Scripture: "How can the scribes say that the Christ is the Son of David?" (v. 35b). The association of the two terms "the Christ" and "the Son of David" is not widespread in first century Judaism, but the expectation that a royal Messiah would be from the line of David was.[145] The scribes, those learned in law, are presented as being of this mind, but Jesus uses a rabbinic-style exegesis of Ps 110:1 to show that they have misinterpreted Scripture. His point of departure is that David, inspired by the Spirit, wrote this psalm which speaks of the God-given victory of the Messiah over all opponents.[146] David spoke of YHWH as κύριος, and of the Messiah as ὁ κύριός μου. God said to the Messiah, "Sit at my right hand, till I put your enemies under your feet" (12:36).[147] David, in the psalm, addressed the Messiah as ὁ κύριός μου. David cannot possibly be the father of the Messiah because he called him his "lord" (v. 37a). A person cannot be "father" of his "lord." Jesus insists that the Messiah, therefore, transcends Davidic expectations.[148]

This brief but subtle argument against Davidic messianic expectation impresses the large crowd, who listen willingly to his teaching. Jesus' presence in the temple, bringing to an end the authority of the leaders of Israel, has been marked by a growing popular support

---

Leben for such strange teaching, and generally read the passage as an affirmation of Jesus as "Lord." See, for example, Taylor, *St. Mark*, 491; Hooker, *St. Mark*, 290–94; Gnilka, *Markus*, 2:169–71; LaVerdiere, *The Beginning*, 2:191.

[145] See, for example, S. Talmon, "The Concepts of *Māšîah* and Messianism in Early Judaism," in *The Messiah: Developments in Earliest Judaism and Christianity* (ed. J. H. Charlesworth; The First Princeton Symposium on Judaism and Christian Origins; Minneapolis: Fortress, 1992), 79–115; L. Schiffman, "Messianic Figures and Ideas in the Qumran Scrolls," in *The Messiah*, 116–29; J. J. Collins, *The Scepter and the Star: The Messiahs of the Dead Sea Scrolls and Other Ancient Literature* (ABRL; New York: Doubleday, 1995); idem, "The Nature of Messianism in the Light of the Dead Sea Scrolls," in *The Dead Sea Scrolls in Their Historical Context* (ed. T. H. Lim, L. W. Hurtado, A. Graeme Auld, and Alison Jack; Edinburgh: T&T Clark, 2000), 199–219; P. R. Davies, "Judaisms of the Dead Sea Scrolls: The Case of the Messiah," in *The Dead Sea Scrolls in Their Historical Context*, 219–32.

[146] On the acceptance of Davidic authorship, and the messianic use of Ps 110:1, see Taylor, *St. Mark*, 492; Nineham, *St. Mark*, 331–32. For J. Marcus (*The Way of the Lord: Christological Exegesis of the Old Testament in the Gospel of Mark* [Louisville: Westminster John Knox, 1992], 132–37), the echatological use of Ps 110 in Jewish tradition and the context of 12:35–37 indicate that Mark uses the psalm to describe "the submission of human and demonic opponents to the divine will embodied in Jesus, and which will become totally and publicly effective at the parousia" (p. 137). This reads too much into the context, both within the narrative, and within the setting of its original readership.

[147] Echoes of Ps 110 appear across the New Testament to give biblical background to Jesus' ascent to glory, despite crucifixion, through the resurrection. See, for example, Acts 2:34–35; Heb 1:13 (direct quotations); Mark 14:62; 1 Cor 15:25; Col 3:1; Heb 1:3. See Pesch, *Markusevangelium*, 2:254; B. Lindars, *New Testament Apologetic: The Doctrinal Significance of the Old Testament Quotations* (London: SCM, 1961), 45–51. On the odd use of the Ps 110:1 in Mark 12:35–37, see pp. 46–47.

[148] For Matera (*The Kingship*, 84–89), the use of κύριος in this setting is another indication of the Markan presentation of Jesus as a royal figure, climaxing the earlier hints that Jesus was a king (see 11:9; 12:6, 10). For the position that Jesus does not deny his Davidic messianic status, but transcends it by means of death and resurrection, see D. H. Juel, *A Master of Surprise: Mark Interpreted* (Minneapolis: Fortress, 1994), 97–99, who claims: "It is as the enthroned 'Lord' that Jesus is the Son of David" (p. 99). But there is little of the enthroned Lord in Mark, especially in 16:1–8. Watts (*New Exodus*, 287–90) sidesteps the issue by affirming Jesus' Davidic sonship in Mark, claiming that this passage adds a further element to this aspect of Markan Christology: he is also David's Lord. But that is precisely what Mark is trying to show is not possible.

and enthusiasm for him and his teaching (see 11:32; 12:12, 37).[149] The crowd has been joined by one of the scribes, who accepted Jesus' word and is not far from the kingdom. The regular insistence upon the positive response of the people, and even one of the scribes, shows the author's concern to include the Jewish people among potential members of the kingdom. It is not Israel that is silenced in 11:27–12:44, but its leaders. These same leaders had entered into conflict with Jesus and began to plot his death in 2:1–3:6.

The veil covering Jesus' messianic status (see 8:29–30) has been further folded back in this exercise in biblical exegesis showing the scribes' faulty understanding of the Messiah. Jesus is the Messiah (see 8:29), but not the one expected by the disciples and their fellow Jews.[150] Jesus' messianic status is to be revealed through the death and resurrection of the Son of Man (see 8:31; 9:31; 10:33–34). He is God's beloved Son (1:11; 9:7). His instruction of the disciples across 8:22–10:52 was marked by an attempt to lead them to true sight, to make them understand and accept that his journey to Jerusalem was not to take possession of a royal city as a Davidic Messiah.[151] Blind Bartimaeus cried out to Jesus as "Son of David," a worker of miracles (10:47–48). Bartimaeus' actions, rather than his words, demonstrate faith and result in his receiving his sight as he joins the way of Jesus.[152] A false messianic hope has been expressed in Jesus as "Son of David" in the acclaim that greeted his ascent to Jerusalem (11:10).[153] Jesus' exegesis of Ps 110:1 now makes the Markan point of view explicit.[154] He transcends the Jewish messianic hopes taught by the scribes and in doing so shows that they are failing in the proper exercise of their function within Israel, the interpretation of Scripture. "It was knowledge alone which gave their power to the scribes."[155] By demonstrating the scribes' faulty exegesis, Jesus destroys their

---

[149] Lagrange (*Saint Marc,* 306) adds a touch of color to this approval: "The people have always loved enjoyable counterarguments."

[150] Lohmeyer, *Markus,* 262–63; Grundmann, *Markus,* 254. Taylor (*St. Mark,* 492–93) argues that this exegesis of the psalm goes back to Jesus, and exposes "the futility of Messianic hopes which do not rise above the earthly and human plane." An unresolvable tension is created when the distinction between the Jesus of history and the Markan theological perspective is not kept; see the survey of scholarly discussion of this passage in Nineham, *St. Mark,* 329–31. Some commentators see this episode as reflecting a "two step" Christology. Both "steps" are present in Rom 1:3. There is a first step presenting Jesus' commitment to the human sphere (reflected in the discussion of Mark 12:36) and a second step associating him with "God for us from eternity past and eternity future" (Schweizer, *Mark,* 258). See also Gnilka, *Markus,* 2:171.

[151] Pesch, *Markusevangelium,* 2:255–56. For Pesch, this is the perspective of the pre-Markan passion narrative. It is also the perspective of the Markan storyteller. Despite Taylor (*St. Mark,* 491) and others, the fact that other New Testament authors accept Jesus' Davidic descent (see Matt 1:1–17; Luke 1:69; 3:23–38; Acts 2:30; Rom 1:3; 15:12; 2 Tim 2:8; Rev 3:7; 5:5; 22:16) does not mean that Mark did. Despite their genealogies, Matthew (22:41–46) and Luke (20:41–44) have versions of Jesus' interpretation of Ps 110:1.

[152] See above, pp. 208–11.

[153] See above, pp. 217–21.

[154] On the Markan correction of a "Son of David" Christology with a "Son of God" Christology, see Telford, *The Barren Temple,* 251–69, and especially Marcus, *The Way of the Lord,* 137–52. Most scholars are unable to let go of a Son of David Christology in Mark. For a representative position, see E. K. Broadhead, *Naming Jesus: Titular Christology in the Gospel of Mark* (JSNTSup 175; Sheffield: Sheffield Academic Press, 1999), 109–15, who concludes: "The Gospel of Mark withdraws from the traditional lines of development without negating the Son of David title" (p. 115). See the brief but accurate assessment of F. J. Matera, *New Testament Christology* (Louisville: Westminster John Knox, 1999), 19–21.

[155] Jeremias, *Jerusalem in the Time of Jesus,* 235. Most interpreters miss the importance of the ongoing theme of Jesus' bringing the authority of religious leaders to an end. It is true that Jesus' teaching in vv. 35–37 transcends all messianic titles (see Ernst, *Markus,* 358–61), but it also rejects a well-established scribal tradition.

authority. As in the debate with the Pharisees and the Sadducees, Jesus has beaten them at their own game.

The false religion of the scribes (12:38–44)

Having silenced the leaders of Israel, Jesus brings his teaching in the temple to an end (12:38; see 11:27; 12:1, 35, 41; 13:1). Analysis of each pericope has shown that Mark has imposed the temple setting upon a number of preexisting traditions to form 11:27–12:44. Such redactional activity does not *lessen* the importance of the setting. Rather, the setting provides crucial implicit commentary for the reader. Jesus has entered Jerusalem and closed down the temple (11:1–25). Never leaving the now silent temple he has systematically closed down the Jewish leadership: the chief priests, the scribes, and the elders (11:27–12:12), the Pharisees (12:13–17), and the Sadducees (vv. 18–27). He has shown that the official interpreters of the Scriptures, the scribes, are wrong in their interpretations (12:35–37). Now (12:38–44) he condemns the hypocrisy of their paraded religion, over against genuine self-gift, exemplified by the widow.[156] As these Jewish leaders are reduced to silence, however, the people's enthusiasm for Jesus has grown (see 11:32; 12:12, 37) and a scribe has approached the kingdom. Israel is not lost. But the only remaining leaders in the story—the chief priests, the scribes, and the elders—will finally resort to a violence that has been in the air from early in the story (3:6).

Continuing to teach in the temple (ἐν τῇ διδαχῇ), Jesus warns against the scribes (v. 38a). The one scribe who has drawn close to the kingdom (vv. 28–34) does not alleviate Jesus' attack upon the scribes as such. The accusations Jesus levels against them are symptomatic of religious leaders of all times and places, and were applicable to the religious élite of first century Judaism. In a society that was theocentric, the persona of the religious figure was surrounded by a certain aura and demanded respect. This led to the situation described by Jesus: the scribes paraded in long robes,[157] expected respectful salutations in the market places where the ordinary folk gathered,[158] and took the positions of honor in both the synagogue gatherings and the temple celebrations of the feasts (vv. 38b–39).[159]

---

[156] Historically, the scribes in the times of Jesus were not a "party," but performed a task as interpreters of the law and "were individuals filling a social role in different contexts rather than a unified political and religious force" (Saldarini, *Pharisees, Scribes and Sadducees*, 276). There were thus scribes from the priestly classes and scribes of the Pharisees. See Jeremias, *Jerusalem in the Time of Jesus*, 233–37; Saldarini, *Pharisees, Scribes and Sadducees*, 241–76; Marcus, *Mark*, 523–24. They are not known to have been particularly corrupt (but see *b. Sot.* 22b; *Ass. Mos.* 7:6). The Markan literary and theological agenda places them in a bad light throughout the Gospel (see 3:22–30; 7:1–5; 11:18, 27–28; 12:12).

[157] This possibly refers to a long version of the outer garment, the *tallith,* worn when at prayer or when involved in religious functions. The clothing of the scribes, however, is not certain; see K. H. Rengstorf, "Die στολαί der Schriftgelehrten: Eine Erläuterung zu Mark 12,38," in *Abraham unser Vater: Juden und Christen im Gespräch über die Bibel. Festschrift für Otto Michel zum 60. Geburtstag* (ed. O. Betz, M. Hengel, and P. Schmidt; AGSU 5; Leiden: Brill, 1963), 383–404; H. Fleddermann, "A Warning about the Scribes (Mark 12:37b–40)," *CBQ* 44 (1982): 54–57.

[158] For a discussion of what these salutations might have been, see Lane, *Mark,* 440; Pesch, *Markusevangelium,* 2:258. On the respect and honor given to the scribes, see Jeremias, *Jerusalem in the Time of Jesus,* 243–45.

[159] One cannot be sure of pre-70 synagogue seating arrangements. However, it appears that there were rows of elevated seats, perhaps with their backs to the Torah shrine, which would have the scribes looking down upon the people. Cranfield (*St. Mark,* 384) confidently asserts, "The πρωτοκαθεδρία was the bench in front of the ark (containing the scriptures) and facing the people."

Such parading of religious superiority, and the haughty acceptance of the honors that accompanied it, is undeserved because this external show does not match the quality of their lives. Longstanding legal, prophetic, and wisdom traditions in Israel called for the respect and protection of widows (see, e.g., Exod 22:21–24; Deut 24:17, 19–22; 27:19; Isa 1:17; Jer 7:6; 22:3; Zech 7:10; Mal 3:5; Ps 146:9; Prov 15:25). The woman without a husband was particularly fragile and open to physical, social, and financial abuse.[160] Jesus accuses the scribes of taking advantage of the widows' financial and social weakness while feigning religion in the form of long and meaningless prayers (καὶ προφάσει μακρὰ προσευχόμενοι). It is possible that προφάσει ("for a pretense") suggests an ulterior motive. Most evidence shows that scribes were generally from the poorer classes, and hospitality to them was seen as an act of piety.[161] Jesus accuses them of false piety with long prayers to "sponge on the hospitality of people of limited means"[162] (the widows), reducing them to a state of penury.[163] This hypocritical parading of religion accompanied by a ruthless and sinful lifestyle will merit a very severe final condemnation, whatever their present honors (v. 40).[164]

The reference to the scribes' sinful treatment of the widows leads directly into the concluding episode.[165] Jesus sits down opposite the treasury, still in the temple, watching the crowds put money into the treasury coffers (v. 41a).[166] Two approaches to this responsibility of all pious Jews are described: the many rich people who make large contributions (v. 41c), and a single poor widow.[167] She puts in two λεπτά that amount to one κοδράντης

See Taylor, *St. Mark*, 494–95; Grundmann, *Markus*, 256; Pesch, *Markusevangelium*, 2:258–59. However, there may be a more Markan theme here, directed to the disciples, called to be servants of all (see 9:35; 10:31, 43–44). See Fleddermann, "A Warning," 57–61.

[160] Lagrange, *Saint Marc*, 307; G. Stählin, "χήρα," *TDNT* 9:444–47.

[161] Jeremias, *Jerusalem in the Time of Jesus*, 111–16.

[162] Lane, *Mark*, 440–41. See also Grundmann, *Markus*, 256; Cranfield, *St. Mark*, 385; Hooker, *St. Mark*, 295.

[163] This accusation is made against the Pharisees by Josephus, *Ant.* 17.41–45. This is the most likely explanation of v. 40a, as it is otherwise difficult to trace how scribes "devoured" widow's houses. See Gnilka, *Markus*, 2:174–75.

[164] The severity of the condemnation indicates its eschatological nature; Gnilka, *Markus*, 2:175. The instruction of disciples continues. See Fleddermann, "A Warning," 61–66.

[165] Whether the two passages came to Mark already joined by the term "widow," or whether they have been joined by Mark, cannot be determined with any certainty. Verses 38–40 may have had a complex prehistory (see, for example, Lohmeyer, *Markus*, 263), while vv. 41–44 are more homogeneous (see Lohmeyer, *Markus*, 265). See also Schweizer, *Mark*, 259; Hooker, *St. Mark*, 296. They are closely related in their present place in the Gospel; Grundmann, *Markus*, 257. On the need to associate the two passages, see A. G. Wright, "The Widow's Mites: Praise or Lament?—A Matter of Context," *CBQ* 44 (1982): 256–65, and especially E. S. Malbon, "The Poor Widow in Mark and Her Poor Rich Readers," *CBQ* 53 (1991): 595–601. Malbon rightly links the account of the poor widow to a number of contexts, both textual and literary, from earlier parts of the Gospel (including 12:38–40). This essay is now available in Malbon, *In the Company of Jesus*, 166–88.

[166] On the treasury, its location in the temple area, and the thirteen trumpet-shaped collection baskets for offerings, see Schürer, *The History of the Jewish People*, 2:281 n. 30. Such reconstructions, however, are speculative, and based on post-70 texts. As Nineham (*St. Mark*, 335) comments: "St. Mark himself may have had no very clear idea what *treasury* was intended." Later Jewish traditions claim that one was not allowed to sit in the temple, and thus some witnesses have Jesus "standing" (ἑστώς: Washington, Tbilisi, Sinaitic Syriac, and Origen). As Grundmann (*Markus*, 258) points out, this is an attempt by the scribes to conform the account to later Jewish tradition, and should be rejected.

[167] In v. 41 the word for "money" is καλκός, an expression which refers to copper coins in general. While the wealthy put in fistfuls of these coins, the poor widow gave only two tiny ones. See Lagrange, *Saint Marc*, 308.

(v. 42).[168] The condemnation of the scribes, who abuse the widows while parading their religiosity, continues with the wealthy who parade their large sums, in contrast with the poverty of the poor widow. Jesus' comment upon the episode is solemnly introduced: καὶ προσκαλεσάμενος τοὺς μαθητὰς αὐτοῦ εἶπεν αὐτοῖς. He opens with the formula ἀμὴν λέγω ὑμῖν (v. 43a). There is a sense of finality in his condemnation of the leaders. The wealthy have merely given out of their surplus (12:44). The reader is reminded of the scribes condemned by Jesus (vv. 39–40). Reversing yet another established understanding of religious respectability, Jesus affirms that the large quantities of coins cast into the treasury have been surpassed by the widow. She has put 'in more than all the others. Her gift surpasses their gifts (v. 43b). They look good, but appearances may be deceiving. The woman's gift is superior because she has given from her poverty, all that she had, described as ὅλον τὸν βίον αὐτῆς (v. 44). There is a double meaning in this expression. It may simply mean that she has given up all she has to live on, and "livelihood" is the usual meaning of the use of the term βίος. But it can also mean life itself, and Jesus' climactic comment instructs the disciples on the price of discipleship: she has given her very life (see 8:31–33; 10:45). The double meaning is intended, for in doing one she has done the other.[169]

The vocation of the first disciples (1:16–20) and of Levi (2:13–14), along with Jesus' instructions to the disciples in 8:22–10:52, must inform the interpretation of 12:41–44. Those who wished to follow Jesus were initially called away from their human and financial support structure: nets, boats, hired hands, father, and tax office. Later, they were challenged to self-gift unto death for the sake of Jesus and the gospel (see 8:34–9:1; 10:35–40), to humble service and receptivity (9:33–37; 10:41–44). They are followers of the Son of Man who came to serve and to give his life (10:42–45). This is the true religion established by the teaching, the life, and the oncoming death and resurrection of Jesus. Unlike the rich man, whose wealth kept him from accepting Jesus' call to discipleship (see 10:21–22), the widow gives her whole life and becomes a model for the disciples of Jesus.[170] "Discipleship

---

[168] The *lepton* was the smallest coin in Roman currency. Two of them formed a *quadrans*, four *quadrantes* formed an *assarius*, and sixteen *assarii* formed a *denarius*, the salary of a laborer for a day; see Schürer, *The History of the Jewish People*, 2:62–66. The widow's two *lepta* were worth one-sixty-fourth of a day's salary. The reference to western coins leads to claims for a western (Roman) readership; see Taylor, *St. Mark*, 497. However, as Taylor also wants to claim that the episode is historic, he rightly points out that "the credibility of the story is in no way effected by the fact that Gk and Roman coins are mentioned" (p. 497). See also Lohmeyer, *Markus*, 266, and especially Pesch, *Markusevangelium*, 2:262. Schürer (*The History of the Jewish People*, 2:67) observes: "Greek and Roman names and items are encountered at every turn."

[169] Malbon, "The Poor Widow," 596. Grundmann (*Markus*, 258–59) sees the double meaning, but interprets the giving of her life as her unconditional love of God.

[170] Lane, *Mark*, 443; L. Simon, "Le sou de la veuve. Marc 12/41–44," *ETR* 44 (1969): 115–26; Painter, *Mark's Story*, 169; Pesch, *Markusevangelium*, 2:263–64, and especially Malbon, "The Poor Widow," 595–601. The location of the episode in the narrative and its relationship to Jesus' instruction to the disciples, solemnly drawn into the episode in v. 43 through the "amen" saying, must be respected. The passage becomes more than "a reminder to Mark's readers that the humblest and poorest of them can make a worthy offering to God" (Hooker, *St. Mark*, 196), or an indication that the good news is proclaimed to the poor (Ernst, *Markus*, 364–66). Gnilka (*Markus*, 2:177–78) points to the solemnity of the introduction and the use of the pericope as instruction for the disciples. But he agrees with Lohmeyer (*Markus*, 267) that the pericope "presents a beautiful example of 'Jewish humanity.'" Equally unacceptable is LaVerdiere (*The Beginning*, 2:194): "Jesus' disciples must never do to a poor widow what the scribes were doing." See also Lührmann, *Markusevangelium*, 212.

involves absolute surrender to and trust in the will of God to whose will and purpose Jesus is about to commit himself absolutely in his passion."[171]

The passage (vv. 38–44) is directed against the scribes, and serves to instruct the disciples.[172] As the concluding passage in a narrative section dedicated to the end of the institutional leadership of Israel, however, it also looks back across 11:27–12:44. Disciples of Jesus, especially the disciples reading or listening to this story, are told that the follower of Jesus is to imitate the widow who gave her all. The religious establishment of Israel has been silenced, and the readers and listeners are now part of a new temple, of which Jesus is the cornerstone (12:10–11). The members of the Markan community hear of wars and rumors of wars (see 13:7), and the destruction of the temple (see 13:2, 14–20). Many false prophets making claims to be the definitive intervention of God in those troubled times challenge them (see 13:5–6; 21–22). But in 11:27–12:44 they have been instructed that, symbolically, Israel and its leadership, now destroyed by the Roman armies, came to an end proleptically with Jesus' presence in the temple.

Disciples have been well prepared for their present situation, and must not be overwhelmed by the dramatic events that have happened in Jerusalem. They are called to be followers of Jesus in an in-between time which stretches from the fall of Jerusalem until the gospel has been preached to all nations (see 13:10). Only then will the Son of Man send out the angels to summon the elect from the four corners of the earth (see 13:26–27). In 13:1–37 Jesus tells disciples all these things before they happen (13:23), so that all disciples might be prepared, ready and watching, when they do happen (see 13:32–37).

The End of Jerusalem (13:1–23)

In Mark 13:1–2 Jesus moves away from the city of Jerusalem for the first time since 11:27. He leaves the temple, responds to his disciples' comments about the beauty of the stones and buildings (vv. 1b–2), and sits down on the Mount of Olives, opposite the temple area (v. 3a). In this provocative setting, looking across the valley toward the splendid temple, Peter, James, John, and Andrew ask privately when the destruction of the temple will take place, together with further questions on the sign and time of the end of all things (vv. 3b–4). Jesus' response to his three closest disciples (see 3:16–18; 5:37; 9:2–8), with Andrew (see 1:16–20), runs from 13:5 to 13:37, where the words spoken to the four are broadened into an exhortation for all (ὃ δὲ ὑμῖν λέγω πᾶσιν λέγω, γρηγορεῖτε).[173]

The literary and theological function of 13:1–37

At no stage throughout the discourse is Jesus' voice interrupted. This is rare in the Gospel of Mark, matched only by the parable discourse in 4:1–34. A summary of the debates

---

[171] Anderson, *Mark*, 287. Nineham (*St. Mark*, 334–35) concludes: "Its teaching that the true gift is to give 'everything we have' (v. 44) . . . sums up what has gone before in the Gospel and makes a superb transition to the story of how Jesus 'gave everything' for men."

[172] See Fleddermann ("A Warning," 52–67) on vv. 38–40. The instruction continues into vv. 41–44 (see v. 43).

[173] I would like to give credit to my dear friend, Dr. Barbara Stead, RSM, whom the Lord called prematurely in 1999, for much of what follows. Although Barbara did not publish on Mark 13, we frequently discussed this passage, and as I write I have fifteen pages of her handwritten reflections in front of me.

over the sources, redaction history, and interpretation of Mark 13 fills a volume in its own right.[174] The hermeneutical principles directing this study, i.e., the determining role of context, the function of textual markers in the discourse, and in this rare case, the direct intervention of the author into the narrative (see 13:14b), are crucial to the interpretation proposed. In response to Jesus' prediction of the destruction of the temple (13:2), Peter, James, John, and Andrew ask three questions (13:3–4). These questions determine Jesus' two-staged response in 13:5–37. In 13:5–23 Jesus tells of the future destruction of Jerusalem, opening and closing his words with the textual marker "take heed" (βλέπετε, vv. 5 and 23). Between these two imperatives, he twice warns of the danger that false prophets might lead the believers astray. The section 13:5–23 is thus carefully constructed around an elegant inclusion:

[A] The need to take heed (βλέπετε) (13:5)

[B] Many who will lead astray (πλανήσουσιν) (13:6)

[B′] False prophets and false christs who will try to lead astray (ἀποπλανᾶν) (13:22)

[A′] Warning to take heed (βλέπετε) (13:23)

His words, "But take heed, I have told you all things beforehand" (v. 23), mark the close of the first half of the discourse.

A second section opens with: "But in those days, *after that tribulation*" (13:24a). The discourse on the destruction of Jerusalem has ended, and Jesus moves to the disciples' questions concerning the end of time which, although not unrelated to the end of Jerusalem and its temple, will be accomplished *after that tribulation* (vv. 24–37).[175] He introduces it with an Old Testament expression associated with the end time: "in those days" (ἐν ἐκείναις ταῖς ἡμέραις). It is composed of apocalyptic scenes that tell of the "signs" that the disciples requested (vv. 24–31; cf. v. 4b) and warnings that point to the end of time, the accomplishment of all these things (vv. 32–37; cf. v. 4c).[176] The final section opens and closes with two warnings, using two different verbs to tell his disciples to "take heed," and to "watch" (βλέπετε, v. 33; γρηγορεῖτε, v. 37; see also vv. 34, 35).[177] But the discourse of

---

[174] Two such volumes exist. A survey of discussions of the background and sources for Mark 13, from the "little apocalypse" theory (see below) to the contributions of contemporary redaction critics, is available in G. R. Beasley-Murray, *Jesus and the Last Days: The Interpretation of the Olivet Discourse* (Peabody: Hendrickson, 1993), 1–349. More recently, a systematic engagement with all the critical issues surrounding the interpretation of Mark 13, and some important new contributions to the analysis of the passage, has appeared. See K. D. Dyer, *The Prophecy on the Mount: Mark 13 and the Gathering of the New Community* (ITS 2; Bern: Peter Lang, 1998).

[175] See Beasley-Murray (*Last Days,* 370) for the suggestion that "after that tribulation" comes from Mark's hand, thus "effectively separating the parousia from the ruin of the temple."

[176] The division of the discourse into three major sections is widely accepted. See the survey in Beasley-Murray, *Last Days,* 364–65. There are differences in the allocation of the material in vv. 24–37. For the interpretation that follows, the focus upon things that the disciples will "see" unites vv. 24–31 (see vv. 26, 29) around the question of "the sign," asked in v. 4c. The discussion of "the hour" in vv. 32–37 responds to the disciples' questions concerning "when" all would be accomplished in v. 4c.

[177] For a similar overall structure of 13:5–37, see J. Lambrecht, *Die Redaktion der Markus-Apokalypse: Literarische Analyse und Strukturuntersuchung* (AnBib 28; Rome: Biblical Institute Press, 1967), 286; R. Pesch, *Naherwartung: Tradition und Redaktion in Mk 13* (Düsseldorf: Patmos Verlag, 1968), 74–82; Gnilka, *Markus,* 180; van Iersel, *Reading Mark,* 159–60; V. Balabanski, *Eschatology in the Making: Mark, Matthew and the Didache* (SNTSMS 97; Cambridge: Cambridge University Press, 1997), 72–75. As we will have occasion to see, the two verbs have different meanings.

13:24–37 is as much a response to the questions raised by the four disciples in 13:4 as was his discourse on the destruction of Jerusalem in 13:5–23. The link between the disciples' questions and the answer from Jesus is carefully indicated by the disciples' concern over the accomplishment of "all these things" (ταῦτα . . . πάντα, v. 4c). Jesus tells them, at the heart of his discourse on the end of time (vv. 29–31), that they will see *all these things* (ταῦτα πάντα, v. 30).

In Mark 13:1–37, in a discourse on the end of Jerusalem and the end of the world, Jesus brings to a close the various "endings" that have characterized 11:1–13:37. The Markan community, and all subsequent readers of this story of Jesus, are living in a period between those two endings: Jerusalem is destroyed, but the end of the world is yet to come. Mark, however, was not the first to tell a story of a hero about to face death, issuing final instructions to disciples. The Markan use of preexisting eschatological themes and apocalyptic language in the final composition of Jesus' final discourse is unique.[178] Scholars have long debated the existence of an early Christian "little apocalypse," a document which predated the fall of Jerusalem, and which served Mark as the basis for his more fully developed treatment of this issue in 13:1–23 (or 13:1–27).[179] Mark certainly used sources, and perhaps some pre-Markan "little Apocalypse,"[180] but 13:1–37 has a character of its own. Such passages as Gen 47–50 (Jacob), Deut 31–34 (Moses), Josh 23–24 (Joshua), 1 Sam 12 (Samuel), 1 Kgs 2:1–10 (David), Tobit 14:3–11 (Tobit), and 1 Macc 2:49–70 (Mattathias), provided good Old Testament background for the literary phenomenon of the "farewell discourse." In the New Testament the same form is found in Luke 22:24–38, Acts 20:17–35, and John 13–17. The *Testaments of the Twelve Patriarchs,* although subjected to Christian editing in transmission, show that the genre was widespread within Judaism in the pre-Christian and the early Christian era. Such discourses are final words to those whom the hero of the story will leave behind, instructing them and encouraging them regarding the suffering, conflicts, and failures they will experience in the future.[181]

---

[178] A survey of the never-ending debate about the pre-Markan source and the Markan redaction of 13:1–37 is beyond the scope of this study. It has already been expertly done by Lambrecht, *Redaktion,* 261–94, and exhaustively in Beasley-Murray, *Last Days,* 162–349. I endorse Beasley-Murray's affirmation: "The balance of eschatological anticipation and parenetic statement in part inheres in the material at Mark's hand, but the maintenance of the balance from the first word of the discourse to its last sentence in no small measure is due to Mark's redactional work. In addition the welding of available groups of sayings and individual logia into the form now exhibited in the discourse is due to Mark's structuring of the material" (*Last Days,* 364). See also Gnilka, *Markus,* 179–80. For a schematic presentation of various redactional theories, see Dyer, *The Prophecy,* 311–20.

[179] The "little apocalypse" theory was first proposed by T. Colani in 1864 (two editions). He advocated a Jewish Christian apocalypse. It became popular when C. Weiszäcker, also in 1864, proposed that it was Jewish. It subsequently received the authoritative approval of Bultmann (*History,* 122). For the antecedents and subsequent development of the theory, see Beasley-Murray, *Last Days,* 1–161. On Colani and Weiszäcker, see pp. 13–20, 32–35.

[180] My two former students in Australia, now colleagues, who have worked intensely on this question have both recently concluded that Mark is using a pre-Markan apocalyptic source, although they differ on what generated the source, its nature, and its length. See Balabanski, *Eschatology,* 88–97; Dyer, *The Prophecy,* 153–84. For a recent restatement of the case against it, see A. Y. Collins, *The Beginning of the Gospel: Probings of Mark in Context* (Minneapolis: Fortress, 1992), 73–91. As Balabanski and Dyer have shown, acceptance of an apocalyptic source does not necessarily detract from Markan literary and theological creativity, as Collins (among others) seems to suggest.

[181] For a fuller description of the genre and its function, see F. J. Moloney, *Glory not Dishonor: Reading John 13–21* (Minneapolis: Fortress, 1998), 4–7. For an introduction, an annotated text, and

The function of 13:1–37 as a "farewell discourse" of the Markan Jesus has been well described by W. L. Lane:

> The primary function of Ch. 13 is not to disclose esoteric information but to promote faith and obedience in a time of distress and upheaval. With profound pastoral concern, (the Markan) Jesus prepared his disciples and the Church for a future period which would entail both persecution and mission. The discourse clearly presupposes a period of historical development between the resurrection and the parousia.[182]

The passage is poised between the account of the ministry (1:14–12:44) and the account of the death and resurrection of Jesus (14:1–16:8).[183] The situation on the Mount of Olives and the questions of 13:4, followed by Jesus' discourse of 13:5–37, serve as Jesus' instructions to his disciples on how they are to live in the time between the destruction of Jerusalem and the end of the world as we know it.

The structure of Mark 13:1–23

A common Markan literary pattern reappears in Mark 13 (see, for example, 2:1–3:6; 4:1–34; 5:1–20).[184] The setting is carefully arranged and the issues are raised by the characters in the story, in this case, Jesus and the disciples (13:1–4). The discourse on the end of Jerusalem follows in the form of a chiasm, with 13:9–13 at its center. The passage can be structured as follows:

13:1–4   Introduction: the setting and questions determining the issues Jesus will address during the discourse

13:5–23   Discourse on the end of Jerusalem

   [A] 13:5–6 False prophets

      [B] 13:7–8 Wars and rumors of wars

         [C] 13:9–13 Mission

      [B'] 13:14–20 Wars and rumors of wars

   [A'] 13:21–23 False prophets

Themes raised in 13:5–6 and 7–8 are developed with more specific reference to the destruction of Jerusalem in vv. 14–20 and 21–23.[185] Those reading and hearing the discourse are

---

further bibliography on the *Testaments of the Twelve Patriarchs,* see H. C. Kee, "Testaments of the Twelve Patriarchs," in *The Old Testament Pseudepigrapha* (ed. J. H. Charlesworth; 2 vols.; New York: Doubleday, 1983), 1:775–828. For a survey of scholarship, and a study of Mark 13 as an example of the genre of a farewell discourse, see Dyer, *The Prophecy,* 233–66.

[182] Lane, *Mark,* 446–47, parenthesis added. Lane suggests that the discourse as a whole came to Mark and has a good claim to have come from Jesus. I think this unlikely, and thus I have modified his claim for Jesus as "the Markan Jesus." See also Lührmann, *Markusevangelium,* 215–16.

[183] For recent reflections on the place of Mark 13 within the literary and theological structure of the Gospel of Mark, see van Iersel, *Reading Mark,* 158–70; M. A. Tolbert, *Sowing the Gospel: Mark's World in Literary-Historical Perspective* (Minneapolis: Fortress, 1989), 257–70; T. J. Geddert, *Watchwords: Mark 13 in Markan Eschatology* (JSNTSup 26; Sheffield: Sheffield Academic Press, 1989), 177–97; Balabanski, *Eschatology,* 58–69.

[184] On this literary pattern across the Gospel, see the critical survey of Dewey, *Markan Public Debate,* 131–80.

[185] The link between events described in 13:5–23 and the fall of Jerusalem is hotly debated. Some support them enthusiastically, e.g., J. Marcus, "The Jewish War and the *Sitz im Leben* of Mark,"

aware of the horrors that are happening, or have just happened (see v. 14b), in Jerusalem. Jesus' description of the destruction of Jerusalem on the eve of his passion is a *vaticinium ex eventu*. Many in the Markan community, living in reasonably close geographical and chronological proximity to the events in Jerusalem, might conclude that this is the end of time, and that the Messiah would soon appear. Jesus insists that it is not yet the time. "The gospel must be preached to all nations" first (v. 10).[186]

Introduction (13:1–4)

Jesus has removed himself from the temple (v. 1a) and then from the city of Jerusalem, and he now sits on the Mount of Olives (v. 3a). This marks a turning point in the narrative. Jesus has been in the temple since 11:27. Now he detaches himself from that setting, and from the issues and the people associated with it, all duly dealt with and brought to an end in 11:1–12:44. In a new setting, a brief dialogue with the disciples raises the question of the end of Jerusalem and its temple. The disciples look back at the temple they have just left, and an unnamed disciple comments upon the beauty of the stones and buildings (v. 1b).[187] Jesus accepts that they are indeed great buildings to behold, but prophesies that they will be totally destroyed.[188] Not even one stone will remain upon another stone, so thorough will be the "throwing down" (v. 2).[189] Jesus predicts the destruction of the

---

JBL 111 (1992): 446–48; idem, *Mark*, 33–37; W. A. Such, *The Abomination of Desolation in the Gospel of Mark: Its Historical Reference in Mark 13:14 and Its Impact in the Gospel* (Lanham: University of America Press, 1999). Others deny them with equal enthusiasm, e.g., M. Hengel, *Studies in the Gospel of Mark* (London: SCM Press, 1985), 14–28. The context provided by vv. 1–4 must determine the meaning of the discourse of vv. 5–23. Jesus foretells the total destruction of the temple in v. 2, and the disciples ask "when?" in v. 4a. The desire to match every detail of vv. 5–23 with evidence for the events of 66–70 C.E., from Josephus or any other source, should not determine the interpretation of this passage. It is Jesus' discourse on the destruction of Jerusalem, responding, in his own fashion (ignoring the question of "when"), to the question of the disciples in v. 4a.

[186] Much analysis of Mark 13 (e.g., Schweizer, *Mark*, 260–67) concludes that the discourse is a poorly controlled collection of sources, and that it is of little importance in Mark's overall literary scheme. Schweizer asserts that "chapter 13 can hardly be claimed as the high point of his book" (p. 262). He then proposes that, after the introduction (vv. 1–4), vv. 14–20 come from the "little apocalypse," vv. 21–23 are a digression applying everything to the readers, and vv. 5–15 and vv. 24–27 describe the end time. For the contemporary reversal of this position, see, for example, Geddert, *Watchwords*, 177–97; Balabanski, *Eschatology*, 58–69.

[187] This is the only place in the Gospel of Mark where an unnamed disciple asks a question of Jesus. It prepares for Jesus' response in v. 2. See Lohmeyer, *Markus*, 268. By addressing Jesus as διδάσκαλε (v. 1b) the disciple shows that the journey to Jerusalem has not led to a full understanding of Jesus' person and role (see 4:38; 9:17, 38; 10:17, 20, 35; 12:14, 19, 32). It is not, as LaVerdiere (*The Beginning*, 2:196) suggests, a reflection of "the Gospel's catechetical interest."

[188] On the wonder of the disciple's statement and the surprise of Jesus' answer, see Taylor, *St. Mark*, 500–501. Much has been made of the fact that Jesus' words are not exactly correct. The destruction of Titus in 70 C.E. and even Hadrian's salting of the city in 135 C.E. left large sections of the retaining walls of the temple in place. They are still in place today, and archaeological work is steadily uncovering more of pre-70 Jerusalem. For Lane (*Mark*, 451–53), this is indication enough that v. 2 comes from Jesus and is not a *vaticinium ex eventu*. But the point is the complete destruction of Jerusalem and its temple, and it does not matter that some details in the rhetoric used to describe that destruction are not precise descriptions of how things actually happened. For a similar rhetoric, see Josephus, *J.W.* 7.1–4, also a description of the destroyed city. The search for *scientifically controllable parallels* to a highly rhetorical passage is a "blind alley" in the interpretation of Mark 13.

[189] Scholars have long debated the relationship between Mark 13:2 and 14:58, and the possibility that Jesus' words are reported here or that one of these sayings has been developed from another. See the full report of the discussion in Beasley-Murray, *Last Days*, 376–79.

temple, the city, and the nation, using prophetic traditions that threaten God's abandoning the temple and subsequent destruction of the city (see Amos 9:1; Jer 7:1–20; 26:17–19; Ezek 9–11; Mic 3:12).[190]

The words addressed to all the disciples in 13:2 become more focused in 13:3–4. Both the setting (v. 3) and the questions (v. 4) are used by Mark to set the agenda for the discourse in 13:5–37.[191] Jesus is outside the city, seated somewhere on the Mount of Olives, a place traditionally associated with an oracle of judgment against Jerusalem (see Zech 14:4; Josephus, *Ant.* 20.169; *J.W.* 2.262). The three disciples who have been most intimate with him, Peter, James, and John, approach Jesus (see 3:17–17; 5:37; 9:2–8). They are joined by Andrew.[192] They ask him privately for further information concerning the timing of the destruction and the sign that will mark its final accomplishment (v. 4).[193] The scene and the themes have been set. Jesus has departed from the city and its now defunct institutions, and looks back upon it from a place associated with oracles of judgment. He begins his discourse with a partial response to the first of the three questions asked by Peter, James, John, and Andrew. He tells of the destruction of Jerusalem, but focuses upon how the disciples are to understand that dramatic event, rather than disclosing the timing of the event. Whatever the sources behind the discourse which follows (vv. 5–37), the "timing" of the destruction of Jerusalem was an irrelevant question for the Markan community. It was happening, and they were hearing about it (see v. 7). The crucial issue is how they are to respond to such news. The second and third questions, a description of the signs and an indication of the time when "all these things" will be accomplished, will be dealt with when Jesus goes on to tell them of the end of the world (vv. 24–37).[194]

---

[190] The closest parallel to Mark 13:2 is Luke 19:44. Both sayings probably developed independently in the tradition. See J. Dupont, "Il n'en sera pas laissée pierre sur pierre (Mc 13,2; Luc 19,44)," *Bib* 52 (1971): 301–20.

[191] On vv. 3–4 as a Markan introduction to the discourse, see Beasley-Murray, *Last Days*, 384–86; Lührmann, *Markusevangelium*, 217–18. Kelber (*Kingdom*, 112–13) claims that the entire discourse hangs on Jesus' word against the temple in v. 2. It is the combination of Jesus' word and the questions asked in v. 4 that serve as the agenda for the discourse. For convincing support for this position, despite my different reading of the discourse and its relationship to v. 4, see Such, *The Abomination of Desolation*, 17–52.

[192] With the addition of Andrew, the group comprises the first four disciples to be called (1:16–20). See Painter, *Mark's Gospel*, 170.

[193] On the private nature of a disclosure that tells of the future, see 4:34; 9:2, 9. See LaVerdiere, *The Beginning*, 2:197 n. 30.

[194] On the separation of ταῦτα, referring back to the destruction of the temple (v. 2), and the ταῦτα . . . πάντα as looking forward, see Lagrange, *Saint Marc*, 311–12; Taylor, *St. Mark*, 502; Anderson, *Mark*, 291; Kelber, *Kingdom*, 113. I am treating vv. 5–37 as a tripartite response to the three questions. Although apocalyptic language is used in vv. 5–23, its point of reference is the destruction of Jerusalem, and thus looks back to the statement of v. 2 (the first ταῦτα of v. 4), not the end of the world (the ταῦτα . . . πάντα of v. 4). Lane (*Mark*, 447–48) makes a similar case. Many think that only two questions are asked: the time of the destruction of Jerusalem and the signs of the end of the world. See, for example, Kelber, *Kingdom*, 113; Anderson, *Mark*, 291; LaVerdiere, *The Beginning*, 2:198; Painter, *Mark's Gospel*, 171. However, as we shall see, vv. 24–31 will deal with "signs" and vv. 32–37 will deal with the accomplishment. Many claim that vv. 24–27 belong to vv. 5–23, and that they were part of the "little apocalypse"; see Taylor, *St. Mark*, 502–3, and especially Such, *The Abomination of Desolation*, 17–52, for surveys. For Such, the σημεῖον of v. 4 points to the abomination in v. 14. He argues that this relationship determines the larger units of vv. 5–27 (made up of vv. 5–8, 9–13, 15–18, 18–23 and 24–27) and vv. 28–37.

[A] False prophets (13:5–6)

The discourse begins with a typical Markan introduction: "And Jesus began to say to them." The issue at the heart of the discourse is immediately broached: "Take heed (βλέπετε) lest anyone lead you astray" (v. 5). Mark's readers are under threat and are warned to "watch." Mark uses this word, which has the basic meaning of "look," extensively and consistently links it with a call to discernment.[195] It is used to open and close 13:5–23 and "is a call to see past the externals and recognize the deceptions that lurk beneath the persuasive words and deceptive signs."[196] There are some who would lead them astray, and they will do this by coming in the name of Jesus. Such people are from Christian ranks (v. 6), maybe even from the Markan community. They claim to come as the final appearance of the Messiah.[197] Their language reflects the prophetic revelation of God, but they claim to be the final appearance of the Messiah, coming to mark the end of time. They use an expression which is at the one time a prophetic identification of God in history (see especially Isa 43:10; 45:18),[198] and a claim to self-identity as the final appearance of the Messiah: "I am he" (v. 6a). They are to be ignored. Such claims, within the context of the dramatic collapse of Jerusalem and its destruction by Rome, are false and will lead astray the many who accept them (v. 6b).[199] The readers and listeners to these words are aware of a number of such impostors. They are merely sketched at this stage of the narrative, but well documented in Josephus's record of the end of Jerusalem (see *J.W.* 2.433–34, 444, 652; 6.313; 7.29–31).[200] Their claims will be more fully developed in 13:21–23.

[B] Wars and rumors of wars (13:7–8)

A new theme is introduced as Jesus issues another warning: "do not be alarmed" (μὴ θροεῖσθε) when they hear of wars and rumors of wars (v. 7).[201] The news of events that are happening, or have happened recently, in the city of Jerusalem is a threat to the Markan view of history.[202] The stories of the war reaching the ears of the members of the Markan

---

[195] Geddert, *Watchwords*, 81–87.

[196] Ibid., 86.

[197] Not all scholars agree that the false prophets are Christians, but coming in the name of Jesus seems to imply that; see Kelber, *Kingdom*, 114–15. The claim that they may belong to the Markan community is speculative. It is generally accepted that the false prophets are not claiming to be the return of Jesus, but the final appearance of the Messiah; see Taylor, *St. Mark*, 503–4; Cranfield, *St. Mark*, 395; Lane, *Mark*, 456; Anderson, *Mark*, 292.

[198] Gnilka, *Markus*, 2:186–87, also H. Zimmerman, "Das absolut Ἐγώ εἰμι als neutestamentliche Offenbarungsformel," *BZ* 4 (1960): 54–69, 266–76. On the relationship between the prophetic use of "I am he" and its use in the Pentateuch, see W. Zimmerli, "Ich bin Jahwe," in *Geschichte und Altes Testament: Albrecht Alt zum siebzigsten Geburtstag* (ed. G. Ebeling; BHT 16; Tübingen: J. C. B. Mohr [Paul Siebeck], 1953), 179–209.

[199] There is an elegant balance to vv. 5b–6, opening with πλανήσῃ πολλοί, and closing with πολλοὺς πλανήσουσιν. Whatever the source of the discourse, it is carefully presented in its Markan dress.

[200] See Marcus, "Jewish War," 457–59, and especially C. H. Williams, *I Am He: The Interpretation of ʾAnî Hûʾ in Jewish and Early Christian Literature* (WUNT 2. Reihe 113; Tübingen: J. C. B. Mohr [Paul Siebeck], 2000), 229–41.

[201] The verb θροέω is used in 2 Thess 2:2 in a warning not to be alarmed by false rumors that the day of the Lord had arrived. See Kelber, *Kingdom*, 116–17.

[202] The link with Jerusalem made here (see also Gnilka, *Markus*, 2:184–88), is not universally accepted. Many take it as a general indication of the end time, which Mark must correct; see, for

community could be understood as part of the turmoil which would herald the end time (see Jer 4:16–17; Zech 14:2; 4 Ezra 8:63–9:3). They are warned not come to this conclusion. These events are part of God's larger design: δεῖ γενέσθαι ("it *must* take place"). Another major theme of 13:5–23 is stated in 13:7c: "The end is not yet." Mark is not writing an eschatological discourse, or indulging in apocalyptic speculation.[203] He is establishing a sense of history that reaches beyond the events of 66–70 C.E., the wars and rumors of wars. There is a shift between 13:7, which refers to the events taking place in Jerusalem, and the prophecies in 13:8, which point to a troubled future.[204] After the destruction of Jerusalem any number of further disasters will take place: wars between nations and kingdoms, and the natural disasters of earthquake and famine (v. 8bc). There is no need to identify the exact events that may or may not lie behind Jesus' prophecy.[205] The readers of the Gospel knew of wars and natural disasters, and they are also part of language associated with prophetic pronouncements and apocalyptic expectation (see Isa 19:2; 4 Ezra 13:31 [wars]; Isa 13:13; Jer 4:24; *1 En.* 1:6–7 [earthquakes]; Isa 14:30; *2 Bar.* 27:6 [famine]).[206] But the point established at this stage of the discourse is that the history of sin, chaos, and tragedy will continue *after* the destruction of Jerusalem. The disciples, and through them the readers, must understand that the events in Jerusalem were but the beginnings of the birth pangs (ἀρχὴ ὠδίνων ταῦτα). Despite its syntactic distance from "wars and rumors of wars" in 13:7, the ταῦτα refers to the events in Jerusalem, and not to the subsequent wars and the natural disasters. The wars and rumors of wars (v. 7) were the beginnings of the birth pangs (v. 8d). But much is yet to be endured before the final end (v. 8abc).

A more detailed description of the horrors of the "wars and rumors of wars" in Jerusalem will be given in 13:14–20. But Mark must insist that the history of tragedy and sin will continue after the destruction of the Holy City. The expression "birth pangs" is often found in prophetic and apocalyptic literature (see Isa 26:17–18; 66:8–9; Hos 13:13; Mic 4:9–10), and indicates that history, which will not come to an end with the destruction of Jerusalem, is still working its painful way to a final end.[207] In this sense 13:5–23 is not un-

---

example, Hooker, *St. Mark,* 308, and especially Beasley-Murray, *Last Days,* 395–96. For Hengel (*Studies,* 21–28), all the allusions here can be fitted into a Roman background, from Nero and the following twelve months, marked by the disastrous rule and slaying of four kings (68–69 C.E.).

[203] As Beasley-Murray (*Last Days,* 365–70) insists, the discourse is not "apocalyptic," but is "to inspire faith, endurance and hope in face of the impending sufferings of the Church and of the Jewish nation" (p. 367), and "to warn Christians against false teachings concerning the end" (p. 368). See Lohmeyer, *Markus,* 285–86; Grundmann, *Markus,* 261; M. D. Hooker, "Trial and Tribulation in Mark XIII," *BJRL* 65 (1982): 78–99; F. Neirynck, "Le discours anti-apocalyptique de Mc. XIII," *ETL* 45 (1969): 154–64; Anderson, *Mark,* 287–90; Dyer, *The Prophecy,* 123–31; Balabanski, *Eschatology,* 70–72.

[204] Against, among many, Beasley-Murray (*Last Days,* 394–98), who interprets v. 7 in the light of v. 8, and thus rejects any association of v. 7 with the events of the Jewish War. For documentation linking vv. 6–8 with events from the War, see Such, *The Abomination of Desolation,* 169–71.

[205] But see Hengel, *Studies,* 14–28. This dramatic period within Roman history, marked by volcanic eruptions and "the year of the four kings," would have provided material for the Markan rhetoric. However, the Markan view looks beyond any immediate events to a history of such events that still lay *ahead* of the Christian community. Reference is regularly made to such events as the earthquake which partially destroyed Pompeii in 62 C.E. See, for example, Hooker, *St. Mark,* 308; Gnilka, *Markus,* 188. As Taylor (*St. Mark,* 505) rightly remarks, "the predictions may be quite general."

[206] See Beasley-Murray, *Last Days,* 394–98.

[207] Later rabbinic teaching speaks of a suffering that will precede the final end as "the birth pangs of the Messiah." One cannot be sure if such an idea was present at the time of the Gospel of Mark, but see Nineham, *St. Mark,* 346; Anderson, *Mark,* 292–93.

connected with 13:24–37. The destruction of Jerusalem (vv. 5–23) is the first of many cata-
clysms that will take place between the "now" of the Markan community and the "not yet"
of the traditional end time. For the moment Mark is concerned to insist that there will be a
period after the destruction of Jerusalem. That event is not the end (v. 7), but the beginning (v. 8) of a period which will come to an end in God's good time (see vv. 24–37).

[C] Mission (13:9–13)

The second use of βλέπετε opens another element in Jesus' discourse on the end of Jerusalem. In 13:5 the verb was used to warn the disciples about others. In 13:9 it tells them
to "watch themselves, to ensure on the one hand that they do not fail to grasp the profound import of their mission to the world, and on the other that they do not fail in their
faith and in their task."[208] Having established that a long history will follow the fall of Jerusalem, he foretells the future of the disciples. Not only will the period of history following
the destruction of Jerusalem be marked by wars and natural disasters (v. 8abc), but Christians will be persecuted. Reflecting the experience of Markan Christians, a *vaticinium ex
eventu* warns the disciples of their future suffering. The people who will be responsible
for the trials and persecutions are never named. Indeed, given the extent of the trials and
persecutions, they cannot be named, as they will be myriad. They will "deliver up"
(παραδώσουσιν ὑμᾶς) the Christians to both trial and suffering at the hands of Jewish
(συνέδρια, συναγωγάς) and Gentile (ἐπὶ ἡγεμόνων καὶ βασιλέων σταθήσεσθε) authorities
(v. 9).[209] Mission is already contained in the naming of these authorities.[210] Jesus, addressing his four disciples, points to the presence of suffering believers in Israel and beyond,
warning them of a future when followers of Jesus will be put on trial and punished for his
sake (ἕνεκεν ἐμοῦ). In a time after the death of Jesus, and after the destruction of Jerusalem, disciples will be tried and tested because of Jesus, and they will bear witness to him
before both Jew and Gentile (εἰς μαρτύριον αὐτοῖς).[211]

---

[208] Beasley-Murray, *Last Days*, 400.

[209] The verb παραδίδωμι (see also v. 11) has already been used in Jesus' passion predictions (see
9:31; 10:33) and is often repeated in the passion narrative (see 14:10–15:15). Similarly, in v. 11 the
time of trial is call "that hour" (ἐν ἐκείνῃ τῇ ὥρᾳ) for the disciples, as it is for Jesus (see 14:41). The
future experience of the disciples repeats the suffering of Jesus; see Lightfoot, *Gospel Message*, 45–59,
also Beasley-Murray, *Last Days*, 399, and the further references provided in n. 69 of that page, and
pp. 370–72. D.-A. Koch ("Zum Verhältnis von Christologie und Eschatologie im Markusevangelium," in *Jesus Christus in Historie und Theologie: Neutestamentliche Festschrift für Hans Conzelmann zum 60. Geburtstag* [ed. G. Strecker; Tübingen: J. C. B. Mohr (Paul Siebeck), 1975], 395–408)
has drawn a convincing parallel between 8:29–9:1, which presents Jesus as the Son of Man, suffering
death for the kingdom of God and its returning Lord, and 13:9–13.

[210] Bultmann, *History*, 122; Lohmeyer, *Markus*, 272; Grundmann, *Markus*, 264.

[211] The expression is ambiguous. It could mean testimony to them, or testimony against
them; see Beasley-Murray, *Last Days*, 401–2. The missionary context suggests that it means "tes-
tifying to them about the gospel." On the nature of courts and trials in Palestine and in the Gentile
world, see D. R. A. Hare, *The Theme of Jewish Persecution of Christians in the Gospel according to St.
Matthew* (SNTSMS 6; Cambridge: Cambridge University Press, 1967), 101–9. Although he now fa-
vors a Roman setting for the Gospel, J. R. Donahue (*Are You the Christ? The Trial Narrative in the
Gospel of Mark* [SBLDS 10; Missoula: Society of Biblical Literature, 1973], 217–24) links the trials of
v. 9 with the mock trials run by the Zealots once they took over the besieged city of Jerusalem. Such
(*The Abomination of Desolation*, 173–77) also documents experiences from the period of the Jewish
War which match vv. 9–13, and suggests that Jesus' trial before the Sanhedrin is also based upon this
prediction.

The central theme of 13:5–23 is stated in v. 10: "And the gospel must first be proclaimed to all nations."[212] Jesus has told his listeners not to be led astray by false claims of eschatological figures (vv. 5–6) and has warned them against reading the news they are hearing of the destruction of Jerusalem as a sign that history was coming to a close. On the contrary, the end is not yet (vv. 7–8). First, before the end, in the in-between time, the gospel must be preached to all the nations. But the use of πρῶτον ("first") maintains the tension between the missionary activity of the disciples and the inevitable end of the world, which will come. Jesus' insistence that the events dealt with in 13:5–23 are not "the end," does not detract from the relationship between the destruction of Jerusalem and 13:24–37, where the end of the world is the subject of his discourse.[213] The period between the destruction of Jerusalem and the end of the world will be marked by human violence and natural disasters, all of which must be experienced and understood by the disciple of Jesus (v. 8). But it will also be a period marked by the bold witness of disciples of Jesus, and the proclamation of the gospel, in the face of trial and abuse, to the four corners of the world, to all the nations (vv. 9–10).

The remaining words of Jesus continue the theme of trial and persecution, but also promise the guidance of the Holy Spirit. The trial and delivery of 13:9 are repeated, but the disciples are told that they should have no cause for anxiety as they face trial. Those on trial, as they go through their own "hour," will be inspired by the Holy Spirit. This is not a promise that they will avoid suffering, but that even in their suffering they will proclaim the gospel, for the Spirit will be present. The process of betrayal is indicated, possibly reflecting what was happening in a community under scrutiny and persecution.[214] However, the perspective of 13:9–13 is toward the future. There is no need to find events reported from the Jewish War which match *everything* raised in 13:9–13. It is sufficient that there be a general awareness and fear, from the widespread knowledge of the world of the time, that believers will be slain, not because they will be hunted down by the authorities, but because family members will betray one another. Perhaps Mic 7:6 was the catalyst for these words of Jesus: "For the son treats the father with contempt, the daughter rises up against her mother, the daughter-in-law against her mother-in-law; a man's enemies are the men of his own house." Brothers will betray brothers, fathers will betray their children, and children will turn against their parents. These processes will

---

[212] Many commentators find this verse an intrusion, and some have suggested a different punctuation, to make it less directed to the Gentile mission; see Nineham, *St. Mark,* 347–48; Hooker, *St. Mark,* 310–12. It is not arbitrary, but a Markan addition to pre-Markan tradition, set at the heart of vv. 5–23. See Lohmeyer, *Markus,* 272; Taylor, *St. Mark,* 507; Gnilka, *Markus,* 2:189. It thus expresses the Markan point of view: disciples are sent into a mission to proclaim the gospel in the in-between time. For an important study of the centrality of the theme of mission in the Gospel of Mark as a whole, see D. Senior, "The Struggle to be Universal: Mission as Vantage Point for New Testament Investigation," *CBQ* 46 (1984): 63–81. For Such (*The Abomination of Desolation,* 139–62), the destruction of Jerusalem and the command to flee to the mountains in v. 14 is the historical basis for the Markan theology of a new community, founded on the rejected cornerstone, preaching the gospel to all the nations.

[213] Gnilka, *Markus,* 2:191.

[214] Hooker (*St. Mark,* 312) remarks: "No doubt it will have corresponded all too closely to the experience of many first-century Christians." The lack of direct evidence for the persecution of Christians during the Jewish War is seen as the weakest point in the argument for setting the Gospel at that time. For an attempt to find some relevant evidence, see Kelber, *Kingdom,* 117–19; Marcus, *Mark,* 34; and especially Donahue, *Are You the Christ?* 212–24. But the future orientation of the rhetoric must be respected.

lead to death.[215] Indeed, there will be an intense hatred in the larger community on account of the disciples' belief in the gospel and commitment to the person of Jesus (cf. 1 Pet 4:14).

Throughout this section of Jesus' discourse, where the focus is on the destruction of Jerusalem, the future experience of the disciples, and the challenge of preaching the gospel in the midst of hatred, trial, persecution, and death, the promise of an end time is always present. The end is not yet, but it will come (v. 7), and the in-between time will be marked by birth pangs which usher in the end time (v. 8). The gospel must be proclaimed to all the nations *before* the end time comes, but its coming is inevitable (v. 10). The discourse is an exhortation to disciples on how they are to live in the in-between time, waiting with patience and endurance for the end (εἰς τέλος).[216] Patient endurance of hatred, misunderstanding, and even death will lead to final salvation (v. 13). Jesus' teaching in 8:34–38 is close at hand: "Whoever wishes to save his life will lose it, but whoever will lose his life for my sake and the gospel will save it." This section of the discourse (vv. 9–13) forms the centerpiece of the chiasm developed by Mark to address excessive concern about the cataclysmic events happening in Jerusalem. A mission lies ahead of the disciples, between the fall of Jerusalem and the end of time. They will suffer and die for the gospel and in the name of Jesus, but the Holy Spirit will direct them through the in-between time. Those who persevere with enduring patience (ὁ δὲ ὑπομείνας) will be saved at the end of time (see Dan 12:12; 4 Ezra 6:25; 7:27).[217]

[B′] Wars and rumors of wars (13:14–20)

Despite the reservations of many, the collection of sayings in 13:14–20, which had a complicated pre-history,[218] is to be related to the experience of the Jewish people in and about Jerusalem at the time of the Jewish War.[219] What was sketched in 13:7 as "wars and rumors of wars" is more fully described in 13:14–20. The author's direct appeal to the reader in 13:14b, "Let the reader understand," should be given its obvious meaning. This

---

215 On Mic 7:6 as the source for Mark 13:12–13, see Lambrecht, *Redaktion,* 141. L. Hartman (*Prophecy Interpreted: The Formation of Some Jewish Apocalyptic Texts and of the Eschatological Discourse Mark 13 Par.* [ConBNT 1; Lund: Gleerup, 1966], 168–69) has drawn attention to the even more pertinent development of the MT in the Targum of Mic 7:6. For Hengel (*Studies,* 222–26), Mark 13:11–13 is to be related to the Neronic persecutions and Tacitus's description of Christians as "odium humani generis" (*Annals* 15:44.2.4). Trajan recommended to Pliny in 112 that he encourage disaffected Christians and family members to inform on one another. Trajan is too late to be directly involved in the Markan experience, but the practice may not have been invented by him. See W. H. C. Frend, *The Rise of Christianity* (London: Darton, Longman & Todd, 1984), 148–51. None of this demands that the Markan community was located in Rome. Such sentiments and practices were possible anywhere in the Empire. For the Roman interpretation, see Lane, *Mark,* 463–64.

216 The expression εἰς τέλος can also have a qualitative meaning, "completely, consummately" (cf. John 13:1). However, within this context, and especially in the light of the use of τὸ τέλος in v. 7, it has the chronological meaning of "to the end."

217 The verb ὑπομένω basically carries the idea of being patient. But it also has the sense of waiting. It may even be linked to Mic 7:6. See Hartman, *Prophecy Interpreted,* 168; Pesch, *Markusevangelium,* 2:286. *Mutatis mutandis,* there are many links between this "farewell discourse" in Mark 13:5–23 and its Johannine counterpart. On living in the in-between time, the name of Jesus, and the presence of the Spirit, especially in John 14 and 16, see F. J. Moloney, "The Johannine Paraclete and Jesus," in *Dummodo Christus annuntietur: Studi in onore di Prof. Jozef Heriban* (ed. A. Strus and R. Blatnicky; BibSciRel 146; Rome: LAS, 1998), 213–28.

218 For the discussion, and his own contribution, see Dyer, *The Prophecy,* 153–84.

219 For objections to this claim, see Hengel, *Studies,* 16–17; Beasley-Murray, *Last Days,* 407–8.

insertion into the discourse did not come from a pre-Markan source, but is a comment from the narrator. People who know what Jesus is talking about are reading the story. When one event happens, then another should follow.[220] The event is the installation of the desolating sacrilege, standing where he ought not be (v. 14a). This is a direct reference back to "the desolating sacrilege" of Dan 9:27, 11:31, and 12:11. The historical background for the event is supplied by 1 Macc 1:54–59. Returning to Syria after his victory in Egypt in 168 B.C.E., Antiochus Epiphanes stopped all sacrifice in the Jerusalem temple. He ordered that observance of the ancestral laws should cease, and he destroyed and burned copies of the book of the covenant. He set up a pagan altar, a desolating sacrilege, on top of the altar of burnt offerings. On the twenty-fifth day of Chislev, unclean sacrifice was offered on the desolating sacrilege, set up on top of the altar of YHWH. In Dan 9:27, however, there is evidence that an image of Zeus, made in the likeness of Antiochus, was raised in the temple. Reflecting prophecies of Jeremiah and Ezekiel about the desecration of the temple and the devastation of the nation, Dan 9:24–27 "has in view the coming of one who acts both blasphemously and destructively, causing devastation to the city and the temple and horror among the people."[221] Between that experience and the period of the Jewish War, Caligula threatened a similar desecration by raising a massive statue of himself within the Temple in 39–40 C.E. Mark 13:14 has been shaped by these events. What happened under Antiochus Epiphanes (and was again threatened in 39–40 C.E.) is rendered more concrete for the situation in Jerusalem in 70 C.E. by means of the masculine participle ἑστηκότα, "standing" where *he* ought not.[222]

Jesus utters a *vaticinium ex eventu* concerning a recent event that has taken place in Jerusalem and its temple, and the narrator reminds the readers that they should know what he is talking about.[223] Ceaseless debate rages around the link between the Danielic and the Markan "desolating sacrilege." The Markan insistence that the sacrilege will be a male human figure "standing where *he* ought not" determines my acceptance of the suggestion that the "he" is the Roman commander Titus himself, amid the planting of Roman standards, accompanied by his idolatrous acclamation as *imperator* (αὐτοκράτορα), within the temple area (Josephus, *J.W.* 6.316).[224] What was claimed for the Danielic "desolating sacrilege" (Dan

---

220 Gnilka, *Markus,* 195.

221 Beasley-Murray, *Last Days,* 411. See his presentation of the biblical background and scholarly debate, summarized above, on pp. 408–11.

222 Such, *The Abomination of Desolation,* 81–87. Josephus (*Ant.* 10.263–281) associates Daniel and the Roman devastation of Jerusalem. Many advocates of a "little apocalypse" claim that it may have been written during the threat from Caligula. See, for example, Grundmann, *Markus,* 266; Schweizer, *Mark,* 263; and especially Such, *The Abomination of Desolation,* 53–79. For others (e.g., Gnilka, *Markus,* 2:211; Balabanski, *Eschatology,* 86–97), the Jewish War itself generated the *Flugblatt* (Gnilka) or Judean oracle (Balabanski).

223 Some attempt to sidestep this issue by regarding v. 14b as words of Jesus, and then placing them within the prophetic, and especially Danielic, tradition (see Dan 8:15–17; 9:22–23; 11:33; 12:10). The saying reminds hearers of their responsibility to recognize and understand prophetic (and apocalyptic) revelations (see also Rev 13:18; 17:9). See, for example, Beasley-Murray, *Last Days,* 411. Others avoid a specific link with an event during the Jewish War by interpreting v. 14a as a more general reference to the antichrist; see, for example, B. H. Branscomb, *The Gospel of Mark* (MNTC; London: Hodder and Stoughton, 1937), 237–38; Lohmeyer, *Markus,* 276; Grundmann, *Markus,* 266–67; Kelber, *Kingdom,* 119–20; Anderson, *Mark,* 296; Gnilka, *Markus,* 2:195–96. But as Taylor (*St. Mark,* 511) points out, the terms and the parallel with 2 Thess 2:3–10 "suggest that the manifestation of Anti-Christ in expected historical events is contemplated."

224 Such (*The Abomination of Desolation,* 92–102) usefully discusses the many identifications suggested.

9:24–27) can also be claimed for 13:14a. Mark "has in view the coming of one who acts both blasphemously and destructively, causing devastation to the city and the temple and horror among the people."[225] The Markan readers have news of this event ("wars and rumors of wars," v. 7), and the author recalls the image used by the prophet Daniel to describe a similar desecration by Antiochus Epiphanes (v. 14a). The narrator reminds the readers that, if the "desolating sacrilege" has reappeared in the temple, a dramatic final moment for Jerusalem and its temple has taken place (v. 14b). As a result of the presence of the Roman army, its idolatrous standards planted in the temple area, and the acclamation of Titus as *imperator,* the people of Jerusalem are to experience flight and untold suffering (vv. 14c–20).

Further critical problems arise in 13:14c. After the narrator's comment in 13:14b, Jesus instructs those who are in Judea to flee to the mountains. Objections have been raised concerning the linking of this command with any situation in the Jewish War. From 66–70 C.E. the Roman armies had taken control of almost all of Judea, and there appears little sense in urging a flight into the hands of the Roman forces.[226] It is also regularly remarked that a flight from Jerusalem, itself a "mountain," would not be spoken of as a flight to the mountains.[227] These objections have received further support from the recent rejection of the tradition of a flight to Pella, an episode reported in Eusebius, *Historia ecclesiastica* 3.5.3, and Epiphanius, *Panarion* 29.7.7–8; 30.2.7; *De mensuris et ponderibus* 15.[228] Scholars differ concerning the reasons for the invention of the tradition of the flight, and the sources used for its development in the second century.[229] Balabanski has recently mounted a convincing defense of the so-called Pella tradition by driving a wedge between these differing opinions. She has shown that the tradition of the flight is pre-Markan and that it should be linked with Mark 13:14.[230] Her careful analysis of Eusebius and

---

[225] Beasley-Murray, *Last Days,* 411.

[226] For an aggressive argument along these lines, see Hengel, *Studies,* 16–17. See also Beasley-Murray (*Last Days,* 407–8), who remarks: "There is not a syllable which reflects knowledge of events which took place in the Jewish War, still less of the actual destruction of the city and temple." Against this see, among many, Lührmann, *Markusevangelium,* 221–23. Lührmann does not decide for any specific incident or person behind v. 14, but explains the context as "something that actually took place during the Roman siege of Jerusalem in the Jewish War" (p. 222).

[227] See, for example, Hengel, *Studies,* 16–17. As Balabanski has pointed out (with reference to 1 Macc 2:28, where flight to the mountains marked the beginning of resistance), the expression had become a *topos.* "A Jerusalemite could make use of this phrase as much as a 'lowlander' in order to spread an injunction to flee from the city while maintaining the anonymity afforded by a known *topos*" (*Eschatology,* 120).

[228] Gerd Lüdemann has been the sternest critic of the tradition. See, for example, G. Lüdemann, "The Successors of Pre-70 Jerusalem Christianity: A Critical Evaluation of the Pella Tradition," in *Jewish and Christian Self-Definition* (ed. E. P. Sanders; 3 vols.; London: SCM, 1980), 1:161–73. For Lüdemann, the Pella tradition arose in the second century among Jewish Christians in Pella who wished to legitimize themselves via a connection to the Jerusalem church. It has been defended by C. Koester, "The Origin and Significance of the Flight to Pella Tradition," *CBQ* 51 (1989): 90–106; Hengel, *Studies,* 18 n. 111; Pesch, *Markusevangelium,* 2:292; idem, "Markus 13," in *L'Apocalypse johannique et l'apocalyptique dans le Nouveau Testament* (ed. J. Lambrecht; BETL 53; Leuven: Leuven University Press, 1980), 355–68. Against the theory, see J. Verheyden, "The Flight of the Christians to Pella," *ETL* 66 (1990): 368–84, and F. Neirynck, "Marc 13: Examen critique de l'interprétation de R. Pesch," in *L'Apocalypse johannique,* 369–401. For a summary, see Balabanski, *Eschatology,* 101–5; Beasley-Murray, *Last Days,* 412–13.

[229] For example, Lüdemann rejects any contact with gospel traditions, while Verheyden and Beasley-Murray argue for them.

[230] For Balabanski, behind Mark 13:14–27 lie two sources, an apocalyptic source (pp. 94–95) and a Judean oracle (p. 91); see *Eschatology,* 86–97. The link between Mark 13:14 and the Pella tradition

Epiphanius leads her to conclude that these reports depend upon different sources. Eusebius's source claimed that the flight oracle was given to members of the Jerusalem church before the war, while Epiphanius linked the Ebionites and Pella.[231] After a thorough analysis of Eusebius and Epiphanius and their dependence upon earlier gospel traditions of a Judean flight, including Mark 13:14, Balabanski convincingly concludes:

> There was indeed a flight of Jewish Christians from Jerusalem in the winter of 67 C.E. I have also argued that the Pella tradition did not originate with Eusebius nor with Epiphanius, and that Epiphanius' sources included a source other than Eusebius and Eusebius' source. These traditions associate the flight both with Pella specifically, and with Perea more generally. This information, combined with the fact that Mark and his community gained early access to the Judean oracle, permits me to postulate that a single unified flight to Pella was a piece of systematizing fiction behind which a true historical kernel is evident. There was indeed an exodus of at least a considerable number of Jewish Christians from Jerusalem; some of those who escaped went to Pella, some to other localities in Perea, and some north to Syria.... Thus the Synoptic flight oracle (the Judean oracle) and the Pella flight tradition permit a glimpse of the way in which a historical event gave rise to a variety of traditions.[232]

Jesus' reference to the "desolating sacrilege" in 13:14a and his command that the disciples flee to the mountains are both *vaticinia ex eventu*. The background is the turmoil of the Jewish War, but two different moments have been joined. The call to flee to the mountains (v. 14c) came from an earlier time in the war, when such flight was possible,[233] while the reference to the "desolating sacrilege" was associated with the Roman desecration of the temple. Gathering material from the "rumors of wars" (v. 7), Mark has composed v. 14 on the basis of two events from the Jewish War (v. 14a, v. 14c), and added his own remark on the need for his readers to be aware of these dramatic events (v. 14b). The message the members of the Markan community are receiving about "wars and rumors of wars" (v. 7) is correct: Jerusalem and its temple are being destroyed (v. 14). The more general remarks of vv. 7–8 are being filled out with details of events in Jerusalem and their consequences in vv. 14–20. What follows in vv. 15–20 (with the exception of the reference to winter in v. 18), has no direct link with specific events from 66–70 C.E., but comes from more general biblical and apocalyptic language used to describe the experience of destruction.

---

is not direct, but via the so-called Judean oracle. For the purposes of the present reading, there is no call to accept every detail of this proposal. I agree that the tradition of a flight was pre-Markan, and that it was formative in v. 14c. It is not, as Kelber (*Kingdom*, 120–22) argues, "an eschatological exodus out of the land of Satan into the promised land of the kingdom" (p. 121).

[231] Balabanski, *Eschatology*, 105–12. Such (*The Abomination of Desolation*, 117–37) also defends the historicity of a flight. However, he does not have recourse to the Pella tradition. He gathers evidence to show that the vigorous persecution of Jews in the period after September 70 was the background for a Markan injunction to Christians to flee from the region of Jerusalem (e.g., Lydda). "In the immediate aftermath of Jerusalem's destruction Mark held an expectation of a future imminent catastrophe for Christians" (p. 126). The Eusebian Pella tradition may reflect this background (see p. 132 n. 21).

[232] Balabanski, *Eschatology*, 133–34. For the discussion of the relationship between the Pella tradition and the New Testament, see pp. 122–34.

[233] For the reconstruction, largely from Josephus, of this situation in the winter of 67, see Balabanski, *Eschatology*, 122–32. She suggests that once Phanias was installed as high priest, anti-Zealot groups revolted. In the winter of 67, as the Zealots were temporarily confined to the inner court of the temple, escape was possible. According to Josephus (*J.W.* 4.99), at that time a number of groups saw that they must escape. Lane (*Mark*, 466–69) agrees that the appointment of Phanias generated a flight. However, he regards Phanias as the "desolating sacrilege."

The dramatic nature of the situation is indicated in 13:15–16.[234] Whoever is praying, resting, or working on the flat roof of their house should not take the time to reenter the house to select what they might need for their flight. Immediate departure is called for (v. 15). Similarly, the worker stripped for action in the field should not return home to gather a more adequate form of clothing for the journey (v. 16). Whoever and wherever they might be, and whatever they might be doing, all must depart directly from their present location, either on the roof or in the fields.[235] A similar concern for the drama and difficulty of the events happening in Jerusalem, still cast in the future for the purposes of the Markan appeal to his disciples, is found in the words directed to pregnant women and nursing mothers (v. 17). Haste is difficult for women with child or nursing a child, but haste is called for and thus they will be disadvantaged (see Josephus, *Ant.* 14.354; *4 Ezra* 6:21).[236] The mention of the timing of the flight from Jerusalem in the depths of winter points back to the warning in 13:14c. There is a close logical link between v. 17 and v. 18, regardless of the contact with v. 14. The need for haste, and the difficulties facing pregnant and nursing women, will be rendered even more problematic during the winter, in the rain and cold winds, the muddy tracks and the swollen wadis. But, as was noted in the discussion of the command to flee to the mountains, a flight took place in late 67 C.E. in the depths of winter. Jesus' words, "Pray that it may not happen in winter," take on further poignancy in the knowledge it was indeed during the winter that people have fled from the disasters, both inside and outside the walls of Jerusalem.[237]

The language of 13:15–16 appears to have been associated with apocalyptic writing prior to the Gospel of Mark (see Luke 17:31), but it has been historicized by its association with 13:14 and, to a lesser extent, with 13:18. The same process continues into 13:19–20. Apocalyptic language abounds as Jesus looks forward to "those days" and describes them as a time of "tribulation" (θλῖψις). Both expressions are stock words in apocalyptic writings (see especially Dan 12:1), but Jesus places the days and the tribulation within a historical framework.[238] He speaks of them as being the most difficult days from creation until the present moment. The two levels of the discourse continue to intersect. As Jesus speaks to disciples on the Mount of Olives, looking across at the city and the temple whose destruction he is predicting, the Markan community is reeling under the shock of the destruction at present taking place and wondering what it might mean.[239] Jesus warns them their concern is well-placed; never has there been such tribulation, through the whole of

---

[234] For Such (*The Abomination of Desolation,* 30–36, 177–78), vv. 14–27 point to an unrealized future, and do not reflect events from the period of the war. They "launch the end time" (p. 30).

[235] For the details of people on the roof and workers in the field, see Gnilka, *Markus,* 2:196. A similar saying is found in Luke 17:31, but it appears to have come from Q and not Mark. Thus, this command to leave immediately must have been associated with end-time language prior to Mark and Luke; see Beasley-Murray, *Last Days,* 417. For Mark, however, its link with v. 14 renders it more historical than apocalyptic.

[236] It is always possible that these details also came from recent reports to the Markan community, but there is no way of proving this.

[237] For the details, see Balabanski, *Eschatology,* 122–32. Coming to the same conclusion concerning the flight and its timing, but on different grounds, see Dyer, *The Prophecy,* 221–31. Against any attempt to link the flight to a specific winter, see Gnilka, *Markus,* 2:196–97.

[238] Gnilka, *Markus,* 2:197.

[239] Some have attempted to associate the θλῖψις of v. 19 with the sufferings of persecuted Roman Christians. See, for example, Pesch, *Naherwartung,* 151–54; Taylor, *Mark,* 514; Grundmann, *Markus,* 267. The close association of vv. 19–20 with vv. 15–18, and the background of apocalyptic language makes this unlikely; see Beasley-Murray, *Last Days,* 418.

human history, and there will never again be such an event. The cataclysm normally associated only with the end time has been drawn back into history and associated with the end of Jerusalem and its temple. But however cataclysmic the events in Jerusalem were, they took place in the period of history running from creation until now. There will be a future time, during which such horrific events will not be repeated. Jesus tells the disciples, and Mark his readers, that the end is "not yet."

The motif of the shortening of the days (v. 20) has analogies in apocalyptic literature, but there is no real parallel to Mark's use of it.[240] The Markan idea of God as the Lord of history has determined these final words of Jesus on the "wars and rumors of wars" (vv. 7–8; vv. 14–20). However, this is not the end of God's care for his people. If the process had been allowed to go on by the Lord of history, then all without exception would have been destroyed, so total and so terrible have the events taking place in Jerusalem become to the minds of those hearing of wars and rumors of wars. But God will not allow this. For that reason, even the destruction of the Holy City of Jerusalem and its sacred place, the temple, comes to an end in God's design. The faithful will not be destroyed, and for their sake God "shortens the days." The disciples listening to the words of Jesus, and the members of the Markan community, themselves disciples of Jesus, are evidence that the time has been shortened. They survive these events which do not mark the end of the world, because "the end is not yet" (v. 8) and the gospel must first be preached to all the nations (v. 10). The existence of the Gospel of Mark is proof that God shortens the days so that the chosen ones might preach the gospel. If that had not happened, there would be no Markan community and no Gospel of Mark. Nevertheless, Christian disciples are still living in an in-between time. However focused this passage might be upon the destruction of Jerusalem, the reality of a definitive end of time is always present.[241]

[A'] False prophets (13:21–23)

False messianic claims, already mentioned in 13:5–6, return. As with the relationship between 13:7–8 and 13:14–20, 13:21–23 gives further detail to the indications of 13:6, and bring the section dedicated to the destruction of Jerusalem and its temple to a close in 13:23. In 13:6 the disciples were warned against those who came in the name of Jesus, claiming, in the first person singular, "I am he." The eschatological heat of the end of Jerusalem and its association with the expected end of the world, highlighted by the coming of the Messiah, generated such claims. In 13:21–22, however, a third person points to the false messiah. A figure visible to all who would like to look will be pointed to, indicated as "the Christ." The false messiahs have their advocates, but they are not to be believed.[242] The theme at the center of 13:5–23, the denial of the coming of the end time and the need to preach the gospel to all nations, in the midst of persecution, suffering, and death (vv. 9–13), continues to determine Mark's message. The false prophets and false messiahs

---

240 For an analysis of the motif in Jewish literature, and the denial that it forms a genuine parallel, see Beasley-Murray, *Last Days,* 419 n. 124.

241 As Gnilka (*Markus,* 2:198) comments on the "shortening of the days": "For the community this means trust, but not absolute security. Some individuals will not be spared the trial."

242 In the setting of the Q version of this saying (Matt 24:26; Luke 17:23) these words answer a question concerning how one knows a false messiah, and the answer is given that the Messiah will come suddenly like a flash of lightning (see Matt 24:27/Luke 17:24). Beasley-Murray (*Last Days,* 393) suggests that Mark 13:21 may have had the same setting and that "the true Messiah is hidden not on earth but in heaven, and the revelation of his presence is comparable to that of the divine glory made known in the exodus and at Sinai, and awaited in the last day."

will have certain powers (see also 2 Thess 2:1–12). They will show signs and do wonders,[243] but they are not to be accepted as the harbingers of the end of time. God has shortened the days of the disasters that afflicted the faithful in the destruction of Jerusalem for the sake of the elect (v. 20). The elect must live on into the period of history that stretches before them, thanks to God's merciful intervention. If the elect (v. 21) were to be seduced by the errors of the false prophets and false messiahs God's design would be thwarted. As this section of the discourse draws to a close, the consistency of the message is maintained. Gazing at the wonders of Jerusalem and its temple (vv. 1–3), Jesus has explained to Peter, James, John, and Andrew the significance of his prophecy concerning the destruction of the wonderful stones and the wonderful buildings (v. 3; see v. 2). The disciples asked "when" this would happen, but for the Markan community that question is no longer relevant. It has happened, and they have knowledge of it (vv. 7–8, vv. 14–20; see v. 14b). What is most important is that they do not read these events as the end of time, nor listen to those who make such claims (vv. 5–6, 21–22). The gospel must first be preached to all the nations (vv. 9–13).[244]

In an elegant closure, Jesus repeats the imperative with which he began his discourse: "take heed" (βλέπετε, v. 23; see v. 5).[245] Adopting the temporal perspective established in 13:1–4, Jesus instructs his four disciples that there must be no failure to observe all he has told them. They have been privileged to hear "all things" before they take place. They are to lead other disciples through troubled times into a future on the other side of the destruction of the wonderful buildings and stones, so that the gospel might be preached. The Markan community is thus informed that it exists because the foundational disciples (see 1:16–20: Peter, James, John, and Andrew), despite all the failure that has marked their journey with Jesus to this point in the story, have not misread the signs of the times. They have paid attention to the word of Jesus, and thus the community exists, after the dramatic events that have taken place in Jerusalem, preaching the gospel to all nations. By means of the gospel, Jesus instructs the members of a Christian community that "the end is not yet" (v. 7). Consistent with Jewish and Christian thought, they know the end will come. They are living in the time between the discourse of Jesus on false understandings of the end (vv. 5–23), and that time when the Son of Man will come in the glory of the Father with the holy angels (see 8:38). The four foundational disciples (see 1:16–20) have also asked Jesus about that time: what will be the sign (v. 4b) and when it will be accomplished (v. 4c). It is to those two questions that Jesus now directs his discourse (vv. 24–37).

The End of the World As We Know It (13:24–37)

The discourse changes focus in 13:24.[246] An adversative ἀλλά opens the first sentence, separating it from what has gone before. The next words, "in those days," are traditional in

---

[243] On "sign prophets," see Josephus, *Ant.* 19.162; 20.167–172, 188; *J.W.* 2.258–263; 6.285–286. See the summary of further Jewish background to sign-working prophets in Marcus, *Mark*, 498–99.

[244] It is unnecessary to distinguish between the "elect" in v. 22 and those addressed in v. 23. This is sometimes suggested to accommodate a Roman readership. See, for example, Beasley-Murray, *Last Days*, 421–22.

[245] See Lambrecht, *Redaktion*, 172; Beasley-Murray, *Last Days*, 420–21; Lane, *Mark*, 473. On the Markan nature of this conclusion, see Taylor, *St. Mark*, 517; Lambrecht, *Redaktion*, 171–72; Pesch, *Naherwartung*, 155.

[246] The relationship between vv. 24–27 and vv. 5–23 is debated; see Taylor, *St. Mark*, 517–21. Many wish to see the events of v. 14 (or even the whole of vv. 5–23) as preparatory to vv. 24–27. See

apocalyptic writing. Jesus indicates that he is addressing the disciples on the period that will come after the tribulations described in 13:5–23 (μετὰ τὴν θλῖψιν ἐκείνην).[247] His response to the question of "the sign" asked by the four disciples in v. 4b (vv. 24b–25) opens with two Old Testament citations (Isa 13:10; 34:4). They are told what a future generation *will see* (vv. 24–27; see v. 26). They are instructed that they must learn the lesson of the fig tree and *see the signs* of the end of time (vv. 28–31; see v. 29). The question of "the sign" in 13:4b is answered by Jesus' instruction on what they will see (vv. 24–27) and their need to recognize the signs of the end (vv. 28–31).[248] In 13:4c the disciples asked *when* all these things would be accomplished. Jesus concludes his discourse with a response to that question. He opens by remarking that only the Father knows "of that day or that hour" (v. 32), and exhorting the disciples to watch and be prepared, as they do not know "when the time will come" (v. 33).[249] As the question of "the sign" (v. 4b) has been answered, Jesus next instructs the disciples on the "when" of the end time and the need for them to watch and wait for it (vv. 32–37; see v. 4c). However, these divisions are not without considerable overlap. Jesus' initial response to the disciples' question concerning "when" all these things will be fulfilled (v. 30; cf. v. 4c) is particularly important, as he brings his response to "the sign" (v. 4b) to closure. He will develop the meaning of 13:30 in his more detailed treatment of the question in 13:32–37.

The structure of Mark 13:24–37

The outline of the argument provided above already furnishes all the textual indicators which determine the structure of Jesus' discourse on the end of the world as we know it. It unfolds as follows:

13:24–27   The sign of the coming of the Son of Man.

13:28–31   Reading the signs of the inevitable and imminent end time.

13:32–37   The unknown day and hour, and the need to watch.

Jesus' promise that this generation will not pass away before "all these things take place" (ταῦτα πάντα γένηται, v. 30) looks back to the disciples' question concerning the accom-

---

especially Such, *The Abomination of Desolation,* 17–52, but also, Lagrange, *Saint Marc,* 322; Beasley-Murray, *Last Days,* 426–27; Lane, *Mark,* 479; Lohmeyer, *Markus,* 279; Grundmann, *Markus,* 268–69; Schweizer, *Mark,* 275–76; Gnilka, *Markus,* 2:199–200, 202, 205. For some (e.g., Lohmeyer, Grundmann, Schweizer, and Gnilka), vv. 24–27 are part of the "little apocalypse."

[247] As Anderson (*Mark,* 298) rightly remarks, "There is no linear connexion . . . between the cosmic portents of vv. 24–25 and the historical oracle relating to 'the desolating sacrilege set up where it ought not to be' of vv. 14ff." See also Painter, *Mark,* 177–79. Dyer (*The Prophecy,* 123–52) has worked impressively with the syntax of Mark 13 to show that vv. 24–27 are a Markan compilation of Septuagintal allusions, independent of vv. 5–23. This section of the discourse may not be as free of pre-Markan elements as Dyer suggests (see Balabanski, *Eschatology,* 86–88), but its independence from the prophecies of vv. 5–23 emerges clearly.

[248] Lührmann (*Markusevangelium,* 218, 224–25) agrees that vv. 5–23 reflect the destruction of Jerusalem and its temple, and that vv. 24–27 point to the signs of the end of the world. However, he suggests that vv. 28–37 deal with the attitude to be adopted as the believer waits for the end time.

[249] Many commentators follow the textual marker of the βλέπετε in v. 33 to divide the final two sections into vv. 28–32 and vv. 33–37; e.g., Taylor, *St. Mark,* 523; Kelber, *Kingdom,* 126; Anderson, *Mark,* 301; Gnilka, *Markus,* 2:208. Because of the obvious response to the question of time (v. 32: "that day or that hour") asked in v. 4c, I make v. 32 the first verse in the final section (vv. 32–37); so also Lagrange, *Saint Marc,* 325; Lane, *Mark,* 481; Hooker, *St. Mark,* 322.

plishment of all these things (ταῦτα συντελεῖσθαι πάντα, v. 4c). Jesus' discourse on the end of time is not without its tensions, especially regarding the sense of the imminence of the Parousia. The sources behind this section of the discourse and the eschatology of Mark and his community must be respected in an attempt to resolve these tensions.

The sign of the coming of the Son of Man (13:24–27)

The discourse on the end of Jerusalem and its temple repeatedly spoke of the end time, differentiating it from the destruction of the Holy City (see vv. 7, 8, 10, 13). In 13:24 "those days" of the end time, after the tribulation and false eschatological hopes generated by the destruction of Jerusalem (vv. 5–23), become the focus of the discourse. Jesus cites Isa 13:10 and 34:4, two passages used by the prophet to describe the wrath which will over-take the world on the day of the Lord. A series of visual images depicts the end of the estab-lished world: the darkening of the sun, the failure of the moon to give light at night, the falling of the stars from heaven (vv. 24b–25). These cosmic events are not to be taken liter-ally, but in the sense in which they were originally uttered by Isaiah. They incorporate com-mon apocalyptic symbolism to indicate that the world as we know it is coming to an end (see Isa 13:2–10; Joel 2:10–3:4; 4:15–16; Amos 8:8–9; Rev 6:12–13; 8:10; *T. Mos.* 10:5; *4 Ezra* 5:4; *1 En.* 80:4–7; *Sib. Or.* 3:796–797, 801–803; 5:512–531).[250] What the signs point to is very real—the end of the world as we know it. However, they must not be read as concrete prophecies of what will physically happen when that time comes.[251]

Those who will witness the end of time will see "the Son of Man coming on the clouds with great power and glory." The end of time will be marked by the coming of the Son of Man, descending in the clouds which at one and the same time conceal and reveal his glory (see Exod 34:5).[252] Jesus' words *against* false messiahs (vv. 21–23) are closely related to the summons to watch for the coming of the Son of Man (vv. 24–27). The Jewish War gener-ated false messiahs, but (ἀλλά, v. 24) the true Messiah, the vindicated Son of Man (see 8:31, 38; 9:31; 10:33–24), will yet come. Jesus takes up the prophecy of Dan 7:13–14, which speaks of the vindication of the holy ones of God, to conclude what has been said concern-ing the Son of Man to this point in the narrative. In 2:10 and 2:28 Jesus spoke enigmati-cally of the authority of the Son of Man to forgive sin and the authority of the Son of Man over the Sabbath. Since then, the expression has been used to speak of Jesus' forthcoming death *and resurrection* (8:31; 9:9, 12, 31; 10:33–34, 45). In 8:38 a first indication of the final authority of the Son of Man was given. He will come at the end of time in the glory of his Father with the angels. The reader can now look back and better comprehend the gap cre-ated in the narrative by the use of the Son of Man in 2:10, 28. Jesus' earthly ministry re-flects the authority of the eschatological Son of Man.[253] In his coming death at the hands

---

[250] Lane (*Mark*, 474) remarks, "No other section of the eschatological discourse is more in-debted to scriptural imagery and language." See the table of the many parallels and allusions in Hartman, *Prophecy Interpreted*, 156–57. See also LaVerdiere (*The Beginning*, 2:204–7). Lambrecht (*Redaktion*, 177–78) suggests that Joel 2:10–3:4; 4:15–16, rather than Isa 34:4, has influenced the Markan text.

[251] See especially Pesch, *Naherwartung*, 158–66, also Hooker, *St. Mark*, 318–19; Beasley-Murray, *Last Days*, 423–27. Gnilka (*Markus*, 2:200) comments: "Its language lies between meta-phoric and realistic."

[252] The coming on the clouds indicates that the one who comes belongs to the heavenly sphere; Gnilka, *Markus*, 2:201; Beasley-Murray, *Last Days*, 429–30.

[253] Whatever the background and original meaning of "the Son of Man," for the Markan reader Jesus is the Son of Man.

of the leaders of Israel, Jesus will submit himself to the necessary loss of self for God so that all authority and glory may be given to him in the resurrection (8:31; 9:9, 12, 31; 10:33–34, 45). The Markan Jesus has applied the Danielic "one like a son of man" (Dan 7:13) to speak of himself as the glorious Son of Man, the final judge and vindicator of the faithful ones. For the believing reader, Jesus is the Son of Man, the authoritative, human, self-giving, suffering, glorified, and final hope of the faithful. "For Mark's readers, this passage is an assurance that, whatever sufferings they may have to endure, their faithfulness to Jesus will be rewarded on the Last Day when they are acknowledged by the Son of Man. This is the other half of the picture painted in 8:38."[254]

The gathering of the remnant from the four corners of the earth, to bring them back to Judea, is found in the Old Testament (see especially Isa 11:11, 16; 27:12; 38:8–9; 43:6; Ezek 39:27–28; Zech 10:6–11). Jesus transforms the image. The Son of Man does not gather a remnant, but the elect, and there is no mention of a place in which they will be gathered. The end time will be marked by the gathering of a new community of God, made up of those who have faithfully lived through the sufferings which marked the time between the first and the second appearance of the Son of Man (see vv. 20–23). This gathering transcends the Jewish expectation that all would come to Judea and Jerusalem, because the new community of God will exist only because the disciples have heard and obeyed Jesus' words in 13:10: "First the gospel must be preached to all the nations." This is the significance of the sending of the angels to gather the elect from the four winds (see Zech 2:6), from the ends of the earth to the ends of heaven (see Deut 13:7; 30:4). The imagery is overwrought, but its overstated universality takes for granted that the gospel has been preached to all the nations between the two comings of the Son of Man. All nations have heard the gospel (v. 10), and the angels will gather the faithful elect from all those nations at the end of time (v. 27).[255]

Reading the signs of the inevitable and imminent end time (13:28–31)

The issue of what will be "seen," responding to the disciples' question about the sign (v. 4b), continues into the lesson to be learned from the fig tree (vv. 28–29).[256] Taking an example from everyday life in Palestine, Jesus exhorts the disciples to learn from their knowledge of the inevitable approach of summer when the branch of the fig tree becomes tender and the tree puts forth its leaves (v. 28).[257] In a parallel fashion, when they see these

---

[254] Hooker, *St. Mark,* 319. See Beasley-Murray, *Last Days,* 430, also Broadhead, *Naming Jesus,* 134: "Operating within the realm of the narrative, the Son of Man title also becomes the vehicle through which the narrative moves beyond itself and its own limitations."

[255] As Lane (*Mark,* 477) suggests, this combination of Old Testament images "means 'everywhere.'"

[256] A number of recent scholars wish to link this generic parable about fig trees with the earlier use of the fig tree to frame Jesus' presence in bringing to an end the temple practices in 11:12–21. If the cursing of the fig tree signified the end of the temple, could not the sign of the budding fig tree signify the coming of the new temple? See, for example, Kelber, *Kingdom,* 124; Telford, *The Barren Temple,* 216–17; Tolbert, *Sowing,* 231–32, 267; Geddert, *Watchwords,* 147; Balabanski, *Eschatology,* 64–65; LaVerdiere, *The Beginning,* 2:208. The link is suggestive but tenuous; it is rejected in Gnilka, *Markus,* 2:205, and the fully documented discussion of Beasley-Murray, *Last Days,* 441–42.

[257] The fig tree is very common in Palestine, and not an evergreen. It is thus an obvious harbinger of summer; see Lagrange, *Saint Marc,* 324; Taylor, *St. Mark,* 520. On v. 28 as a similitude, see Lohmeyer, *Markus,* 280. Among its many uses, it is also found in Jewish literature to symbolize the joys of the messianic age; see Telford, *The Barren Temple,* 128–204.

things, then they will know that the Son of Man is at the gates. There is a level of ambiguity in this exhortation. The need to read the signs of the coming end of time, marked by the presence of the Son of Man, is clear. But what are "these things" (ταῦτα) that are to parallel the knowledge generated by the tender branch and the growing leaves of the fig tree indicating the imminence of summer? The ταῦτα could look back to the apocalyptic symbols of the end of the world taken from Isa 13:10; 34:4 in 13:24a–25, or it could look further back to the description of the end of Jerusalem in 13:5–23. The ambiguity is generated by Mark's use of this pre-Markan fig tree tradition as a "lesson" that expands upon Jesus' response to the disciples' request for "the sign" of the end (v. 4b).[258] The context determines the point of reference for "these things." Coming hard on the heels of the use of Isaianic symbols that will indicate the imminent end of time, "these things" must link 13:28–31 with 13:24–27. Furthermore, the sight of "these things" will betray the truth that "he is near, at the very gates" (ἐγγύς ἐστιν ἐπὶ θύραις).[259] The link between the signs of 13:24b–25 and the subsequent (see v. 26a: καὶ τότε ὄψονται) coming of the Son of Man and gathering of the elect in 13:25–26 is matched by "seeing these things take place" (v. 29a) and the approach of the Son of Man, at the very gates (v. 29b).[260]

Further critical difficulties emerge with 13:30: "Truly, I say to you, this generation (ἡ γενεὰ αὕτη) will not pass away before all these things (ταῦτα πάντα) take place." Interpreters struggle with this saying, and many attempts have been made to interpret "this generation" in a way that eases the impression of Jesus' support for the imminent return of the Son of Man.[261] If Jesus told his contemporaries that the end would come about in their time, then we have a prophecy from Jesus that did not come true. Attempts to avoid the obvious meaning of "this generation" are not convincing. Similarly the reference to the imminence of the end of the world must be maintained.[262] As with 13:28–29, this is another originally independent pre-Markan saying of Jesus, inserted into this context because of the link words ταῦτα in 13:29 and ταῦτα πάντα in 13:30.[263] The reference to "all these

---

[258] We cannot be sure what "these things" referred to in the original setting of this tradition. A Lukan text which approximates v. 29 (12:54–56) takes Jesus' listeners to task for their inability to recognize the approach of the kingdom of God in the activity of Jesus (see also Luke 11:20). The Lukan parallel to Mark 13:29 (Luke 21:31) identifies "these things" with "the kingdom of God." This may have been its original setting; see Taylor, *St. Mark*, 520; Grundmann, *Markus*, 270; Hooker, *St. Mark*, 320–21. On this complex of sayings and their probable original association with the kingdom, see Anderson, *Mark*, 299–300.

[259] The translation "he is near," with reference to coming of the Son of Man in vv. 26–27, is not the only one possible. It could also mean "it is near," with reference to the kingdom of God (see 1:15). As suggested in the previous note, this may have been the original reference point for this group of sayings, but in their present Markan context, they look back to vv. 24–27. The Son of Man is the "he" who is near.

[260] Hooker (*St. Mark*, 319) disagrees, since vv. 26–27 were "the climax to the period of waiting." I agree, but would suggest that in v. 29a "these things" look back to vv. 24a–25, and the final coming of the Son of Man (vv. 26–27) is paralleled in v. 29b.

[261] Others claim that "these things" refers to something other than the end time. For example, Lagrange (*Saint Marc*, 324–25) and Hartman (*Prophecy Interpreted*, 222–26) argue that it refers to the destruction of the temple. After a lengthy and informative discussion, Beasley-Murray (*Last Days*, 443–49) claims that it refers to the prophecies in vv. 1–27. See also Cranfield, *St. Mark*, 407–8.

[262] See Nineham, *St. Mark*, 359–60, and especially Such, *The Abomination of Desolation*, 163–69.

[263] On the "catchwords" which have generated vv. 28–37, see Taylor, *St. Mark*, 519–20; Nineham, *St. Mark*, 358. For fuller speculations on the pre-Markan tradition, see Gnilka, *Markus*, 2:203–4. Balabanski (*Eschatology*, 82–86) provides an interesting analysis of the oral characteristics of vv. 28–32.

things" in 13:30, however, also looks back to the Markan introduction, and the questions raised by the disciples. They asked when all these things will be accomplished (ταῦτα . . . πάντα, v. 4c). Jesus, having dealt explicitly with "the sign" (see v. 4b) in 13:24–29, brings that discussion to closure and begins to face the question of "when" (see v. 4c). This question will be dealt with in more detail in 13:32–37, but for the moment he tells his listeners, and the Gospel narrative tells its readers, that the end may be very close.

The *Markan* question of 13:4b is answered by the *Markan* Jesus through a collection of originally independent *pre-Markan* sayings (vv. 28–29). The link word ταῦτα has led Mark to add another *pre-Markan* saying in 13:30 which moves the discourse away from the question of "the sign" (v. 4b), toward the question of "when" (v. 4c). This juxtaposition of Markan and pre-Markan passages, and the shift from a response to "the sign" (v. 4b) to "when" (v. 4c), creates a tension. But it is not impossible to grasp Mark's meaning.[264] Jesus will open his final words on "when" this will all be accomplished by frankly admitting that neither he nor the angels in heaven know (v. 32). The discourse on the end of Jerusalem (vv. 5–23) repeatedly insisted that the destruction of the Holy City was not the end of time, but that the end would surely come. The Markan Jesus, despite 13:30, has no idea how long the time between the two events will be (see v. 32). However, for Mark and his community there is every possibility that it will be very brief. "The Jesus who encounters the hearer in this saying . . . does not so much fix an exact terminal date for the end as fill the hearer's present moment with urgency and make it impossible for him to postpone or evade decision indefinitely."[265] This is the central message of 13:32–37.

Another independent pre-Markan saying closes 13:28–31, joined to 13:30 by means of the link word "pass away" (οὐ μὴ παρέλθῃ, v. 30; παρελεύσονται, v. 31). This is a forceful claim from Jesus that whatever the end of the world as we know it may bring, his word will never pass away. It formally closes Jesus' response to the question of "the sign" (v. 4b; cf. vv. 24–29), even though he has already begun to respond to the question of "when" (v. 4c; cf. v. 30). The background to Jesus' words is biblical: "The grass withers, the flower fades, but the word of our God will stand forever" (Isa 40:8). The sentiments expressed in Second Isaiah, however, have been radically transformed in Jesus' discourse on the end of the world. It is not a question of grass withering and flowers fading, but the total annihilation of the world as we know it: the passing away of all that is above ("heaven") and all that is below ("earth"). Nor is it a question of the word of God, but the word of Jesus. The Markan Christology continues to draw Jesus into a closeness with God (see 1:1, 11; 9:7; 15:39; see also 5:19–20; 11:2–3, 27–33; 12:6). There can be no quibbles with what Jesus has said in response to the questions raised by the disciples in 13:4. His words have an authority and a life that transcends God's creation of the heaven and the earth, and all the events of human history. The emphasis is not on the traditional apocalyptic prediction that heaven and earth will pass away. Rather, the saying is an eloquent reminder that in all the difficulties and dangers through the in-between time, the community has comfort and guidance in the enduringly authoritative words of Jesus. He is the bearer of the good news of the ultimate vindication of all who are prepared to take the risk of following his way and his word.

---

[264] Once again, "all the things" that will take place may well have had an original reference to the coming of the kingdom, and not to the end time (see Mark 9:1; Matt 16:28); Hooker, *St. Mark,* 321.

[265] Anderson, *Mark,* 300. See also Nineham, *St. Mark,* 360; Schweizer, *Mark,* 282; Hooker, *St. Mark,* 321.

The unknown day and hour, and the need to watch (13:32–37)

Jesus has spoken of the imminent coming of the end time in 13:30, but modifies that saying in 13:32. However imminent it may be, the knowledge of "when" such an event will take place (see v. 4c) is reserved to the Father. Not even the celestial powers of the angels, nor even the Son, knows when "that day" or "that hour" will be.[266] The reference to "that day" echoes warnings in the Old Testament about "the Day of the Lord" (see Isa 2:12; Amos 5:18; see also 2 Thess 1:10), and it remains a time *of the Lord*.[267] Jesus' confidence of 13:30, juxtaposed with his confession of ignorance of 13:32, reflects the different origins of these independent pre-Markan sayings, but there is no contradiction. One can be confident that something will take place within a certain period of time (v. 30) without being certain of the exact time when it will take place (v. 32). The reader is warned about the urgency of the coming end of time (v. 30), but informed that the hour when this will take place is in the unknowable design of God.[268] Urgency and mystery are carefully combined as Jesus instructs upon the need to be prepared for God's decisive action, bringing the world as we know it to an end. Jesus' response to the disciples' question of "when" all these things would be accomplished (v. 4c), initiated in 13:30, is now resumed, and is the concern of 13:32–36, leading to Jesus' final exhortation (v. 37) that all must watch.

If Jesus is unable to tell the disciples "when" all things will be brought to their end, then the disciples must also remain in ignorance (v. 33b). In the tension created by knowledge *that* it will take place (v. 30), and ignorance about *when* it will happen, the disciples are told, for the last time, that they must take heed and watch (βλέπετε).[269] The commands to watch (vv. 5, 9, 23) have been associated with the need for the disciples to read with discernment the signs that are going on around them, and not allow themselves to be swept away by false expectations. It retains that sense here, as the disciples are warned that they must be watchful in the in-between time. The warnings against false signs and false voices (vv. 5–23) are still present in Jesus' command of 13:33a.[270]

A brief similitude is added to develop the theme of the responsibility of the disciples in the time between Jesus' departure and his return. A person who leaves on a journey gives responsibilities to his servants. He expects these responsibilities to be discharged. A particular responsibility is given to the doorkeeper. He is charged "to be on the watch" (ἵνα γρηγορῇ, v. 34). Jesus shifts from the use of βλέπειν to γρηγορεῖν as he describes the responsibility of the doorkeeper. The doorkeeper is not warned against the potential falsity and

---

[266] There has been endless discussion over the possibility that Jesus' words in v. 32 are *ipsissima verba Jesu*. See the survey in Taylor, *St. Mark*, 522–23. For a survey of patristic reflection, see Lagrange, *Saint Marc*, 326–27. On the one hand, it is unlikely that the early church would create a saying that predicated Jesus' ignorance. On the other hand, with the exception of Matt 11:27/Luke 10:22, Jesus never uses "the Son" to speak of himself outside the Fourth Gospel; see Gnilka, *Markus*, 2:207. This question does not concern us, but it is possible that an authentic saying of Jesus confessing ignorance of the end-time may have been modified in the tradition through the addition of the title; see C. R. Kazmierski, *Jesus, the Son of God: A Study of the Marcan Tradition and Its Redaction by the Evangelist* (FB 33; Würzburg: Echter Verlag, 1979), 139–50; Hooker, *St. Mark*, 323. On the important christological subordination of the Son to the Father, see Schweizer, *Mark*, 283; Anderson, *Mark*, 302.

[267] Lane, *Mark*, 481.

[268] Ibid., 482: "The parousia is not conditioned by any other consideration than the sovereign decision of the Father, which remains enveloped with impenetrable mystery."

[269] There is support for the addition of "and pray" in v. 33a, but this extra imperative has probably crept into the text through accommodation with 14:38.

[270] On the use of βλέπειν, see Geddert, *Watchwords*, 81–87.

danger that others might bring. The verb βλέπειν has been used to call the disciples to a careful discernment of what is going on around them, to heed rightly the voices and read the signs that they hear and see. The introduction of γρηγορεῖν into the discourse shifts the nuance behind the commands to watch which occur so regularly in 13:5–37 (βλέπετε, vv. 5, 9, 23, 33; γρηγορεῖτε, vv. 35, 37). This verb calls the doorkeeper to perform with care and exactness the mission entrusted to him (v. 34c). Jesus uses the verb γρηγορεῖν to command disciples to watch. They were called to follow him (1:16–20) and instructed on the implications of discipleship as they journeyed to Jerusalem (8:22–10:52). They are to perform the mission for which they were appointed (see 3:14–19; 6:7–13) in the period between Jesus' departure and his return.[271]

Another element in the application of the similitude to the disciples (v. 35) is its association with the night. The theme of the lack of knowledge of the disciples, first stated in 13:33, returns. The times when the master of the house might return are taken from the watches of the night according to Roman reckoning: the evening, midnight, cock crow, and the morning. Neither the doorkeeper in the similitude (v. 34) nor the disciples in Jesus' application (v. 35) will receive warning of when the master of the house might return. They do not know when the master of the house is coming.[272] There can be no doubt that he is coming. Indeed he may be close at hand (v. 30), but they—like Jesus and the angels—do not know when he will come (vv. 32–33). The darkness of the night makes the call to perform their duty even more urgent and difficult.[273] They are warned lest the master come suddenly and find them asleep (v. 36).[274]

The warning of 13:36 links the farewell discourse with the passion narrative that follows. Jesus' passion takes place around the four watches of the night mentioned in 13:35, and three of them are explicitly mentioned. The events leading up to Jesus' passion and the final meal with his disciples take place in the evening (14:17). The experience of Gethsemane, the arrest, and the Jewish trial take place in the middle of the night (14:32–65). At cock crow, Peter will deny Jesus three times (14:72), and the trial before Pilate takes place in the morning (15:1).[275] Ironically, in the light of Jesus' warning in 13:36, when at Gethsemane he will ask Peter, James, and John (cf. 13:4) to watch, the master will come and find them sleeping (γρηγορεῖτε, 14:34, 38; οὐκ ἴσχυσας . . . γρηγορῆσαι, cf. v. 37). Throughout the Markan story of Jesus the disciples who initially responded so well (see 1:16–20; 2:13–14) have failed to accept or even understand his demands. The passion of Jesus will open with further failures: the disciples sleeping when the master comes (14:32–42; see 13:36), Judas's betrayal (14:43–50; see 13:35), and Peter's denials (14:66–72; see 13:35). The possibility of failure does not lessen Jesus' insistence that disciples be what they were

---

[271] For this meaning of γρηγορεῖν, see Geddert, *Watchwords,* 89–111. On the elements in vv. 33–36 which indicate that Jesus' words are addressed to the Christian community, see Grundmann, *Markus,* 271–72.

[272] On the importance of "not knowing" in vv. 33–36, see Gnilka, *Markus,* 2:209.

[273] Hooker (*St. Mark,* 323) comments: "A man going on a journey in Palestine in the first century AD would not travel at night, and his servants could hardly be blamed for not waiting up for him." On these grounds, she finds the similitude odd. Rather than odd, it is the link with the forthcoming passion and the Markan rhetoric that makes this night journey important for the similitude and its application; see Lohmeyer, *Markus,* 284–85.

[274] On the Christian importance of remaining "awake," see Lohmeyer, *Markus,* 284; Schweizer, *Mark,* 283.

[275] The evening (14:17), cock crow (14:72), and morning (15:1) are explicitly mentioned. However, 14:32–65 is set across the middle of the night, even though this time frame is never explicitly mentioned; see Lightfoot, *Gospel Message,* 53.

appointed to be: his chosen ones who do what he has done (3:14–19; 6:7–13). Broadening his audience beyond the four foundational disciples who have been the recipients of this discourse (13:37a), he commands all disciples, those in the story and those reading the story (πᾶσιν λέγω), to watch (γρηγορεῖτε, v. 37b). Mark "is concerned not about apocalyptic instruction *for the few* but the demeanor *of the whole Church* that must await the future God will bring."[276]

Disciples are the privileged recipients of Jesus' message concerning the end of Jerusalem (vv. 5–23) and the end of the world as we know it (vv. 24–37). The authoritative word of Jesus (v. 31) has instructed them on their future experiences in the in-between time (vv. 9–13). The many false signs and voices they will see and hear, in that time marked by trial and suffering, must not mislead them (βλέπετε, vv. 5, 9, 23, 33). They must faithfully perform the task for which they were appointed by Jesus (γρηγορεῖτε, vv. 34, 35, 36), so that before the end of time the gospel will be preached to all the nations (v. 10). Only when this is done will the Son of Man come and gather the faithful from the four corners of the earth (vv. 26–27). However, Jesus is about to depart, through his death and resurrection. The association of the evening, midnight, cock crow, and morning (v. 35) with the oncoming passion of Jesus (14:17, 72, 15:1) indicates that the passion is also in some sense eschatological. This does not remove the traditional Jewish expectation of a final "Day of the Lord." However, as the passion account will show, Jesus' death and resurrection introduce an "eschatological" era. The challenge of living in the in-between time as a new temple, an eschatological people taking the gospel to all nations, outlined in Jesus' farewell discourse (13:5–37), lies squarely in the hands of fragile and sinful disciples. But they have been assured: "Heaven and earth will pass away, but my words will not pass away" (v. 31).

Conclusion

Jesus' approach to Jerusalem and entry into the temple (11:1–11) trigger a series of encounters between Jesus and fundamental aspects of Jewish life and worship. He brings temple worship to a standstill, as Israel has not recognized the time of the coming of the kingdom. In place of the rituals of the Jerusalem temple he established a new way to God, marked by faith, prayer, and forgiveness (11:12–25). The leaders of Israel—the chief priests, the scribes, the elders, the Pharisees, and the Sadducees—are systematically subjected to Jesus' scrutiny and found wanting. After a series of encounters with these leaders, he reduces them to silence (12:34), and points to a different form of "leadership." The widow who gives her all has becomes the model of the true disciple of Jesus (11:26–12:44). Leaving the temple, he sits with his disciples on the Mount of Olives, looks back at the splendid buildings, tells of its future destruction (13:1–4), and warns his disciples that they must not read the events surrounding the destruction of Jerusalem and its temple as the end of time. First the gospel must be preached to all the nations (13:5–23; see v. 10). But there will be an end of the world as we know it. Although the exact timing of this event is not known, not even by the angels in heaven nor the Son, it is an essential part of God's design (v. 32). The followers of Jesus must watch carefully, reading the signs of the end, performing their tasks as his chosen disciples (13:24–37).

The temple rituals come to an end, the institutions of Israel come to an end, the city and its temple will soon come to an end, and the world will come to an end. What

---

[276] Anderson, *Mark*, 301; see also Lane, *Mark*, 483–84.

survives? At the end of the encounter with each of the elements fundamental to Jewish life and belief, Jesus looks to the future. He tells of a new community based on faith, prayer, and forgiveness (11:22–25). He points to the woman who gives her life (12:41–44), and he prophesies the preaching of the gospel to the whole world (13:10) by faithful disciples who are watching and waiting for the final coming of the Son of Man (13:32–37). Jesus' discourse on the end of Jerusalem and the end of the world is aimed at the disciples. It instructs them on the need to endure suffering, as Jesus will endure it (see 13:9–13). However, the discourse is not only introduced by the example of the widow who gave her whole life (12:44), but it is framed by the account of another woman whose action in anointing Jesus' body will be remembered wherever the good news is preached (14:9).[277] The "framing" of the eschatological discourse by the two women, one who gives her life and the other who shares in the death of Jesus, highlights the fact that 13:1–37 is aimed at the disciples. The framing also introduces hope in the face of increasing opposition to Jesus (11:27–28; 12:12, 13), and the disciples' increasing inability to understand and accept Jesus' invitation to give their all and follow him through suffering and death to resurrection (8:22–10:52).

The reader of the Gospel of Mark knows that Jesus' life ended in an execution, but that a Christian community, waiting for the final coming of the Son of Man, still reads and listens to the story of Jesus. The answer to the question asked above—"What survives?"—is found in Jesus' use of Ps 118:22–23, promising: "The very stone which the builders rejected has become the head of the corner; this was the Lord's doing, and it is marvelous in our eyes" (12:10–11). The apparent rejection and destruction of Jesus lies in the immediate future. However strange this may appear to be, it is part of God's design. This is the Lord's doing, and on the foundation stone of the rejected one a believing, praying, forgiving, group of followers, who give themselves unconditionally (see 12:44), will preach the gospel to the ends of the earth (see 14:9), watching and waiting for the final coming of their Lord. The Markan account of the passion of Jesus (14:1–15:47), and an epilogue which returns to themes from the prologue (16:1–8), tell the story of the rejection of Jesus, and challenge the Christian community to life in the in-between time, as a new temple, the ongoing presence of God, built upon the cornerstone of the rejected one. Jesus will build a new temple in place of the destroyed temple. But Mark's story of Jesus tells the reader that his earthly ministry is only the beginning (see 1:1) of the process. The passion narrative will be the last trial prior to its realization, but the realization is still in the future (see 16:7–8).

---

[277] E. S. Malbon, "The Major Importance of the Minor Characters in Mark," in *In the Compan of Jesus: Characters in Mark's Gospel* (Louisville: Westminster John Knox, 2000), 202, 215–17.

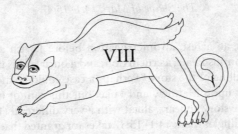

VIII

THE PASSION OF JESUS (MARK 14:1–15:47)

The single most difficult fact that the members of the earliest Christian church had to face was that Jesus of Nazareth, who they believed was the Christ, had been ignominiously crucified. Some twenty years after the event of Jesus' crucifixion, Paul confesses: "We preach Christ crucified, a stumbling block to Jews and folly to Gentiles" (1 Cor 1:23). The death and resurrection of Jesus was the turning point in the history of the relationship between God and the creation that determined his theological vision. What had been lost by the disobedience of Adam has been superabundantly restored by the unconditional obedience of Jesus in his self-gift on the cross (see Rom 3:21–26; 5:12–21). God's raising Jesus from among the dead establishes a new creation (see Gal 6:15; 2 Cor 5:17). Jesus becomes the firstborn of the many who will follow him into death and be raised with him (see 1 Cor 15:12–28; Rom 6:1–11).

Paul's was not the only voice in the early church to preach the crucified Jesus of Nazareth as the Christ, the Son of God (see Mark 1:1, 11). The Markan storyteller could not sidestep the end of his story. He had to write a narrative that told of those events.[1] However, like Paul and other early Christians, he was not interested in simply recording the "brute facts." They would have to be told, but in such a way that convinced the readers and listeners that Jesus was the Christ, the Son of God. Mark was surely the recipient of traditions that carried the narrative of Jesus' passion from the first to the second generation. We cannot be sure of the extent and the details of a pre-Markan passion narrative.[2] Each of the four Gospels displays considerable independence in reporting Jesus' ministry,[3] but they are at one when narrating the end of the story. All describe Jesus' final evening with his

---

[1] See Grundmann, *Markus*, 272–74; G. S. Sloyan, *Jesus on Trial: The Development of the Passion Narratives and Their Historical and Ecumenical Implications* (ed. J. Reumann; Philadelphia: Fortress, 1973), 1–3. As Taylor (*St. Mark*, 525), paraphrasing K. L. Schmidt, remarks: "The Passion Narrative . . . is the oldest and most notable document in the garland of the acts of martyrs." B. M. F. van Iersel (*Reading Mark* [Collegeville: The Liturgical Press, 1988], 171) highlights the Gospel's focus by pointing out "that it devotes about ten times as much space to the arrest, trial and execution as it does to the resurrection."

[2] For an excellent summary of research into the pre-Markan passion narrative, see M. L. Soards, "The Question of a PreMarcan Passion Narrative," Appendix IX in R. E. Brown, *The Death of the Messiah: From Gethsemane to the Grave: A Commentary on the Passion Narratives in the Four Gospels* (2 vols; ABRL; New York: Doubleday, 1994), 2:1492–1524. See also J. R. Donahue, "Introduction: From Passion Traditions to Passion Narrative," in *The Passion in Mark* (ed. W. H. Kelber; Philadelphia: Fortress, 1976), 1–20; A. Y. Collins, *The Beginning of the Gospel: Probings of Mark in Context* (Minneapolis: Fortress, 1992), 92–118. For a brief summary of the proposed situations in the life of the early church which may have generated a passion narrative, see Schweizer, *Mark*, 284–86.

[3] This is as much the case for the so-called Synoptic Gospels (Mark, Matthew, and Luke), which are literally related, as it is for the Gospel of John. Matthew and Luke had access to the Gospel of Mark, but each evangelist has told the story in an original fashion, even in the passion narrative. See the useful study of F. J. Matera, *Passion Narratives and Gospel Theologies: Interpreting the Synoptics through Their Passion Stories* (Theological Inquiries; New York: Paulist Press, 1986).

disciples, Gethsemane, an arrest, an interrogation before Jewish authorities, before the Roman authority of Pontius Pilate, a crucifixion, and a burial. This unity cannot be the result of Mark's initial telling of the story.[4] Perhaps a case could be mounted for the formative influence of Mark upon Matthew and Luke, but this cannot be said for the Fourth Gospel, where the same story appears, albeit with a very differently theological message.[5]

The following reading of Mark 14:1–15:47 takes for granted that Mark's passion narrative was part of a larger storytelling tradition, but was shaped for its own purposes.[6] The Markan story as a whole moves steadily toward this climax. However much Mark's readers already knew, his account of Jesus' death and resurrection provides an unexpected conclusion to a story that began by announcing who Jesus was (see 1:1–13). Initial successes (1:14–45) led to increasing opposition, and Jesus foretold his death and resurrection in Jerusalem (8:31; 9:31; 10:33–34). As the end loomed, the initially enthusiastic disciples (see 1:16–20; 2:13–14; 6:7–13), were more afraid and increasingly unable to understand whom they were following to Jerusalem, and why they were with him (8:22–10:52).

The Shape of Mark 14:1–15:47

The sequence of events in the Markan passion narrative was probably determined by pre-Markan traditions: the anointing (14:1–9), a final meal (14:10–31), Gethsemane (14:32–42), the arrest (14:43–52), the Jewish trial (14:53–72), the Roman trail (15:1–20), the crucifixion (15:21–41), and the burial (15:42–47). But to say that the sequence of events was determined by the tradition is to fail to do justice to Mark's careful blending of his own point of view with that tradition. We have seen throughout this reading of the Gospel of Mark that the author has the habit of "intercalating" episodes (see 3:20–35; 4:1–34; 5:21–43; 6:7–30; 11:12–26; 13:5–23).[7] If we divide the material in the Markan passion nar-

---

[4] It is an overstatement to claim "It is impossible to conclude from the Gospels what sequence of events brought Jesus to the cross"; G. S. Sloyan, *The Crucifixion of Jesus: History, Myth, Faith* (Minneapolis: Fortress, 1995), 40. See pp. 40–43 for the reasons for Sloyan's skepticism. The claim is true for the step-by-step detail, but not for the overall process, found in the same sequence across at least two traditions: Mark (followed by Matthew and Luke), and John. For Sloyan, Luke's use of a special source (*Jesus on Trial*, 89, 94–95, 109) could make it three traditions.

[5] Lührmann, *Markusevangelium*, 227–32. But see the study of M. Lang, *Johannes und die Synoptiker: Eine redaktionsgeschichtliche Analyse von Joh 18–20 vor dem markanischen und lukanischen Hintergrund* (FRLANT 182; Göttingen: Vandenhoeck & Ruprecht, 1999). See also Brown, *Death*, 1:77–85. The following study focuses upon the *Markan* passion narrative. My interest is primarily literary and theological; see Sloyan, *The Crucifixion*, 25–27. I will only touch upon long-debated historical questions, and ongoing discussions of the Markan redaction of a pre-Markan narrative. Regular reference will be made to Brown, *Death*, for those interested in investigating these issues further. This recent encyclopedic work is a balanced guide to contemporary scholarly discussion. See also the introductory analysis of each pericope in Gnilka, *Markus*.

[6] As Soards ("The Question," 2:1523–24) concludes: "We may safely conclude that Mark uses a source in writing his PN (passion narrative). We know that source, however, only as incorporated in Mark. The greatest challenge that lies before us is not the separation of tradition from Marcan redaction; for . . . that task may finally be an impossible one" (parenthesis mine). For a briefer survey, coming to the same conclusions, see also Brown, *Death*, 1:53–57.

[7] See, among many, J. R. Donahue, *Are You the Christ? The Trial Narrative in the Gospel of Mark* (SBLDS 10; Missoula: Society of Biblical Literature, 1973), 58–63. The following suggestion is a development of Donahue's work on 14:53–65. G. S. Sloyan ("Recent Literature on the Trial Narratives of the Fourth Gospel," in *Critical History and Biblical Faith: New Testament Perspectives* [ed. T. J. Ryan; The College Theology Society Annual Publication Series; Villanova: College Theology Soci-

rative into two major blocks, the first dealing with Jesus, his disciples, and the Jewish leaders (14:1–72), and the second dealing with Jesus and his execution by Roman crucifixion (15:1–47), two variations of the same literary pattern emerge.

The pattern can be described as the steady reporting of scenes, shifting systematically from a focus upon other characters in the story (A) to a focus upon Jesus (B). In 14:1–72 the "other characters" are always the disciples.[8] In several of these episodes (see vv. 17–21, 26–31) Jesus is present and is the speaker. However, he speaks of the future failures of Judas, Peter, and all the disciples. Similarly, Peter, James, and John are present (although absent, as they are not able to "watch") in Gethsemane (vv. 32–42). The focus of the episode is the prayer of Jesus to the Father. In this sequence, the disciples move dramatically toward their final failure in 14:50. Full of fear they flee, and the narrator adds a parable to comment upon their fear and flight in vv. 51–52. As a group they do not reappear in the story. The sequence dealing with Jesus, the disciples, and the Jewish leaders (14:1–72) unfolds as follows, with (A) sections focusing mainly upon the disciples and (B) sections focusing upon Jesus.

[A] The Jewish leaders plot to kill Jesus (14:1–2).

    [B] *Jesus* is anointed at Bethany (14:3–9).

[A] *Judas, one of the Twelve,* joins the plot of the Jewish leaders (14:10–11).

    [B] *Jesus* sees to the preparations for a Passover meal (14:12–16).

[A] Jesus predicts his betrayal *by Judas, one of the Twelve* (14:17–21).

    [B] *Jesus* shares the meal, giving bread and wine to *the disciples* (14:22–25).

[A] Jesus predicts the future denials of *Peter* and the flight of *all the disciples* (14:26–31).

    [B] *Jesus* prays in Gethsemane (14:32–42).

[A] *Judas, one of the Twelve,* brings representatives of the Jewish leaders, who arrest Jesus, and *all the disciples* flee (14:43–52).

    [B] *Jesus* reveals himself at the Jewish hearing (14:53–65).

[A] *Peter* denies Jesus three times (14:66–72).

---

ety, 1979], 136–76) draws back from his earlier purely redaction-critical approach in *Jesus on Trial,* and espouses the need to follow the literary creativity of Mark. In this, he is influenced by Donahue's intercalated structure (see pp. 142–45). See also X. Léon-Dufour (*Sharing the Eucharistic Bread: The Witness of the New Testament* [trans. M. J. O'Connell; New York: Paulist Press, 1987], 187–88), who identifies this pattern as the "juxtaposition of light and darkness," but carries it only as far as v. 31. Van Iersel (*Reading Mark,* 172) recognizes a series of "sandwich constructions." Taylor (*St. Mark,* 526, 562) identifies these scenes, but divides them into two blocks: 14:1–52, events leading to the arrest, and 14:53–15:47, events leading to the crucifixion and the burial. LaVerdiere (*The Beginning,* 2:217–23) offers an overview of the sections of 14:1–16:8, claiming that the narrative is so closely knit that "most commentators have all but given up looking for major divisions in the story." For a survey which shows that this is the case, see O. Genest, *Le Christ de la Passion: Perspective structurale: Analyse de Marc 14,53–15,47 des parallèles bibliques et extra-bibliques* (Recherches 21 Théologie; Tournai: Desclée, 1978), 29–34, 57–58, 97–98. Most simply divide the material into large narrative blocks. See, for example, Lührmann (*Markusevangeliuum,* 231–71), who works with 14:1–11, 12–25, 26–42, 43–52, 53–72; 15:1–20a, 20b–41; 15:42–16:8. All changes of scene, time, characters, and action are subordinated to this larger scheme.

    [8] In making this claim, I am aware that the disciples are not present when the chief priests and the scribes plot in vv. 1–2. However, in vv. 10–11, Judas joins that plot. There is nothing forced in the division of 14:1–72 into these eleven scenes. They exactly represent, for example, the division of the text in Ernst, *Markus,* 397–451.

The eleven brief scenes in this arrangement shift systematically from portrayals or predictions of disciples' failures to a presentation of the person of Jesus. Poignantly, and importantly for the Markan understanding of discipleship, at the very center, in the sixth scene (vv. 22–25), the failing disciples and Jesus share a meal.[9]

The pattern repeats in the second half of the narrative (15:1–47). It is dominated by Roman process, from the trial to the crucifixion. However, the chief priests and the scribes, leaders of the Jews, are always present, lurking in the background, inciting the crowd against Jesus. The disciples, having left the scene in 14:50, do not appear. The narrative continues from 14:66–72 (A), so the Roman sequence must open with a focus upon Jesus (B). It unfolds as follows:

[B] *Jesus* reveals himself as the Roman hearing begins (15:1–5).

[A] Barabbas is released rather than Jesus (15:6–11).

[B] Pilate proclaims *Jesus* innocent and ironically styles him king as the Roman hearing closes (15:12–15).

[A] The Roman soldiers ironically proclaim the truth as they mock Jesus (15:16–20a).

[B] *Jesus* is crucified (15:20b–25).

[A] Passersby and the Jewish leaders ironically proclaim the truth as they mock Jesus (15:26–32).

[B] When *Jesus* dies, a centurion proclaims him Son of God (15:33–39).

[A] The women watch the crucifixion from a distance (15:40–41).

[B] *Jesus* is buried (15:42–47).

In a way that parallels the eleven scenes of 14:1–72, in which the central (sixth) scene was the meal with Jesus (14:21–25), the crucifixion of Jesus (15:21–25) is the central (fifth) scene of the nine episodes that form the Roman sequence.[10] As we have seen, 14:1–72 focuses strongly upon the disciples, their failure, and Jesus' unconditional commitment to them. One of them is present, denying Jesus, in the final scene (14:66–72). The Roman sequence brings Mark's christological proclamation to its high point. The disciples do not appear, and thus at its center is the crucified Christ.[11]

---

[9] F. J. Moloney, *A Body Broken for a Broken People: Eucharist in the New Testament* (rev. ed.; Peabody: Hendrickson, 1997), 44–54.

[10] The division into nine "scenes" across 15:1–47 is not as obvious as the eleven-fold division across 14:1–72. Many would unite vv. 1–15 and vv. 20b–41 (see, for example, Ernst, *Markus*, 451, 462–63). See below for the case for the divisions proposed.

[11] In two rich studies, J. P. Heil ("Mark 14,1–52: Narrative Structure and Reader Response," *Bib* 71 [1990]: 305–32, and "The Progressive Narrative Pattern of Mark 14,53–16,8," *Bib* 73 [1992]: 331–58) has also developed a structure on the basis of similarly related scenes. I differ radically, however, from his approach for two basic reasons. In a literary approach major characters must play a role in the determination of structure. In his attempt to produce two balanced structures of nine scenes (three sets of three intercalated scenes) in 14:1–52, repeated in 14:53–16:8, Heil associated the Peter scenes (14:53–54, 66–72) with the Roman process, the crucifixion, and the resurrection (14:53–16:8). This separates Peter from a narrative that has been dominated by disciples, in which Peter's denials are the culmination (14:1–72). A parallel problem emerges with the association of 16:1–8 with 14:53–15:47; the unspoken main character of 16:1–8 is God, and this looks back to 1:1–13. My second major difficulty is Heil's placement of the meal scene (14:22–25) and the crucifixion (15:16–32) as flanking episodes in the central sandwich. Eleven scenes in 14:1–72, on the

This rapid movement from one brief scene to another adds urgency to the narrative. It enables the storyteller to describe the unfailing presence of Jesus, Messiah, Son of the Blessed, Son of Man (14:61b–62), and Prophet (v. 65) to a consistently failing group of disciples. Nowhere is this more poignantly highlighted than in the final meal he shares with them before they betray him, deny him, and flee, as he said they would (14:1–72; see vv. 17–31). The pattern continues to throw into relief the christological climax of the Gospel in the description of the unrelenting suffering of the innocent Jesus, King of the Jews (15:2, 9, 12, 14, 18, 26), the Christ, the king of Israel (15:32), and Son of God (15:39). Paradoxically, on the cross the claims made by the narrator for Jesus in 1:1–13 are shown to be true (15:1–47). In the midst of the rejection and the suffering, new characters appear, "outsiders" like Simon of Cyrene (15:21), the centurion at the cross (15:39), the women (15:40–41, 47), and Joseph of Arimathea (15:43–46). They are the first hint of a newer generation of disciples whose following (15:21), commitment (15:40–41, 47), belief (15:39), and courage (15:43–46) have their beginnings at the cross.[12]

Jesus, the Disciples, and the Jewish Leaders (14:1–72)

[A] The plot of the Jewish leaders (14:1–2)

All the disciples have been exhorted to watch (13:37). Now the passion narrative opens with a plot that signals the approaching crisis.[13] Mark sets the story of Jesus' passion within the context of the Passover, the Feast of the Unleavened Bread (v. 14a).[14] Two days before the celebration the chief priests and the scribes hatch the plot to have Jesus arrested by stealth and kill him.[15] Various combinations of chief priests, elders, and scribes are regarded by

---

basis of the presence of the disciples and nine in 15:1–47 on the basis of Roman action (and see the culmination of 15:39, roughly parallel to Peter's denials) places the meal and the crucifixion at the center of each setting. The fact that, over the years, Heil has found the same structure in three of the four passion and resurrection narratives makes one suspicious. Cf. J. P. Heil, *The Death and Resurrection of Jesus: A Narrative-Critical Reading of Matthew 26–28* (Minneapolis: Fortress, 1991); idem, *Blood and Water: The Death and Resurrection of Jesus in John 18–21* (CBQMS 27; Washington D.C.: The Catholic Biblical Association, 1995). Genest (*Le Christ de la Passion*) has used structuralism to trace the shape of 14:53–15:1, 15:1–21, and 14:65, 15:17–20b, 29–32c. No overarching structure for the whole passion narrative is attempted.

[12] The evidence points to a well-articulated assembly of pre-Markan traditions and more original Markan contributions. Attempts to trace a pre-Markan passion narrative, with judgments that certain sequences "do not fit," or "follow smoothly" (Collins, *Beginning*, 104), "do not follow coherently" (ibid., 105), "disturb the context" (ibid., 108), and so on destroy the theological and literary unity of Mark 14–15. The multiplicity of opinions (reflected in Collins' excellent overview) indicates the speculative nature of the criteria used to determine what is Markan and pre-Markan.

[13] The use of δέ as the second word in v. 1 indicates the author's desire to connect the closing command to watch (13:37) with the passion that follows.

[14] At the time of Jesus two originally separate celebrations had been joined, one coming from a pastoral setting and the other recalling the exodus; Taylor, *St. Mark*, 527–28; LaVerdiere, *The Beginning*, 2.223 n. 3. The following reading of the passion narrative will focus entirely upon the Markan perspective, for which the Passover context is important. This is not the case in all four Gospels. On the historical question, see the fully documented discussion in Brown, *Death*, 2:1350–78.

[15] Even within the Markan account, the chronology can be difficult to follow. Most likely the "two days" mentioned here would mean twenty-four hours, as a day was counted on each appearance of the daylight. The evening of one day and the morning of the next would be "two days." The following tentative scheme is suggested by the narrative: plot and anointing (Wednesday), preparations and the Passover meal (Thursday), Gethsemane, arrest, and Jewish hearing (during the night

Mark as the Sanhedrin. The evil nature of the plan to slay Jesus is indicated by the secrecy of the plan, although their deadly opposition to Jesus is not new (see 3:6; 11:18: 12:12).[16] It cannot be done in the broad light of day. The many times during the story when they were unable to move against Jesus because of his popularity with the people are echoed (see 2:6–12; 11:32; 12:12, 37) as they decide that the plan must not be put into operation *during* the feast.

Historically, the celebration of the major feasts were times of great tension during the period of Roman occupation (cf. Josephus, *Ant.* 17.213–218; 20.105–112; *J.W.* 2.255; 2.280–281; 5.244).[17] A tumult from among the people at this time of the year was to be avoided. The Jewish leadership, therefore, set no precise time for the death of Jesus. This will be resolved for them in 14:10–11 when one of Jesus' disciples joins their plot. There is irony here. The chief priests and the scribes have decided that this Passover, a celebration that recalled God's liberation of Israel from its slavery, will not be marked by the death of Jesus. The Christian community reading of the plot on the part of the leadership knows that Jesus' saving death transformed the Passover.[18]

[B] The anointing of Jesus (14:3–9)

Jesus is anointed in a most extravagant fashion as he sat at table, somewhere outside the city, at the house of a previously unknown character, Simon the leper (14:3).[19] The account of the anointing is sparse. The woman is not described, but everything about her action is extravagant. The flask containing the ointment is made of alabaster, the ointment itself is a precious commodity, pure nard.[20] She destroys the flask by breaking it and pours the precious ointment over the head of Jesus.[21] The irony surrounding the mention of the

---

between Thursday and Friday), Roman hearing, crucifixion, and burial (Friday). An empty tomb is thus discovered "after three days" = end of daylight on Friday, daylight on Saturday, morning light on Sunday; cf. 8:31; 9:31; 10:34). See Hooker, *St. Mark*, 325–26. Gnilka (*Markus*, 2:217–18, 220) points out that this scheme can generate "seven days" and suggests it is Markan. For Pesch (*Markusevangelium*, 2:323–28), the chronology is determined by the pre-Markan passion narrative, beginning from Jesus' arrival in Jericho (10:46) and Jerusalem (11:1–11).

[16] D. Senior, *The Passion of Jesus in the Gospel of Mark* (Passion Series 2; Wilmington: Michael Glazier, 1984), 20–28. For an exhaustive study of the historical background to the Sanhedrin's composition, its legal status under Roman governance, its capacity to condemn to death and execute, and a suggestion concerning the thorny question of Jewish "responsibility" (not "guilt") for the death of Jesus, see Brown, *Death*, 1:328–97. Brown concludes that the Sanhedrin, whose composition was broader than the Markan chief priests, elders, and scribes, had authority to recommend execution, but that this had to be ratified by Roman authority. Jesus of Nazareth was a figure whose words and actions could be understood as deserving of punishment, and thus he prompted a reaction from the Jewish leadership. See also E. Schürer, *The History of the Jewish People in the Age of Jesus Christ (175 B.C.–A.D. 135)* (ed. G. Vermes, F. Millar, and M. Black; 3 vols.; Edinburgh: T&T Clark, 1973–1987), 2:199–226.

[17] Lane, *Mark*, 490; van Iersel, *Reading Mark*, 173.

[18] LaVerdiere, *The Beginning*, 2:226. It may thus express a Markan point of view, and not be a clumsy remnant from the pre-Markan traditions, as many suppose; e.g., Hooker, *St. Mark*, 326. On the scholarly discussion of when the Jewish leaders planned Jesus' arrest and subsequent death, complicated by some minor textual variants, see Taylor, *St. Mark*, 528–29.

[19] Painter (*Mark's Gospel*, 181) suggests that the mention of Simon and his house, otherwise unknown, exemplifies Jesus' command to stay in the one house while on mission (cf. 6:10).

[20] Nard oil was made from the roots of Indian plants, and was thus rare and costly. The word translated "pure" (πιστικῆς) is obscure, and this translation comes from its association with πιστός (trustworthy/faithful). For the discussion, see BDAG, 818, s.v. πιστικός; Taylor, *St. Mark*, 530–31.

[21] Gnilka (*Markus*, 2:223) reads the destruction of the jar as a sign of the unconditional devotion of the woman to Jesus; cf. Lane, *Mark*, 493, Painter, *Mark's Gospel*, 181.

Passover feast in 14:1–2 continues, but with less subtlety. In contrast to the plot to slay Jesus, the woman's gesture indicates a royal anointing. The theme of Jesus as a king, unmentioned to this point in the narrative, is broached. It will gather momentum as the passion narrative develops.[22] The gesture, and thus also its significance, is rejected by others at the gathering. They are not named, and an association with the disciples should be assumed. It is interesting, however, that Mark does not mention them. They grumble angrily among themselves about the waste of the precious commodity, claiming that it could have been sold for about three hundred times the wage for a day's work. The money could have then been distributed among the poor.[23] They turn on the woman in reproach (vv. 4–5). There is no malice in this judgment, but a total lack of recognition of the christological significance of the woman's gesture.

Jesus must explain why she is to be left alone, and in doing so he gives a further interpretation of her gesture. Jesus' first words look back to the royal anointing. The misunderstanding must be corrected, and they have no right to disturb her because what she has done is correct (καλὸν ἔργον).[24] She is the only one at the gathering who has correctly read the events surrounding Jesus' presence in the vicinity of Jerusalem (v. 6). The presence of Jesus must be understood as a unique moment in the coming of God's kingdom (see 1:14–15). There will be a long history of poor and oppressed people, and the followers of Jesus will always have the opportunity and the responsibility to care for them. However, this is the moment for the recognition of who Jesus is and what he is doing.[25] Only the woman has done so (v. 7). The episode recalls the earlier example of the widow who gave her all and was presented as a model of discipleship (12:41–44). Like the widow, this unnamed woman has also done everything possible (14:8a). Jesus' discourse to the disciples (13:1–37), summoning them to watchfulness (βλέπετε) and to act worthily of their call (γρηγορεῖτε), is framed by two women who serve as models of true discipleship.[26] In the light of later events, as Jesus will be rushed into a tomb without anointing (15:46), Jesus adds a further interpretation. The woman recognizes that Jesus is on his way to death, and the anointing of his body is a proleptic honoring of the body of Jesus for its burial (v. 8). Jesus' speaking of his oncoming burial links this episode with the literary frame of the plot (vv. 1–2) and Judas' joining the chief priests and the scribes

---

[22] Gnilka, *Markus*, 2:223–24. The sudden appearance of this new christological category (as well as the name Simon the leper) is an indication that Mark is influenced by pre-Markan traditions. However, he uses them for his own ends. For a summary of the widespread agreement that the theme of Jesus as "king" is from the pre-Markan traditions, see Soards, "The Question," 1510–12. F. J. Matera (*The Kingship of Jesus: Composition and Theology in Mark 15* [SBLDS 66; Chico: Scholars Press, 1982], 67–91) disagrees. He argues that the royal theme has been anticipated across chapters 11–12 (see 11:9; 12:6, 10; 35–37). "In chapters 11–12 Mark has been developing a royal theme which prepares the reader for the royal theology of chapter 15" (p. 91). He does not consider the anointing of Jesus in 14:3.

[23] Almsgiving was seen as an important part of the celebration of Passover; Gnilka, *Markus*, 2:224; Pesch, *Markusevangelium*, 2:332.

[24] The expression καλὸν ἔργον is generally interpreted as a "beautiful" or "splendid" deed. D. Daube (*The New Testament and Rabbinic Judaism* [London: Athlone, 1956; repr. Peabody: Hendrickson, 1994], 315–17) suggests that it reflects a technical expression for a charitable work. The context, where others question the point of her action, is defended by Jesus as a "correct" deed, and in this sense "good." For this meaning, see BDAG, 504, s.v. καλός, par. 2b. Her interpretation of Jesus' presence in Jerusalem at the time of Passover is correct, while that of the others is incorrect.

[25] Taylor, *St. Mark*, 532; Gnilka, *Markus*, 2:224–25; Senior, *The Passion*, 46.

[26] E. S. Malbon, "The Major Importance of the Minor Characters in Mark," in *In the Company of Jesus: Characters in Mark's Gospel* (Louisville: Westminster John Knox, 2000), 202, 215–17.

(vv. 10–11). "Readers . . . learn from Jesus' own lips that the efforts of the authorities to kill him will be successful."[27]

The reader and the disciples are aware that the gospel must first be preached to the whole world (see 13:10). The action of the woman will be part of the "good news" because the action itself is gospel. She has recognized that Jesus' death is at hand and has provided a royal anointing (v. 3) that prepares his body for its burial (v. 8). To do so, like the widow, she has given her all. The recognition of the significance of Jesus' death and an unconditional acceptance of all that it means define discipleship for Mark. The disciples in the story are far from any such recognition. By telling the story of the woman's anointing of the body of Jesus, the "good news" of discipleship will be proclaimed wherever the gospel is preached (v. 11).[28] But it is not only a question of discipleship. This episode announces, at the beginning of the passion narrative, that Jesus is king, and that his crucifixion, death, and burial will point to that truth.[29]

[A] Judas, one of the Twelve, joins the plot against Jesus (14:10–11)

An intimate link is forged among the chief priests and the scribes who planned Jesus' death (14:1–2) and Judas Iscariot, who was one of the Twelve (v. 10).[30] In 3:14 Jesus appointed Judas as one of the Twelve, so that he might be with him. He now turns away from that intimacy by scheming to "hand Jesus over" (ἵνα αὐτὸν παραδοῖ). Judas's handing over of Jesus is a betrayal of what it means to be a disciple (i.e., to be with Jesus), as his betrayal means a willing, violent, and physical separation from him who appointed him to the Twelve. There is also a paradoxical connection between Judas's act and God's design; the passion predictions have already said that Jesus *must* (δεῖ, 8:31) be handed over (παραδίδοται, 9:31; παραδοθήσεται, 10:33).[31] The chief priests and the scribes, who earlier were perplexed concerning when they might trap Jesus, are delighted to have the complicity of an intimate follower of Jesus, and the promise of money links Judas with the shame of a plot that began in stealth (v. 1). Judas now joins Jesus' enemies, seeking an opportunity to betray him.[32]

[B] Jesus prepares for the Passover meal (14:12–16)

The first day of the passion narrative begins a series of intercalations. The enemies of Jesus plot to slay Jesus (vv. 1–2) and one of the Twelve joins them (vv. 10–11). Between

---

27 Brown, *Death*, 1:119.

28 Hooker (*St. Mark*, 330) remarks: "The story is itself a proclamation of the good news." It is not a reference to the worldwide preaching of the gospel, as Taylor (*St. Mark*, 533–34) points out. But see Nineham, *St. Mark*, 372; Gnilka, *Markus*, 2:225–26.

29 Hooker, *St. Mark*, 328. K. E. Corley (*Private Women, Public Meals: Social Conflict in the Synoptic Tradition* [Peabody: Hendrickson, 1993], 102–6) shows that the woman could be judged as promiscuous, but Mark has subordinated any such suggestion to the theological themes of discipleship and the cross.

30 Within the broader structure outlined above, 14:1–16 forms an impressive sandwich construction in its own right: conspiracy—unconditional love—betrayal. See Schweizer, *Mark*, 290; Grundmann, *Markus*, 276.

31 Senior, *The Passion*, 48–49; Gnilka, *Markus*, 2:229. In the predictions the verb is the divine passive. Judas is the one who actively hands Jesus over. For a good study of the relationship of the passion predictions to the passion narrative, see Matera, *Kingship*, 96–97.

32 What motivated this historically certain betrayal, and what "opportunity" offered itself, is impossible to determine. For Mark, the opportunity will be his ability to lead the representatives of the chief priests and the scribes to Jesus in Gethsemane, and to identify Jesus (14:43–45).

these reports the reader has encountered the proclamation of the gospel: the recognition of who Jesus is and the preparation of the body of the king for his burial (vv. 3–9). On the following day, "the first day of the Unleavened Bread, when they sacrificed the passover lamb,"[33] the focus returns to Jesus (vv. 13–16). The disciples show their dependence upon him by asking where they should go to prepare for the celebration of Passover (v. 12).[34] The instructions that follow closely match Jesus' earlier words to his disciples as they were about to enter Jerusalem (14:13–15; see 11:1–6).[35] The details are different, but the same theological perspective is maintained: Jesus is in command of the situation as he arranges for the celebration of the Passover meal. He instructs his disciples where they should go, whom they will meet. He exactly identifies him whom they should follow as a man carrying a pitcher of water (v. 13). On following him to the householder, they are to state that "the teacher" asks for the room where he will celebrate the Passover with his disciples (v. 14). Without question, the householder will show them a large upper room, where they are to prepare for the supper (v. 15).[36] The likelihood of such a series of events is not strong, especially at a time of the year when many pilgrims were pouring into Jerusalem. However, that only serves to heighten the point made by the storyteller.[37] The events that are about to happen transcend the expected, and Jesus goes into them knowing what lies ahead, and makes suitable arrangements for the first of the events of his passion.[38] Everything takes place exactly as Jesus had said, and the disciples prepare the Passover meal (v. 16). Following hard on the heels of Judas's joining the plot to slay Jesus (vv. 10–11), Jesus knowingly provides "the opportunity" for Judas (v. 11) by going into the city of Jerusalem in the company of his disciples to celebrate Passover.[39] Despite what lies ahead, Jesus is the master of the situation as he responds unconditionally to God's will.[40]

---

[33] For the chronological indications, see above, note 15. But problems emerge. The lambs were slaughtered on 14th Nisan, and the first day of Unleavened Bread was the day of the Passover meal, 15th Nisan. Further difficulties emerge from the indications in vv. 12–16 that the meal celebrated with the disciples was a Passover meal; see Gnilka, *Markus,* 2:232–33. It appears most likely that the Johannine dating of the death of Jesus as the day before the feast, as the Passover lambs were slain (see John 18:28; 19:14), is correct, despite the many attempts to explain away the fact that this means that Jesus was tried and crucified on a Holy Day; see especially J. Jeremias, *The Eucharistic Words of Jesus* (trans. N. Perrin; London: SCM, 1966), 15–88, and A. Jaubert, *The Date of the Last Supper* (trans. I. Rafferty; Staten Island; St. Paul, 1965). Despite the improbability of Jesus' being slain on the day of the Passover, Mark has dated these events in this way for theological reasons; J. P. Meier, *A Marginal Jew: Rethinking the Historical Jesus* (3 vols; ABRL; New York: Doubleday, 1991–2001), 1:386–401.

[34] Mark's Passover scheme is driven by theological concerns (see the previous note), but he does not exploit the link with the Passover later in the narrative. This is strange, as is probably best explained by Senior: "In these preparatory scenes he brings that rich theological symbol of liberation and hope emphatically before the reader" (*The Passion,* 51).

[35] The similarity between the two passages extends even to details. Eleven consecutive words in 14:13 are identical with 11:1–2. See the chart in Taylor, *St. Mark,* 536.

[36] On the description of the room, see Gnilka, *Markus,* 2:233–34; Lane, *Mark,* 500.

[37] Nineham (*St. Mark,* 375–77) lists a number of incongruities in the passage, suggesting that it was not part of the original narrative. If it was added by Mark (on the basis of 11:1–6), it serves his literary and theological agenda well.

[38] Against Taylor (*St. Mark,* 537–39), who strains to show the basic historicity of these events.

[39] As Hooker (*St. Mark,* 335) comments: "There is no suggestion that Jesus is in hiding, or that the preparations are being carried out in secret; anyone could have followed the disciples, just as they followed their guide." Oddly, Senior (*The Passion,* 52) describes this moment as a "quiet, almost guarded, entry."

[40] Lohmeyer (*Markus,* 300) comments on vv. 12–16: "It creates only an example for the thought that stands over the whole passion account." See also Grundmann, *Markus,* 279.

[A] Jesus predicts the betrayal of Judas, one of the Twelve (14:17–21)

The interpretation of 14:17–21 depends upon its place within the overall literary structure of 14:1–72. The reader has arrived at the first of three scenes that dominate the central section of this part of the narrative. In 14:22–25 Jesus will share the meal with his disciples. Before the meal (vv. 17–21) he will prophecy the betrayal of Judas, and after the meal (vv. 26–31) he will prophecy the denials of Peter and the flight of all the disciples. The narrator opens the episode by setting the event in the evening and locating Jesus with "the Twelve" (v. 17). The disciples have prepared everything for the meal, following Jesus' instructions (vv. 12–16). He comes to the upper room (v. 15) with a group of people whom he chose and appointed to be "with him" in a special way (3:14). A further setting is provided for the words of Jesus: "as they were at table eating" (v. 18a). The verb ἀνακειμένων indicates that they were "reclining" at table. This posture was taken at the particularly solemn Passover meal, but was not normal for everyday Jewish meal settings.[41] It also adds a further level of intimacy to the setting. Jesus now speaks about his betrayer at the meal table, a sacred place among friends.[42]

There is a link with the earlier meal scenes in 6:31–44 and 8:1–9. The disciples expressed a desire to exclude others from the table of the Lord (see 6:35–36; 8:4). In this meal setting (14:17–21), Jesus announces that one of the Twelve will break the exclusive fellowship he established with them in 3:14–19. With the solemn "Amen, I say to you," he makes the shocking connection between one who is about to betray him, and the fact that this person is sharing a meal with him, alluding to Ps 41:9 (v. 18bc; cf. Ps 55:12–14).[43] Sorrow overcomes the Twelve, and they begin to ask, in turn, "Is it I?" The question, μήτι ἐγώ expects a negative response.[44] They are hoping that their sorrow will be eased by Jesus' assurance to each one of them that he is not the betrayer. Jesus does not identify Judas, but announces that it is "one of the Twelve," and heightens the paradox of the betrayer's presence at the table by noting that they both reach into the same dish (v. 20).[45] The contrast between intimacy and betrayal is powerfully stated, and the deliberate betrayal of that intimacy generates Jesus' harsh judgment in 14:21. There is an inevitability about the oncoming suffering, death, and ultimate vindication of the Son of Man. It is a necessary, although paradoxical, part of God design, the fulfillment of what was written of the Son of Man (v. 21a).[46] The reader is aware of this from the passion predictions, which used the expres-

---

[41] Hooker, *St. Mark,* 336.

[42] On the importance of meals in the biblical tradition, see Léon-Dufour, *Sharing the Eucharistic Bread,* 35–38.

[43] Gnilka, *Markus,* 2:236–37. These Psalms are part of an Old Testament theme of the suffering of the Just One. This complex of ideas played a role in the development of the Christian story of Jesus' suffering and death (especially in Matthew and Luke). For a presentation of this theme and its relationship to the passion accounts, see L. Ruppert, *Jesus als der leidende Gerechte? Der Weg Jesus im lichte eines alt- und zwischen-testamentlichen Motivs* (SBS 59; Stuttgart: Katholisches Bibelwerk, 1972). On Ps 41:9 in Mark 14:18, see D. J. Moo, *The Old Testament in the Gospel Passion Narratives* (Sheffield: The Almond Press, 1983), 237–40.

[44] See BDF, 220–21, par. 427.

[45] V. K. Robbins, "Last Meal: Preparation, Betrayal, and Absence," in *The Passion in Mark: Studies on Mark 14–16* (ed. W. Kelber; Philadelphia: Fortress, 1976), 29–34. Robbins highlights these elements in the story, but underestimates the positive presentation of Jesus' presence to the failing disciples.

[46] Daniel 7 remains the essential scriptural reference. The "one like a son of man" of 7:14 is the corporate representative of the holy ones of God who must undergo suffering and even martyrdom under Antiochus IV, in the firm belief that God will have the last word.

sion "the Son of Man" to speak of Jesus' oncoming death and resurrection (see 8:31; 9:31; 10:33–34). The divine necessity, however, does not lessen the tragedy of the fact that "one of the Twelve," a disciple specially chosen and appointed by Jesus to be with him (3:14–19) and to continue his mission (see 6:7–13), has broken the bond. "The plan and purpose of God find expression here without exonerating the betrayer."[47] Judas's deliberate separation from Jesus is read by Mark, and by the early church as a whole, as worthy only of the worst condemnation. It would be better if he had never been born (v. 21bc).[48]

[B] Jesus shares the meal with the Twelve (14:22–25)

The description of Jesus' celebration of the meal with the Twelve, the centerpiece of 14:1–72, is terse. The context of the meal is recalled (v. 22a), but very little is reported of Passover meal practices.[49] However, the sharing of a cup of wine and the reference to the covenant in 14:23–24 link the meal with those practices. The focus is entirely upon the gift of the bread, identified as the body of Jesus (v. 22), and the gift of the cup, the blood of the covenant, poured out for many (vv. 23–24). The passage concludes solemnly with an "amen" saying, a word of confidence that this meal, despite Jesus' words about his body and his blood (vv. 22, 24), is not the end of Jesus' sharing in the delights of God's kingdom. The two points of reference in the actions of the supper are Jesus and the disciples. As with the earlier bread miracles, the language and ritual of a eucharistic celebration are recalled. Taking (λαβών, 14:22; cf. 6:41; 8:6) bread (ἄρτον, 14:22; ἄρτους, 6:41; 8:6), he blessed, broke and gave (εὐλογήσας ἔκλασεν καὶ ἔδωκεν, 14:22; εὐλόγησεν καὶ κατέκλασεν . . . καὶ ἐδίδου, 6:41; εὐχαριστήσας [εὐλογήσας, 8:7] ἔκλασεν καὶ ἐδίδου, 8:6). Behind all three narratives lie the eucharistic practices of the Markan community, but the thrust of the narrative is not to "institute" the Eucharist. Unlike the Lukan (Luke 22:14–20) and the Pauline (1 Cor 11:23–26) tradition, there is no command to go on doing these things in memory of Jesus (cf. Luke 22:19; 1 Cor 11:24–25).[50]

Taking, blessing, breaking, and giving the bread is primarily a symbolic statement interpreted by Jesus in his words: "Take, this is my body" (v. 22). The broken bread is the broken body of Jesus given to the disciples. The primary point of reference is Jesus' coming death, but this death is interpreted as *for others*. The same must be said for the sharing of the cup. The cup is interpreted by Jesus as his spilt blood, poured out for many (v. 24).[51] What was sug-

---

[47] Painter, *Mark's Gospel*, 185.

[48] Taylor (*St. Mark*, 547) asserts: "The 'Woe' pronounced over him is not a curse, but a cry of sorrow and anguish: 'Alas! for that man,' and the saying 'It were better, etc.' is not a threat, but a sad recognition of facts."

[49] It is widely accepted that this passage, with its cultic background and sacrificial tone, developed independently and was only subsequently accepted into the pre-Markan (or Markan) passion story; see, for example, Lohmeyer, *Markus*, 302–3; Schweizer, *Mark*, 300–303; Grundmann, *Markus*, 283–84; Gnilka, *Markus*, 2:240–43. La Verdiere (*The Beginning*, 2:234–39) would agree, but shows how well the passage sits in its present Markan context. See also Gnilka, *Markus*, 2:249.

[50] Lührmann, *Markusevangelium*, 238–40. Given the importance of the table of the Lord in Christian tradition, a large amount of scholarly literature has been dedicated to Mark 14:22–25; Matt 26:26–29; Luke 22:14–20; John 6:51–58; 1 Cor 11:23–26. As well as Jeremias, *The Eucharistic Words;* Léon-Dufour, *Sharing the Eucharistic Bread;* and Moloney, *Body Broken,* an excellent summary of the discussion is found in J. Kodell, *The Eucharist in the New Testament* (Zacchaeus Studies: New Testament; Wilmington: Michael Glazier, 1989). A helpful bibliographical compendium of specialized works can be found in Léon-Dufour, *Sharing the Eucharistic Bread*, 311–21.

[51] Wine was not customary at all shared Jewish meals at this time, but it was an essential part of the Passover ritual. The remark that drinking blood would be "regarded . . . with horror" (Hooker,

gested concerning the broken body *for others* is made explicit in the spilt blood *for many*. Jesus' words to the disciples in 10:45 are being further explained: "For the Son of Man also came, not to be served, but to serve, and to lay down his life as a ransom for many." The use of "many" reflects a Semitic form of inclusiveness and refers to the vastness of the number of recipients of Jesus' self-gift unto death.[52] It does not mean that he will break his body and spill his blood for some but not for others. However, the Passover setting, associating the forthcoming death of Jesus with the liberating experience of the exodus and the subsequent relationship established with God, is not entirely neglected. Jesus interprets the pouring out of his blood as the establishment of a covenant (v. 24).[53] This description recalls Moses' ratifying the covenant between YHWH and the people of Israel, taking the blood of sacrificed oxen and sprinkling half of it on the altar and the other half on the people with the words, "Behold the blood of the covenant which the Lord has made with you in accordance with all these words" (Exod 24:8).[54] Verses 22–24, within their literary context, tell of Jesus' breaking bread and sharing wine as a sign of his gift of self unto death *for others,* establishing a covenant of freedom and oneness with God: "and they all drank of it" (v. 23b).[55]

The eucharistic practice of the Markan community is taken for granted, and its language used to convey the message of Jesus' willing self-gift unto death for "the many." But within the Markan story, who are the *others* to whom Jesus gives the broken bread and with whom he shares the wine? Within the larger literary pattern of intercalations which shapes 14:1–72, Jesus' presence at the table, sharing bread and wine with his disciples (vv. 22–25) is set between vv. 17–21 and 26–31. The *others* are represented at the table by the betrayer, whose actions have been prophesied in 14:17–21, and Peter and the disciples, whose future denials and flight will be foretold in 14:26–31.[56] The dramatic presentation of Jesus and the disciples continues with the solemn promise of v. 25, again introduced with "Amen, I say to you." Jesus' broken body (v. 22) and spilt blood may appear to be the end of his story (v. 24), but they will not be the end of the presence of Jesus and the kingdom of God. This is the final festive meal that Jesus will celebrate with his disciples. He will not drink again of the fruit of the vine (v. 25b) *until* that day when he will drink a new wine in the kingdom of God (v. 25c).[57] The word "until" has a temporal function that forces the reader to look beyond the coming death of Jesus.[58] At each passion prediction,

---

St. Mark, 342) overlooks the fact that this narrative was generated in a Christian community already celebrating the Eucharist. What Jesus actually said to his disciples is difficult to establish.

[52] Hooker (*St. Mark,* 343) observes: "The 'many' stand in contrast to the 'one' who gives up his life." For strong links with 10:45 and Isa 53, see R. E. Watts, *Isaiah's New Exodus and Mark* (Tübingen: J. C. B. Mohr [Paul Siebeck], 1997), 349–65. See also J. Marcus, *The Way of the Lord: Christological Exegesis of the Old Testament in the Gospel of Mark* (Louisville: Westminster John Knox, 1992), 186–87. For Suffering Servant imagery in Mark, especially regarding the notion of Jesus' saving death, see ibid., 186–98.

[53] Some manuscripts have "my blood of the *new* covenant," a theologically satisfying statement for the Christian tradition, but doubtless imported from Luke 22:20 and 1 Cor 11:25. It is lacking in, among others, Sinaiticus, Alexandrinus, Ephraem Rescript, Regius, Koridethi, and Athos.

[54] Taylor, *St. Mark,* 545–46; Nineham, *St. Mark,* 385–86.

[55] Anderson (*Mark,* 313–14) asserts: "The solitary narrative detail that intrudes in the description of Jesus' actions and words, **they all drank of it,** could have been a reminder to the Church that all, however reprobate (even the betrayer?), were admitted to the fellowship of Jesus and were offered the mercy and love of God in and through him" (bold in original).

[56] On the "dialogue" between Jesus and the disciples present at the table, who do not actually speak, see Léon-Dufour, *Sharing the Eucharistic Bread,* 60–62, 117–18, 130–32, 195–96.

[57] The "fruit of the vine" is regularly used as a poetic expression for "wine." Cf. Num 6:4; Isa 32:12; Hab 3:7.

[58] Gnilka, *Markus,* 2:246–47.

Jesus confidently affirmed a resurrection on the third day (see 8:31; 9:31; 10:34). This is repeated here as he speaks of a time after his death when he will drink the new wine of the messianic banquet (cf. Isa 25:6; *2 Bar.* 29:5–8; Matt 8:11; Luke 14:15; John 2:1–11; Rev 19:9). The disciples will prove themselves to be extremely fragile (vv. 17–21, 26–31), but the kingdom promised by the advent of Jesus (1:14–15) will be established, not destroyed, by his death.

> Mark has given us an account of Jesus' gift of himself unto death so that he could set up a new and lasting kingdom with the very people who frame the narrative of the meal. The meal that Jesus shared was not a meal for the worthy ones (vv. 22–25). *It was a meal for those people who were closest to Jesus but who, faced with the challenge to love him even unto death, betrayed and abandoned their Lord* (vv. 17–21, 26–31).[59]

The Markan version of Jesus' final meal with his disciples is as much about his relationship with the disciples as it is about his self-sacrifice in death, "seen as the new act of redemption, establishing a covenant between God and his people which supersedes the old covenant between God and Israel."[60]

[A] Jesus predicts the future denials of Peter and the flight of all the disciples (14:26–31)

Often regarded as a Markan addition to his source, 14:26 tells of the singing of a hymn and the departure from the upper room to the Mount of Olives. It serves as a connecting link between the events in the upper room (vv. 17–25) and the scenes in Gethsemane (vv. 32–52).[61] A deliberate Markan link between the meal and the celebration of Passover is often suggested in the claim that the hymn was the final part of the Hallel (Pss. 114–118), associated with the closing of the Passover meal. But we cannot be sure that ὑμνεῖν can be identified so specifically.[62] The passage leads the reader away from the upper room toward the Mount of Olives, the place where Jesus delivered his farewell discourse (13:1–37). The indications that Jesus is about to be betrayed (vv. 17–21) and the prophecy of his death (vv. 22–24) perhaps recall David's ascent of the Mount of Olives in 2 Sam 15:30, fleeing from Absalom, the son who betrayed him.[63] However, there is no sense of flight in Jesus' journey with the disciples. On the contrary, he speaks of *their* future flight.

The disciples are told that they will fall away (σκανδαλισθήσεσθε, 14:27). This failure links the whole group with Peter, the "satan," the stumbling block (σκάνδαλον, 8:33; cf. Matt 16:23), and also places them among the ranks of those who would be ashamed of Jesus and his words when challenged to give themselves unconditionally for Jesus and the

---

[59] Moloney, *Body Broken,* 54. Stress in original.

[60] Hooker, *St. Mark,* 340. See also Lohmeyer, *Markus,* 304–5; Senior, *The Passion,* 61–62. For a perceptive reading of the meaning of Jesus' self-gift in vv. 21–25, relating this message to other parts of the Gospel as the resolution of the mystery of Jesus, see van Iersel, *Reading Mark,* 193–97.

[61] Some (e.g., Lohmeyer, *Markus,* 310–11) mistakenly separate vv. 26–31 from vv. 22–25, suggesting that it is an introduction to Gethsemane.

[62] Many regard the reference to the Hallel as certain; see, e.g., Anderson, *Mark,* 316; Hooker, *St. Mark,* 344; Senior, *The Passion,* 62. Taylor (*St. Mark,* 548) is not sure ("It is commonly held . . ."). Brown (*Death,* 1:122–23) rejects the identification as depending upon later Passover practices. He suggests, probably correctly, "one should recognize more simply and surely that *hymnein* indicates a prayerful context as the meal closed" (p. 123). See also Schweizer, *Mark,* 307.

[63] For this possibility, see Brown, *Death,* 1:125–26.

gospel (see 8:35–38).[64] An earlier passage comes to the mind of the reader: in the explanation of the parable of the sower (4:14–20), Jesus described disciples who initially respond with joy, but when tribulations arise on account of the word they immediately fall away (εὐθὺς σκανδαλίζονται, 4:17). The parable has become prophecy in 14:27. Yet, like the betrayal of Judas (see 14:21), their flight paradoxically fulfills God's design. The disciples' falling away was foretold in the Scriptures.[65] The initiative of God is highlighted by Mark's alteration of the use of the imperative in the Hebrew text of Zech 13:7 ("Strike the shepherd!") to the first person future singular: "I will strike" (πατάξω). God's design lies behind the death of Jesus, and it has the necessary consequence of the scattering of the sheep. There is a further important alteration of the Hebrew in Mark's simple juxtaposing of the striking of the shepherd and the scattering of the sheep. In Zech 13:7 the command to strike the shepherd is *so that* the sheep would be scattered. "The disciples' failure is a consequence, but not the purpose of Jesus' death."[66] The use of Zech 13 introduces the familiar image of a shepherd (see Ezek 34; Num 27:17; Ps 23) which, despite the difficulties traced by many scholars in establishing the history of this brief but important collection of sayings,[67] leads easily into Jesus' promise of 14:28. As with great compassion he looked upon the great throng of sheep without a shepherd beside the sea of Galilee (6:34, 39, 42),[68] he will deal similarly with his scattered disciples.

The disciples have been told that Jesus will be raised (8:31; 9:31; 10:33–34; cf. 9:9–10). After that has taken place, Jesus will go before them into Galilee. The use of the verb προάγειν is open to several interpretations. It could mean "to go before," in the sense of arriving in Galilee before they do. However it could also mean "to go before" in the sense of "to lead" the disciples into Galilee. Within the present context, in the light of the use of the image of the shepherd and the scattered sheep from Zech 13:7 in v. 27, the second sense is to be preferred.[69] A crucial Markan theme has been stated: Jesus will be slain, and his death will lead to the scandalizing and the scattering of the disciples. They will all flee (v. 27). But he will not abandon them. As the risen one he will gather his scattered disciples and lead them, as a shepherd leads his sheep, into Galilee (v. 28). The promise of a future "leading" of the scattered disciples to Galilee recalls Jesus' earlier "leading" them toward Jerusalem. In 10:32 the narrator reported: "And they were on the road, going up to Jerusalem, and Jesus was leading them (ἦν προάγων αὐτοὺς ὁ Ἰησοῦς)." On that occasion they were full of fear, but the reader suspects that once Jesus has been raised the journey back to Galilee will be accompanied by different sentiments. That the journey is not reported is one of several

---

[64] The verb is different in 8:38 (ἐπαισχύνομαι), but the idea of an inability to accept Jesus' challenge is the same in both situations. On the link with Peter's "satanic" role, see Brown, *Death,* 1:133–34.

[65] On Zech 13:7 in Mark 14:27, see Moo, *Old Testament,* 182–87.

[66] Senior, *The Passion,* 64.

[67] See Brown, *Death,* 1:126–33, 142–45 for various reinterpretations of Zech 13:7 in Jewish traditions, its importance in the Markan context, and the scholarly discussion of the history of the early Christian traditions involved here. The major difficulty is created by v. 28, which is repeated in 16:7. These two verses are crucial to the Markan theological agenda. Are they *both* redactional? Was one original and the other constructed from it? It is difficult to be certain, and a decision is not called for in this reading of the Gospel.

[68] On Ps 23 as background for some of the imagery used in 6:31–44, see above, pp. 129–33.

[69] Marcus, *The Way of the Lord,* 161–63. Taylor (*St. Mark,* 549) and Schweizer (*Mark,* 308) reject this meaning because it cannot have the same meaning in 16:7. But the context of each use of προάγειν can determine its meaning (see also 6:45; 10:32; 11:9), and thus 16:7 need not come into play at this stage of the story. See Hooker, *St. Mark,* 345; Gnilka, *Markus,* 2:253.

surprises that awaits the reader at the end of the story. For the moment, the disciples are in-structed that they are heading for a God-designed failure, and Jesus will see to it that they will be restored to his company.[70] Promise of this is made in 14:27–28. Very shortly the prophecy of 14:27 will be fulfilled (see v. 50). The fulfillment of the promise of 14:28, how-ever, is more problematic, as the reader will discover on encountering 16:7–8.[71]

Peter becomes the center of attention as he swears allegiance to Jesus, strongly denying the possibility that he would join all the other disciples in their failure (εἰ καὶ πάντες σκανδαλισθήσονται, 14:29).[72] This confident assertion prompts Jesus to prophecy Peter's forthcoming triple denial (v. 30). The prophecy is solemn, opening with ἀμὴν λέγω σοι, di-rected straight to Peter (second person singular), and Jesus' knowledge is so total that he is able to indicate the time span: "this very night, before the cock crows twice."[73] In the midst of tragedy, Jesus is still exercising authority and showing his knowledge. The details pro-vided by Jesus will become significant later in the narrative, but for the moment, the con-nection with 8:34–38 continues. Peter is told that, in a moment of danger, unlike the true disciple who denies himself (ἀπαρνησάσθω ἑαυτόν, 8:34), takes up the cross, and follows Jesus, he will deny Jesus three times (τρίς με ἀπαρνήσῃ). The prophecy of Peter's denials heightens the tragic separation between Jesus and the disciples as a group, foretold in 14:27–28. The unity established in 3:14–19 will be broken, but Peter will not hear the word of Jesus (v. 31). Again looking back to the model of discipleship proposed by Jesus in 8:34–38, he insists that, if necessary (ἐὰν δέῃ με, 14:31),[74] he will be prepared to lay down his life for the sake of Jesus (see 8:35–37). The remark from the narrator in 14:31c must be given its full weight.[75] The walk from the upper room to the Mount of Olives began with Jesus' foretelling the falling away of the disciples as a group (v. 27). It ends with that same group joining Peter's words of commitment unto death (v. 31b). Jesus tells the disciples that the model of discipleship he taught them in 8:34–38 is about to be totally abandoned as they fall away, flee, and deny him. They will not take up the cross and follow him (8:34). It is not only Peter who says that he will not fall away (see 14:29) or deny Jesus (v. 31b). All the disciples said the same (v. 31c). The disciples with whom Jesus has shared a meal (vv. 22–25), telling them that he is drawing them into the saving and liberating experience of his broken body and spilt blood, will betray him (vv. 17–21), fall away, and deny him (vv. 26–31). In the midst of his predictions of their failure, flight, and denials, Jesus has

---

[70] Grundmann (*Markus,* 287–88) rightly points to this passage as an instruction for all believ-ers. However, he highlights the possibility of their failure. I agree that it is addressed to all believers, but suggest that more than failure is involved.

[71] In 16:7 the promise of 14:28 is repeated as the women are commissioned to tell the disciples and Peter that Jesus is leading them into Galilee. However, in v. 8 the women flee and do not execute the commission. This element in the Markan story is not given sufficient attention by Marcus (*The Way of the Lord,* 154–64) in his study of the use of Zech 9–14 in the passion narrative.

[72] As Brown (*Death,* 1:133) points out, the use of εἰ καί does not deny the fact that the disciples will fall away. Peter affirms that he will be an exception to this failure.

[73] On the variations on the cock-crowing prediction and fulfillment across the Gospels, see Brown, *Death,* 1:136–37.

[74] The use of δέῃ, a form of δεῖ, links Peter's promise with Jesus' first passion prediction ("The Son of Man *must* [δεῖ] go up to Jerusalem . . . ," 8:31). "Peter, who once strongly rejected the neces-sity of that suffering (Mark 8:31–33) is now more strongly professing his willingness to share it; but alas he is no more realistic in one reaction than the other" (Brown, *Death,* 1:138).

[75] Most commentators gloss over this final remark from the narrator. See, for example, the scant attention given to it in the usually exhaustive treatments of Taylor (*St. Mark,* 550) and Pesch (*Markusevangelium,* 2:383). Better is the treatment in Gnilka, *Markus,* 2:254–55.

sounded a note of hope. He has presented himself as the shepherd who will lead his fragile disciples into Galilee (v. 28). The reader has every reason to believe in Jesus' prophecies as he is even able to tell Peter the details of the timing of his threefold denial (v. 30). What is about to happen is not the result of uncontrolled fate. The theme of Jesus' unfailing presence to ever-failing disciples dominates 14:17–31, the centerpiece of 14:1–72, a long section composed of passages focusing alternately upon Jesus and his disciples.

[B] The prayer of Jesus in Gethsemane (14:32–42)

The passion of Jesus begins with this episode.[76] It continues themes from the Gospel to this point and provides a christological key for much that follows as Jesus is arrested, tried, and crucified.[77] Jesus' presence in Gethsemane is dominated by his relationship with God, whom he calls "Abba," while the failure of Peter, James, and John is a submotif. The episode can be divided into three moments (14:32; 14:33–40; 14:41–42), with the central section having its own internal subdivision:[78]

[A] Introduction: Jesus and the disciples in Gethsemane (14:32)

   [B] Jesus, Peter, James, and John (14:33–34)

      [C] The prayer of Jesus to the Father (14:35–36)

         [D] Jesus, Peter, James, and John (14:37–38)

      [C'] The prayer of Jesus to the Father (14:39)

   [B'] Jesus, Peter, James, and John (14:40)

[A'] Conclusion: "The hour has come" to leave Gethsemane (14:41–42)

This pattern shows the narrator's focus upon Jesus' lament, at once fearful yet trusting God, set against the increasing weakness of Peter, James, and John. In 13:35–37 these three disciples had been instructed to "watch" (γρηγορεῖτε) across the hours of the evening, midnight, cock crow, and morning.

Introduction: Jesus and the disciples in Gethsemane (14:32)

The journey from the upper room, begun in 14:26, reaches its conclusion on the Mount of Olives at a place called Gethsemane. The word means "oil press," and the cultivation of olives on the hill opposite the temple area is well attested.[79] Jesus separates himself from the disciples, whom he commands to sit down, so that he might pray (ἕως προσεύξωμαι). The location is evocative, opposite the temple area with the city before him

---

[76] Scholars have found tensions and contradictions in vv. 32–42, and have thus developed complex source theories; see Schweizer, *Mark,* 309–11; Grundmann, *Markus,* 290–91; Gnilka, *Markus,* 2:256–58. For a survey, defending the narrative unity of the final form of the passage, see Brown, *Death,* 1:216–27.

[77] R. Feldmeier, *Die Krisis der Gottessohnes: Die Gethsemaneerzählung als Schlüssel der Markuspassion* (WUNT 2. Reihe 21; Tübingen: J. C. B. Mohr [Paul Siebeck], 1987), 233–36.

[78] See also Feldmeier, *Die Krisis,* 112–22; Brown, *Death,* 1:202–3, for similar suggestions. Many (e.g., Lohmeyer, *Markus,* 313–14; Feldmeier, *Die Krisis,* 123–25) see a pattern of "threes" across the passage: a threefold movement into solitary prayer (vv. 32–34), three moments of prayer interspersed with visits to the failing disciples (vv. 35–41), three moments as Jesus turns toward his arrest (vv. 41–42).

[79] Gnilka, *Markus,* 2:258–59; Brown, *Death,* 1:148–49.

and the Judean waste behind him.[80] However, not only is the setting established with this scene, but also the purpose of Jesus' presence at Gethsemane: prayer.

Central section: Jesus' prayers (14:33–40)

Jesus, Peter, James, and John (14:33–34). Peter, James, and John are singled out from the larger group, which has been instructed to sit nearby (v. 32). From the moment of the vocation of the Twelve, these men have been associated with Jesus in a special way. In 3:16–17 Jesus gave them special names. Since then, he has drawn them into other privileged moments: the raising of Jairus's daughter (5:37), the transfiguration (9:2), and along with Andrew, they have heard Jesus' words on the end of Jerusalem and the end of time (see 13:3). They have been instructed that the timing of the events that will mark the end is unknown to anyone but God (see 13:32), but they must stay awake and be watchful (vv. 35–37). Earlier in the story all three have boasted of their willingness and ability to share in his suffering: see 10:35–40 (James and John); 14:29–31 (Peter). The link between 13:35–37 and Jesus' command to the three disciples to "watch" (γρηγορεῖτε, 14:44) as they gather for prayer in the evening (see 13:35) hints at something final about to happen.[81] This is a critical moment. They are now to do as they were instructed in Jesus' discourse when they were last together on the Mount of Olives (13:3): "Watch!"

The critical nature of the moment is made apparent in that Jesus' words are entirely uncharacteristic of his teaching and instructions throughout the Gospel to this point (14:34). He announces that his soul is very sorrowful, even unto death. The intensity of Jesus' sense of his oncoming passion and his awareness of the imminent scattering of the disciples "is enough to kill him, and he will ask God to be delivered from such a fate."[82] He uses words and expressions reflecting Israel's psalms of lament (see especially Pss 30:8–10; 40:11–13; 42:6, 11–12; 43:1–2, 5; 55:4–8; 61:1–3; 116:3–4; cf. John 12:27; Heb 5:7).[83] The original Psalm, like almost all the psalms of lament, comes from someone in a situation of suffering, abandonment, hopelessness, and violated innocence. But through all the expressions of fear, suffering, and hopelessness, and the questions put to God, a profound trust is expressed in the ultimate victory of God over the source of evil (see, e.g., Pss 42:5b, 8, 11b;

---

[80] There are good reasons to accept that historically Jesus prayed a troubled prayer before his death; see Gnilka, *Markus,* 2:264. The event is well supported across a number of different New Testament witnesses, as well as the Synoptic Tradition (and Luke may have a different source for the scene); see John 12:27; 14:31; 18:11; Heb 5:7. For this case, see Hooker, *St. Mark,* 346–47, and the full discussion in Feldmeier, *Die Krisis,* 9–63, 133–39. See also Brown, *Death,* 1:227–34, and S. R. Garrett, *The Temptations of Jesus in Mark's Gospel* (Grand Rapids: Eerdmans, 1998), 104–15, with particular attention to the contribution of Heb 5:7. For Taylor (*St. Mark,* 551–57), the passage as a whole depends upon an authentic Petrine tradition.

[81] For further discussion of the links between the presence of the three disciples at Gethsemane and earlier scenes in the Gospel, see Brown, *Death,* 1:151–52.

[82] Brown, *Death,* 1:156. Brown rightly draws this conclusion, in close association with the prayer which follows in v. 36, after a long discussion of the many interpretations of what is meant by sorrow "unto death" (pp. 153–56). See also S. E. Dowd, *Prayer, Power and Suffering: Mark 11:22–25 in the Context of Markan Theology* (SBLDS 105; Atlanta: Scholars Press, 1988), 153.

[83] See the discussion of Mark's use of these psalms in Moo, *The Old Testament,* 240–42. See also Marcus, *The Way of the Lord,* 172–86 (for an association between the Markan community and the righteous sufferer), and Feldmeier, *Die Krisis,* 148–62. Feldmeier (pp. 161–62) correctly points out that the use of these psalms that have their origins in the laments of the righteous sufferer must not distract from the Markan presentation of Jesus as the Messiah and Son of God.

43:2a, 4, 5b).[84] At no earlier time in the narrative, as he pointed forward to his death, were the sentiments of anxiety, sorrow, or fear expressed. It is often claimed that this uniqueness reflects the historicity of the episode, as it is out of tune with the Markan presentation of Jesus.[85] This is not necessarily the case. The passion has begun, and these words of lament and anxiety point forward to the horror of the events that will follow. Jesus' sudden change of attitude indicates the unrelenting nature of the suffering that he is about to endure. However, it does not take away from him the trust that—whatever may happen to him—God will have the last word.[86] Those sentiments have regularly been part of his passion predictions (8:31; 9:31; 10:33–34). The disciples should be able to hear the change in Jesus' sentiment, and do as he is asking of them: "watch." "The time of testing has already begun."[87]

The prayer of Jesus to the Father (14:35–36). Jesus now distances himself from the three chosen disciples (v. 35) and takes up an extreme position of prayer. He has prayed earlier (see 1:35; 6:46), but nothing was said about his adopting a physical position (cf. John 17:1). Here he collapses on the ground. The narrator paraphrases Jesus' prayer. What was suggested in Jesus' words to the disciples (v. 34) is now made explicit; Jesus prays that God might release him from the coming events. These events are summed up in the expression "the hour" (ἡ ὥρα), a traditional expression that points to the unique moment of God's design (cf. vv. 37, 41). Jesus has used "the hour" in 13:32 to speak of the final, eschatological intervention of God that closes history. The death of Jesus will take place in history, but it forms part of the larger conflict between God and a rebellious world that will slay God's Son.[88] Jesus' "final prayer" allows the reader into the heart of the person praying. For all his unconditional commitment to God's design, so amply shown throughout the Gospel, the reader is allowed into the inner recesses of Jesus' mind and heart, to find two things: terror and a determination to accept whatever God wants. Even in 14:35, the request that the hour might pass is accompanied by the rider "if it were possible."

The paraphrase is replaced with the words of Jesus in 14:36. Jesus addresses God as "Abba," a Hebrew and Aramaic address normally directed to one's own father.[89] This is the only appearance of this affectionate term in any of the Gospels. Here it heightens the sense

---

[84] Senior, *The Passion,* 70–73.

[85] See, for example, R. Barbour, "Gethsemane in the Tradition of the Passion," *NTS* 16 (1969–1970): 231–52; W. Kelber, "Mark 14:32–42: Gethsemane Passion Christology and Discipleship Failure," *ZNW* 63 (1972): 166–87; idem, "The Hour of the Son of Man and the Temptation of the Disciples," in *The Passion in Mark* (ed. W. Kelber; Philadelphia: Fortress, 1976), 41–60.

[86] As Senior (*The Passion,* 69) remarks: "The text betrays few jagged edges and, indeed, fits smoothly into the ongoing narrative of Mark." On the function of the Gethsemane scene within the Gospel as a whole, see Feldmeier, *Die Krisis,* 233–36.

[87] Hooker, *St. Mark,* 348.

[88] Brown (*Death,* 1:167–68) concludes: "While for Mark the death of Jesus is involved in 'the hour,' the death is part of a struggle with sinners that is an aspect of the coming of the Kingdom. Mark is presenting a moment that is both historical and eschatological." See also Feldmeier, *Die Krisis,* 185–86. On the language of "eschatological testing" across vv. 32–42, see Garrett, *The Temptations,* 91–95.

[89] It is possible that this intimate address to God was regularly used by Jesus in his prayer (see also Rom 8:15; Gal 4:6). For a fully documented discussion, see Brown, *Death,* 1:172–75, and especially the important broadening of this discussion by M. M. Thompson, *The Promise of the Father: Jesus and God in the New Testament* (Louisville: Westminster John Knox, 2000), 20–86.

of trust and unity between Jesus and God, but also makes a serious christological claim. Jesus prays to God as a son to a father. These words are Jesus' first implicit claim to be the Son of God, a theme that will come to a climax in the events of the passion. The narrator translates the expression for the Greek reader: "Abba, Father" (v. 36a). The prayer has three parts. Jesus initially confesses his belief in the absolute power of God: "all things are possible to you" (v. 36b). The prayer, opening with a call to God as "Abba" and a statement of unconditional belief in God's ultimate authority, is shot through with obedient trusting.[90] Only on the basis of trust, obedience, and confidence in God's ability to do whatever God desires can Jesus formulate the second part of his prayer.

Jesus moves from praise to petition. He uses the imagery of a cup or a chalice, an image found in the biblical tradition to describe God's righteous punishment poured out upon a sinful people (see see Isa 51:17, 22; Jer 25:15–16; 49:12; 51:7; Lam 4:21; 23:31–32; Ezek 23:33; Hab 2:16; Pss 11:6; 75:9). The same image is also found in Jewish literature to speak of the experience of suffering.[91] Jesus used the image of a cup to challenge the sons of Zebedee in their desire to occupy special places in the kingdom (10:38), and this suggests that not only wrath but also the experience of suffering may be part of the meaning of the image. The request that God might allow the hour to pass from Jesus is deepened by means of the image. Jesus' "hour" of suffering and death is to heal the rebellious relationship between God and the creation. Aware of the significance of this action, and of his role in God's design, the Markan Jesus nevertheless trembles and hesitates as it approaches, and asks that the God for whom all things are possible might change his plans for the role of this sorrowful human being (v. 36b; cf. v. 34). This poignant prayer is an important moment in the Markan presentation of the saving action of God through the obedient, yet fragile and fearful human being, Jesus of Nazareth.[92] The exalted claims of the voice from heaven (1:10–11; 9:7) and the confessions of the vanquished demons (1:24; 3:11; 5:7) might appear to be in question as Jesus calls out in fear and pain. However, the enigma of the Gospel of Mark lies in the truth that the man, Jesus of Nazareth, who suffered so much is the Christ and Son of God (see 1:1, 11). "Now the communion between Father and Son is acclaimed by Jesus himself, not in the swirl of the epiphany, or in the homage of the supernatural, but in the stark fear of approaching death."[93]

The final part of the prayer is an act of self-abandonment: "yet not what I will, but what you will" (v. 36d).[94] The sentiments expressed thus far in the prayer are subordinated to a Christology of unconditional openness to the design of God which has been the hallmark of the Gospel story in its entirety. Thus, the final part of the prayer flows inevitably and

---

[90] Feldmeier, *Die Krisis*, 169–71.

[91] See Gnilka, *Markus*, 2:260–61; Feldmeier, *Die Krisis*, 175–85; Brown, *Death*, 1:169.

[92] Garrett, *The Temptations*, 96–98. Thompson (*The Promise of the Father*, 89–90) rightly insists that Jesus' use of Abba is not about endearment or intimacy. For a discussion of the seeming contradiction between Jesus' passion predictions and his request that "the hour" pass from him, see Brown, *Death*, 1:166–67. The Markan point of view is aptly summarized by Painter (*Mark's Gospel*, 190): "Mark reinforces the reader's awareness of the plan and purpose of God in the events about to be narrated, but without diminishing awareness of the human stress and strain involved in the fulfilment."

[93] Senior, *The Passion*, 74.

[94] Many have noticed the similarity between this petition and the petition found in the Matthean version of the Lord's prayer (Matt 6:10); S. van Tilborg, "A Form Criticism of the Lord's Prayer," *NovT* 14 (1972): 94–105; Brown, *Death*, 1:175–78. Mark may well have been in touch with traditions about Jesus' prayer, as is indicated by the use of "Abba" in v. 36a, the acceptance of God's will in v. 36d, and the warning about entering into temptation in v. 38.

logically (for the Markan Jesus) from the earlier affirmation of God's ultimate authority (v. 36a).[95] As with the use of the image of the cup (10:38), the episode of the request of the sons of Zebedee is recalled. Unable to understand their vocation to discipleship, they stated in 10:35: "Teacher, we want you to do for us whatever we ask of you" (θέλομεν ἵνα ὃ ἐὰν αἰτήσωμέν σε ποιήσῃς ἡμῖν). In accepting his role as the Son of God (v. 36b), Jesus reverses this expression as he prays to his Father: οὐ τί ἐγὼ θέλω ἀλλὰ τί σύ.

> The Markan narrative demands at every point that the power and willingness of God to eliminate human suffering be held in dialectical tension with the persecution, suffering, and death of God's beloved Son and of those who follow him.[96]

This brief paraphrase of Jesus' prayer and then Jesus' own words, set the tone for Jesus' presence in the events that follow. None of it is to be taken lightly. For Mark, the reader must understand that Jesus' shameful treatment at the hands of both Jewish and Roman authorities and the cruel and unjust crucifixion of this innocent man is a travesty of justice, and terrible agony. He cries out to the Father in anguish at the onset of the hour (vv. 35–36), and he will cry out to the Father again as it closes (15:35; see also 15:37a). Jesus' prayer in Gethsemane, reported in 14:35–36, will be prayed three times: 14:35–36, 14:39, and implicitly in 14:41. The succinct statements of vv. 39 and 41 recall the content of vv. 35–36 with all its depth and intensity.

Jesus, Peter, James, and John (14:37–38). The command "to watch," given to Peter, James, and John in 14:34, has not been obeyed. Returning to the disciples Jesus finds them asleep. The favorite Markan literary technique of intercalation continues as Jesus' unconditional commitment to the Father, cost him what it may (vv. 35–36), is matched by the failure of the disciples (vv. 33–34, vv. 37–38). The intercalation is more than mere rhetoric. It is a powerful way of setting the light of Jesus' response to God's design against the increasing darkness of the disciples' response to Jesus. Jesus' reprimand is directed to Peter, but meant for all three disciples, and through them to all disciples. However, it will be Peter who will later fail again, further fulfilling the prophecies of Jesus. Not only at Gethsemane does he fail to be the disciple he was called to be.[97] For the moment Peter, James, and John have been asked to watch with Jesus for but one hour of the night (see 13:35). They have not been able to do so. Jesus therefore issues a larger warning which is based upon widespread human experience, but which will also be exemplified very soon in the narrative by Peter's denials.

Disciples are urged to watch and pray (γρηγορεῖτε καὶ προσεύχεσθε), that they might not enter into temptation (εἰς πειρασμόν, 14:38). Earlier in the Gospel Jesus taught the disciples that the new community, founded upon the rejected cornerstone (see 12:10–11), will be marked by a new approach to God, through faith, prayer, and forgiveness (11:22–25). In this situation Satan and his allure are to be resisted. Jesus' prayer of 14:35–36 offers Mark's readers and listeners a model of faith and prayer. The disciples have been repeatedly exhorted to watchfulness, that they might behave as disciples of Jesus (13:35–37; 14: 34, 37, 38).[98] It is on the example of Jesus' lonely presence "watching" in

---

95 Dowd, *Prayer,* 157; Brown, *Death,* 1:165–67.

96 Dowd, *Prayer,* 161.

97 For this meaning of Mark's use of γρηγορεῖτε, see T. J. Geddert, *Watchwords: Mark 13 in Markan Eschatology* (JSNTSup 26: Sheffield: Sheffield Academic Press, 1989), 90–94. Without reference to Geddert, Brown (*Death,* 1:156) agrees: "*Grēgorein* here does involve staying physically awake, but it also has a sense of religious alertness."

98 LaVerdiere, *The Beginning,* 2:246–47.

prayer that the community will be built, as the spirit is very willing but the flesh is weak. Not only at the end of the Gospel story has Jesus shown the way to resist "temptation" (πειρασμός). His very first appearance in the Gospel told of his encounter with Satan, the power of evil who could be a stumbling block to the accomplishment of God's design (1:12–13). He was "tested" (πειραζόμενος), but resisted Satan's attempt to maintain control of the human story, and instead reestablished in his person the original order of God's creative design.[99] Disciples of Jesus are called to continue this rejection of the great "temptation" (14:38: πειρασμός). Jesus uses a well-known understanding of the human condition, importantly (but not only) portrayed in the biblical tradition.[100] It is true that all human beings are caught between the aspirations of the spirit and the attractions of the flesh, but this saying of Jesus will soon prove to be the case for Peter specifically. Despite his massive "spiritual" affirmations of loyalty to Jesus (14:29–31), he will fail to put his life where his words are when challenged at the Jewish trial. He will deny that he is a disciple of Jesus. His spirit is willing, but his flesh is weak, and he has failed to "watch" with Jesus in Gethsemane (v. 38; cf. vv. 66–72).[101]

The prayer of Jesus to the Father (14:39). The Markan literary technique of intercalation demands that Jesus return to the prayer of 14:35–36. Briefly the narrator reports Jesus' going away from the sleepy disciples (v. 39a), and what has been evoked for the reader in both 14:34–35 and 14:35–36 is present as the narrator states that Jesus prayed "saying the same words." Weak the disciples may be, and discouraging may also be this lack of preparedness of those whom he has called (1:16–20), chosen (3:14–19), formed (8:22–10:52), and uniquely associated with himself (5:37; 9:2–8; 13:3; 14:33). Yet Jesus' unconditional commitment to the Father, cost him what it may, remains steadfast. His threefold prayer has been met by the threefold silence of God. Alone and in silence Jesus raised his voice to God, but there was no answer, just as at the moment of his death he will raise his voice to God, and again be met by silence (15:35, 37a). But Jesus goes through his passion because he recognizes that God, his Father who can do all things, wishes Jesus, his Son, to establish a new community of God on the basis of a cornerstone that will be rejected.[102] This is God's deed, and it is remarkable to behold (cf. 12:10–11).

Jesus, Peter, James, and John (14:40). Mark repeats his rhythmic intercalation between Jesus and the disciples. The prayer of Jesus, briefly reported as "saying the same words" and summoning up 14:35–36 for the reader, is matched by Jesus' second discovery of his sleeping disciples (v. 40). The indication that their "eyes were heavy" is further proof of Jesus' earlier words, "the flesh is weak" (v. 38). At the transfiguration the same three disciples demonstrated their inability to grasp the significance of what was going on around them. The narrator commented that Peter "did not know what to say" (9:6). Now all three disciples are at a loss for words: "and they did not know what to answer him." Jesus has insisted that they watch and overcome the weaknesses of the flesh. He has shown a

---

99 For this interpretation of 1:12–13, see above pp. 37–40. For a fuller discussion of the Gethsemane scene as a crucial moment in the great πειρασμός, see Brown, *Death,* 1:157–62, 197; Taylor, *St. Mark,* 554–55.

100 Feldmeier, *Die Krisis,* 202–8; Senior, *The Passion,* 78–79, and the references on p. 79 n. 42. See also Gnilka, *Markus,* 2:261–62; Brown, *Death,* 1:198–200.

101 Garrett (*The Temptations,* 94–95) rightly points out that the spirit and the flesh of Jesus are also tested here. The outcome, however, will be different from the testing of Peter and the disciples.

102 Feldmeier, *Die Krisis,* 187–91.

preparedness to face whatever future God may have in store for him (vv. 35–36). But the disciples sink deeper into failure, not watching (vv. 34, 37, 38), overcome by the weakness of the flesh (v. 38). The contrast between Jesus and his disciples is extreme.

Conclusion: "The hour has come" to leave Gethsemane (14:41–42)

There is a sense in which this "conclusion" is also a continuation of the intercalation between responses of Jesus and the disciples to the πειρασμός, the coming of "the hour." Particularly important is Jesus' third return to the sleeping disciples, explicitly identified as "the third time" (v. 41a), a number indicating "completion." It must be tacitly assumed that between the second and the third visit to the disciples, Jesus has prayed to the Father "saying the same words" (v. 39; cf. vv. 35–36). The disciples have failed to correspond to the command to "watch" (v. 34; cf. vv. 37–38).[103] Once this narrative is detached from the "historical," its power can be sensed. These details take on a poignant significance, especially evocative once the use of intercalation is recognized. As the disciples have not accepted the command to watch but have instead taken their "fleshly" (v. 38) time for sleep and rest (v. 41b), their opportunity to associate themselves intimately with Jesus' moment of unconditional self-gift has passed them by.[104] Jesus will go to the cross alone because the disciples have not been able to "watch." Nevertheless, as he rises to face his betrayer, he asks them to come with him (v. 42). They will not be able to meet this challenge (vv. 50–52).[105]

In some ways the disciples become redundant in "the hour" in which the Son of Man is delivered into the hands of sinners (14:41; cf. especially 9:31).[106] They have not supported Jesus in the first moment of his agony (vv. 35–36), and they will not be there from this moment on. Jesus' teaching about the preparedness of the disciple to follow him, the Son of Man, into death and to resurrection (8:31; 10:33–34) has fallen on deaf ears (8:31–38; 10:35–45). Nevertheless, Jesus' design to associate them with "the hour" remains. Showing an awareness of what is to follow, and in a special way the determining presence of Judas in the immediately following episode (v. 42b), Jesus asks them to join him as he rises from his position of humble prayer to face what lies ahead: "Arise, let us go from here" (v. 42a). The Gethsemane episode is at an end. Other agents, including the betrayer, one of the Twelve, will determine the events that follow (see vv. 43–52), necessitating Jesus' movement to another place (see v. 53).[107]

The association of the disciples with Jesus on his journey to the cross, despite their consistent inability to understand who he is and what he asks from them, is one of the major features of the Markan narrative. It intensifies in the episodes that lead to the crucifixion, and climaxes in the arrest and flight that follow. His arrest, at the instigation of one of the Twelve (v. 43), will lead to the flight of the disciples (v. 50) and a commentary upon

---

[103] Lane, *Mark*, 518.

[104] There are three fateful forces in play: "the hour has come," "the Son of Man is handed over," "the betrayer is at hand." See Senior, *The Passion*, 79–80.

[105] Brown, *Death*, 1:213–15.

[106] This is the first time "the Son of Man" appears in the passion narrative. It continues the themes gathered around it throughout the earlier parts of the Gospel, and highlights the eschatological nature of "the hour" (vv. 37, 41). See Lohmeyer, *Markus*, 318–19. For a fuller discussion of its function in v. 41, see Brown, *Death*, 1:210–13.

[107] The use of ὁ παραδιδούς to refer to Judas looks back to earlier uses of the verb παραδίδωμι to speak of Jesus' coming passion (see 3:19; 9:31; 10:33; 14:10, 11, 18, 21) and forward to the next episode and the death that will follow. See Feldmeier, *Die Krisis*, 128–31, 216–24; Garrett, *The Temptations*, 100–104.

it (vv. 51–52). This event, however, is a fulfillment of Jesus' words in 14:27: "I will strike the shepherd and the sheep will be scattered." It is tragic, but somehow part of God's design. The reader must wait for a resolution to the tension between the disciples' mission and their total inability to understand the significance of Jesus' death.

[A] Judas and representatives of the Jewish leaders arrest Jesus, and all the disciples flee (14:43–52)

Mark links the arrival of Judas and emissaries of the chief priests, scribes, and elders with his urgent εὐθύς. Bearing swords and clubs, the band arrives while Jesus was still speaking, inviting his disciples to join him as he goes to meet his betrayer (v. 43; cf. v. 42). The chief priests, scribes, and elders appeared in the discussion over Jesus' authority in 11:27–33. Since then Jesus has reduced the Pharisees and the Sadducees to silence (see 12:34). The chief priests and the scribes have plotted Jesus' death (14:1–2) and have been joined by Judas (14:10–11). The cluster of leaders (chief priests, scribes, and elders) will represent Israel's leaders throughout the passion narrative (see 14:47, 53, 54, 55, 60, 61, 63, 66; 15:1, 3, 10, 11, 31). But they send their representatives, suitably armed, to arrest Jesus.[108] The figure of Judas, explicitly named as "one of the Twelve," dominates the opening moments of the arrest.[109] Jesus had made several prophecies across the Gospel about future events, and this is the first of them to be fulfilled (cf. 14:17–21). Dramatic irony marks the sign with which Judas, now called "the betrayer" (ὁ παραδιδοὺς αὐτόν, v. 44), identifies Jesus (a kiss: v. 44), and the title with which he salutes Jesus ("Master": ῥαββί, v. 45). The reader is outraged by this betrayal.[110] The one Judas kisses is to be arrested (v. 44). He calls him by a title of respect, kisses him (v. 45), and he is violently arrested: "They laid hands on him and seized him" (v. 46).

In the confusion "one of those who stood by" draws a sword and cuts off the ear of the slave of the high priest (v. 47). The unnamed character will become Peter in the Johannine story (John 18:10). The reader supposes that it must be one of the disciples, but he is from a group now called οἱ παρεστηκότοι: "those who stood by." This is a deliberate and subtle change of direction on the part of the storyteller.[111] As those who have been known throughout the Gospel as "the disciples" (οἱ μαθηταί) approach their final appearance in the story (v. 50), they are no longer regarded as "disciples." Their failure to learn from the way and word of Jesus relegates them to the position of "those who stood by."[112] The

---

[108] The arresting party is a group sent formally by the leaders, and not a "rabble" as is sometimes suggested; e.g., Taylor, *St. Mark,* 558; Hooker, *St. Mark,* 351. See Lane, *Mark,* 524; Brown, *Death,* 1:247; Painter, *Mark's Gospel,* 191.

[109] Many suggest that the phrase "one of the Twelve" was added to a pre-Markan passion narrative. However, Brown is more likely correct as he comments, "Already in the tradition this fixed designation vocalized Christian distress that Jesus was betrayed by one of his chosen Twelve" (*Death,* 1:246).

[110] The use of the compound verb καταφιλέω rather than the simple verb φιλέω for "to kiss" accentuates the treacherous duplicity; Schweizer, *Mark,* 317. For other treacherous uses of the kiss in Jewish and other literature, see Pesch, *Markusevangelium,* 2:400; Senior, *The Passion,* 81–82. See especially 2 Sam 15:5; 2 Sam 20:8–10; Prov 27:6. For the Markan presentation of Judas, see Brown, *Death,* 1:241–42, and on the use of the kiss, see ibid., 1:252–55.

[111] Most regard the bystander as not a disciple; Taylor, *St. Mark,* 559–60; Senior, *Passion,* 82–83; Brown, *Death,* 1:266–67; and especially LaVerdiere, *The Beginning,* 2:251–52. Hooker (*St. Mark,* 351) remarks: "In Mark the incident is something of an intrusion into the narrative."

[112] But see Gnilka, *Markus,* 2:270.

expression οἱ μαθηταί does not return to the story until the young man at the empty tomb promises the women that Jesus is going ahead of Peter and the disciples to Galilee (16:7).

Jesus' response initiates another theme that will recur across the passion story: his innocence. The violence of the arrest and the parallel violence of the one who responds with a sword thrust are out of place.[113] There is a slight incongruity between the beginning of the account of the arrest, where a sign is needed in order to identify Jesus, and its close, where Jesus points back to his regular coming and going and teaching in the temple (cf. 11:11–12:44).[114] His opponents know who he is. Indeed, he has silenced them with his teaching, and has caused the people to be astonished at his teaching (11:18) and to respect him (12:12, 37; cf. 11:32). The presence of his opponents wielding weapons (14:43) and violently laying hands upon him (v. 46) matches the behavior of those who capture a robber (ὡς ἐπὶ λῃστὴν ἐξήλθατε, v. 48). In his initial presence in the temple in 11:15–19 Jesus taught that his house had been made into "a den of robbers" (σπήλαιον λῃστῶν, v. 17, citing Jer 7:11). The readers and listeners to the story know that Judas and his colleagues are the guilty characters in this encounter. It is not Jesus who is the robber.[115] Later the chief priests will exacerbate their guilt by stirring up the people to ask that a brigand be freed and Jesus crucified (15:6–15). However, this is not the time for apportioning guilt. It is "the hour" which is subject to the design of God, and thus the actions of the arresting party and the violent response of one of those standing by are to be understood as somehow necessary. The scriptures, the authoritative revelation of the divine will, must be fulfilled. It is not possible to identify any particular scriptural passage fulfilled by this arrest. However, the general background of the suffering of the righteous one is sufficient for Jesus' indications that his violent arrest is the fulfillment of scripture.[116]

The disciples, no longer privileged with that title (v. 47), abandon Jesus (v. 50). This flight brings to a climax the steady drift away from Jesus that has highlighted the behavior and the response of the disciples from 4:41 on. They began so well, responding wordlessly to his call (1:16–20; 2:13–14). They were called to be "with him," so that they might do what he does (see 3:13–19), and they successfully involved themselves in his mission. But in 4:41 they indicate their inability to understand who Jesus is, and in 6:30, on their return from a successful mission, they have not understood who they are in relation to Jesus. The way to Jerusalem (8:31–10:45) has been highlighted by their increasing fear and inability

---

[113] B. T. Viviano ("The High Priest's Servant's Ear: Mark 14:47," *RB* 96 [1989]: 71–80) has made too much of the wounded figure as the slave of the high priest. The high priest is rendered unfit for service by physical deformity, not the δοῦλος τοῦ ἀρχιερέως. For a detailed discussion of the historical and theological issue of the cutting off of the servant's ear, see Brown, *Death,* 1:271–74. There is an interesting parallel, never mentioned in these discussions, in Tacitus (*Histories* 3.84), who tells of Vitellius's German supporter's cutting off the ear of the tribune as the ex-emperor was led off to execution. This passage (written ca. 109–110), reporting events of December 69, makes interesting reading in the light of Mark 14:47.

[114] The incoherence is no doubt the result of the placing side by side of several episodes, the core of which remains Jesus' arrest (vv. 43–46); Hooker, *St. Mark,* 351. It is hard to decide whether this editorial activity was pre-Markan, or the work of the author. The final result, however, is a crucial Markan passage that says a great deal about the disciples, as well as telling of Jesus' arrest. Indeed, in my reading of the text, the portrait of the disciples is Mark's main literary and theological concern.

[115] Hooker (*St. Mark,* 352) makes an interesting link with 7:1–13. There the Pharisees accused Jesus of being a lawbreaker. Here, those accused by Jesus in 11:15–19 as behaving like robbers treat him as if he were a robber. They are the real lawbreakers.

[116] Senior, *Passion,* 83–84.

to follow Jesus in his response to God. His teaching on the cross, humble receptivity, and service has fallen on deaf ears, and they have become more and more afraid (10:32). As the passion begins, and the physical reality of the cross looms, they all forsake him and flee (14:50). The disciples as a group never again appear in the narrative. This passage opened with the fulfillment of Jesus' prophecy on Judas (14:43–46; cf. 14:17–21); it closes with the fulfillment of the prophecy that the shepherd will be struck and they will all fall away (14:50; cf. 14:27–31).[117] The reader now waits for the fulfillment of a further prophecy: before the cock crows twice, Peter will deny Jesus three times (14:66–72).

This crucial moment in the account of the disciples' relationship with Jesus calls for further comment. It is provided in the parabolic story of 14:51–52. The enigmatic episode of the young man (νεανίσκος) who followed him (συνεκολούθει αὐτῷ) has been the source of much interest. Many have attempted to identify the young man with a historical figure, and some suggest that the young man was the evangelist Mark. Such explanations miss the relationship of 14:51–52 and the flight of the disciples in 14:50.[118] The young man, a follower of Jesus, is dressed only with a linen cloth (σινδόνα ἐπὶ γυμνοῦ).[119] After the description of the young follower of Jesus, two events take place. Those who had seized Jesus (ἐκράτησαν αὐτόν, 14:46) also seize the young man (κρατοῦσιν αὐτόν, 14:51c). He shares the experience of Jesus. However, his response to the threat that he may "follow" Jesus further into the violence of the passion is to join the flight of the disciples: he fled (v. 52). The young man is a model of the disciples as a group. His association with the disciples is indicated by Mark's use of the prefix συν- in the verb συνηκολούθει, found only in Mark 5:37 and Luke 23:49 in the rest of the New Testament. However, he is not only "with" the disciples in following Jesus, but also with them in their flight. He leaves the linen cloth behind and flees naked.

The nakedness of the young man comments upon the situation of the disciples whom he represents.[120] Called to share in the life, ministry, and destiny of Jesus, and claiming that

---

[117] Brown, *Death*, 1:286–87.

[118] For a survey of interpretations of this strange passage, see Taylor (*St. Mark*, 561–62), who argues for its historicity. See also Lohmeyer, *Markus*, 323–24; Anderson, *Mark*, 324; Pesch, *Markusevangelium*, 2:402, and Brown, *Death*, 1:294–304. For a complete bibliography of the discussions, see ibid., 2:238–39, and for a documented survey of traditional commentary on the passage, see F. Neirynck, "La fuite du jeune homme en Mc 14,51–52," in *Evangelica: Gospel Studies—Etudes d'évangile* (ed. F. Van Segbroeck; BETL 60; Leuven: Leuven University Press, 1982), 227–31. Hooker (*St. Mark*, 352) represents the mainstream opinion that the story "has no obvious theological significance." See also Nineham, *St. Mark*, 396–97. Its present location in the narrative and the use of the verbs "to follow" and "to flee" are hints that it is associated with the Markan theology of discipleship. For Lührmann (*Markusevangelium*, 246–47), it adds to the christological message that Jesus must die abandoned. Recourse is often had to Amos 2:16, where the prophet describes a day of judgment so fierce "he who is stout of heart among the mighty shall flee away naked in that day"; see, for example, Lane, *Mark*, 527–28. The association of the "stout of heart" with the young man (even as a symbol of the disciples) is hard to establish.

[119] The early church already struggled to comprehend this passage, and early textual variants attempt to smooth it out. Some omit ἐπὶ γυμνοῦ. For a discussion of the variants, and a defense of the text as read above, see Neirynck, "La fuite du jeune homme," 233–37; Brown, *Death*, 1:294–95.

[120] Gnilka, *Markus* 2:271–72; Neirynck, "La fuite du jeune homme," 215–38; H. Fleddermann, "The Flight of a Naked Young Man (Mark 14:51–52)," *CBQ* 41 (1979): 412–17; Brown, *Death*, 1:302–4. Many interpretations look forward to the σινδών in 15:46 and the return of a νεανίσκος in 16:5 for the interpretation of 14:51–52. Those possible associations, in a narrative reading of the Gospel, will be discussed when we arrive at the later passages. Is the reader expected to recall 14:51–52 as Jesus is buried (15:46) and a young man is found in an empty tomb (16:5)? That remains to be seen.

they had left everything to follow him (10:28), the disciples in their flight separate them-selves from Jesus. The parabolic commentary of the young man, who flees from a sharing in the suffering of Jesus, applies to all the disciples. In both the biblical and Greco-Roman world nakedness is a symbol of nothingness, of exile, slavery, poverty, misery, and the loss of all one has and is (cf. Matt 25:36; John 21:7; James 2:15; Rev 3:17; 16:15).[121] The flight of the disciples, as with the parabolic commentary of the flight of the young man, may make good sense in terms of the preservation of one's life. But the follower of Jesus is called to lose life for the sake of Jesus and the Gospel (see 8:34–38). At this point of the story, the dis-ciples have failed to accept that challenge, and must be judged, in the light of the parabolic comment of the experience of the young man, to be naked in their nothingness as they flee from their share in the destiny of Jesus.[122]

[B] The self-revelation of Jesus at the Jewish hearing (14:53–65)

Now subject to the authority of his opponents, Jesus is led away from the garden to an assembly of the Jewish leaders: the gathering of the chief priests, the elders, and the scribes. Peter, who follows "at a distance,"[123] is also there, sitting with the temple guards (14:53–54). Within this setting, a hearing before Jewish authorities takes place, leading to Jesus' self-revelation and condemnation (14:51–64). It closes with abuse from the temple guard (14:65). The careful Markan arrangement of the material produces the following structure:[124]

14:53–54   Introduction: the setting and the characters: leaders, Peter, and the guards

14:55–61a   False charges

14:61b–62   Jesus' self-revelation

14:63–64   False condemnation

14:66   Conclusion: abuse from the guards and a challenge that Jesus prophesy

The passage is framed by a setting and characters who become crucial in the episode which follows (14:66–72), where Jesus' prophecy that Peter would deny him (v. 30) is fulfilled. At

---

[121] Brown (*Death*, 1:303) suggests that the σινδών would have been of great value (see Prov 31:24; Judg 14:12), adding force to the loss which follows the flight. See also Gnilka, *Markus*, 2:271. The symbolic value of the nakedness also explains the heavy-handed use of the word γυμνός—twice in two verses (vv. 51, 52). Some scholars see in the cloth a symbol of baptism and the passage as a symbolic abandoning of one's baptismal commitment to share in Jesus' cross; see LaVerdiere, *The Beginning*, 2:252–55, and the literature cited there.

[122] As Grundmann (*Markus*, 297) comments: "The evangelist wants to say that the scattering of the followers of Jesus was so complete that the last person still near him had to flee naked."

[123] He may have interrupted his flight (v. 50) to resume his following, but "at a distance" indi-cates his increasing separation from Jesus; see Gnilka, *Markus*, 2:278.

[124] A Jewish hearing or trial was certainly part of the pre-Markan passion narrative, and ele-ments of that earlier tradition appear in 14:53–65. The above arrangement, however, is a good indi-cation of the Markan reworking of the earlier tradition. For a recent survey of discussions of the trial and the nature of the pre-Markan passion narrative at this point, see Donahue, *Are You the Christ?* 4–51. More recent scholarship is surveyed in Brown, *Death*, 1:548–60. Brown suggests that Mark has pulled together three or four items that were originally separate in the tradition, and in doing so has produced "the clarity and force of the unified trial (which) has moved and been re-membered by millions" (p. 560; parenthesis mine).

the center of the passage, set between false charges and an unjust condemnation, Jesus reveals himself as the Christ, the Son of God and Son of Man.[125]

Introduction (14:53–54)

Jesus is no longer the master of the situation as he is led to an assembly of the chief protagonists in the plot to slay him, all the chief priests and the elders and the scribes (14:53; cf. 8:31; 10:33; 11:18, 27; 14:1–2, 10, 43).[126] Peter is introduced into the scene, an event that sits clumsily side by side with the description of the flight of all the disciples in 14:50 and the comment upon it in 14:51–52. Two remarks explain Peter's presence. First, Peter's denials are one of the most certain historical facts that we know about Jesus' final days. They must be reported. Second, the Markan theological agenda demands that Jesus' prophecy about Peter's denial (v. 30) be fulfilled. In a typically Markan fashion, Peter is introduced "with the temple guards" (μετὰ τῶν ὑπηρετῶν, 14:54) as the first part of a sandwich construction. One who was appointed to be "with Jesus" in 3:14 is shifting his allegiance.[127] After the intercalation of 14:55–64, and the introduction in 14:65 of the request from the abusing "temple guards" (ὑπηρέται) that Jesus prophesy, Peter will return in 14:66–72 and Jesus' prophecy will be fulfilled.[128]

False charges (14:55–61a)

The theme of Jesus' innocence continues as the Jewish hearing opens with a series of general statements indicating that there is no case against Jesus. The chief priests and the whole Sanhedrin seek testimony (μαρτυρία) of Jesus' offenses to help realize their plan to put him to death (cf. 14:1–2).[129] Since 11:18 the verb "to seek" (ζητεῖν) has been used to describe the efforts of the Jewish leadership to destroy Jesus. They began *seeking* to destroy him (11:18), they *sought* to seize him (12:12), they *sought* in stealth to seize and kill him (14:1), and Judas *sought* how to give him over (14:11). Now that they have him in their hands, they *seek* testimony against him (14:56),[130] but they are unable to trump up any evidence (14:55). For Mark, the process is marked by false accusations and is a betrayal of justice from the start. A series of people bear false witness against Jesus, but this ploy

---

[125] Donahue (*Are You the Christ?* 67–68) claims that the two Peter scenes form a sandwich construction. Brown (*Death*, 1:426–28) supports my suggestion that vv. 53–54 serve as an introduction to the Sanhedrin proceeding, and that Peter's association with that event was pre-Markan. This does not detract from Markan literary creativity in the present shape of the narrative. He writes the narrative as "an elaborate interweaving of the Jewish interrogation with Peter's denials in order to achieve simultaneity" (p. 432). See also D. H. Juel, *Messiah and Temple: The Trial of Jesus in the Gospel of Mark* (SBLDS 31; Missoula: Scholars Press, 1977). After a survey of the historical (pp. 7–20) and redaction critical (pp. 20–39) explanations of the trial, Juel cogently argues (pp. 41–58) that it must be read as "literary in the proper sense." It is marked by the literary features of irony and double-level meaning, arguing that Jesus is the Messiah-King and the Messiah who will build an eschatological people. See also Senior, *Passion*, 87–88.

[126] On the composition of the Sanhedrin and its responsibility for the death of Jesus, see above, note 16. The theological and literary significance of the Markan grouping to represent Jewish leadership is missed by overhistorical readings. See, for example, Taylor, *St. Mark*, 564–65.

[127] LaVerdiere, *The Beginning*, 2:259.

[128] On the use of ὑπηρέται in the trials, see Brown, *Death*, 1:402–3. On their being "temple guards," see Taylor, *St. Mark*, 565.

[129] The association of ὅλον τὸ συνέδριον with the chief priests lines up official Judaism against Jesus.

[130] Brown, *Death*, 1:432–33.

fails as well.[131] The different testimonies do not agree, and thus no condemnation can be laid against Jesus (v. 56; see Deut 17:6; 19:15).[132] "Ironically the trial against Jesus has violated the Law against false testimony (Exod 20:16; Deut 5:20)—one of the Ten Commandments, reiterated by Jesus in Mark 10:19."[133] These general statements are rendered concrete in a false charge which reports words of Jesus: "I will destroy this temple that is made with hands, and in three days I will build another, not made with hands" (14:57–58).

This saying of Jesus appears here for the first time in the Gospel of Mark. It is repeated by Matthew (Matt 26:61) and also found in a Johannine version (John 2:19). A saying in Q (Luke 13:35 // Matt 23:38–39) records similar sentiments, and the Acts of the Apostles indicates that the relationship between the early church and the temple was important, but at times uneasy (Acts 2:46, 49; 3:1; 19:46; 24:53).[134] A number of critical questions surround the temple saying, but they need not detain us here.[135] In terms of the Markan narrative, which *must* be taken as the norm for an appreciation of the reader's response to this statement from the witnesses, Jesus has *never* made this statement. Mark states explicitly that the accusation that Jesus has said these words is false testimony. There is a double edge to the untruthfulness of this witness, and deep irony enters the narrative. As the Markan Jesus has never uttered these words, whatever may be the case with other New Testament documents,[136] the witness is not true. The reader recalls Jesus' symbolic bringing to an end of the cultic functioning of the temple in 11:15–19, with its accompanying "frame" of the withered fig tree in 11:12–14, 20–25. This passage was closely followed by the citation of Ps 118:22–23 and his comment upon it in 12:11–12. After the prophecy of the destruction of the wicked tenants of the vineyard (12:9), Jesus spoke of a new building, constructed upon the stone rejected by the builders. Read and heard in the aftermath of the destruction of the Jerusalem temple in 70 C.E., the Markan community is conscious of being a temple of God, built upon the person of the risen Jesus, rejected and slain by the leaders of Israel.[137] A similar idea lies behind Jesus' prediction of the coming destruction of Jerusalem and its temple in 13:1–23, and the establishment in 13:24–37 of a "watching" community in an in-between time.

The irony in 14:57–58 is that Jesus, having *never* made the claim brought against him by the false witnesses on the destruction and the rebuilding of the temple, is falsely ac-

---

[131] The Old Testament theme of the plotting and accusation of the evil against the just one continues; see Moo, *Old Testament*, 247–49; Brown, *Death*, 1:434; Senior, *Passion*, 90.

[132] Gnilka, *Markus*, 281.

[133] Brown, *Death*, 1:435.

[134] For a documented discussion of these passages, see Brown, *Death*, 1:434–38.

[135] There are two fundamental questions. Did Jesus of Nazareth actually speak of the future destruction and rebuilding of the Jerusalem temple (Mark 14:58; John 2:19; Luke 13:35 // Matt 23:38–39)? How is it that for Mark and Acts (Acts 2:46, 49; 3:1; 19:46; 24:53) this affirmation is regarded as false, while for Matthew (Matt 26:61) and John (2:19) it is correct? For a thorough investigation of both issues, see Brown, *Death*, 1:434–60.

[136] Among many, see D. Lührmann, "Markus 14,55–64: Christologie und Zerstörung des Tempels im Markusevangelium," *NTS* 27 (1980–1981): 457–74; idem, *Markusevangelium*, 249.

[137] Several meanings are possible for the accusation that Jesus would build another temple "in three days" (διὰ τριῶν ἡμερῶν). The use of διά gives the idea of something that Jesus would do "within" the brief period of three days. All three passion predictions speak of resurrection "after (μετά) three days" (see 8:31; 9:31; 10:34). Probably irony is again present. For the false accusers, the former is intended: Jesus claimed that he would raise the temple from ruins in a brief period of time, but for the Markan readers, the "three days" recall the resurrection. See the discussion in Hooker, *St. Mark*, 359, and Brown, *Death*, 1:443–44.

cused, yet the reader knows that the relationship between Jesus and the temple in Jerusalem is at best ambiguous, and that there will indeed be a new temple, not built by human hands, but constructed upon the cornerstone of the rejected one (11:22–25; 12:11–12; 13:24–37).[138] The theme of the destruction of the temple will return as the passion progresses. Jesus will again be abused as one who claimed to destroy the temple and rebuild it in three days in 15:29. In 15:38, at his death, the temple curtain before the Holy of Holies tears from top to bottom, and immediately the centurion confesses that Jesus was Son of God (15:39). In this sense, although the witnesses in their misunderstanding and lies bring false and contradictory evidence (14:59), they articulate a truth that will be acted out as the story unfolds. Unable to agree on what Jesus said (v. 59), the prescriptions of Num 33:30, Deut 17:6, 19:15 remain unfulfilled, and no condemnation can follow from such false and confused testimony. Yet the words and actions of Jesus have already indicated that there will be a new temple (11:12–25; 12:11–12; 13:1–37), and the community is aware that Titus has destroyed the temple made by human hands. The members of that community are aware that another temple, not made by human hands, has emerged from the chaos.[139]

To this point, Jesus has been silent, as all the evidence has been in his favor. The Jewish legal tradition supports his innocence (Deut 17:6; 19:15). There is no call for him to respond to confused and contradictory witnesses (14:55–59). Nevertheless, the high priest attempts to badger Jesus into some form of response. He asks what answer he would make in the light of all the contradictory and false witnesses that have been leveled against him.[140] What is needed is a word from Jesus that will incriminate him, and that is the point of the question from the high priest (14:60). Jesus is an innocent man, not guilty of all that has been said about him by a variety of witnesses who are unable to agree and have not understood the significance of what he has said about a new temple, built upon the rejected

---

[138] The temple "built by human hands" (χειροποίητον) refers to the Jerusalem temple, while the "one not built by human hands" (ἀχειροποίητον) is yet to be fully identified. For the suggestion that Mark uses a term ("built by human hands"), which comes from LXX language for idols, to criticize the temple, see Brown, *Death,* 1:438–40. For a list of suggestions concerning the identity of the temple not built by human hands, see Brown, *Death,* 1:440–43. There is no need to make that decision at this stage of the story. It is a prolepsis, a gap in the narrative, and the reader looks forward to its resolution. There are already sufficient hints, however, in 11:12–25; 12:11–12; and 13:1–37, that the followers of Jesus form this new structure built upon the rejected cornerstone.

[139] These paragraphs reflect the conclusions of the fine study of Juel (*Messiah and Temple,* 127–215). See also E. S. Malbon, *Narrative Space and Mythic Meaning in Mark* (New Voices in Biblical Studies; San Francisco: Harper & Row, 1986), 120–26. For a detailed and fully documented discussion of the Markan use of this saying as false, see Brown, *Death,* 1:448–54. Brown explains the Markan strategy historically, tracing the ambiguous development of the relationship between the early Christian church and the temple (see pp. 450–53). A similar approach is found in Donahue, *Are You the Christ?* 103–84. Donahue argues that the accusation in 14:58, which had an earlier independent existence, was inserted by Mark into a larger insertion of vv. 56–59. Donahue traces the anti-temple theme in Mark, and explains the insertion of v. 58 as a Markan presentation of Jesus as someone who was opposed to the temple in his lifetime (pp. 103–38). The saying also addresses the Markan community, a new temple after the destruction of the Jerusalem temple in 70 C.E. These are helpful studies, but not enough is made of the profound irony of a false accusation that the reader knows will prove to be true. This aspect of the temple saying is admirably developed by Juel and Malbon. For briefer reflections on the irony, see Senior, *Passion,* 91–94; LaVerdiere, *The Beginning,* 2:261–64.

[140] The Markan use of the preposition κατά and verbs containing the expression as a prefix highlights the attempts of the high priest to bring Jesus down (14:55, 60, 64); see Brown, *Death,* 1:463.

stone. They have quoted words of Jesus that, in the Gospel of Mark, have never been said. Ironically, their accusation will prove to be true, and the Markan readers are aware of that level of truth. However, they are inventing words Jesus never said to articulate his relationship to the temple. There is no call for him to respond to false and contradictory testimony, and thus he remains silent (14:61a). "The emphatic silence of the Marcan Jesus is a contemptuous rebuke for the low quality of the charade."[141]

Jesus' self-revelation (14:61b–62)

Unable to raise a response to the false accusations, the high priest changes the direction of the process. The use of "again" (v. 61b) to introduce his next words indicates this change of direction.[142] He asks a question which takes the reader back to the opening verse of the Gospel (1:1): "Are you the Christ, the Son of the Blessed?" The high priest uses the circumlocution of "the Blessed" to avoid mentioning the word "God," and asks Jesus whether he is the Christ, the Son of God. To this point in the story Jesus has avoided any messianic acclaim (8:29–30; 11:1–11), has commanded silence subsequent to deeds which could be understood as messianic (1:44; 3:12; 5:43; 7:36; 8:26; 9:9), and even disassociated himself from the Davidic line (12:35–37). The only term he has used to speak of himself is "the Son of Man," mainly to refer to his future suffering (see 8:31; 9:31; 10:33–34), but also as the source of his authority (see 2:10, 28). As his ministry drew to a close, further developing a promise made in 8:38, Jesus spoke of the Son of Man providing the key to all his uses of the expression. The Son of Man will come on the clouds at the end of time for the gathering of the elect (13:24–27). In the midst of the suffering of the holy ones of the Most High at the hands of Antiochus IV of Syria, Daniel is promised that final authority will be given to "one like a son of man" (Dan 7:13). But the question of the high priest goes beyond Jesus' self-revelation as the Son of Man. He asks Jesus to accept or refuse what the reader knows to be true of this central character in the good news about Jesus Christ, Son of God (1:1, 11).[143]

Only now, as the passion is under way, can Jesus accept these titles of honor, and associate them with the more customary "Son of Man." His response, "I am" (ἐγώ εἰμι) is an unqualified acceptance of his messianic sonship.[144] The story of Jesus has pointed forward to the suffering and death of the Son of Man. The enigma is, however, that in his suffering he exercises his messianic sonship. The story of Jesus is not only of a suffering Christ, Son of God and Son of Man. The promise of Dan 7:13, and the description of the Son of God seated at the right hand of the Father developed in the early church's reading of Ps 110:1,

---

[141] Brown, *Death,* 1:463. Hooker (*St. Mark,* 357) comments: "It is not Jesus who is breaking the Law, but his opponents, who claim to uphold it!" On interpretations of Jesus' silence—e.g., royal, eschatological, Suffering Servant (see Isa 53:7)—see Brown, *Death,* 1:463–64.

[142] Brown, *Death,* 1:465.

[143] On the need to locate the meaning of these titles within the framework of the Christology of the Markan community—i.e., what "Christ" and "Son of God" meant to them, with reference back to 1:1—see Brown, *Death,* 1:467–70. On the links between the historical Jesus and these titles, see pp. 473–83.

[144] Some (e.g., Nineham, *St. Mark,* 408) suggest that Jesus' response remains ambiguous. Despite the possibility that Jesus' use of ἐγώ εἰμι in 6:50 is to be associated with the traditional language of a theophany, this is not the case here (as, for example, in John 18:5). As the passion starts, Jesus proclaims that he is the Christ, the Son of God; see Taylor, *St. Mark,* 568–69; Hooker, *St. Mark,* 360–61; Brown, *Death,* 1:488–89; and the comprehensive study of C. H. Williams, *I Am He: The Interpretation of 'Anî Hû' in Jewish and Early Christian Literature* (WUNT 2. Reihe 113; Tübingen: J. C. B. Mohr [Paul Siebeck], 2000), 242–51.

points beyond Jesus' suffering and death.[145] This first and only *self*-revelation of Jesus as the Christ and the Son of God in the Gospel of Mark is a christological high point of the narrative.[146] Jesus is Christ, Son of God, and Son of Man in his suffering and on the cross. It is as the crucified one that he will reveal himself as Christ and Son of God, but through the cross he will establish himself at the right hand of Power, and exercise ultimate authority as the Son of Man at the gathering of the elect.[147] All acceptable notions of the Christ and the Son of God are dismantled as Jesus makes this claim. Betrayed by Judas, abandoned by his disciples, put on trial by the leaders of his people, Jesus is finally in a position to reveal who he is: the Christ, the Son of God, the vindicated Son of Man, the one seated at the right hand of God, to whom all authority will be given (v. 62).[148]

False condemnation (14:63–64)

The high priest has achieved his goal. He responds to Jesus' *correct* self-revelation with a public gesture used to express horror at blasphemy: he tears his clothes (see 2 Kgs 18:37–19:4).[149] But his question shows that he is circumventing due process: "Why do we still need witnesses?" (v. 63). The attempt to bring witness against Jesus that might lead to his death (v. 55) has led nowhere. The high priest bypasses all need for witnesses and condemns Jesus on the basis of his self-revelation and declares Jesus' acceptance of such titles a blasphemy. Irony pervades the narrative as the reader knows Jesus has told the truth, and

---

[145] Brown (*Death,* 1:496–500) rightly highlights the two "positions" in which the sanhedrists will see the Son of Man: seated at the right of Power and coming on the clouds. There is a blend of the present authority of the risen Lord and the final coming of the Son of Man with authority at the Parousia. See Hooker, *St. Mark,* 361–62.

[146] Senior (*Passion,* 94) comments: "These are perhaps the most condensed christological statements in Mark and represent the culmination of motifs that run the length of the Gospel." On the buildup across the Gospel toward this statement, see pp. 95–99. See also Lührmann, *Markusevangelium,* 249–50.

[147] D. H. Juel (*Master of Surprise: Mark Interpreted* [Minneapolis: Fortress, 1994], 94) rightly remarks that the promise of the future sight of the Son of Man "does not represent a qualification of the messianic epithets but a promise that the claim will be vindicated." For the detailed analysis which lies behind this affirmation, see Juel, *Messiah and Temple,* 77–107. See also C. R. Kazmierski, *Jesus, the Son of God: A Study of the Marcan Tradition and Its Redaction by the Evangelist* (FB 33; Würzburg: Echter, 1979), 165–89, and Marcus, *The Way of the Lord,* 164–71. Marcus suggests that 14:62, read in the suffering Markan community, also predicts their future vindication. Matera (*Kingship,* 93–116) also sees the use of Son of Man in 14:62 as pointing to ultimate vindication. He claims too much, however, in his identification of the Son of Man as an eschatological king (see pp. 100–116). For the unacceptable argument that "the Son of Man" is the climactic and "title *par excellence* for his Christology" (p. 182), see Donahue, *Are You the Christ?* 138–87. Donahue's position represents a school of thought associated with Norman Perrin in Chicago that regarded Mark's use of "the Son of Man" as a "correction" of false Christologies emerging in the Markan community. See N. Perrin, "Mark 14:62: The End Product of a Christian Pesher Tradition?" in *A Modern Pilgrimage in New Testament Christology* (Philadelphia: Fortress, 1974), 10–22. For Perrin and his followers, 14:62 is evidence for the early Christian development of the Son of Man title, the result of a pesher of Dan 7:13 in the light of Ps 110:1. It is used over against all titles which may smack of a θεῖος ἀνήρ Christology. See the supportive summary of this process in Sloyan, *Jesus on Trial,* 49–61. For a full discussion and a sound rejection of this thesis, see J. D. Kingsbury, *The Christology of Mark's Gospel* (Philadelphia: Fortress, 1983); see esp. pp. 157–76. The use of the expression "Power" as a circumlocution for God highlights the authority with which Jesus, the Son of Man, will come as judge. Gnilka (*Markus,* 2:282) suggests that "you will see" suggests Wis 5:2, and even Zech 12:10: "They will look upon the one whom they have pierced" (cf. John 19:37).

[148] Lane, *Mark,* 535–37.

[149] On the background to this gesture, see Gnilka, *Markus,* 2:282–83; Brown, *Death,* 1:517–19.

thus does not deserve condemnation, while the high priest claims he has blasphemed (v. 64a).[150] He turns to the Sanhedrin and asks for their decision concerning Jesus' guilt (v. 64b), and they are unanimous in their agreement that Jesus should be slain (v. 64c). The high priest matches the *false* use of *false* witnesses (vv. 55–61a), which preceded Jesus' revelation of *the truth* (vv. 61b–62), as he and the Sanhedrin come to a *false* judgment, finding Jesus worthy of death on the basis of his truthful claim (vv. 63–64).

Conclusion (14:65)

Physical abuse and suffering begin as the Jewish hearing comes to a close. Some members of the Sanhedrin begin to vent their rage against Jesus by spitting on him (cf. Isa 50:6–7). They place a cover over his face so he will be unable to see his assailants, and strike him. Blows rain upon him as a result of his self-revelation as the Christ, the Son of God, the Son of Man, the one who will be seated at the right hand of God and who will come with power. The irony of the situation deepens as they demand that he prophesy. If he is all he claims to be, then they demand that he give them some sign. This demand is related to his being blindfolded and unable to know from where the blows come.[151] They make a mockery of him, insisting that he prophesy who will strike him, and from where the blow will come. But the reader is aware he has long prophesied that this moment would come (8:31; 9:31; 10:33–34), and the very next scene will be another fulfillment of a recent prophecy (14:66–72; cf. 14:30).[152] The reader recalls that Peter had followed Jesus into the courtyard of the high priest, and that he was seated there with the temple guards (μετὰ τῶν ὑπηρετῶν), warming himself at their fire (14:54). The temple guards (οἱ ὑπηρέται) join the abusive action against Jesus expressing their opposition to him with blows.[153] Peter is with this group, and this reference to the temple guards closes the description of the Jewish hearing by looking back to its introduction (vv. 53–54), reminding the reader of the presence of Peter, whose denials will dominate the following episode (vv. 66–72). Ironically, those opposing and abusing Jesus are unaware that he has already prophesied what is happening to him, and the denials which are about to follow also fulfill prophesy.[154]

---

[150] Brown, *Death,* 1:519–20. As Brown points out, Raba's principle of *b. Sanh.* 9b, prohibiting self-incrimination, should not be introduced here. It is too late and reflects later legal processes. The major Markan theme is that Jesus is condemned by people telling lies, while he tells the truth. For a detailed discussion of every possible explanation for the charge of blasphemy, historically (at a Jewish hearing) and theologically (according to each evangelist), see Brown, *Death,* 1:520–47. See also the survey of scholarly discussion of this question in Juel, *Messiah and Temple,* 95–106. Brown concludes that historically Jesus took stances and said things that could be regarded by his opponents as blasphemy. This is reflected in the Gospel reporting of the Jewish trial. However, as Schweizer (*Mark,* 331) remarks: "Since only those cases were regarded as blasphemy when the most holy Name was uttered, the sentencing of Jesus to death for this statement ("I am") can hardly be thought to be justified" (parenthesis mine).

[151] See Brown (*Death,* 1:573–76) for a discussion of the blindfolding and the spitting, coming to the conclusion adopted above.

[152] For a complete chart showing the links between the Servant in Isa 50 and 53, the passion predictions, and Jesus' passion, see Brown, *Death,* 1:570–71.

[153] Discussion surrounds the meaning of the guards' "receiving" (ἔλαβον) Jesus, especially as Jesus is still under the control of the chief priests, the elders, and the scribes in 15:1. See the discussion in Brown, *Death,* 1:576–77. Brown helpfully suggests that it has the meaning expressed in colloquial English as "to get someone" in a violent or angry sense. He thus renders the expression: "they got him with slaps" (p. 568). See also Taylor, *St. Mark,* 571. This interpretation lies behind my paraphrase "express their opposition to him."

[154] This is seldom noticed. See, for example, Lohmeyer, *Markus,* 330; Nineham, *St. Mark,* 408–9. Senior (*Passion,* 101) remarks: "The Christian reader is reminded again that Jesus' power is

[A] Peter denies Jesus three times (14:66–72)

The account of Peter's denial of Jesus came to Mark in the tradition, but the Markan use of the tradition is subtle and skillful.[155] The Jewish hearing closed with reference to the temple guards (οἱ ὑπηρέται, 14:65), already mentioned at the beginning of the episode in association with Peter (v. 54).[156] Peter's link with these opponents of Jesus who have received him with blows (v. 65) is carried into the following episode in 14:66a. The narrator recalls that Peter was in the courtyard (κάτω ἐν τῇ αὐλῇ), the place where he had sat with the temple guards (εἰς τὴν αὐλήν), warming himself at their fire (v. 54).[157] As Peter's final scene in the Gospel of Mark opens, he is portrayed as moving away from Jesus toward those who arrested and now abuse him (v. 65b). A further character comes onto the scene, a maidservant of the high priest, the person who has falsely condemned Jesus to death (vv. 61–64). Jesus' opponents and their associates gather, and Peter is with them (v. 66). The narrator recalls Peter's presence at the fire with the temple guards (v. 67a; cf. v. 54), and reports that the maid looks closely at Peter (v. 67a) and makes a statement that the reader recognizes as true. She does not interrogate Peter, but states he was "with" the Nazarene, Jesus (μετὰ τοῦ Ναζαρηνοῦ, 14:67b). Being "with" Jesus was the fundamental element in the establishment of the Twelve (3:14) and their association with the ministry of Jesus (3:15; 6:7–13). The unusual description of Jesus as "the Nazarene, Jesus" identifies him as someone from Galilee, an issue that becomes important in the third denial, where Peter is identified as "a Galilean" (v. 70). For the moment, however, Peter's first denial is not a denial of Jesus, but he denies (ὁ δὲ ἠρνήσατο) the truth of the woman's affirmation. He is not able to know or understand what she is talking about (v. 68a).[158] Peter refuses to acknowledge his "being with" Jesus.

---

not exercised according to the world's pattern." The affirmation is true, but is not the point of the ironic demand that Jesus prophesy. However, see Brown (Death, 1:577), who makes a link with Isa 50:6–7 in the spitting on the face of v. 65a and the action of the guards in v. 65b. At the center (v. 65b) one finds the command to prophesy. "In the center of the Marcan scene, then, is the challenge to Jesus to prophesy, issued at the very moment that he is being shown to be a true prophet. Framing him on either side are the echoes of Isaiah the prophet." See also the excellent treatment of the irony of v. 65 in Juel, Messiah and Temple, 68–72. On Jesus as a prophet in Mark's Gospel, see E. K. Broadhead, Naming Jesus: Titular Christology in the Gospel of Mark (JSNTSup 175; Sheffield: Sheffield Academic Press, 1999), 43–60.

155 Extensive scholarly debate surrounds this issue. Two contrasting factors must be assessed: the high level of improbability that the early church would have invented an account of Peter's denial of Jesus on the one hand, and the very different fashions in which the denials are presented across the fourfold Gospel tradition, on the other. The threefold form of the denials (see the chart in Brown, Death, 1:589–90) would have been formed in the pre-Markan and pre-Johannine traditions by creatively building upon elements from authentic historical tradition. As Brown comments: "The survival of the story without a basis in fact seems incredible; yet the Gospel narratives reflect strongly an imaginative storytelling style. Basic fact and imaginative description, however, are not an impossible combination" (Death, 1:621). See the similar remarks in Gnilka, Markus, 2:294–95. For a full-scale treatment of the question, see Brown, Death, 1:610–26. For a narrative study of the passage, see A. Borrell, The Good News of Peter's Denial: A Narrative and Rhetorical Reading of Mark 14:54.66–72 (trans. S. Conlon; University of South Florida International Studies in Formative Christianity and Judaism; Atlanta: Scholars Press, 1998).

156 On the intercalation of Jesus' witness to the truth (vv. 55–65) between Peter's presence in the courtyard (v. 54) and his denials (vv. 66–72), see Borrell, The Good News of Peter's Denial, 120–45.

157 On the use of αὐλή to mean an exterior courtyard, see Brown, Death, 1:593–94. Unlike the Roman process, the Jewish hearing is conducted in a place cut off from Peter and the temple guards. See Taylor, St. Mark, 572; Gnilka, Markus, 2:292.

158 Mark's Greek οὔτε οἶδα οὔτε ἐπίσταμαι σὺ τί λέγεις is technically ungrammatical. See the discussion in Brown, Death, 1:600. However, it is most likely determined by Mark's desire to insist

Peter's first denial is followed by a movement out to the gateway to avoid the scrutiny of the woman who associated him with Jesus. This change of location also places him in a position where a rapid escape may be possible if events turn against him (v. 68b).[159] However, he cannot escape the maidservant, who looks at him again, and begins to share her impressions with other bystanders (v. 69a). The word spreads as she continues to speak to the bystanders.[160] It is not explicitly stated, but the only bystanders present thus far have been the temple guards. It is to Peter's erstwhile companions (v. 54) that the woman speaks, shifting her focus away from Peter's association with Jesus to his association with the other disciples. She insists Peter is "one of them" (v. 69b). Not only has Peter denied (ἠρνήσατο: aorist tense) knowledge of what she claims about his association with Jesus (v. 68), but as the truth spreads, he steadily continues to deny (ἠρνεῖτο: imperfect tense) his association with those whom Jesus has called and who have followed him (v. 70a). Having denied that he had been "with Jesus" (v. 67), he now continues his rejection of all that Jesus had done in creating a group of followers by denying that he was "one of them." Peter's original denial (v. 67) of his being "with" Jesus looked back to 3:14. In rejecting his association with Jesus' other followers, he disassociates himself from the Twelve who, along with Peter, had been appointed to "be with him" (3:14–19).

After a brief period of time the bystanders, probably those with whom he has associated around the fire in the courtyard (see v. 54, 65: οἱ ὑπηρέται), who most likely recall his accent, his Galilean dialect of Aramaic,[161] restate, on firmer evidence, the second affirmation of the woman. They are certain he is one of them, because he is a Galilean (v. 70b). Only now does Peter deny his knowledge of the man whom he swore he would follow unto death (14:31). The significance of the third denial is highlighted by its weighty introduction. Peter calls down a curse upon himself as he swears an oath to the truthfulness of what he is about to say (v. 71a).[162] His words go beyond anything called for by the affirmation of the bystanders. They did not ask about Jesus, but about those who belonged to Jesus' party. But Peter denies knowledge of Jesus: "I do not know this man of whom you speak." They had not spoken of Jesus! The denials have moved steadily from a denial of any understanding of the maidservant's accusation that he had been "with Jesus," to a further denial of his association with the Twelve and the other followers of Jesus (see 3:14–19). Finally, although the bystanders continue to insist that he must be "one of them," he rejects all knowledge of Jesus (v. 71b).[163]

In the light of Jesus' prophecy of 14:30, the reader is not surprised to hear what follows: immediately (εὐθύς) the cock crowed a second time (v. 72a).[164] This is Peter's final

---

upon the disciple's lack of knowledge. On this theme, see below for my comment upon Peter's final denial: "I do not know this man of whom you speak." On the strength of the verb ἀρνέομαι, see Taylor, *St. Mark,* 573.

[159] Taylor, *St. Mark,* 574; Brown, *Death,* 1:602.

[160] The use of the imperfect ἤρξατο followed by an infinitive, widely used by Mark, here indicates that she did not make the statement recorded in v. 69b once, but went on repeating it.

[161] On this possibility see, among many, Taylor, *St. Mark,* 575; Senior, *Passion,* 102–3. This is made explicit in Matt 26:73.

[162] On the oath formula, see the discussion in Brown, *Death,* 1:604–5. Some have suggested that it is a cursing of Jesus, but this is not called for. Hooker (*St. Mark,* 365) correctly remarks: "We should probably understand it as meaning that he invoked a curse upon himself if he is lying."

[163] On Peter as the personification of the disciples' rejection of their call to be "with Jesus," see Borrell, *The Good News of Peter's Denial,* 145–70.

[164] On the chronological and possible literary background to the use of the cockcrow, see Brown, *Death,* 1:605–7.

appearance in the Markan story. All the disciples have fled at the arrest (v. 50), and from this point on, only women who have been with him from Galilee follow Jesus to the cross and the grave (15:40–41, 47, 16:1–8). Peter's final action in the story is to remember (v. 72b). There is much to recall: Jesus' prophecy of 14:30, which has been fulfilled, despite his oath that he would rather die than abandon Jesus (14:31).[165] Words of Jesus from the end of his discourse on the Mount of Olives also lie behind this moment. The disciples were told to be attentive to their responsibilities as followers of Jesus (γρηγορεῖτε) as they do not know when the master of the household is coming. He may come at cock crow (13:35). The irony of the Markan Christology continues to emerge as the passion of Jesus unfolds. The master of the house is the suffering Jesus, coming at cock crow and fulfilling his prophecies. Peter has repeatedly claimed he neither knows nor understands what he is being asked (v. 68), and finally swears he does not know Jesus (v. 71: οὐκ οἶδα τὸν ἄνθρωπον). The language of knowing and understanding has been an important part of Jesus' teaching on discipleship (4:11–13) and part of their increasing failure (6:52; 9:6; 9:32). Peter's first and third denials bring this lack of knowledge and understanding to a climax.[166] It is with such memories that Peter collapses (ἐπιβαλών) with anguish and begins to weep (v. 27c).[167] Despite the tragedy of the moment, there is hope as Peter recalls the prophetic words of Jesus and recognizes his role in its fulfillment. With profound sorrow and tears, not arrogance, Peter leaves the scene. He may not reappear in person within the confines of Mark 1:1–16:8, but the reader has good reason to suspect that the last word in Peter's story has not been said (see 16:7).[168]

The Roman Trial, Crucifixion, Death, and Burial of Jesus (15:1–47)

Changes of location mark turning points within the overall structure of the passion narrative. It opened with Jesus in Bethany (14:3). From there he went to the upper room (14:12–16) and to Gethsemane after the final meal (14:32). Arrested in Gethsemane, he is led to the house of the high priest (14:53). The passion narrative is heading for dénouement. Only three locations remain: he will be led to Pilate (15:1), to Golgotha (15:22), and to a grave (15:46). Across these three locations, however, the steady movement from a focus upon Jesus to a focus upon other agents in the action is maintained over nine brief scenes: [B] 15:1–5: Jesus, [A] 15:6–11: Barabbas, [B] 15:12–15: Jesus, [A] 15:16–20a: the soldiers, [B] 15:20b–25: Jesus, [A] 15:26–32: passersby and leaders, [B] 15:33–39: Jesus, [A] 15:40–41: the women, [B] 15:42–47: Jesus. At the center of this rhythmic shift from character to character one finds the central scene of the crucifixion of Jesus, Messiah and Son of God (15:20b–25).

---

165 Brown, *Death*, 1:624.

166 Senior, *Passion*, 103–4, and especially Borrell, *The Good News of Peter's Denial*, 83–117. This literary and theological motif has created the clumsy Greek of Peter's first denial in v. 67: οὔτε οἶδα οὔτε ἐπίσταμαι σὺ τί λέγεις.

167 The use of ἐπιβάλλειν here is very obscure. It can have a passive or intransitive meaning. See the survey of difficulties and possibilities in Brown, *Death*, 1:609–10. I suggest that a sense of desperate sorrow is communicated by this verb, which can have a strong meaning of being physically taken over (Brown's option [b], which he does not accept).

168 See the elegant comment of Grundmann (*Markus*, 305): "Thus he stands, a man who can no longer believe, between an inability to believe and yet a necessity to believe."

[B] The self-revelation of Jesus as the Roman hearing begins (15:1–5)

A change of time, already heralded by the cockcrow, accompanies the change of place.[169] First thing in the morning the Jewish leaders, the chief priests, the elders, the scribes (cf. 8:31; 10:33; 11:18, 27; 14:1, 10, 43, 53, 55), and the whole Sanhedrin (cf. 14:55) having declared that Jesus deserves death (14:64), hold further counsel (cf. 3:6). The result of this consultation is that Jesus is bound and led to Pilate, the Roman authority.[170] The narrator's use of the verb παρέδωκαν for the "handing over" of Jesus, associates the Jewish leaders with Jesus' being handed over unto death (cf. 9:33; 10:33; 14:10, 1, 18, 21, 41). "The Jews here, and Pilate in v. 15, are in some mysterious way agents of God's plan to 'deliver up' his Son for the salvation of the world."[171] The Jewish leaders will never be far away, and for Mark they are responsible for Jesus' death.[172] The remaining action against Jesus is the result of decisions taken by the Roman authority, including the final confession of faith by a Roman centurion (15:39). The first three scenes take place in the praetorium. Three distinct issues are developed: Jesus' self-revelation (15:1–5), the question of Barabbas (15:6–15), and the ironic mockery of Jesus as King of the Jews (15:16–20a).

As one would expect from a Roman authority, Pilate raises the political question of Jesus' royal status: "Are you the King of the Jews?"[173] Paralleling his acceptance of the high priest's question concerning his status as Messiah and Son of God with ἐγώ εἰμι, Jesus accepts Pilate's description with the enigmatic words: "You have said so" (σὺ λέγεις). The expression can be taken as an attempt to sidestep the question,[174] but the parallel with the question of the high priest, whose entourage returns immediately in 15:3, and the fact that the Roman authority asks the question, point to Jesus' words as a conditional acceptance. Never in the Gospel has Jesus claimed to be a king, despite suggestions to the contrary from others (11:9–10). His only association with kingly language has been his claim to be bringing in the kingdom *of God* (1:15; 4:11, 26, 30; 9:47; 10:14–15, 23, 24, 25; 12:34; 14:25).

---

[169] The cockcrow links the end of the Jewish process (14:72) with the beginning of the Roman hearing (15:1); see Painter, *Mark's Gospel*, 198.

[170] The nature of this morning consultation is the subject of considerable historical reflection. See the summary of the problems and discussions in Taylor, *St. Mark*, 578; Hooker, *St. Mark*, 354–57. In Luke 22:66–71, the hearing recorded by Mark as taking place during the night (14:53–65) takes place in the morning. In Matt 26:66, Jesus is judged as "deserving of death" during the night hearing, but it is not until the morning that he is "judged" (see 27:1). On the relationship between the trial of Jesus and the Mishnaic Law, see Brown, *Death*, 1:357–63. One cannot be certain of the "time" of the Jewish hearing, as Mark has formed it from a number of elements which existed in the pre-Markan tradition; see Nineham, *St. Mark*, 410–11. It is unlikely that Luke is working with a better historical tradition, as some would suggest, e.g., Sloyan, *Jesus on Trial*, 89, 94–95, 109; see now idem, "Recent Literature on the Trial Narratives of the Fourth Gospel," in *Critical History and Biblical Faith: New Testament Perspectives* (ed. T. J. Ryan; The College Theology Society Annual Publication Series; Villanova: College Theology Series, 1979), 139–40, 164. He is, rather, reshaping the Markan material into a more "orderly account" (see Luke 1:1–4). See the remarks of Brown, *Death*, 1:527–30.

[171] Nineham, *St. Mark*, 415.

[172] Hooker (*St. Mark*, 366) observes: "The responsibility of the Jews for the whole affair is stressed." She points to vv. 1, 3, 11, 13–14 as evidence. She then concludes: "In contrast, Pilate is astonished by Jesus (v. 5), attempts to release him (vv. 5ff.), and declares him innocent (v. 14)."

[173] "It is a Greco-Roman formulation of the question which the high priest asked of Jesus in a Jewish version in 14:61" (Schweizer, *Mark*, 336). See also Anderson, *Mark*, 336; Juel, *A Master of Surprise*, 95.

[174] See Lohmeyer, *Markus*, 335, Grundmann, *Markus*, 307, and the summary of possibilities in Nineham, *St. Mark*, 415. Pesch (*Markusevangelium*, 2:458) rightly points out that the narrative presumes that Pilate regards Jesus' response as an acceptance of kingship in 15:9, 12.

Having accepted his messianic status in the Jewish hearing, and further explaining what this meant in terms of the final vindication of the suffering Son of Man (14:61–62), Jesus accepts that he is King of the Jews, but not in a way that Pilate would understand. In other words, Jesus' enigmatic response indicates that Pilate has the words right, but does not understand the full meaning of his own question.[175] Jesus' royalty will be exercised from a cross. "For Mark the title, king of the Jews, legitimately reveals the crucified one."[176] This explanation is beyond Pilate's ken. Thus Jesus accepts Pilate's words (σὺ λέγεις), but what those words mean is yet to be acted out, and Pilate will see to it that they are.[177]

Mark continues to include the Jewish leaders in the process: "And the chief priests accused him of many things" (15:3).[178] The ambiguity of Jesus' reply to Pilate opens the door for them to bring their accusations to Pilate's attention, but it also enables Mark to continue his presentation of Jesus as the righteous sufferer, surrounded by enemies who lie and hate (cf. Ps 109:2–3).[179] Pilate has heard Jesus' ambiguous acceptance of his kingship but oddly interrogates no further on that crucial political issue. It is the "many things" of the chief priests that causes Pilate to ask Jesus why he makes no response to the charges they bring (v. 4). He calls Jesus' attention to the seriousness of the accusations with the expression "behold" (ἴδε), creating the impression that he is on Jesus' side and is warning him of unsubstantiated charges leveled against him. "One gets the impression that Pilate takes the many other charges no more seriously than Jesus does."[180] The silence of Jesus before the charges of the chief priests repeats his earlier silence in the face of the false accusations brought against him during the Jewish hearing (14:60–61a; see also Isa 53:7 on the silence of the Servant). He has nothing more to say, as the truth has already been proclaimed, via Jesus' response to the high priest's question: he is the Christ, the Son of God and the Son of Man (14:61b–62). Pilate has also heard the truth in his ambiguous

---

[175] Brown (*Death*, 1:732–33) also suggests that Jesus accepts the title, and makes a link with 14:61b–62. He claims, however, that the Markan reader would regard Jesus' enigmatic response as an indication that the response of 14:61b–62 is more important: "Marcan readers would have to assume that Jesus is more the Messiah than King of the Jews." (p. 733). It is also often pointed out that "King of the Jews" is a more political title than "King of Israel," which has more religious connotations, associated with "the Christ" in 15:32. See, among many, Senior, *Passion*, 108–9. This certainly is the case, but not to be underestimated is the ambiguous, ironic importance of Pilate's proclamation of Jesus as "King of the Jews" in v. 2 and its rejection by the crowd, goaded by the leaders, in vv. 9 and 12.

[176] Painter, *Mark's Gospel*, 199. Brown (*Death*, 1:729–32) suggests that this Roman question about Jesus' claim to royalty may be the oldest strata of the trial narratives. Among others, N. A. Dahl (*The Crucified Messiah and Other Essays* [Minneapolis: Augsburg, 1974], 10–36) suggests that the certain fact of the title on the cross, "Jesus of Nazareth, King of the Jews" (Mark 15:36), provides the origins for this tradition.

[177] Lohmeyer (*Markus*, 335) catches this meaning with his suggestion that σὺ λέγεις is a half-yes, understood by the believer, but mysterious to the unbeliever. This is not oversubtle, as Taylor (*St. Mark*, 579) claims. It is part of the overall Markan use of irony.

[178] The Markan limiting of the group to the chief priests (see the larger groups involved in Matt 27:12; Luke 23:1–2; John 18:31, 35) is an indication of his desire to point to Jewish leadership as Jesus' chief opponents. Unlike the Johannine narrative (John 18:28–19:16a), where Pilate and Jesus move from a public place before the crowds and Jesus' accusers, in Mark (and also Matthew and Luke) the Roman process takes place with Jesus' opponents present and able to intervene; see Brown, *Death*, 1:705. There is some discussion about the meaning of πολλά. Did the chief priests accuse Jesus of "much" or "many things"? In favor of the latter, see Brown, *Death*, 1:734.

[179] Gnilka, *Markus*, 2:300.

[180] Brown, *Death*, 1:735.

acceptance of the suggestion that he is "the King of the Jews" (15:2). Nothing more needs to be said. Pilate is left wondering, puzzled (15:5).[181]

[A] The question of Barabbas (15:6–11)

Verses 6–8 introduce the theme of 15:6–11.[182] Mark invokes a practice he claims was habitual for Pilate: he used to release one prisoner at the request of the people (v. 6). It is impossible to find evidence for this practice (cf. Matt 27:15). However, it is found in the Johannine passion narrative (John 18:39).[183] The narrator describes a character currently held in prison, named Barabbas. He is one of a group of rebels (μετὰ τῶν στασιαστῶν), a murderer who had slain people during a recent insurrection.[184] As no indication is given of which revolt is intended, by simply stating "in the revolt" (ἐν τῇ στάσει), the narrator takes for granted that the reader understands. In a most unlikely sequence of events, almost ignoring for the moment that Pilate is hearing a charge that merits execution (vv. 1–5), the crowd appears out of nowhere.[185] They do not ask explicitly for Barabbas, but that Pilate free a prisoner on the occasion of the Passover feast, as has been his custom

---

[181] Senior (*Passion,* 109–10) suggests that the astonishment of many and kings shutting their mouths at the sight of the Suffering Servant in Isa 52:14–15 may lie behind Pilate's wondering; see also Hooker, *St. Mark,* 368. Brown (*Death,* 1:699–705) attempts to reconstruct the character of Pilate on the basis of six major events from Pilate's period as prefect. The evidence points to a man who was capable of caving in to strong demands when, in his estimation, the overall order would be better preserved by such weakness. Mark's account supports this assessment, beginning with the fact that he never again returns to his question about Jesus' kingship (which is, above all, a Markan theological affirmation), but remains somewhat bewildered (θαυμάζειν) by Jesus' silence in the face of false Jewish accusations. As he concludes his investigation of the nature of the Roman trial and the decision to hand Jesus over to be crucified, Brown records: "Jesus had not met either the best or the worst of Roman judges" (*Death,* 1:722). See also Sloyan, *Jesus on Trial,* 19–35; idem, *The Crucifixion,* 31–33. For a different, very negative, assessment of Pilate, the friend of the anti-Jewish Sejanus, see Gnilka, *Markus,* 2:299.

[182] Pesch (*Markusevangelium,* 2:461) divides vv. 6–15 into vv. 6–8 (introduction), a three-stepped main section (vv. 9–11, 12–13, 14), with a conclusion in v. 15. I am suggesting that vv. 6–8 introduces the Barabbas question which concludes in v. 11 with the request that he be freed. The issue of Jesus' destiny emerges with Pilate's question in v. 12, and the request that Jesus be crucified. He is then handed over to flogging and crucifixion in v. 15. This creates two scenes: vv. 6–11 (Barabbas) and vv. 12–15 (Jesus).

[183] Despite the confidence of some (e.g., Lane, *Mark,* 552–53), it is impossible to trace the annual practice of freeing a prisoner at Passover. But the association with the freeing of Barabbas during Jesus' passion is ancient and most likely took place. On both issues, see Pesch, *Markusevangelium,* 2:467; Gnilka, *Markus,* 2:304–5; Brown, *Death,* 1:793–95. For attempts to find some background for the custom, which would hardly have been invented by Christian tradition, see Taylor, *St. Mark,* 580–81; Lagrange, *Saint Marc,* 414; Lohmeyer, *Markus,* 337; LaVerdiere, *The Beginning,* 2:278–79; and especially Brown, *Death,* 1:814–20.

[184] Gnilka (*Markus,* 2:301) claims the description of Barabbas suggests that he was the leader of the revolt. He also suggests that there is a deliberate play on the name Barabbas, which means "son of the father," as Jesus is Son of the Father. Against this, see LaVerdiere, *The Beginning,* 2:279, and especially Brown, *Death,* 1:796–800, 811–14. It is a reasonably common name; see Lagrange, *Saint Marc,* 387. Some manuscripts and early translations call him "Jesus Barabbas," but this has been imported into Mark 15:7 from a stronger (but also doubtful) reading found in Matt 27:16–17.

[185] Hooker (*St. Mark,* 369) points out that this cannot be the same "crowd" which worried the leaders in 14:2. Within the present context, "For Mark, the significance of the crowd is that it represents the Jews." They reject their King and ask for Barabbas. Against a number of commentators (e.g., Cranfield, *St. Mark,* 450), who guess that the crowd is a group of supporters of Barabbas.

(v. 8). Jesus is not present in the story; the reader hears only of Barabbas (v. 7), Pilate, and the crowd (v. 8). At the end of the passage, the chief priests enter, but Jesus is never present or active in this passage. It concludes with the request that Barabbas be released (v. 11).[186]

Pilate suggests the release of "the King of the Jews" (15:9). He has accepted Jesus' self-revelation (v. 2), despite his perplexity over the silent king facing many charges from the leaders of his people, and has his own political assessment of Jesus' royal claim (vv. 4–5).[187] Pilate offers to free Jesus to the crowd, not to the leaders, for he perceived that the chief priests had delivered Jesus up (παραδεδώκεισαν; cf. v. 1) "out of envy" (διὰ φθόνον). Pilate is working at a political and not a theological level. He has accepted that Jesus is the King of the Jews and judges that Jesus is a threat to the current religious and political leadership of the priests. It is as a politician that Pilate offers "the crowd" their king.[188] This is his way of circumventing the designs of the leaders of the Jews who are the driving force behind Jesus' arrest (14:43) and condemnation (14:64). The Markan agenda is strongly at work here. There is little likelihood a Roman prefect would desire to free a figure whom he believed to be a king of a subjugated people.[189] The guilt for what is about to happen to Jesus is shifted away from Pilate and placed squarely upon the leadership of the Jews.[190] Pilate not only accepts Jesus' self-revelation of Jesus as "King of the Jews" (v. 2), but also judges that he is innocent, and attempts to set him free, via the supposedly customary practice of freeing a prisoner on the occasion of the feast (v. 6).[191]

The second theme, the responsibility of the leaders of the Jews, is highlighted as the narrator reports that the chief priests stir up the crowd to reject Pilate's offer to free Jesus,

---

[186] My division of vv. 6–15 into vv. 6–11 (Barabbas) and vv. 12–15 (Jesus as a suffering and insulted king) may appear strange. It is made on the basis of Jesus' absence in vv. 6–11, where the focus is upon Barabbas, and his presence in vv. 12–15 where "your king" (v. 12) is rejected and handed over for flogging and crucifixion (v. 15). There is no indication where Jesus was as Pilate spoke with "the crowd" about his release in vv. 6–11. He is present, however, in vv. 12–15 as the crucifixion is demanded and Pilate hands him over. Jesus is led "inside the palace" in v. 16 (ἔσω τῆς αὐλῆς), indicating that in vv. 12–15 he was "outside" with Pilate and the crowd. But there is no such indication in vv. 6–11 where Pilate talks with a crowd and the Jewish leaders lurk in the background.

[187] This proclamation by Pilate could also be regarded as a problem to my structure (see previous note). I have claimed that vv. 1–5 were marked by Jesus' veiled self-revelation as "king." The same christological theme returns in vv. 6–11. Thus it could be claimed, although absent, he is not "off the scene." The ironic proclamation of the truth continues, but Jesus never appears in vv. 6–11. He is evaluated by Pilate, the crowd, and the leaders of the Jews. The crucial point of comparison is the other character in the pericope: Barabbas. A further moment in the proclamation of Jesus as king will come in vv. 12–15 when, in Jesus' presence (see v. 15), the crowd's earlier acclamation of his messianic royalty is recalled (see 11:9–10).

[188] Lohmeyer, *Markus,* 339; Lane, *Mark,* 554–55; Pesch, *Markusevangelium,* 2:464. Gnilka (*Markus,* 2:302) makes little of this, simply suggesting Pilate has heard that the Jewish trial was a sham. Nothing in the text suggests this. The issue is Jesus' being a rejected king. For a broad discussion of the possible meanings of φθόνος here, with no reference to the above suggestion concerning political authority, see Brown, *Death,* 1:801–3. Lagrange (*Saint Marc,* 388) makes the interesting remark that Pilate was trying to be politically adroit, but really did not understand the machinations of the Jewish hierarchy.

[189] Hooker (*St. Mark,* 368) rightly remarks, "the notion that a Roman official would release any particular prisoner whom they requested is incredible." It is even more incredible that he would release someone who claimed to be king.

[190] Anderson, *Mark,* 337.

[191] Doubtless the historical Pilate would not have behaved in this fashion or treated Jesus as a king in any way. But it misses the Markan irony to suggest that Pilate is sarcastically baiting the crowd as, for example, LaVerdiere (*The Beginning,* 2:280–81); Brown (*Death,* 1:824).

and to ask for the freedom of Barabbas (v. 11). Mark wishes to present to his hearers and readers the false choice made by the leaders of the people. The association of Barabbas with revolt and murder is linked to many other parallel events familiar to the reader (cf. 13:14: "Let the reader understand"). It is possible a choice was offered and Barabbas was chosen, but the careful description of Barabbas in 15:1–3, associated with Pilate's presentation of Jesus as the King of the Jews, is a further example of Markan irony. The revolutionary and the murderer will be freed and the innocent king slain.[192] But the readers know from the events of 65–70 that revolt and murder have produced the destruction of the people and their leadership.

[B] Pilate proclaims Jesus innocent and ironically styles him king (15:12–15)

The decision to crucify Jesus is not taken by Pilate. He defers to the crowd, asking them what he should do with "the man whom you call the King of the Jews" (v. 12). The narrative progresses with the steady use of "the King of the Jews" across 15:1–15. In 15:2 Pilate asked if Jesus were such a figure, and received an answer. In 15:9, responding to the crowd's request that a prisoner be freed, he offered them Jesus, "the King of the Jews." Pilate's third use of the expression associates the crowd with Jesus' claim to royal status: "the man whom you call King of the Jews."[193] However partial, and political, his understanding of Jesus' royalty (vv. 2, 9), he recognizes that the people call him King of the Jews (v. 12). They will have their understanding of "the King of the Jews" from their history, religion, and messianic hopes. It is to this understanding of "King of the Jews" that Pilate now appeals.[194] The crowd who had earlier cried out its acclamation of Jesus as the one who comes in the name of the Lord, bringing in the kingdom of their father David (11:9–10), is challenged. They have acclaimed Jesus as their king. If they ask for the freedom of Barabbas, what is Pilate to do with the man they call the King of the Jews? The Roman prefect may have a faulty understanding of Jesus' royalty (cf. vv. 2, 9) but he recognizes that the Jewish crowd accepts Jesus is "the King of the Jews" in a messianic and royal sense (v. 12).[195]

---

[192] The unjust trial of an innocent Jesus announces the future experience of the Christian community, as Jesus has already told the disciples in 13:9–11. "Mark presents Jesus as the first in a long line of those who would suffer unjust accusations and be brought to trial for the sake of the Gospel" (Senior, *Passion*, 110).

[193] The transmission of the text is confused here. Some manuscripts (Alexandrinus, Bezae, Koridethi, an eighth-century uncial, and some early translations) insert θέλετε to read "what therefore *do you wish* that I do . . ." However, it is omitted by the major witnesses (Sinaiticus, Vaticanus, Ephraem Rescript, Freer Gospels, Families 1 and 13, and a number of versions). It is to be excluded as an assimilation from 15:9. The specification of Jesus as "*whom you call* (ὅν λέγετε) King of the Jews" is missing in Alexandrinus, Bezae, Freer Gospels, Koridethi, Families 1 and 13, and a number of versions. It is found in Sinaiticus, Ephraem Rescript, Athos, and a number of versions. As well as the slight superiority of the external evidence, the Matthean rewriting of this passage (Matt 27:22: τὸν λεγόμενον Χριστόν) appears to presuppose the ὅν λέγετε of Mark 15:12. Internally, the "whom you call" is required for the subtle development of the use of the title "the King of the Jews," as explained in the interpretation suggested above. It is not to be interpreted as Pilate's attempt to lay the onus for the use of the title on the Jews; see, for example, Taylor, *St. Mark*, 582–83.

[194] Pilate does not disassociate himself with Jesus as a king. It is the Jews who make the claim. See Taylor, *St. Mark*, 582–83.

[195] As Lagrange, *Saint Marc*, 389 remarks: "Pilate gives in to the temptation to allow the Jews to contradict themselves."

The response from the crowd is immediate: they ask Pilate to execute Jesus by means of the most painful death in Roman legal process: crucifixion (15:13).[196] In a final attempt to free Jesus, Pilate asks the ironic question: "What evil has he done?" (v. 14a). The irony comes from the fact that the reader knows Jesus has done no evil. It is clear that the Jewish process leading to the decision that Jesus be executed (14:53–65), and handed over to the Roman authority (15:1), was a sham. However, the reader is also aware that the third passion prediction had foretold that the leaders of the Jews would hand Jesus over to the Gentiles, and would slay him (10:34). The ironic demand from Jesus' captors in 14:65 that Jesus prophesy continues to be fulfilled as the crowd shouted (ἔκραξαν) their insistence that Pilate crucify Jesus (v. 14b). In 11:9 the crowd kept on shouting (ἔκραζον) "Hosanna!" Now they shout, "Crucify him."[197] Pilate has reminded the people that they are judging their king, but they ask for his death by crucifixion. This is the first time (vv. 13–14) the verb "to crucify" (σταυρόω) is used. In his passion predictions (8:31; 9:31; 10:33–34) Jesus never spoke of crucifixion, but stated that he would be put to death (ἀποκτείνω). Earlier, the Herodians and the Pharisees decided together that he must be destroyed (ἀπόλλυμι, 3:6). Jesus will be an innocent, crucified King of the Jews (v. 12), slain by the Romans at the explicit request of the Jewish crowd (vv. 13–14), goaded on by the leaders of the Jews (v. 11).

The death of John the Baptist comes to mind as the narrator gives the motive for Pilate's delivering (παρέδωκεν) Jesus to be crucified: his desire to satisfy the crowd.[198] There is no hint that Pilate finds Jesus guilty of any crime. Like Herod, who wondered about the Baptist (6:16; cf. 15:5) and had no desire to slay him but gave in to pressure (6:26), Pilate goes against his own convictions and, also giving in to public pressure, hands Jesus over to be crucified (15:15). Before the crucifixion, however, the request is granted that a revolutionary and a murderer, Barabbas, be released (v. 15b). As the king goes to his death, a representative of those who brought Israel to its destruction is set free. As most commentators remark, there are parallels between the Jewish hearing and the process before Pilate, despite the brevity of the latter.[199] Jesus has proclaimed the truth in unique moments of self-revelation (14:61–62a; 15:2), yet he has been unjustly judged as a blasphemer and worthy of death (14:64), handed over to death without any condemnation (15:15).[200] Those who

---

[196] Commentators note that the use of πάλιν in v. 13 is strange, as they do not call out "again." This is the first time they have asked for Jesus' crucifixion. Schweizer, *Mark,* 338, rightly remarks: "Perhaps this is a device to express the stubborn and repeated rejection of Jesus." For the details of crucifixion, see M. Hengel, *Crucifixion in the Ancient World and the Folly of the Cross* (trans. J. Bowden; London: SCM, 1977); J. A. Fitzmyer, "Crucifixion in Ancient Palestine, Qumran Literature, and the New Testament," *CBQ* 40 (1979): 493–513; Sloyan, *The Crucifixion,* 9–23; Brown, *Death,* 2:945–52.

[197] Gnilka, *Markus,* 2:302; Brown, *Death,* 1:824. Taylor (*St. Mark,* 581) attempts in vain to explain why the crowd has changed its opinion of Jesus.

[198] On this, see Matera, *Kingship,* 97–100. Gnilka (*Markus,* 2:302) produces evidence from instructions to representatives of Rome that they must never give in to public opinion. This continues Gnilka's argument that Pilate was an incompetent and guilty party in Jesus' death. Brown's assessment is probably correct: "The Marcan Pilate is not exculpated: He is not so malevolent as the chief priests, but he is a poor excuse for Roman justice" (*Death,* 1:754). On the lack of a formal Roman "Abi ad crucem" ("You shall go to the cross") judgment, see Brown, *Death,* 1:853–55. For a reading of 15:1–15 as a demonstration of "perversity and blindness of the Romans," see Garrett, *The Temptations,* 127–29.

[199] See, for example, Senior, *Passion,* 109.

[200] Mark offers no legal reason why Pilate handed Jesus over to crucifixion; see Brown, *Death,* 1:850–51. For speculation upon what those reasons might have been, see Brown, *Death,* 1:717–19.

hold him abuse him. The blindfolding, spitting, and striking of 14:65 is repeated in the brief report of Jesus' scourging in 15:15c.[201] However, the mocking recognition of Jesus as a prophet in 14:65 is more fully developed in 15:16–20a. In 15:12–15 Pilate, the Roman authority, has reminded the crowd that Jesus is the innocent King of the Jews. Both leaders and people reject their innocent king and ask for his crucifixion.[202] In 15:16–20a Roman soldiers, in their mockery of Jesus, will ironically confirm the truth proclaimed by Pilate.

[A] The Roman soldiers ironically proclaim the truth as they mock Jesus (15:16–20a)

Roman involvement with Jesus' ongoing suffering is assured by the identification of his aggressors as "soldiers" and the location of the insults that follow as the praetorium. Similarly, "the whole cohort" gathers together.[203] Jesus is present but the active characters in this scene are the soldiers who lead him into the praetorium. The calling together of the whole cohort introduces a scenario of major abuse. The mock coronation follows: the clothing in a purple cloak, the plaiting of a crown of thorns and placing it upon him (v. 17).[204] Such behavior of Roman soldiers with a prisoner condemned to death was commonplace.[205] They are the unwitting lead figures in the brief episode that follows. Mark uses them to continue the proclamation of the truth: Jesus is King of the Jews in his suffering.[206] The soldiers recognize this with their mocking salutation: "Hail, King of the Jews" (v. 18). In this caricature of the Roman salute to the emperor, "Ave Caesar,"[207] the reader

---

[201] In the Roman provinces the horrible practice of flogging before crucifixion took place only at the execution of slaves. On the crucifixion of slaves, see Hengel, *Crucifixion*, 51–63. See Gnilka, *Markus,* 2:303, and especially Brown, *Death,* 1:851–53 on Roman floggings.

[202] Senior, *Passion,* 112.

[203] On the Roman nature of the characters and events of v. 16, see Taylor, *St. Mark,* 585; Brown, *Death,* 1:864–65. Most agree that a full cohort (about six hundred soldiers) is probably not intended; see, for example, Cranfield, *St. Mark,* 452.

[204] On the color purple as a sign of royalty, see, among many, Pesch, *Markusevangelium,* 2:472.

[205] See the fundamental study of R. Delbrueck, "Antiquarisches zu den Verspottung Jesu," *ZNW* 41 (1942): 124–45, and the further copious documentation in support of this affirmation in Brown, *Death,* 1:873–77. Brown points out that the Markan pairing of both Jewish mockery (14:64–65) and Roman mockery (15:16–20a) shows "the equally negative portrayal of the two sets of mockers" (p. 877). Despite the Markan focus upon the responsibility of the Jewish leadership, the Romans also bear their share of guilt in Jesus' suffering. Some (e.g., Anderson, *Mark,* 338) have suggested that 15:16–20a is composite, and that it may have been added to the pre-Markan narrative. The narrative flows on from v. 15b to v. 20b very smoothly. See the summaries of the scholarly discussion of this question in Pesch, *Markusevangelium,* 2:468–69; Gnilka, *Markus,* 2:306; Brown, *Death,* 1:871–73. The parallel between the two mockings must be noted; see Schweizer, *Mark,* 540–41. Matera (*Kingship,* 21–34) links the mockeries of 15:16–20a, 27–32, and 35–36. He considers 14:65 as the result of Markan editorial work on a pre-Markan tradition (pp. 32–33) but does not make a literary link between this earlier mockery and 15:16–20a.

[206] Brown (*Death,* 1:866) mentions that Christian piety and iconography have accentuated the suffering involved in the crown of thorns. On the development of popular passion piety, see the rich study of Sloyan, *The Crucifixion,* 123–44. But as Brown rightly remarks: "In the Gospels, however, there is no stress on torture, and the crown is part of the royal mockery, like the robe and the sceptre" (*Death,* 1:866). On the ironic royalty of the clothing and the gestures, see LaVerdiere, *The Beginning,* 2:284. Hooker (*St. Mark,* 370) reports a suggestion that the thorns may have pointed outward "and that it was a deliberate caricature of the radiate crown (imitating the rays of the sun-god) with which 'divine' rulers were portrayed on the coins of the period." See also Brown, *Death,* 1:867.

[207] Gnilka, *Markus,* 2:308.

recognizes that the truth is proclaimed: the suffering Jesus is the King of the Jews. The blend of suffering and proclamation of the truth continues into v. 19. The soldiers strike him on the head and spit upon him. The humiliation and pain are extreme, but as they inflict suffering upon the crowned king, dressed in a purple cloak, they kneel down in homage. This may be mockery, a caricature of the traditional approach to a Hellenistic leader,[208] but homage on bended knee is a powerfully ironic recognition of Jesus' royalty.[209] The soldiers are unwittingly saying and doing things that the reader recognizes as the truth.

For Mark, however, it is more than irony. It is not only that people who do not recognize what they are saying or doing proclaim a royal figure. For the Markan Christology it is *in the moment of suffering, insult, humiliation, and finally death* that Jesus is king (cf. 10:45).[210] A crowd of people who mistakenly wished to install a new Davidic Messiah in Jerusalem (11:9–10) have unwittingly accepted their role in God's design by seeing to it that their king will be handed over to the Gentiles and slain by crucifixion (10:34; 15:12–13). The Gentiles have clothed and crowned him as a king and have bent their knee in homage, even as they outrageously insult and injure him (10:33; 15:17–19). "Jesus *is* a King, but as the taunts and mockeries of Jesus' opponents unwittingly affirm, *not* a king in the human mode of power."[211] But the mockery comes to an end; Jesus' royal garb, the cloak and the crown, are taken from him and he is again dressed in his own clothes (v. 20a).[212] Jesus turns toward the cross (v. 20b).[213]

[B] The crucifixion of Jesus (15:20b–25)

There is scant agreement among scholars on the limitations of this pericope. Some run the passage on to 15:26, where the inscription placed upon the cross is described,[214] others to 15:27, to include the two robbers.[215] Some would go as far as 15:32, embracing the whole scene before Jesus' death (cf. vv. 33–39),[216] while others regard 15:20b–41 to be so tightly interwoven that it is impossible to discover different scenes.[217]

---

[208] Gnilka, *Markus*, 2:309.

[209] Brown, *Death*, 1:869.

[210] See Senior, *Passion*, 113–14; Lührmann, *Markusevangelium*, 257. "There is no coincidence that the kingship of Jesus and his status as son of God should be bound up with his crucifixion and death" (Painter, *Mark's Gospel*, 201).

[211] Senior, *Passion*, 108 (stress in original).

[212] In normal Roman practice, after the prisoner was convicted and insulted he would carry a cross to the place of crucifixion naked. Brown (*Death*, 1:870) suggests that there may have been a Roman concession to the Jewish abhorrence of public nudity.

[213] Gnilka (*Markus*, 2:308) comments: "The grim *game* is over, to make way for the grimmer *reality*."

[214] E.g., Schweizer, *Mark*, 342; Anderson, *Mark*, 339–42.

[215] E.g., Brown, *Death*, 2:902, 935; Gnilka, *Markus*, 2:314. On pp. 309–14, Gnilka reviews theories of identifiable sources in vv. 20b–41, concluding that it is difficult to break this material into sections. He suggests a basic pre-Markan passion narrative which has been further developed with the addition of apocalyptic elements and themes from the OT figure of the righteous sufferer, especially with the help of Ps 22. If there is a division of the material, Gnilka suggests that it should be vv. 20a–27 (way of the cross and crucifixion), vv. 29–32 (insults), vv. 33–41 (death and its consequences).

[216] E.g., Lagrange, *Saint Marc*, 396 (for vv. 20b–22 as a unit), 399 (for vv. 23–32 as a unit); Nineham, *St. Mark*, 420–21; Lohmeyer, *Markus*, 341; Lane, *Mark*, 560–62; Hooker, *St. Mark*, 371–72.

[217] Taylor, *St. Mark*, 587; Grundmann, *Markus*, 311–12.

Three major literary factors point to 15:20b–25 as a unit, and 15:26–32 as a separate unit.[218] Scholars agree that the passage opens with v. 20b: "And they led him out to crucify him." The events described in vv. 21–25 are entirely concerned with things done by the Romans to Jesus as he is led to Golgotha (vv. 21–22) and crucified (vv. 23–25). No direct speech is recorded, and the subject of every major verb is the third person plural, "they," i.e., the Roman soldiers (v. 20b: "they led," v. 21: "they compelled," v. 22: "they brought," v. 23: "they offered," v. 24: "they crucified," "they divided," v. 25: "they crucified"). Mark renders most of these verbs in the historic present: "they led" (v. 20b), "they bring" (v. 22), "they crucify" (v. 24), "they divide" (v. 24). This Greek construction is used to make the past more vivid.[219] The passage concludes, looking back to the purpose of the soldiers' leading Jesus out in v. 20b: "It was the third hour, and they crucified him (καὶ ἐσταύρωσαν αὐτόν). The verb σταυρόω appears only three times in the passage: once at the beginning and twice at the end. In 15:24–25 the soldiers did what they set out to do in 15:20b. The literary form and content of 15:26–32 differ from 15:20b–25. Verses 26–32 are highlighted by direct speech (vv. 26, 29b–30, 31b–32a) as Jesus is abused, and the truth is ironically proclaimed. The passage opens with a reference to the two robbers who were crucified on either side of Jesus (v. 27), and it closes by returning to them (v. 32b). Finally, in the overall scheme I have suggested for Mark 14:1–15:47,[220] 15:20b–25 focuses upon something that happens *to Jesus:* he is crucified. The following passage (vv. 26–32) is dominated by others: the inscription, those who passed by, the chief priests and the scribes, and the robbers who all hurl abuse at Jesus.[221]

The Roman soldiers continue to control events as they lead Jesus out of the praetorium, and presumably out of the city limits to crucify him (v. 20b).[222] They are also the agents who compel a passerby, Simon of Cyrene, who happened to be there as he came in from the fields, to carry the cross of Jesus (v. 21).[223] It is possible that Simon of Cyrene was a revered figure, as he is referred to as "the father of Alexander and Rufus." No explanation is given, and apparently none is needed. Alexander and Rufus might have been two personalities well known to the original readers and hearers of the story, possibly members of the Markan community,[224] and their father has been singled out for a special honor. The forc-

---

[218] See also Pesch, *Markusevangelium,* 2:474–75, although I would not share his confidence about this literary shape already being in place in a pre-Markan passion narrative.

[219] See BDF, 167, par. 321: "The historic present can replace the aorist indicative in a vivid narrative at the events of which the narrator imagines himself to be present; the *Aktionsart* usually remains punctiliar in spite of the present tense form."

[220] See above, pp. 275–79.

[221] On the possibility of recovering the pre-Markan primitive core for the Markan crucifixion account, see Brown, *Death,* 2:904–5. He skeptically concludes: "Here as elsewhere one may detect early traditions (shared independently by the Gospels) but . . . we cannot reconstruct with serious probability a preMarcan narrative, even if we have good reason to think one existed" (pp. 904–5).

[222] This accords with both Jewish and Roman practice; see Brown, *Death,* 2:912–13.

[223] A number of unresolvable puzzles surround Simon. Cyrene is in North Africa, and thus he must be regarded as, at best, a diaspora Jew, possibly in Jerusalem for Passover. But if this were indeed the eve of Passover, what was he doing in the fields? For a discussion of these issues, see the brief but accurate remarks of Nineham, *St. Mark,* 422; Pesch, *Markusevangelium,* 2:477; and the detailed treatment of Brown, *Death,* 2:915–16. For a defense of the historicity of Simon and his witness, see Taylor, *St. Mark,* 588; Lohmeyer, *Markus,* 341–42.

[224] See Lagrange (*Saint Marc,* 397–98). We cannot, of course, be sure of that detail. However, they were sufficiently well known to the original recipients of this gospel to be simply alluded to, though they are otherwise unknown. A reference to a "Rufus" is found in Rom 16:13, but the name is too common to insist that the Rufus of Rom 16 and Mark 15 are the same person (but see Taylor,

ing of a passerby to help Jesus with the carrying of the cross, understandable after the flogging and the abuse to which he was subjected,[225] has been turned into a description of the model disciple. Simon of Cyrene is transformed into a true disciple after the flight of the Twelve and the complete abandonment of Jesus (see 14:50–52). He alone carries the cross of Jesus (v. 21c). Perhaps it is not oversubtle to see a double meaning in the words τὸν σταυρὸν αὐτοῦ. Within its immediate context, the expression refers back to Jesus: Simon carries Jesus' cross. However, it can also suggest that he carries his own cross, as Jesus has asked of all disciples (8:34).[226]

Jesus is led to the place of execution, a place called Golgotha, an Aramaic word that Mark renders into Greek for his readers: "the skull-place" (v. 22).[227] Without any indication of a change of subject, the narrator reports that "they" offered him a mixture of wine and myrrh. This is the only hint of compassion on the part of the Romans: they offer a form of drug to deaden some of the excruciating pain associated with being nailed to a cross, dropped into a hole in the ground, and left there in agony until death. The evidence, however, points to this practice as Jewish. Many commentators suggest that women from Jerusalem make this offering to Jesus, following the recommendations of Prov 31:6–7 (see also b. Sanh. 43a). It is strange, however, that this detail is not mentioned, and the third person plural subject "they" dominates the passage. The natural reading of the Markan text is that the Romans were responsible, whatever the prehistory of the episode.[228] Jesus, who has declared his preparedness to accept everything that the will of the Father asks from him (14:36), refuses this chance to avoid his agony.[229] The Gospel has moved steadily toward the moment of Jesus' crucifixion, and the event is described twice, each time in the same two words, expressed in different Greek tenses. In 15:24, the narrator continues to use the historic present tense that has dominated the passage since 15:20b, a technique vividly conveying the tragedy of the event: σταυροῦσιν αὐτόν. In 15:25, looking back upon the description of 15:24 and recalling that it took place at the third hour, he more properly uses the aorist tense to recall the horror of what they did: ἐσταύρωσαν αὐτόν. For all its simplicity, this is dramatic writing.[230]

St. Mark, 588, for the opposite opinion). For a survey of attempts to identify these figures, see Brown, Death, 2:916.

[225] See Brown (Death, 2:914–15), who suggests that this is the reason for the Romans' making an exception to their practice that the condemned man carried at least the cross beam (the patibulum). The upright was often already at the place of crucifixion; see Gnilka, Markus, 2:315.

[226] Grundmann, Markus, 313; Cranfield, St. Mark, 455; Schweizer, Mark, 343; Lührmann, Markusevangelium, 259; Senior, Passion, 116; Malbon, "Minor Characters," 203. This position is developed in B. K. Blount, "A Socio-Rhetorical Analysis of Simon of Cyrene: Mark 15:21 and Its Parallels," Sem 64 (1993): 173–80. The suggestion is rejected, among others, by Anderson, Mark, 340.

[227] Most agree that the place received its name from its shape; see Brown, Death, 2:937.

[228] For the suggestion that women from Jerusalem are responsible, see Lagrange, Saint Marc, 399; Nineham, St. Mark, 423; Lohmeyer, Markus, 342; Lane, Mark, 564; Anderson, Mark, 341; Hooker, St. Mark, 372–73.

[229] For the details of the practice, and the above interpretation of the passage, see Grundmann, Markus, 313; Brown, Death, 2:941–42; Gnilka, Markus, 2:316. Cranfield (St. Mark, 455) and LaVerdiere (The Beginning, 2:291) suggest that Jesus' words at the supper, that he would not drink wine until he drank it new in the kingdom (14:25), may be involved here. It has also been suggested that there may be a veiled reference to Ps 69:22 (so Schweizer, Mark, 344; Painter, Mark's Gospel, 203), but see the discussion in Pesch, Markusevangelium, 2:478 rejecting any link with the psalm.

[230] It is, however, one of the indications (along with the repeated insults of vv. 26–32) used by many to trace two editions of the passion narrative which have been combined, thus producing these repetitions. For a summary, see Gnilka, Markus, 2:310–11. Lohmeyer (Markus, 342–43), commenting on the verbs, remarks: "It is as if the crucifixion were an ever-present action."

The event is accompanied by another practice common among Roman soldiers: they divide his garments by casting lots to decide what each would take.[231] Subtly, Mark associates the vivid, rapid description of the physical crucifixion of Jesus in 15:24a and 15:25b with a passage from the Old Testament in 15:24b. The major part of the narrator's description of the soldiers' behavior makes extensive use of Ps 22:19.[232] Dramatic tragedy the crucifixion might be, but it fulfills scripture and is thus part of God's design. Allusions to the righteous sufferer permeate the passion narrative, and Ps 22 is an important element in the biblical tradition that portrays this figure.[233] Mark will further exploit the possibilities of Ps 22 as Jesus dies (15:34). By indicating that the crucifixion took place "at the third hour," Mark begins his careful setting of the time periods that will highlight Jesus' agony. In 15:33, darkness will descend upon the whole land "at the sixth hour," and in 15:34 a section begins in which Jesus will cry out to God and die "at the ninth hour." This steady passing of three sets of three hours indicates that none of these events is mere chance, something that fatalistically fell upon Jesus. Jesus' crucifixion at the third hour (v. 25), the apocalyptic signs which surrounded his agony at the sixth hour (v. 33), and his death at the ninth hour (v. 34) show "how carefully God took care of the events surrounding the death of the Son."[234]

This simple but eloquent description of Jesus' crucifixion by the Romans "at the third hour," fulfilling the Scriptures, forms the centerpiece of 15:1–47. The fifth of nine scenes, it is not only the culmination of much that has been anticipated by the Gospel as a whole, but 15:1–20a has also prepared particularly for it, and the events and words reported in 15:26–47 depend upon it. The brutal starkness of the scene is imposing.[235] No one speaks as the Roman soldiers lead Jesus out to crucify him and systematically go about their gruesome task. The steady use of the historic present adds immediacy to the narrator's report. The silence, so much in contrast with the scenes that surround the passage, where chatter

---

[231] Lagrange, *Saint Marc*, 400; Taylor, *St. Mark*, 589.

[232] The use of the psalm is obvious, but rather haphazard. Mark's direct borrowing from the psalm is underlined: LXX 22:19: <u>διεμερίσαντο τὰ ἱμάτιά</u> μου ἑαυτοῖς καὶ ἐπὶ τὸν ἱματισμόν μου <u>ἔβαλον κλῆρον</u>. The places where he diverges can be explained by the Markan context. Only John 19:24 cites the LXX of the psalm as an explicit fulfillment of scripture, while the Synoptics use it rather loosely within their particular context, without any claim that the action of the soldiers fulfills scripture (Matt 27:35; Luke 23:34). See the discussion in Moo, *Old Testament*, 252–57; Brown, *Death*, 2:953–54. There is no need to resort to the theory that Mark may have been using a translation of a Semitic *Textvorlage;* Gnilka, *Markus*, 2:316–17. The strong presence of Ps 22 in Mark 14–15 has led some to suggest that it provided the basis for the original pre-Markan passion narrative. See the survey of this discussion in Matera, *Kingship*, 127–29.

[233] Grundmann, *Markus*, 312–13.

[234] Brown, *Death*, 2:960. See also Gnilka, *Markus*, 2:317; Hooker, *St. Mark*, 373. A number of literary and historical questions emerge from these "hours." Is it possible to harmonize the hours mentioned by Mark and John (cf. John 19:14, where Jesus stands before Pilate "at the sixth hour")? See the summary of attempts to do so in Brown, *Death*, 1:959. Each evangelist must be allowed to go his own way, and harmonization proves to be impossible. Lane (*Mark*, 566–67), whose excellent commentary defends the historicity of most events reported in the Gospel, must uncharacteristically suggest that "at the third hour" is a gloss. It is more likely that the Johannine timing, which would have Jesus hung on the cross in the early afternoon, is preferable to Mark's "third hour," which would see Jesus already crucified at 9:00 AM. It is sometimes suggested that the Markan use of "the third hour" comes from the early Christian practice of praying three times in the day (*Did.* 8:3; see Nineham, *St. Mark*, 424; Anderson, *Mark*, 342; LaVerdiere, *The Beginning*, 2:292). This, however, is speculative, as LaVerdiere's note admits.

[235] It is perhaps this starkness which has led many to the surprising conclusion that "these verses lack the sort of unity which may be expected" (Cranfield, *St. Mark*, 453).

and insult can be found (vv. 16–20a, 26–32), highlights the fact that Jesus is alone as he submits to the actions of the Roman soldiers. The only ray of light comes from the allusion to Ps 22:19, and the first indication that this took place "at the third hour." These hints promise the reader that, in a mysterious way, God's design is being worked out in this brutal murder (cf. 10:45; 14:36).

[A] Passersby and the Jewish leaders ironically proclaim the truth as they mock Jesus (15:26–32)

Elements in 15:26–32 indicate that the section, in its canonical shape,[236] is intended as a literary unit, dedicated to the proclamation of the crucified Jesus as king, savior, and Christ. The passage opens with the kingship of Jesus proclaimed in the title on the cross (v. 26) and the information that two robbers were crucified on either side of Jesus (v. 27).[237] It closes with a development of v. 26 in the final proclamation that Jesus is the Christ, the king of Israel (v. 32a), and a remark from the narrator that the two robbers joined in the abuse of Jesus (v. 32b). Between the frame of vv. 26–27 and 32 passersby recall the sayings about the construction of a new temple of God (v. 29) and demand that Jesus show his authority by *coming down from the cross* (v. 30). The Jewish leaders acknowledge Jesus' saving presence among others, but answer the request of the passersby by telling them that he cannot save himself (v. 31). They will see and believe in Jesus' claim to be the Christ and the king of Israel (see 14:61–62a; 15:2) only if he *comes down from the cross* (v. 31a). The literary form of 15:26–32 is markedly different from the somber, wordless reporting of the crucifixion of Jesus in 15:20b–25 and the description of the death of Jesus in 15:33–39. "The terse understatement of the crucifixion scene gives way to a cascade of abuse."[238]

The Roman practice of placing a sign upon the instrument of execution, indicating the reason for the death sentence, lies behind 15:26.[239] We cannot be certain about the exact words of what was most likely a crude indication of Jesus' crime, but the Romans repeat the confession that Pilate extracted from Jesus in 15:2 in the inscription, "the King of the Jews."[240] The ambiguity of the ironic proclamation of the truth in 15:2 (cf. 15:9, 12) is repeated in 15:26. As far as the Roman executioners are concerned, this is a political pretender, executed by the ruling authority for making unacceptable political claims.[241] As far as the reader is concerned, however, Jesus' royalty is being exercised now that he has been crucified. Unlike any other king, Jesus is King of the Jews in his annihilation. The narrator adds that two "robbers" (δύο λῃστάς) were also crucified, one on either side. Jesus had

---

[236] As always, there are suggestions concerning the pre-Markan tradition behind vv. 26–32, and the Markan editing of it; see Nineham, *St. Mark,* 425; Schweizer, *Mark,* 348–49; Anderson, *Mark,* 343; and the survey in Pesch, *Markusevangelium,* 2:482.

[237] Brown (*Death,* 2:968) claims that the use of the historic present here, "and with him they crucify two bandits," forms an inclusion with the similar use of the historic present in v. 24, "and they crucify him." But what of the inclusion between v. 27 and v. 32b?

[238] Senior, *Passion,* 117.

[239] It was not always practiced, but done sometimes to discourage the general public from performing similar crimes; see Brown, *Death,* 2:963. On the sign on the cross as "solid historical fact," see Lane, *Mark,* 567–68. But on the difficulty of exactly establishing the inscription, see Pesch, *Markusevangelium,* 2:485.

[240] For a study of the possible historical background to the events reported at the cross, see Brown, *Death,* 2:1026–29.

[241] Lagrange (*Saint Marc,* 401) remarks: "Pilate knew the Jews but not Israel."

protested at his arrest that his opponents were dealing with him as if he were a ληστής (14:38), and now he is crucified among them.[242] The indication of the location of the two malefactors, "one on his right and one on his left," repeats the request of the sons of Zebedee, who sought positions of authority as Jesus and his entourage journeyed toward Jerusalem (10:37).[243] They believed they were following the one who would restore Israel's royal splendor, but Jesus instructed them that he was able to offer them only a share in his suffering (10:39). Positions on either side of Jesus in Jerusalem are not positions of power, but a sharing in his suffering.

Passersby, newcomers to the rejection of Jesus, call out insults, but the description of their approach to Jesus recalls Ps 22. Their words come from the psalms of lament (v. 29a), and their charge against Jesus recalls the theme of the new temple (v. 29b). The taunting gesture of wagging the head recalls Ps 22:7: "All who see me mock at me, they make mouths at me, they wag their heads," and the derisive expression "Aha" echoes the lament Ps 35:21: "They open wide their mouths against me; they say, 'Aha! Aha! Our eyes have seen it' " (see also Pss 40:15; 70:4). Jesus, the righteous and innocent sufferer, is ironically recognized as the abuse is mouthed (v. 29a).[244] The irony continues as they take up the false accusation brought against Jesus during the Jewish hearing (14:58): "You who would destroy the temple and build it in three days" (15:29b). Here, however, it is not an accusation, but a statement of what the reader knows to be true. Jesus never made the claims his false accusers leveled against him in 14:58. But he had spoken, on the occasion of his bringing the temple cult to an end, of a new way to God by faith, prayer, and forgiveness (see 11:22–25). He developed this theme further in his angry encounter with the Jewish leaders, telling them of the wondrous act of God that would be a new temple built upon the rejected cornerstone (12:10–11). He also predicted the end of Jerusalem and its temple, but instructed his disciples that this was not the end. They were to take the gospel to all nations (13:5–23; see v. 10). The reader is aware that there is a new temple, constructed upon the foundation of the crucified and risen Christ. The believing reader forms part of that new temple and thus is aware that everything the passersby say is true: Jesus is the innocent righteous sufferer, and despite the fact that the Romans have destroyed Jerusalem and its temple, he has constructed a new temple in three days.

Ironically, the only mistake the passersby make is to ask Jesus to save himself by coming down from the cross. Again Ps 22 forms the background for the narrative: "He hoped in the Lord, let him deliver him; let him save him because he wants him" (v. 9; cf. Wis

---

[242] Brown, *Death,* 2:969. One is tempted to make a link with Barabbas, via the word ληστής, which can mean both "robber" and "revolutionary"; see, for example, Lohmeyer, *Markus,* 343; Senior, *Passion,* 118. This is not called for, however, as Barabbas (unlike John 18:40, where the identity of Barabbas as a ληστής is important), is connected with insurrection via the term στασιαστής (see 15:7). As the interpretation of v. 32b will indicate, the significance of the two criminals does not lie in their being revolutionaries, but malefactors who reject Jesus. Early scribes (Greek, Latin, and Syriac) attempted to make a link between this scene and Isa 53:12 by inserting v. 28: "And the scripture was fulfilled which says, he was reckoned with the transgressors." The evidence is late and the style un-Markan; see Lagrange, *Saint Marc,* 401–2.

[243] See also Painter (*Mark's Gospel,* 204), who questions this suggestion because of the different words for "left" in each instance, and the fact that the malefactors insult Jesus. But see Senior, *Passion,* 118, and LaVerdiere, *The Beginning,* 2:293. The broader context, especially the return of the two malefactors in v. 32b, support the above interpretation. On v. 32b, see below.

[244] Brown, *Death,* 2:988–99. A number of commentators also trace Lam 2:15 as the reference to the passersby; see, e.g., Grundmann, *Markus,* 314; Pesch, *Markusevangelium,* 2:486; Hooker, *St. Mark,* 375. For a contrary view, see Cranfield, *St. Mark,* 456.

2:17–18).[245] The reader knows that it is only *on the cross* that Jesus is able to respond to the design of God, and Ps 22:9 expresses the hope that God will deliver Jesus. He will not *save himself.* Jesus' earlier words to the disciples act as intertext: "Whoever wishes to save his life will lose it, and whoever loses his life for my sake and the gospel's will save it" (8:35). The reader is aware that the mistake of the passersby is fundamental. The request that Jesus save his own life and come down from the cross is totally alien to the logic of the Gospel of Mark. It is *on the cross* that Jesus is the innocent righteous sufferer, the one who will build a new temple in three days. The identical mistake will be made by the Jewish leaders (v. 32a).

Further abuse is heaped upon Jesus (ἐμπαίζοντες) by the Jewish leaders, the chief priests who chatter among themselves and with the scribes (v. 31a).[246] They have never been far from center stage (see 8:31; 10:33; 11:18, 27; 14:1, 10, 43, 53, 55; 15:10–11), and theirs is the last voice raised in ironic insult. Their first reported comment is to respond to the request of the passersby, that Jesus save himself (see v. 30). They unwittingly condemn themselves as they admit that Jesus has indeed saved others (v. 31b). This remark looks back across the story of Jesus reported in the Gospel and recalls Jesus' saving actions: his releasing of those possessed by demons (1:21–28; 5:1–20; 7:24–30; 9:14–29, and the summaries in 1:32–34; 3:11–12; see also 3:20–27), his healing miracles (1:29–31, 40–45; 2:1–12; 3:1–6; 5:24b–34; 7:31–37; 8:22–26; 10:46–52, and the summaries in 1:31–34; 3:10; 6:2, 53–56), and his raising from death itself (5:21–24a, 35–43). The verb σῴζειν has been connected explicitly with these actions of Jesus in 5:23, 28; 6:56, and 10:52.[247] Implicitly, the words of the Jewish leaders, "He saved others," accept that Jesus has done these deeds *for others.* But, they tell the passersby, "He cannot save himself" (v. 31b). They continue to misread the agenda of Jesus, as it is reported in the Gospel. "For the Son of Man came, not to be served, but to serve, and to give his life as a ransom for many" (10:45). As we have seen, the same theme was central to the Markan presentation of Jesus' final meal with his disciples (14:22–25).[248] In his unconditional response to the will of God (see 14:36), who is well pleased with his beloved Son (see 1:11; 9:7), he gives himself *for others,* and not *for himself.* Again, there is a sense in which the Jewish leaders ironically proclaim the truth: *he cannot* save himself, as this would be contrary to what the Father asks of his Son.[249]

During the Jewish hearing Jesus was condemned for acknowledging that he was the Christ, the Son of the Blessed (see 14:61–62a), and during the Roman trial he was questioned on his claim to be king.[250] Now crucified, those responsible for the Roman action

---

[245] Brown, *Death,* 2:994–95. On the chain of allusions to Ps 22 across vv. 29–31, see Moo, *The Old Testament,* 257–60.

[246] There is a sense of an accumulation of insult generated by the use of different verbs for the abuse of the passersby (ἐβλασφήμουν) and the Jewish leaders (ἐμπαίζοντες). This piling up of verbs will continue into v. 32b. For Gnilka (*Markus,* 2:320), the talking among themselves is a sign of their distance from Jesus. For similar sentiments, see Lagrange, *Saint Marc,* 402: "They maintain their distance, grumbling among themselves." Lane (*Mark,* 569) suggests that, after all they have done to bring about Jesus' death, they are now congratulating themselves. The historicity of Jewish leaders at the execution, and the originality of vv. 31–32a, are often questioned. See, for example, Hooker, *St. Mark,* 374, and the summary of earlier discussion in Taylor, *St. Mark,* 591–92.

[247] As Senior (*Passion,* 120) comments, these words are "an ironic distillation of Jesus' entire mission." See also LaVerdiere, *The Beginning,* 2:295–96.

[248] See above, pp. 285–87.

[249] On this double-meaning of οὐ δύναται, see Cranfield, *St. Mark,* 457. On suffering and the will of God in Mark, see Dowd, *Prayer,* 133–36.

[250] As Brown (*Death,* 2:987–88) points out, the two charges leveled against Jesus at the Jewish hearing (temple and Christ) have returned.

(15:10–11) proclaimed him the Christ and king of Israel. There is a subtle blend of both the Jewish and Roman trials in the final ironic mockery.[251] The Jewish leaders state the truth as they mockingly salute Jesus as "the Christ, the King of Israel."[252] Pilate questioned Jesus about his being "King of the Jews" (v. 2), and he presented Jesus to the crowd as "King of the Jews" (vv. 9, 12). The sign on the cross repeats this title (v. 26). There is an ambiguity in it, resolved in the ironic confession of faith by the Jewish leaders. Placed in apposition with "the Christ," the title "the King of Israel" associates Jesus with the religious hopes of the nation, and not just with a possible royal figure who might restore the political freedom of the Jews.[253] Fastened securely to the cross, in the midst of abuse, Jesus is proclaimed Christ and king of Israel. Repeating the mistake of the passersby, the Jewish leaders lay down a condition. If he performs a wonderful miracle and saves himself by *coming down from the cross,* then they will see for themselves that he is the Christ, the king of Israel, and they will believe. The request is at cross-purposes with the theological agenda of the Gospel: Jesus is the Christ and the king of Israel *on the cross.* It is as the crucified one that the Son responds to the design of the Father. The only place where anyone, including the Jewish leaders, can "see" the Christ, the king of Israel, is *on the cross.*

The irony of the Jewish leaders' claim that they will see and believe if Jesus comes down from the cross runs deep.[254] The theme of blindness was first struck in 8:18, when Jesus asked the disciples if it was blindness that rendered them incapable of understanding the meaning of the bread miracles. It was continued in the two miracles which opened and closed the central section of the Gospel: the blind man at Bethsaida (8:22–26), and blind Bartimaeus (10:46–52). The theme of the partial sight of the disciples emerged at Caesarea Philippi (8:27–30), and continued across 8:31–10:45. The disciples have now abandoned Jesus (14:50–52), and in their place we find the Jewish leaders who ask that Jesus come down from the cross that they might see and believe. Like the disciples, they have their understanding of who the Messiah and king of Israel must be and what he must do. Only when Jesus corresponds to *their expectations* will they see and believe. They continue to adopt the stance they took over against Jesus in 8:11–12, seeking from him a sign from heaven.[255] But they are profoundly mistaken. Jesus, Messiah and king of Israel, must be seen and believed as he hangs on the cross.[256]

The narrator closes the abuse scene deftly by circling back to its beginning: the two malefactors who were crucified, one on the right and one on the left of Jesus (v. 32b; see v. 27). Even those executed with him reject him.[257] There is irony, however, in the apparently laconic remark: "Those who were crucified with him also reviled him" (v. 32b). Jesus asked his disciples to take up their cross (8:34–35) and told them that the only glory he could offer them was a sharing in his experience of the cross (10:38–40). Ironically, the two

---

[251] See Brown's discussion in *Death,* 2:992–93.

[252] There are no conditions, as in Matt 27:40: "If you are the Son of God," and Luke 23:35b: "If he is the Christ of God, his Chosen One." It is an ironic statement of fact: Jesus is the Christ, the king of Israel.

[253] Senior, *Passion,* 120–21.

[254] Lohmeyer, *Markus,* 344; C. D. Marshall, *Faith as a Theme in Mark's Narrative* (SNTSMS 64; Cambridge: Cambridge University Press, 1989), 200–208.

[255] Hooker, *St. Mark,* 374.

[256] On the Markan transformation of the Jewish tradition of Christ and Son of God, see Broadhead, *Naming Jesus,* 145–54 (the Christ), and 116–23 (Son of God).

[257] This may be a further allusion to Ps 22: "All who see me mock at me" (v. 7); see Senior, *Passion,* 121; Brown, *Death,* 2:999. Gnilka (*Markus,* 2:321) remarks: "Even the criminals whose fate Jesus has taken upon himself do not spare him."

robbers are in privileged positions, one on the left and one on the right (v. 27), "crucified with Jesus" (v. 32b).[258] But they reject this privilege and join the passersby and the Jewish leaders in heaping abuse upon him.[259] The readers, also in a situation of persecution, failure, and suffering (13:9–13), are challenged by these two figures, one at the right and the other at the left of Jesus. They too have the positions asked for by the sons of Zebedee (10:37). Are they willing to understand and accept their sharing in the cross of Jesus Christ? Are they able to drink the cup and be baptized with the baptism with which Jesus is baptized (10:38)? Or will they join "those who were crucified with him" at the skull-place, rejecting Jesus, along with his other opponents (v. 32b)?

[B] The death of Jesus, proclaimed Son of God (15:33–39)

The second reference to time, "and when the sixth hour had come" (15:33), introduces the dramatic and densely theological report of the three hours that lead to the death of Jesus "at the ninth hour" (15:34). It closes with the confession of the Roman centurion, "seeing" Jesus breathing his last breath: "Truly this man was the Son of God" (15:39).[260]

The period between the sixth hour (midday) and the ninth hour (three o'clock in the afternoon) is marked by "darkness over the whole land." This detail, introduced as a deliberate allusion to Amos 8:9, focuses upon the eschatological nature of the events reported. The original setting of the prophecy was already eschatological, introduced by the formula "on that day," widely used across the prophetic traditions to indicate God's final and decisive intervention into human affairs. The death of Jesus is not just any death. The reader is aware that the moment of God's definitive intervention into the human story has arrived.[261] "Mark sees this day as a climactic day for all peoples and the whole earth."[262] The

---

[258] I agree with Taylor (*St. Mark*, 592): "συνσταυροῦμαι is manifestly not used in its Pauline sense (Rom vi. 6, Gal ii. 20) of being crucified with Christ." This does not exclude the possibility that there is an allusion to earlier Markan teaching on the relationship between discipleship and the cross. See also Schweizer, *Mark*, 351; LaVerdiere, *The Beginning*, 2:296.

[259] Yet another verb is added to the list of words for abuse: ὠνείδιζον αὐτόν. On the importance of these three words to indicate abuse, see Painter, *Mark's Gospel*, 205. All verbs come from the vocabulary of abuse directed at the righteous sufferer; see Pesch, *Markusevangelium*, 2:486 (v. 29), 487 (v. 31), 489 (v. 32b).

[260] There are a number of theories concerning the history of the composition behind vv. 33–39; see Brown, *Death*, 2:1083–88. Again there is no agreement on the literary unity of the passage in its present form. Some would bring the scene to a close at Jesus' death in v. 37; e.g., Lohmeyer, *Markus*, 344–45; Brown, *Death*, 2:1032–33. Many add vv. 40–41 as a form of conclusion; e.g., Nineham, *St. Mark*, 426; Lane, *Mark*, 570–71; Senior, *Passion*, 131–32; Hooker, *St. Mark*, 374–75; Painter, *Mark's Gospel*, 206–8; LaVerdiere, *The Beginning*, 2:296–98. The centurion's confession, and his sight of Jesus' expiring, links vv. 38–39 to vv. 33–37. The leapfrog use of the women in vv. 40–41, 47, 16:1 suggests that their role as characters in the narrative calls for its own focus. See also Schweizer, *Mark*, 351–52; Pesch, *Markusevangelium*, 2:491–92; Anderson, *Mark*, 344–45.

[261] There is little point in trying to establish what physical phenomena might have created three hours of darkness from midday until 3:00 PM (but see Lagrange, *Saint Marc*, 403–4; Taylor, *St. Mark*, 593; Cranfield, *St. Mark*, 457–58). It is true that the deaths of other notables in antiquity have been marked by similar phenomena; see Grundmann, *Markus*, 315; Pesch, *Markusevangelium*, 2:493–94; Gnilka, *Markus*, 2:321. But for Mark the obvious allusion to Amos 8:9 provides the eschatological meaning of the darkness: "On that day" says the Lord God, "I will make the sun go down at noon, and darken the earth in broad daylight." Brown (*Death*, 2:1035–36) extends the allusion to Amos further, tracing the theme of darkness in Gen 1:2–3; Exod 10:21–23; Jer 15:9; 33:19–21; Wis 5:6; Zeph 1:15; Joel 2:2; 3:4. See also Lane, *Mark*, 571–72.

[262] Brown (*Death*, 2:1036), claiming that ἐφ' ὅλην τὴν γῆν should be given its theologically universal meaning, rather than what was astronomically possible.

events that follow in rapid succession from 15:34–39, "at the ninth hour" (v. 34a), take place in this eschatological darkness. The first of those events are the reported words of Jesus, crying out with a loud voice the opening words of Ps 22 in Aramaic, which the evangelist translates into Greek as "My God, my God, why have you forsaken me" (15:34b; cf. Ps 22:1).[263] The use of Ps 22, the lament par excellence of the righteous sufferer which has dominated the Markan passion account (see 14:17; 15:24, 29, 30–31), reaches its climax and high point in these final words of Jesus in the Gospel.[264]

Christian reflection has long struggled with the suggestion that Jesus' final words on the cross could have been words of such dereliction, made even more dramatic by the loud scream as he dies, deliberately reprising his earlier loud crying out (v. 37; cf. v. 34). There have been numerous attempts to overcome this scandal. Many have argued that Jesus' citation of the first verse of Ps 22 is an implicit citation of the complete psalm.[265] Thus it would include the psalm's later expression of confidence and thanksgiving for the saving action of God and the universal proclamation of God's eschatological dominion (vv. 23–32).[266] The sense of abandonment, and the intensity of the question that Jesus asks in death, must be maintained to capture fully the Markan presentation of the crucified Christ. It must not be softened or sidestepped in any way.[267] The Gospel has steadily affirmed that Jesus is the Son of God (1:1, 11; 9:7; 14:61b–62).[268] The cry from the cross is final confirmation that only as the crucified savior, Christ and king of Israel (15:30, 31, 32), Jesus reveals himself to be the Son of God. There can be no easing of that theological agenda, which has been building

---

[263] On the transliteration of the Aramaic, the translation, and textual difficulties that this process has produced, see Brown, *Death*, 2:1051–58.

[264] Some suggest that the use of the Aramaic may reflect Mark's use of a primitive passion source, still in Aramaic, which was already based upon Ps 22. See, for this possibility, Senior, *Passion*, 123. Against this, however, is the misunderstanding of the Aramaic by the bystanders in v. 36. This presupposes that the whole scene is constructed in Greek, as the confusion involved in the play upon ελωι and Ἠλία would hardly take place in a Semitic context; see Hooker, *St. Mark*, 376; Brown, *Death*, 2:1061–63, esp. p. 1062 n. 86.

[265] E.g., Gnilka, *Markus*, 2:322; LaVerdiere, *The Beginning*, 2:301–3.

[266] Matera, *Kingship*, 132–35. Senior (*Passion*, 123–24) asserts: "There can be no question that these words are an expression of *faith*, not despair or bitterness. The opening line of the Psalm should not be separated from its context of prayer." But Senior wants it both ways. He goes on to say: "At the same time, however, the fact that Mark makes Jesus' last words a *lament* must not be downplayed" (p. 124; stress in original). See also Pesch, *Markusevangelium*, 2:494–95. I agree that this is not "bitterness" but neither is it, as Senior claims, an "affirmation of his unbroken trust in his Father," with reference to Gethsemane (p. 124). Jesus' final cry is not a *parallel* with 14:36, but the *consequence* of 14:36. In support of the interpretation adopted above, see Brown, *Death*, 2:1045–47. See further pp. 1047–51, for a survey of attempts to adopt a kinder understanding of Jesus' cry. Brown concludes: "I find no persuasive argument against attributing to the Jesus of Mark/Matt the literal sentiment of feeling forsaken expressed in the psalm quote" (p. 1051). See also Lohmeyer, *Markus*, 345 (who also stresses that even in his sense of having been abandoned, he addresses God as "my" God); Taylor, *St. Mark*, 594; Lane, *Mark*, 572–74; Hooker, *St. Mark*, 375; Garrett, *The Temptation*, 130–33.

[267] The temptation to soften Jesus' final utterance parallels the requests of the passersby and the Jewish leaders that Jesus *come down from the cross* that they might see and believe (15:30, 32)!

[268] Affirmation of Jesus' sonship has come from the most authoritative voices in the narrative: the narrator (1:1), God (1:11; 9:7), and Jesus himself (14:61b–62). There are also the well-known admissions of his sonship from the demonic world (see 1:24, 34; 3:11; 5:7). These subtly communicate the truth to the reader. The demons attempt to overcome Jesus by using his correct name, as the reader recognizes. But Jesus' authority transcends this culturally conditioned agenda. Lührmann (*Markusevangelium*, 263) suggests that Jesus' calling upon Elijah reminds the reader of the transfiguration (9:2–7), where Elijah was present to Jesus, the Son of God (v. 7).

since Jesus' first indication that the bridegroom would be taken away (2:20) and the first plotting to destroy Jesus (3:6). Although not explicit in the text, the reader is aware that it is as "Son" that Jesus cries out "my God."[269] This leads to a further important feature in the logic of the Markan narrative. Jesus' question leads the reader to wonder: if this is the way God deals with his Son, what kind of God is this? The answer to that question will not be found within the passion narrative. The mystery of the crucified Christ, king of Israel and Son of God, will be resolved as the centurion makes his confession of faith (15:39), but the question Jesus poses to God in 15:34 leads into the telling of the action of God in 16:1–8. There, although never explicitly mentioned, God is the main protagonist.

Jesus' cry to God is completely misunderstood. Hearing ελωι on the lips of Jesus, some of the bystanders, unable to accept that Jesus may be addressing himself to God, claim he is crying to Elijah, the traditional Jewish figure who comes to the help of those beyond all help (v. 35).[270] An unnamed individual (v. 36a) runs, fills a sponge full of vinegar, puts it on a reed to give Jesus something to drink, and comments: "Wait, let us see whether Elijah will come to take him down" (v. 36b).[271] The profound misunderstanding of who Jesus is, and what God is doing in this eschatological event, continues. Jesus' focus is entirely upon God, however desperate his cry (v. 34). The attending figure does not listen to what Jesus says (v. 34), but only to the interpretation of some of the bystanders (v. 35). In what is possibly the final use of a psalm of lament (Ps 69:22), he attempts to rouse the dying man from his last moments by offering him a pungent drink of vinegary wine (ὄξος).[272] His gesture and words suggest that with some help Jesus may remain alive and Elijah might still come to Jesus' aid by taking him down from the cross.

The bystanders and this individual have understood neither the signs that surround Jesus' last moments, nor his use of Ps 22:1. As Jesus cried out ελωι, ελωι, they understood him to be crying out for help from Ἠλίας. The apocalyptic and eschatological context created by the three-hour long darkness over the whole land (vv. 33–34a), and Jesus' cry to

---

[269] The accumulation of information about Jesus is so rich at this stage of the narrative, that the reader needs no prompting by means of an explicit reference to Jesus as "Son" to recognize that it is as "Son" that he cries out to God. The fact that he does not use the expression "Father" as he did in Gethsemane (14:36; cf. 8:38; 13:32) is determined by the use of Ps 22:1; see also Brown, *Death*, 2:1046–47.

[270] See the beginnings of this tradition in 1 Kgs 17:1–24, and its later development in *b. Ber.* 58a; *b. Abod. Zar.* 17b, 18b; *Esth. Rab.* 10.9. See also Brown, *Death*, 2:1062–63. Brown rightly highlights the irony of the statement, as Elijah is not only the help of the helpless, but also figures largely in many eschatological scenarios—but here, "Ironically, while Elijah will not intervene on Jesus' side, soon God will, and in a very visible way that all will see" (p. 1063). Matera (*Kingship*, 122–25) attempts to construe the misinterpretation as ironically royal. The evidence hardly supports this case.

[271] Commentators discuss whether the unnamed figure is a Roman soldier or a Jew. In the light of the Elijah speculation, the latter is to be preferred, however unlikely it is that the Romans would allow such movement around a crucified criminal; see Cranfield, *St. Mark*, 459; Pesch, *Markusevangelium*, 2:496; Brown, *Death*, 2:1064. Taylor (*St. Mark*, 594–96) resolves the problem by having the wine offered by a Roman and the words spoken by a Jew. This is an unlikely reading of v. 36. Nineham (*St. Mark*, 429) suggests that v. 36a and v. 36b may come from two separate pre-Markan traditions. See also Anderson, *Mark*, 346–47.

[272] Different from the οἶνος of v. 23, the low quality red wine ὄξος is closer to vinegar than wine; see Lane, *Mark*, 573–74; Brown, *Death*, 1059 n. 79. An allusion to Ps 69:22 is not certain. The close proximity of Ps 22:1 (v. 34), despite the lack of verbal and contextual contact between Mark and Ps 69:22 ("And they gave for my bread gall and for my thirst they gave me to drink vinegar"), suggests that this psalm of lament from the righteous sufferer may be allusively present in Mark 15:36. See the discussion in Brown, *Death*, 2:1058–60.

God (v. 34b), have been trivialized. The actions of the unnamed bystander, and the understanding by a number of people of Jesus' words as a plea to Elijah to save him in his hour of desperation, express the belief that Jesus has claim to acceptance only if he *comes down from the cross* (v. 36b). As with the Jewish leaders, the bystander wants to "see" if Elijah will resolve Jesus' situation as the crucified (v. 36b; cf. vv. 30, 32).[273] He may be beyond "saving himself" (vv. 30–31), as death is obviously at hand, but maybe Elijah will come and *take him down from the cross,* and that "sight" will resolve doubts about Jesus (v. 36b). At this point in the story, those present at his death have ignored or completely misunderstood Jesus' turning to God (v. 34) and the importance of his being *on the cross* (vv. 30, 32).[274] There is further irony for the reader, however. Elijah may be the patron of hopeless cases in Jewish thought, but Jesus has already told Peter, James, and John that John the Baptist was Elijah, the prophet of the end time. "His (John the Baptist's) rejection, imprisonment and violent death had pointed the way to the destiny of the Son of Man."[275]

The report of Jesus' death is stark: "And Jesus uttered a loud cry (φωνὴν μεγάλην) and breathed his last (ἐξέπνευσεν)" (v. 37). The link with Jesus' earlier loud cry (v. 34: φωνῇ μεγάλη) is clear, and this wordless scream is Mark's final and dramatic statement on the crucifixion.[276] In the Gospel of Mark, Jesus of Nazareth, the Christ, the king of Israel and Son of God (14:61a–62; 15:2, 9, 12, 26, 32), dies on a cross, abandoned by his disciples (14:50), alone, in agony, with a terrible question on his lips (15:34, 37). "No New Testament text more boldly expresses the reality of Jesus' humanity or the manner of his dying."[277] *Immediately following* the death of Jesus, two events take place which indicate the beginning of a new era. The eschatological nature of the death of Jesus, symbolized by the darkness over the whole land between the sixth and the ninth hour, becomes clear. As he dies the separation between the inner Sanctuary, once the preserve only of the priestly cast of Israel, is torn from top to bottom (v. 38), and a Gentile, the Roman centurion, confesses: "Truly this man was the Son of God" (v. 39). The death of Jesus marks the turning point of the ages.

God enters the story in the tearing apart of the curtain of the temple which "was rent apart" (ἐσχίσθη, v. 38). At the beginning of the story the heavens were rent apart (σχιζομένους, 1:10) to allow the Spirit of God to descend while the voice of God declared, "You are my beloved Son." Now, at Jesus' death, the veil of the sanctuary is rent asunder, and it will lead to the centurion's confession: "Truly this man was the Son of God" (15:39).

---

[273] The words ἄφετε ἴδωμεν are to be read as "do let us see," and not as "leave him alone. Let us see." See Taylor, *St. Mark,* 595, against Brown, *Death,* 2:1065.

[274] Senior, *Passion,* 124–25. The words are not spoken in mockery, as some suggest (see, e.g., Lohmeyer, *Markus,* 346; LaVerdiere, *The Beginning,* 2:303–5; and especially Matera, *Kingship,* 29–32), but in profound misunderstanding.

[275] Senior, *Passion,* 125 (parenthesis mine).

[276] The sense of final abandonment and obedient self-gift must not be lost. For some (e.g., Schweizer, *Mark,* 354; Gnilka, *Markus,* 2:323; Pesch, *Markusevangelium,* 2:497–98), the loud cry may be a theological statement from the early church, indicating that Jesus' death was an eschatological judgment. Brown (*Death,* 2:1044–45) develops this argument at length, linking the loud cry with Old Testament and Jewish literature. He makes a strong case for its being related to the eschatological theme of "the final battle with evil." K. Stock ("Das Bekenntnis des Centurio. Mk 15,39 im Rahmen des Markusevangelium," *ZKT* 100 [1978]: 290–94) argues that the cry is a part of Jesus' epiphany as the Son of God. Closely related to this is the claim of Matera (*Kingship,* 137): "The centurion did not make his confession because he saw a man die in utter abandonment, but because the crucified one dies with a messianic cry." See also LaVerdiere, *The Beginning,* 2:308.

[277] Senior, *Passion,* 126.

This is the first indication (but there will be others; see 16:1–8) that God has not forsaken his Son. The reference to "the curtain of the temple" (τὸ καταπέτασμα τοῦ ναοῦ, v. 38a) is vague, and several "curtains" have been suggested.[278] However, the mounting theme of the new temple, replacing the now defunct temple of Jerusalem (11:12–25), whose destruction Jesus has already foretold (13:5–23), constructed upon the rejected cornerstone (see 12:10–11), points to the veil which separated the inner sanctum of the Sanctuary from its outer chambers. The accusation leveled against Jesus by false witnesses, that he would destroy the temple made by human hands and in three days raise up another, not made by human hands (14:58), repeated in the abuse of the passersby as Jesus hung upon the cross (15:29), is ironically fulfilled. Once it was sacred, penetrated only by the High Priest, the privileged representative of the people of Israel, on Yom Kippur. Now the veil hiding the inner sanctum of the temple from public gaze is completely torn apart, and the temple is open to all who might look.[279]

The first "to look" is a Gentile, a Roman centurion. With great care, the centurion is located in the most advantageous position, standing facing the crucified Jesus (v. 39). He "sees" the way Jesus dies.[280] What happens with the Roman centurion is the complete reversal of the expectations of the passersby (vv. 39–30) and the Jewish leaders (31–32a).[281] In statements that rejected the Markan understanding of God's action in and through

---

[278] See, e.g., Lohmeyer, *Markus*, 347; Lane, *Mark*, 575; Donahue, *Are You the Christ?* 201–3; and the survey of earlier scholars in Taylor, *St. Mark*, 596. They suggest the outer veil, hung over the doors by Herod (Josephus, *Ant.* 8.75), whose rending would expose the whole temple to the view of the outsider. For a comprehensive review (and rejection) of the many proposals, especially that of the "outer veil," see Brown, *Death*, 2:1106–13. He insists that τὸ καταπέτασμα refers to the inner veil of the sanctuary. See also the good analysis in Taylor, *St. Mark*, 596, coming to the same conclusion. For subsequent interpretations of the veil (especially in Josephus, *J.W.* 6.293–296 and *b. Yoma* 39b), see Brown, *Death*, 2:1113–18. See also Juel, *Messiah and Temple*, 140–42. Like several other commentators (e.g., Lohmeyer, *Markus*, 347; Pesch, *Markusevangelium*, 2:498; Gnilka, *Markus*, 2:323–24), Juel claims that "final decision about the precise interpretation is perhaps impossible" (p. 142).

[279] For a discussion of the possible "positive" or "negative" interpretations of the veil, see Senior, *Passion*, 126–29. The categories are perhaps unfortunate. It is a negative judgment upon the Jerusalem temple, destroyed by the time this gospel is read and heard. But it is positive insofar as it addresses the universal availability of God, once reserved to a chosen people. For a similar combination of the negative and positive interpretations, see Grundmann, *Markus*, 316; Hooker, *St. Mark*, 377–78; Gnilka, *Markus*, 323–24; Anderson, *Mark*, 347; P. Lamarche, "La Mort du Christ et la voile du temple selon Marc," *NRTh* 106 (1974): 583–99; J. P. Heil, "The Narrative Strategy and Pragmatics of the Temple Theme in Mark," *CBQ* 59 (1997): 76–100; Garrett, *The Temptations*, 119–24. For a "negative" interpretation, see Brown, *Death*, 2:1101–2, who sees the rending of the veil as a sign that God has departed from the Sanctuary. In the time between the death of Jesus and the destruction of Jerusalem, as this gospel is being written, "the building that continued to stand there was not a holy place" (p. 1102). See also Schweizer, *Mark*, 344–45; Juel, *Messiah and Temple*, 141–42; Matera, *Kingship*, 137–40; Lührmann, *Markusevangelium*, 264.

[280] There is an element of verisimilitude in the location and the seeing of the centurion. He is presumably there to witness the execution. This is verified by Pilate's summoning him to see whether Jesus was dead in v. 44; see Taylor, *St. Mark*, 597.

[281] Matera (*Kingship*, 21–34) proposes that Mark has used three mockeries (15:16–20a, 27–32, 35–36) "to build up the passion narrative of chapter 15" (p. 34). On pp. 135–37 he proposes that the confession of the centurion is set in deliberate contrast to the first of these mockeries, also from Roman soldiers (vv. 16–20a). I have suggested that vv. 35–36 are more a profound misunderstanding than a mockery, and that the mockery of 14:65 is neglected in this scheme. Nevertheless, the contrast between the Roman mockery in vv. 16–20a and the Roman confession in v. 39 is worthy of notice. See the interesting structuralist study of these mockeries in Genest, *Le Christ de la Passion*, 123–43.

Jesus crucified, they demanded that the crucified Jesus come down from the cross. The Jewish leaders had gone so far as to say that when they "saw" him come down, then they would "believe" (v. 32b). It is the way Jesus breathes his last (v. 39), crying out to God in loud desperation (v. 34) and screaming in final agony (v. 37), that leads the Roman centurion to make his confession: "Truly this man was the Son of God (υἱὸς θεοῦ ἦν).[282] The Gospel has come full circle. It began with an affirmation from God that Jesus was his beloved Son (1:11), and it closes with a confession from a Gentile that this man is the Son of God (15:39). A new temple is built on the destroyed body of Jesus as privileged access to the old temple comes to an end (v. 38).[283] A Gentile recognizes that the Son of God can be found in the crucified Jesus (v. 39).[284]

One could justifiably claim that the Christology of the Gospel of Mark has received its full articulation.[285] Other minor themes will emerge in the final episodes of the passion

---

[282] The Greek for "Son of God" has no article, yet I have consistently translated it "the Son of God." Many suggestions have been made to explain what might be meant by the anarthrous use of "Son of God" in 15:39. A human being cannot confess "the Son of God" in Mark; it means "a son of god," like other famous human beings; a Roman soldier cannot be expected to confess the religious title "the Son of God." See the summary of these arguments in Brown, *Death,* 2:1146–50, leading to the conclusion, which most share, that "there is no convincing objection to the thesis that the predicate in the confession of the Marcan centurion meant 'the Son of God' in the full sense of the term" (p. 1150). On "the Son of God" as a royal messianic title in Mark, explaining the full meaning of King of the Jews, Christ, and king of Israel, see Kazmierski, *Son of God,* 191–204; Stock, "Das Bekenntnis," 294–98; Matera, *Kingship,* 140–45; Schweizer, *Mark,* 356–59. A number of contemporary scholars link the anarthrous use of υἱὸς θεοῦ in 1:1 and 15:39, suggesting that, despite its Jewish origins, the Gospel appeals to Greco-Roman converts, readers who would have read the title in the light of their awareness that Caesar was called *divi filius.* The title in 1:1 and 15:39 retains its crucial role in the Markan Christology, but appeals to both Jewish and Greco-Roman readers. See T. H. Kim, "The Anarthrous υἱὸς θεοῦ in Mark 15,39," *Bib* 79 (1998): 221–41; A. Y. Collins, "Mark and His Readers: The Son of God among Jews," *HTR* 92 (1999): 393–408; idem, "Mark and His Readers: The Son of God among Greeks and Romans," *HTR* 93 (2000): 85–100; C. A. Evans, "Mark's Incipit and the Priene Calendar Inscription: From Jewish Gospel to Greco-Roman Gospel," *Journal of Greco-Roman Christianity and Judaism* 1 (2000): 67–81.

[283] Malbon, *Narrative Space,* 137–40.

[284] Brown (*Death,* 2:1144–45) strains to argue that the centurion's confession is also associated with his "sight" of the sundered temple veil. To the objection that a soldier at the "skull-place" standing in front of Jesus could not see the tearing of the inner veil of the Sanctuary, he responds that this would not have been a problem for the Markan readers. I suggest that it would, but it also unnecessarily shifts the focus away from the Christology of the crucified Son of God. The link between ἐξέπνευσεν in v. 37 cannot be separated from the οὕτως ἐξέπνευσεν in v. 39 by an association of the centurion's confession with the events described in v. 38. See Lohmeyer, *Markus,* 347–48, and Stock, "Das Bekenntnis," 290–91. A similar objection must be raised against Matera (*Kingship,* 135–37), who concludes, on the basis of his royal interpretation of Jesus' use of Ps 22:1: "The centurion did not make his confession because he saw a man die in utter abandonment, but because the crucified one dies with a messianic cry" (p. 137). See also LaVerdiere, *The Beginning,* 2:308. Senior (*Passion,* 131) links the centurion with the many "outsiders" who have come to faith, while Jesus' disciples, his family, and the Jewish leaders have not. He lists Levi (2:13–14), the Syrophoenician woman (7:24–30), Bartimaeus (10:46–52), the scribe (12:28–34), the widow (12:41–44), and the woman at Bethany (14:3–9). In terms of the narrative, however, they do not play the same crucial role as the Roman centurion; see Stock, "Das Bekenntnis," 298–301.

[285] Thus, Senior (*Passion,* 121) correctly comments: "The death scene is the summit of Mark's narrative, the final resolution of the christological issues apparent throughout the Gospel." See also Nineham, *St. Mark,* 431. For a recent rejection of this, see E. S. Johnson, "Is Mark 15:39 the Key to Markan Christology?" *JSNT* 31 (1987): 3–22. Parallels are often drawn between the Pauline and the Markan presentation of the cross. For the suggestion that Mark is interacting with Pauline thought,

narrative. The women from Galilee will watch (vv. 40–41, 47), and Joseph of Arimathea will take courage, ask for the body of Jesus, and enclose it in a tomb (vv. 42–47). Lesser characters appear to replace the now absent disciples, watching and attending to the crucified Christ. However, two major themes remain frustratingly unresolved. First, is there a future for the disciples of Jesus, to whom the secrets of the kingdom of heaven have been given (4:11), and who have been authorized to share in the ministry of Jesus (3:14–15; 6:7–13)? The journey to Jerusalem has been highlighted by the inability to accept and understand what it means to follow Jesus, but he has never abandoned them (8:31–10:52). The night before he died he told the Twelve of Judas's betrayal, Peter's denials, and their proximate abandonment of their stricken shepherd (14:17–21, 27–31). Yet he has shared a meal, breaking bread and sharing a cup with them, explaining that the meal is a sign of his body broken and blood poured out "for many" (14:22–26). Is their flight the end of the story for the disciples, who promised so much (see 1:16–20; 2:13–14; 3:13–19)? Second, and even more critical, is the question contained in Jesus' final words in the story: "My God, my God, why have you forsaken me?" (15:34). Has God abandoned Jesus? The tearing of the temple veil is a first sign that God has not been absent. But more is needed, especially in the light of Jesus' confident and consistent prophecy of resurrection in the passion predictions (8:31; 9:31; 10:33–34). The Christology of the Gospel of Mark may be satisfactorily resolved as the veil of the temple tears asunder and a Roman centurion, gazing upon Jesus in his moment of death, confesses his faith in Jesus as the Son of God (15:38–39). Yet the narrative cries out for a more satisfactory dénouement: what of the disciples, and what of God?

[A] The women at the cross (15:40–41)

A new set of characters is introduced in 15:40–41. The reader is told the names of three women: Mary Magdalene, Mary the mother of James the younger and of Joses, and Salome (v. 40b).[286] Other women are mentioned (v. 41b). Information is also provided about both the past and the present relationship between these women and Jesus. The three named women, and the larger group, have been associated with Jesus from his time in Galilee.[287] This links the women with the earlier teaching and ministry of Jesus. They are called "followers" and "servants." They followed him (ἠκολούθουν αὐτῷ) and they ministered to him (διηκόνουν αὐτῷ) during that time (v. 41b).[288] At the cross, they are described as "looking on from afar." The language used for both the past and present

---

giving the Pauline theology of the cross a historical and narrative basis, see R. P. Martin, *Mark: Evangelist and Theologian* (Exeter: Paternoster Press, 1972), 156–62. See also W. R. Telford, *The Theology of the Gospel of Mark* (New Testement Theology; Cambridge: Cambridge University Press, 1999), 164–69, and especially J. Marcus, "Mark—Interpreter of Paul," *NTS* 46 (2000): 473–87.

[286] The introduction of these names, without explanation, and especially the reference to James and Joses, also without explanation, could indicate that the women and the two sons were known to the community. See, for example, Lagrange, *Saint Marc*, 410; Taylor, *St. Mark*, 598; Anderson, *Mark*, 348–49. This does not necessarily mean, as Lane (*Mark*, 577), among others, would argue, that their presence substantiates the historicity of details of the Markan cross scene; see Nineham, *St. Mark*, 431. Pesch (*Markusevangelium*, 2:505–7) makes the unlikely claim that there are two separate mothers: one of James and the other of Joses, making a total of four women identified.

[287] The syntax of vv. 40–41 could indicate that the larger group of unnamed women were not to be included under the description of "following" and "serving" Jesus during his time in Galilee. However, this is not necessarily the case; see Brown, *Death*, 2:1155.

[288] The use of the imperfect tense indicates the *durative* aspect of their following and serving; see Pesch, *Markusevangelium*, 2:508.

activities of the women sets them in marked contrast with the other disciples, and especially the Twelve, but associates them with the vacillating Peter as Jesus began his passion.[289]

The disciples had been called to "be with" Jesus (3:14), "to follow" him (1:16–20; 2:13–14; 8:34), and they have been described as "following" throughout the narrative (6:1; 10:28, 32; 11:9). Followers of the Son of Man who came to serve and not be served (10:45), the disciples have also been called to service (9:35; 10:43). But the narrative has presented them as gradually decreasing in their attachment to Jesus as fear and misunderstanding increased (4:41; 6:30; 6:50; 8:17–21, 32; 9:6, 28–29, 32, 33–34, 38 10:32, 35–41). The Twelve were last encountered fleeing from Jesus, leaving him to face his destiny alone (14:50), naked in their fear and separation from Jesus (14:51–52). Peter alone remained at hand. As Jesus was led to the high priest, Peter continued to follow him (καὶ ὁ Πέτρος . . . ἠκολούθησεν, 14:54). But like the women (15:40) he follows only "from a distance" (ἀπὸ μακρόθεν, 14:54). He has separated himself with his denials and departed from the story in tears (14:66–72). The women's watching "from a distance" suggests that, like Peter following Jesus to the high priest (14:54), there are limits to their association with the crucified, but their past following and service indicate that they are genuine disciples of Jesus.[290] Nothing more is said. The reader is made aware of the presence of the women at the cross, and expects to hear more of them. The expectation will be fulfilled as they play an increasingly active role in the last episodes of the story: at the burial (15:47) and at the empty tomb (16:1–8).

[B] The burial of Jesus (15:42–47)

The final episode in the Markan passion narrative serves as a bridge. It closes the story of Jesus' suffering and crucifixion and points the reader toward the day following the Sabbath (15:42; 16:1). Jesus is dead (15:37, 44–45), but what happens to his body is the myopic focus of this brief narrative. After an introduction, indicating the time and the presence of Joseph of Arimathea (vv. 42–43a), the action is entirely determined by decisions concerning Jesus' dead body (vv. 43b, 44, 45, 46). Even the introduction of the women (v. 47), leapfrogging from vv. 40–41 and leading into 16:1–8, retains this focus. They see where the body of Jesus was laid. Thus, by focusing upon his burial, this final passage is more concerned about *Jesus* than any other character. It fittingly brings to a close a series of epi-

---

[289] On the irony, see Painter, *Mark's Gospel*, 208. The following and the serving must be given their full Markan meaning. The storyteller wants the reader to associate the women's past activities with Jesus' teaching on discipleship; see Schweizer, *Mark*, 360; Senior, *Passion*, 131; and especially Gnilka, *Markus*, 2:326. Against Grundmann (*Markus*, 317) and Brown (*Death*, 2:1153 n. 29), who claims that the verb "to serve" here "probably means to take care of material needs, particularly food and drink."

[290] Brown (*Death*, 2:1155–57) claims, against some who make exaggerated claims for the women, that Mark would probably have regarded the women as "disciples," but not as μαθηταί in the strict sense of that term. They are sent to the μαθηταί in 16:7, and are thus not part of that group. This distinction is not called for as the reader is given plenty of hints that the women who watch, follow, and serve must be regarded as "disciples." See E. S. Malbon, "Fallible Followers: Women and Men in the Gospel of Mark," *Sem* 28 (1983): 40–43; W. Munro, "Women Disciples in Mark?" *CBQ* 44 (1982): 230–36; Corley, *Private Women: Public Meals*, 84–86. Malbon's essay is now available in Malbon, *In the Company of Jesus: Characters in Mark's Gospel* (Louisville: Westminster John Knox, 2000), 41–69. Brown (*Death*, 2:1157–58) correctly points to the limitations in the women's discipleship, as do Malbon and Munro. Brown suggests that the "from afar" may even be an allusion to Ps 38:12: "Those who are close to me stood from a distance." In the psalm, a suffering figure describes how he gets no help from those closest to him. See also Gnilka, *Markus*, 2:325. Without reference to the psalm, Pesch (*Markusevangelium*, 2:505) claims that the expression "from afar" continues the use of righteous sufferer language. The allusion to the psalm is subtle, as Lohmeyer (*Markus*, 348) points out.

sodes, encompassing the entire passion narrative, that have focused alternately upon Jesus and other characters. Twenty brief scenes have filled 14:1–15:47, shifting the reader's attention from others to Jesus, as the narrative unfolded. The passion narrative comes to an end with the burial of Jesus, but points the reader forward, seeking an answer to the question raised by the dying Jesus: has God abandoned his Son (15:34)?[291]

The coming of evening on the day of preparation (παρασκευή) for the Sabbath generates the need for Jesus to be buried (v. 42).[292] The law prohibits burial once the time of preparation for a Sabbath begins (Deut 21:22–23; cf. Josephus, *J.W.*, 4.317; *Ant.*, 4.264; Philo, *Spec. Laws* 3.152). The Markan readers hear of the timing of the burial of Jesus, aware that "after three days" he will rise (see 8:31; 9:31; 10:33–34). They are most likely already celebrating the day after the Jewish Sabbath as the day of the Lord's resurrection. However, in context the mention of time provides the motivation for Joseph of Arimathea's actions (v. 43). Jesus is reported to have died at about three o'clock in the afternoon ("the ninth hour"). Something must be done with his body before the setting of the sun, lest it be left hanging on the cross during a Sabbath.[293]

Joseph of Arimathea is not mentioned elsewhere in the Gospel of Mark, although (as well as in Matthew and Luke) he is associated with the burial of Jesus across the synoptic tradition and John (John 19:38).[294] His background is sketched. He is a respected "member of the council" (βουλευτής)[295] and is described as a figure "looking for" the kingdom of God. This does not make him a disciple, but someone in search of the fulfillment of God's promise of eschatological intervention.[296] The death of Jesus generates a law-abiding response from Joseph, a righteous Jew. He must attend to the dead body of Jesus so that the law not be offended.[297] Mark notes that this action calls for courage (v. 43).[298] Pilate had

---

[291] Pesch, *Markusevangelium*, 2:511.

[292] The word παρασκευή came to be the Jewish word for "Friday," the day before the Sabbath day (Josephus, *Ant.*, 16:163; *Did.*, 8.1); see Gnilka, *Markus*, 2:332.

[293] On the calculation of the time of the day, on the basis of the "ninth hour" (v. 34) and ἤδη ὀψίας γενομένης (v. 42), and the need for a certain haste to bury the body before sunset, see Brown, *Death*, 2:1211–12. Mark 14:12–16 suggests that the meal of vv. 22–26 was that of Passover, which would make the day of the crucifixion the day of the Passover celebration, but that fact has disappeared from Mark's calculations. See Nineham, *St. Mark*, 433; Hooker, *St. Mark*, 380.

[294] For a detailed study of his function in the Markan narrative, see I. Broer, *Die Urgemeinde und das Grab Jesu: Eine Analyse der Grablegungsgeschichte im Neuen Testament* (SANT 31; Munich: Kösel-Verlag, 1972), 123–200. For Broer he was a historical character, but originally hostile. His sympathetic presentation in vv. 43–46 developed as an empty tomb became part of the Easter kerygma (see pp. 280–94). This skepticism is not universally accepted. There are many similarities across the burial traditions, including the Johannine. Brown (*Death*, 2:1238–41, 1270–79) attempts to lay bare what might have been a pre-Gospel account of the burial used by all evangelists. See also Gnilka, *Markus*, 2:331–32. Pesch (*Markusevangelium*, 2:509–10) argues strongly for vv. 42–47 as part of an original pre-Markan passion narrative. For speculation concerning the origins of Joseph, see Brown, *Death*, 2:1213 n. 17.

[295] The "council" does not necessarily mean the Sanhedrin; Brown, *Death*, 1:340–48. But in the light of 15:1, where the Sanhedrin held a "consultation" (συμβούλιον), Mark probably means that Joseph of Arimathea belonged to the Sanhedrin. See Brown, *Death*, 2:1213–14.

[296] Brown, *Death*, 2:1214–16; Senior, *Passion*, 133. Brown (p. 2:1215) and Senior (p. 133) rightly draw a parallel between Joseph and the scribe who was "not far from the kingdom of God" in 12:34. For a nuanced and very helpful study of the "minor characters" and their function in the narrative, see Malbon, "Minor Characters," 189–225.

[297] Brown, *Death*, 2:1216–17; Hooker, *St. Mark*, 381.

[298] On Roman and Jewish practices in dealing with the bodies of condemned criminals, see Brown, *Death*, 2:1207–10. LaVerdiere (*The Beginning*, 2:314) argues that courage was required because Joseph was flaunting the Sanhedrin's opposition to Jesus.

handed Jesus over to be scourged and crucified (v. 15). Roman authority remains responsible for the crucified criminal, and the mention of Joseph's need for courage indicates that
he is crossing the line between the governor and those governed. How will he be judged as
he asks for the body of someone the Romans have executed under the title, "The King of
the Jews" (v. 26)?[299] The actions of Joseph, described above, portray him as a righteous Jew,
giving Jesus the burial which he believed was in accordance with the law, even at some personal risk. However, at another level the reader senses that Joseph is more than a pious Jew.
This hitherto unknown character can be contrasted to the frightened and fleeing disciples
(14:50). "Mark portrays Joseph as doing something the disciples had feared to do: he associates himself with the crucified Jesus."[300]

But Joseph is not the focus of the passage. He asks Pilate "for the body of Jesus"
(v. 43b). In 15:44–45 the interest shifts to the body of Jesus. Pilate wonders (ἐθαύμασεν)
that Jesus should have died so quickly.[301] Pilate's response to Jesus' self-revelation was wonder (see v. 5), and this emotion is repeated when he hears of Jesus' death (v. 44a).[302] He
calls upon the witness of the centurion who had stood directly facing Jesus as he breathed
his final breath (v. 44b; cf. v. 39a). Pilate is assured that Jesus is dead by the person the
reader has already met as the most truthful witness to Jesus in the narrative thus far (v. 45a;
cf. v. 39b). On the assurance of the centurion, Pilate responds positively to the request of
Joseph (v. 43b) and permits the handing over of "the dead body" to Joseph (v. 45b).[303] The
body has been requested (v. 43b), the once living Jesus is certainly now a corpse
(vv. 44–45a) and is handed over to Joseph (v. 45b).

The description of a hurried burial follows.[304] There is no washing of the body and no
embalming. Jesus is taken down from the cross,[305] wrapped in a newly bought linen cloth

---

[299] See Pesch, *Markusevangelium*, 2:513–14; Brown, *Death*, 2:1217.

[300] Senior, *Passion*, 133, cf. Painter, *Mark's Gospel*, 209. This does not make Joseph into a disciple, but forces the above response from a discerning reader.

[301] This passage, reporting Pilate's amazement and ascertaining that Jesus is really dead, is not
found in Matthew and Luke. A number of commentators (see, for example, Lohmeyer, *Markus*, 350;
Taylor, *St. Mark*, 599; Schweizer, *Mark*, 362; Hooker, *St. Mark*, 381) suggest that they were added to
Mark by a redactor, and that the original Mark (as reflected in Matthew and Luke) did not contain
it. For a detailed rejection of this and similar proposals, see Brown, *Death*, 2:1219–22.

[302] Brown, *Death*, 2:1220. For an understanding of his wonder as religious awe, see Gnilka,
Markus, 2:333.

[303] The use of σῶμα in v. 43b and πτῶμα in v. 45 shifts from a word which is used in general of a
human body (v. 43b) to another word used only for a corpse (v. 45). See Gnilka, *Markus*, 2:333.

[304] Brown (*Death*, 2:1209–10) shows that Jewish tradition would not permit an honorable burial
to anyone found guilty in a Jewish court. He then suggests (pp. 1243–44) that the Markan account,
where the body is neither washed nor anointed, could not be regarded as an honorable burial. See also
idem, "The Burial of Jesus (Mark 15:42–47)," *CBQ* 50 (1988): 233–45. For the contrary opinion, see
Grundmann, *Markus*, 319; Gnilka, *Markus*, 2:334–36. Pesch (*Markusevangelium*, 2:515) suggests that
the washing and the anointing are omitted for literary reasons: they make possible the visit of the
women to anoint the body (16:1). A critical historical question emerges. According to many (e.g.,
Lohmeyer, *Markus*, 351–52) there were two burial traditions. One has Jesus buried as a common
criminal; e.g., Acts 13:29: "they took him down from the tree and they laid him in a tomb"; the
"they" refers to "those who live in Jerusalem and their rulers" (v. 27). Against this, Mark has developed
a tradition in which Jesus is buried with honor, and his tomb is well known. Cf. Loisy's position on
this matter described in Lagrange, *Saint Marc*, 414. For a dismissal of this suggestion, with reference
to 1 Cor 15:3–5, Rom 6:4, and Col 2:12, claiming that it finds "no support in the Gospel text or in the
primitive Christian tradition," see Brown, *Death*, 2:1206–7. See also Bultmann, *History*, 274, who concludes that the basic story is "an historical account which creates no impression of being a legend."

[305] The verb καθαιρέω is the correct technical term for taking a dead body down from a cross;
see Lagrange, *Saint Marc*, 413. There is some debate on who "took down" Jesus' body: was it Joseph,

(σινδόνι) and laid in a tomb.[306] The report of the tomb indicates a cavelike cutting into a rock face, and with a large rock door to be rolled across the aperture. Such burials were not for the common people, but the respected and influential Joseph buries Jesus in a fashion that looks forward to the resurrection story (16:3–4).[307] Two of the women who stood looking at the crucified Jesus, Mary Magdalene and Mary the mother of Joses (cf. v. 40), are in attendance at this burial, but for the moment they are not important agents in the story.[308] They see where Jesus was laid (v. 47).

The focus of 15:42–47 is upon the dead body of Jesus and its being laid in a tomb. But a number of incidents tell the reader that this is not the end of the story. The timing of the episode points the reader to the day after the Sabbath (15:42; cf. 16:1). The body is not properly prepared for burial, and women who saw him die (15:40–41) have also watched to see where he was hurriedly buried (15:47; cf. 16:1). Jesus is wrapped in a σινδών, the same type of covering found in the description of the young man who fled from Gethsemane—a parabolic comment upon the flight of the disciples. Another young man will appear in the empty tomb (16:5; cf. 14:50, 51–52). Most of all the reader, who has followed the death of the Son of God and the burial of his body, waits for God's further response to Jesus' question in 15:34. The Christian reader is aware that God did not abandon his Son (cf. 16:6).[309]

Conclusion

The Markan passion narrative is the result of a carefully wrought use of pre-Markan traditions to produce a unique story of the suffering and death of Jesus. Composed in two major sections, the first (14:1–72) is a continuous interplay between Jesus and the disciples. As Jesus moves steadily toward his ironic condemnation by the Jewish leaders, the

---

or did others do it? In 16:6 the young man will ask the women to look at the place where "they" laid him; see Brown, *Death*, 2:1245–46. Note the implications of this debate for the issue raised in the previous note. A number of commentators (e.g., Lagrange, *Saint Marc*, 413; Taylor, *St. Mark*, 602; Lane, *Mark*, 580) remark that Joseph would have needed helpers to do this task. See, however, the warning against such conclusions in Gnilka, *Markus*, 2:333.

[306] Joseph is presented as a man of some means, able to purchase the σινδών and to place Jesus in a rich man's tomb; Senior, *Passion*, 133. On the cloth, its size, cost, and how it could be purchased late in the afternoon of the day of preparation, see the detailed treatment in Brown, *Death*, 2:1244–45. I doubt such questions ever crossed the minds of the Markan readers. Similarly, LaVerdiere's attempt to associate the shroud (via 14:51–52) with baptism is far-fetched (*The Beginning*, 2:315).

[307] Senior, *Passion*, 134–35. For speculations on the tomb, its shape, what it was like inside, the stone that was rolled in front of it, and how Joseph had the immediate access to a tomb, see Brown, *Death*, 2:1247–51. While quaintly interesting, I suspect that Mark never asked such questions, nor did he expect his readers to ask them.

[308] Brown (*Death*, 2:1251) correctly insists that the women were present, but not involved. Their involvement is to follow shortly (16:1–8). The difference in the names of the women in v. 47, compared with v. 40 and 16:1, has led to numerous textual variations; see Taylor, *St. Mark*, 602. Schweizer (*Mark*, 361) comments: "This lack of correspondence is evidence of the fact that this account actually was based upon the testimony of a few women and was not fabricated later to explain how in 16:1 the women knew where Jesus was buried." Thus also Anderson, *Mark*, 349–50. See above, note 294.

[309] On the forward looking nature of vv. 42–47, see Pesch, *Markusevangelium*, 2:514–16; Lührmann, *Markusevangelium*, 268; Gnilka, *Markus*, 2:336–37.

disciples' failure intensifies. In the end, Jesus is proclaimed Christ, Son of God, whose suffering will be vindicated by the coming of the Son of Man (14:61–62). The disciples flee, fearful and naked in their separation from Jesus (14:50–52). Only Peter remains, following at a distance. But he associates himself with Jesus' enemies and denies him three times (14:53–54, 66–72). Yet, at the center of 14:1–72, in the sixth of eleven scenes (vv. 22–25), Jesus shares a meal with his fragile and failing disciples. The disciples do not reappear as active characters in the narrative, but they are promised that, despite their fear and flight, Jesus will go before them into Galilee. There they will see him (14:28).

The second section (15:1–47) is a further interplay of other characters with Jesus. Romans, however, replace the disciples as Jesus' major dialogue partners throughout this section, although the Jewish leaders are never far away. The ironic christological proclamation of the Jewish trial (14:61–62) is extended into the Roman hearing and the crucifixion. Jesus is proclaimed "the King of the Jews" by Pilate (15:2, 9), by the crowd (15:12, indirectly), by the Roman soldiers (15:18), and in the title the Romans place on the cross (15:26). Alone in his agony, he is proclaimed savior by the passersby (15:30) and by the Jewish leaders (15:31), and ironically recognized as the Christ, the king of Israel, in the mockery of the Jewish leaders (v. 32). The reader is made aware that it is only *on the cross* that Jesus can lay claim to be savior, Christ, and king of Israel, as his enemies demand that he come down from the cross that they might see and believe (15:30, 32). Crying out an anguished question of abandonment to his God (15:34), Jesus screams and expires (15:37). The christological high point of the Gospel arrives as a consequence of Jesus' agonizing death: the temple of Jerusalem is symbolically destroyed, and the sanctuary once reserved to the Jewish priests is laid open for all to see. A new temple, built upon the rejected cornerstone, is founded (cf. 12:10–11), and the Roman centurion, standing before Jesus and seeing the manner of his death, is the first of many to proclaim that Jesus is the Son of God (15:38–39). The promise of the voice from heaven in 1:11 has been realized in 15:39. Women watch, and Jesus is hurriedly buried in scenes which bring the traditional passion story to an end. But they point the reader toward the resurrection promised by Jesus during his journey to Jerusalem (8:31; 9:31; 10:33–34), and demanded by Jesus' question of God in his moment of death (15:34). At the center of 15:1–47, the fifth of nine scenes (vv. 20b–25) relates the silent and merciless account of Jesus' crucifixion, the event so long anticipated by the Gospel of Mark (cf. 2:20; 3:6).

As the first half of the passion narrative closed, the disciples moved tragically toward the denials of Peter (14:66–72). As the second half ends, the Romans' participation in Jesus' agony closes with one of them accepting that Jesus is the Son of God (15:39). The simplicity of the literary structure, combined with the depth of the dramatic irony used to proclaim the truth of Jesus, Christ, King and Son of God on the cross, reflect a finely tuned Christian author. The figure that created literary history by inventing the literary form "gospel" did more than edit the received tradition. The narrative has prepared the reader for the Gospel's climax: the much-anticipated account of the resurrection of Jesus. There, one would expect, the failure of the disciples and the apparent failure of Jesus will be resolved. God will become the major actor in what follows, but there is a twist at the end of the tale. God will show that he has never abandoned his Son (cf. 15:34), but the expected restoration of discipleship to the fearful and frightened men who fled from Jesus at Gethsemane (14:50) will receive something of a setback. Even the women, who have remained with Jesus from Galilee to the cross (15:40–41) and the tomb (v. 47), will join the disciples in fear and flight (16:8).

SECTION 4

EPILOGUE

MARK 16:1–8

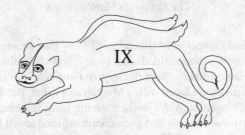

IX

THE EPILOGUE (MARK 16:1–8)

The account of the events that took place on the day after the Sabbath is closely linked with the story of Jesus' passion. The indication of time, by means of the genitive absolute, "And when the Sabbath was passed (καὶ διαγενομένου τοῦ σαββάτου)" of 16:1a looks back to 15:42: "It was the day of preparation, that is, the day before the Sabbath (ὅ ἐστιν προσάββατον)." The explicit naming of the characters, Mary Magdalene, Mary the mother of James, and Salome (16:1b), brings back on stage all the women mentioned watching the death of Jesus from afar (15:40). Two of them, Mary Magdalene and Mary the mother of Joses, had also seen where the body of Jesus was laid (15:47).[1] On the basis of this connection the conclusion to the Gospel of Mark is articulated in three steps:[2]

16:1–4   The setting: an empty tomb

16:5–7   The Easter proclamation

16:8   The failure of the women

Each of these narrative steps bristles with critical problems, but the major concern of this commentary is to trace the Markan narrative and theological strategies that have determined the conclusion to the Gospel.[3]

---

[1] The temporal association of 16:1–8 with the events reported in 14:1–15:47 is the work of Mark. The question of Mark's use of sources (e.g., the names of the women; see note 3) is hotly debated, but there can be no questioning the *Markan intention* to link the account of the events at the empty tomb with the crucifixion and death of Jesus. See G. Lüdemann, *The Resurrection of Jesus: History, Experience, Theology* (London: SCM, 1994), 111–14.

[2] See Pesch, *Markusevangelium*, 2:527–28. Pesch detaches v. 1 as an introduction, but then divides the rest of the narrative into vv. 2–4, 5–7, 8.

[3] The fundamental critical problem comes from the debate whether Mark 16:1–8 is built upon pre-Markan traditions (e.g., the names of the women, their plan to anoint Jesus' dead body, an empty tomb, the appearance of the young man [angel], the command to the women), with links to events that took place, or is a Markan composition in its entirety. For the classical form-critical approach to these questions, see R. Bultmann, *History of the Synoptic Tradition* (trans. John Marsh; Oxford: Basil Blackwell, 1968), 284–91. For an exhaustive survey of attempts to reconstruct the pre-Markan sources that lie behind 16:1–8, see F. Neirynck, "Marc 16,1–8. Tradition et rédaction: Tombeau vide et angélophanie," in *Evangelica: Gospel Studies—Etudes d'évangile: Collected Essays* (ed. F. van Segbroeck; BETL 60; Leuven: Leuven University Press, 1982), 239–71, further updated in an additional note in *Evangelica II. 1982–91: Collected Essays* (ed. F. van Segbroeck; BETL 99; Leuven: Leuven University Press, 1991), 796–97. For briefer surveys see also P. Perkins, *Resurrection: New Testament Witness and Contemporary Reflection* (Garden City: Doubleday, 1984), 115–16; A. Y. Collins, *The Beginning of the Gospel: Probings of Mark in Context* (Minneapolis: Fortress, 1992), 129–34; and Lüdemann, *Resurrection*, 115–21. Perkins opts for a pre-Markan tradition, Lüdemann for a Markan reworking of some traditional elements, and Collins insists that 16:1–8 is entirely the result of Markan literary and theological creativity (pp. 134–38). A consequence of the latter

But did the original Gospel of Mark end with 16:8? Our present printed texts, with a number of possible continuations added after 16:8, reflect difficulties that emerged in the earliest days of Christian tradition. Once the written Gospel texts were passed from generation to generation, scribes were faced with a Markan story that, unlike the Gospels of Matthew, Luke, and John, closed with the women fleeing from the empty tomb (16:8). They had heard the Easter message (16:6) and been commissioned to tell Peter and the disciples of Jesus' going before them into Galilee, as he had promised (16:7; cf. 14:28). Scribes provided more satisfactory endings to make the Gospel of Mark conform to the concluding stages of the Gospels of Matthew, Luke, and John. In Matthew and Luke, women receive the Easter message and report it to the disciples (Matt 28:1–10; Luke 24:1–12). In the Gospel of John, there is only one woman, Mary of Magdalene, but the story of the empty tomb is reported to Peter and the Beloved Disciple (John 20:1–3). Most English editions of the Gospel of Mark include either a longer ending (Mark 16:9–20), or a shorter ending (16:9–10). Some provide both.[4] The imaginative gathering of a number of Easter appearance stories from the other Gospels and the Acts of the Apostles generated the longer ending (vv. 9–20).[5] The shorter ending merely affirms that the women reported the message, and from then on salvation was proclaimed from east to west (vv. 9–10). However, these are only two of several textual traditions that have come down to us, and none of them has serious claim to authenticity. They are the work of scribes, unhappy with the silence of the women in v. 8.[6] The *textual* problem was created by a *theological* problem. Is it possible that, for Mark, the women did not proclaim the Easter message, with the result that the relationship between Jesus and the faltering disciples was never restored?

Given the universal agreement that the present endings are the work of later scribes, those who claim that the original Gospel of Mark did not end at 16:8 suggest that the original ending was lost.[7] In the light of the promise of a future encounter in Galilee (v. 7), and

---

position (shared by many) is that the story of the Easter morning was the invention of Mark, and has no basis in history (pp. 138–48). Lüdemann (*Resurrection,* 121) also bluntly concludes his analysis of the Markan reworking of some traditional elements: "In all honesty we can discover absolutely nothing from the story about what really happened in history." Pesch (*Markusevangelium* 2:519–28) also believes that 16:1–8 is a unified narrative, but takes the opposite position: it came to Mark *as a whole* from the pre-Markan passion narrative and is a witness to the earliest Christian kerygma (cf. 1 Cor 15:3–5). I will touch upon these questions in the notes, and pursue a reading of the Markan narrative in the text.

[4] The longer ending (vv. 9–20) is found in most of the extant manuscripts of the Gospel, but is missing from Sinaiticus, Vaticanus, the Old Latin Bobiensis, Sinaitic Syriac, and other manuscripts. Clement of Alexandria and Origen show no knowledge of it, and Eusebius and Jerome regarded them as unauthentic. The shorter ending (vv. 9–10) is found in a considerable number of manuscripts of the seventh to the ninth century, generally as a preface to the longer ending. A third ending, called the "Freer Logion," is a gloss on 16:14 (in the longer ending) and is quoted by Jerome. See the discussion of the Freer Logion in Taylor, *St. Mark,* 614–15. For a commentary on 16:9–20, see chapter 10 below, pp. 355–62.

[5] See the discussion of the longer endings of Mark in the Appendix. For a useful list of the borrowings from other New Testament documents in Mark 16:9–20, see B. M. F. van Iersel, *Reading Mark* (Collegeville: The Liturgical Press, 1988), 214.

[6] On the textual traditions, see Metzger, *Textual Commentary,* 102–7, and the more extensive treatments of Lagrange, *Saint Marc,* 426–39; Lane, *Mark,* 601–11; and especially J. Hug, *La finale de l'Evangile de Marc (Mc 16,9–20)* (EBib; Paris: Gabalda, 1978), 187–215. The discussion of this issue is succinctly documented in T. E. Boomershine, "Mark 16:8 and the Apostolic Commission," *JBL* 100 (1981): 225 n. 2.

[7] See, for example, Taylor, *St. Mark,* 609–10; Cranfield, *St. Mark,* 1963, 470–71; N. Q. Hamilton, "Resurrection Traditions and the Composition of Mark," *JBL* 84 (1965): 415–21; C. J. Reedy, "Mk

the agreement of Matthew, Luke, and John that the women announced the Easter message, these scholars claim that there must have been a further page to resolve the tension created by 16:7–8. However, the suggestion of a lost ending creates more difficulties than it resolves. The "lost ending" solution depends upon a number of well-nigh impossible hypotheses. Perhaps the original ending was contained in a self-standing page in what we call a codex, an ancient form of a book, with pages sewn together, like a modern book. As with our books, wear and tear may detach the first or last page. But it is unlikely that the Gospel of Mark was originally written in a codex. That form used for the preservation of texts came into Christian usage very early, but probably not for the original autographs of the New Testament texts.[8]

Very likely the very first "Gospel of Mark" was written on a scroll, not a codex.[9] Is it possible that the last part of the original manuscript, a scroll, was torn off, as the last page of a codex might have become detached? Although more difficult than losing the last page of a codex, wear and tear of a much-used scroll may have damaged its final several inches. We must then consider the possibility that the loss of the closing section of the scroll would have taken place *with the original autograph of the Gospel of Mark*. It is unlikely that the community that received the original scroll containing the Gospel of Mark would inadvertently allow the ending to disappear.[10] It is difficult to imagine that before even a single copied version existed of the original Gospel of Mark, the ending of the original was inadvertently torn off, and nothing was done to retrieve it. If only one copy of the original Mark containing the so-called "lost ending" existed, some trace of that ending would be present in the ancient manuscript tradition. But we have no such evidence.[11] The original Gospel of Mark ended at 16:8, and the interpreter must make sense of Mark's literary and theological reasons for closing his Gospel with the fear, flight, and silence of the women (16:8).[12]

8:31–11:10 and the Composition of Mark," *CBQ* 34 (1972): 188–97; Schweizer, *Mark*, 365–67; E. Linnemann, "Der (wiedergefundene) Markusschluss," *ZTK* 66 (1969): 255–87. A full discussion of the history of scholarship can be found in Hug, *La finale*, 11–32. For an accurate and succinct survey of the arguments for and against the Gospel's ending at 16:8, see Anderson, *Mark*, 351–54. See also Hug, *La finale*, 177–85; A. Lindemann, "Die Osterbotschaft des Markus: Zur theologischen Interpretation von Mark 16.1–8," *NTS* 26 (1979–1980): 298–300.

[8] There is some discussion concerning the use of the scroll and the codex in the early church. Most argue (as above) that the autographs would have been on scrolls, but that Christians used the codex very early, perhaps even toward the end of the first century; see, e.g., B. M. Metzger, *The Text of the New Testament: Its Transmission, Corruption, and Restoration* (2d ed.; Oxford: Clarendon Press, 1968), 5–8; J. Finegan, *Encountering New Testament Manuscripts: A Working Introduction to Textual Criticism* (London: SPCK, 1975), 27–29. See, however, K. and B. Aland, *The Text of the New Testament: An Introduction to the Critical Editions and to the Theory and Practice of Modern Textual Criticism* (trans. E. F. Rhodes; Grand Rapids: Eerdmans, 1987), 75: "Apparently from the very beginning Christians did not use the scroll format for their writings, but rather the codex." See also pp. 101–2.

[9] It was not called "The Gospel of Mark" at that stage. The titles ascribing authors to the Gospels are generally regarded as second century, although Hengel (*Mark*, 64–84) disputes this. He claims that once more than one "gospel" existed, each single Gospel was attached to an author. Thus "according to Mark" would have been attached to the title before the end of the first Christian century.

[10] Nineham, *St. Mark*, 440–41.

[11] Lüdemann, *Resurrection*, 110. As Taylor (*St. Mark*, 610) admits: "How the original ending disappeared is . . . obscure." Hug's study, *La finale*, shows conclusively that 16:9–20 is the product of a Hellenistic missionary situation in the second half of the second century. See also J. A. Kelhoffer, *Miracle and Mission: The Authentication of Missionaries and Their Message in the Longer Ending of Mark* (WUNT 2. Reihe 112; Tübingen: J. C. B. Mohr [Paul Siebeck], 2000).

[12] Many of the scholars who insist that there must have been a lost ending (see above, note 7) are reacting against the suggestions of Lohmeyer (*Markus*, 355–58) that the ending points to a

The Setting: An Empty Tomb (16:1–4)

The link between the time and the characters in the passion account, and the events that take place "when the Sabbath was past," has already been noticed.[13] The narrator reports that they brought spices so that they might go to anoint Jesus' dead body. Joseph of Arimathea had buried Jesus without the usual washing and anointing of the body in 15:46. Jesus had hinted at his burial without anointing in his interpretation of the unknown woman's gesture in 14:8: "She has anointed my body beforehand for burying." However, the notion of returning, some thirty-six hours after a death by crucifixion, to anoint a body that has been entombed without embalming has been seized upon by the critics as an indication of the implausibility of the motivation for the women's visit to the tomb.[14] Historically speaking, the objection is sound, and the issue of the anointing disappears imme-

---

Markan community waiting in Galilee for the Parousia. This claim has been further developed by Marxsen (*Mark,* 75–92) and a number of more recent redaction critics in the United States who have accepted the conclusions of Lohmeyer and Marxsen. See, for example, T. Weeden, *Traditions in Conflict* (Philadelphia: Fortress, 1971), 111–16; W. Kelber, *The Kingdom in Mark: A New Place and a New Time* (Philadelphia: Fortress, 1974), 129–47; J. D. Crossan, "Empty Tomb and Absent Lord (Mark 16:1–8)," in *The Passion in Mark* (ed. W. H. Kelber; Philadelphia: Fortress, 1976), 135–52; N. Perrin, *The Resurrection Narratives: A New Approach* (London: SPCK, 1977), 17–40. This position, which stresses a community living in the absence of Jesus and waiting for the Parousia, does not do justice to the message of the Gospel as a whole. See Best, *Mark,* 72–78; and especially J. D. Kingsbury, *The Christology of Mark's Gospel* (Philadelphia: Fortress, 1983), the whole book, and esp. 25–45; and the summary in Marcus, *Mark,* 75–79. However, their insistence that the original Gospel closed with 16:8 is correct. A study coming to the same conclusion by the use of literary and rhetorical criteria can be found in P. L. Danove, *The End of Mark's Story: A Methodological Study* (BibIntS 3; Leiden: Brill, 1993), 119–31.

[13] Critics have attempted to isolate different stages of the tradition in the changing situation and names in 15:40, 47, and 16:1. See especially I. Broer, *Die Urgemeinde und das Grab Jesu: Eine Analyse der Grablegungsgeschichte* (SANT 31; Munich: Kösel-Verlag), 87–137; L. Oberlinner, *Historische Überlieferung und christologische Aussage: Zur Frage der "Bruder Jesu" in der Synopse* (FB 19; Stuttgart: Katholisches Bibelwerk, 1975), 97–120; Lüdemann, *Resurrection,* 111–12. See also Bultmann, *History,* 284–85; Lohmeyer, *Markus,* 353; Grundmann, *Markus,* 319–20); R. H. Fuller, *The Formation of the Resurrection Narratives* (London: SPCK, 1972), 52; Anderson, *Mark,* 354; Hooker, *St. Mark,* 383, and the summary in Perkins, *Resurrection,* 116–17. Early scribes also attempted to smooth out the difficulties; see Lane, *Mark,* 582 n. 1. The subtle changes may have been intended. Mary Magdalene is present throughout (15:40, 47; 16:1). Salome is present at the cross and at the grave (15:40; 16:1). Mary is identified as the mother of both James and Joses in 15:40, as the mother of Joses in v. 47, and as the mother of James in 16:1. It is the same Mary, identified by both her sons (15:40), and then by each one singly (15:47, 16:1). This careful swapping of characters and names, with the presence of Mary Magdalene throughout, introduces simple but subtle variety. As Collins (*The Beginning of the Gospel,* 130) remarks: "It is true that the references to them are not verbally identical. But the differences may be explained perfectly well as stylistic variations that avoid monotonous repetition." But this does *not* mean that the names are a Markan invention, as Collins seems to suggest (p. 135). It is one thing to recognize Markan literary activity, and another to attribute everything said in 16:1–8 to the fruit of his literary and theological creativity. Mark works creatively with earlier traditions. It is, of course, naïve to claim that "It reads like an eye-witness account, not a dramatization of a religious conviction" (Cranfield, *St. Mark,* 463). See the judicious remarks of Taylor (*St. Mark,* 602): "The narrative is constructed by Mark himself on the basis of tradition, although not that of an eyewitness." The fact that it is impossible to recover the pre-Markan tradition does not prove that Mark was not using earlier sources, as Crossan ("Empty Tomb," 136–38) would claim. See the balanced assessment in Lindemann, "Die Osterbotschaft des Markus," 302–10.

[14] Schweizer, *Mark,* 364. Lane attempts to overcome this problem by suggesting that the women merely wished to pour oil on the head as a sign of devotion, and not anoint (*Mark,* 585).

diately from the narrative. Both Matthew (28:1) and Luke (24:1) eliminate the bringing of spices *to anoint the body,* although Luke retains a reference to spices. A motivation flowing from the narrative (14:8; 15:46) has most likely been introduced by Mark to bring the women to the site of Jesus' burial.[15] The history of the tradition ultimately escapes us, but Mark has the women come to the tomb to render respect to the person whom they have seen slain (15:40–41) and buried (15:47), and in this they show that they are not prepared for what they discover. "For all its strangeness, from the Marcan standpoint this notice serves to show that motivated as they were by ordinary desires, they had not the slightest expectation from the human side of the amazing divine sequel."[16]

The women proceed to the site of the tomb "very early on the first day of the week (λίαν πρωὶ τῇ μιᾷ τῶν σαββάτων, 16:2)."[17] The day is Sunday, thus fulfilling the repeated use of "third day" language across the Gospel (8:31; 9:31; 10:34; 14:58; 15:29).[18] The time of the day is just after sunrise: "when the sun had risen" (v. 2).[19] The remark about the inbreak of daylight may be more than an innocent remark to inform the reader on the time of day. The rising of the sun might indicate that something more than the women imagine, quite outside their control, is about to be revealed. This suggestion is made in the light of the Johannine account of the unbelieving Mary Magdalene at the empty tomb. Mary's journey to the tomb is accompanied by the remark, "while it was still dark" (John 20:1).[20] Mark 16:2 gives the readers their first hint that the darkness that enveloped the earth during the crucifixion (15:33–37) has been overcome. Darkness prevailed while the Son, in agony, asked the Father why he had abandoned him. Light now dawns as God enters the story.[21] On their way to the tomb the women ask one another who will roll away

---

[15] Collins, *Beginning,* 134–35. For others, the visit to the tomb to anoint the body reflects a pre-Markan tradition. It was the original motivation for the visit to the tomb, clumsily retained by Mark, and without further consequence to the Markan narrative.

[16] Anderson, *Mark,* 354.

[17] The expression is clumsy due to a Hebraism; see Gnilka, *Markus,* 2:341; Anderson, *Mark,* 354–55; Perkins, *Resurrection,* 117–18.

[18] Pesch, *Markusevangelium,* 2:530–31; Lührmann, *Markusevangelium,* 269; Gnilka, *Markus,* 2:341. Many have attempted to see seven days in Mark 11:1–16:8, concluding with the explicit mention of Sunday, the day after the Sabbath; the seven days are said to represent an early form of a Christian "Holy Week." For a detailed survey, and cautious rejection of the suggestion, see F. Neirynck, "ΑΝΑΤΕΙΛΑΝΤΟΣ ΤΟΥ ΗΛΙΟΥ," in *Evangelica: Gospel Studies* (ed. F. van Segbroeck; BETL 60; Leuven: Leuven University Press, 1982), 206–13.

[19] The double notation of time ("very early . . . when the sun had risen") has created numerous hypotheses of redactional activity, and several textual variations. See the exhaustive survey and a defense of the Markan nature of this indication of time in Neirynck, "ΑΝΑΤΕΙΛΑΝΤΟΣ," 191–202. Painter (*Mark's Gospel,* 210) is probably correct in suggesting: "Perhaps he meant that they set out after dark but arrived after sunrise." See also Lagrange, *Saint Marc,* 415–16.

[20] This suggestion does not presuppose a literary connection between the Markan and Johannine resurrection accounts. But see M. Lang, *Johannes und die Synoptiker: Eine Redaktionsgeschichtliche Analyse von Joh 18–20 vor dem markanischen und lukanischen Hintergrund* (FRLANT 182; Göttingen: Vandenhoeck & Ruprecht, 1999), 259–79, and F. J. Moloney, "Where Does One Look? Reflections on Some Recent Johannine Scholarship," *Salesianum* 62 (2000): 238–48. The similarity suggests that the early church rapidly developed an interpretation of the day of resurrection that reached beyond the transmission of a received tradition.

[21] See Grundmann, *Markus,* 322, and with reservations, Gnilka, *Markus,* 2:341. For a detailed survey of the question, see Neirynck, "ΑΝΑΤΕΙΛΑΝΤΟΣ," 181–214. On the symbolic reading of the appearance of light, see pp. 203–4, and n. 123 on p. 203. Early commentators and scribes saw the importance of the light. See for example, the gloss in the Codex Bobiensis and the interpretation of the *Gospel of Peter* 35–44, reported in Lane, *Mark,* 582 n. 3; see also p. 585 n. 10.

the stone covering the opening of the tomb (v. 3; cf. 15:46). Why did they not ask this question before they set out on their journey with the express purpose of anointing the body (16:1)?[22] The narrative will provide the answer in 16:4: if three women were aware that they would not be able to roll back the stone, it must have been very large.[23] The narrator will announce that such was the case (see v. 4b).

God's action has already overcome the women's difficulty. Raising their eyes they saw that the stone *had been rolled back* (v. 4a: ἀποκεκύλισται). The passive form of the perfect tense of the verb indicates that God had decisively entered the story. There is no one else who could have rolled back the stone, and thus the divine passive is used to extend the first hint provided by the rising of the sun as the women went to the tomb. The pleonastic use of two verbs to tell of the women's raising their eyes and seeing (ἀναβλέψασαι θεωροῦσιν) heightens the solemnity of the moment. This is no ordinary seeing. The women may not be aware of it, but the reader senses in this exaggerated "seeing" the hint of a sight of the revelation of God's action. The narrator then confirms what the reader suspected on overhearing the women's discussion over who would roll back the stone: "it was very large" (v. 4b; cf. v. 3). The event of God's intervention is in the past. The women see what God has already done. The scene is set for the second step in the Markan resurrection account. The most important character has entered the narrative.[24] God, implied by the divine passive, has overcome the darkness and has opened the seemingly impossible (vv. 2–4).

The Easter Proclamation (16:5–7)

Three stages mark the central section of the brief narrative: a description of the young man in the tomb and the women's reaction (v. 5), the proclamation that God has raised Jesus (v. 6), and the women's commission to tell the disciples that Jesus is going before them into Galilee (v. 7).[25] On penetrating the tomb, the women see a young man (νεανίσκον) seated on the right side of the tomb, dressed (περιβεβλημένον) in a white robe. The response of the women is amazement (ἐξεθαμβήθησαν). This strengthening of the verb "to be amazed" by adding a prefix heightens the impression of the women's response. They are literally "amazed out of themselves." The sense of the numinous is conveyed as the women's reaction matches traditional responses to a theophany. The young man, and only the young man, present on the right side of the tomb announces that the tomb is empty.[26] They do not find the body of Jesus, but a young man.

---

[22] Hooker, *St. Mark,* 384.

[23] J. Ernst, *Das Evangelium nach Markus* (RNT; Regensburg: Pustet Verlag, 1981), 485–86.

[24] Gnilka, *Markus,* 2:341; Ernst, *Markus,* 486. Schweizer (*Mark,* 371) comments: "For man the large stone closes the tomb now and forever, and this makes the miraculous intervention of God which has already occurred so much more impressive." The strength of this point is missed if, in the light of Matt 28:2, the angel of v. 5 is regarded as responsible for rolling back the stone. See, e.g., Perkins, *Resurrection,* 118; Lüdemann, *Resurrection,* 112.

[25] A number of scholars have suggested that the angelophany (vv. 5–7) was not original; see Bultmann, *History,* 290. For a summary and support for this case, E. L. Bode, *The First Easter Morning: The Gospel Accounts of the Women's Visit to the Tomb of Jesus* (AnBib 45; Rome: Pontifical Biblical Institute, 1970), 165–71. See also Neirynck, "Mark 16,1–8," 255–58.

[26] The origin of an empty tomb tradition is at the heart of many debates surrounding Mark 16:1–8. Did Mark receive a tradition of an empty tomb, or did he invent it? For a full discussion, proposing that the Jerusalem community did not know of an empty tomb, an element in the resurrection kerygma developed in the pre-Markan tradition, see Broer, *Die Urgemeinde und das Grab Jesu*

It is almost universally accepted that the young man dressed in a white robe is an angelic figure (cf. 2 Macc 3:26, 33; Tob 5:9; Mark 9:3; Acts 1:10; 10:30; Rev 6:11; 7:9, 13; Josephus, *Ant.* 5.277).[27] He is a messenger from God. This is no doubt true, but the reader recalls the earlier reference to the young man (νεανίσκος) in 14:51–52. He was a symbol of the failed disciples who fled in fear, naked in their nothingness as they separated themselves from Jesus when he was arrested at Gethsemane. Unable to deny themselves, take up the cross, and follow him (see 8:34), despite their protestations that they would die for him (14:31), they abandon Jesus to his solitary death. The clothing of the young man in 16:5 is different. The young man in the parable on the disciples left a linen cloth (τὴν σινδόνα, 14:52) in the hands of Jesus' assailants. The young man in the tomb is dressed in a white robe (στολὴν λευκήν, 16:5). But the dead body of Jesus was wrapped in a σινδών (15:46), and now there is no sign in the tomb of this garment of death. The young man in the garden was initially clothed (περιβεβλημένος, 14:51) but ran away naked (γυμνός, 14:52). The young man in the tomb is also clothed (περιβεβλημένος, 16:5), and there is no indication that his white robe will be snatched from him.

The verbal links are too many, and the passages follow one another too closely within the story to be irrelevant (14:51–52; 15:46; 16:5). No doubt the primary meaning of the text is that the women encounter a heavenly figure in an empty tomb, and this figure announces the Easter message to them (v. 6). However, it also contains a hint that the disciples, whose flight and fear have been conveyed in the parable of the young man who fled naked in 14:51–52, have not been dismissed from the story. God has entered the story, and his messenger, dressed in a white robe, will announce what God has done to the one who had been laid in the tomb (v. 6). The figure recalls the parable on the disciples who abandoned their crucified Messiah (14:51–52). As God has transformed the death of Jesus by raising him from the dead, discipleship may be reestablished and nakedness covered. The reader will find that the disciples and Peter are named in 16:7, called to "see" Jesus in

---

(esp. 280–94). As is regularly pointed out, an empty tomb does not generate Easter faith. However, biblical anthropology demands that a risen Jesus means an empty tomb; see Gnilka, *Markus,* 2:345–46, and especially G. Stemberger, *Der Leib der Auferstehung: Studien zur Anthropologie und Eschatologie des palästinischen Judentums im neutestamentlichen Zeitalter (ca. 170 v.Cr.—100 n.Chr)* (AnBib 56; Rome: Biblical Institute Press, 1972). Does this mean that the empty tomb tradition was born of an anthropological notion, and may have no relation to an actual tomb in Jerusalem? See the careful study of Anton Vögtle, coming to this conclusion, in A. Vögtle and R. Pesch, *Wie kam es zum Osterglauben?* (Düsseldorf: Patmos-Verlag, 1975), 85–98. This is not the place to resolve the debate. The evidence points to the antiquity of an empty tomb tradition; see Schweizer, *Mark,* 368–71; Anderson, *Mark,* 356–57; and the thorough but polemical study of W. L. Craig, "The Historicity of the Empty Tomb of Jesus," *NTS* 31 (1985): 39–67. For a more complete list of opinions, see G. O'Collins, "The Resurrection: The State of the Questions," in *The Resurrection: An Interdisciplinary Symposium on the Resurrection of Jesus* (ed. S. T. Davis, D. Kendall, and G. O'Collins; Oxford: Oxford University Press, 1997), 13–15. The Jewish and Christian apologetic "myths" of Matt 27:62–28:20 are rarely discussed. Matthew reports that the story is abroad that Jesus' disciples stole the body ("The story has been spread among the Jews to this day": Matt 27:15), but it is the result of corruption and lies (27:62–66; 28:11–15) because Jesus has been raised and seen (28:1–10, 16–20). However recent the *apologetic* might be, earlier *events* generated it. Both the Christian (risen Jesus) and the Jewish (stolen dead body) apologetic presuppose that there had been an empty tomb. The Matthean story is late (*circa* 85 C.E.), but it is generated by something other than Matthew's use of Mark 16:1–8. Could that "something" be the need for both Jews and Christians to explain an empty tomb? See the summary dismissal of this line of argument in Vögtle and Pesch, *Wie kam es?* 89.

[27] See the evidence for this assembled in R. E. Brown, *The Death of the Messiah: From Gethsemane to the Grave: A Commentary on the Passion Narratives in the Four Gospels* (2 vols; ABRL; New York: Doubleday, 1994), 1:299–300.

Galilee, just as he promised they would in the midst of their earlier confusion and failure (14:28). The case must not be overstated, as the function of the young man is not to act as a symbol of "restored discipleship," but a hint that God's action can reverse failure. As God has done with the apparent failure of Jesus, so he can do for the failed disciples.[28]

The young man announces an Easter message that focuses upon the transforming power of God. Paralleling biblical theophanies, he urges the women not to be afraid (v. 6a). The pre-Easter Jesus, known by the women who followed him from Galilee and who watched his death (15:40–41), is described in a carefully constructed sentence: "You are seeking Jesus, the Nazarene, who was crucified" ('Ιησοῦν ζητεῖτε τὸν Ναζαρηνὸν τὸν ἐσταυρωμένον, 16:6a).[29] But that situation has changed. Two of them also watched the burial and saw where they laid him (15:47). They are asked to look again: "He is not here, see the place where they laid him" (ἴδε ὁ τόπος ὅπου ἔθηκαν αὐτόν, 16:6c). At the center of the proclamation, explaining the transformation of the women's experience of the death (15:40–41) and the burial (15:47), lies the action of God: "He has been raised!" (ἠγέρθη, 16:6b). The aorist tense of the verb announces that God had entered the story of Jesus before the women appeared on the scene. Human experience and expectation have been transcended by the action of God.[30]

The question asked of God by Jesus from the cross, "My God, my God, why have you forsaken me?" (15:34), has been answered. Jesus has not been forsaken. Unconditionally obedient to the will of God (14:36), Jesus has accepted the cup of suffering. On the cross he is Messiah, king of Israel and Son of God (15:32, 39). God's never failing presence to his obedient Son leads to the definitive action of God: he has been raised! The apparent failure of Jesus has been reversed by the action of God, who has raised Jesus from death. The women are told to look at the place where they laid him. The opponents of Jesus crucified him, and he has been placed in a tomb. It could appear that they have had their victory, but they have been thwarted.[31] He has been raised, and the existence of Mark's Gospel indi-

---

[28] This is nothing more than a hint. As too much is sometimes read into the parallels between 14:51–52 and 16:5 (Brown, *Death*, 1:299: "flights of imagination"), mainstream scholarship tends to reject any connection. See, for example, Bode, *First Easter Morning*, 26–27; Perkins, *Resurrection*, 118–19. Many have attempted to link the uses of the young man in 14:51–52 and 16:5 with baptismal symbolism. For a survey of these opinions, and a rejection of them, see Neirynck, "La fuite du jeune homme," 215–19. For a resumption of a baptismal reading of the passage, see LaVerdiere, *The Beginning*, 2:320–22.

[29] Lohmeyer (*Markus*, 354–55) points out that the verb ζητεῖν often has a negative meaning in Mark. The women are seeking the dead, and are thus in error. Pesch (*Markusevangelium*, 2:531–35) also plays upon this idea of mistaken and correct "seeking." On the use of "the Nazarene" across the Gospel, culminating in this presentation of Jesus as the crucified, see E. K. Broadhead, *Naming Jesus: Titular Christology in the Gospel of Mark* (JSNTSup 175; Sheffield: Sheffield Academic Press, 1999), 31–42.

[30] Although many translate "He has risen," full strength must be given to the passive mood: "He has been raised." Against Cranfield (*St. Mark*, 466), who suggests that the use of the passive of ἐγείρω must not be pressed, see Lohmeyer, *Markus*, 355, 357–58; Gnilka, *Markus*, 2:342–43; Hooker, *St. Mark*, 385; Ernst, *Markus*, 487; Lührmann, *Markusevangelium*, 269–70. As Lindemann ("Die Osterbotschaft des Markus," 304–6) rightly points out, Mark's focus is upon the proclamation that God has raised Jesus, not on the fact of the empty tomb. See also H. Paulsen, "Mk XVI 1–8," *NovT* 22 (1980): 158–61.

[31] The instruction to "look at the place where they have laid him" has been used by some to suggest that the origin of the empty tomb tradition can be found in the Jerusalem Christian community's practice of venerating the tomb of Jesus. On interest in tombs, see Perkins, *Resurrection*, 142 n. 36. Among many, see especially L. Schenke, *Auferstehungsverkündigung und leeres Grab: Eine traditionsgeschichtliche Untersuchung von Mk 16,1–8* (SBS 33; Stuttgart: Katholisches Bibelwerk, 1968), 56–93. Attempts to locate the origin of an empty tomb tradition in the cultic practice of the

cates that there is a community of believers whose coming into being depends upon God's action. Jesus' prophecy that the rejected stone has become the foundation stone of a new temple of God has proved true (12:11–12; 14:58; 15:29).

The new temple depends upon those who have carried the story of Jesus to the Markan community. During the life and ministry of Jesus the disciples were commissioned for that task (3:13–14; 6:7–13), and told that before the end of time the gospel would be preached to all nations (13:10).[32] They have disappeared from the story, fleeing in fear, naked in their nothingness (14:50–52). The young man commissions the women to announce a message to the failed disciples. The promise of the restoration of the failed disciples was first made by Jesus to his disciples as they walked away from their last meal: "After I am raised up, I will go before (future tense: προάξω) you into Galilee" (14:28). A hint that this promise would be realized was found in the presence of a young man in the empty tomb (16:5), reversing the parabolic comment upon the fleeing disciples (14:50) in the episode of the young man who fled in fear, naked (14:51–52). The future tense of 14:28 is now rendered as a present tense in the young man's instruction to the women. They are to tell the disciples of Jesus (τοῖς μαθηταῖς αὐτοῦ) and Peter that "he is going (present tense: προάγει) before you into Galilee, as he told you" (v. 7). In 10:32 the reader learned that the disciples were headed toward Jerusalem because Jesus was going before them (ἦν προάγων), leading them to the place of his passion, death, and resurrection. His promise, that he would lead them away from the city of their fear and failure (14:28), will be fulfilled (16:7).[33] The stage is set for an encounter in Galilee where failure will be forgiven and discipleship restored.[34] Despite their fear (4:40; 6:50; 9:32; 10:32), failure (4:35–41; 5:16, 31;

Jerusalem church are thoroughly surveyed in Neirynck, "ΑΝΑΤΕΙΛΑΝΤΟΣ," 181–91. Neirynck does not deny the possibility that the tradition developed in this context, but asks what came first, history or liturgy (pp. 190–91).

[32] Gnilka (*Markus*, 2:343–44, 347) rightly points to the Markan insistence that the disciples are to leave Jerusalem as that is not where they are to exercise their ministry. They will be witnesses to the risen Jesus in Galilee, and this leads them into a Gentile mission; see also Fuller, *Resurrection Narratives*, 59–62; Painter, *Mark's Gospel*, 212–13; and especially D. Senior, "The Struggle to Be Universal: Mission as Vantage Point for New Testament Investigation," *CBQ* 46 (1984): 63–81.

[33] Too much is sometimes made of the verb προάγειν. See the survey of the earlier discussion in Fuller, *Resurrection Narratives*, 58–62. Since then it has been pressed by Best in an attempt to counter the Lohmeyer-Marxsen-Perrin-Weeden-Kelber suggestion that the disciples are gathered in Galilee, waiting for the Parousia in the absence of Jesus. For example, E. Best (*Following Jesus: Discipleship in the Gospel of Mark* [JSNTSup 4; Sheffield: JSOT Press, 1981], 199–203) claims that the verb has the idea of "to go at the head of," and thus (via 14:27–28) "shepherding." The risen Jesus is once again with and caring for the disciples (3:14). See also Broadhead, *Naming Jesus*, 94–96. Its primary meaning is to "lead forward" or to "go before"; BDAG, 864, s.v. προάγω. LSJ, 1466, s.v. προάγω, also gives examples from classical literature of "escort on their way," but the meaning of "leading" is primary. That is what Jesus does in 10:32, promises to do in 14:28, and is announced as doing in 16:7 (cf. 6:45; 11:9). See the helpful assessment of E. S. Malbon, *Narrative Space and Mythic Meaning in Mark* (New Voices in Biblical Studies; San Francisco: Harper & Row, 1986), 68–71. She rightly comments: "*Hodos* and *proagein* signal not so much one place among others as a way between places, a dynamic process of movement" (p. 71). In a number of publications, Best rightly strains against the popularity of the Lohmeyer-inspired theory of Mark's proclamation of the "absence of Jesus." But he reads too much into the Markan use of "house" as a community "household," the community as a "ship," shepherded by Jesus, but without any group or member with special responsibility for others; see, e.g., Best, *Following Jesus*, 226–45; idem, *Mark: The Gospel as Story* (Edinburgh: T&T Clark, 1983), 55–65.

[34] Most commentators note that the singling out of Peter in v. 7 looks back to his denials, and thus highlights the theme of failure; e.g., Taylor, *St. Mark*, 607; Cranfield, *St. Mark*, 467; Hooker, *St. Mark*, 385. For Bode (*First Easter Morning*, 28–31), it also shows an awareness of Peter's role as a

6:7–30, 35–36, 45–52; 8:4, 14–21, 31–33; 9:5–6, 28–29, 32–34, 38–41; 10:35–41; 11:9–10), and flight (14:50), they will see him there, as he had promised (16:7; cf. 14:28).[35]

The Failure of the Women (16:8)

Jesus' promise appears to be thwarted by the last line of the Gospel: "And they went out and fled from the tomb; for trembling and astonishment had come upon them; and they said nothing to anyone, for they were afraid" (v. 8). The women, who had overcome the scandal of the cross by looking on from afar as Jesus died (15:40–41), and had watched where he was buried (15:47), have not been able to overcome the scandal of the empty tomb and the Easter proclamation. They have joined the disciples in flight (ἔφυγον; cf. 14:50, 52) and fear (ἐφοβοῦντο γάρ; cf. 4:41; 6:50; 9:32; 10:32). Like Peter, they have degenerated from following "from a distance" (ἀπὸ μακρόθεν, 15:40; cf. 14:54) to final failure (16:8; cf. 14:66–72). Does this mean that there is, in Mark's view of things, no vision of the resurrected Jesus, and that the disciples are still waiting for his return?[36] The very existence of the Markan community, receiving and passing on this gospel story, makes that option unlikely.[37] Many have suggested that the silence of the women is a form of Markan apolo-

---

witness to the resurrection (cf. 1 Cor 15:5). See also Fuller, *Resurrection Narratives,* 57–58, and Bode, *First Easter Morning,* 31, for the suggestion Peter is given special prominence. The women are to tell the disciples "and especially Peter."

[35] The tradition history of 14:28 and 16:7 is widely debated. In their present Markan setting, these two verses are closely related. But the disobedience and the failure of the women in v. 8 is greatly lessened when v. 7 is removed. See the survey in Neirynck, "Marc 16,1–8," 245–47. This has led many to suggest that both are the result of Markan redaction. Bultmann (*History,* 285, 287) regards 14:28 and 16:7 as Markan footnotes "to prepare the way for a Galilean appearance of Jesus" (p. 285). Many have followed him, e.g., Bode, *Easter Morning,* 35–37; Lüdemann, *Resurrection,* 116–17. However, a good case can be made for 16:7 as the reworking of a pre-Markan word on the announcement of the resurrection to Peter; see Gnilka, *Markus,* 2:338–39; Neirynck, "Marc 16,1–8," 258–71; and especially Lindemann, "Die Osterbotschaft des Markus," 306–8. If this was the case, 14:28 has developed from a more original pre-Markan form of 16:7. In the end, however, both 14:28 and 16:7 are important elements in the Markan narrative and theological agenda. Neirynck's exhaustive study shows that, as with the passion account, the interpreter is faced with signs that pre-Markan elements helped form 16:1–8. But in the end, we have only Mark to work with, and the reconstruction of Mark's *Vorlage* proves to be highly speculative. The account is not an unambiguously Markan invention, but it features a unity created by Mark's work as an author; see Neirynck, "Marc 16,1–8," 271, and especially Paulsen, "Mk XVI 1–8," 145–65. Paulsen argues for a pre-Markan tradition of 16:1–6, 8b, dominated by the proclamation ἠγέρθη (v. 6), but insists that the passage must be understood in the light of the Markan theological perspective reflected in 14:28 and 16:7.

[36] So Lohmeyer, *Markus,* 355–56; Marxsen, *Mark the Evangelist,* 75–92; Nineham, *St. Mark,* 446; and a number of contemporary scholars; see above, note 12. Following Lohmeyer, much weight is given to the interpretation of the future tense of the verb "to see" (ὄψεσθε) as an indication of an eschatological "sight" at the Parousia; see especially Weeden, *Traditions in Conflict,* 111–16; Perrin, *The Resurrection Narratives,* 17–40. The evidence is slight, and is contradicted by the use of the same verb elsewhere to refer to Easter appearances (1 Cor 9:1; Matt 28:17; John 20:18, 25, 29); see Taylor, *St. Mark,* 608; R. H. Stein, "A Short Note on Mark xiv.28 and xvi.7," *NTS* 20 (1973–1974): 445–52; Best, *The Gospel as Story,* 76–78. For a survey of the various attempts, both literary and theological, to explain v. 8, see Bode, *First Easter Morning,* 39–41; Lindemann, "Die Osterbotshaft des Markus," 308–10.

[37] W. R. Telford (*The Theology of the Gospel of Mark* [New Testament Theology; Cambridge: Cambridge University Press, 1999], 149–51) joins G. H. Boobyer, C. F. Evans, E. C. Hoskyns, and J. Schreiber in seeing 14:28 and 16:7 as a message to the Gentile church. The risen Jesus will be found in Galilee of the Gentiles. This suggestion gives due importance to the ongoing mission of the post-

getic, allied to the idea of the messianic secret. On the basis of the Pauline evidence (e.g.,
1 Cor 15:3–5), it is claimed that nothing was known of the empty tomb in earlier traditions. Mark invented the silence of the women to explain this lack of knowledge.[38] Others
have focused upon the emotional experience of the women, "trembling and astonishment
(τρόμος καὶ ἔκστασις) had come upon them." These emotions often accompany the experience of the grandeur of the divine. In this understanding, the fear and flight are an indication of holy awe in the face of the numinous wonder of the resurrection.[39]

The women's sharing of the fear and flight of the disciples must be given its full importance. The disciples before them grew steadily more fearful (4:41; 5:36; 6:50; 9:32; 10:32),
and they broke their oneness with Jesus when they fled (14:50). The association of the experience of the women with that of the disciples is too important and too obvious to be
subsumed into the themes of the absence of Jesus, an apologetic for general ignorance concerning the tomb, or the more theological explanation of fear and trembling in the face of
the action of God in Jesus. There is doubtless an important element of the numinous in
the reaction of the women to the words of the young man in 16:6–7, but there can be no
missing Mark's primary intention. The odd, but dramatic, ending of a book with the
words ἐφοβοῦντο γάρ is not an indication that there must have been a longer ending.[40] It
drives home, with considerable force, the women's sharing in one of the fundamental aspects of the disciples' failure to follow Jesus to the cross: fear (cf. 4:41; 6:50; 9:32; 10:32).
Mark indicates that, in the end, the women who have followed Jesus through the experience of the cross to the grave, finally join the other disciples in the fear and flight of their
failure (14:50–52).[41]

Does that mean that the Gospel ends in unresolved failure on the part of all who have
followed Jesus? In one sense, such is the case, but to read this failure independently of the
earlier parts of the story would lead to a misunderstanding of the Gospel of Mark.[42] The
ending of the Gospel must be understood in the light of the story as a whole, and especially
as a return to the prologue (1:1–13). As the Gospel opened, the reader was provided with
all the information necessary to understand who Jesus was, and what God was doing for
humankind. The prologue to the Gospel is unashamedly full of confessions of faith in the
person of Jesus of Nazareth. However, *the reader* is the only one who hears these confessions. The characters from the story are not standing by, listening. The narrator tells *the*

Easter Markan community, but he discounts any link between the disciples *in the story* and the readers *of the story*. As Telford says elsewhere, "As in all else, his original Jewish disciples didn't get the
message!" (idem, *Mark* [NTG; Sheffield: Sheffield Academic Press, 1995], 149).

[38] So, e.g., Grundmann, *Markus*, 322–23. For a survey of this proposal, and a critique of it, see
Neirynck, "Marc 6,1–8," 247–51.

[39] This is the traditional solution to the problem, generally with reference back to the fear of the
disciples at the transfiguration (see 9:6); see, e.g., Lagrange, *Saint Marc*, 418; Taylor, *St. Mark*, 609;
Lightfoot, *Gospel Message*, 96–97; Cranfield, *St. Mark*, 469–70; Nineham, *St. Mark*, 447–48; Lane,
Mark, 590–92; Pesch, *Markusevangelium*, 2:535–36; Ernst, *Markus*, 489–90; Lührmann, *Markusevangelium*, 271; Gnilka, *Markus*, 2:344 (but see below). For a well-documented survey of suggestions concerning the Markan function of v. 8, see Boomershine, "Mark 16:8," 227–34.

[40] It has often been claimed that a book could not end with the word γάρ ("for"). It is certainly a
strange ending, but should not be taken as impossible. Among many, see R. H. Lightfoot, *The Gospel
Message of St. Mark* (Oxford: Clarendon Press, 1950), 80–97; T. E. Boomershine and G. L.
Bartholomew, "The Narrative Technique of Mark 16:8," *JBL* 100 (1981): 213 n. 4.

[41] Perkins, *Resurrection*, 121–22; van Iersel, *Reading Mark*, 203–4. See also the chart of the distribution of Mark's vocabulary of fear and astonishment in Bode, *First Easter Morning*, 38.

[42] This case has been consistently argued by Best. See, for example, his approach to the question
of Markan disciples in *Following Jesus*, passim, and in his *The Gospel as Story*, 128–33.

reader that Jesus is the Christ (1:1), the Lord (v. 3), the mightier one (v. 7), the one who will baptize with the Holy Spirit (v. 8), the beloved Son in whom God is well pleased (v. 11). Only the reader recognizes that Jesus' presence in the wilderness, with the wild animals and served by angels, recalls God's original design for humankind, as told in the story of Adam and Eve. God's original created order has been restored in the person of Jesus of Nazareth (vv. 12–13).

The beginning (1:1–13) and the end (16:1–8) of the Gospel of Mark address the reader. Throughout the story the reader has followed the disciples as they steadily fell further from the design God had for his Son and for those who follow him (see 8:34–9:1). They have abandoned him (14:50), betrayed him (14:43–45), and denied him (14:66–72). They have ignored Jesus' command to "watch" with him across the passion (13:35–37). Jesus has unflinchingly accepted God's will, cost what it may (14:36). The voice of God, summoning the disciples to listen to his obedient Son (9:7), has gone unheeded. Only the women, who have been with him since his days in Galilee, have been present at the cross (15:40–41), at the burial (15:47), and at the empty tomb (16:1–7). But in the end they join the disciples in their trembling, astonishment, fear, and flight (16:8; see 14:50). In the light of the information provided in 1:1–13 the *Christian reader* is asked to reassess God's design, outlined in 1:1–13, on arrival at the conclusion of the story of Jesus in 16:1–8.[43] If 1:1–13 served as a prologue to the Gospel of Mark, 16:1–8 is its epilogue. The action and the design of God are again at center stage.[44]

Mark 16:1–8 is the masterstroke of a storyteller who, up to this point, has relentlessly pursued the steady movement toward failure of all the male disciples.[45] The evidence of the tradition (seen in the Gospels of Matthew, Luke, and John) indicates that women were the first witnesses of the Easter event, and reported an Easter message to the unbelieving and discouraged disciples.[46] This was well known by members of early Christian commu-

---

[43] Boomershine and Bartholomew ("The Narrative Techique," 213–23) have shown that the Gospel contains a number of literary features which are repeated in 16:8. Thus, 16:8 "seems particularly appropriate for the ending of a story which brings to a close the Gospel narrative as a whole" (p. 223). See also J. L. Magness, *Sense and Absence: Structure and Suspension in the Ending of Mark's Gospel* (Semeia Studies; Atlanta: Scholars Press, 1986), 87–105.

[44] This is well caught by Anderson (*Mark*, 358): "The *silent* fear with which Mark's record closes need not be taken as an editorial insertion on Mark's part . . . to account for the lateness of the empty tomb tradition, nor yet as an implicit condemnation of the women's craven-heartedness or blindness. Rather their fearful silence eloquently enough proclaims the truth that the first word and the last word of the good news is not anything men or women can think or say or do, but *God's own witness to his Son*" (stress in original). See also van Iersel, *Reading Mark*, 210–11.

[45] On Mark as a storyteller, using the young man in 14:51–52 and 16:6 and the ending at 16:8 as examples, see the provocate reflections of F. Kermode, *The Genesis of Secrecy: On the Interpretation of Narrative* (Cambridge: Harvard University Press, 1979), 49–73. Even Bultmann (*History*, 286) recognizes this: "Yet Mark's presentation is extremely reserved. . . . His construction is impressive: the wonder of the women v. 3, the surprised sight of the rolled-away stone and the apperance of the angel vv. 4f., the masterly formulated angelic message v. 6 and the shattering impression in v. 8."

[46] Against Bode, *First Easter Morning*, 151–75. Bode's reconstruction of "the reality of the empty tomb" concludes "that some Christian women visited the tomb of Jesus on the first day of the week, found it empty, left perplexed and apparently kept the matter to themselves" (p. 175). This historicization of the Markan subversion of the tradition misses the point of 16:7–8. As is often argued, the fact that women were the primary witnesses to the resurrection would have been such an embarrassment to the early church that it could not have been created; so, e.g., Lane, *Mark*, 588–89; Cranfield, *St. Mark*, 464. See, however, the softening of this widely held principle in T. Ilan, *Jewish Women in Greco-Roman Palestine* (Peabody: Hendrickson, 1996), 163–66. The role of the women in

nities. In this, Matthew, Luke, and John, each in their own way, are closer to what happened on that Sunday morning. *But Mark has changed the story.*[47] Why has Mark taken a well-known tradition and altered it so radically? There is something profoundly Pauline in what Mark is trying to do as he takes away all initiative from human beings and places it with God.[48] As with the promises of Jesus' forthcoming death and resurrection (8:31; 9:31; 10:33–34), the promises of 14:28 and 16:7 will be fulfilled. *What Jesus said would happen, will happen.* Jesus was challenged by his enemies to prophesy (14:65); the failure of the disciples (14:50; cf. v. 27), the betrayal of Judas (14:43–46; cf. vv. 17–21), and the denials of Peter (14:66–72; cf. vv. 30–31), his arrest, his trials, and his crucifixion have all shown that Jesus' predictions come true.[49] The *reader* has every reason to believe that the promises of 14:28 and 16:7 *have already come true.* But Jesus' meeting with the disciples and Peter in Galilee does not take place within the limitations of the story. It cannot, because the women do not obey the word of the young man. They, like the disciples, fail; they flee in fear (16:8).[50]

When and how does Jesus' meeting with the failed disciples, women and men, take place? The answer to that question cannot be found *in the story,* but the very existence *of the story* tells the reader that *what Jesus said would happen, did happen.* The Gospel of Mark, with its faith-filled prologue telling of God's design for the human situation in the gift of his Son (1:1–13), addresses a believing community. This indicates that the disciples and Peter did see Jesus in Galilee, as he had promised (14:28; 16:7). As Jesus' prophecies

---

15:42–47 and then in 16:1–8 also suggests that the Jerusalem community knew where the grave was; see Gnilka, *Markus,* 2:346.

[47] This affirmation depends upon the belief that behind 14:28 and 16:7 lies the Markan awareness of earlier traditions surrounding Jesus' resurrection and appearances. Not all would accept this; see the discussion in Telford, *The Theology of the Gospel of Mark* (New Testament Theology; Cambridge: Cambridge University Press, 1999), 137–51.

[48] Fundamental to Pauline thought is the belief that God has saved sinful humankind by his free gift of grace, made available in and through the death and resurrection of Jesus Christ (cf. Rom 3:21–26). It is not so much a question of how good the believer might be, or how well he or she performs (although a life modeled on that of Jesus is demanded; see the "ethical excursus" of Rom 5:1–8:39). What ultimately changes the relationship between God and the human story, lost since the fall of Adam, is the boundless goodness of God (Rom 5:12–21), made visible in Jesus Christ (Rom 8:31–39). For an excellent analysis of the similarities between Pauline and Markan thought, without suggesting literary dependence, see Marcus, *Mark,* 73–75; Painter, *Mark's Gospel,* 213. For a less convincing study that returns to the suggestion of G. Volkmar (*Die Religion Jesu* [Leipzig: Brockhaus, 1857]), that Mark is an allegory, using the Jesus story, of the Pauline gospel, see P. N. Tarazi, *The New Testament Introduction: Paul and Mark* (New York: St. Vladimir's Seminary Press, 1999), 111–237. J. Marcus ("Mark—Interpreter of Paul," *NTS* 46 [2000]: 473–87) has recently highlighted the parallels between the Pauline and Markan presentations of the cross. Marcus suggests that this is but the beginning of his interest in the Pauline-Markan relationship (pp. 474–76). My reading of Mark 16:1–8 finds a narrative presentation of the resurrection of Jesus that repeats a message fundamental to the Pauline gospel. See above, p. 330 n. 285.

[49] See also Lindemann ("Die Osterbotschaft des Markus," 310–14), who adds to the fulfillment of the prophecies of the passion, and the indications of 14:28 and 16:7, the proleptic revelation of Jesus in the transfiguration (9:2–13) and the proclamation of Jesus as the Christ and Son of God in 14:61–62, vindicated in the coming of the Son of Man. The reader arrives at 16:8 with all this in place. See also Fuller, *Resurrection Narratives,* 66–70, especially the fulfillment of 9:9; Boomershine, "Mark 16:8," 232–39; Paulsen, "Mk XVI 1–8," 169–74; Magness, *Sense and Absence,* 108–13.

[50] For an interpretation of the alternate endings of Mark's Gospel, added at a later stage, see chapter 10. Interested readers will find full-scale studies of vv. 9–20 in Hug, *La finale,* and Kelhoffer, *Miracle and Mission.* For helpful briefer studies, consult Schweizer, *Mark,* 373–79; Pesch, *Markusevangelium,* 2:544–59; Gnilka, *Markus,* 2:351–58; Hooker, *St. Mark,* 387–91.

come true (8:31; 9:31; 10:32–34; 12:11–12; 14:17–21, 27–31), the believing reader accepts that the promise of 14:28 and 16:7 also came true. There is no record of any such encounter *within the narrative.* It is not required, as the believing community has the word itself: "Jesus has been raised" (16:6). If the promise of 14:28 and 16:7 had been thwarted, there would be no Christian community, and thus no Gospel of Mark, read and heard within the community.[51] "This is the end of Mark's story, because it is the beginning of discipleship."[52]

Conclusion

The explanation of the enigma of the failure of the women in 16:8 lies in Mark's desire to instruct his readers that the encounter between the risen Jesus and the failed disciples did not take place because of the success of the women. As the disciples failed (14:50–52), so also the women failed (16:8). In the end, *all human beings fail* . . . but God succeeds. God has raised Jesus from the dead (16:6); the Father has not abandoned the Son (15:34). The same God will also raise the disciples, men and women, from their failure. They will see the risen Lord in Galilee, but not because the disciples or the women succeed. The event that bridged the gap between the end of the Gospel of Mark and the community which heard it and read it took place because of the initiative of God, and not the success of men or women. The Christian community that produced and received the Gospel of Mark existed because of the initiative of God.[53] The promise of the Gospel's prologue (1:1–13) is fulfilled in the action of God described in its epilogue (16:1–8) and experienced by believing readers of the Markan story.

The epilogue to the Gospel of Mark maintains its relevance. The Easter proclamation, "He has been raised" (v. 6),[54] the promise that Jesus was going before his disciples into Gali-

---

[51] Gnilka (*Markus*, 2:344) asserts: "Complete understanding lies beyond 16:8. The 'image' of the silent women permits no historical reconstruction of rival communities but refers to the reader or hearer of the Gospel and his or her faith."

[52] Hooker, *St. Mark*, 394. See also Lindemann, "Die Osterbotschaft des Markus," 314–17; Paulsen, "Mk XVI 1–8," 165–75; Magness, *Sense and Absence*, 107–25; E. S. Malbon, "Text and Contexts: Interpreting the Disciples in Mark," *Semeia* 62 (1993): 90–96, now available in idem, *In the Company of Jesus: Characters in Mark's Gospel* (Louisville: Westminster John Knox, 2000), 100–130; Danove, *The End of Mark's Story*, 203–30.

[53] For an excellent synthesis of the ongoing relevance of the post-Easter Markan community, gleaned from a reading of the Gospel, see K. Scholtissek, "Nachfolge und Autorität nach dem Markusevangelium," *TTZ* 100 (1991): 56–74.

[54] This is not the place to evaluate what might have been meant by "resurrection" in the earliest church. Mark's terse narrative offers no help. For a survey, see F. J. Moloney, "Faith in the Risen Jesus," *Salesianum* 43 (1981): 305–16. Scholarly opinion varies from those who argue for the physical presence of the pre-Easter Jesus alive among his disciples (e.g., W. Pannenberg, "Did Jesus Actually Rise from the Dead?" *Dialog* 4 [1965]: 18–35; idem, *Grundzüge der Christologie* [Gutersloh: Gerd Mohn, 1964], 85–103), to an experience among the disciples that they had been forgiven (so E. Schillebeeckx, *Jesus: An Experiment in Christology* [London: Collins, 1979], 115–319), a mysterious awareness that "the Jesus thing goes on" (W. Marxsen, *The Resurrection of Jesus of Nazareth* [London: SCM, 1970]), the expected fulfillment of the disciples' recognition of the pre-Easter Jesus as the Mosaic eschatological prophet (R. Pesch, "Zur Entstehung des Glaubens an die Auferstehung Jesu," *TQ* 153 [1973]: 201–28), or the resolution of the experiences of the righteous sufferer (Lührmann, *Markusevangelium*, 270). Recently Adele Collins has revived the suggestion (see M. Goguel, *La foi à la résurrection de Jésus dans le christianisme primitif* [Paris: E. Leroux, 1933], 215–22) that ancient, Jewish, and especially Greco-Roman ideas of a translation to heaven have been used by Mark to

lee (v. 7), and the failure of the women to speak to anyone because they, like the disciples before them, fled in fear (16:6–8; cf. 14:50), point beyond the limitations of the Markan story to the existence of a believing Christian community. The prologue to the Gospel (1:1–13) informed the reader that Jesus was the Christ (1:1), the Lord (v. 3), the mightier one (v. 7), one who would baptize with the Holy Spirit (v. 8), the beloved Son of God (v. 11), restoring God's original creative design (vv. 12–13). The original Markan community accepted this confession of faith, and attempted to live as authentic disciples of Jesus, taking up their cross as receptive servants of all in imitation of Jesus (8:31–10:44), who came to serve and not be served, and to lay down his life (10:45). Yet, in human terms, the disciples, both men and women, fail to follow Jesus through the cross to resurrection. In the same human terms, even Jesus failed, crying out in anguish from the cross (15:34). But Jesus' apparent failure is his victory. On the cross he is King, Messiah, and Son of God (15:26, 31–32), and God has entered the story by raising his Son from the dead: "He has been raised" (ἠγέρθη, 16:6b). He is no longer in the place where they laid him (v. 6c).

The author believes and wishes to communicate that the exalted christological claims of the prologue (1:1–13) have been vindicated by the story of the suffering and crucified Jesus, especially by means of the Easter proclamation of the epilogue (16:1–8). The affirmation of God's project by means of the prologue (1:1–13) and the epilogue (16:1–8) also points to God's vindication of failed disciples. The original readers of the Gospel of Mark, aware of their fragility, were encouraged by a story which told of the inability of the original disciples, men and women, to overcome their fear and follow Jesus through the cross to resurrection (14:50; 16:8). But as God has transformed the failure of Jesus by the resurrection (16:6), his promise to the failing disciples of a meeting in Galilee (14:28; 16:7) has also eventuated. God, and not human beings, generated the new temple, built upon the rejected cornerstone (12:10–11; 14:57–58; 15:29, 38). The existence of the Gospel and its original intended readership are proof of that fact.[55]

The realization of Jesus' promises is not found *in the text*. The existence of the Markan community and its story of Jesus indicate that it is taking place *among the readers of the text*, in the experience of the original readers and hearers of the Gospel of Mark. But that is not the end of the process. The proclamation of the Gospel of Mark in fragile Christian communities, experiencing their own versions of fear and flight, for almost two thousand years suggests that the accomplishment of the promise of 14:28 and 16:7 continues in the

---

present his understanding of the absence of the risen Jesus (*Beginning,* 138–48); also idem, "The Empty Tomb in the Gospel according to Mark," in *Hermes and Athena* (ed. E. Stump and T. P. Flint; Notre Dame: University of Notre Dame Press, 1993), 107–40; Lüdemann, *Resurrection,* 119–21. For Collins's broader agenda concerning the Markan readership and its Greco-Roman context, see A. Y. Collins, "Mark and His Readers: The Son of God among Greeks and Romans," *HTR* 93 (2000): 85–100. For a strenuous rejection of any Greco-Roman influence on the Markan resurrection account, see O'Collins, "The State of the Questions," 15–17. Danove, *The End of Mark's Story,* provides a literary and rhetorical study of the Gospel that finds little or no evidence of Greco-Roman influence.

[55] On the perennial nature of the Markan message of the tension between success and failure among disciples, both women and men, see H.-J. Klauck, "Die erzählerische Rolle der Jünger im Markusevangelium: Eine narrative Analyse," *NovT* 24 (1982): 1–26; E. S. Malbon, "Fallible Followers: Women and Men in the Gospel of Mark," *Sem* 28 (1983): 29–48, now available in idem, *In the Company of Jesus,* 41–69; R. C. Tannehill, "The Disciples in Mark: The Function of a Narrative Role," in *The Interpretation of Mark* (ed. W. R. Telford; IRT 7; Philadelphia: Fortress, 1985), 134–57; F. J. Moloney, "The Vocation of the Disciples in the Gospel of Mark," in *"A Hard Saying": The Gospel and Culture* (Collegeville: The Liturgical Press, 2001), 53–84.

Christian experience of the subsequent readers and hearers of the Gospel. What Jesus promised (14:28; 16:7) happened for the Markan community and continues to happen among generations of fragile followers of Jesus. As Christian disciples continue to fail and flee in fear, they are told that God's action in and through the risen Jesus overcomes all such failure.[56] Jesus is going before them into Galilee. There they will see him. The conclusion to Mark's Gospel is not a message of failure,[57] but a resounding affirmation of God's design to overcome all imaginable human failure (16:1–8) in and through the action of God's beloved Son (1:1–13). The words addressed to the struggling disciples at the transfiguration are addressed to all who take up this gospel: "Listen to him" (9:7).

---

[56] For similar suggestions, see Boomershine, "Mark 16:8," 234–39; R. C. Tannehill, "The Gospel of Mark as Narrative Christology," *Sem* 16 (1980): 82–84; S. R. Garrett, *The Temptations of Jesus in Mark's Gospel* (Grand Rapids: Eerdmans, 1998), 137–69.

[57] Against, for example, Schweizer (*Mark*, 373): "No joy is visible—only fear. In comparison with God's unprecedented action man has nothing to show except a complete lack of understanding." Particularly important has been the influential study of Weeden *(Traditions in Conflict)*. Not only is the Markan church experiencing the absence of Jesus, awaiting the Parousia, but the disciples (the characterization of the heresy that produced the Gospel) are judged as having failed totally: "Mark is assiduously involved in a vendetta against the disciples. He paints them as obtuse, obdurate, recalcitrant men who at first are unperceptive of Jesus' messiahship, then oppose its style and character, and finally totally reject it. As a *coup de grace,* Mark closes his Gospel without rehabilitating the disciples" (pp. 50–51).

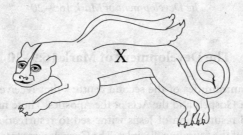

THE APPENDIX (MARK 16:9–20)

The commentary on Mark 16:1–8 argued that the original Gospel of Mark closed, surprisingly, with the flight of the frightened women in 16:8. The textual, literary, and theological arguments in defense of this position have been provided during the course of the commentary.[1] Paradoxically, although it is certain that the author of Mark 1:1–16:8 played no part in the composition of 16:9–20, many Christian lectionaries use this passage each year as the Gospel lection for the Feast of St. Mark on April 25![2] Such usage calls for a brief comment upon the passage, despite the fact that this study, the tracing of the literary and theological argument of the Gospel of Mark, reached its conclusion with the analysis of 16:1–8.[3]

---

[1] See above, pp. 339–54, and the scholarly discussions found in notes 4–11. For a comprehensive discussion of the textual problems, see K. Aland, "Bemerkungen zum Schluss des Markusevangeliums," in *Neotestamentica et Semitica: Studies in Honour of Matthew Black* (ed. E. E. Ellis and M. Wilcox; Edinburgh: T&T Clark, 1969), 157–80, and idem, "Der wiedergefundene Markusschluss? Eine methodologische Bemerkung zur textkritischen Arbeit," *ZTK* 67 (1970): 3–13 (a response to the study of E. Linnemann; see above, p. 341 n. 7]). Comprehensive bibliographies can be found in F. Neirynck, J. Verheyden, F. Van Segbroeck, G. Van Oyen, and R. Corstjens, eds., *The Gospel of Mark: A Cumulative Bibliography 1950–1990* (BETL 102; Leuven: Leuven University Press, 1992), 620. See also C. A. Evans, *Mark 8:27–16:20* (WBC 34b; Nashville: Thomas Nelson, 2001), 540–43. This fine volume, which completes Robert Guelich's Word Biblical Commentary on the Gospel of Mark, appeared too late for inclusion in my study of the Gospel. This Appendix, added later at the request of my publishers, offers an opportunity to recognize Evans's important contribution to Markan scholarship. The valuable study of J. A. Kelhoffer, *Miracle and Mission. The Authentication of Missionaries and Their Message in the Longer Ending of Mark* (WUNT 2. Reihe 112; Tübingen: J. C. B. Mohr [Paul Siebeck], 2000) is not mentioned by Evans, no doubt because it appeared after he completed his commentary. The only contemporary scholar who has suggested that vv. 9–20 might be original is W. Farmer, *The Last Twelve Verses of Mark* (SNTSMS 25; Cambridge: Cambridge University Press, 1974). Farmer has long insisted that Mark is an abbreviated compilation of Matthew and Luke. This is the only place in the Gospel of Mark where the text actually supports such a claim. For a history of the interpretation of Mark 16:9–20, see J. Hug, *La finale de l'évangile de Marc (Marc 16:9–20)* (EBib; Paris: Gabalda, 1978), 11–24; Kelhoffer, *Miracle and Mission*, 1–46.

[2] On authorship, see above, pp. 11–15. We may not be sure who "Mark" was, but the existence of the Gospel long attached to this name merits the liturgical celebration.

[3] There are a number of "endings," among which vv. 9–20 is probably the oldest, and has been most widely accepted. In 1546 it was declared part of the Catholic canon of sacred Scriptures at the Council of Trent. See the discussion of the relevance of this declaration in LaVerdiere, *The Beginning*, 2:332–33. See the classical discussion, from a Roman Catholic point of view, of the long ending's "canonical authenticity" (assessed positively) and "literary authenticity" (assessed negatively) in Lagrange, *Saint Marc*, 433–37. The so-called "shorter ending" is sometimes found immediately after v. 8, thus concluding the Gospel, or as a final conclusion to the "longer ending," i.e., after v. 20. It reflects an attempt to overcome the women's silence, although no resurrection appearance is supplied. The universal mission of the Christian community and the description of the gospel as

The Development of Mark 16:9–20

The Christian communities of the second century that received the Gospel of Mark also received the other Gospels and the Acts of the Apostles. These narrative proclamations of the life, death, and resurrection of Jesus witnessed to resurrection appearances and to Jesus' commissioning of the founding disciples. The Gospels were transmitted from one generation to another, and from one location to another, in an oral form, as many early Christians would not have been "readers" in the modern sense of their being able to read texts (if they could afford to have them). However, the abundant evidence of a textual tradition that reaches back to the second century shows that, in imitation of the scribes found in both the Jewish and the Greco-Roman world, the documents of the New Testament were copied by scribes, initially onto papyrus rolls, and increasingly into large codices, sewn at the back, able to be opened and used as we open and use a modern book.[4] The desire to preserve and transmit texts regarded as important to the emerging Christian church sometimes led to the further desire on the part of the copyists to improve upon or "correct" the text. It must be said, however, that most textual variants resulted from human error, inevitable given the arduous task of copying a long document by hand. At worst, they reflect the desire of a scribe to make the text grammatically or logically more consistent.[5] Indeed, Mark 16:9–20 appears to be the only example of such an interpretative addition to any of the Gospels.[6]

The author not only selected from across the other Gospels, but also delved into passages and themes from the Acts of the Apostles. In this way he developed a synthetic description of a variety of actions of the risen Lord, the response of the disciples, a final commission, and a report of Jesus' ascension, and even a summary description of the success of the disciples' mission, and the validating signs that accompanied it.[7] The most obvious elements are:

"the sacred and imperishable proclamation of eternal salvation" reflect an author familiar with Hellenistic thought. See Hooker, *St. Mark*, 388–89. It is replete with non-Markan vocabulary and syntax; Taylor, *St. Mark*, 614. An English version of the text runs as follows: "They reported all these instructions briefly to Peter's companions. Afterwards, Jesus himself sent out through them, from east to west, the sacred and imperishable proclamation of eternal salvation. Amen."

[4] For excellent introductions to the science of textual criticism, see J. Finegan, *Encountering New Testament Manuscripts: A Working Introduction to Textual Criticism* (Grand Rapids: Eerdmans, 1974), and K. and B. Aland, *The Text of the New Testament: An Introduction to the Critical Editions and to the Theory and Practice of Modern Textual Criticism* (trans. E. F. Rhodes; Grand Rapids: Eerdmans, 1987). On the earliest texts, see Finegan, *Encountering*, 85–100; K. and B. Aland, *The Text*, 56–64. For a stimulating history of New Testament textual criticism, see B. M. Metzger, *The Text of the New Testament: Its Transmission, Corruption and Restoration* (2d ed.; Oxford: Clarendon Press, 1968).

[5] See K. and B. Aland, *The Text*, 275–92.

[6] Some might suggest that John 21:1–25 is an "appendix," added to a narrative that originally closed with John 20:1–31. This is not the case. There is no convincing textual evidence that the Gospel of John ever circulated without 21:1–25. See K. and B. Aland, *The Text*, 292. In my opinion, it was added to a narrative that concluded with 20:30–31, by those responsible for the final form of John 1:1–20:31, before the Gospel ever appeared. It is, therefore, more of an epilogue than an appendix. For a full discussion of this question, and the interpretation of John 21 as an epilogue, see F. J. Moloney, *The Gospel of John* (SP 4; Collegeville: The Liturgical Press, 1998), 545–68.

[7] For an attempt to reconstruct the tradition history of vv. 9–20, with a survey of other such attempts, see Pesch, *Markusevangelium*, 2:546–48. Pesch (among others) suggests that the passage is a combination of an older resurrection tradition (vv. 9–15, 19) to which the author has added his major concern, that of mission (vv. 16–18, 20). Recent scholarship, however, vigorously defends the literary and theological unity of vv. 9–20. See especially, Hug, *La finale*, 173–76, and especially

16:9	The appearance to Mary Magdalene alone (cf. John 20:11–18), and her description as "from whom he (Jesus) had cast out seven demons (cf. Luke 8:2)
16:10	The mourning of the disciples, whose hopes have been dashed (cf. Luke 24:19–24)
16:11	The disciples display lack of belief in the risen Lord (cf. Luke 24:11, 41; Matt 28:17)
16:12	Two disciples on the road (cf. Luke 24:13–35)
16:14	Jesus reproaches the disciples for their lack of belief (cf. Luke 24:25, 37; John 20:19, 26)
16:15	Jesus gives the disciples a commission (cf. Matt 28:19; Luke 24:46–49; Acts 1:8; see also John 20:21–23)
16:16	Belief brings salvation and unbelief leads to condemnation (cf. John 3:18, 36; 12:44–50; 20:22–23, and passim)
16:17	Jesus promises the gift of tongues to future missionaries (cf. Acts 2:4; 10:46)
16:18	Jesus promises that they will be protected against the dangers of serpents and poisoning (cf. Acts 28:3–5)
16:19	Jesus ascends (cf. Luke 24:51; Acts 1:2, 9)
16:20	A general summary of the activity of the missionaries that betrays knowledge of Acts (see Acts 2:5–13; 28:3–5, and the many similarities across Acts as a whole)[8]

A close analysis of the parallels between Mark 16:12–13 and Luke 24, and a further analysis of the parallels between Mark 16:15–17 and Matt 28:18–20, show convincingly that the Lucan Emmaus story and the Matthean Great Commission have played an important role in the development of vv. 9–20.[9] In addition to this systematic exploitation of the themes of failure, presence of Jesus to those who are failing, and the commission, which have their origins in Luke 24 and Matt 28, there are also indications of contact with a number of details found only in John 20.[10]

The Purpose of Mark 16:9–20

The author did more than simply cull episodes from other narrative material in the New Testament.[11] In vv. 9–20 he has extended certain themes that appeared regularly

---

Kelhoffer, *Miracle and Mission*, 158–69. Thus, vv. 9–20 belong to an "author" and should not be regarded simply as a scribal addition. For a comprehensive study of the characteristics of the passage that display an author's deliberate attempt to bring the Gospel of Mark to a satisfactory conclusion in conformity with Matthew, Luke, and John, see Kelhoffer, *Miracle and Mission*, 177–244. Given the culture of the time, I will refer to the author throughout as "he."

[8] This list has been developed from Evans, *Mark*, 546. See also Pesch, *Markusevangelium*, 2:544–46; Metzger, *Textual Commentary*, 122–28, and especially the comprehensive analysis of Kelhoffer, *Miracle and Mission*, 65–122. For a summary and an excellent chart, see pp. 121–22. Kelhoffer argues convincingly (against Hug) that the author had the other Gospels in front of him, and was not simply using traditions from those Gospels.

[9] See Evans, *Mark*, 546–47. For further detail on the influence of these and other New Testament texts upon the formation of vv. 9–10, see pp. 547–50.

[10] See also Kelhoffer, *Miracle and Mission*, 123–50.

[11] However, as Painter (*Mark's Gospel*, 215), remarks: "Whoever compiled this ending does not display Mark's dramatic skills."

across the Gospel of Mark. Most obvious are the themes of the failure and lack of faith of the disciples (vv. 11, 13, 14),[12] and the theme of mission (vv. 15–18, 20). However close to Matt 28:19 Jesus' words in Mark 16:15 may appear, they continue (with a Matthean flavor), the words of the Markan Jesus: "First the gospel must be preached to all the nations" (Mark 13:10). A further, perhaps more subtle theme that continues into the conclusion is the ultimate success of Jesus' never-failing presence to the ever-failing disciples (v. 20).[13]

In the light of this data, one can suggest that there were at least three major "purposes" for the construction and addition of Mark 16:9–20:

1. The most fundamental purpose was to overcome the scandal of the flight and the silence of the women. Matthew, Luke, and John all report the commission given to women (one woman in John) at the tomb (in Luke by two men, in Matthew and John by Jesus himself). In all cases the women fulfill their commission: they announce the Easter message. The absence of this sequence of events in the Gospel of Mark was felt to be unacceptable. It was clear from the other Gospels, and from Paul (1 Cor 15:3–8) that Mark's ending, as it came to a second-century author, was factually incorrect. The author resolved the problem by means of the addition of 16:9–20.[14]

2. Although he has continued themes from the Gospel of Mark (mission, the fragile disciples) with some skill, he is strongly constrained by his own situation in a second-century Christian church increasingly involved in the Gentile mission. The silence of the women in v. 8 had to be transformed to give authoritative missionary instruction from the risen Jesus to fragile disciples now involved in that mission.[15]

3. The missioners must be encouraged. For this reason the Gospel of Mark, as handed on by the author of vv. 9–20, concludes with a passage that reports three resurrection appear-

---

[12] As the commentary on Mark 1:1–16:8 has shown, this theme is central to the Markan theology of discipleship. It is most developed in 8:22–10:52.

[13] This theme too is developed across 8:22–10:52 but finds its most dramatic expression, in my reading of the Gospel of Mark, in 14:1–72 and 16:1–8.

[14] It must be recalled that the addition of vv. 9–20 was not the *only* answer. There are four: (i) the shorter ending, attached to 16:8; (ii) the shorter ending attached to v. 20 of the longer ending; (iii) the longer ending attached to 16:8; and (iv) the addition of the Freer Logion after v. 14 in the longer ending (see below, note 18). These are the endings that come down to us in the extant manuscript tradition. There may have been others that have been lost. On the patristic use of vv. 9–20, see Lagrange, *Saint Marc*, 427–32. For a well-documented survey of the possible dates for the origins of the longer ending (at the latest by the middle of the second century, for it was known to Justin, Tatian, and Jerome) and the shorter ending (by the end of the second century), see especially Kelhoffer, *Miracle and Mission*, 169–77, and the shorter summaries of Lane, *Mark*, 602–05, and Grundmann, *Markus*, 324–25. Grundmann accepts the proposal that vv. 9–20 are the work of a certain Ariston, at the turn of the first and second centuries. See also Lohmeyer, *Markus*, 360–61. However, the evidence for this figure as the author is slight: see Lagrange, *Saint Marc*, 436–37; Kelhoffer, *Miracle and Mission*, 20–22. There is general agreement on the dating. Some would date the shorter ending later; e.g., Painter, *Mark*, 215 (fourth century).

[15] On the nature of the longer ending as an exhortation to missionaries, see the major studies by Hug, *La finale*, 217–20, and Kelhoffer, *Miracle and Mission*, 473–80. Both these works, separated by time and method, and differing considerably on the question of sources (see Kelhoffer, *Miracle and Mission*, 130–37), come to the same conclusion concerning the purpose of the longer ending. As LaVerdiere, *The Beginning*, 2:336, succinctly comments: "It tries to convince any readers who may have been wavering that their belief in Jesus' resurrection and their mission was well-founded." See also W. R. Telford, *The Theology of the Gospel of Mark* (New Testament Theology; Cambridge: Cambridge University Press, 1999), 144–45: "While the text has Jesus upbraid the disciples for their unbelief and hardness of heart, it has him commission the twelve (*sic*) nevertheless, and give them authority to carry out a mission to all the world, to Jews and Gentile alike."

ances, but which is articulated in five stages, all ultimately directed to the missionary situation of the second century church:

(i)   Jesus appears to Mary Magdalene, but the the disciples do not believe (vv. 9–11).

(ii)   Jesus appears a second time, to two disciples on the road in the country, but the disciples still fail to believe (vv. 12–13).

(iii) Jesus appears to the disciples and upbraids them for their continuing failure (v. 14).

(iv)   At this final appearance, Jesus commissions his disciples for a universal mission, promising salvation, charismatic gifts, and protection for all who believe (vv. 15–18).

(v)   Jesus ascends to heaven, to the right hand of the Father, and the disciples go forth to preach everywhere, supported by Jesus (vv. 19–20).

The Message of Mark 16:9–20[16]

Fundamental to the missionary activity of the early church was the conviction that the missionaries were doing the work of the Lord.[17] Thus, the first step in addressing the missionary church was to show that contrary to the silence and flight of 16:8, the conclusion to the Gospel of Mark established contact between the risen Lord and the disciples, however fragile they have appeared to be across the Gospel of Mark as a whole. The result is at once clumsy and skillful. The clumsiness comes from the author's dependence upon already existing Gospel narratives. But the theological relevance of vv. 9–11 and the repetition of the motif of appearance, announcement, and failure in vv. 12–13 must not be undervalued. These two reports of appearances of the risen Jesus address second-century missionaries—and no doubt Christian missionaries of all time—who struggle with their failures of faith and the ambiguities of the mission itself. Not even the disciples of Jesus believed in the proclamation that Jesus was alive, risen from the dead. Borrowing from Johannine (John 20:19, 26) and perhaps Lukan (Luke 24:25, 37; Acts 1:10–11) traditions, the author reports that these disciples are so caught up in their mourning and weeping that they do not believe the proclamation of Mary Magdalene to whom Jesus first appeared. They will not believe that he is alive and has been seen (vv. 9–11). This must have

---

[16] For more extended commentaries on vv. 9–20, see Hug, *La finale,* 39–162; Lagrange, *Saint Marc,* 419–26; Taylor, *St. Mark,* 610–14; Lohmeyer, *Markusevangelium,* 360–64; Schweizer, *Mark,* 373–78; Grundmann, *Markus,* 326–29; Pesch, *Markusevangelium,* 2:544–56; LaVerdiere, *The Beginning,* 334–59.

[17] The movement into genuine "missionary activity," taking the early Christian communities out of their original Jewish-Christian setting and into the Gentile world, faced many problems, both internal and external. This is not the place to discuss these complex and highly debated issues. A fundamental reason, however, for the existence of such "missionary material" in the New Testament as accounts of Jesus' presence to the Gentiles, commissions from the risen Jesus sending the disciples into the Gentile world, and the literary and theological arguments in defense of mission in Acts and Paul, was the need to authorize the early churches' missionary activity by citing the pre-Easter and risen Jesus as having sent the disciples on mission. On the general question, see the fundamental studies of J. Jeremias, *Jesus' Proclamation to the Nations* (trans. S. H. Hooke; London: SCM, 1958), and F. Hahn, *Mission in the New Testament* (trans. F. Clarke; SBT 47; London: SCM, 1965). On the formative function of "memory" in the early church, see the valuable collection of N. A. Dahl, *Jesus in the Memory of the Early Church* (Minneapolis: Augsburg, 1976), esp. pp. 167–75 on "The Early Church and Jesus."

been an important matter as the author penned these lines; initial failure to believe in an authentic witness to the risen Lord is not necessarily ultimate failure. Using characters from the Lukan tradition, the author reports a second time that the first disciples fail to believe that Jesus was alive, this time announced by two disciples who meet Jesus while they are walking in the country (vv. 12–13; cf. Luke 24:13–35). The adroit repetition of appearance, proclamation, and unbelief in vv. 9–11 and 12–13 indicates the importance of faith that Jesus "was alive" (v. 11). The use of repetition makes the point forcibly: Jesus *is risen*, he *is alive* and *has appeared* to certain witnesses. However, the original disciples of Jesus do not believe in these "first" witnesses (v. 9: πρωΐ, v. 12: μετὰ δὲ ταῦτα).

Jesus comes to the eleven (the Twelve, less Judas) while they are at table. The scene recalls the Lukan and the Johannine resurrection appearances (Luke 24:36–43: an appearance and a meal in a room; John 20:19–23: an appearance in a room; 21:9–14: an appearance and a meal by the side of the lake). The theme of the failure of the disciples, already highlighted twice (vv. 11–13), appears here for a third time. There may well be a reminiscence of the disciples' response to Jesus' appearance to them on the mountain in Galilee in Matt 28:17: "And when they saw him they worshiped him, but some doubted." The persistence of this theme, so central in the Gospel of Mark, into these verses added both to close the Gospel and to encourage and exhort missionaries reflects the ever-present reality of failure among believers (v. 14). As the addition of the so-called Freer Logion indicates,[18] its presence in vv. 9–20 may reflect concern over the ongoing presence of sin, despite the saving events reported in the Gospel of Mark. Not only do the disciples refuse to believe in the witnesses of Jesus' resurrection, but succeeding generations refuse to believe as well.[19]

The commissioning of the disciples, reported in different forms across all other Gospels (Matt 28:16–20; Luke 24:44–49; Acts 1:8; John 20:19–23), now follows. The command to go into the whole world and to preach the gospel to all creation is close to Matt 28:16–20, where the universal lordship of the risen Lord lies behind the mandate to go out and teach everyone what Jesus has taught them (v. 15). Matthew 28 is under the eyes of the author who penned these verses, as baptism is seen as an important element in the response to the preaching of the gospel. However, baptism is seen as something more than an initiation rite; it is an expression of belief.

---

[18] At this point, the so-called "Freer Logion," found in Greek only in the fifth-century manuscript W (in the Freer Museum in Washington) appears. Jerome also cites part of it (*Pelag.*, 2.15 [PL 22:576]). The Greek is obscure, but may be roughly translated as follows: "And they excused themselves saying, 'This age of lawlessness and unbelief is under Satan, who by means of the unclean spirits does not allow the true power of God to be comprehended. Therefore,' they said to Christ, 'reveal your righteousness now.' And Christ replied to them, 'The limit of the years of Satan's power has been completed. But other terrible things draw near, even for the sinners for whom I was delivered to death that they might turn back to the truth and sin no more, in order that they might inherit the spiritual and imperishable glory of righteousness which is in heaven'" (see Hooker, *St. Mark*, 390). Reflecting a thought world distant from the Gospel of Mark, the Logion offers an explanation for the failure of the disciples, and for ongoing unbelief, despite Jesus Christ's life, death, and resurrection. This leads the disciples to ask for the Parousia, but the risen Jesus points elsewhere. The text expresses confidence in the final victory of God's righteousness over the power of Satan. See further, Taylor, *St. Mark*, 614–15; Lane, *Mark*, 606–11; Anderson, *Mark*, 359–60.

[19] On this theme as a continuation of an important Markan issue, see Schweizer, *Mark*, 375, who concludes: "Witnessing, proclamation, grace and salvation exist only as the result of God's action in the face of all human resistance." See also Grundmann, *Markus*, 329–30; Pesch, *Markusevangelium*, 2:551.

Again the second century missionary activity of the church would have influenced the risen Lord's indication to the disciples of the fruits of their mission. There is a Johannine ring to his words concerning the salvation of those who believe and whose faith is manifested in baptism. They will be saved, while those who do not believe will be condemned (cf., e.g., John 3:11–21, 31–36; 12:44–50). As vv. 9–20 will conclude with Jesus' departure from the disciples, his commission must also assure the missionaries, by means of signs, that despite his physical absence they are acting with his authority.[20] These signs are not unknown in the rest of the New Testament. Phenomena reported in the ministry of the disciples in Mark 6:7–13 (healing and casting out demons), the experience of Paul in Acts 28:3–5 (picking up serpents), the charismatic experiences of early Christian communities reflected in 1 Cor 12–14 (speaking in tongues), and other parallel experiences reported in the Acts of the Apostles (cf. Acts 2:5–13), are described in vv. 17–18. Faith enables believers to cast out demons and to speak in tongues, and to be unaffected by the poisonous bite of the serpent and the poisonous potions made by human beings.[21] Faith produces a security that only the risen Lord can assure. As with the rest of the long ending, the language and experiences may come from the experience of missionaries in the second Christian century, but the relevance is ongoing.[22]

Aware that Jesus is no longer present to them as he was during his days on earth, the author tells of his departure to heaven (cf. Acts 1:1–2, 9), to sit at the right hand of God (see Ps 110:1; Mark 12:36; 14:62). From this position Jesus exercises the authority of his universal lordship and assures the ultimate success of those who believe in him (v. 19). Thus, there is a logical link between the statement about Jesus' ascension to the right hand of God in v. 19 and the report of the success of the preaching of the disciples "everywhere" (πανταχοῦ). Jesus may be absent, but his fragile disciples are empowered by signs that are evidence of the authority of the risen Lord, enabling them to perform successfully what they have been commanded to do. This is possible only because their absent Lord (v. 19) is, in fact "working with them" (v. 20). Looking back to vv. 17–18, the author recalls the prodigious signs that the believers were able to do, and indicates that the authority of the absent Lord to his missionary church is certified by these and other signs (v. 20).[23]

---

[20] For extensive documentation indicating that miracles performed by believers, under instruction by the apostles, were viewed as authentication of the kerygma of the missionaries, see Kelhoffer, *Miracle and Mission*, 245–338. Kelhoffer shows that the link with the apostles waned in the late second century and into the third as the focus shifted away from the apostles to the wonders performed by the believers.

[21] For a survey of Greco-Roman, Jewish, and early Christian literature on picking up snakes without harm, see Kelhoffer, *Miracles and Mission*, 340–416. On drinking deadly substances with impunity, see ibid., 417–72.

[22] Schweizer (*Mark*, 377) points out that the listing of these charismatic gifts "is indicative of a church which was still rather flexible."

[23] Schweizer (*Mark*, 378) remarks: "What Luke does in Acts may be seen in embryo here." See also Pesch, *Markusevangelium*, 2:555. As Gnilka (*Markus*, 2:358) remarks: "It is decisive . . . that the 'everywhere' remains part of the assignment to preach the gospel, and that precisely and only in the fulfillment of this assignment can the cooperating help of the exalted Lord, who remains with his church, be experienced." A number of later manuscripts, no doubt under the influence of the shorter ending, which concluded with a solemn "Amen," have added "Amen" to v. 20. As already mentioned, some manuscripts add the shorter ending to v. 20, thus providing an "Amen" to show that the Gospel of Mark, as they wish to hand it down, has come to an end. The evidence for the shorter ending as a conclusion to 16:8 is stronger than the evidence for its appearance after vv. 9–20. See Lane, *Mark*, 602–3; Hug, *La finale*, 213–14.

Conclusion

The author responsible for vv. 9–20 must have spoken effectively to the Christian communities of the second century, or this ending would not have survived. Among several candidates, this ending is most widely represented in the textual tradition and accepted into the Christian canon. Its success is due to the fact that it did what it set out to do: it resolved the enigmatic ending of the Gospel of Mark; it continued central themes of the Gospel, especially disciples, failure, and mission; and, finally, it spoke effectively to a missionary church of the second century. The enigmatic silence of the women is replaced by Jesus' appearances to Mary Magdalene, two disciples, and then the eleven. Despite the weakness of their belief (vv. 9–14), vv. 9–20 assured success, the ongoing authority of the risen and ascended Jesus, and his constant protection for themselves and their converts (vv. 15–20). This is a comforting message.

Considerable skill is evident in the author's use of existing accounts of the appearances, the commissions, and the missionary activity of the early church to speak to the missionaries of his own time. There is good reason, on both literary and theological grounds, for the presence of vv. 9–20 as the most successful attempt to resolve the enigma of 16:8. But the author has betrayed one of the fundamental purposes of Mark, the original evangelist, whose version of the story of Jesus closed with the fear, flight, and silence of the women in 16:8. Rather than ask the *readers of the Gospel* to "fill the gap" left by the failure of the women in 16:8, especially by means of the promises of Jesus in 14:27 and 16:7, he provides all the "filling" that second-century readers might have wanted. As I trust my above comments indicate, the message of vv. 9–20 is not without significance in the contemporary Christian church. But it catches only part of what Mark wished to say to the church by ending the Gospel at 16:8. The flight and silence of the women force readers to ask where they stand, relying only upon the action of God to make divine sense of human nonsense. This message is challenging, and not particularly comforting in the light of our repeatedly failing attempts to determine our own future and God's ways within that future. It would be more appropriate if we looked elsewhere in the Gospel of Mark for a lection that might better represent the shadowy figure behind this story of Jesus' life, teaching, death, and resurrection as we celebrate the feast of St. Mark in our liturgies.

BIBLIOGRAPHY

Reference Works and Sources

Aland, B., K. Aland, J. Karavidopoulos, C. M. Martini, and B. M. Metzger, eds. *The Greek New Testament.* 4th ed. Stuttgart: United Bible Societies, 1993.

Aland, K., and B. Aland, eds. *Novum Testamentum Graece.* 26th ed. Stuttgart: Deutsche Bibelstiftung, 1979.

———. *The Text of the New Testament: An Introduction to the Critical Editions and to the Theory and Practice of Modern Textual Criticism.* Translated by E. F. Rhodes. Grand Rapids: Eerdmans, 1987.

Bietenhard, H. *Midrasch Tanhuma B. R. Tanhuma über die Tora, genannt Midrasch Jelammenedu.* 2 vols. Judaica et Christiana 5–6. Bern: Peter Lang, 1980–1982.

Blass, F., and A. Debrunner. *A Greek Grammar of the New Testament and Other Early Christian Literature.* Revised and translated by R. W. Funk. Chicago: Chicago University Press, 1961.

Boismard, M.-E., and A. Lamouille. *Synopsis graeca quattuor evangeliorum.* Leuven/Paris: Peeters, 1986.

Braude, W. G. *Pesiqta Rabbati: Discourses for Feasts, Fasts, and Special Sabbaths.* Yale Judaica Series. 2 vols. New Haven & London: Yale University Press, 1968.

Brown, F., S. R. Driver, and C. A. Briggs. *A Hebrew and English Lexicon of the Old Testament with an Appendix Containing the Biblical Aramaic.* Oxford: Clarendon Press, 1907.

Brown, R. E., J. A. Fitzmyer, and R. E. Murphy, eds. *The New Jerome Biblical Commentary.* Englewood Cliffs: Prentice Hall, 1989.

Charlesworth, J. H., ed. *The Old Testament Pseudepigrapha.* 2 vols. London: Darton, Longman, and Todd, 1983–1985.

Danby, H. *The Mishnah: Translated from the Hebrew with Introduction and Brief Expository Notes.* Oxford: Clarendon Press, 1933.

Danker, F. W. *A Greek-English Lexicon of the New Testament and Other Early Christian Literature.* 3d ed. Chicago: University of Chicago Press, 2000.

Dio Cassius. *Roman History.* Translated by E. Cary. 9 vols. Loeb Classical Library. Cambridge: Harvard University Press, 1919–1927.

Elliger, K., and K. Rudolph. *Biblia Hebraica Stuttgartensia.* Stuttgart: Deutsche Bibelgesellschaft, 1983.

Epstein, I., ed. *The Babylonian Talmud.* 35 vols. London: Soncino, 1948–1952.

Eusebius. *The Ecclesiastical History.* Translated by K. Lake and J. E. L. Oulton. 2 vols. Loeb Classical Library. Cambridge: Harvard University Press, 1926–1932.

Finegan, J. *Encountering New Testament Manuscripts: A Working Introduction to Textual Criticism.* London: SPCK, 1975.

Freedman, H., and M. Simon, eds. *Midrash Rabbah: Translated into English with Notes, Glossary and Indices.* 10 vols. London: Soncino, 1939.

García Martínez, F. *The Dead Sea Scrolls Translated: The Qumran Texts in English.* Leiden: E. J. Brill, 1996.

Guillaumont, A., H.-Ch. Puech, G. Quispel, W. Till, and Yassah 'Abd Al Masih. *The Gospel according to Thomas: Coptic Text Established and Translated.* Leiden: E. J. Brill, 1959.

Hennecke, E., and W. Schneemelcher. *New Testament Apocrypha.* 2 vols. London: Lutterworth, 1963–1965.

Jastrow, M. *Dictionary of the Targumim, the Talmud Babli and Yerushalmi, and the Midrashic Literature.* 2 vols. New York: Pardes, 1950.

Josephus. Translated and edited by H. St. J. Thackeray et al. 9 vols. Loeb Classical Library. Cambridge: Harvard University Press, 1926–1965.

Juvenal and Perseus. Translated by G. G. Ramsay. Loeb Classical Library. Cambridge: Harvard University Press, 1918.

Kittell, G., and G. Friedrich, eds. *Theological Dictionary of the New Testament.* 10 vols. Grand Rapids: Eerdmans, 1964–1976.

Lake, K., trans. and ed. *The Apostolic Fathers: With an English Translation.* 2 vols. Loeb Classical Library. Cambridge: Harvard University Press, 1912–1913.

Lauterbach, J. Z. *Mekilta de-Rabbi Ishmael: A Critical Edition on the Basis of the Manuscripts and Early Editions with an English Translation, Introduction, and Notes.* 3 vols. The Jewish Publication Society Library of Jewish Classics. Philadelphia: The Jewish Publication Society of America, 1933–1935.

Levertoff, P. *Midrash Sifre on Numbers.* New York: Macmillan, 1926.

Liddell, H., R. Scott, and A. S. Jones. *A Greek-English Lexicon.* Oxford: Clarendon Press, 1968.

Lohse, E., ed. *Die Texte aus Qumran: Hebräisch und Deutsch.* 3d ed. Munich: Kösel-Verlag, 1981.

Metzger, B. M. *The Text of the New Testament: Its Transmission, Corruption, and Restoration.* 2d ed. Oxford: Clarendon Press, 1968.

_____. *A Textual Commentary on the Greek New Testament.* Stuttgart: Deutsche Bibelgesellschaft, 1994.

Moulton, J. H., W. F. Howard, and N. Turner. *A Grammar of New Testament Greek.* 4 vols. Edinburgh: T&T Clark, 1909–1976.

Neirynck, F., J. Verheyden, F. Van Segbroeck, G. Van Oyen, and R. Corstjens, eds. *The Gospel of Mark 1950–1990.* BETL 102. Leuven: Leuven University Press, 1992.

Neusner, J. *Sifra: An Analytical Translation.* Brown Judaic Studies 138. Atlanta: Scholars Press, 1988.

Philo. Translated and edited by F. H. Colson et al. 12 vols. Loeb Classical Library. Cambridge: Harvard University Press, 1929–1953.

Pirot, L., A. Robert, and H. Cazelles, eds. *Dictionnaire de la Bible Supplément.* Paris: Letouzey, 1928–.

Pliny. *Natural History.* Translated by H. Rackham and W. H. S. Jones. 10 vols. Loeb Classical Library. Cambridge: Harvard University Press, 1938–1969.

Powell, M. A., C. G. Gray, and M. C. Curtis. *The Bible and Modern Literary Criticism. A Critical Assessment and Annotated Bibliography.* New York: Greenwood, 1992.

Rahlfs, A. *Septuaginta. Id est Vetus Testamentum Graece iuxta LXX Interpretes.* 2 vols. 8th ed. Stuttgart: Württemburgische Bibelanstalt, 1965.

Robinson, J. M., Paul Hoffmann, and J. S. Kloppenborg, eds. *The Critical Edition of Q: Synopsis Including the Gospels of Matthew and Luke, Mark, and Thomas with English, German, and French Translations of Q and Thomas.* Managing editor, M. C. Moreland. Minneapolis: Fortress Press, 2000.

Schwab, M., ed. *Le Talmud de Jérusalem.* 11 vols. Paris: Maisonneuve, 1878–1890.

Strack, H., and P. Billerbeck. *Kommentar zum Neuen Testament aus Talmud und Midrasch.* 6 vols. Munich: C. H. Beck, 1922–1961.

Suetonius. *Lives of the Caesars: Lives of Illustrious Men.* Translated by J. C. Rolfe. 2 vols. Loeb Classical Library. Cambridge: Harvard University Press, 1913.

Tacitus. *The Histories.* Translated by C. H. Moore. 2 vols. Loeb Classical Library. Cambridge: Harvard University Press, 1925.

Temporini, H., and W. Hasse, eds. *Aufstieg und Niedergang der Römischen Welt.* Berlin: Walter de Gruyter, 1981–.

Zerwick, M. *Biblical Greek Illustrated by Examples.* Rome: Biblical Institute Press, 1963.

Commentaries

Anderson, H. *The Gospel of Mark.* New Century Bible. London: Oliphants, 1976.

Branscomb, B. H. *The Gospel of Mark.* The Moffatt New Testament Commentary. London: Hodder and Stoughton, 1937.

Cranfield, C. E. B. *The Gospel according to St. Mark.* Cambridge Greek Testament Commentary. Cambridge: Cambridge University Press, 1959.

Ernst, J. *Das Evangelium nach Markus.* Regensburger Neues Testament. Regensburg: Pustet Verlag, 1981.

Evans, C. A. *Mark 8:27–16:20.* Word Biblical Commentary 34b. Nashville: Thomas Nelson, 2001.

Gnilka, J. *Das Evangelium nach Markus.* 5th ed. Evangelisch-katholischer Kommentar zum Neuen Testament II/1–2. 2 vols. Zürich/Neukirchen/Vluyn: Benziger Verlag/Neukirchener Verlag, 1998.

Grundmann, W. *Das Evangelium nach Markus.* 6th ed. Theologischer Handkommentar zum Neuen Testament 2. Berlin: Evangelische Verlagsanstalt, 1973.

Guelich, R. A. *Mark 1–8:26.* Word Biblical Commentary 34a. Dallas: Word Books, 1989.

Gundry, R. H. *Mark: A Commentary on His Apology for the Cross.* Grand Rapids: Eerdmans, 1993.

Hooker, M. D. *The Gospel according to St. Mark.* Black's New Testament Commentary. London: A. & C. Black, 1991.

Lagrange, M.-J. *Evangile selon Saint Marc. Etudes bibliques.* Paris: Gabalda, 1920.

Lane, W. L. *Commentary on the Gospel of Mark.* The New International Commentary on the New Testament. Grand Rapids: Eerdmans, 1974.

LaVerdiere, E. *The Beginning of the Gospel: Introducing the Gospel according to Mark.* 2 vols. Collegeville: The Liturgical Press, 1999.

Lohmeyer, E. *Das Evangelium des Markus.* 17th ed. Meyers Kommentar. Göttingen: Vandenhoeck & Ruprecht, 1967.

Lührmann, D. *Das Markusevangelium.* Handbuch zum Neuen Testament 3. Tübingen: J. C. B. Mohr (Paul Siebeck), 1987.

Marcus, J. *Mark 1–8.* The Anchor Bible 27. New York: Doubleday, 2000.

Myers, C. *Binding the Strong Man: A Political Reading of Mark's Story of Jesus.* Maryknoll: Orbis Books, 1990.

Nineham, D. E. *The Gospel of St. Mark.* Pelican New Testament Commentaries. Harmondsworth: Penguin Books, 1963.

Painter, J. *Mark's Gospel: Worlds in Conflict.* New Testament Readings. London: Routledge, 1997.

Pesch, R. *Das Markusevangelium.* Herders theologischer Kommentar zum Neuen Testament II/1–2. 2 vols. Freiburg: Herder, 1976–1977.

Schweizer, E. *The Good News according to Mark.* London: SPCK, 1971.

Swete, H. B. *The Gospel according to St. Mark.* London: Macmillan, 1909.

Taylor, V. *The Gospel according to St. Mark.* 2d ed. London: Macmillan, 1966.

Other Studies

Abrahams, I. *Studies in Pharisaism and the Gospels*. First Series. Cambridge: Cambridge University Press, 1917.

Achtemeier, P. J. "The Origin and Function of the Pre-Markan Miracle Catenae." *Journal of Biblical Literature* 91 (1972): 198–221.

_____. "Toward the Isolation of Pre-Markan Miracle Catenae." *Journal of Biblical Literature* 89 (1970): 265–91.

Aland, K. "Bemerkungen zum Schluss des Markusevangeliums." Pages 157–80 in *Neotestamentica et Semitica: Studies in Honour of Matthew Black*. Edited by E. E. Ellis and M. Wilcox. Edinburgh: T&T Clark, 1969.

_____. "Die wiedergefundene Markusschluss? Eine methodologische Bemerkung zur textkritischen Arbeit. *Zeitschrift für Theologie und Kirche* 67 (1970): 3–13.

Albertz, M. *Die synoptische Streitgespräche*. Berlin: Trowitsch & Sohn, 1919.

Allison, D. C. "Psalm 23 (22) in Early Christianity: A Suggestion." *Irish Biblical Studies* 5 (1983): 132–37.

Ashton, J. *Understanding the Fourth Gospel*. Oxford: Clarendon Press, 1991.

Athanasius. *Life of Anthony*. Translated by R. C. Cregg. Classics of Western Spirituality. London: SPCK, 1980.

Aune, D. E. *The New Testament in Its Literary Environment*. Philadelphia: The Westminster Press, 1987.

Aus, R. *Water into Wine and the Beheading of John the Baptist: Early Jewish-Christian Interpretation of Esther 1 in John 2:1–11 and Mark 6:17–29*. Brown Judaica Studies 150. Atlanta: Scholars Press, 1988.

Baarlink, H. *Anfängliches Evangelium: Ein Beitrag zur näheren Bestimmung der theologischen Motive im Markusevangelium*. Kampen: J. H. Kok, 1977.

Balabanski, V. *Eschatology in the Making: Mark, Matthew, and the Didache*. Society for New Testament Studies Monograph Series 97. Cambridge: Cambridge University Press, 1997.

Banks, R. *Jesus and the Law in the Synoptic Tradition*. Society for New Testament Studies Monograph Series 28. Cambridge: Cambridge University Press, 1975.

Barbour, R. "Gethsemane in the Tradition of the Passion." *New Testament Studies* 16 (1969–1970): 231–52.

Barrett, C. K. "The Background of Mark 10.45." Pages 1–18 in *New Testament Essays: Studies in Memory of T. W. Manson*. Edited by A. J. B. Higgins. Manchester: Manchester University Press, 1959.

_____. *The Gospel according to St. John*. 2d ed. London: SPCK, 1978.

_____. *The Holy Spirit in the Gospel Tradition*. London: SPCK, 1970.

_____. "The House of Prayer and the Den of Thieves." Pages 13–20 in *Jesus und Paulus: Festschrift für Werner Georg Kümmel zum 70. Geburtstag*. Edited by E. Ellis and E. Grässer. Göttingen: Vandenhoeck & Ruprecht, 1975.

_____. *New Testament Background: Selected Documents*. London: SPCK, 1956.

Bauckham, R., ed. *The Gospel for All Christians: Rethinking the Gospel Audiences*. Grand Rapids: Eerdmans, 1998.

Bauer, W. *Orthodoxy and Heresy in Earliest Christianity*. London: SCM Press, 1972.

Beasley-Murray, G. R. *Jesus and the Last Days. The Interpretation of the Olivet Discourse*. Peabody: Hendrickson, 1993.

Beavis, M. A. *Mark's Audience: The Literary and Social Setting of Mark 4:11–12*. Journal for the Study of the New Testament: Supplement Series 33. Sheffield: Sheffield Academic Press, 1989.

Belo, F. *A Materialist Reading of the Gospel of Mark*. Maryknoll: Orbis Books, 1981.

Berger, K. *Die Amen-Worte Jesu: Eine Untersuchung der Legitimation in Apokalyptischen Rede.* Beihefte zur Zeitschrift für die neutestamentliche Wissenschaft 39. Berlin: Walter de Gruyter, 1970.

_____. *Die Auferstehung des Propheten und die Erhöhung des Menschensohnes: Traditions-geschichtliche Untersuchungen zur Deutung des Geschickes Jesu in frühchristlichen Texten.* Studien zur Umwelt des Neuen Testaments. Göttingen: Vandenhoeck & Ruprecht, 1976.

Best, E. *Disciples and Discipleship: Studies in the Gospel according to Mark.* Edinburgh: T&T Clark, 1986.

_____. *Following Jesus: Discipleship in the Gospel of Mark.* Journal for the Study of the New Testament: Supplement Series 4. Sheffield: JSOT Press, 1981.

_____. "Mark iii.20, 21, 31–35." *New Testament Studies* 22 (1975–1976): 309–19.

_____. *Mark: The Gospel as Story.* Edinburgh: T&T Clark, 1983.

_____. "The Role of the Disciples in Mark." *New Testament Studies* 23 (1976–1977): 377–401.

_____. *The Temptation and the Passion: The Markan Soteriology.* 2d ed. Society for New Testament Studies Monograph Series 2. Cambridge: Cambridge University Press, 1990.

Betz, H. D. *Nachfolge und Nachahmung Jesu Christi im Neuen Testament.* Beiträge zur historischen Theologie 39. Tübingen: J. C. B. Mohr (Paul Siebeck), 1967.

Bilezikian, G. *The Liberated Gospel: A Comparison between the Gospel of Mark and Greek Tragedy.* Grand Rapids: Baker, 1977.

Black, C. C. *The Disciples according to Mark: Markan Redaction in Current Debate.* Journal for the Study of the New Testament: Supplement Series 27. Sheffield: Sheffield Academic Press, 1989.

_____. *Mark: Images of an Apostolic Interpreter.* Studies on Personalities of the New Testament. Columbia: University of South Carolina, 1994.

_____. "The Quest of Mark the Redactor: Why Has It Been Pursued, and What Has It Taught Us?" *Journal for the Study of the New Testament* 22 (1989): 19–39.

_____. "Was Mark a Roman Gospel?" *The Expository Times* 105 (1993–1994): 36–40.

Blackburn, B. *Theios Anêr and the Markan Miracle Traditions: A Critique of the Theios Anêr Concept as an Interpretative Background to the Miracle Traditions Used by Mark.* Wissenschaftliche Untersuchungen zum Neuen Testament 2. Reihe 40. Tübingen: J. C. B. Mohr (Paul Siebeck), 1991.

Blount, B. K. "A Socio-Rhetorical Analysis of Simon of Cyrene: Mark 15:21 and Its Parallels." *Semeia* 64 (1993): 171–98.

Bode, E. L. *The First Easter Morning: The Gospel Accounts of the Women's Visit to the Tomb of Jesus.* Analecta Biblica 45. Rome: Biblical Institute Press, 1970.

Boismard, M.-E. *Le martyre de Jean l'apôtre.* Cahiers de la Revue Biblique 35. Paris: Gabalda, 1996.

Boomershine, T. E. "Mark 16:8 and the Apostolic Commission." *Journal of Biblical Literature* 100 (1981): 225–39.

Boomershine, T. E., and G. L. Bartholomew. "The Narrative Technique of Mark 16:8." *Journal of Biblical Literature* 100 (1981): 213–23.

Booth, R. *Jesus and the Laws of Purity: Tradition History and Legal History in Mark 7.* Journal for the Study of the New Testament: Supplement Series 13. Sheffield: JSOT Press, 1986.

Booth, W. C. *The Rhetoric of Fiction.* 2d ed. Chicago: University of Chicago Press, 1983.

Boring, M. E. "Mark 1:1–15 and the Beginning of the Gospel." *Semeia* 52 (1991): 43–81.

Bornkamm, G. *Jesus of Nazareth.* Translated by I. and F. McLuskey with J. Robinson. London: Hodder & Stoughton, 1963.

_____. "Πνεῦμα ἄλαλον: Eine Studie zum Markusevangelium." Volume 4, pages 21–36 in *Geschichte und Glaube.* Beiträge zur evangelischen Theologie 53. 4 vols. Munich: Kaiser Verlag, 1971

Bornkamm, G., G. Barth, and H. J. Held, *Tradition and Interpretation in Matthew.* Translated by P. Scott. London: SCM Press, 1963.

Borrell, A. *The Good News of Peter's Denial. A Narrative and Rhetorical Reading of Mark 14:54.66–72.* Translated by S. Conlon. University of South Florida International Studies in Formative Christianity and Judaism. Atlanta: Scholars Press, 1998.

Boucher, M. *The Mysterious Parable: A Literary Study.* Catholic Biblical Quarterly Monograph Series 6. Washington: The Catholic Biblical Association of America, 1977.

Breck, J. *The Shape of Biblical Language: Chiasmus in the Scriptures and Beyond.* New York: St. Vladimir's Seminary Press, 1994.

Broadhead, E. K. *Naming Jesus: Titular Christology in the Gospel of Mark.* Journal for the Study of the New Testament: Supplement Series 175. Sheffield: Sheffield Academic Press, 1999.

Broer, I. *Die Urgemeinde und das Grab Jesu: Eine Analyse der Grablegungsgeschichte im Neuen Testament.* Studien zum Alten und Neuen Testament 31. Munich: Kösel-Verlag, 1972.

Brown, P. *The Body and Society: Men, Women, and Sexual Renunciation in Early Christianity.* London: Faber & Faber, 1988.

Brown, R. E. *The Birth of the Messiah: A Commentary on the Infancy Narratives of Matthew and Luke.* New York: Doubleday, 1977.

―――. "The Burial of Jesus (Mark 15:42–47)." *Catholic Biblical Quarterly* 50 (1988): 233–45.

―――. *The Death of the Messiah: From Gethsemane to the Grave: A Commentary on the Passion Narratives in the Four Gospels.* 2 vols. Anchor Bible Reference Library. New York: Doubleday, 1994.

Brown, R. E., and J. P. Meier. *Antioch and Rome: New Testament Cradles of Catholic Christianity.* New York: Paulist Press, 1983.

Buchanan, G. W. "Mark 11:15–19: Brigands in the Temple." *Hebrew Union College Annual* 30 (1959): 169–77.

Bultmann, R. *History of the Synoptic Tradition.* Translated by John Marsh. Oxford: Basil Blackwell, 1968.

―――. "Is Exegesis without Presuppositions Possible?" Pages 145–53 in *New Testament Mythology and Other Basic Writings.* Edited by S. M. Ogden. Philadelphia: Fortress Press, 1984.

―――. *Theology of the New Testament.* Translated by K. Grobel. 2 vols. London: SCM Press, 1952–1955.

Burkett, D. R. *The Son of Man Debate: A History and Evaluation.* Society for New Testament Studies Monograph Series 107. Cambridge: Cambridge University Press, 2000.

Byrne, B. J. *'Sons of God—Seed of Abraham': A Study of the Idea of the Sonship of God of All Christians in Paul against the Jewish Background.* Analecta Biblica 83. Rome: Biblical Institute Press, 1979.

Campenhausen, H. von. "The Events of Easter and the Empty Tomb." Pages 42–89 in *Tradition and Life in the Church: Essays and Lectures in Church History.* Translated by A. V. Littledale. London: Collins, 1968.

―――. *The Formation of the Christian Bible.* London: A. and C. Black, 1972.

Cangh, J.-M. van. *La multiplication des pains et l'eucharistie.* Lectio divina 86. Paris: Cerf, 1975.

Capel Anderson, J., and J. Staley, eds. "Taking it Personally: Introduction." *Semeia* 72 (1995): 7–18.

Casey, M. *Son of Man: The Interpretation and Influence of Daniel 7.* London: SPCK, 1979.

Charlesworth, J. H. "The Son of David: Solomon and Jesus." Pages 72–87 in *The New Testament and Hellenistic Judaism.* Edited by P. Borgen and S. Giversen. Peabody: Hendrickson, 1997.

Charlesworth, J. H., ed. *The Messiah: Developments in Early Judaism and Christianity.* The First Princeton Symposium on Judaism and Christian Origins. Minneapolis: Fortress Press, 1992.

Chatman, S. *Story and Discourse: Narrative Structure in Fiction and Film.* Ithaca: Cornell University Press, 1978.

Collins, A. Y. *The Beginning of the Gospel: Probings of Mark in Context.* Minneapolis: Fortress Press, 1992.

_____. "The Empty Tomb in the Gospel according to Mark." Pages 107–40 in *Hermes and Athena*. Edited by E. Stump and T. P. Flint. Notre Dame: University of Notre Dame Press, 1993.

_____. "Mark and His Readers: The Son of God among Greeks and Romans." *Harvard Theological Review* 93 (2000): 85–100.

_____. "Mark and His Readers: The Son of God among Jews." *Harvard Theological Review* 92 (1999): 393–408.

Collins, J. J. "The Nature of Messianism in the Light of the Dead Sea Scrolls." Pages 199–219 in *The Dead Sea Scrolls in Their Historical Context*. Edited by T. H. Lim, L. W. Hurtado, A. Graeme Auld, and Alison Jack. Edinburgh: T&T Clark, 2000.

_____. *The Scepter and the Star: The Messiahs of the Dead Sea Scrolls and Other Ancient Literature*. Anchor Bible Reference Library. New York: Doubleday, 1995.

Conzelmann, H. *An Outline of the Theology of the New Testament*. Translated by J. Bowden. London: SCM Press, 1969.

_____. *The Theology of St. Luke*. Translated by G. Buswell. London: Faber & Faber, 1961.

Corley, K. E. *Private Woman, Public Meals: Social Conflict in the Synoptic Tradition*. Peabody: Hendrickson, 1993.

Corsini, E. *The Apocalypse: The Perennial Revelation of Jesus Christ*. Translated and edited by F. J. Moloney. Good News Studies 5. Wilmington: Michael Glazier, 1983.

Cotter, W. "The Markan Sea Miracles: Their History, Formation, and Function in the Literary Context of Greco-Roman Antiquity." Ph.D. dissertation, University of St. Michael's College, Toronto School of Theology, 1991.

_____. "The Markan Stilling of the Storm (Mk 4:35–41): Context and Claims." Unpublished paper delivered at the Annual Meeting of the Catholic Biblical Association, Loyola-Marymount University, Los Angeles, August 2000.

_____. *Miracles in Greco-Roman Antiquity: A Sourcebook for the study of New Testament Miracle Stories*. London: Routledge, 1999.

Cousar, C. B. "Eschatology and Mark's *Theologia Crucis:* A Critical Analysis of Mark 13." *Interpretation* 24 (1970): 321–35.

Craghan, J. F. "The Gerasene Demoniac." *Catholic Biblical Quarterly* 30 (1968): 522–36.

Craig, W. L. "The Historicity of the Empty Tomb of Jesus." *New Testament Studies* 31 (1985): 39–67.

Crossan, J. D. *The Dark Interval: Towards a Theology of Story*. Niles: Argus Communications, 1975.

_____. "Empty Tomb and Absent Lord (Mark 16:1–8)." Pages 135–52 in *The Passion in Mark*. Edited by W. H. Kelber. Philadelphia: Fortress Press, 1976.

_____. *In Parables: The Challenge of the Historical Jesus*. New York: Harper & Row, 1973.

_____. "The Parable of the Husbandmen." *Journal of Biblical Literature* 90 (1971): 451–65.

_____. "The Seed Parables of Jesus." *Journal of Biblical Literature* 92 (1973): 256–57.

Cullmann, O. *Baptism in the New Testament*. Translated by J. K. S. Reid. London: SCM Press, 1950.

Culpepper, R. A. "Mark 10:50: Why Mention the Garment?" *Journal for Biblical Literature* 101 (1982): 131–32.

Cunningham, P. J. *Mark: The Good News Preached to the Romans*. New York: Paulist Press, 1998.

Dahl, N. A. *The Crucified Messiah and Other Essays*. Minneapolis: Augsburg Press, 1974.

_____. *Jesus in the Memory of the Early Church*. Minneapolis: Augsburg, 1976.

Dalman, G. *Sacred Sites and Ways: Studies in the Topography of the Gospels*. London: SPCK, 1935.

Danove, P. L. *The End of Mark's Story: A Methodological Study*. Biblical Interpretation Series 3. Leiden: E. J. Brill, 1993.

Daube, D. *The New Testament and Rabbinic Judaism*. London: Athlone, 1956. Repr. Peabody: Hendrickson, 1994.

Davies, P. R. "Judaisms of the Dead Sea Scrolls: The Case of the Messiah." Pages 219–32 in *The Dead Sea Scrolls in Their Historical Context.* Edited by T. H. Lim, L. W. Hurtado, A. Graeme Auld, and Alison Jacks. Edinburgh: T&T Clark, 2000.

Davies, W. D., and D. C. Allison. *A Critical and Exegetical Commentary on the Gospel according to Saint Matthew.* International Critical Commentary. 3 vols. Edinburgh: T&T Clark, 1988–1997.

Deines, R. *Die Pharisäer: Ihr Verständnis im Spiegel der christlichen und jüdischen Forschung seit Wellhausen und Graetz.* Wissenschaftliche Untersuchungen zum Neuen Testament 101. Tübingen: J. C. B. Mohr (Paul Siebeck), 1997.

Delbrueck, R. "Antiquarisches zu den Verspottung Jesu." *Zeitschrift für die neutestamentliche Wissenschaft und die Kunde der älteren Kirche* 41 (1942): 124–45.

Derrett, J. D. M. *Law in the New Testament.* London: Darton, Longman & Todd, 1970.

Dewey, J. "The Literary Structure of the Controversy Stories in Mark 2:1–3:6." *Journal of Biblical Literature* 92 (1973): 394–401.

———. "Mark as Interwoven Tapestry: Forecasts and Echoes for a Listening Audience." *Catholic Biblical Quarterly* 53 (1991): 221–36.

———. *Markan Public Debate: Literary Technique, Concentric Structure, and Theology in Mark 2:1–3:6.* Society of Biblical Literature Dissertation Series 48. Chico: Scholars Press, 1980.

Dibelius, M. *From Tradition to Gospel.* Translated by B. L. Woolf. Library of Theological Translations. Cambridge & London: James Clarke, 1971.

Dobschütz, E. von "Zur Erzählerkunst des Markus." *Zeitschrift für die neutestamentliche Wissenschaft und die Kunde der älteren Kirche* 27 (1928): 193–98.

Dodd, C. H. *The Parables of the Kingdom.* London: Collins, 1936.

Donahue, J. R. "A Neglected Factor in the Theology of Mark." *Journal of Biblical Literature* 101 (1982): 563–94.

———. *Are You the Christ? The Trial Narrative in the Gospel of Mark.* Society of Biblical Literature Dissertation Series 10. Missoula: Society of Biblical Literature, 1973.

———. "Introduction: From Passion Traditions to Passion Narrative." Pages 1–20 in *The Passion in Mark.* Edited by W. H. Kelber. Philadelphia: Fortress Press, 1976.

———. "The Quest for the Community of Mark's Gospel." Volume 2, pages 819–34 in *The Four Gospels 1992: Festschrift Frans Neirynck.* Edited by F. van Segbroeck, C. M. Tucker, G. van Belle, and J. Verheyden. 3 vols. Biblioteca ephemeridum theologicarum lovaniensium 100. Leuven: Leuven University Press, 1992.

———. "Recent Studies on the Origin of 'Son of Man' in the Gospels." *Catholic Biblical Quarterly* 48 (1986): 484–98.

———. "Tax Collectors and Sinners. An Attempt at Identification." *Catholic Biblical Quarterly* 33 (1971): 49–61.

———. "Windows and Mirrors: The Setting of Mark's Gospel." *Catholic Biblical Quarterly* 57 (1995): 1–26.

Donaldson, J. " 'Called to Follow.' A Twofold Experience of Discipleship." *Biblical Theology Bulletin* 5 (1975): 67–77.

Donfried, K. P. "The Feeding Narratives and the Marcan Community." Pages 95–103 in *Kirche: Festschrift für Günther Bornkamm zum 75. Geburtstag.* Edited by D. Lührmann and G. Strecker. Tübingen: J. C. B. Mohr (Paul Siebeck), 1980.

Dowd, S. E. *Prayer, Power, and the Problem of Suffering: Mark 11:22–25 in the Context of Markan Theology.* Society of Biblical Literature Dissertation Series 105. Atlanta: Scholars Press, 1988.

Dreyfus, F. "L'argument scripturaire de Jésus en faveur de la résurrection des morts (Marc XII, 26–27)." *Revue Biblique* 66 (1959): 213–24.

Drury, J. "Mark." Pages 402–17 in *The Literary Guide to the Bible.* Edited by A. Alter and F. Kermode. London: Collins, 1987.

Dunn, J. D. G. *Jesus and the Spirit: A Study of the Religious and Charismatic Experience of Jesus and the First Christians As Reflected in the New Testament.* London: SCM Press, 1975.

_____. "Mark 2:1–3:6: A Bridge Between Jesus and Paul in the Question of the Law." *New Testament Studies* 30 (1984): 395–415.

Dupont, J. "Il n'en sera pas laissée pierre sur pierre (Mc 13,2; Luc 19,44)." *Biblica* 52 (1971): 301–20.

Dwyer, T. *The Motif of Wonder in the Gospel of Mark.* Journal for the Study of the New Testament: Supplement Series 128. Sheffield: Sheffield Academic Press, 1996.

Dyer, K. D. *The Prophecy on the Mount: Mark 13 and the Gathering of the New Community.* International Theological Studies 2. Bern: Peter Lang, 1998.

Edwards, J. R. "Markan Sandwiches: The Significance of Interpolations in Markan Narratives." *Novum Testamentum* 31 (1989): 193–216.

Ernst, J. "Johannes der Täufer und Jesus von Nazareth in historischer Sicht." *New Testament Studies* 43 (1997): 161–83.

Evans, C. A. "Jesus' Action in the Temple: Cleansing or Portent of Destruction?" *Catholic Biblical Quarterly* 51 (1989): 237–70.

_____. "Mark's Incipit and the Priene Calendar Inscription: From Jewish Gospel to Greco-Roman Gospel." *Journal of Greco-Roman Christianity and Judaism* 1 (2000): 67–81.

_____. *To See and Not Perceive: Isaiah 6.9–10 in Early Jewish and Christian Interpretation.* Journal for the Study of the Old Testament: Supplement Series 64. Sheffield: Sheffield Academic Press, 1989.

Farmer, W. R. *The Last Twelve Verses of Mark.* Society for New Testament Studies Monograph Series 25. Cambridge: Cambridge University Press, 1974.

_____. "Modern Developments of Griesbach's Hypothesis." *New Testament Studies* 23 (1976–1977): 275–95.

Feldmeier, R. *Die Krisis des Gottessohnes: Die Gethsemaneerzählung als Schlüssel der Markuspassion.* Wissenschaftliche Untersuchungen zum Neuen Testament 2. Reihe 21. Tübingen: J. C. B. Mohr (Paul Siebeck), 1987.

Feneberg, W. *Der Markusprolog: Studien zur Formbestimmung des Evangeliums.* Studien zum Alten und Neuen Testaments 36. Munich: Kösel-Verlag, 1974.

Finegan, J. *Encountering New Testament Manuscripts: A Working Introduction to Textual Criticism.* Grand Rapids: Eerdmans, 1974.

Fitzmyer, J. A. "The Aramaic Qorbān Inscription from Jebel Ḥallet eṭ-Ṭûri and Mark 7:11/Matt 15:5." *Journal of Biblical Literature* 78 (1959): 60–65.

_____. "Crucifixion in Ancient Palestine, Qumran Literature and the New Testament." *Catholic Biblical Quarterly* 40 (1979): 493–513.

_____. "4Q246: The 'Son of God' Document in Qumran." *Biblica* 74 (1993): 153–74.

_____. "The Matthean Divorce Texts and Some New Palestinian Evidence." *Theological Studies* 39 (1976): 196–226.

_____. "The Priority of Mark and the 'Q' Source in Luke." Pages 3–40 in *To Advance the Gospel: New Testament Studies.* New York: Crossroad, 1981.

Flanagan, P. J. *The Gospel of Mark Made Easy.* New York: Paulist Press, 1997.

Fleddermann, H. "A Warning about the Scribes (Mark 12:37b–40)." *Catholic Biblical Quarterly* 44 (1982): 52–67.

_____. "The Flight of a Naked Young Man (Mark 14:51–52)." *Catholic Biblical Quarterly* 41 (1979): 412–17.

Fowler, R. M. *Let the Reader Understand: Reader-Response Criticism and the Gospel of Mark.* Minneapolis: Fortress Press, 1991.

_____. *Loaves and Fishes: The Function of the Feeding Stories in the Gospel of Mark.* Society of Biblical Literature Dissertation Series 54. Chico: Scholars Press, 1981.

Frei, H. W. *The Eclipse of Biblical Narrative: A Study in Eighteenth and Nineteenth Century Hermeneutics.* New Haven: Yale University Press, 1974.

Frend, W. H. C. *The Rise of Christianity*. London: Darton, Longman, and Todd, 1984.

Freund, E. *The Return of the Reader: Reader-Response Criticism*. New Accents. London: Methuen, 1987.

Freyne, S. *The Twelve: Disciples and Apostles. A Study in the Theology of the First Three Gospels*. London: Sheed and Ward, 1969.

Fuller, R. H. *The Formation of the Resurrection Narratives*. London: SPCK, 1972.

Gadamer, H.-G. *Truth and Method*. New York: Seabury Press, 1975.

Garrett, S. R. *The Temptations of Jesus in Mark's Gospel*. Grand Rapids: Eerdmans, 1998.

Geddert, T. J. *Watchwords: Mark 13 in Markan Eschatology*. Journal for the Study of the New Testament: Supplement Series 26. Sheffield: Sheffield Academic Press, 1989.

Genest, O. *Le Christ de la Passion: Perspective structurale. Analyse de Marc 14,53–15,47 des parallèles bibliques et extra-bibliques*. Recherches 21 Théologie. Tournai/Montréal: Desclée/Bellarmin, 1978.

Genette, G. *Narrative Discourse: An Essay in Method*. Ithaca: Cornell University Press, 1980.

_____. *Narrative Discourse Revisited*. Ithaca: Cornell University Press, 1988.

George, A., and P. Grelot, eds. *Introduction à la Bible. Tome III: Le Nouveau Testament*. 7 vols. Edition nouvelle. Paris: Desclée, 1976–1986.

Gerhardsson, B. "The Parable of the Sower and Its Interpretation." *New Testament Studies* 14 (1967–1968): 165–93.

Gibson, J. B. "Jesus' Refusal to Produce a 'Sign' (Mk 8.11–13)." *Journal for the Study of the New Testament* 38 (1990): 37–66.

_____. "Jesus' Wilderness Temptation according to Mark." *Journal for the Study of the New Testament* 53 (1994): 3–34.

_____. *The Temptations of Jesus in Early Christianity*. Journal for the Study of the New Testament: Supplement Series 112. Sheffield: Sheffield Academic Press, 1995.

Gnilka, J. "Bräutigam—spätjüdisches Messiasprädikat?" *Trierer theologische Zeitschrift* 69 (1960): 298–301.

_____. "Die essenischen Tauchbäder und die Johannestaufe." *Revue de Qumran* 3 (1961): 185–207.

_____. *Jesus of Nazareth: Message and History*. Translated by S. S. Schatzmann. Peabody: Hendrickson, 1997.

Goguel, M. *La foi à la résurrection de Jésus dans le christianisme primitif*. Paris: E. Leroux, 1933.

Goulder, M. D. *Luke: A New Paradigm*. 2 vols. Journal for the Study of the New Testament: Supplement Series 20. Sheffield: Sheffield Academic Press, 1989.

Haenchen, E. "Die Komposition von Mk vii 27—ix 1 und Par." Pages 1–29 in *The Composition of Mark's Gospel: Selected Studies from Novum Testamentum*. Edited by D. E. Orton. Brill's Readers in Biblical Studies 3. Leiden: E. J. Brill, 1999.

Hahn, F. *Mission in the New Testament*. Translated by F. Clarke. Studies in Biblical Theology 47. London: SCM Press, 1965.

_____. *The Titles of Jesus in Christology*. Translated by H. Knight and G. Ogg. London: Lutterworth Press, 1969.

Hahn, F., ed. *Der Erzähler des Evangeliums: Methodische Neuansätze in der Markusforschung*. Stuttgarter Bibelstudien 118–119. Stuttgart: Katholisches Bibelwerk, 1985.

Hamilton, N. Q. "Resurrection Traditions and the Composition of Mark." *Journal of Biblical Literature* 84 (1965): 415–21.

Hanson, K. C., and D. E. Oakman, *Palestine in the Time of Jesus: Social Structures and Social Conflicts*. Minneapolis: Fortress Press, 1998.

Hare, D. R. A. *The Son of Man Tradition*. Minneapolis: Fortress Press, 1990.

_____. *The Theme of Jewish Persecution of Christians in the Gospel according to St. Matthew*. Society for New Testament Studies Monograph Series 6. Cambridge: Cambridge University Press, 1967.

Hartman, L. *Prophecy Interpreted: The Formation of Some Jewish Apocalyptic Texts and of the Eschatological Discourse Mark 13 Par.* Coniectanea biblica: New Testament Series 1. Lund: Gleerup, 1966.

Harvey, A. E. *Jesus and the Constraints of History.* London: Duckworth, 1982.

Hedrick, C. W. "The Role of 'Summary Statements' in the Composition of the Gospel of Mark: A Dialog with Karl Schmidt and Norman Perrin." *Novum Testamentum* 26 (1984): 289–311 (now available in *The Composition of Mark's Gospel: Selected Studies from* Novum Testamentum [ed. D. E. Orton; Brill's Readers in Biblical Studies 3; Leiden: Brill, 1999], 121–43).

Heil, J. P. *Blood and Water: The Death and Resurrection of Jesus in John 18–21.* The Catholic Biblical Quarterly Monograph Series 27. Washington: The Catholic Biblical Association, 1995.

_____. *The Death and Resurrection of Jesus: A Narrative-Critical Reading of Matthew 26–28.* Minneapolis: Fortress Press, 1991.

_____. "Mark 14,1–52: Narrative Structure and Reader Response." *Biblica* 71 (1990): 305–32.

_____. "The Narrative Strategy and Pragmatics of the Temple Theme in Mark." *Catholic Biblical Quarterly* 59 (1997): 76–100.

_____. "The Progressive Narrative Pattern of Mark 14,53–16,8." *Biblica* 73 (1992): 331–58.

_____. "Reader-Response and the Narrative Context of the Parables about Growing Seed in Mark 4:1–34." *Catholic Biblical Quarterly* 54 (1992): 271–86.

Hengel, M. *The Charismatic Leader and His Followers.* Translated by J. Greig. Studies of the New Testament and Its World. New York: Crossroad, 1981.

_____. *Crucifixion in the Ancient World and the Folly of the Cross.* Translated by J. Bowden. London: SCM Press, 1977.

_____. "Das Gleichnis von den Weingärtnern Mc 12,1–12." *Zeitschrift für die neutestamentliche Wissenschaft und die Kunde der älteren Kirche* 59 (1968): 1–39.

_____. "Mk 7,3 πυγμῇ: Die Geschichte einer exegetischen Aporie und der Versuch ihrer Lösung." *Zeitschrift für die neutestamentliche Wissenschaft und die Kunde der älteren Kirche* 60 (1969): 182–98.

_____. *Studies in the Gospel of Mark.* London: SCM Press, 1985.

_____. *Was Jesus a Revolutionist?* Philadelphia: Fortress Press, 1971.

_____. *The Zealots: Investigations into the Jewish Freedom Movement in the Period from Herod I to 70 A.D.* Edinburgh: T&T Clark, 1989.

Henten, J. W. van. "The First Testing of Jesus: A Rereading of Mark 1:12–13." *New Testament Studies* 45 (1999) 349–66.

Hoehner, H. W. *Herod Antipas: A Contemporary of Jesus Christ.* Grand Rapids: Zondervan, 1980.

Holladay, C.H. *Theios anēr in Hellenistic Judaism: A Critique of the Use of This Category in Christology.* Society of Biblical Literature Dissertation Series 40. Missoula: Scholars Press, 1977.

Holtzmann, H. J. *Die synoptischen Evangelien: Ihr Ursprung und geschichtlicher Charakter.* Leipzig: Wilhelm Engelmann, 1863.

Hooker, M. D. *Beginnings: Keys That Open the Gospels.* Valley Forge: Trinity Press International, 1998.

_____. "In His Own Image?" Pages 28–44 in *What About the New Testament? Studies in Honour of Christopher Evans.* Edited by M. D. Hooker and C. Hickling. London: SCM Press, 1975.

_____. "Is the Son of Man Problem Really Insoluble?" Pages 155–68 in *Text and Interpretation: Studies in the New Testament Presented to Matthew Black.* Edited by E. Best and R. McL. Wilson. Cambridge: Cambridge University Press, 1979.

_____. *Jesus and the Servant: The Influence of the Servant Concept of Deutero-Isaiah in the New Testament.* London: SPCK, 1959.

_____. *The Message of Mark.* London: Epworth Press, 1983.

_____. *The Son of Man in Mark: A Study of the Background of the Term "Son of Man" and Its Use in St. Mark's Gospel.* London: SPCK, 1967.

_____. "Traditions About the Temple in the Sayings of Jesus." *Bulletin of the John Rylands University Library of Manchester* 70 (1988): 7–19.

_____. "Trial and Tribulation in Mark XIII." *Bulletin of the John Rylands University Library of Manchester* 65 (1982): 78–99.

_____. "What Doest Thou Here, Elijah?" Pages 59–70 in *The Glory of Christ in the New Testament: Studies in Christology in Memory of George Bradford Caird.* Edited by L. D. Hurst and N. T. Wright. Oxford: Oxford University Press, 1987.

Hug, J. *La finale de l'Evangile de Marc (Mc 16,9–20). Etudes bibliques.* Paris: Gabalda, 1978.

Iersel, B. M. F. van. "Die wunderbare Speisung und das Abendmahl in der synoptischen Tradition (Mk VI 35–44, par.; VIII 1–10, par.)." *Novum Testamentum* 7 (1964): 167–94.

_____. *Reading Mark.* Collegeville: The Liturgical Press, 1988.

Ilan, T. *Jewish Women in Greco-Roman Palestine.* Peabody: Hendrickson, 1996.

Iser, W. *The Act of Reading: A Theory of Aesthetic Response.* London: Routledge & Kegan Paul, 1978.

_____. *The Implied Reader: Patterns of Communication in Prose Fiction from Bunyan to Beckett.* Baltimore: Johns Hopkins University Press, 1978.

Jaubert, A. *The Date of the Last Supper.* Translated by I. Rafferty. Staten Island: St. Paul, 1965.

Jeremias, J. *The Eucharistic Words of Jesus.* Translated by N. Perrin. London: SCM Press, 1966.

_____. *Jerusalem in the Time of Jesus: An Investigation into Economic and Social Conditions during the New Testament Period.* Translated by F. C. and C. H. Cave. London: SCM Press, 1969.

_____. *Jesus' Promise to the Nations.* Translated by S. H. Hooke. London: SCM Press, 1967.

_____. *New Testament Theology.* Translated by J. Bowden. London: SCM Press, 1971.

_____. "Paarweise Sendung im Neuen Testament." Pages 136–43 in *New Testament Essays: Studies in Memory of Thomas Walter Manson 1893–1958.* Edited by A. J. B. Higgins. Manchester: Manchester University Press, 1959.

_____. *The Parables of Jesus.* Translated by S. H. Hooke. London: SCM Press, 1963.

Johnson, E. S. "Is Mark 15:39 the Key to Mark's Christology?" *Journal for the Study of the New Testament* 31 (1987): 3–22.

Johnson, L. T. *The Letter of James.* Anchor Bible 37a. New York: Doubleday, 1995.

_____. *Religious Experience in Earliest Christianity.* Minneapolis: Fortress Press, 1998.

Juel, D. H. *A Master of Surprise: Mark Interpreted.* Minneapolis: Fortress Press, 1994.

_____. *Messiah and Temple: The Trial of Jesus in the Gospel of Mark.* Society of Biblical Literature Dissertation Series 31. Missoula: Scholars Press, 1977.

Kazmierski, C. R. "Evangelist and Leper: A Socio-Cultural Study of Mark 1.40–45." *New Testament Studies* 38 (1992): 37–50.

_____. *Jesus, the Son of God: A Study of the Marcan Tradition and Its Redaction by the Evangelist.* Forschung zur Bibel 33. Würzburg: Echter Verlag, 1979.

Kealy, S. P. *Mark's Gospel: A History of Its Interpretation.* New York: Paulist Press, 1982.

Keck, L. "The Introduction to Mark's Gospel." *New Testament Studies* 12 (1965–1966): 352–70.

_____. "Mark 3,7–12 and Mark's Christology." *Journal of Biblical Literature* 84 (1965): 341–58.

_____. "The Spirit and the Dove." *New Testament Studies* 17 (1970–1971): 41–67.

Kee, H. C. *Community of the New Age: Studies in Mark's Gospel.* Philadelphia: Westminster, 1977.

_____. "The Terminology of Mark's Exorcism Stories." *New Testament Studies* 14 (1968): 232–46.

Kelber, W. "The Hour of the Son of Man and the Temptation of the Disciples." Pages 41–60 in *The Passion in Mark.* Edited by W. Kelber. Philadelphia: Fortress Press, 1976.

_____. *The Kingdom in Mark: A New Place and a New Time.* Philadelphia: Fortress Press, 1974.

_____. "Mark 14:32–42: Gethsemane Passion Christology and Discipleship Failure." *Zeitschrift für die neutestamentliche Wissenschaft und die Kunde der älteren Kirche* 63 (1972): 166–87.

_____. *Mark's Story of Jesus.* Philadelphia: Fortress Press, 1979.

_____. *The Oral and Written Gospel: The Hermeneutics of Speaking and Writing in the Synoptic Tradition, Mark, Paul, and Q.* Philadelphia: Fortress Press, 1983.

Kelber, W. H. ed. *The Passion in Mark.* Philadelphia: Fortress, 1976.

Kelhoffer, J. A. *Miracle and Mission: The Authentication of Missionaries and Their Message in the Longer Ending of Mark.* Wissenschaftliche Untersuchungen zum Neuen Testament 2. Reihe 112. Tübingen: J. C. B. Mohr (Paul Siebeck), 2000.

Kermode, F. *The Genesis of Secrecy: On the Interpretation of Narrative.* Cambridge: Harvard University Press, 1979.

Kim, T. H. "The Anarthrous υἱὸς θεοῦ in Mark 15,39." *Biblica* 79 (1998): 221–41.

Kingsbury, J. D. *The Christology of Mark's Gospel.* Philadelphia: Fortress Press, 1983.

_____. *Conflict in Mark: Jesus, Authority, Disciples.* Minneapolis: Fortress Press, 1989.

Klauck, H.-J. "Die erzählerische Rolle der Jünger im Markusevangelium: Eine narrative Analyse." *Novum Testamentum* 24 (1982): 1–26.

Koch, D.-A. "Inhaltliche Gliederung und geographischer Aufriss im Markusevangelium." *New Testament Studies* 29 (1983): 145–66.

_____. "Zum Verhältnis von Christologie und Eschatologie im Markusevangelium." Pages 395–408 in *Jesus Christus in Historie und Theologie: Neutestamentliche Festschrift für Hans Conzelmann zum 60. Geburtstag.* Edited by G. Strecker. Tübingen: J. C. B. Mohr (Paul Siebeck), 1975.

Kodell, J. *The Eucharist in the New Testament.* Zacchaeus Studies: New Testament. Wilmington: Michael Glazier, 1989.

Koester, C. "The Origin and Significance of the Flight to Pella Tradition." *Catholic Biblical Quarterly* 51 (1989): 90–106.

Koester, H. *Ancient Christian Gospels: Their History and Development.* Philadelphia: Trinity Press International, 1990.

Kramer, W. *Christ, Lord, Son of God.* Translated by B. Hardy. Studies in Biblical Theology 50. London: SCM Press, 1966.

Kuhn, H.-W. *Ältere Sammlungen im Markusevangelium.* Studien zur Umwelt des Neuen Testaments 8. Göttingen: Vandenhoeck & Ruprecht, 1971.

Kümmel, W. G. "Das Gleichnis von den bösen Weingärtnern (Mk. 12:1–9)." Volume 1, pages 207–17 in *Heilsgeschehen und Geschichte: Gesammelte Aufsätze 1933–1964.* Edited by E. Grässer, O. Merk, and A. Fritz. 2 vols. Marburger Theologische Studien 3. Marburg: Elwert, 1965.

Kuthirakkattel, S. *The Beginning of Jesus' Ministry according to Mark's Gospel (1,14–3,6): A Redaction Critical Study.* Analecta Biblica 123. Rome: Biblical Institute Press, 1990.

Lamarche, O. "La Mort du Christ et la voile du temple selon Marc." *La nouvelle revue théologique* 106 (1974): 583–99

Lambrecht, J. *Die Redaktion der Markus-Apokalypse: Literarische Analyse und Strukturuntersuchung.* Analecta Biblica 28. Rome: Biblical Institute Press, 1967.

_____. "Jesus and the Law: An Investigation of Mk 7,1–23." *Ephemerides theologicae lovanienses* 53 (1977): 24–82.

_____. *Once More Astonished: The Parables of Jesus.* New York: Crossroad, 1983.

_____. "The Relatives of Jesus in Mark." Pages 85–102 in *The Composition of Mark's Gospel: Selected Studies from* Novum Testamentum. Edited by D. E. Orton. Brill's Readers in Biblical Studies 3. Leiden: E. J. Brill, 1999.

Lang, M. *Johannes und die Synoptiker: Eine redaktionsgeschichtliche Analyse von Joh 18–20 vor dem markanischen und lukanischen Hintergrund.* Forschungen zur Religion und Literatur des Alten und Neuen Testaments 182. Göttingen: Vandenhoeck & Ruprecht, 1999.

Lentzen-Deis, F.-L. *Die Taufe Jesu nach den Synoptikern: Literarkritische und Gattungsgeschicht-liche Untersuchungen.* Frankfurter theologische Studien 4. Frankfurt: Josef Knecht, 1970.

Léon-Dufour, X. *Sharing the Eucharistic Bread: The Witness of the New Testament.* Translated by M. J. O'Connell. New York: Paulist Press, 1987.

Lightfoot, R. H. *The Gospel Message of St. Mark.* Oxford: Clarendon Press, 1950.

_____. *History and Interpretation in the Gospels.* The Bampton Lectures 1934. London: Hodder and Stoughton, 1935.

Lindars, B. *Jesus Son of Man: A Fresh Examination of the Son of Man Sayings in the Gospels.* London: SPCK, 1983.

_____. *New Testament Apologetic: The Doctrinal Significance of the Old Testament Quotations.* London: SCM Press, 1961.

Lindemann, A. "Die Osterbotschaft des Markus: Zur theologischen Interpretation von Mark 16.1–8." *New Testament Studies* 26 (1979–1980): 298–317.

Linnemann, E. "Der (wiedergefundene) Markusschluss." *Zeitschrift für Theologie und Kirche* 66 (1969): 255–87.

Longstaff, T. R. W. *Evidence of Conflation in Mark? A Study in the Synoptic Problem.* Society of Biblical Literature Dissertation Series 28. Missoula: Scholars Press, 1977.

Loos, H. van der. *The Miracles of Jesus.* Supplements to Novum Testamentum 9. Leiden: E. J. Brill, 1965.

Lövestam, E. *Jesus and "This Generation": A New Testament Study.* Coniectanea biblica: New Testament Series 25. Stockholm: Almqvist & Wiksell, 1995.

Lüdemann, G. *The Resurrection of Jesus: History, Experience, Theology.* Translated by J. Bowden. London: SCM Press, 1994.

_____. "The Successors of Pre-70 Jerusalem Christianity: A Critical Evaluation of the Pella Tradition." Volume 1, pages 161–73 in *Jewish and Christian Self-Definition.* Edited by E. P. Sanders. 3 vols. London: SCM Press, 1980.

Lührmann, D. "Markus 14,55–64: Christologie und Zerstörung des Tempels im Markus-evangelium." *New Testament Studies* 27 (1980–1981): 457–74.

Luz U. "Kann die Bibel heute noch Grundlage für die Kirche sein?" *New Testament Studies* 44 (1998): 317–39.

Magness, J. L. *Sense and Absence: Structure and Suspension in the Ending of Mark's Gospel.* Semeia Studies. Atlanta: Scholars Press, 1986.

Malbon, E. S. "Disciples/Crowds/Whoever: Markan Characters and Readers." *Novum Testamentum* 28 (1986): 104–30.

_____. "Echoes and Foreshadowings in Mark 4–8: Reading and Rereading," *Journal of Biblical Literature* 112 (1993): 211–30

_____. "Fallible Followers: Women and Men in the Gospel of Mark." *Semeia* 28 (1983): 29–48.

_____. *In the Company of Jesus: Characters in Mark's Gospel.* Louisville: Westminster John Knox, 2000.

_____. "The Jesus of Mark and the Sea of Galilee." *Journal of Biblical Literature* 103 (1984): 363–77.

_____. "The Jewish Leaders in the Gospel of Mark: A Literary Study of Marcan Characterization." *Journal of Biblical Literature* 108 (1989): 259–81.

_____. "The Major Importance of the Minor Characters in Mark." In *In the Company of Jesus: Characters in Mark's Gospel.* Louisville: Westminster John Knox, 2000

_____. *Narrative Space and Mythic Meaning in Mark.* New Voices in Biblical Studies. San Francisco: Harper & Row, 1986.

_____. "The Poor Widow in Mark and Her Poor Rich Readers." *Catholic Biblical Quarterly* 53 (1991): 589–604.

_____. "Text and Contexts: Interpreting the Disciples in Mark." *Semeia* 62 (1993): 81–102.

Manek, J. "Fishers of Men." *Novum Testamentum* 2 (1957–1958): 138–41.

Manns, F. "Le thème de la maison dans l'évangile de Marc." *Recherches de Science Religieuse* 66 (1992): 1–17.

Mansfield, M. R. *"Spirit and Gospel" in Mark.* Peabody: Hendrickson, 1987.

Manson, T. W. *The Teaching of Jesus.* Cambridge: Cambridge University Press, 1967.

Marcus, J. "Blanks and Gaps in the Parable of the Sower." *Biblical Interpretation* 5 (1997): 1–16

———. "The Jewish War and the *Sitz im Leben* of Mark." *Journal of Biblical Literature* 111 (1992): 441–62.

———. "Mark 4:10–12 and Markan Epistemology." *Journal of Biblical Literature* 103 (1984): 557–74.

———. "Mark—Interpreter of Paul." *New Testament Studies* 46 (2000): 473–87.

———. *The Mystery of the Kingdom of God.* Society of Biblical Literature Dissertation Series 90. Atlanta: Scholars Press, 1986.

———. *The Way of the Lord: Christological Exegesis of the Old Testament in the Gospel of Mark.* Louisville: Westminster John Knox, 1992.

Marshall, C. D. *Faith as a Theme in Mark's Narrative.* Society for New Testament Studies Monograph Series 64. Cambridge: Cambridge University Press, 1989.

Martin, R. P. *Mark: Evangelist and Theologian.* Exeter: Paternoster Press, 1972.

Martyn, J. L. *History and Theology in the Fourth Gospel.* Rev. and enl. ed. Nashville: Abingdon, 1979.

Marxsen, W. *Mark the Evangelist: Studies on the Redaction History of the Gospel.* Nashville: Abingdon, 1969.

———. *The Resurrection of Jesus of Nazareth.* London: SCM Press, 1970.

Massaux, E. *The Influence of the Gospel of Saint Matthew on Christian Literature before Saint Irenaeus.* Translated by N. J. Belval and S. Hecht. Edited by A. J. Bellinzoni. New Gospel Studies 5. Macon: Mercer, 1993.

Masuda, S. "The Good News of the Miracle of the Bread: The Tradition and Its Markan Redaction." *New Testament Studies* 28 (1982): 191–219.

Matera, F. J. "The Incomprehension of the Disciples and Peter's Confession (Mark 6,14–8,30)." *Biblica* 70 (1989): 153–72.

———. *The Kingship of Jesus: Composition and Theology in Mark 15.* Society of Biblical Literature Dissertation Series 66. Chico: Scholars Press, 1982.

———. *New Testament Christology.* Louisville: Westminster John Knox, 1999.

———. *Passion Narratives and Gospel Theologies: Interpreting the Synoptics Through Their Passion Stories.* Theological Inquiries. New York: Paulist Press, 1986.

———. "The Prologue as the Interpretative Key to Mark's Gospel." *Journal for the Study of the New Testament* 34 (1988): 3–20.

Mauser, U. *Christ in the Wilderness.* Studies in Biblical Theology 39. London: SCM Press, 1963.

McKnight, E. V. *Post-Modern Use of the Bible: The Emergence of Reader-Oriented Criticism.* Nashville: Abingdon, 1988.

McLaren, J. *Turbulent Times? Josephus and Scholarship on Judea in the First Century C.E.* Journal for the Study of the Pseudepigrapha: Supplement Series 29. Sheffield: Sheffield Academic Press, 1998.

Meier, J. P. "The Brothers and Sisters of Jesus in Ecumenical Perspective." *Catholic Biblical Quarterly* 54 (1992): 1–28.

———. "The Circle of the Twelve: Did It Exist During Jesus' Public Ministry?" *Journal of Biblical Literature* 116 (1997): 635–72.

———. *A Marginal Jew: Rethinking the Historical Jesus.* 3 vols. Anchor Bible Reference Library. New York: Doubleday, 1991–2001.

Michaelis, W. "Zum jüdischen Hintergrund der Johannestaufe." *Judaica* 7 (1951): 81–120.

Minear, P. "The Needle's Eye: A Study in Form Criticism." *Journal of Biblical Literature* 61 (1942): 157–69.

Minette de Tillesse, G. *Le secret messianique dans l'Evangile de Marc.* Lectio Divina 47. Paris: Editions du Cerf, 1968.

Moloney, F. J. "Adventure with Nicodemus: An Exercise in Hermeneutics." Pages 259–79 in *"A Hard Saying": The Gospel and Culture.* Collegeville: The Liturgical Press, 2001.

_____. *Beginning the Good News: A Narrative Approach.* Collegeville: The Liturgical Press, 1995.

_____. *Belief in the Word: Reading John 1–4.* Minneapolis: Fortress Press, 1993.

_____. "Biblical Reflections on Marriage." *Compass Theological Review* 28/1 (1994): 10–16.

_____. *A Body Broken for a Broken People: Eucharist in the New Testament.* Rev. ed. Peabody: Hendrickson, 1997.

_____. "The End of the Son of Man?" *The Downside Review* 98 (1980): 280–90.

_____. "Faith in the Risen Jesus." *Salesianum* 43 (1981): 305–16.

_____. "The Fourth Gospel and the Jesus of History." *New Testament Studies* 46 (2000): 42–58.

_____. *Glory Not Dishonor. Reading John 13–21.* Minneapolis: Fortress Press, 1998.

_____. *The Gospel of John.* Sacra Pagina 4. Collegeville: The Liturgical Press, 1998.

_____. "The Gospel of John: A Tale of Two Paracletes." Pages 149–66 in *"A Hard Saying": The Gospel and Culture.* Collegeville: The Liturgical Press, 2001.

_____. "Jesus Christ: The Question to Cultures." Pages 183–209 in *"A Hard Saying": The Gospel and Culture.* Collegeville: The Liturgical Press, 2001.

_____. "The Johannine Paraclete and Jesus." In *Dummodo Christus annuntietur: Studi in onore di Prof. Jozef Heriban.* Edited by A. Strus and R. Blatnicky. Biblioteca di scienze religiose 146; Rome: LAS, 1998, 213–28.

_____. *A Life of Promise: Poverty-Chastity-Obedience.* Wilmington: Michael Glazier, 1984.

_____. "Mark 6:6b–30: Mission, the Baptist, and Failure." *CBQ* 63 (2001): 663–79.

_____. "Matthew 19,3–12 and Celibacy: A Redactional and Form Critical Study." *Journal for the Study of the New Testament* 2 (1979): 42–60.

_____. "Narrative Criticism of the Gospels." Pages 85–105 in *"A Hard Saying": The Gospel and Culture.* Collegeville: The Liturgical Press, 2001.

_____. *Signs and Shadows: Reading John 5–12.* Minneapolis: Fortress Press, 1996.

_____. "To Teach the Text: The New Testament in a New Age." *Pacifica* 11 (1998): 159–80.

_____. "The Vocation of the Disciples in the Gospel of Mark." In *"A Hard Saying": The Gospel and Culture.* Collegeville: The Liturgical Press, 2001, 53–84.

_____. "Where Does One Look? Reflections on Some Recent Johannine Scholarship." *Salesianum* 62 (2000): 223–51.

Montague, G. T. *Mark: Good News for Hard Times.* Ann Arbor: Servant Books, 1981.

Moo, D. J. *The Old Testament in the Gospel Passion Narratives.* Sheffield: The Almond Press, 1983.

Moule, C. F. D. "From Defendant to Judge—and Deliverer." Pages 82–99 in *The Phenomenon of the New Testament.* Studies in Biblical Theology. Second Series 1. London: SCM Press, 1967.

_____. "Neglected Features in the Problem of 'the Son of Man.'" Pages 413–28 in *Neues Testament und Kirche: Festschrift für Rudolf Schnackenburg.* Edited by J. Gnilka. Freiburg: Herder, 1974.

_____. *The Origin of Christology.* Cambridge: Cambridge University Press, 1977.

Munro, W. "Women Disciples in Mark?" *Catholic Biblical Quarterly* 44 (1982): 225–41.

Murphy-O'Connor, J. "John the Baptist and Jesus: History and Hypotheses." *New Testament Studies* 36 (1990): 359–74.

Neirynck, F. "ΑΝΑΤΕΙΛΑΝΤΟΣ ΤΟΥ ΗΛΙΟΥ." Pages 206–13 in *Evangelica: Gospel Studies—Etudes de l'évangile.* Edited by F. van Segbroeck. Bibliotheca ephemeridum theologicarum lovaniensium 60. Leuven: Leuven University Press, 1982.

_____. "La fuite du jeune homme en Marc 14,51–52." *Ephemerides theologicae lovanienses* 55 (1979): 43–66.

_____. "Le discours anti-apocalyptique de Mc. XIII." *Ephemerides theologicae lovanienses* 45 (1969): 154–64.

_____. "Marc 13: Examen critique de l'interprétation de R. Pesch." Pages 369–401 in *L'Apocalypse johannique et l'apocalyptique dans le Nouveau Testament.* Edited by J. Lambrecht. Bibliotheca ephemeridum theologicarum lovaniensium 53. Leuven: Leuven University Press, 1980.

_____. "Marc 16,1–8: Tradition et rédaction. Tombeau vide et angélophanie." Pages 239–71 in *Evangelica: Gospel Studies—Etudes d'évangile. Collected Essays.* Edited by F. van Segbroeck. Bibliotheca ephemeridum theologicarum lovaniensium 60. Leuven: Leuven University Press, 1982.

_____. "Marc 16,1–8: Tradition et rédaction. Tombeau vide et angélophanie." Pages 796–97 in *Evangelica II. 1982–91. Collected Essays.* Edited by F. Van Segbroeck. Bibliotheca ephemeridum theologicarum lovaniensium 99. Leuven: Leuven University Press, 1991.

Neirynck, F., T. Hansen, and F. van Segbroeck. *The Minor Agreements of Matthew and Luke against Mark, with a Cumulative List.* Bibliotheca ephemeridum theologicarum lovaniensium 37. Leuven: Leuven University Press, 1974.

Oakman, D. E. "Cursing Fig-Trees and Robbers' Dens: Pronouncement Stories Within Social Systemic Perspective. Mark 11:12–25 and Parallels." *Semeia* 64 (1993): 253–72.

Oberlinner, L. *Historische Überlieferung und christologische Aussage: Zur Frage der "Brüder Jesu" in der Synopse.* Forschung zur Bibel 19. Stuttgart: Katholisches Bibelwerk, 1975.

O'Collins, G. "The Resurrection: The State of the Questions." Pages 5–28 in *The Resurrection: An Interdisciplinary Symposium on the Resurrection of Jesus.* Edited by S. T. Davis, D. Kendall, and G. O'Collins. Oxford: Oxford University Press, 1997.

Orchard, O., and T. R. Longstaff, eds. *J. J. Griesbach: Synoptic and Text-Critical Studies.* Society for New Testament Studies Monograph Series 34. Cambridge: Cambridge University Press, 1978.

Orton, D. E., ed. *The Composition of Mark's Gospel: Selected Studies from Novum Testamentum.* Brill's Readers in Biblical Studies 3. Leiden: Brill, 1999.

Osborne, B. A. E. "Peter: Stumbling-Block and Satan." *Novum Testamentum* 15 (1973): 187–90.

Oyen, G. van. *The Interpretation of the Feeding Miracles in the Gospel of Mark.* Collectanea Biblica et religiosa antiqua 4. Brussels: Wetenschappelijk Comité voor Godsdienstwetenschappen Koninklijke Vlaamse Academie van België voor Wetenschappen en Kunsten, 1999.

Painter, J. *Just James: The Brother of Jesus in History and Tradition.* Studies on Personalities of the New Testament. Columbia: University of South Carolina, 1997.

_____. "When Is a House Not a Home? Mark 3:13–35." *New Testament Studies* 45 (1999): 498–513.

Pannenberg, W. "Did Jesus Actually Rise from the Dead?" *Dialog* 4 (1965): 18–35.

_____. *Grundzüge der Christologie.* Gutersloh: Gerd Mohn, 1964.

Parrott, R. "Conflict and Rhetoric in Mark 2:23–28." *Semeia* 64 (1993): 117–37.

Patsch, H. "Abendmahlsterminologie ausserhalb der Einsetzungsberichte." *Zeitschrift für die neutestamentliche Wissenschaft und die Kunde der alteren Kirche* 62 (1971): 210–31.

Paulsen, H. "Mk XVI 1–8." *Novum Testamentum* 22 (1980): 138–75.

Perkins, P. *Resurrection: New Testament Witness and Contemporary Reflection.* Garden City: Doubleday, 1984.

Perrin, N. "The Christology of Mark: A Study in Methodology." *Journal of Religion* 51 (1971): 173–87.

_____. "Mark 14:62: The End Product of a Christian Pesher Tradition?" Pages 10–22 in *A Modern Pilgrimage in New Testament Christology.* Philadelphia: Fortress Press, 1974.

_____. *Rediscovering the Teaching of Jesus.* London: SCM Press, 1967.

_____. *The Resurrection Narratives: A New Approach.* London: SPCK, 1977.

_____. "Towards an Interpretation of the Gospel of Mark." Pages 1–78 in *Christology and a Modern Pilgrimage.* Edited by H. D. Betz. Claremont: Society of Biblical Literature, 1971.

_____. "The Use of *(Para)didonai* in Connection with the Passion of Jesus in the New Testament." Pages 94–103 in *A Modern Pilgrimage in New Testament Christology.* Philadelphia: Fortress Press, 1974.

_____. *What Is Redaction Criticism?* London: SPCK, 1970.

Pesch, R. "Berufung und Sendung, Nachfolge und Mission: Eine Studie zu Mk 1,16–20." *Zeitschrift für katholische Theologie* 91 (1969): 1–31.

_____. "Levi–Matthäus (Mk 2,14/Mt 9,9; 10,3). Ein Beitrag zur Lösung eines alten Problems." *Zeitschrift für die neutestamentliche Wissenschaft und die Kunde der älteren Kirche* 59 (1968): 40–56.

_____. "Markus 13." Pages 355–68 in *L'Apocalypse johannique et l'apocalyptique dans le Nouveau Testament.* Edited by J. Lambrecht. Bibliotheca ephemeridum theologicarum lovaniensium 53. Leuven: Leuven University Press, 1980.

_____. *Naherwartung: Tradition und Redaktion in Mk 13.* Düsseldorf: Patmos Verlag, 1968.

_____. "Zur Entstehung des Glaubens an die Auferstehung Jesu." *Theologische Quartalschrift* 153 (1973): 201–28.

Petersen, P. *Literary Criticism for New Testament Critics.* Philadelphia: Fortress Press, 1978.

Pilch, J. J. *Healing in the New Testament: Insights from Medical and Mediterranean Anthropology.* Minneapolis: Fortress Press, 2000.

Quesnell, Q. *The Mind of Mark: Interpretation and Method through the Exegesis of Mark 6,52.* Analecta Biblica 38. Rome: Pontifical Biblical Institute, 1969.

Rabinowitz, P. J. "Whirl without End: Audience-Oriented Criticism." Pages 81–100 in *Contemporary Literary Theory.* Edited by C. D. Atkins and L. Morrow. London: Macmillan, 1989.

Räisänen, H. "Jesus and the Food Laws: Reflections on Mark 7,15." *Journal for the Study of the New Testament* 16 (1982): 79–100.

Reedy, C. J. "Mk 8:31–11:10 and the Gospel ending." *Catholic Biblical Quarterly* 34 (1972): 188–97.

Rengstorf, K. H. "Die στολαί der Schriftgelehrten: Eine Erläuterung zu Mark 12,38." Pages 383–404 in *Abraham unser Vater: Juden und Christen im Gespräch über die Bibel. Festschrift für Otto Michel zum 60. Geburtstag.* Edited by O. Betz, M. Hengel, and P. Schmidt. Arbeiten zur Geschichte des Spätjudentums und Urchristentums 5. Leiden: E. J. Brill, 1963.

Rhoads D., J. Dewey, and D. Michie. *Mark as Story: An Introduction to the Narrative of a Gospel.* 2d ed. Philadelphia: Fortress Press, 1999.

Rigaux, B. "Die Zwölf in Geschichte und Kerygma. " Pages 468–86 in *Der historische Jesus und der kerygmatische Christus. Beiträge zum Christusverständnis in Forschung und Verkündigung.* Edited by H. Ristow and K. Matthiae. Berlin: Evangelische Verlagsanstalt, 1962.

Rimmon-Kenan, S. *Narrative Fiction: Contemporary Poetics.* New Accents. London: Methuen, 1983.

Robbins, V. K. "Last Meal: Preparation, Betrayal, and Absence." Pages 29–34 in *The Passion in Mark: Studies on Mark 14–16.* Edited by W. Kelber. Philadelphia: Fortress Press, 1976.

Robinson, J. A. T. *Redating the New Testament.* London: SCM Press, 1976.

Robinson, J. M. *The Problem of History in Mark.* Studies in Biblical Theology 21. London: SCM Press, 1957.

Rohde, J. *Rediscovering the Teaching of the Evangelists.* Translated by D. M. Barton. London: SCM, 1968.

Rohrbach, R. I. "The Social Location of the Markan Audience." *Biblical Theology Bulletin* 23 (1993): 114–27.

Ruppert, L. *Jesus als der leidende Gerechte? Der Weg Jesus im Lichte eines alt-und zwischentestamentlichen Motivs.* Stuttgarter Bibelstudien 59. Stuttgart: Katholisches Bibelwerk, 1972.

Saldarini, A. J. *Pharisees, Scribes, and Sadducees in Palestinian Society.* Wilmington: Michael Glazier, 1988.

Sanders, E. P. *Jesus and Judaism.* Philadelphia: Fortress Press, 1985.

Schenke, L. *Auferstehungsverkündigung und leeres Grab: Eine traditionsgeschtichtliche Untersuchung von Mk 16,1–8.* Stuttgarter Bibelstudien 33. Stuttgart: Katholisches Bibelwerk, 1968.

Schiffman, L. "Messianic Figures and Ideas in the Qumran Scrolls." Pages 116–29 in *The Messiah: Developments in Earliest Judaism and Christianity.* Edited by J. H. Charlesworth. The First Princeton Symposium on Judaism and Christian Origins. Minneapolis: Fortress Press, 1992.

Schildgen, B. D. *Power and Prejudice: The Reception of the Gospel of Mark.* Detroit: Wayne State University Press, 1999.

Schillebeeckx, E. *Jesus: An Experiment in Christology.* London: Collins, 1979.

Schmidt, K. L. *Der Rahmen der Geschichte Jesu: Literarkritische Untersuchungen zur ältesten Jesusüberlieferung.* Darmstadt: Wissenschaftliche Buchgesellschaft, 1964.

Schnelle, U. *The History and Theology of the New Testament Writings.* Translated by M. E. Boring. Minneapolis: Fortress Press, 1998.

Scholtissek, K. " 'Er ist nicht ein Gott der Toten, sondern der Lebenden' (Mk 12,27): Grundzüge der markanische Theo-logie." Pages 71–100 in *Der lebendige Gott: Studien zur Theologie des Neuen Testaments. Festschrift für Wilhelm Thüsing zum 75. Geburtstag.* Edited by Th. Söding. Neutestamentliche Abhandlungen. Neue Folge 31. Münster: Aschendorff, 1996.

_____. "Nachfolge und Autorität nach dem Markusevangelium." *Trierer theologische Zeitschrift* 100 (1991): 56–74.

Schulz, A. *Nachfolgen und Nachahmen: Studien über das Verhältnis der Neutestamentlichen Jüngershaft zur Urchristlichen Vorbildethik.* Studien zum Alten und Neuen Testaments 6. Munich: Kösel, 1962.

Schürer, E. *The History of the Jewish People in the Age of Jesus Christ (175 B.C.–A.D. 135).* Revised and edited by G. Vermes, F. Millar, and M. Black. 3 vols. Edinburgh: T&T Clark, 1973–1987.

Schüssler-Fiorenza, E. *In Memory of Her: A Feminist Theological Reconstruction of Christian Origins.* London: SCM Press, 1983.

Schweitzer, A. *The Quest of the Historical Jesus.* Translated by W. Montgomery. London: A. and C. Black, 1910.

_____. *The Quest of the Historical Jesus.* First Complete Edition. Edited by J. Bowden. London: SCM Press, 2000.

Schweizer, E. *Jesus.* Translated by D. E. Green. London: SCM Press, 1971.

_____. "Mark's Theological Achievement." Pages 42–63 in *The Interpretation of Mark.* Edited by W. Telford. Issues in Religion and Theology 7. Philadelphia: Fortress Press, 1985.

Scroggs, R. *The Last Adam: A Study in Pauline Anthropology.* Oxford: Blackwell, 1966.

Selvidge, M. J. "Mark 5:25–34 and Leviticus 15:19–20: A Reaction to Restrictive Purity Regulations." *Journal of Biblical Literature* 103 (1984): 619–23.

Senior, D. "The Eucharist in Mark: Mission, Reconciliation, Hope." *Biblical Theology Bulletin* 12 (1982): 67–72.

_____. *The Passion of Jesus in the Gospel of Mark.* The Passion Series 2. Wilmington: Michael Glazier, 1984.

_____. "The Struggle to Be Universal: Mission as Vantage Point for New Testament Investigation." *Catholic Biblical Quarterly* 46 (1984): 63–81.

_____. " 'With Swords and Clubs . . .'—The Setting of Mark's Community and His Critique of Abusive Power." *Biblical Theology Bulletin* 17 (1987): 10–20.

Shepherd, T. "The Narrative Function of Markan Intercalation." *New Testament Studies* 41 (1995): 522–40.

Simon, L. "Le sou de la veuve: Marc 12/41–44." *Etudes théologiques et religieuses* 44 (1969): 115–26.

Sloyan, G. S. *The Crucifixion of Jesus: History, Myth, Faith.* Minneapolis: Fortress, 1995.

———. *Jesus on Trial: The Development of the Passion Narratives and Their Historical and Ecumenical Implications.* Edited by J. Reumann. Philadelphia: Fortress Press, 1973.

———. "Recent Literature on the Trial Narratives of the Fourth Gospel." Pages 136–76 in *Critical History and Biblical Faith: New Testament Perspectives.* Edited by T. J. Ryan. The College Theology Society Annual Publication Series. Villanova: College Theology Society, 1979.

Smith, D. E. "Narrative Beginnings in Ancient Literature and Theory." *Semeia* 52 (1991): 1–9.

Smith, S. H. "The Literary Structure of Mark 11:1–12:40." Pages 171–91 in *The Composition of Mark's Gospel: Selected Studies from* Novum Testamentum. Edited by D. E. Orton. Brill's Readers in Biblical Studies 3. Leiden: E. J. Brill, 1999.

Snodgrass, K. R. "The Parable of the Wicked Husbandmen: Is the Gospel of Thomas Version the Original?" *New Testament Studies* 21 (1974–1975): 142–44.

Soards, M. L. "The Question of a PreMarcan Passion Narrative." Volume 2, pages 1492–1524 in R. E. Brown, *The Death of the Messiah: From Gethsemane to the Grave: A Commentary on the Passion Narratives in the Four Gospels.* 2 vols. Anchor Bible Reference Library. New York: Doubleday, 1994.

Standaert, B. *L'Evangile selon Marc: Composition et genre littéraire.* Brugge: Sint-Andriesabdij, 1978.

Stegemann, E. W., and W. Stegemann, *The Jesus Movement: A Social History of Its First Century.* Minneapolis: Fortress Press, 1999.

Stein, R. H. "The Proper Methodology for Ascertaining a Markan Redaction History." Pages 34–51 in *The Composition of Mark's Gospel: Selected Studies from* Novum Testamentum. Edited by D. E. Orton. Brill's Readers in Biblical Studies 3. Leiden: E. J. Brill, 1999.

———. "A Short Note on Mark xiv.28 and xvi.7." *New Testament Studies* 20 (1973–1974): 445–52.

Stemberger, G. *Der Leib der Auferstehung: Studien zur Anthropologie und Eschatologie des palästinischen Judentums im neutestamentlichen Zeitalter. (ca. 170 v.Cr.—100 n.Chr).* Analecta Biblica 56. Rome: Biblical Institute Press, 1972.

Sternberg, M. *The Poetics of Biblical Narrative: Ideological Literature and the Drama of Reading.* Indiana Literary Biblical Series. Bloomington: Indiana University Press, 1985.

Stock, A. *Call to Discipleship: A Literary Study of Mark's Gospel.* Good News Studies 1. Wilmington: Michael Glazier, 1982.

Stock, K. *Boten aus dem Mit-Ihm-Sein: Das Verhältnis zwischen Jesus und den Zwölf nach Markus.* Analecta Biblica 70. Rome: Biblical Institute Press, 1975.

———. "Das Bekenntnis des Centurio: Mk 15,39 im Rahmen des Markusevangeliums." *Zeitschrift für katholische Theologie* 100 (1978): 289–301.

Stoldt, H.-H. *History and Criticism of the Markan Hypothesis.* Edinburgh: T&T Clark, 1980.

Such, W. A. *The Abomination of Desolation in the Gospel of Mark: Its Historical Reference in Mark 13:14 and Its Impact in the Gospel.* Lanham: University Press of America, 1999.

Talmon, S. "The Concepts of Māšîaḥ and Messianism in Early Judaism." Pages 79–115 in *The Messiah: Developments in Earliest Judaism and Christianity.* Edited by J. H. Charlesworth. The First Princeton Symposium on Judaism and Christian Origins. Minneapolis: Fortress Press, 1992.

Tannehill, R. C. "The Disciples in Mark: The Function of a Narrative Role." Pages 134–57 in *The Interpretation of Mark.* Edited by W. Telford. Issues in Religion and Theology 7. Philadelphia: Fortress Press, 1985.

———. "The Gospel of Mark as Narrative Christology." *Semeia* 16 (1980): 57–95.

Tarazi, P. N. *The New Testament Introduction: Paul and Mark.* New York: St. Vladimir's Seminary Press, 1999.

Telford, W. R. *The Barren Temple and the Withered Tree: A Redaction-critical Analysis of the Cursing of the Fig-Tree Pericope in Mark's Gospel and Its Relation to the Cleansing of the Temple Tradition.* Journal for the Study of the New Testament: Supplement Series 1. Sheffield: JSOT Press, 1980.

_____. *Mark.* New Testament Guides. Sheffield: Sheffield Academic Press, 1995.

_____. "The Pre-Markan Tradition in Recent Research 1980–1990." Volume 2, pages 695–723 in *The Four Gospels 1992: Festschrift Frans Neirynck.* Edited by F. van Segbroeck, C. M. Tucker, G. van Belle, and J. Verheyden. 3 vols. Biblioteca ephemeridum theologicarum lovaniensium 100. Leuven: Leuven University Press, 1992.

_____. *The Theology of the Gospel of Mark.* New Testament Theology. Cambridge: Cambridge University Press, 1999.

Telford, W. R., ed. *The Interpretation of Mark.* Issues in Religion and Theology 7. Philadelphia: Fortress Press, 1985.

Theissen, G. *The First Followers of Jesus: A Sociological Analysis of Earliest Christianity.* London: SCM Press, 1978.

Thissen, W. *Erzählung der Befreiung: Eine Exegetische Untersuchung zu Mk 2,1–3,6.* Forschung zur Bibel 21. Würzburg: Echter Verlag, 1974.

Thompson, M. M. *The Promise of the Father: Jesus and God in the New Testament.* Louisville: Westminster John Knox, 2000.

Tiede, D. L. *The Charismatic Figure as Miracle Worker.* Society of Biblical Literature Dissertation Series 1. Missoula: Society of Biblical Literature, 1972.

Tilborg, S. van. "A Form Criticism of the Lord's Prayer." *Novum Testamentum* 14 (1972): 94–105.

Tödt, H. E. *The Son of Man in the Synoptic Tradition.* Translated by D. M. Barton. London: SCM Press, 1965.

Tolbert, M. A. *Sowing the Gospel: Mark's World in Literary-Historical Perspective.* Minneapolis: Fortress Press, 1989.

Tuckett, C. M. *Q and the History of Early Christianity: Studies on Q.* Peabody: Hendrickson, 1996.

_____. *The Revival of the Griesbach Hypothesis.* Society for New Testament Studies Monograph Series 44. Cambridge: Cambridge University Press, 1982.

_____. *Reading Mark.* Collegeville: The Liturgical Press, 1988.

Verheyden, J. "The Flight of the Christians to Pella." *Ephemerides theologicae lovanienses* 66 (1990): 368–84.

Vermes, G. *Jesus the Jew. A Historian's Reading of the Gospels.* London: Collins, 1973.

Vielhauer, P. "Jesus und der Menschensohn: Zur Diskussion mit Heinz Edward Tödt und Eduard Schweizer." *Zeitschrift für die neutestamentliche Wissenschaft und die Kunde der älteren Kirche* 60 (1963): 133–77.

Viviano, B. T. "The High Priest's Servant's Ear: Mark 14:47." *Revue Biblique* 96 (1989): 71–80.

Vögtle, A., and R. Pesch, *Wie kam es zum Osterglauben?* Düsseldorf: Patmos-Verlag, 1975.

Volkmar, G. *Die Religion Jesu.* Leipzig: Brockhaus, 1857.

Waetjen, H. C. *A Reordering of Power: A Socio-Political Reading of Mark's Gospel.* Minneapolis: Fortress Press, 1989.

Wahlberg, R. C. *Jesus according to a Woman.* New York: Paulist Press, 1975.

Wansbrough, H. "Mark 3,21: Was Jesus Out of His Mind?" *New Testament Studies* 18 (1971–1972): 234–35.

Watts, R. E. *Isaiah's New Exodus and Mark.* Wissenschaftliche Untersuchungen zum Neuen Testament 2. Reihe 88. Tübingen: J. C. B. Mohr (Paul Siebeck), 1997.

Weeden, T. *Mark: Traditions in Conflict.* Philadelphia: Fortress Press, 1971.

Weihs, A. "Die Eifersucht der Winzer zur Anspielung auf LXX Gen 37,20 in der Parabel von der Tötung des Sohnes (Mk 12,1–12)." *Ephemerides theologicae lovanienses* 76 (2000): 5–29.

Wenham, D. "The Meaning of Mark iii.21." *New Testament Studies* 21 (1974–1975): 296–97.

White, K. W. "The Parable of the Sower." *Journal of Theological Studies* 15 (1964): 300–307.

Williams, C. H. *I Am He: The Interpretation of 'Anî Hû' in Jewish and Early Christian Literature.* Wissenschaftliche Untersuchungen zum Neuen Testament 2. Reihe 113. Tübingen: J. C. B. Mohr (Paul Siebeck), 2000.

Witherington, B. *Women in the Ministry of Jesus: A Study of Jesus' Attitudes to Women and Their Roles as Reflected in His Earthly Life.* Society for New Testament Studies Monograph Series 51. Cambridge: Cambridge University Press, 1984.

Wrede, W. *The Messianic Secret.* Translated by J. C. G. Greig. Cambridge & London: James Clarke, 1971.

Wright, A. G. "The Widow's Mites: Praise or Lament?—A Matter of Context." *CBQ* 44 (1982): 256–65.

Xeravitis, G. "The Early History of Qumran's Messianic Expectations." *Ephemerides theologicae lovanienses* 76 (2000): 113–21.

Zimmerli, W. "Ich bin Jahwe." Pages 179–209 in *Geschichte und Altes Testament: Albrecht Alt zum siebzigsten Geburtstag.* Edited by G. Ebeling. Beiträge zur historischen Theologie 16. Tübingen: J. C. B. Mohr (Paul Siebeck), 1953.

Zimmerman, H. "Das absolute Ἐγώ εἰμι als neutestamentliche Offenbarungsformel." *Biblische Zeitschrift* 4 (1960): 54–69, 266–76.

Zimmermann, J. *Messianische Texte aus Qumran. Königliche, priesterliche und prophetische Messiasvorstellung in der Schriften von Qumran.* Wissenschaftliche Untersuchungen zum Neuen Testament 2. Reihe 104. Tübingen: J. C. B. Mohr (Paul Siebeck), 1998.

INDEX OF MODERN AUTHORS

INDEX OF ANCIENT SOURCES

JEWISH WRITINGS